Archaeology of the Mid-Holocene Southeast

The Ripley P. Bullen Series

Florida Museum of Natural History

ARCHAEOLOGY OF THE MID-HOLOCENE SOUTHEAST

EDITED BY
KENNETH E. SASSAMAN
AND
DAVID G. ANDERSON

UNIVERSITY PRESS OF FLORIDA
Gainesville/Tallahassee/Tampa/Boca Raton
Pensacola/Orlando/Miami/Jacksonville

Library of Congress Cataloging-in-Publication Data
Archaeology of the Mid-Holocene southeast / edited by Kenneth E. Sassaman
and David G. Anderson.
    p. cm. — (The Ripley P. Bullen series)
    Includes bibliographical references (p.   ) and index.
    ISBN 0-8130-1855-2
    1. Indians of North America—Southern States—Antiquities.
2. Southern States—Antiquities.   I. Sassaman, Kenneth E.
II. Anderson, David G., 1949–.   III. Series.
E78.S65A77   1996   95-45466
975'.01—dc20   CIP

Figure 4-7 reprinted from *Early Pottery in the Southeast: Tradition and Innovation in Cooking Technology* by Kenneth E. Sassaman. Copyright © 1993 by The University of Alabama Press. Reprinted by permission of the publisher.
Figure 12-4 reprinted from "The Tomoka Mound Complex in Northeast Florida," *Southeastern Archaeology* 4, no. 2 (1994):109–18, by Bruce Piatek, by permission of the journal editor.

University Press of Florida
15 Northwest 15th Street
Gainesville, FL 32611

The University Press of Florida is the scholarly publishing agency for the State University System of Florida, comprised of Florida A & M University, Florida Atlantic University, Florida International University, Florida State University, University of Central Florida, University of Florida, University of North Florida, University of South Florida, and University of West Florida.

Contents

Section I. Mid-Holocene Environments   1

Section II. Technology   39

Section III. Subsistence and Health   97

Section IV. Regional Settlement Variation   155

Section V. Regional Integration and Organization   219

TABLES

Figures

SERIES EDITOR'S FOREWORD

As this volume amply demonstrates, our knowledge of the precolumbian Native American cultures of the southeastern United States has undergone immense growth in the last few decades. New generations of scholars armed with data derived from recent interdisciplinary archaeological investigations are literally rewriting the past, providing much fuller accounts and explanations of human cultures and their adaptations to their natural and social environments.

Several decades ago when I took my first college undergraduate course in southeastern archaeology, the cultures of the Archaic period, the mid-Holocene from 8000 to 3000 B.P., were presented as egalitarian hunter-gathering bands living in relative isolation from one another. Over time as modern forests came to dominate the landscape, Archaic bands developed a ground tool technology that allowed them to make extensive use of forest products, especially nuts; they also gathered and ate huge quantities of freshwater shellfish that had begun to flourish in many of the southeastern rivers. Archaic groups did not live in large villages, did not inhabit the coasts, and did not build or use mounds. The only exception to the last was the Poverty Point culture of the Lower Mississippi Valley, an anomaly no one could successfully explain except by saying it was different from what was known about other Archaic cultures.

In that course, five thousand years of history were compressed into one textbook chapter and a week's lectures. No small wonder that I and other archaeologists opted to spend our careers investigating the seemingly more interesting cultures that preceded or developed out of those of the mid-Holocene.

But all that has changed. With this important volume, Kenneth Sassaman and David Anderson and their colleagues serve notice that old characterizations of the cultures of the Archaic period have been buried under the back dirt of new excavations and new interpretations. A host of specialists utilizing data from paleoenvironmental studies, biological anthropology, archaeobiology, and archaeology offer exciting, fresh perspectives on the Southeast and the cultures that lived there during the mid-Holocene epoch.

Topical and regional syntheses recount the geological and vegetative histories of the mid-Holocene. Against that backdrop of changing and regional natural settings, the volume's contributors examine Archaic economic patterns, social organization, technology, group interactions, health, and regional and temporal variations in architecture and settlement systems. We learn that Archaic cultures inhabited large expanses of the southeast coast and some built mounds for ceremonial purposes. And the Poverty Point culture, once so enigmatic, is rein-terpreted in the context of these new perspectives.

Emphasizing the regional and chronological cultural variations that existed within the mid-Holocene, *Archaeology of the Mid-Holocene Southeast* places the Archaic cultures squarely at the forefront of archaeological theory.

Jerald T. Milanich
General Editor

PREFACE

The archaeology of the mid-Holocene Southeast is a burgeoning subject that lacks focus. Research has progressed rapidly in the last several decades, diversifying to include the specialties of bioarchaeology, paleoethnobotany, and faunal analysis. Under the purview of cultural resource management, the volume of sites investigated has risen dramatically, and the cumulative stack of contract reports would exceed the height of Monks Mound. Repositories are filled with mid-Holocene artifacts and ecofacts, local journals boast numerous contributions, and a number of new dioramas depict life as a mid-Holocene hunter-gatherer.

Indeed, the amount of information about mid-Holocene archaeology is now immense, but conceptual frameworks for interpreting this information have not kept pace. Few attempts at regional synthesis have appeared since the 1950s when James Griffin's (1952a) *Archaeology of Eastern United States* was issued (see Morse [1967], Phelps [1964] and Rolingson [1967] for notable exceptions); Caldwell (1958) published his treatise, *Trend and Tradition;* Lewis and Kneberg's (1959) summary of the Midsouth Archaic appeared in *American Antiquity;* and William S. Webb put to paper but never published his life's work on the Archaic. Granted, there have been a number of recent subregional or local syntheses, usually embedded within full accounts of prehistory (e.g., Anderson and Joseph 1988; Chapman 1985a; Jenkins and Krause 1986; Milanich 1994; Milanich and Fairbanks 1980; Walthall 1980); and at least two panregional syntheses, by Smith (1986) and Steponaitis (1986), have brought us up to date on Archaic research since the 1950s. Otherwise, research on the mid-Holocene Southeast has been reported in topically focused volumes, numerous contract reports, and papers with limited distribution. To compound the problem, we do not see the level of interaction and cross-fertilization among mid-Holocene specialists that existed in the 1950s. Whereas researchers working on the Mississippi period are confronted by a greater volume of information than are their mid-Holocene counterparts, the flow of information among Mississippian specialists is seemingly more efficient, partly because they enjoy greater leadership, direction, and focus. One might suggest, in fact, that Mississippian researchers work within an integrated hierarchy, compared to Archaic enthusiasts who are disintegrated and autonomous.

The metaphor we introduce here embodies a major shortcoming in the way we view much of prehistory. The divide between hunter-gatherer societies and food producers carries with it a tremendous amount of conceptual baggage. If we set apart food-producing societies as something socially and politically as well as economically distinct from nonfood producers, one has little to do with the other, and we are led to division of labor in anthropology wherein specialists on either side of the conceptual divide have little to say to one another. This divide has, of course, a long history in archaeology. It became codified for the Southeast when Joseph Caldwell, in *Trend and Tradition,* characterized Archaic prehistory as a ladder of evolutionary development. The top rung for hunter-gatherers was achieving "primary forest efficiency." Only food production and its associated levels of cultural complexity remained, and once that threshold was reached there was no turning back.

The teleology of Caldwell's model persists today in virtually every summary of southeastern prehistory written for contract reports or the lay audience. It is a simple, straightforward depiction of the past, without loose or ragged edges. It persists in many circles despite trenchant criticism on several fronts. The collection of papers in Price and Brown's recent compendium aimed to educate archaeologists about the diversity of economic and social formations called hunter-gatherer (Price and Brown 1985a). It included a paper by William Marquardt (1985) that discussed the social complexity and scale of the Shell Mound Archaic. That same year Barbara Bender (1985) brought her social perspective on hunter-gatherer complexity to bear on the midwestern Late Archaic. On the global front, a debate was astir among ethnographers on the historical validity of hunter-gatherers. Many books and papers appeared that undermined the attribution of classic hunter-gatherer features with an isolated ecological adaptation (e.g., Headland and Reid 1989; Ingold et al. 1988; Leacock and Lee 1982; Schrire 1984; Wilmsen 1983). These showed that hunters-gatherers had histories of long-term interaction with food producers and could be understood only as products of such interaction.

This recent conceptual work seems to have had little impact in studies of the southeastern Archaic. This is not to say that recent research on the Archaic has been insignificant or atheoretical. It does suggest, however, that much work continues to be bogged down in the anachronistic conceptual framework that portrays mid-Holocene hunter-gatherers as isolated, locally adapted, and ecologically constrained populations frozen in an evolutionary moment between the big-game hunters of the late Pleistocene and food producers of the late Holocene. At worst, such a perspective homogenizes these populations into autonomous, self-contained egalitarian societies; at best, it attributes variation among them to environmental differences alone.

The lack of recent synthesis on the mid-Holocene Southeast is both symptom and cause of the conceptual mire in which we find ourselves. This volume is offered as a dose of remedy. We do not pretend to have the only conceptual insight to lift Archaic studies from its mire, nor do we suggest that everyone agrees with our characterization of the situation. But we believe that the papers included here highlight the considerable diversity that existed among populations of the mid-Holocene Southeast and present a variety of new perspectives that will help us to interpret this newfound diversity.

The impetus for this project came from ongoing efforts to synthesize South Carolina prehistory for resource management purposes. Beginning in 1991, the Council of South Carolina Professional Archaeologists sought funding from the South Carolina Department of Archives and History to conduct a series of symposia and to publish the proceedings as Historic Contexts for the state. That year, we, along with Christopher Judge, organized a symposium on the Paleoindian and Early Archaic periods (Anderson et al. 1992). Arguing that the archaeology of these periods in South Carolina could be understood only in its regional context, we invited contributors from across the Southeast. The regional scope was successful in that it allowed for broad-based comparisons and contrasts, but it was constrained by a lack of data and by the barriers of modern geopolitical boundaries.

In the second year of the synthesis project, we revised the framework to introduce topical approaches to synthesis. Most of the contributors to this volume were solicited for their expertise on particular aspects of the mid-Holocene record, not necessarily on particular pieces of geography. Subregional spatial boundaries are inherent to some of the topics presented here, though by and large contributors draw on data from across the southeastern United States to synthesize knowledge about particular subjects. It is our belief that this approach transcends both the site-specific format of Phillips and Brown's *Archaic Hunters and Gatherers in the American Midwest* (1983), and the state-specific focus of our first synthesis volume (Anderson et al. 1992), to summarize and interpret mid-Holocene prehistory at the regional scale.

By synthesis we mean more than just a summary of knowledge to date. Syntheses are intended to provide conceptual frameworks for organizing the cumulative body of knowledge about a subject. They are thus theoretical as well as substantive. We realize that not all attempts at synthesis are explicitly theoretical, nor should they be. But we suggest that any attempt to organize and communicate a body of information is guided by theory, however implicit and unassuming it may be. This volume is not guided by one overarching theoretical perspective; it is, in fact, a showcase for alternative readings of the mid-Holocene archaeological record. Regardless of the particular bent that individual contributors take, however, all recognize diversity in this record, and it is our goal to display data on diversity and offer a variety of approaches to explain it. Some contributors view diversity as a product of local adaptation, others as responses to regional-scale processes of interaction, but none repaint the picture of homogeneous foragers so entrenched in the modern literature.

For our purposes, the mid-Holocene is defined in deliberately broad terms. Chronostratigraphic boundaries for the mid-Holocene are generally limited to the Climatic Optimum of about 8000–5000 B.P. The onset of this period of environmental change is well documented, and it marks some rather dramatic changes in the way hunter-gatherer populations in the Southeast made a living and related to one another. The changes are not all that apparent across the entire region, yet the intensive riverine settlements of the interior Southeast are a conspicuous departure from the preceding millennia, and these responses arguably affected the entire Southeast through processes of interaction and group fissioning.

The close of the mid-Holocene may be equally well documented by environmental data, but this is not at all apparent in the archaeological record. Many of the features attributed to Late Archaic adaptations associated with the transition to modern conditions after 5000 B.P. had precedents in the Middle Archaic. Contributors to this volume document some of these early trends and show that they were rarely unilineal or irreversible. Thus, the beginning of the Late Archaic period at about 5000 B.P. is becoming increasingly blurred as we open our eyes to the fact that not all of human prehistory is reduced to responses to broad-based environmental change.

Our closure here at 3000 B.P. is difficult to defend for the same reasons noted for the division between the Middle and Late Archaic periods. The traits that traditionally divided the Archaic and Woodland periods at 3000 B.P. are totally ambiguous. Pottery, mound building, social differentiation, mortuary ceremonialism, long-distance trade, and plant domestication all existed long before 3000 B.P. Sassaman (1993a) has suggested that a panregional process of disintegration and fissioning occurred at about 3000 B.P., facilitated in part by the widespread adoption of pottery. We may thus be justified in drawing a temporal line at 3000 B.P., although it would remain unjustifiable to sever the historical connections between Archaic and Woodland populations on sociopolitical grounds alone. Some chapters transcend this temporal boundary to describe continuity and change in the Early Woodland period. In keeping with a perspective on historical contingency, this is justified and necessary, and it goes to show that any analytical division of time is somewhat arbitrary.

The spatial boundaries for the project are saddled with similarly arbitrary parameters. We define the Southeast as all continental land east of the Mississippi River and south of the Ohio River valleys. Cultural connections across these boundaries are apparent in the paneastern patterns of particular cultural behaviors and flows of materials and personnel. Several chapters introduce the archaeological records from the Midwest and Middle Atlantic to situate southeastern archaeological data further within a macroscale arena of historical influences and interactions. Other papers have geographical foci that were more or less restricted by the subject matter involved. The juxtaposition of different scales of analysis in this volume underscores the importance of multiscalar approaches to studies of process (Marquardt 1992a; Marquardt and Crumley 1987; Nassaney and Sassaman 1995), reminding us that detailed empirical records are built from the ground up, but need to be conceptualized from the sky down.

It is indeed an exciting time for mid-Holocene research in the Southeast. Mounting evidence for ceremonialism, exchange, and intergroup strife, combined with greater appreciation for detailed local histories of subsistence and technology, are lifting Archaic period studies to a new level of anthropological relevance. It is no longer feasible to characterize Archaic hunter-gatherers in generalized terms; variation is what characterizes the record of their existence, and it is variation that we must explain. Changes in our scales of analysis—from site-specific to regional, from synchronic to diachronic—will allow different perspectives on variation, so it is essential that detailed site analyses continue alongside macroscale comparative studies. Armed with new questions and new conceptions, extant collections gain new significance. We trust that some scholars, particularly young scholars, may be inspired to reexamine the vast Archaic collections housed at the universities of Alabama, Tennessee, Kentucky, and Florida and elsewhere. Ongoing fieldwork will of course continue to add new sites and artifacts to the inventory of the mid-Holocene record, and we hope that some of the issues discussed herein will inspire research designs for their investigation. Above all, we hope that the arbitrary dividing line between Archaic and Woodland can be lifted forever to reveal the historical processes transcending the temporal boundaries we have imposed, to dissolve the analytical impasse that keep hunter-gatherers in a category separate from food producers, and to gain the attention of scholars whose interests are fixed on so-called complex societies.

This volume is one of several products resulting from efforts on the part of the Council of South Carolina Professional Archaeologists to synthesize South Carolina prehistory from a regional perspective. Funding for the project was provided by the National Park Service, Department of the Interior, through a Survey and Planning Grant administered by the South Carolina Department of Archives and History (SCDAH). Matching funds were provided by the South Carolina Institute of Archaeology and Anthropology (SCIAA), University of South Carolina, and its Savannah River Archaeological Research Program (SRARP). Gratefully acknowledged are the personal efforts and support of Mary Edmunds, Nancy Brock, Stephen Skelton, Lee Tippett, and Niels Taylor of SCDAH; Bruce Rippeteau and Sherry Bailey of SCIAA; Mark Brooks and Richard Brooks of SCIAA-SRARP; and SRARP sponsor Andrew Grainger of the U.S. Department of Energy–Savannah River. Additional support was provided by National Park Service, Interagency Archeological Services Division–Atlanta, under the direction of John Ehrenhard.

Artwork for this volume was expertly produced by Julie Barnes Smith (chaps. 5 and 14), Stephanie Brown (chap. 4), and others acknowledged in individual chapters. Christopher Gillam is thanked for some last minute computer graphics for chapter 1.

The staff and affiliates of the University Press of Florida deserve special recognition for the professional and thorough attention given to this project. We are grateful to our copyeditor Sally Antrobus, editors Judy Goffman and Walda Metcalf, director Kenneth Scott, the UPF production staff, and especially Bullen series editor Jerry Milanich, for support and encouragement throughout the project.

Our thanks to reviewers of an earlier version of the manuscript—Jerry Milanich, Patty Jo Watson, and Jim Brown—for their thoughtful suggestions and encouragement. We also acknowledge the intellectual debt to the numerous colleagues who have contributed to our thinking on the mid-Holocene Southeast and whose influence is evident in many chapters. Finally, we thank our families and friends for encouragement and inspiration, particularly our wives, Cherry and Jenalee, who continue to suffer patiently and with good humor through our long absences and manic episodes.

SECTION I

MID-HOLOCENE ENVIRONMENTS

It is no exaggeration to claim that archaeologists have looked to climatic conditions of the mid-Holocene as *the* primary influence on Middle Archaic cultural adaptations. Recent and ongoing paleoenvironmental research is exposing the complexities of data on human-land relations, documenting both regularities and variation that do not always coincide with cultural developments.

In chapter 1, Joseph Schuldenrein reviews geoarchaeological analyses of landscape evolution to draw inferences about mid-Holocene climate and human land use. His detailed study of the Rucker's Bottom site in the upper Savannah River valley provides a basis of comparison with previous work in the Haw River and Little Tennessee River valleys. Schuldenrein concludes that despite variable stream dynamics and channel morphology among the study areas, Archaic period floodplain development assumed a cyclic pattern of progressive sedimentation followed by intervals of stabilization. Importantly, panregional evidence for soil formation at the Early to Middle Archaic interface (ca. 8000 B.P.) marks the onset of floodplain stabilization at a time when climatic conditions may have encouraged prehistoric populations to cluster at riverine locations. Such was apparently the case in the Midwest and Midsouth, where shell middens and other riverine midden sites began to form after 7500 B.P. However, the lack of similar cultural developments in the South Atlantic Slope points to historical divergences that cannot be attributed to riverine dynamics alone.

The mid-Holocene was time of punctuated global warmth in post-Pleistocene climate. The particular manifestations of the climatic maximum in the Southeast, and its effects on human occupation, have been subjects of considerable deliberation. In their interpretation of pollen and sediment data from the Atlantic Coastal Plain in chapter 2, William A. Watts, Eric C. Grimm, and T. C. Hussey argue that the availability of surface water and variation in water table depth had profound implications for distributions of Archaic populations. As their data on the onset of sedimentation in Florida and the Southeast Coastal Plain show, changes in these variables were neither synchronous nor uniform. Similarly, the shift from oak-to pine-dominated forests was an uneven process that apparently began in the South Atlantic Slope as early as 8500 B.P. but did not begin in south Florida until after 7000 B.P. Likewise, the time it took pine to reach local maxima varied, with rates much faster in the Carolinas than in south Georgia and Florida. Although vegetational and water table changes were nowhere so quick as to be perceived in a single lifetime, the differences in rates of change are indeed significant to our reading of long-term archaeological records, especially patterns of regional settlement, demography, and subsistence technology.

1

Geoarchaeology and the Mid-Holocene Landscape History of the Greater Southeast

JOSEPH SCHULDENREIN

The period between 8000 and 3000 B.P. is perhaps the most critical in understanding coeval trends in landscape history and prehistoric settlement across continental North America. Early Holocene climates and hydrographic changes (12,000–8000 B.P.)—expressed by extensive glacial features, lakes, and undulating terrain in northern latitudes and by wide and deep valley trenches and broad plains in the central and southern parts of the continent—account for a prehistoric record that is spotty and uneven. Evidence suggests that the majority of early archaeological sites (i.e., Paleoindian and Early Archaic) have either been severely eroded or remain deeply buried as a result of hydrographic overhauls, broad-scale resculpting of terrain, and mobilization of great masses of Pleistocene sediment. Conversely, by the end of the mid-Holocene largely modern environments had been established and, not surprisingly, upper Late Archaic sites abound almost everywhere across North America. Accordingly, later prehistoric site alignments "map onto" contemporary plots of favorable resource and subsistence zones.

It follows that the 5000-year interval of mid-Holocene time was the "window of adjustment" during which postglacial environments stabilized, stream channels adjusted to renascent floodplains, hill and slope sedimentation rates diminished, and critical resource zones emerged. Along the coastal plains, estuaries, and inlets, sea level rise slowed appreciably and littoral-marine habitats assumed their present configurations. A systematic understanding of the prehistoric geography of the mid-Holocene is the key to explaining broad diachronic changes in paleoecology.

Current research converges around the complexity of climatic, biotic, and edaphic factors to explain the general thrust of southeastern mid-Holocene environmental change (Webb et al. 1993). For example, although it has been established that the 3000-year southward incursion of pine, beginning around 8000 B.P., realigned biotic communities, the reasons for the incursion are unclear; stadial or cyclical advances may have been regulated by changes in evapotranspiration (i.e., climatic causes) or by variability in soil types (Watts 1980; Watts et al., this volume; Webb et al. 1993; Wright 1983). Clearly, the effects of the midcontinental Altithermal, which produced warming and drying trends, were a contributing factor. Yet, while in middle Tennessee species-poor, xeric plant communities emerged at this time (Delcourt 1979), to the south and east wetland species began to dominate, perhaps due to Gulf Coast circulation patterns enhanced by rising sea levels (Delcourt and Delcourt 1985). Paleovegetation maps remain the most widely cited sources of data used for generating late Quaternary reconstructions for the southeastern United States. Geomorphic and geoarchaeological sources and observations are here drawn upon to provide an alternative perspective on mid-Holocene ecological variability. To date, no comprehensive landscape or stratigraphically based models have been advanced because the extant record is limited and poorly documented. Geoarchaeological research designs have not yet become standard tools even in larger scale archaeological investigations. Where regionally applied, however, they have furnished important new insights on questions of prehistoric and environmental succession.

In this review I abstract geoarchaeological interpretations from a variety of published sources as well as from my primary research in select subregions of the greater Southeast. Appropriate studies from cultural resource management (CRM) reports are utilized as well. Landscape sequences include only those preserving linked and stratified prehistoric and geological successions. Expectedly, as elsewhere in the Eastern Woodlands, landscape histories are developed from alluvial chronologies in trunk drainages, supplemented by several coastal and estuarine records. Finally, limited interpretations of upland sites are offered that integrate key periods of aeolian sedimentation and soil formation. Advances in process geomorphology underscore the potential of slope and wind-borne deposits for correlating mid-Holocene cycles of landscape evolution and occupation in nonalluvial settings. Unfortunately such approaches have not yet been widely applied to archaeological sites (although see Van Nest 1993), and until recently they have not been attempted in the Southeast.

Several regions of the Southeast remain incompletely understood geomorphologically. In particular, the Florida peninsula's diverse coastal settings are the product of active but asynchronic sedimentation processes during the Holocene (Davis et al. 1992). Landscape histories remain fragmentary and archaeological stratigraphies are only now being integrated with the marine and terrestrial chronologies of the past 10,000 years (Milanich 1994; Purdy 1992).

Regional Investigations

A survey of archaeological research spanning the area east of the Mississippi, south of the Ohio valley, to the Atlantic Coast and Gulf of Mexico discloses that broadly based settlement and landscape work has been undertaken in four key physiographic divisions (fig. 1-1; Fenneman 1938; Hunt 1974): (1) Lower Mississippi Valley and Embayment (Tennessee, Kentucky, Arkansas, Mississippi, and Louisiana); (2) Southeast Piedmont (Georgia and the Carolinas); (3) Southeast Coastal Plain (Georgia and the Carolinas); (4) Interior Appalachian Plateau drainages (Tennessee and Kentucky). This geographic bias in the investigative record is a function of contemporary landscape modification projects that have selectively subjected the above divisions to extensive CRM research. Most typically, reclamation and planning projects have involved dam and recreational lake construction.

The indirect impetus behind ecologically based prehistoric studies derives from the River Basin surveys in the middle part of the century. Especially prominent were the Lower Mississippi Valley surveys of the 1930s and 1940s, which demonstrated the relationships between changing floodplain geography and differential prehistoric settlement (Phillips et al. 1951; Phillips 1970). At the same time, pioneering late Quaternary investigations cautioned archaeologists that the Mississippi channel had undergone severe channel modifications in "prehistoric time" (Fisk 1944), a theme that was subsequently developed by Saucier (1964, 1974, 1981, 1994) in models of changing man/land distributions of the Lower Mississippi Valley and Delta. To a lesser degree, research in the Ohio and Tennessee basins of the Appalachian Interior (Webb 1946, 1950a; Webb and DeJarnette 1942) and the Carolina Piedmont (Coe 1964) alerted researchers to the strong links between landform successions and prehistoric settlement.

Over the past 20 years, more focused interdisciplinary research has isolated time-transgressive trends in the archaeological and geomorphic records. In the Lower Mississippi Valley, mid-Holocene alluvial sequences have been developed for the St. Francis basin (Guccione et al. 1988; Saucier 1964) and the Red River drainage (DeBusschere et al. 1989; Pearson 1986). More complex treatments have examined intricate base-level changes dictating tidal estuarine and stream successions in the Amite River basin (Autin 1993) and the deltaic lowlands (Britsch and Smith 1989; Frazier 1967; Penland et al. 1988). Models of human mobility, settlement logistics, and patterned variablility in the preservation record have been integrated into many of these landscape constructions.

In the Interior Appalachian Plateau, tributaries to the Tennessee have been exposed to extensive geoarchaeological treatments, beginning with the work of Chapman (1977), who exposed deeply buried Middle Archaic soils along the Little Tennessee. Long-term studies along the Duck River initially produced a detailed alluvial stratigraphy, replete with terrace and soil sequences, followed by a model of differential settlement and riverine resource utilization (Brakenridge 1984; Turner and Klippel 1989). The trunk stream immediately to the south, the Cumberland, was characterized by systematic erosional "gaps" during the middle Holocene, in response to changing channel geometry (Leach and Jackson 1987).

The southeastern Piedmont has been the location of some of the largest CRM projects undertaken in the eastern United States. Along the Savannah River, the

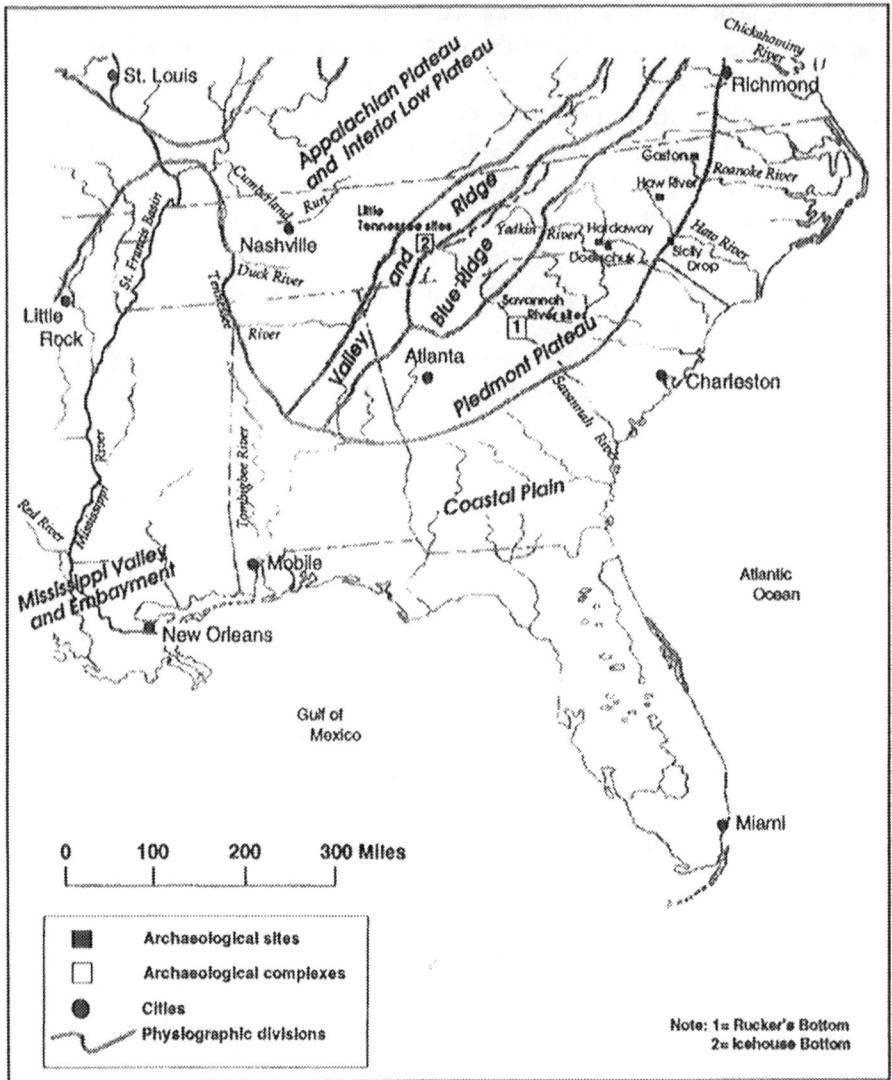

Fig. 1-1.   The southeastern United States showing physiographic divisions and sites mentioned in text.

Richard B. Russell Reservoir project produced three separate perspectives on Holocene landscape development and archaeology; these ranged from pedological (Foss et al. 1985) to geomorphological (Segovia 1985) and geoarchaeological (Anderson and Schuldenrein 1985; Schuldenrein and Anderson 1988). The Savannah River area has yielded one of few integrated archaeostratigraphic sequences spanning the entire range of known prehistoric occupation in eastern North America. A second deeply stratified succession was documented along the Haw River in North Carolina (Claggett and Cable 1982; Larsen and Schuldenrein

1990). Here a sealed mid-Holocene sequence facilitated comparisons and contrasts with earlier and later Holocene sedimentation regimes. Along the Roanoake River in the Virginia Piedmont, recent investigations have identified a buried fragipan ("Btx horizon") separating Early and Late Archaic horizons in mid-Holocene alluvium. The paleosol's pedogenic characteristics contrast with the underlying early and capping late Holocene profiles to signal a unique weathering environment for the period 8000–3000 B.P. (Blanton et al. 1994). Extensive work coupled with optimal archaeostratigraphic preservation accounts for the well-indexed Holocene sequences across the Piedmont and Appalachian provinces.

Conversely, Holocene profiles of the southeastern Coastal Plain are considerably less diagnostic. This is because much of the record is either submerged on the coastal shelf or inaccessible due to depth and groundwater problems. Typically, Holocene sediment accumulations are on the order of only 1–2 m and the isolation of riverine, estuarine, and littoral facies is often imperceptible in compressed stratigraphies. However, several offshore projects have produced dated sequences along the Gulf Coast (Coastal Environments, Inc. 1977). On the Savannah River, Coastal Plain models linking stream dynamics, Holocene sea level fluctuations, and settlement data have been applied from composite site records (Brooks et al. 1986; Goodyear and Foss 1992) and in detail at the Pen Point site (Brooks and Sassaman 1990). A variant of this model has been applied to the upper Southeast, in the Chesapeake Bay and Chickahominy drainage in eastern Virginia (Blanton, this volume; Schuldenrein and Blanton n.d.). Comparisons to Middle Atlantic and northeastern sea level and settlement data are warranted since reduced rates of sea level rise after 5000 B.P. implicate progressively less dynamic and more homogeneous shoreline changes along the length of the eastern continental shelf (Bloom 1983; Fletcher and Wehmiller 1992: Part II).

Figure 1-2 summarizes principal mid-Holocene valley histories across the four physiographic divisions, in geographic sequence from west to east. These are indexed against the culture chronology and the climatic episodes bracketing the interval (9000–2000 B.P.). For purposes of this study the onset of the mid-Holocene is equated with the upper Early Archaic and terminates with the Early Woodland period. Climatic episodes include the Atlantic and Sub-Boreal. Trends in valley history were assembled from dated alluvial, terrace, shoreline, and bay-mouth stratigraphies, benchmark soil chronologies, and reconstructed vegetation successions.

Only the most widely registered diachronic trends are highlighted for each division. It is stressed that correlation of valley trends between divisions must be tempered by appreciation of the geomorphic processes unique to each. Such processes reflect the interaction and limitations of regionally endemic physiographic, hydrographic, climatic, and edaphic mechanisms. In the Mississippi Valley and Embayment, extensive stream migrations are the product of broad drainage networks of numerous higher order streams that converge in distributary nets and

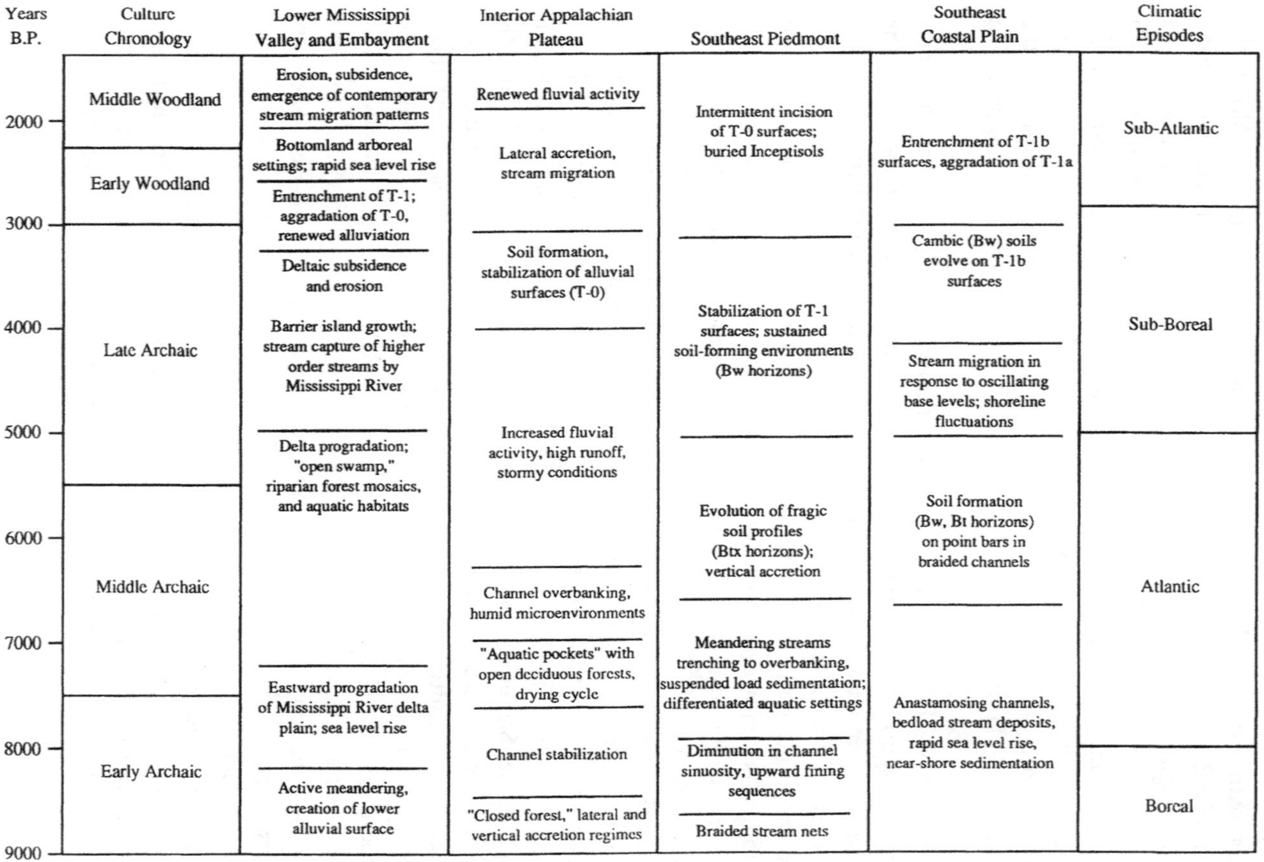

Years B.P.	Culture Chronology	Lower Mississippi Valley and Embayment	Interior Appalachian Plateau	Southeast Piedmont	Southeast Coastal Plain	Climatic Episodes
2000	Middle Woodland	Erosion, subsidence, emergence of contemporary stream migration patterns	Renewed fluvial activity	Intermittent incision of T-0 surfaces; buried Inceptisols	Entrenchment of T-1b surfaces, aggradation of T-1a	Sub-Atlantic
3000	Early Woodland	Bottomland arboreal settings; rapid sea level rise / Entrenchment of T-1; aggradation of T-0, renewed alluviation	Lateral accretion, stream migration		Cambic (Bw) soils evolve on T-1b surfaces	Sub-Boreal
4000	Late Archaic	Deltaic subsidence and erosion / Barrier island growth; stream capture of higher order streams by Mississippi River	Soil formation, stabilization of alluvial surfaces (T-0)	Stabilization of T-1 surfaces; sustained soil-forming environments (Bw horizons)	Stream migration in response to oscillating base levels; shoreline fluctuations	
5000		Delta progradation; "open swamp," riparian forest mosaics, and aquatic habitats	Increased fluvial activity, high runoff, stormy conditions	Evolution of fragic soil profiles (Btx horizons); vertical accretion	Soil formation (Bw, Bt horizons) on point bars in braided channels	Atlantic
6000	Middle Archaic		Channel overbanking, humid microenvironments			
7000		Eastward progradation of Mississippi River delta plain; sea level rise	"Aquatic pockets" with open deciduous forests, drying cycle	Meandering streams trenching to overbanking, suspended load sedimentation; differentiated aquatic settings		
8000	Early Archaic	Active meandering, creation of lower alluvial surface	Channel stabilization	Diminution in channel sinuosity, upward fining sequences	Anastamosing channels, bedload stream deposits, rapid sea level rise, near-shore sedimentaion	
9000			"Closed forest," lateral and vertical accretion regimes	Braided stream nets		Borcal

Fig. 1-2. Principal mid-Holocene valley histories across four physiographic divisions of the southeastern United States.

deltaic plains of a magnitude without parallel elsewhere. Appalachian stream systems are dominated by turbulent flow across steep thalwegs that produces
extreme erosional gradients and thick, consequent depositional basins over relatively short distances. Along the Coastal Plain, stream mouth sedimentation and
near-shore deposition may be active and convergent, but since net sedimentation
rates are low, the dynamism of the geomorphic system may be obscured. Finally,
Piedmont systems typically conform to the most direct model of graded upstream
erosion and downstream deposition, since fewer extrinsic controls are exerted on
these systems than on the others.

Division-specific constraints notwithstanding, several convergent and synchronic trends typify the mid-Holocene valley histories across the Southeast:

(1) The mid-Holocene (ca. 8500 B.P.) is signaled by a transition to lower-energy
    channel environments as braided streams give way to meandering rivers and
    stabilization of base levels; bedload sequences are succeeded by lateral accre-
    tion profiles.
(2) During the early mid-Holocene, sea level continued to rise rapidly as the Mis-
    sissippi River Delta prograded eastward; channel sinuosity diminished and
    stream beds in narrower valleys stabilized within their channels.
(3) After 7500 B.P. aquatic biomes emerged in the deciduous forests of the south-
    eastern interior; streams were progressively entrenched in their channels
    (even in broader floodplains of the Gulf and south Atlantic coasts); sus-
    pended load sedimentation dominated; systematic preservation of alluvial
    sites is registered (Interior Appalachian province).
(4) By 6000 B.P., near contemporary meander belts are established in most
    provinces with the exception of the Mississippi Valley, where open swamps
    emerge on the margins of prograded deltas; deep and strong to moderately
    weathered soil profiles preserved in the Piedmont and Coastal Plain ("Bw,"
    "Bt," and "Btx" horizons); second and first terrace surfaces (T-2 and T-1)
    have been downcut, depending on breadth and configuration of alluvial
    landscape; initial Late Archaic occupations.
(5) Renewed alluviation by 4000 B.P. in south-central divisions (Mississippi
    Valley, Interior Appalachians); fluvial dynamism accompanied by barrier
    island growth on the Gulf Coast and stream capture of high-order flow lines
    by the Mississippi; accelerated runoff and stormy climates; stream migration
    in response to oscillating base levels along the Atlantic coast; extensive Late
    Archaic habitation.
(6) At 3000 B.P. there is ongoing soil formation and stablization of 2–3 m valley
    surfaces (T-1 and T-0) everywhere but the Mississippi Valley; the latter is
    characterized by deltaic subsidence and entrenchment of T-1 and alluviation
    along emergent floodplains (T-0) within and beyond the trunk system;
    extensive and well-preserved alignments of Late Archaic sites with contem-
    porary drainage lines are present everywhere but in the Mississippi Valley.

(7) The late Holocene cycle of cutting and filling (2500–1500 B.P.) is character-
    ized by lateral accretion of new T-o surfaces (T-1a in Southeast Coastal
    Plain); Inceptisol profiles; bottomland arboreal environments (Mississippi
    Valley); a pulse in sea level rise promoting meandering and anastamosing
    channels at estuarine and delta mouths (Gulf and upper southeast Atlantic
    coasts); and by widespread but locally variable settlement of valley bottoms
    by Woodland populations.

(8) Contemporary valley surfaces emerge after 1000 B.P., variously capped by
    accumulations of postsettlement alluvium (PSA) in response to historic
    plowing and working of fertile bottomlands, accelerated slope erosion, and
    dam-regulated sedimentation; admixture of historic and late prehistoric
    assemblages in plowzone (Ap) horizons and coarse upper sands capping low-
    lying alluvial terraces and floodplains.

The role of climate in accounting for divisional variability in the mid-Holocene
alluviation and general landscape records remains multifaceted and is beyond the
scope of this paper. However, Knox (1983:31) underscores the significance of
regional edaphic systems during this pivotal interval when annual temperatures
were at their maximum (i.e., the Altithermal). Regional vegetation is perhaps the
single most critical factor, since the extent, density, and depth of cover are linked
to flood frequency and erosional regimes. Accordingly, mean annual sediment
yields and sediment concentrations responded differently to vegetation shifts by
region, because mean annual sediment yield is a function of flood frequency,
while annual sediment concentration reflects the efficacy of the vegetation cover
in retarding erosion. Since the largest order fluvial responses to biotic succession
occurred in the early Holocene, middle Holocene variability between regional
alluvial systems may be crudely gauged by reconstructions of paleo–storm systems
(indicative of discharge frequencies) and syntheses of pollen records. Elsewhere,
Knox (1983) has argued for increased occurrences of large floods in the northern
Midwest after 6000 B.P. This activity would presumably have been magnified
along the trunk stream (i.e., Mississippi River) in a downstream direction and is
consistent with arguments for mid-Holocene stream capture and realignments of
higher order tributary systems (fig. 1-2). The pollen record is equivocal, as Watts
et al. (this volume) note that climatic interpretations are uncertain for the Piedmont and Coastal Plain because the oak/herb to pine/swamp succession was stag-
gered and characterized by differential responses to climatic change. Webb et al.
(1993: fig. 17.17) are more direct and propose that across the Southeast generally,
there was a time-transgressive trend to desiccation between 9000 and 6000 B.P.
that advanced southward before reversing after 3000 B.P.

As the above discussion implies, the complexities of large-scale paleoclimatic
and landscape reconstruction do not converge around a comprehensive, integrated model of southeastern human paleoecology. I propose that the most compelling strategy for isolating linked landscape and occupation successions is

inductive. It begins with the landform sequence and archaeological stratigraphy of the Georgia–South Carolina Piedmont along the Savannah River; radiates outward to explore analogous spatial and vertical relations between sites and sediment columns within the same division (i.e., Piedmont); and then offers some guidelines for structuring investigations between divisions.

Mid-Holocene Geoarchaeology of the Savannah River Piedmont

Rich archaeological assemblages stratified within alluvial soils and sediments of the Savannah River first terrace (T-1) were investigated at seven archaeological sites (fig. 1-1; see Anderson and Schuldenrein 1985). Most sites preserved evidence for alluviation and soil formation for discrete, stratified components (table 1-1). The Paleoindian record is sparse and is confined to limited artifact assemblages. For the succeeding Early Archaic in situ contexts documenting the late Pleistocene–Holocene interface are Rucker's Bottom (9EB91) and Gregg Shoals (9EB259). The latter site contains a deeply stratified sequence, formed largely as a result of the high sedimentation rates occurring at the confluence of an alluvial fan with the primary stream (Tippitt and Marquardt 1984). It is not typical of primary depositional activity. More indicative of the valley sedimentation regime is Rucker's Bottom.

Terminal Pleistocene through Holocene Events

Figure 1-3 crosscuts Rucker's Bottom and illustrates the major sedimentation events and soil-forming periods along the floodplain terrace (T-1/T-0). The key disclosure was the succession of three major Archaic horizons spanning 7500 years in lithostratigraphic articulation. Since the total sediment accumulation from the base of the Early Archaic component—the lowest marker horizon—to the top of the sequence is only on the order of 1.3 m, it was possible to monitor the compressed Archaic succession carefully in the field. The Savannah, as a braided stream over the duration of the Holocene, differentially eroded and deposited sediment on altimetrically equivalent surfaces, often obscuring the significance of surficial relief. To control for lateral and vertical stratigraphic variability, the distribution and depths of the individual Archaic horizons were followed out.

The disposition of buried surfaces—most notably those defined by the terminal Pleistocene and mid-Holocene soils—does not diverge significantly from the contemporary ridge (fig. 1-3). Subsurface probes did, however, suggest microtopographic variations in the substrate, as, for example, over the Early Archaic component, which appeared at depths ranging from 80 to 130 cm. These discrepancies are attributable to localized recession of floodwaters and perhaps slight displacement of artifact provenance along graded slopes of the crest (Anderson and Schuldenrein 1985).

Table 1-1. Summary of prehistoric components and geoarchaeological contexts

Site	Prehistoric components	Geoarchaeological contexts and archaeostrata[a]
38AB22	Mississippian, Early Woodland, Late Archaic, Middle Archaic	Mississippian midden in buried context on outer levee (2); Early Woodland in terminal floodplain deposits (1, 2) on inner level; Late Archaic associated with inner levee Cambic paleosol (3a). Middle Archaic articulates with lamellar units (3b).
9EB75	Middle/Late Woodland	Cultural materials housed in interdigited buried A horizon and weak sheet midden on terrace-levee (2).
9EB382	Mississippian, Middle/Late Woodland, Early Woodland, Late Archaic, Middle Archaic, Early Archaic	Surficial manifestations on exhumed late Pleistocene terrace.
9EB76	Mississippian, Middle/Late Woodland, Late Archaic	Mississippian in disturbed (i.e, plowzone) context (1); Woodland and Archaic associated with terrace-levee Cambic paleosol and swale edge (2, 3a).
38AB288	Mississippian, Middle/Late Woodland, Early Woodland, Late Archaic, Middle Archaic	Mississippian and Woodland materials in disturbed or recently sealed alluvial contexts (1, 2); stratified Late Archaic assemblages preserved in both classic slackwater and ponding deposits and in underlying Cambic paleosol developed on low-energy flood silts (3a); Middle Archaic associated with Argillic paleosol in slough and lower-energy elevations and with silty bank sediments at outer levees (3b).
38AB91	Mississippian, Middle/Late Woodland, Early Woodland, Late Archaic	Mississippian and Woodland in matrix of stabilized floodplain surface sediments (1, 2); Late Archaic housed in Cambic paleosol (3a).
9EB91	Mississippian, Middle/Late Woodland, Early Woodland, Late Archaic, Middle Archaic, Early Archaic, Paleoindian (?)	Mississippian articulates with both extensive sheet midden and activity-specific features assignable to discrete occupational phases (1, 2) across terrace-levee and into swale edge; Woodland deposits are spatially localized on terrace-levee (2); extensive Late Archaic distributions on Cambic B profile documenting stabilized floodplain surface (3a); Middle and Early Archaic distributions on surfaces indicative of dynamic geomorphic imbalances, alternately registering episodes of soil formation (lamellae) and channel activity (vertical and lateral aggradation) (3b, 3c); Paleoindian associated with early Holocene gravel flow.

a. Refers to archaeostratigraphy for the Savannah River/Richard B. Russell sites (see fig. 1-3; Anderson and Schuldenrein, 1985).

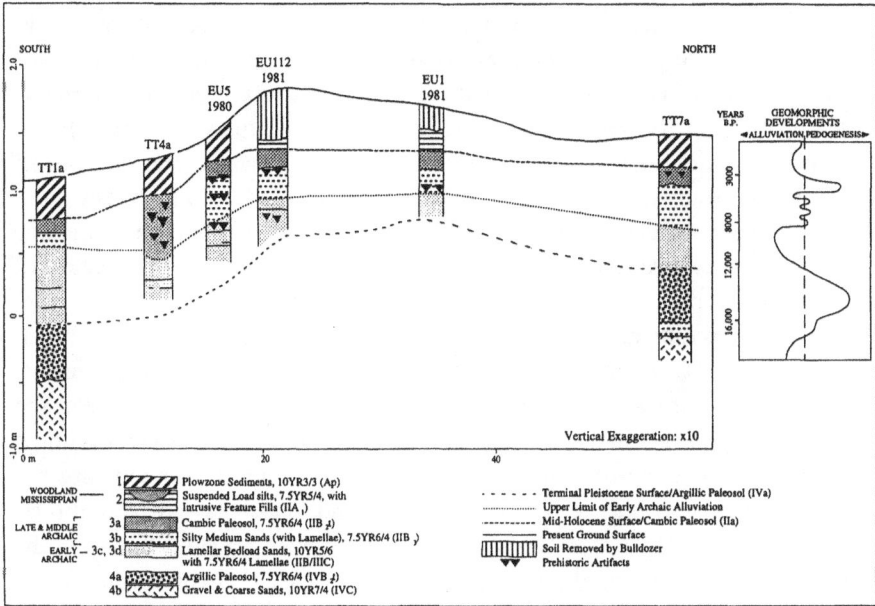

Fig. 1-3.   Geoarchaeological transect, the Archaic block at Rucker's Bottom (terrace-levee).

The most striking aspect of the earliest Holocene fills was their homogeneity, lateral extent, and consequently their long-term potential for stratigraphic correlation. They all occur in medium- to coarse-grained sands, not visibly bedded but reasonably well sorted and apparently tied to the same depositional regime and interval. Additionally, these sands occur below a distinct zone of laterally extensive mineralized bands. These "lamellae" are prolific at Rucker's Bottom and at most other floodplain sites along the Russell Reservoir (table 1-1). Stratification of lamellae suggests that if banding is pedogenic, a mid-Holocene (i.e., post–Early Archaic) interval of environmental stability is implicated. The uniform presence of bedload sediments at all Early Archaic exposures at Rucker's Bottom implies vigorous channel activity immediately prior to, or penecontemporaneous with, soil formation.

Middle Archaic profiles were also widely exposed across the sites with depths ranging from 50 to 155 cm. Bedding structures suggested that mid-Holocene stream flow was extremely sinuous and diagnostic of an expansive floodplain. Archaeostratigraphic indications were for a diffuse Middle Archaic occupation on a series of gently undulating floodplain rises and depressions. Variable entrenchment of the channel into underlying coarse Early Archaic deposits characterized a period of lateral planation. Subsequently, meandering and accompanying suspended load deposition established a new channel morphology and sedimentation pattern trending to long-term overbanking.

It was the Middle Archaic horizons that registered the most clustered distributions of the mineralized clay lamellae; these occurred as abrupt beds varying in thickness from 2 or 3 cm to as much as 10 cm. Landform support of pedogenic origins for the lamellae was the systematic expansion of level floodplain surfaces, upward fining of the sediment matrix, the broader confines of a meandering floodplain, and diminished vertical accretion. Collectively the ramifications of these changes translate into broader, more diversified, and simultaneously more stable surfaces on which soil formation proceeded. The floodplain habitat became increasingly attractive to more specialized prehistoric groups over the course of the mid-Holocene.

Subsequent sedimentation slowed appreciably and began resembling contemporary trends by Late Archaic times. These strata overlie Middle Archaic units by 10–25 cm. A systematic increase in the silt component and the redder hue of the sediment matrix suggested a more sustained pedogenetic interval than was noted for any previous prehistoric period. An extensive Cambic B horizon caps the mid-Holocene alluvium at Rucker's Bottom and underlies later prehistoric midden deposits. The upper Late Archaic soil/sediment graded diffusely to the parent material. Truncated surfaces, marked in Middle Archaic lamellae by sharper contacts, were absent. Progressive stabilization of occupation surfaces seemed a logical prerequisite to Late Archaic settlement systems since larger populations and more specialized activities had to be supported by the environment of exploitation.

The succession of alluviation, lamellar formation, and pedogenesis over the protracted period of Archaic floodplain occupation is replicated everywhere across the broad T-1/T-0 surface of Rucker's Bottom and is reinforced at other multicomponent Archaic sites along the Savannah River Piedmont (Anderson and Joseph 1988). To assess the changing energy of the alluvial environment through time, the differential sedimentation rates for each of the Archaic phases were measured at representative sections of 9EB91. Over the 7500-year interval of Archaic time, from 10,000 to 2500 B.P., net sedimentation was 75 cm, or an average of 1 cm/100 years. The results of segregating these data according to the separate Archaic components were as follows:

(1) Late Archaic: 20.0 cm/2000 yrs.   (1.0 cm/100 yrs.)
(2) Middle Archaic: 22.5 cm/2500 yrs.   (0.9 cm/100 yrs.)
(3) Early Archaic: 25.0 cm/1500 yrs.   (1.7 cm/100 yrs.)

It is noted that these results are site-specific, generic indices. They are measures of net sedimentation only (i.e., irrespective of differential erosion and degradation rates in the past, etc.) and lack precise radiometric controls. A general decrease in aggradation is observed up the sequence—to Middle and Late Archaic times—that broadly mirrors the synchronous trend to lateral accretion and stability through time. A corollary to these results is that sedimentation rates at Rucker's Bottom are slow, and that the propensity for preservation of largely in situ archaeological materials is correspondingly high.

Evidence from site sedimentological analyses confirms field observations and is illustrated in figure 1-4, a composite profile of site archaeostratigraphy. As shown, each cultural stratum presents a unique geoarchaeological signature, but up the 2 m profile, fully 1.3 m of bedload (below 3b) documents the earliest and most active sedimentary phases, from 14,000 to 8000 B.P. This is the signal indicator that overall channel behavior evolved within the alluvial landscape of the Pleistocene and early Holocene channel belt and that flow vectors did not diverge significantly in prehistoric time, despite changes in channel geometry.

The stratigraphic column is subdivided into four depositional units (1–4) offset by two paleosols (3a and 4a). Progressive fining characterizes the discrete depositions up the sequence. Unit 3 is the most pervasive and thickest accumulation, spanning Paleoindian to Late Archaic times. Minor soil-forming episodes are distinguished by the thin and crenulated red-brown lamellae. As noted, their origins are a function of pedogenetic transformations on discrete alluvial units (Dijkerman et al. 1967; Larsen and Schuldenrein 1990). Mineralogical enrichment proceeded on well-sorted medium- to fine-grained sands. The lamellae are the sole indicators of even limited soil formation over the 7000-year period of the early to mid-Holocene. Otherwise the entire central portion of the sequence records gentle but episodic floodplain accretion. Over this duration, sedimentation dominates over pedogenesis. The optimal period of soil formation dates to around 15,000–12,000 B.P., the age of the lower paleosol, unit 4a. The Rucker's Bottom sequence is a more detailed version of the Russell Reservoir–wide model outlined in figure 1-2 (see also table 1-1).

In terms of archaeological stratification, the distributions of the Archaic assemblages are relatively diffuse. This is a function of the mildly acidic composition of the substrate. Leaching of the prehistoric A horizons and their susceptibility to stripping would have degraded features and eliminated their sedimentary integrity and consistence. Localized displacement of artifacts by winnowing and recession of periodic floodwaters enhanced this trend. Only the later Woodland-Mississippian features preserved intact, organic cultural residues. Pre–Late Archaic components are more disjunct horizontally and vertically. A distinctive pre–Late Archaic anthrosol cannot be distinguished on sedimentological grounds.

Both sedimentological and pedological properties are highlighted by the graphs in figure 1-4. Acid-base balances (pH readings) remained fairly consistent and mildly acidic for the duration, but the organic matter curve displays significant variation with time. Values are high for upper (i.e., Late Archaic and subsequent) occupations housing preserved features; the fine-grained sandy matrix supported a forest cover and thin leaf litter horizon that resulted in rapid leaching at the level of the Cambic B horizon. Subsequent declines in lower Archaic levels attest to the poorly developed soil covers that were apparently subject to more inundation and sediment reworking. Organic values rise only in the Argillic B

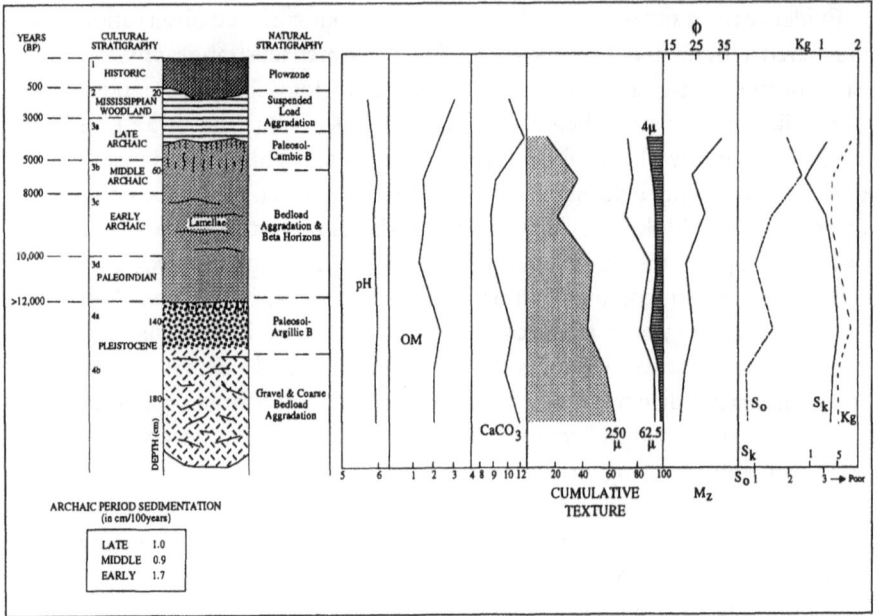

Fig. 1-4.   Composite stratigraphy, Archaic block at Rucker's Bottom.

horizon, supporting the terminal Pleistocene and erosional surface, which was a long-term and therefore stable marker horizon.

Perhaps the most telling index of change in the depositional regimen is the granulometric data illustrating the transition from bedload to suspended load aggradation up the column. Principal shifts occur in the relative proportions of the fine and medium sand grades (at 250 μ). By the end of Late Archaic times, finer grade sands and silts begin to dominate the sediment load. This marks a transition toward progressive floodplain stabilization, underscored also by the scaled reduction in sedimentation rates over the course of the Archaic (fig. 1-4). Mean particle sizes decrease to the top of the prehistoric column. The only bulges in the clay fraction occur in the paleosols, where illuviation was the dominant process. Sorting data show that sediment uniformity was the rule until over-banking and differential settling altered the depositional pattern around 8000 B.P.; sorting is best in the bedload aggradation units and worst in pedogenic units and overbank strata.

A final consideration involves the paleoclimatic implications of the alluviation phases, which peak during the intervals 10,000–8000 B.P., 5000–4000 B.P., and at 1500 B.P. Fluvial geomorphologists are divided as to whether high-level sedi-mentation attests to intensification or retardation of precipitation and attendant runoff. Most recent research suggests that in humid temperate provinces, cooler and wetter climates may result in reduced sediment yields and consequent erosion and incision of primary channels, or at least channel enlargement (see Schumm 1977: table 5-2). Conversely, in situations with increased sediment yield, such as those implicated by the two alluviation peaks, slightly drier and warmer conditions than those favoring soil formation would have prevailed. The major alluviation cycles bracket the Altithermal (8000–5000 B.P.). If that phase reliably dates a warm-dry peak, then the pattern of climatic changes recorded by the floodplain stratigraphy at the Rucker's Bottom terrace-levee may best be viewed as a continuum with optimal warm-moist conditions prevalent in pedogenesis phases and alluviation bridging a transition to cooler and drier environments.

Perspective on the Mid-Holocene

It is the Late Archaic Cambic paleosol that is the most pervasive natural sedimentary unit (archaeostratum 3a). The utility of this archaeostratum is that it is a chronostratigraphic benchmark even in the absence of diagnostic archaeological assemblages. Table 1-1 illustrates the pervasiveness of the Cambic soil; it articulates with Late Archaic occupations at five of the seven sites examined along the Russell Reservoir.

Below the paleosol, both the prehistoric and geologic stratigraphies vary the length of the reservoir, in part because of the relative dynamism of the early Holocene channel that differentially eroded selected floodplain segments. Intact Middle Archaic deposits have been noted at four of the sites while the Early Archaic is present at two (table 1-1). In no case did the cultural materials appreciably alter the natural matrix of the alluvial fills or associated weathering profiles. Correlations across sites corroborate the model for an upward fining sequence established at Rucker's Bottom, intermittently disrupted by minor intervals of soil formation over approximately a 6000-year span (10,000–4000 B.P.). As discussed earlier, the primary evidence for soil formation derives from pedomorphic interpretations of lamellae following the emergence of stabilized surfaces on graded beds atop lateral accretion deposits.

The only major period of soil formation across the Savannah River Piedmont occurred between 4000 and 3000 B.P., near the end of the mid-Holocene and at a time consistent with the reversal of Altithermal conditions. These results are consistent with most recent vegetation constructions positing a northward expansion of effective moisture belts in the Southeast (Webb et al. 1993). These are the conditions sustaining the evolution of the Cambic paleosol in midlatitude environments (Birkeland 1984; Bunting 1967; Buol et al. 1988). Weak, moist pulses influencing the shifting pedosedimentary balances during the interval 8000–5000 B.P. are accordingly manifest in the closely spaced lamellae as discussed earlier (see also Foss and Segovia 1984). Previous reconstructions of the prehistoric floodplain at Rucker's Bottom have suggested that by Altithermal times, slowing alluviation regimes promoted by medium energy streamflows and a migrating stream exposed broader floodplain surfaces (Segovia 1985); this promoted expansion of extensive vegetation mats, soil formation, and the proliferation of the lamellae. Research by Knox (1983) across the Eastern Woodlands indicates alluviation rates had slowed in most areas east of the Mississippi River by 8000 B.P. Thus, moderately moist conditions may have persisted in the Southeast. On a finer scale it is suggested that the lamellar pulses may calibrate these developments (Larsen and Schuldenrein 1990).

Regional Correlations:
From the Piedmont to the Appalachian Plateau

As noted, the past ten years have generated both methodological advances in geoarchaeology and an ever increasing database of deeply stratified Archaic sites along major floodplains of the Southeast. The record is most extensive for the two interior divisions, the Piedmont and Interior Appalachian plateaus. Pioneering investigations by Coe (1964) in the Carolina Piedmont and by Broyles (1971) in West Virginia have been supplemented by cultural resource mitigations along the Haw River and Richard B. Russell reservoirs, among others. These studies provide the baseline for expanding the scale of geoarchaeological investigations from local to regional levels.

To examine mid-Holocene developments, three stratified floodplain Archaic complexes were considered: (1) Savannah River Piedmont sites (Anderson and Schuldenrein 1983, 1985); (2) Haw River sites in the North Carolina Piedmont (Claggett and Cable 1982; Larsen and Schuldenrein 1990); (3) Little Tennessee River sites of the Appalachian Plateau (Chapman 1976, 1977). Figure 1-1 illustrates the geographic settings of these complexes. Both the Haw and Savannah River sectors drain the southeastern Piedmont, while the Little Tennessee is in the Ridge and Valley province. The Piedmont streams are aligned south-southeast, emptying onto the Coastal Plain, while the Ridge and Valley lines trend south-southwest into the Mississippi Valley. Piedmont elevations are significantly lower than those of the Ridge and Valley and topography is considerably gentler; the catchment of the Little Tennessee ranges from some 2000 to 700 feet (610–215 m) while the Piedmont basins of both the Haw and Savannah span elevations from 800 to 200 feet (245–60 m).

Physiographic and topographic controls therefore account for significant variability in drainage density, channel dynamics, and alluvial geomorphology and sedimentation patterns. The implications of basinwide and interdrainage differences have been examined by numerous investigators (Butzer 1980; Knox 1983; Leopold et al. 1964; Schumm 1977), who adopt a wide range of views on the merits of broad comparisons. In expanding the level of consideration to the regional scale, however, it is useful to outline measures of commonality and patterning and to explore potential correlations that are often obscured by localized and overly parochial approaches based on site-specific reconstructions.

A case in point is the initial model formulated by Coe (1964) for Piedmont alluvial prehistoric sequences, which was locked into an evaluation of two narrow floodplain segments of the Yadkin–Pee Dee and Roanoke rivers (fig. 1-1). Coe's explanation emphasized *local* deposition and floodplain morphology to explain differential archaeological distributions at the stratified Hardaway, Doerschuk, and Gaston sites. Coe (1964) inferred that since microbasins formed at rock-shielded eddies and preserved features, analogous mechanisms were active across the Piedmont. The shortcomings of such a circumscribed approach were dramatically illustrated at the Haw River, the drainage intermediate between the Roanoake (Gaston site) and Yadkin–Pee Dee (Doerschuk site). Here investigations demonstrated that both the time factor and depositional hydrodynamics along an extensive portion of the drainage must be understood to explain differential sedimentation (C. E. Larsen 1982). Thus, the deeply buried sequence at Haw River occurs in a broad floodplain, a situation essentially precluded by Coe. At Haw River a drainagewide geological investigation was initiated, in which it was found that a major tectonic feature (the Indian Creek Fault Zone) created the depositional basin responsible for accumulation of the alluvium and artifact-preserving fills.

At Icehouse Bottom along the Little Tennessee drainage, Chapman (1976, 1977) also accounted for accelerated sedimentation rates at bottoms locations by implicating "eddy formation" at isolated meander belt constrictions. While this is a similarly local, site-specific argument, it incorporates updated information on paleoclimatic chronology to establish and date the sequence of floodplain events. Most crucial to the explanation of differential preservation, however, is the fact that changing floodplain morphology and stream mechanisms along the length of the Little Tennessee are reflections of active river dynamics that accelerate progressively downstream. It follows that at such steeply graded streams as those of the Ridge and Valley province, extreme erosion and incision upstream correspond to active and abrupt deposition and meandering downstream. Consequently, differential sediment accumulations and optimal conditions for archaeological site preservation document basinwide hydrological changes.

The utility of this basinwide approach in such regional studies is that it facilitates recognition of principal similarities as well as differences among the three drainages. Figure 1-5 shows the relative positions of the site complexes along their changing river gradients. This is a "logistic index" of Archaic site placement. Archaeological site location at a particular river segment provides crude indications of preferential habitats and settlement strategies that simultaneously mirror river dynamics the length of the gradient. Figure 1-5 demonstrates that for each of the site complexes—irrespective of physiographic context—preservation is optimal at gradient inflection points (i.e., note uniform slopes for floodplain segments of Archaic sites). Thus, by examining the site in its general hydrographic setting, it may be possible to piece together those mechanisms of site preservation that have far-reaching implications for settlement reconstruction. On the basis of figure 1-5, some site-locational properties are readily apparent:

Joseph Schuldenrein

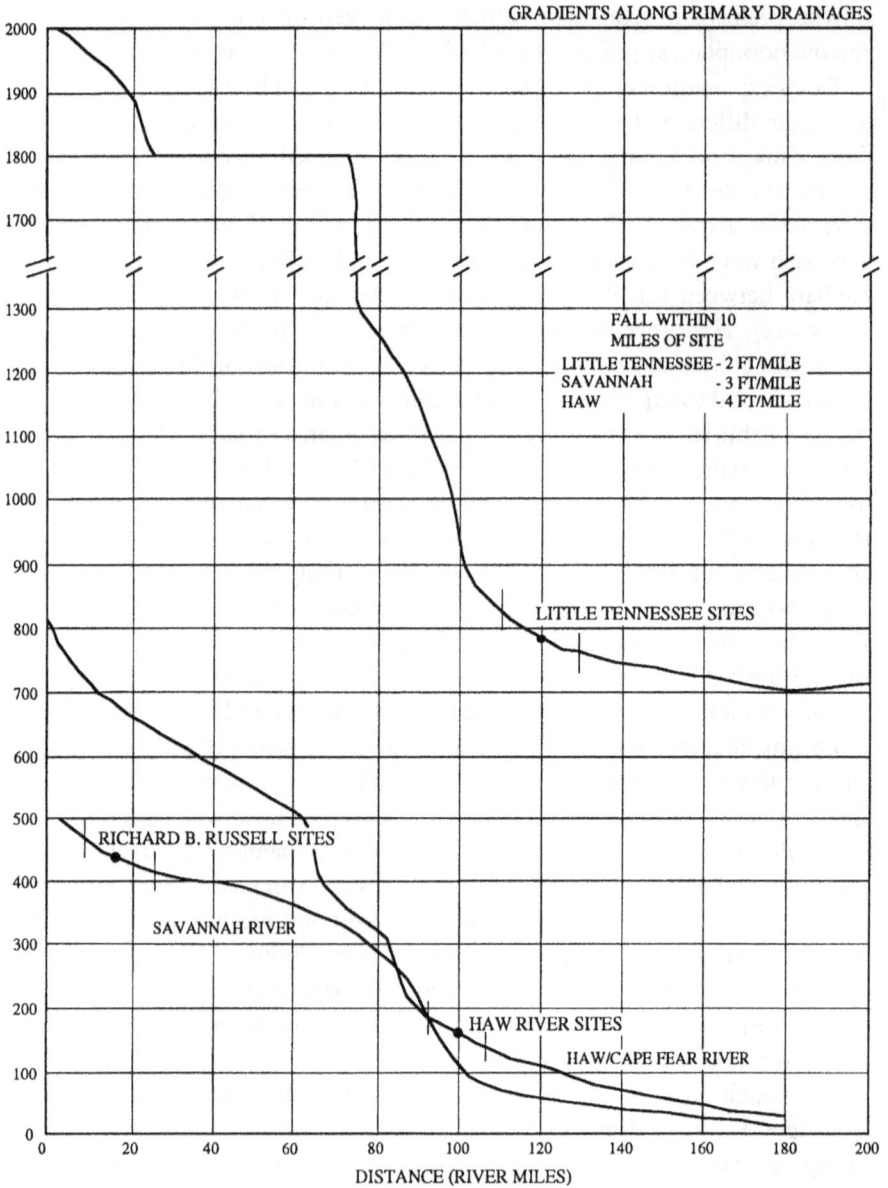

Fig. 1-5. Gradients along primary drainages of three southeastern floodplain sites.

(1) Sites occur where depositional basins are the norm and gradients are sub-
    dued. These pockets are generally downstream, except along the Savannah,
    but here the gradient is uniformly gentle.
(2) Steep fall and erosion compensated by deep downstream sedimentation
    (Appalachian) accounts for more disjunct patterns of site preservation than
    those featured across subdued terrain (Piedmont), where linearly extensive

but vertically reduced sediment thicknesses are the norm. The former dynamic explains the behavior of the Little Tennessee River as it reaches base level and the confluence with the Tennessee. Dramatic morphologic changes can occur abruptly when critical erosional and/or depositional thresholds are exceeded. This is an especially crucial consideration in explaining abrupt, blocklike Archaic sediment accumulations versus the more progressive, gradual, and diminished buildup of the less dynamic Piedmont streams.

As stressed above, regional-scale comparisons necessitate appreciation of a multiplicity of variables including landform configurations, floodplain width, thalweg, channel geometry, runoff patterns, stream dynamics, and vegetation cover. Relationships among these variables are often problematic (Kochel 1988; Leopold et al. 1964; Schumm 1977). For calibrating these often complex relationships chronologically, the most diagnostic parameters available are evidence for: (1) *sedimentation rates* (gauged by time-depth controls using archaeological assemblages as stratigraphic indicators [see Ferring 1986]), and (2) *soil forming processes* (disclosed by the presence of relict features, in this case the lamellae, that overprint sediment matrices containing the mid-Holocene archaeological assemblages under consideration). Both parameters were examined in detail for and aided in the reconstruction of the sequence at Rucker's Bottom on the Savannah River (see discussion above). They are applied to compare the pedosedimentary profiles of the three locales under consideration.

At the Piedmont site complexes, the earliest major diagnostic cultural horizons are Early Archaic and occur in medium- to coarse-grained sands, apparently tied to a relatively uniform depositional regime. These sands are coarsest below the zone of lamellae formation. The presence of bedload sediments at Early Archaic exposures implies vigorous channel activity at this time. Middle Archaic depths, especially at Rucker's Bottom, are the most variable because they are associated with a series of surfaces. Progressive diminution in mean grain size is typical and argues for gentler and probably less competent stream flow. Evidence derived from recognition of paleotopographic gradients implicates variable entrenchment of the channel into underlying coarse Early Archaic deposits and characterizes a period of lateral planation across the floodplain. After this time, meandering and accompanying suspended load deposition resulted in differentiated floodplains that were relatively broad and featured drastically reduced sedimentation levels.

The Middle Archaic horizons mark the appearance of the mineralized clay lamellae. Previously cited arguments for the pedogenic origins of these strata implicated a meandering floodplain and diminished accretion rates, especially toward the top of the sequence. There is no evidence of sustained soil formation (i.e., Bt horizons) in this portion of the Piedmont. More stable floodplain habitats became increasingly attractive to more specialized prehistoric groups. By Late Archaic times, sedimentation rates and patterns slowed appreciably and began resembling contemporary trends.

As discussed, Icehouse Bottom's location in more accentuated terrain and its dynamic fluvial system created a deeper, more pronounced mid-Holocene sequence; more than 3 m of sediment accumulated over 2500 years. Earliest occupation began around 9500 B.P. and floodplain construction continued through the Middle Archaic. The site is located on the first terrace of the south bank of the Little Tennessee River along an extremely sinuous river segment, perhaps signifying a former island setting. Aggradation at Icehouse Bottom is characterized by episodic blocklike depositions with cultural and natural strata displaying more abrupt textural and structural displacements than at the Haw or Savannah River sites, as well as clearer stratification.

Despite dramatic differences among site settings and their fluvial dynamics, and channels, all register analogous vertical successions. These are signified by synchronous breaks in the sedimentation and pedogenic regimes depicted in figure 1-6. Synchroneity in the geoarchaeological record is initially discernible in the recurrent geological cycles registered across all three profiles.

As shown, each site incorporates geologically sealed Archaic occupations buried by progressive fining of sediments up the sequence. Active deposition is cyclically disrupted by pedogenic lamellae. Vertical sediment bodies display alternating intervals of "pedosedimentary equilibrium." This is a concept that has been recently explored by geoarchaeologists assessing the paleoclimatic implications of changing relative dominance of pedogenesis and sedimentation in floodplains (Ferring 1992; Waters 1992). Accordingly, at given stages active net deposition ceases and stabilization ensues, marked by a variable degree of soil development. Stabilization is typically disrupted by an erosional phase, after which deposition resumes. While the magnitude and intensity of any given phase varies among the sites, general trends are parallel through time. Patterned variability and similarities among sites are illustrated by the mid-Holocene/Archaic period pedosedimentary profiles.

In site-specific terms, Rucker's Bottom features the most compressed depositional record with the lowest net sedimentation rates, and while the occupations are tied to the lamellae, the compactness of the profile often blurs the relationship. Fortunately, the geomorphic studies showed that the lamellae were associated with a period when the floodplain was laterally extensive and supported a more differentiated habitat. Lamellae are clustered at the Early/Middle Archaic stratigraphic boundary. Recurrent flooding may have impeded the formation of deep pedogenic profiles (i.e., with Bt horizons).

At Haw River there is a much deeper accumulation and a more complex sequence of lamellae. The most closely spaced and thinnest lamellae are situated at the Early/Middle Archaic interface, coincident with the most crowded occupations. These abundant lamellae are indicators of relatively low sedimentation rates. The data show a major drop-off in Haw River alluviation intensity prior to Middle Archaic times (Larsen and Schuldenrein 1990).

At both Piedmont locations, relatively low sedimentation rates are registered for the Archaic, but it is significant that the Early Archaic, with its bedload-rich

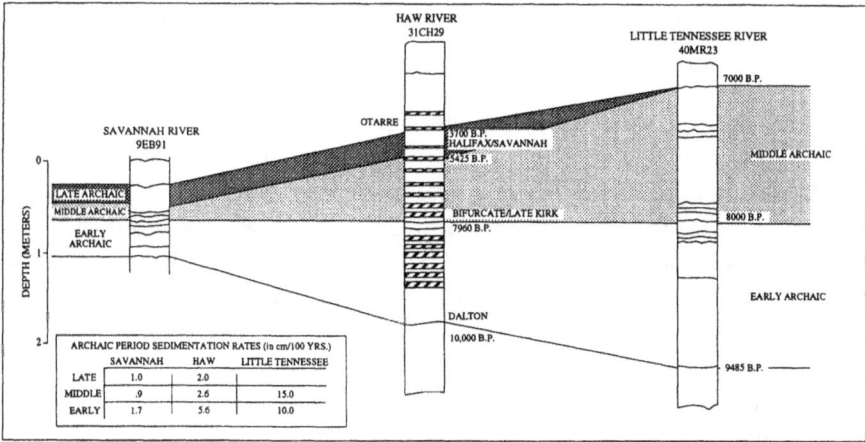

Fig. 1-6. Archaic period pedosedimentary profiles at three southeastern floodplain sites.

sediment load, features twice the deposition of the Middle and Late Archaic periods. This may be an indicator of the desiccation trend documented for the early Holocene across the Eastern Woodlands and would substantiate contemporary hypotheses linking such trends to higher alluviation rates (Knox 1983; Schumm 1977).

At Icehouse Bottom the aggradation rates underscore contrasting trends. Net accumulation is much more rapid than at Piedmont sites and intensifies with time. This may be attributed to a stream regime that is more episodic with a high degree of periodicity. Major thicknesses of sediment are embanked against terrace edges as well as erosional unconformities (Chapman 1977). The evidence signifies more massive, episodic, and punctuated deposition than the subdued but recurrent alluviation along the Haw and Savannah floodplains; the latter, as indicated earlier, were semicontinuous overbank accumulations, intermittently disrupted. Stream behavior along the Little Tennessee was governed by such hydraulic variables as the deepening slope, increased sediment load, and changing entropy or stream energy levels. Episodic deposition on inside banks or point bars resulted in the variable deposition rates along this stretch of the river. It is not surprising then that the stratigraphic column is typified by cultural strata separated by irregularly spaced sterile horizons sometimes including derived cultural materials.

Nevertheless, all sequences converge around the clustering of lamellae in the middle of the sequence where they are distinct but closely spaced vertically. They are also clearly linked with unique occupations. Lamellae clustering may signify increased frequency—and perhaps less intensity—of site occupation. Figure 1-6 suggests that at Icehouse Bottom, as at the Haw and Savannah rivers, lamellar formation is most active at the Early/Middle Archaic interface, or during the lower mid-Holocene, around 8000 B.P. The lamellae disrupt an otherwise rapid rate of deposition.

In summary, three major mid-Holocene trends are evident in alluvial sequences across the southeastern interior:

(1) Sedimentation modes, patterns, and rates along Piedmont streams are, expectedly, different in intensity and magnitude from those of the Appalachian Interior due to variable stream dynamics. Piedmont streams flowing along gentler gradients are distinguished by overbank sedimentation suites over the course of the mid-Holocene. Streams discharged progressively finer sediments. Early Archaic deposition was much greater than that of subsequent periods and was associated with relatively coarse bedload. The Appalachian Interior basin supported high-energy river systems, the dynamics of which were governed by intense upstream erosion and episodic and abrupt downstream aggradation, reflecting sharply defined geomorphic thresholds.

(2) There is a cyclical pattern for mid-Holocene floodplain development that may crosscut physiographic boundaries in the Southeast. Major streams feature sustained but progressively lower-energy sedimentation regimes followed by intervals of stabilization. Cycles end as soil development ensues and is succeeded by erosion. There is a periodicity of floodplain buildup and lamellae formation that diminishes and disappears around 3000 B.P.

(3) The archaeological stratigraphy underscores a clustering of lamellae at the Early/Middle Archaic stratigraphic boundary. This period may have witnessed minimal deposition and floodplain stabilization on an extraregional scale. There is a correlation between the shifting pedosedimentary balance and the prehistoric record. Episodic mid-Holocene alluviation punctuates periods of intensive occupation. The major break in the 5000-year mid-Holocene record is the pervasiveness of a soil at the Early/Middle Archaic boundary, around 7500 B.P. At this time stable and broad floodplains were dominant across much of the southeastern interior.

Consistent with regional observations, this reconstruction supports the hypothesis that the Altithermal was heralded by increasing sedimentation rates as erosional conditions were accelerated and the climate assumed a warming-drying aspect (i.e., by the close of Early Archaic times). New patterns of geomorphic equilibrium set in over the interval 8000–5000 B.P. as floodplains stabilized and shorter term pedogenic-sedimentation cycles dominated. The correlation between lamellae and artifact density at this time may argue that drier conditions encouraged prehistoric groups to cluster at floodplain locales.

Aeolian Environments: Terra Incognita

Only limited research has explored the implications of aeolian sequences for reconstructing landscape history for the past 10,000 years. This is because fossilized dune fields are typically considered the most reliable barometers of paleo-climatic change across ancient environments; most such fields formed during the Pleistocene across North America (McKee 1979). Additionally, archaeological manifestations are seldom geologically sealed. Cyclical deflation commonly causes sites to "collapse down" in indistinguishable multicomponent sediment matrices often composed of residual lags and wind-polished artifact clasts.

The potential of elevated sand sites to inform on prehistoric paleoecology and settlement has recently been explored in a variety of upland settings, chiefly by archaeologists working along the upper Coastal Plain of South Carolina (Taylor et al. 1994), North Carolina (Braley and Benson 1994), and Virginia (Blanton 1994; Pullins 1994). These regions, generally spanning the footslopes of the Pied-mont, are locally referred to as Sandhills and consist of reworked Miocene and Pliocene marine sediments in elongated and parabolic dunes.

A recent geoarchaeological study at a Sandhills site in Hoke County, North Carolina, proposes that a dynamic equilibrium between soil formation and defla-tion may account for at least intermittent, if not widespread, preservation of uplands mid-Holocene sites (Braley and Schuldenrein 1993). Site 31HK140 is a temporary Early to Middle Archaic camp, the integrity of which was largely pre-served by "upbuilding" of a spodic paleosol—a soil type formed in the pine forest environment—for at least 5000 years. Close examination of the weathering pro-file disclosed bisequal horizonation (Buol et al. 1988), a pedogenic sequence in which two stacked but discrete soil successions were separated by an unlike horizon. Figure 1-7 illustrates the relative uniformity of the sedimentological and geochemical signatures of the archaeosedimentary profile. Significantly, how-ever, covarying trends in mobile iron (Fe) and artifact concentrations suggested that while progressive accumulation of sands generally kept pace with weathering and resulted in upward migration of weathering zones, peak soil-forming envi-ronments may coincide with the terminal occupation, perhaps at the close of the Late Archaic (Braley and Schuldenrein 1993:44–46), around 3000 years ago. This is consistent with the turn to moister conditions at the close of the mid-Holocene.

While net sedimentation in this Sandhills environment was minimal, close monitoring of coeval pedogenic and artifact density trends shows promise for merging reconstructions of prehistoric succession and environmental change. The 31HK140 study underscores the potential of microstratigraphy and site for-mation studies to integrate even subtle Holocene occupational histories and landscape chronologies. The stratigraphic backdrop of increasingly refined and comprehensive alluviation records furnishes the much needed benchmark chronology.

Summary and Conclusions

Geoarchaeological research across the southeastern United States is beginning to yield a wealth of information on landscape change, settlement systematics, and

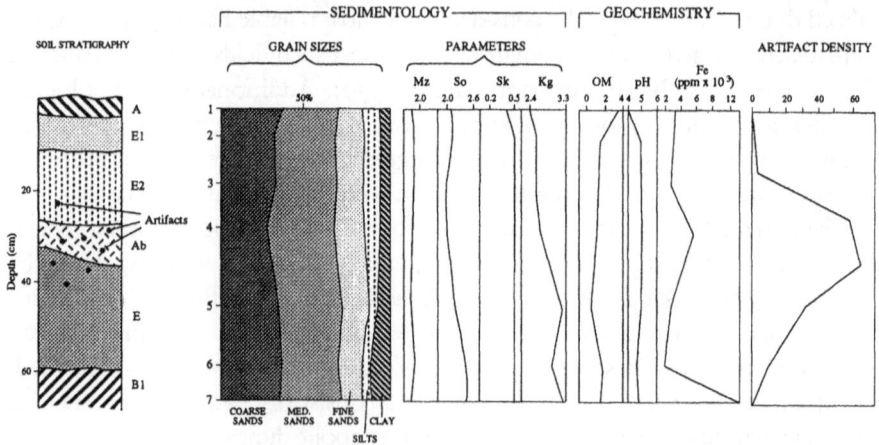

Fig. 1-7.   Results of soil sediment analysis, 31HK140.

archaeological preservation. Correlations between landform and occupational histories are evident for the duration of mid-Holocene time. Earlier investigators attributed coeval trends in the geomorphic and site distribution records to the overriding effects of the Altithermal; the warm and dry interval between 8000 and 5000 B.P. was recognized as the central event dictating human adaptive strategies for confronting environmental stress.

Over the past 20 years, interdisciplinary Quaternary research has been undertaken in many areas not previously investigated. These studies emerged as a result of large-scale cultural resource management programs. A regional focus was adopted in the study of prehistoric and environmental change that suggested that vegetation and landform successions were regionally variable and perhaps even asynchronic across the Southeast. Careful geomorphic models have also been generated, but these feature a dominant regional focus as well. Attempts to synthesize the most compelling earth-science-based paradigms center around the alluviation records and soil-forming profiles of four major provinces: Lower Mississippi Valley and Embayment; Southeast Piedmont; Southeast Coastal Plain; and Interior Appalachian Plateau.

For the mid-Holocene, several synchronous trends are apparent that crosscut physiographic divisions. These may be summarized as follows:

(1) *Onset of mid-Holocene: 8500 B.P.* Postglacial reduction in sea level rise is accompanied by a leveling of stream gradients and diminution of stream competence as braided, bedload-rich streams give way to meandering rivers that feature lateral accretion regimes.

(2) *7500–6500 B.P.* Entrenchment of many stream systems in their present channels occurs as lateral accretion is succeeded by channel overbanking; moderately

weathered soil profiles are characteristic; for trunk streams, Middle Archaic site alignments are traceable over discrete valley segments.

(3) *4000–3000 B.P.* First terrace (T-1) systems are stabilized and Late Archaic settlement complexes proliferate along terraces and floodplains across the Southeast.

(4) *End of mid-Holocene: 2500–1500 B.P.* A new cycle of cutting and filling marks a reduction in base level and development of T-0 surfaces; Woodland populations selectively utilized these surfaces.

Various different lines of evidence suggest that transformations to alluvial systems are a function of changing evapotranspiration budgets, sediment yields, and flood discharge regimes. These mechanisms are largely, but not exclusively, climate forced. Consequently, variability between regional valley systems mitigates against de facto projection of alluviation and soil chronologies and requires finer resolution of regional chronostratigraphies.

Accordingly, a stratified, mid-Holocene geoarchaeological sequence along the Savannah River Piedmont serves as a baseline for modeling stable vs. dynamic events as well as archaeological preservation gradients for this critical region of the Southeast. Results converge around a significant period of soil formation at the transition between the Early and Middle Archaic (7500 B.P.). Soils are recognized by clustered stacks of lamellae.

These lamellae and deeper alluvial packages are present elsewhere in the southeastern interior, specifically in the Appalachian Plateau. This region is topographically and physiographically distinct from the Piedmont. However, the presence of analogous geoarchaeological sequences verifies the effects of climatic transition across regions. Trends in alluviation, discharge, and floodplain construction appear to be regionally regulated, but extrinsic mechanisms trigger threshold changes in these systems. These extrinsic mechanisms appear to be extraregional in scope. Recent studies of archaeological sites in nonalluvial settings (i.e., aeolian mantled uplands, hillslopes, and colluvial margins) offer possibilities of incorporating such successions within the broader frameworks established by alluvial and archaeological chronologies.

It is proposed that an inductive methodology be applied to integrate the growing base of geoarchaeological sequences across the Southeast, with landscape histories emerging from the site-specific to intersite and thence to regional and extraregional levels of investigation. The integration of such data sets is imperative if Quaternary scientists and archaeologists hope to expand the scale of prehistoric research.

2

Mid-Holocene Forest History of Florida and the Coastal Plain of Georgia and South Carolina

WILLIAM A. WATTS, ERIC C. GRIMM, AND T. C. HUSSEY

The history of the Holocene forests of the southeastern United States has been established by pollen-analytical studies of pond and lake sediments from sites in Florida, Georgia, and South Carolina. The method has advantages and limitations. It gives a broad regional picture of the development of the forest cover through the Holocene, but it is less capable of discriminating small-scale local events. It is unlikely to yield specific information about archaeological sites except in the rare cases where a habitation site immediately adjoins a small lake or pond (McAndrews 1988; McAndrews and Byrne 1975). In such cases, evidence of human presence may be provided by pollen and macrofossils of cultivated plants or by charcoal (Clark 1988), concentrated in sediments representing a short period of time. Pollen studies in the Southeast have been carried out in small lakes and ponds rather than in larger lakes, which have the disadvantages of integrating pollen carried in by streams from a wide region and of presenting greater technical difficulties in coring. Studies have also been carried out in peat deposits, where the pollen counts reflect the peat-forming plants growing at the site as well as regional upland vegetation, but where pollen preservation may be unsatisfactory because of peat oxidation during times of low water (Jacobson and Bradshaw 1981).

Lakes and ponds occur commonly in the Florida peninsula and in the Coastal Plain of Georgia and the Carolinas. Most lakes in the region began as limestone sinkholes, but in South Carolina the predominant lake and swamp type is the Carolina bay, the origin of which is still somewhat controversial. The analysis by Thom (1970), which shows that bay formation is related to deflation and shaping of shallow lakes by strong glacial-age winds, is now accepted by most scientists.

The slow sedimentation rates recorded from bays in South Carolina (Frey 1954) means that pollen studies have had relatively low resolution and the possibility of hiatuses. In comparison with the Coastal Plain, the Piedmont (Jackson and Whitehead 1993) and higher mountains of Georgia and the Carolinas have few natural ponds or bogs and there is insufficient material available for study. Finally, although the potential fossil flora is large, in practice the number of species that produce abundant preservable pollen is small, fortunately including the great majority of trees. Unfortunately, three genera, *Pinus* (pine), *Quercus* (oak), and *Taxodium* (bald cypress), as well as being abundant in the field, produce so much pollen that they collectively provide 70–80 percent of the mid-Holocene fossil pollen found, thereby diminishing the resolution that a larger range of genera might provide. *Pinus* and *Quercus* both have numerous species with diverse ecological preferences. Oak, in particular, ranges from small shrubs in well-drained soils to large trees of mesic forest.

The Holocene pollen record from the southeastern Coastal Plain and Florida reveals a simple picture of the replacement of oak and herbs by pine and swamp plants in the mid-Holocene (Watts and Hansen 1988). It is believed that the early Holocene vegetation consisted of oak forest or oak-dominated scrub with low diversity in woody species and occasional openings dominated by herbs with affinities to modern prairie. In the mid-Holocene, expanding pine replaced oak and there was an extensive development of swamps and lakes. The climatic regime under which oak/herb vegetation existed and the type of climatic change that took place in the mid-Holocene must be established in order to understand the environments in which early humans lived.

It is known that most lake basins of sinkhole type in the Southeast were dry in the early Holocene and that only lakes with a substantial water depth today (ca. 20 m) are likely to have contained water and deposited sediments as far back as 10,000 years before present (B.P.). Few lakes with such water depths today are known. The water table was low, as much as 18 m below today's levels in south-central Florida as the Holocene began (Watts and Hansen 1988). The water table rose to begin to fill lake basins from about 8000 B.P. and has continued to rise steadily with some variation in rate to the present day. The ratio of precipitation to evaporation was such as to allow the slow recharge of the water table in the early Holocene but did not permit the development of a complete cover of mesic forest trees. It seems probable that precipitation was less than today's, but the causes are imperfectly known. One cause is certainly the effect of solar radiation differences from the present (Kutzbach and Webb 1993), which tended to result in the early Holocene in warmer summers and colder winters than today, changing to essentially modern values by 6000 B.P. At present the Florida peninsula has predominantly summer rainfall with a dry winter season. It is possible that the seasonal rainfall distribution differed from today's in the early to mid-Holocene but such a distribution has not yet been modeled and would be linked to different ocean-surface temperatures and ocean-current patterns. At first sight the rising sea level may have contributed a water table rise (Watts and Hansen 1994) by reducing the gradient of flow from the aquifers to the sea, but as the vegetation cover has varied independently of sea level, which was still very far down as vegetation changes began to take place (Fairbanks 1989), it seems more probable that vegetation has been responsive to regional climatic change only.

A number of examples illustrate the water level change. At Little Salt Spring (Clausen et al. 1979; fig. 2-1) in southwest Florida, a cenote some 60 m deep, the water level rose from –26 m to approximately present levels between 12,000 and 8500 B.P. It then fell 8 m by 5500 B.P. and subsequently rose to its present level once more. The neighborhood of the cenote was occupied by Archaic period people after 6800 B.P. Peat-forming plant communities began to develop marginal to the cenote after 8500 B.P. (Brown and Cohen 1985), recording the rise of water in the cenote to flood the surrounding land. A drying trend recorded in the peaty sediments began after 8000 B.P. and peaked about 7000 B.P. at Little Salt Spring (Brown and Cohen 1985; Clausen et al. 1979). This has not been observed elsewhere but is not inherently improbable. It requires studies in marginal sediments of lakes—usually the deepest points are chosen for study—to detect sedimentary records of changing lake level (Digerfeldt 1986). There is also evidence for late Holocene water table fluctuation during the development of the Everglades (Gleason and Stone 1994).

Buck Lake in south-central Florida (fig. 2-1) is another cenotelike shaft with deep water today. Water entered the bottom of the shaft shortly before 8270 B.P. and a shallow pool was colonized by water lilies, which deposited peat rich in water lily seeds, especially of *Brasenia* (water shield). The water depth at this time was probably 1–2 m. Subsequently the water level rose to its present depth of 17.4 m and the water lily peat was buried under lake mud that is still forming today. Other sites show similar basal dates to that of Buck Lake. Sedimentation began at 8160 B.P. at Mud Lake, at 8510 B.P. at Lake Louise near the Georgia-Florida state line (Watts 1971), and at 7290 B.P. at Lake Barchampe, also on that border (fig. 2-1).

Lack of surface water in much of the Florida Peninsula and the southern Coastal Plain in the early Holocene has implications for early humans in that it would have been necessary to live beside cenotes, near the shores of what are now deep lakes, or on riverbanks, for the major rivers would still have run, even at lower rates of discharge. It is possible that much archaeological material has been irretrievably buried under lake deposits as lake levels rose.

In South Carolina at Clear Pond (Hussey 1993), sedimentation was uninterrupted from glacial times to the present. The site, noted by Thom (1970), is a small pond, apparently a sinkhole, near to the coast in an area rich in fossil dunes and close to a large concentration of Carolina bays (fig. 2-1). The glacial sediments are sandy, resulting from wind-driven sand in an open environment. The Holocene sediments are lake muds with a proportion of sand and silt. Other sites in the Carolinas and Virginia (Frey 1954; Whitehead 1965, 1981) also have

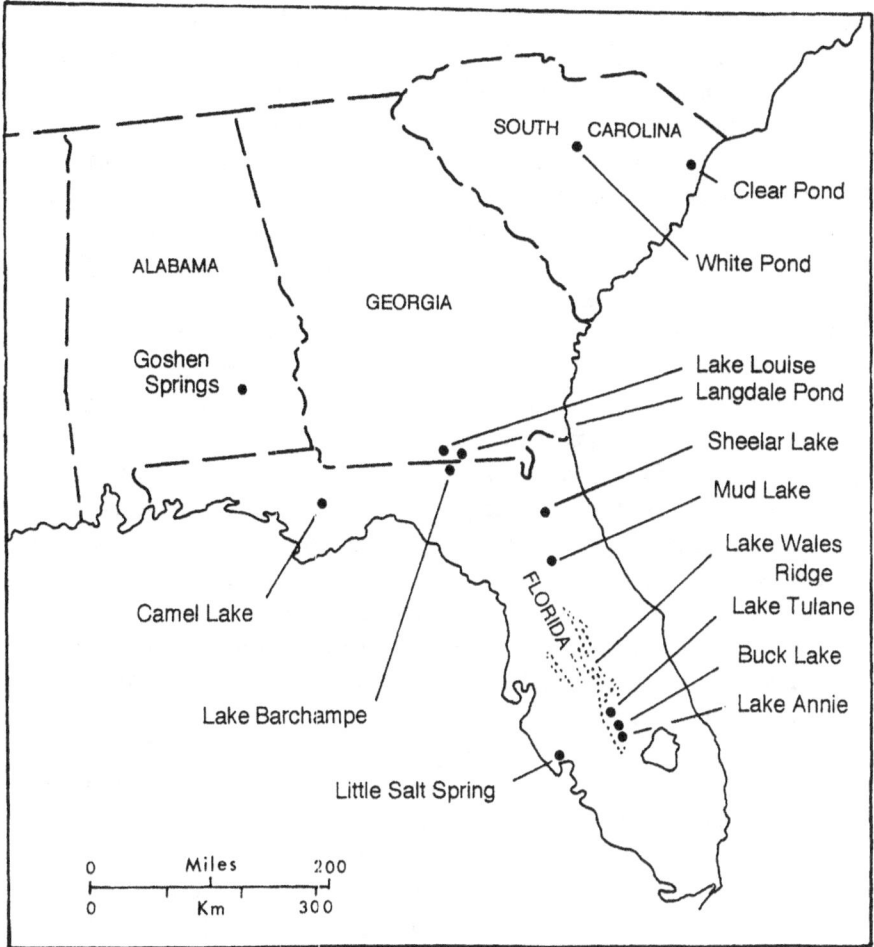

Fig. 2-1. Location of pollen sites reviewed in text.

continuous sedimentation. Evidently, early to mid-Holocene dryness was more pronounced in Florida and the Georgia Coastal Plain than farther north, where climatic conditions today are different with less seasonal differentiation and considerable winter precipitation.

The Pollen Diagrams

The pollen diagrams (figs. 2-2–2-7) are presented in a uniform style, drafted according to the Tiliagraph computer program developed by Grimm (1992). With minor exceptions, the diagrams record the same genera and in the same order at all the sites. This enables comparisons to be made at the cost of some loss of detail due to the omission of infrequent taxa. Uncorrected radiocarbon dates appear in the text as years before present (B.P.). Standard errors can be found on the pollen diagrams. Three sites, Clear Pond, Langdale Pond, and Lake Barchampe, are reported here for the first time. Buck Lake has been referred to briefly (Watts and Hansen 1988), but its pollen diagram has not been published. Mud Lake is substantially redrawn from Watts (1969) and only Lake Louise (Watts 1971), a key site, is repeated with little change. With the exception of Clear Pond, where the base of the diagram is dated to 10,000 B.P., all the sites began sedimentation early in the Holocene. At Lake Louise and Mud Lake, the Holocene sediments are separated by a hiatus from underlying much older organic sediments, possibly of interglacial age.

All the sites begin with a period of oak domination associated with herbs. Grasses (*Poaceae*), ragweed (*Ambrosia*), composites (Asteroideae), and chenopods are characteristic. Hickory (*Carya*) is associated with oak maxima at Lake Louise (fig. 2-2), Lake Barchampe (fig. 2-3), and Clear Pond (fig. 2-4). A scrub species, *Carya floridana,* occurs on sandy soils in south-central Florida, but large tree species also occur throughout the region in both mesic and dry forest. Superficially, Clear Pond is like the Georgia and Florida sites, but its oak maximum is associated with mesic trees such as beech (*Fagus*) and the hornbeams (*Ostrya/Carpinus*). This is a transitional forest from a more mesic predecessor in which beech was abundant before 10,000 B.P. Oak dominance lasted from 10,000 to 8500 B.P. at this site. A similar record is available from White Pond on the upper Coastal Plain of South Carolina (Watts 1980).

Modern analogs for oak/herb pollen spectra are lacking in the Southeast because of the abundance of pines, especially *Pinus palustris* (longleaf pine), which dominated the natural forests at the time of European settlement. The nearest analogs today are to be found in the prairie-forest border in the Midwest, where oak stands are mixed with prairie in vegetation that has evolved under the influence of frequent fires (Grimm 1983; McAndrews 1966). Florida today contains species representative of widespread prairie genera such as *Liatris, Dalea, Eriogonum,* and *Petalostemon,* species now isolated from the great prairies of the central United States but suggesting a biogeographic relationship at some remote time. It is not held to be likely that Florida's climate closely resembled that of the prairie-forest border in Minnesota, but the prairie analog implies a regime of colder winters and drier, hotter summers than at present, as is also indicated by orbital considerations (Kutzbach and Webb 1993). Unfortunately, no studies are yet available of fossil charcoal in lake sediments, which would define fire frequency at this time.

The oak/herb plant communities were replaced by pine forest in the mid-Holocene. Longleaf pine was probably the main forest dominant and largest pollen producer in southern Georgia and northern Florida, but it is rare or absent south of central Florida, where it is replaced by *Pinus elliottii* (slash pine) and, on fossil dunes, by *Pinus clausa* (sand pine). In the Coastal Plain of the Carolinas, *Pinus taeda* (loblolly pine) is common today and probably played an important part in the Holocene forests with longleaf pine and yet other pine species. Natural

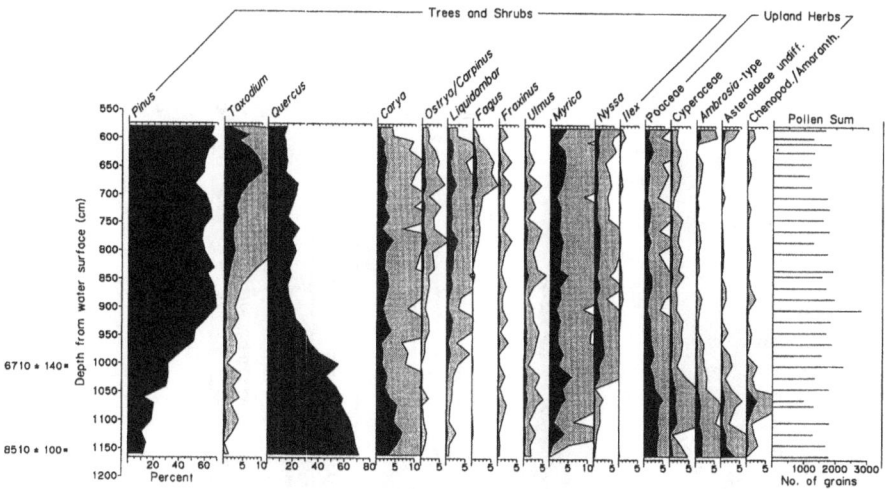

Fig. 2-2.   Pollen diagram for Lake Louise, Lowndes County, Georgia. Analyst: W. A. Watts.

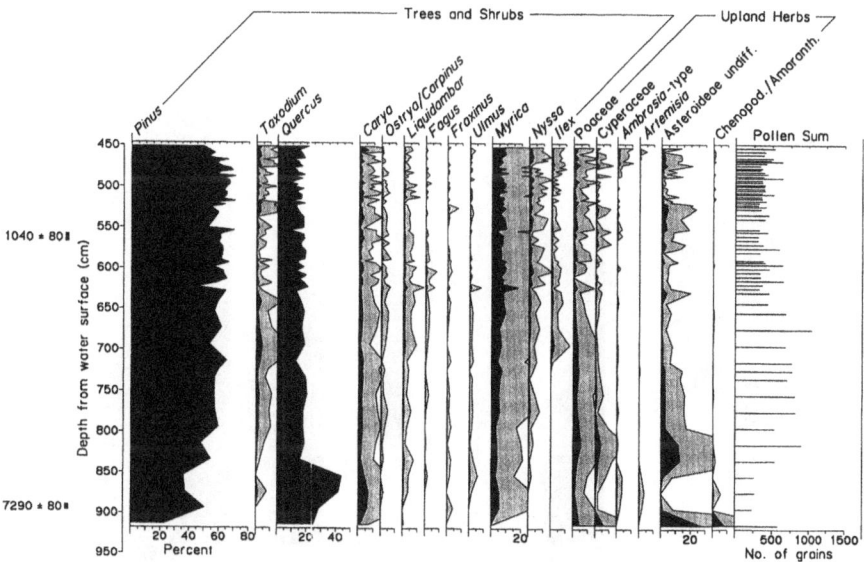

Fig. 2-3.   Pollen diagram for Lake Barchampe, Hamilton County, Florida. Analyst: B. C. S. Hansen.

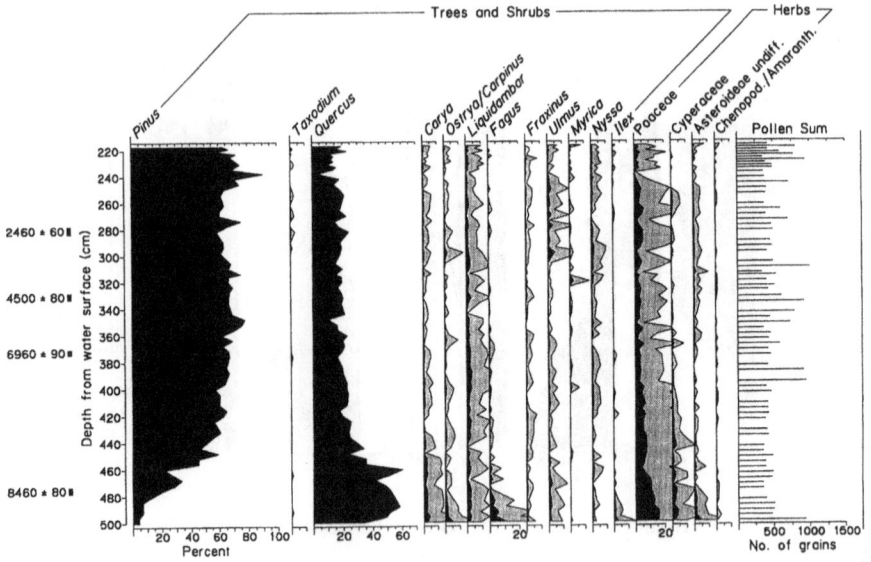

Fig. 2-4.   Pollen diagram for Clear Pond, Horry County, South Carolina. Analyst:
T. C. Hussey.

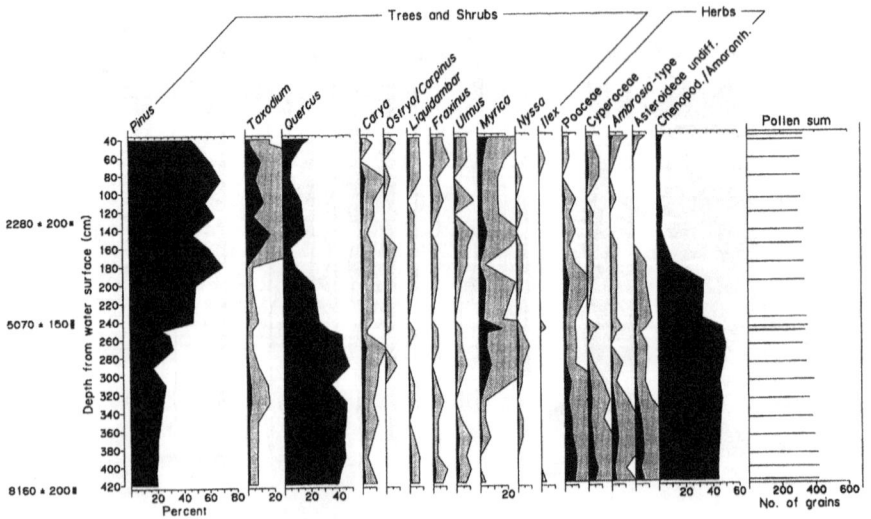

Fig. 2-5.   Pollen diagram for Mud Lake, Marion County, Florida. Analyst:
W. A. Watts.

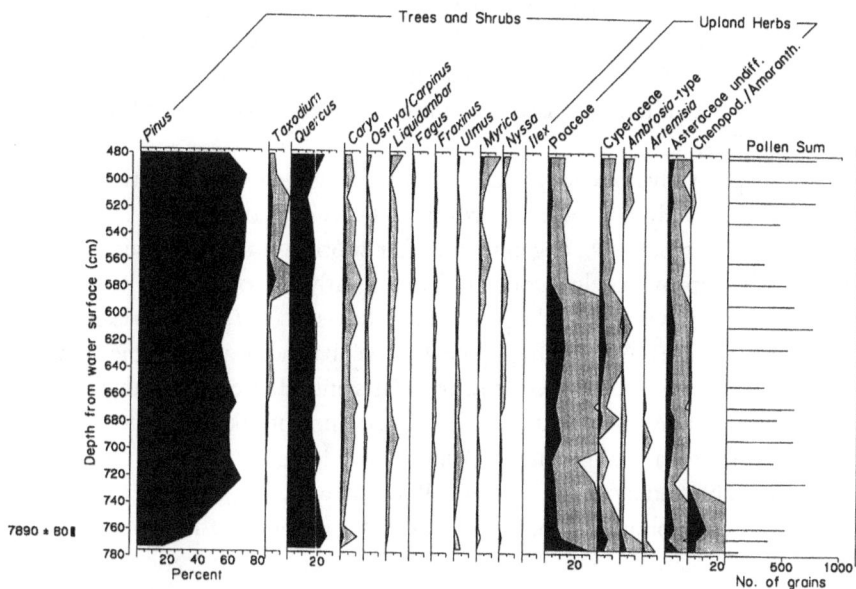

Fig. 2-6.   Pollen diagram for Langdale Pond, Lowndes County, Georgia. Analyst: B. C. S. Hansen.

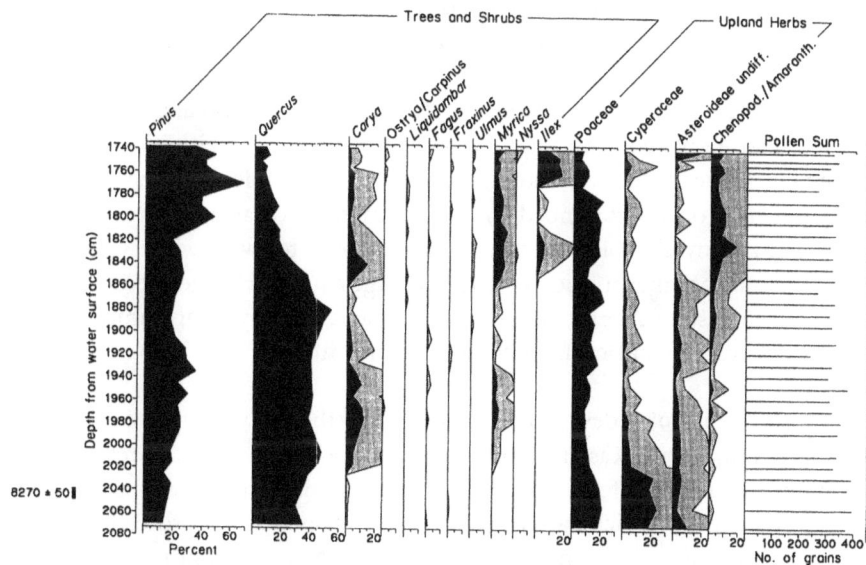

Fig. 2-7.   Pollen diagram for Buck Lake, Highlands County, Florida. Analyst: R. Nickmann.

lightning-caused fires are well known to be important in the maintenance of pine forest ecosystems in the Southeast today. It is probable that present-day radiation levels and seasonality had been achieved by 6000 B.P. (Kutzbach and Webb 1993), bringing warmer winters and cooler summers than in the early Holocene, with high summer precipitation caused by thunder showers accompanied by frequent lightning strikes.

There are probably not enough radiocarbon dates to date the initiation of pine dominance accurately. The best time control, at Clear Pond (fig. 2-4), shows that pine was low at 10,000 B.P., began to rise after 8460 B.P., and had achieved present levels by approximately 8000 B.P. This is early in comparison with Lake Louise, where pine was low at the profile base (8510 B.P.) but began to exceed oak by 6710 B.P. (fig. 2-2). A stable high pine–low oak balance was not achieved until approximately 5000 B.P. At Sheelar Lake (Watts and Hansen 1994) this balance was achieved about 6000 B.P. At Mud Lake the decline of oak is dated to 5070 B.P. (fig. 2-5). At Lake Barchampe (fig. 2-3) and Langdale Pond (fig. 2-6), pine dominance was established by about 7000 B.P. Buck Lake (fig. 2-7) appears to record a long and late oak dominance, but without dates it is possible that sedimentation in the cenotelike site was faster in the early Holocene when aquatic plants were abundant in shallow water than later when deep water was established. At Lake Annie in southern Florida (Watts 1975), pine dominance was established by 4715 B.P. and at Lake Tulane, in the same region (Grimm et al. 1993), a date of 4650 B.P. is available. This suggests that the substitution of oak by pine took place much later in the south than in northern Florida and especially than in the Carolinas.

At Lake Louise and Mud Lake bald and/or pond cypress (*Taxodium distichum/ascendens*) increases at about 3000 B.P. (figs. 2-2, 2-5). At Lake Louise there is a further increase in *Taxodium* in the recent past, perhaps the last 1000 years, suggesting a further rise in the water table. The development of great swamps such as Okefenokee and the Everglades (Cohen 1973; Gleason and Stone 1994) was initiated about 5000 years ago. Large peat-forming swamps in the Southeast resulted from the continuing water table rise of the late Holocene. Their invasion of the upland probably continued until it was limited by drainage works in recent times. The late invasion of beech at Lake Louise points to cooler winters (Huntley 1993) and may be an expression of Little Ice Age climatic change. Beech is most successful in eastern North America where mean January temperatures range from –10°C to 5°C and mean July temperatures from 17°C to 24°C (Huntley 1993).

Jacobson et al. (1987) developed a technique for the study of rates of change in the vegetation cover of eastern North America from 18,000 B.P. to present. The technique can integrate fossil pollen data from a number of sites within a region to reveal the times at which the reorganization of vegetation was proceeding most rapidly in response to climatic change. In eastern North America (Grimm and Jacobson 1992), the middle Holocene appears as a time of slow change in the vegetation cover, without large-scale, short-term events. This is consistent with the evidence, for example, from Lake Louise that the replacement of oak by pine was a slow and steady process occupying up to 3000 years.

Conclusions

The new studies reported above confirm the already well established pattern of oak/herb vegetation being replaced by pine/swamp vegetation in the mid-Holocene of Florida and the Georgia Coastal Plain. The expansion of pine to a new stability was achieved first in South Carolina by about 8000 B.P., last in southern Florida by about 4500 B.P. This suggests a relatively slow change in climate from north to south, but climatic interpretation is open to uncertainty because different species of the common tree genera were involved, and they do not necessarily respond equally to climatic change. There are also site factors such as soil type to be considered and there is not at present a sufficient number of radiocarbon dates for satisfactory chronological control. The rate of change from oak/herb to pine/swamp was slow, probably occupying up to 3000 years at some sites; change, although steady and unfaltering, would probably not have been observable in one human lifetime.

There are major differences between sites in South Carolina and in southern Georgia/Florida. The oak/herb phase occupies less time in the north, so that it becomes the 2000 years or so in which mesic trees had largely disappeared before pine expanded. In contrast, southern Georgia and the Florida peninsula show substantial homogeneity during the more extended time (up to 6000 years) in which oak/herb vegetation was present. South Carolina must be regarded as a distinctive climatic and vegetational province that does not conform to the patterns from farther south.

The oak scrub or forest with prairie openings was ecologically suitable habitat for large game. Most modern lakes were dry, but deep cenotes contained water. Economies based on hunting large game may have been favored at this time. There may have been some lakes or ponds dependent on perched water tables above the main aquifers, and as long as the aquifers were recharged, water would have flowed out as springs, forming rivers as happens today. It is not likely that access to water provided a serious problem for early humans except in very local contexts. As the modern lakes filled in the mid- to late Holocene, all problems of water availability vanished, and new food-gathering, fishing, and hunting economies were increasingly possible as wetland expanded.

The climate of the late Holocene is easy to establish. It is essentially the modern one with abundant summer rainfall derived from thundershowers. The late appearance of beech at Lake Louise may suggest a somewhat lowered winter temperature in recent centuries, but, by and large, the period of pine domination has had a climate similar to today's. The earlier Holocene seems to have had colder winters and warmer summers than today with reduced precipitation. We do not know whether this was a relatively small difference from the modern climate or a large one. Was the seasonality different with reduced summer and increased winter rainfall? We cannot at present state the distinctive local boundary conditions that would enable the early Holocene climate to be modeled. In this context, it would be of interest to know whether early Holocene lake sediments have a lower charcoal frequency than those of the late Holocene. A lesser indication of natural fires would point to a climate in which summer thundershowers were less significant.

One somewhat disappointing feature of the data is the extent to which pollen of pine and oak, representing many species of both, masks the expression of other genera in the fossil record. Future research, in addition to improving time resolution by increased numbers of radiocarbon dates, will need to focus on increasing the resolution of our plant data by larger counts of the less common species and by the study of plant macrofossils. This will enable the distinctive local characteristics of sites to be identified in the fossil record. For example, the slopes around Lake Barchampe are covered by mesic woodland, but the regional abundance of pine pollen masks that woodland's presence in the pollen record. Palynologists will continue to welcome opportunities to link records of early humans to the pollen record where, for example, occupation sites adjoin lakes or ponds. These will help greatly in placing early human occupation in its exact ecological context.

Acknowledgments

We wish to thank Barbara C. S. Hansen for carrying out pollen analyses at Lake Barchampe and Langdale Pond, Rudy Nickmann for his study of Buck Lake, and James Almendinger for his assistance in the field at Lake Barchampe and Langdale Pond. The work was supported in part by grants from Trinity College, Dublin, and by NSF Grant DEB-902265 to E. C. Grimm.

Section II

Technology

The vast majority of items in the material record of Archaic period hunter-gatherers in the Southeast consists of flaked stone tools and the by-products of their manufacture and use. Modern analytical approaches to flaked stone tool technology are the subject of chapter 3 by Daniel S. Amick and Philip J. Carr. Their focus is on organizational studies of Middle and Late Archaic lithic technology, studies built upon the ethnoarchaeological research of Lewis Binford. Amick and Carr describe the conceptual underpinnings of organizational studies, showing how variation in the production, design, and use of stone tools is related to environmental structure, settlement mobility, subsistence strategies, and social organization. They summarize efforts to apply organizational theory and method to lithic assemblages in the Southeast. Despite regional differences in the environmental parameters that influence organizational strategies, they note a consistent shift toward more expedient technologies in the Middle Archaic period, accompanied by use of smaller territories but also by higher rates of residential mobility. This is followed by increased use of curated technologies coupled with a rise in logistical mobility and the use of specific, often nonlocal raw materials. Importantly, this shift, while panregional in scope, was not synchronous, unlike technological changes associated with the Pleistocene-Holocene transition. A more varied, complex picture emerges, one that no doubt will continue to be elucidated through the methods and theory of technological organization.

Innovations are what enable archaeologists to recognize disjunctures in culture history. The development of ground and polished stone tools was long believed to mark the transition from the focused hunting of the late glacial and early postglacial era to the generalized foraging of the mid-Holocene. Bruce Smith (1986) makes a convincing argument to the contrary by showing that mid-Holocene ground and polished stone tools had technological precedents in the Early Archaic period. In chapter 4, however, Kenneth E. Sassaman argues that ground and polished tools became important media for shaping and manipulating interpersonal alliances, and in this sense embodied something of a social innovation. He reviews observations on the form, contexts, and distributions of bannerstones and grooved axes to document patterns that cannot be interpreted in environmental or microeconomic terms alone. This is further manifested in the variegated patterns to the adoption of durable, heat-resistant vessels, one of the more conspicuous innovations of the late mid-Holocene. Across the board, innovations apparently did not emerge spontaneously and simultaneously to meet the local needs for food capture or processing, nor were they patterned strictly after pathways and rates of group interaction. Rather, Sassaman maintains that they arose from social demands that varied among societies of the Southeast, that such demands were embedded in ritual and ceremony, and that such contexts could either inhibit or promote change, depending on circumstances that were independent of tool function or efficiency.

In chapter 5, Sassaman and R. Jerald Ledbetter examine evidence for Middle and Late Archaic architecture. Only recently have we begun to appreciate the range of built structures used during the mid-Holocene, including relatively substantial houses with prepared clay floors, wall posts, and internal hearths or earth ovens. Most of the examples of substantial architecture come from sites with independent evidence of intensive occupation, such as thick midden accumulation, numerous graves, and diverse material culture assemblages. However, many sites with such evidence lack traces of structures, supporting the long-standing notion that mid-Holocene houses were insubstantial affairs that are virtually invisible in the archaeological record. Sassaman and Ledbetter review the now appreciable body of evidence for ephemeral structures, including cases inferred from the indirect evidence of artifact distributions. They also introduce new evidence for upland pithouses dating to the Late Archaic period. The existence of elaborate architecture at upland sites brings into question assumptions about season of occupation, site reuse, and territorial circumscription. Although few definitive conclusions can be reached at this point, there are enough examples of structures to begin addressing issues of seasonality, household size, co-resident size, and community layout. A great deal of variation in structure size, permanence, and positioning is apparent already, and efforts to interpret this variation have only just begun.

3

Changing Strategies of Lithic Technological Organization

DANIEL S. AMICK AND PHILIP J. CARR

The utility of an organizational approach to understanding southeastern lithic technology during the mid-Holocene is the focus of this chapter. This approach is founded largely upon observations of technological behavior gained through ethnoarchaeological research among subsistence hunters. The most valuable contribution of viewing technology in organizational terms is that it provides a body of theoretical knowledge for structuring the analysis of lithic artifacts. Such a strategy emphasizes the development of theory capable of explaining variation in archaeological materials. This theoretical structure for lithic analysis encourages the integration of lithic remains with other types of archaeological data in relation to ecological parameters. Proposed theoretical relationships among technology and prehistoric mobility, land-use strategies, and settlement organization are especially important endowments of the organizational approach. The relationship between organizational and social strategies is explored in some recent research.

Studies of technological organization have resulted in many recent methological and theoretical advances in our understanding of prehistoric lifeways in the southeastern United States. This progress is especially important for discerning patterns of change during the Archaic period, which is often characterized as a period of stability with minimal cultural adjustments. Recent advances in the study of Archaic period lithic technology in the Southeast, which derive from models of technological organization, are reviewed in this chapter. Brief comparison of these patterns of Middle Archaic technological organization suggests widespread changes across the Southeast that may result from regional variation in environmental productivity and human population levels. Some fundamental shifts in the organization of technology are associated with these changes.

Nelson (1991:57) defines studies of the organization of technology as those with a focus on "the selection and integration of strategies for making, using, transporting, and discarding tools and the materials needed for their manufacture and maintenance. Studies of the organization of technology consider economic and social variables that influence those strategies." Koldehoff (1987:154) offers a comparable definition, to which he specifies several relevant domains of investigation: "Some of the key variables or factors a society must take into account in the organization include: (1) the types of raw materials available, (2) the distance to raw material sources, (3) the basic food-getting strategies, (4) the mobility and predictability of biotic resources, (5) the seasonal availability and accessibility of biotic and mineral resources, (6) the group's mobility, and (7) the social relations with neighboring groups (e.g., access to resources in adjacent territories via alliances and exchange networks)." Kelly (1988:717) emphasizes similar goals and variables in his definition of technological organization and adds, "Research on the organization of technology aims to elucidate how changes reflect large-scale behavioral changes in prehistoric society."

Behavioral and dynamic aspects of technology are emphasized under the organizational approach, which provides useful methodological concepts and theoretical goals for lithic studies. The origins of and most substantial contributions to the study of technological organization are found in Binford's ethnoarchaeological work among the Nunamiut Eskimos. His key papers on technological and settlement organization among hunter-gatherers are reprinted in *Working at Archaeology* (Binford 1983a:243–386; also see Binford and O'Connell 1984).

There is a close relationship between Binford's principles of technological organization and the parameters of settlement and mobility. Consequently, most studies of technological organization have also emphasized mobility (e.g., Bamforth 1985, 1986, 1991; Carr 1994a; Chatters 1987; Ebert and Kohler 1988; Kelly 1988, 1992; Parry and Kelly 1987; Shott 1986). The effects of mobility on technology are most directly related to procurement and transport costs (e.g., Ebert 1979; Kuhn 1994; McAnany 1988; Ricklis and Cox 1993). Common methods used to infer patterns of technological organization include investigations into the strategies of raw material use (Amick 1984, 1985a, 1987; Andrefsky 1994; Bamforth 1986; Carr 1994b; Kuhn 1989, 1991); assemblage diversity (Cable 1992; Magne 1989; Shott 1989a; Theime 1991; Thomas 1983:425–431, 1989); tool use-life (Shott 1989b); retooling (Keeley 1982; Torrence 1989a); and tool design (Bleed 1986; Kuhn 1994; Nelson 1991). The roles of energetic efficiency and risk reduction in technology are implicated in the more recent work stemming from this analytical framework (e.g., Bousman 1993; Edmonds 1987; Jeske 1989, 1992; Jochim 1989; Lurie 1989; Torrence 1983, 1989a, 1989b).

However, it is important to recognize the limitations of theoretical relationships between technological and settlement organization that are based on ethnographic evidence alone. Because of its greater time depth, the archaeological record is expected to contain configurations of organizational strategies that are unknown in the ethnographic record. Examples of such cases have been suggested for North American Paleoindians (Amick 1994; Kelly and Todd 1988;

Seeman 1994) as well as from Middle Archaic groups in the Southeast (Carr and Klippel 1993). Mid-Holocene hunter-gatherer archaeology in the Southeast is particularly valuable in this regard because we have few ethnographic analogs for hunter-gatherers in temperate deciduous forest environments.

Major Chronological Changes in Southeastern Technological Organization

Although not directly related to technological organization, many studies of lithic interassemblage variation in the Southeast have pursued similar goals. These studies rely on the assumption that technology is responsive to environment, resources, and mobility. Most notable, Jay Johnson (1981, 1982, 1984, 1989) has used lithic assemblage comparisons effectively in modeling Archaic settlement systems in northeast Mississippi. Similar work has been conducted with lithic assemblages in the Arkansas Ozarks (Raab et al. 1979; Stahle and Dunn 1982), northwest Georgia (Jefferies 1982a), and South Carolina (Canouts and Goodyear 1985; Goodyear et al. 1979; House and Ballenger 1976; House and Wogaman 1978). Such studies are strengthened by explicit modeling of lithic reduction systems to determine functional variation among lithic assemblages that might relate to settlement-subsistence systems.

Johnson (1989:120–121) has reviewed some of the arguments for changes in technological organization in the Southeast. Heavily curated technologies are characteristic of Paleoindian and Early Archaic times. Middle Archaic technologies exhibit a significant shift toward expedience. Technologies emphasize somewhat greater curation during the Late Archaic. Finally, the reduction in residential mobility during Woodland and Mississippian times is associated with increased reliance on expedient technology. However, there is evidence during these later periods of the production of curated tools that are standardized and specialized. The manufacture and distribution of these tools seem to indicate the increasing operation of social and political factors in the technology of more complex societies.

Long-term changes in environment and population growth affected prehistoric cultural systems in the Southeast (Muller 1978; Smith 1986; Steponaitis 1986). Such changes are expected to result in organizational changes as well. It is possible to discuss certain trends in the organization of technologies based on current knowledge. These studies provide a useful baseline for developing theoretical models of technological organization.

Paleoindian and Early Archaic

Late Pleistocene and early Holocene technologies in the Southeast emphasized the production of formal tools as part of a curated toolkit in response to high rates of residential mobility (Anderson 1990; Daniel 1986, 1994; Daniel and Wisenbaker 1987; Daniel et al. 1986; Goodyear 1974, 1979, 1993; Kelly and Todd 1988).

Patterns of raw material use and technological design and behavior also suggest a technology associated with high mobility.

Middle Archaic

Technological change is not evident in traditional views of the mid-Holocene archaeological record of the Southest. "There is, in fact, very little in the archaeological record of the Southeast to suggest that the middle Holocene witnessed an ever increasing inventory of tool types or that any technological innovations of a revolutionary nature took place" (Smith 1986:21). This traditional view places heavy emphasis on artifact types and trait lists in defining change. Under this static framework, emphasis is placed on the evidence for continuous and gradual change during the Archaic. The classic expression of this paradigm of the eastern Archaic is represented in Caldwell's (1958) monograph on "primary forest efficiency."

By contrast, organizational studies of lithic assemblages and settlement patterns imply that significant changes characterize the mid-Holocene. Cable (1982a, 1992) recognizes a shift from logistic mobility and curated technology (Early Archaic) to residential mobility and expedient technology (Middle Archaic) in the North Carolina Piedmont. This change is associated with warmer and more heterogeneous environments during the mid-Holocene.

In addition to significant environmental changes associated with the end of the Pleistocene and the mid-Holocene Climatic Optimum, Middle Archaic populations in the Southeast were required to adjust to increasing demographic packing. Walthall (1980:58) notes "a major trend that clearly accelerated during the middle [*sic*] Archaic was increased territoriality and population growth resulting in much regional stylistic diversity." Steponaitis (1986:372) states: "By the end of the Middle Archaic, there are signs of demographic growth in many parts of the Southeast . . . We may speculate that this population increase may have caused band territories to become smaller and more tightly packed, which in turn may have created a tendency to reoccupy the same sites more frequently or for longer periods of time."

In many cases, regional population increases appear to have constrained mobility. These constraints are not common prior to the mid-Holocene. For example, Nance (1986:26) reports a general absence of occupation during the Early Holocene (ca. 9500–8500 B.P.) in the lower Tennessee-Cumberland-Ohio region. However, the apparent regional abandonment of the lower Little Tennessee River valley between 5000 and 3000 B.P. (Chapman 1985b:149) suggests that complete population packing in the Southeast may not have been achieved until the Late Archaic period. Mobility constraints are expected to cause greater reliance on local raw materials during the Middle Archaic. In addition, reliance on heavily curated formal tools declines in favor of more expedient technology. Hafted biface technology also shows a shift away from strategies that prolong tool use-life (e.g., beveling). Greater emphasis on heat treatment may be expected in the Middle Archaic as an effort to extend the utility of local lithic resources.

Evidence of systematic scavenging and recycling of Early Archaic tools by Middle Archaic peoples is noted in the Duck River basin (Amick 1985b:30; Hofman 1986a:81). This recycling behavior is believed to reflect reduced mobility, lowered energy investment in technology, and frequent erosion of early Holocene sites during the mid-Holocene. Evidence of systematic lithic scavenging is noted also among Woodland groups on the South Atlantic Coastal Plain (Sassaman and Brooks 1990; Sassaman et al. 1990:319–320). Scavenging of lithic debris is increasingly recognized by archaeologists working in arid portions of western North America as an important factor affecting assemblage variation and the organization of lithic technology (Camilli and Ebert 1992; Ebert 1992; Kelly 1988; Wandsnider 1989). Archaeological lithic scatters remain exposed for long periods in desert areas and later occupants often used these old sites as lithic sources. Such scavenging often focused on large pieces of debris and finished formal tools. Although rapid burial and revegetation of sites in the Southeast probably inhibited lithic scavenging, investigation of this behavioral strategy requires greater attention.

Sassaman (1994a) argues that changing strategies of biface production in South Carolina depend on social means of alleviating risk as much as on microeconomic factors. He argues that knowledge about the availability of raw materials and tasks for which tools are used is not sufficient to understand technological organization because tool production is underwritten by the social relations among people that determine use-rights, sharing, risk pooling, and other factors. Sassaman (1991, 1995a) also suggests, based on Marxist and revisionist thinking, that forager and collector societies can exist contemporaneously. Under this view, residentially mobile foragers are expected to characterize marginal environments while dominant collectors control the preferred resources. Although this model resists testing, it suggests the increasingly important role of competition for resources as population levels rise.

Late Archaic

Notable changes in settlement and technology appear to characterize the Late Archaic. This shift is exemplified by Winters' (1969) model of settlement-subsistence. Mobility in this type of system may be termed *entrenched* (Graham and Roberts 1986) where systematic reoccupation usually occurs at a series of sites. Entrenched mobility systems typically develop in response to mobility constraints imposed by regional population growth. The development of entrenched systems of mobility may be rooted in the Middle Archaic in locations where population densities were high relative to subsistence resources.

Entrenched mobility often involves a strategy of task group procurement and logistical mobility to transport resources to consumers. There are fewer opportunities to embed resource procurement in residential moves, which are infrequent and redundant. Logistical procurement of preferred lithic resources and investment in curated tools with long use-life (e.g., bifaces) is an expected response to lowered access to resources. Late Archaic use of logistical procurement strategies is emphasized in the work of numerous researchers in the Southeast. Stockpiling of resources is another expected response to entrenched mobility. Late Archaic use of amorphous cores and expedient technologies appears to support this notion (Johnson 1986, 1987a; Parry and Kelly 1987). Additional technological strategies for coping with reduction in residential mobility could include exchange (Johnson and Brookes 1989; Sassaman 1994a; Sassaman et al. 1988) and the regular use of task groups or part-time specialists in toolstone procurement and tool manufacture (Amick 1985a; Sassaman et al. 1988). The study of Poverty Point blades and microdrills supports localized technological differences among many autonomous but interacting Late Archaic groups (Johnson 1983, 1993a).

Woodland and Mississippian

The increasing role of sedentism and political and social complexity affects technological organization of the Woodland and Mississippian societies. Sedentism results in stockpiling of raw materials and greater use of expedient technology, such as primary flaking tools and amorphous cores (Hilgeman 1985; Johnson 1987a; Parry and Kelly 1987; Teltzer 1991). Increasing political and social complexity results in craft specialization and expanded ideological roles for the production, exchange, and use of stone tools. Morrow (1987) proposes that Hopewellian blade industries function as regional identity (stylistic) markers (cf. Parry 1994). The distributional and use-wear analysis of Middle Woodland bladelets by Odell (1994a) suggests a functional relationship of blade technology with ceremonial activities.

Political organization of labor and control of resources becomes an increasingly important factor in Mississippian technological organization. For example, the impressive large swords and maces manufactured from Dover chert may imply the control of materials related to the production of ceremonial or symbolic artifacts. These artifacts were probably manufactured by expert craftsmen skilled at bifacial manufacture. The role of craft specialization in Mississippian lithic technology is emphasized in Yerkes' (1983, 1987, 1989a) use-wear studies of microdrills and Johnson's (1987a) technological analysis of cores from Carson Mound.

Studies of the Design and Use of Hafted Bifaces in the Southeast

Studies of the resharpening sequence and use-wear patterns of large, stemmed projectile points have contributed significantly to our understanding of tool design in the southeastern United States (Ahler 1971; Ahler and McMillan 1976; Goodyear 1974, 1982; Morse 1973; Morse and Goodyear 1973). These hafted biface tools are commonly viewed as multifunctional projectile point/knives (PP/Ks) or projectile point/hafted cutting tools (PP/HCTs) because of such studies. The long use-life of these tools suggests that they were heavily curated components of personal gear. In fact, some researchers suggest that much of the typological variation among Middle and Late Archaic stemmed points refers to resharpening and rehafting rather than to stylistic differences (Hoffman 1985; Hofman 1986a; Johnson 1981). Investigation of tool function and design remains an important but neglected avenue of research in the study of Archaic technological organization. The recent identification of flake-tipped arrows in the Late Archaic component at Napoleon Hollow (Odell 1988) provides additional reason to reassess current ideas about Archaic hunting behavior and PP/K function.

Christenson (1977) suggests several significant long-term changes in biface and PP/K technology in the chert-poor Sangamon River valley of west-central Illinois. Early Archaic bifaces are characterized by high frequencies of beveling, basal grinding, and serration. Beveling and basal grinding are believed to reflect strategies to extend the use-life of these hafted cutting tools. Experimental replications by Sollberger (1971) support the role of beveling in extending biface use-life.

Wiant and Hassen (1985) extended this study by examining the chronological response of blade beveling to variation in lithic resource distribution. They conclude that throughout the Archaic, blade beveling is used as a way to prolong the use-life of bifaces in regions with scarce lithic resources. Thus, access to lithic resources appears to influence technology during and following the mid-Holocene. However, Early Archaic biface technology shows frequent beveling in lithic-rich regions also. Biface technology before the mid-Holocene is less affected by access to lithic resources. In part, this greater access to lithic resources may reflect the decreased constraints on mobility afforded by lower population densities.

Johnson (1985, 1986, 1987b) demonstrates that the contrasting use of bifaces and multidirectional (amorphous) cores is largely a function of raw material availability. As he explains: "The versatility and relative light weight of bifaces make them a preferred tool, and the degree of their curation is dependent upon the accessibility of the raw material. That is, in areas where biface-quality chert is not available, the bifaces will be conserved and recycled. If there is a local, low-quality chert, one of the ways to conserve bifaces is to substitute an expedient tool for a biface in those tasks where it is possible" (Johnson 1985:162). This pattern is one way in which local resource availability should be expected to affect organizational strategy and assemblage content.

Organizational concepts concerning tool design (e.g., Bleed 1986; Nelson 1991) have the potential to provide new insight regarding hafted biface technology in the Southeast. Although design concepts are often difficult to operationalize (see

Pelto and Pelto 1978:38–53 regarding operationalism in anthropological research), this approach has the potential to provide some alternative ways of interpreting variation among stone tools in the Southeast.

Regional Analyses of Technological Organization

Most work on Middle Archaic technological organization in the Southeast and Midwest is influenced by the observations of Brown and Vierra (1983) on mid-Holocene land-use changes in the lower Illinois River valley. This argument states that Archaic groups in that region responded to mid-Holocene environmental changes by increased sedentism at floodplain locations. Brown and Vierra (1983:169) characterize this shift in settlement organization as "a substitution of residential mobility for logistic mobility." A shift away from expedient tool maunfacture and use is associated with the increased reliance on logistic mobility strategies (Brown and Vierra 1983:186).

In several regions of the greater Southeast, organizational approaches to flaked stone technology have been instrumental in reconstructing and explaining variation in Archaic settlement systems. We review several of these efforts in the subsections that follow; figure 3-1 provides locations for these projects.

South Atlantic Slope

Understanding of Middle Archaic technological organization in the Piedmont and Coastal Plain of the South Atlantic Slope is enhanced by detailed organizational models of the Early Archaic (Anderson and Hanson 1988; Cable 1982a; 1992; Sassaman 1992a; Sassaman et al. 1990). Anderson and Hanson (1988) use geographic patterns of resource availability to build a model of seasonal variation in settlement location and organization. They enlist several archaeological examples in support of their model of macroband territories oriented along major river drainages (cf. Daniel 1992, 1994).

Early Archaic settlement is argued to be primarily logistical, including the use of winter base camps. Early Archaic technology in this region is characterized by a dominance of expedient tools (Anderson and Hanson 1988:262, 274; Cable 1992). These models predict increased residential mobility associated with the development of homogeneous hardwood forests during the early Holocene. The weaknesses of these models (as of most other regional models of the organization of settlement and technology) are a lack of methodological rigor and limited empirical support. In particular, rigorous testing is still needed to evaluate the accuracy of the Anderson and Hanson (1988) model.

Middle Archaic assemblages in the South Atlantic Slope are characterized by expedient technology and highly localized use of lithic raw materials (Blanton 1985; Blanton and Sassaman 1989; Perlman 1981; Sassaman 1991; Sassaman et al. 1988). Blanton and Sassaman (1989:64) describe Middle Archaic stone technology in South Carolina as follows:

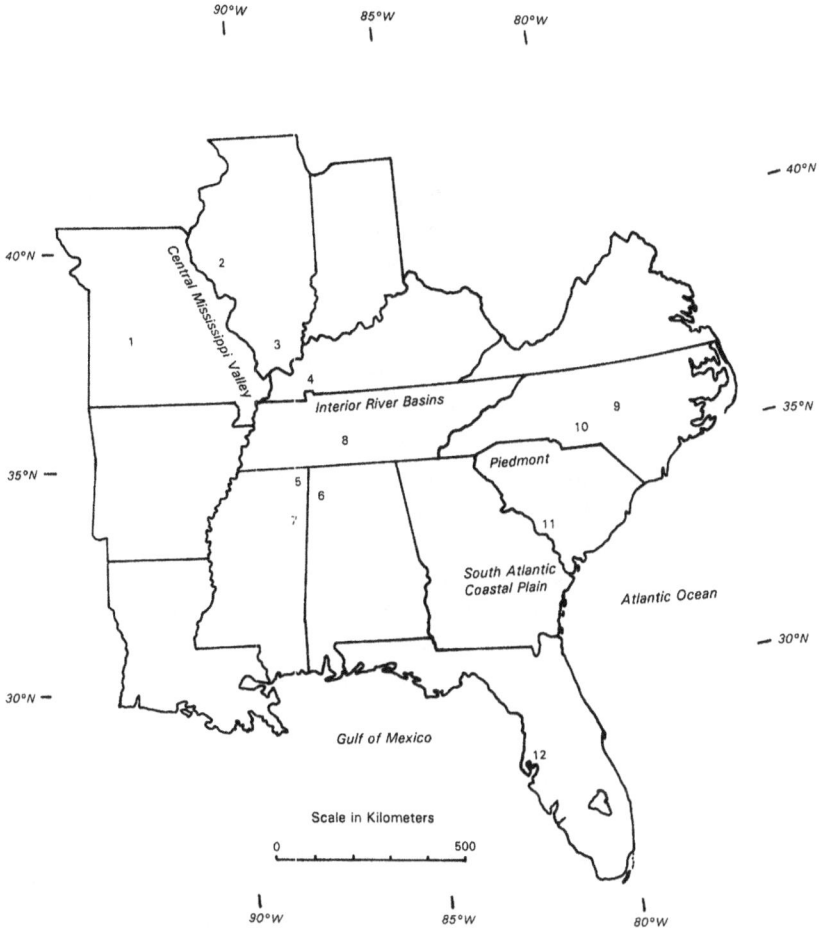

Fig. 3-1.   Primary locations of some intensive research on mid-Holocene technology and major studies of technological organization mentioned in text. *Key:* (1) Rodgers Shelter (Ahler 1971; Ahler and McMillan 1976). (2) Lower Illinois River valley (Brown and Vierra 1983; Lurie 1989; Odell 1985a, 1988, 1989, 1994a, 1994c; Wiant and Hassen 1985. (3) Black Earth (Jefferies 1983; Morrow 1982; Morrow and Jefferies 1989). (4) Lower Cumberland–Tennessee valley (Conaty 1987; Conaty and Leach 1987; Nance 1984, 1986). (5) Yellow Creek (Johnson 1979, 1981, 1982, 1984). (6) Bear Creek (Futato 1983). (7) Upper Tombigbee valley (Lurie 1987). (8) Central Duck River basin (Amick 1984, 1985a, 1986, 1987; Carr 1994b; Hofman 1981, 1984, 1986a, 1986b, 1992; Turner and Klippel 1989). (9) Haw River (Cable 1982a, 1982b, 1992). (10) Hardaway/Morrow Mountain (Daniel 1986, 1992, 1994). (11) Savannah River valley (Anderson and Hanson 1988; Anderson and Schuldenrein 1983, 1985; Blanton 1985; Blanton and Sassaman 1989; Sassaman 1991, 1994a; Sassaman et al. 1988, 1990). (12) Harney Flats (Daniel and Wisenbaker 1987; Daniel et al. 1986).

The overriding trend evident in lithic technology during this period is increasing simplification. Simplification refers in this case to a minimization of elaboration and formalization among tool types designed for use in specific, planned tasks. . . .

Compared to Early Archaic toolkits, the number of recognizable formal tool types present in Middle Archaic toolkits is few. Middle Archaic assemblages from excavated sites throughout the Southeast have yielded a reduced array of formal tools . . . The assemblages from such sites attest to the fact that a higher frequency of tools was produced *ad hoc* at the expense of more formal tools.

More reliance is placed on situational gear than personal gear in these Middle Archaic technologies (Blanton and Sassaman 1989:64–68; Sassaman 1991). Significant range reduction is also indicated during the Middle Archaic, when distinct band ranges seem to correspond to the Coastal Plain and Piedmont (Sassaman et al. 1988). High levels of residential mobility are inferred during the Middle Archaic for Morrow Mountain groups in the Piedmont, who are characterized as foragers (Sassaman 1991). During the Late Archaic, greater sedentism and logistical mobility characterize the settlement system, while the use of specialized lithic sources and curated tool forms (i.e., bifaces) characterizes the technology (Sassaman 1994a). As noted above, Sassaman (1994a) proposes that social factors are responsible for this organizational change.

Interior River Basins

Hofman (1984) points out that Middle Archaic settlement organization in the central Duck River basin (CDRB) probably included a mixture of forager-collector strategies. Amick (1984, 1985a, 1986, 1987) uses patterns of raw material variation in several Middle and Late Archaic lithic assemblages in the CDRB to suggest a local shift from expedient to curated technology and from residential to logistical mobility. Middle Archaic assemblages exhibit heavy reliance on local, poor quality stone while Late Archaic assemblages show a predominance of late stage biface reduction using nonlocal Fort Payne chert. Amick considers this apparent shift in organizational strategy to reflect changing environmental conditions including population increases.

Analysis of systematic survey information supports the argument that Middle Archaic land use differs from the preceding and following periods in the CDRB (Turner and Klippel 1989). However, Amick's conclusions are weakened by failure to examine functional variation among assemblages, which might confound his results. There is a possibility that his Middle Archaic assemblages represent residential camps, while most of the Late Archaic assemblages represent logistical camps (cf. Amick 1986). Carr's (1994b) examination of Middle to Late Archaic flake debris at the Hayes shell midden focuses on patterns of raw material use and stages of manufacture present. Expectations of assemblage content are developed for different site types through a consideration of technological strategies and tool design. Controlling for functional variation, he still finds support for Amick's model of organizational change.

Because the Archaic period appears to exhibit a long-term trend toward increasing logistical organization, the observed differences between Middle and Late Archaic assemblages in the CDRB might result from geographic repositioning of the settlement system (Morey 1988:144–153). Unfortunately, archaeological sampling usually represents only a small portion of prehistoric land-use systems. This problem was recognized in Amick's original work on the CDRB: "Chronological interassemblage content may not reflect changes in system organization, but rather system positioning within the region and annual range changes (Binford 1983b:46–47). Therefore, interassemblage variability may not measure culture change, but only repositioning of the extant system in space" (Amick 1987:73). As a result of these factors, the CDRB may have served primarily as the residential range of Middle Archaic groups and the logistical range of Late Archaic groups.

Systematic knowledge is limited regarding Archaic land use throughout the interior river basins of the southeastern United States, but work at Archaic sites in western Kentucky and northeastern Mississippi provides some basis for regional comparison. In western Kentucky, both Middle and Late Archaic assemblages exhibit an emphasis on expedient strategies using abundant, high-quality local stone (Conaty 1987; Conaty and Leach 1987; Nance 1984, 1986). Because this area contains extremely rich lithic resources, there is little evidence of organizational change.

Yellow Creek is located in northeast Mississippi in the uplands of the western Tennessee River valley, where Fort Payne chert outcrops are abundant. Analysis of these materials is presented in several exemplary works by Johnson (1979, 1981, 1982, 1984, 1985, 1989). Heavy occupation in this area is documented for Middle and Late Archaic groups. Chert procurement and biface manufacture appear to be the major activities conducted at these sites. Late Archaic sites contain longer segments of biface manufacture than do Middle Archaic sites. Johnson interprets this difference to reflect more sedentary and greater residential use of the Yellow Creek uplands by Late Archaic groups. Middle Archaic occupations are characterized by higher mobility.

At the nearby midden mounds on the floodplain of the upper Tombigbee River, Lurie (1987) suggests a pattern of increasing sedentism during the Archaic. Although her results are complicated by variable site functions, Lurie (1987) shows Late Archaic selectivity for Fort Payne chert with an emphasis on logistical mobility and curated technology. Middle Archaic technology is dominated by lesser quality local materials.

Futato (1983) reports similar patterns of raw material use among PP/Ks from the Little Bear Creek watershed located just northeast of the upper Tombigbee River. The frequency of local Tuscaloosa chert gravels is highest among the

Middle Archaic Sykes/White Springs points (*n* = 56, 60.2%). Use of Fort Payne chert from more distant sources is highest among Benton points (*n* = 144, 71.6%), which characterize the succeeding temporal phase. Futato (1983:130) implies that a shift of settlement systems toward greater use of the Tennessee River valley is indicated by elevated use of Fort Payne chert.

Widespread evidence shows a significant focus on Fort Payne chert by late Middle Archaic groups in the Midsouth that begins during the Benton phase, about 5900–4400 B.P. (temporal estimate from Hall et al. [1985]). Johnson and Brookes (1989) have discussed the significance of Benton as a ritualized noncere-monial exchange network. They follow Brose (1979; also see Jefferies, this volume) in viewing such networks as a reflection of increased population density with the development of territorial sedentism. In locations like the CDRB and the upper Tombigbee, removed from direct access to Fort Payne chert sources, regional reliance on Fort Payne during the late Middle Archaic is related to curated technology and logistical mobility. Fort Payne chert appears to have been procured and prepared at distant sources by task groups then transported as bifa-cial preforms for use and further reduction. This activity results in assemblages dominated by biface-thinning debris of Fort Payne chert. Similar specialization in Allendale chert use may be associated with the late Middle Archaic on the South Atlantic Coastal Plain (Blanton and Sassaman 1989; Sassaman et al. 1988).

Central Mississippi Valley

Analysis of the Middle Archaic lithic assemblage at Black Earth shows no signifi-cant difference in the treatment of local and nonlocal cherts (Jefferies 1983, 1990; Morrow 1982; Morrow and Jefferies 1989). This pattern implies that acquisition of nonlocal cherts was not accomplished through trade or direct collection but embedded within seasonal movements. This procurement strategy may imply set-tlement organization based on residential rather than logistic mobility. In addi-tion, technological and functional analysis of Middle Archaic hafted endscrapers from Black Earth demonstrates the frequent use of tool recycling to conserve energy expenditure and chert resources (Jefferies 1990).

Lurie (1989) used the analysis of stone tools at Koster in the lower Illinois River valley to support a model of increased sedentism during the mid-Holocene. She also proposes a shift in settlement organization from residential mobility to logis-tical mobility. Late Archaic groups in the American Bottom are characterized as collectors with curated technology (Emerson and McElrath 1983:239; Phillips and Gladfelter 1983:208; Yerkes 1989b). Odell's (1994b, 1994c) analysis of Archaic through Mississippian lithic assemblages in west-central Illinois also supports a model of increasing sedentism and greater use of logistical strategies following the mid-Holocene.

Analysis of the Middle and Late Archaic lithic assemblages at Napoleon Hollow, also in the lower Illinois River valley, shows a significant shift from reliance on bifacial reduction to the use of flake blanks and edge retouch technologies (Odell 1985a, 1988, 1989:163). These changes are seen to reflect the increased curation of technology in association with greater logistical mobility. Furthermore, Odell (1994c) demonstrates some notable technological responses to increased sedentism and associated reliance on logistical forays. As residential mobility among groups in the lower Illinois River valley decreases, tools are more frequently and carefully hafted to minimize the risk of failure. In addition, tools appear to become more specialized in function.

Summary of Organizational Change

Several characteristics of Middle Archaic organization across the Southeast have been revealed in the foregoing review. Compared to the preceding Early Archaic period, (1) the scale of land use decreased; (2) use of local raw materials increased; (3) technology became more expedient; and (4) residential mobility increased although basic settlement organization should be characterized as logistical. Organizational changes evident in the late Middle Archaic and Late Archaic periods include (1) increased use of specific (nonlocal) raw materials; (2) technology became less expedient with greater reliance on hafting and bifaces; and (3) increased logistical mobility.

Despite variable changes in local environments, comparison of mid-Holocene technology in these three large regions suggests a consistent pattern of technological change. This correspondence indicates that shifts toward residential mobility and the use of less territory cause Middle Archaic technologies to become more expedient. Access to resources is improved by the development of logistical strategies during the late Middle Archaic. The timing of this shift varies across regions and this change most clearly typifies Archaic change in settlement and technology in the mixed deciduous woodlands of the Midcontinent. This change is most evident in regions with limited lithic resources. The roots of this organizational shift in the Midsouth are found in the Benton phase, which may date as early as 5900 B.P.

Prospectus for Organizational Studies of the Southeastern Archaic

The patterns seen by archaeologists are typically the result of long-term stability in the operation of cultural systems. Such patterns include chronological repetition in tool design and toolkits, occupational reuse of the same places, and entrenchment of mobility patterns and raw material procurement strategies. Recognition of these patterns is limited by archaeological methods and sampling in concert with the redundancy of prehistoric behavior. Ingbar (1994) demonstrates some of the potential methodological pitfalls in associating raw material distributions with territorial boundaries.

Change in technological organization between the Early and Middle Archaic appears to have been fundamental, rapid, and widespread. This reorganization suggests that foragers in the Eastern Woodlands may have been responding to significant environmental changes. Investigations of the mid-Holocene archaeological record have the potential to reveal conditions resulting in change and stability among human foraging groups. The emergence and evolution of Middle Archaic systems should reveal much about the factors that constrain foragers in general.

It is necessary to work at larger scales than are currently employed to understand mid-Holocene hunter-gatherer organization in the Southeast. However, as Steponaitis (1986:372) notes, there is a lack of regional support for systemic models of large-scale land use in the Southeast. The development of such models will require the use of typologies and analytical approaches designed to address questions that lie beyond those of the culture historical approaches. Traditional methods of lithic artifact classification are tied to static models of culture history and contribute little to the study of culture change.

Dynamic studies of prehistoric behavior in lithic analysis are evident in the recent use of debitage analysis, biface production models, refitting, and use-wear studies to address processual issues. Johnson (1993b:51–52) notes the inherent appeal of the processual approach for lithic analysis in general. An organizational approach to technological analysis contributes directly to these issues in a manner that emphasizes the dynamics of cultural process. To a large degree, such work assumes an interest in working within the framework of organizational theory. Interest in this theory, largely the product of Binfordian arguments about hunter-gatherer economy and ecology, is not universally shared. However, there are few competing theories and many simply choose to work empirically in a theoretical vacuum. This is an unproductive strategy because it does not require the investigator to reexamine existing conventions. Progress is best achieved when our questions are posed from the standpoint of theoretical knowledge. This strategy does not imply that organizational studies of prehistoric lithic technology are without uncertainty. Ambiguity in the conclusions of organization studies usually relates to the lack of reliable methods for implementing theoretical constructs in concert with archaeological sampling limitations (Odell 1994b).

Several potential avenues for the study of technological organization exist in the Southeast. First, many existing collections should be reexamined in terms suitable to processual analysis (e.g., Collins 1975, 1993; Odell 1980; Sheets 1975). Daniel (1986, 1994) has successfully employed this strategy using the Hardaway assemblage. Second, detailed consideration of design issues in toolkit evolution should prove informative. Finally, the comparison of systemic change in technology over large regions is advocated (see comments by Kelly 1994). The scale of most current studies is severely limited compared to prehistoric land-use systems. Organizational studies require thoughtful consideration of the scale of prehistoric land use in relation to archaeological sampling.

The mid-Holocene archaeological record of the Southeast holds great potential to demonstrate diversity in organizational strategies that may result from environmental change, population packing, and variable configurations of lithic resources. Buried sites are common in the Southeast. Often these sites contain well-preserved community patterns and organic materials suitable for radiocarbon dating and subsistence analysis. Minimally, these sites contain temporally limited samples of technological debris. A considerable baseline on raw material distribution, environmental change, and demographic history now exists for most regions of the Southeast. Few other regions contain such detailed information. The archaeological record of the Southeast presents a unique opportunity to understand hunter-gatherer evolution in a heavily forested, temperate deciduous woodland. Ethnographic analogs to this situation are rare and investigators of the southeastern Archaic should use this opportunity to contribute to general theories of hunter-gatherer behavior and evolution (e.g., Goodyear 1988). Recent studies suggest that gender may play a significant role in structuring lithic assemblage variation (Gero 1991; Sassaman 1992b). The effects of sexual division of labor on prehistoric technology are largely underappreciated. Organizational studies of technology are appropriate avenues for addressing these issues.

The organizational approach challenges southeastern archaeologists to move away from methods that emphasize the normative goals of culture history and classification. Movement is encouraged toward processual studies that focus on understanding the dynamics of technological behavior underlying archaeological variability. It is not possible to achieve processual goals while using methods developed to facilitate the cultural-historical paradigm. Interassemblage comparisons and functional studies of stone tool manufacture, use, and discard are a step in the right direction. The current focus on patterns of raw material procurement and use is also important. However, we need to look at lithics in new ways. Our reliance on standard formal and typological classifications is inadequate for understanding the behavioral dynamics behind technological organization.

Analytical techniques such as artifact refitting (Bergman and Doershuk 1992; Hofman 1981, 1986b, 1992; Lurie 1987:339–340; Sassaman 1993b; Seeman 1994; Yerkes 1989b) and use-wear (Ahler 1971, 1981; Ahler and McMillan 1976; Cable 1982b; Gaertner 1990; Goodyear 1974; Jefferies 1990; Keeley 1980; Lurie 1987; Odell 1985a, 1985b, 1988, 1989, 1994a, 1994b, 1994c; Robertson 1984; Yerkes 1983, 1987, 1989a, 1989b), which are important to processual understanding of technology, remain marginally important to lithic analysts in the Southeast. Johnson (1993b:45) suggests that the lack of use-wear studies in the Southeast reflects the paucity of resident specialists. Site structural analysis (e.g., Doershuk 1989; Kimball 1993; Sassaman 1993b) is another productive avenue for the conduct of organizational studies. Most importantly, lithic analysis needs to be integrated with larger goals in archaeology. The value of integrating several types of analysis in addressing archaeological problems is clear in site structure work. However, these efforts must offer more than an evaluation of postdepositional disturbance or some particularistic reconstruction of behavior.

Conclusions

Progress in archaeological methods will be accomplished through techniques that seek to identify human behavior in the archaeological record. Lithic studies are well positioned to contribute to our understanding of prehistoric human behavior. Stone artifacts can monitor mobility patterns and the relationship of landscape use to technological and subsistence activities. To achieve these goals, we must begin to look at lithic artifacts in novel ways to understand the processes of manufacture, use, and discard. Understanding the record of human behavior in stone artifacts requires an emphasis on dynamic models of assemblage formation. Process-oriented analytical strategies rather than static typologies are needed to improve current methods (see Cable 1992:141–142 for similar recommendations). The recent emphasis on the role of raw materials and reduction sequence analysis has strengthened southeastern lithic studies, but powerful techniques like refitting and use-wear remain severely underrepresented.

Acknowledgments

The comments and assistance of several individuals were invaluable in writing this paper. Special thanks to Chris Bergman, Mike Collins, Randy Daniel, Jay Johnson, and Ken Sassaman for providing references and comments that were critical to the completion of this review. Despite the assistance and advice of these individuals, we remain responsible for the interpretations and opinions expressed.

4

Technological Innovations in Economic and Social Contexts

KENNETH E. SASSAMAN

Mid-Holocene populations of the Southeast have long been noted for developing a variety of innovations to improve the efficiency with which they captured and processed food. Most of the innovations fall under the general categories of ground and polished stone, and include such things as pestles and mortars, nutting stones, stone vessels, grooved axes, and atlatl weights. The purported increase in abundance and variety of ground stone tools has been particularly influential in archaeological characterizations of the mid-Holocene. Greater reliance on ground stone tools is often viewed as evidence for increased dietary reliance on plant foods, which, in the broader sense, marks an evolutionary departure from late Pleistocene and early Holocene predecessors who allegedly specialized in hunting. In this regard, mid-Holocene innovations signify a watershed in Archaic adaptations.

The logic and empirical reality of this scenario has been soundly denounced by Bruce Smith (1986). He notes that there was no increase in the types or perhaps even abundance of tools considered ground stone, especially ones associated with plant processing. "There is, in fact, very little in the archaeological record of the Southeast to suggest that the middle Holocene witnessed an ever increasing inventory of tool types or that any technological innovations of a revolutionary nature took place" (Smith 1986:21). It follows that the conceptual divide between early and mid-Holocene populations is weakened, and we are pressed to see continuity in the archaeological record of the Archaic period.

A pattern of continuity would appear to undermine the whole purpose of this chapter. I agree that many of the innovations attributed to mid-Holocene populations had their origins millennia before and that mid-Holocene economies were not dramatically different from those of the early Holocene. However, there remain three aspects of mid-Holocene technology that warrant in-depth discussion. First, many of the technologies with precedents in the Early Archaic or even Paleoindian periods underwent substantial development over the course of the mid-Holocene, much of which served to increase the efficiency of production and use. Second, these same technologies occupied conspicuous roles in the reproduction of social conditions necessary for labor. And third, the temporal and spatial distributions of innovations were patchy, reflecting not simply differential economic pressures across the region but also patterns in the integration of regional populations. I agree with Smith that mid-Holocene innovations may not have been all that revolutionary in a microeconomic sense, but I think they were revolutionary in social ways that were the very foundation for mid-Holocene economies. Innovations that exemplify these trends are spearthrowers, grooved axes, and durable, heat-resistant containers.

Spearthrowers

A spearthrower is simply a stick, up to a meter in length, with a hook or peg at its end that accepts the end of a spear and enables the user to propel the spear with greater efficiency than would hand propulsion alone (Cotterell and Kamminga 1990:166–167). To be effective as a hunting weapon, a spear has be thrown with accuracy and sufficient kinetic energy to penetrate its target. These two requirements are somewhat at odds: accuracy is best achieved with low trajectories, which in turn puts a limit on the weight of a spear, but heavier spears have higher kinetic energy potential and thus better penetration power. The spearthrower is a good compromise, making it possible to cast a lighter spear at higher velocity (Cotterell and Kamminga 1990:168).

Spearthrowers, or atlatls, to use the Native American term, were widely used in eastern North America during the mid-Holocene. The technology was probably introduced by founding Paleoindian populations, although direct evidence for this is lacking. Spearthrowers used by Upper Paleolithic hunters in Europe and Asia were fully organic, if occasionally elaborate in design, and it is safe to presume that early North American inhabitants used similar items of organic media that have not been routinely preserved in archaeological context. During the mid-Holocene inorganic components, namely atlatl weights, were introduced in eastern North America, and this innovation greatly increased the archaeological visibility of the technology (Webb and Haag 1939:58).

Although few would question the functional superiority of spearthrowers over hand-propelled spears, the role of atlatl weights in spearthrower technology has spawned considerable debate. The idea that these items served as weights for spearthrowers was championed by William S. Webb in a series of site reports (Webb 1946; Webb and DeJarnette 1942:270–286, 1948a; Webb and Haag 1939:51–58) and in a short volume devoted to spearthrower technology (Webb 1957). Drawing from his physics background, Webb argued that the transfer of momentum from spearthrower to spear was maximized when the spear was positioned directly at the center of percussion, or center of oscillation. This was made possible by attaching a weight near the atlatl hook (fig. 4-1, top row), on which a spear rested. Other improvements were made when long hooks were replaced by short hooks, hooks were carved at the proximal end of an antler attachment, weights were offset to a position directly behind hooks, and finally, weights had hooks carved into them (fig. 4-1, bottom row). The composite design of Archaic spearthrowers was also considered efficient in terms of manufacture because it enabled the user to change worn or broken parts without replacing the whole tool.

Webb's data on the chronology of spearthrowers do not thoroughly support his claims, nor do more recent studies employing larger, regionwide samples (e.g., Kwas 1981). Moreover, modern analysts have provided alternative interpre-

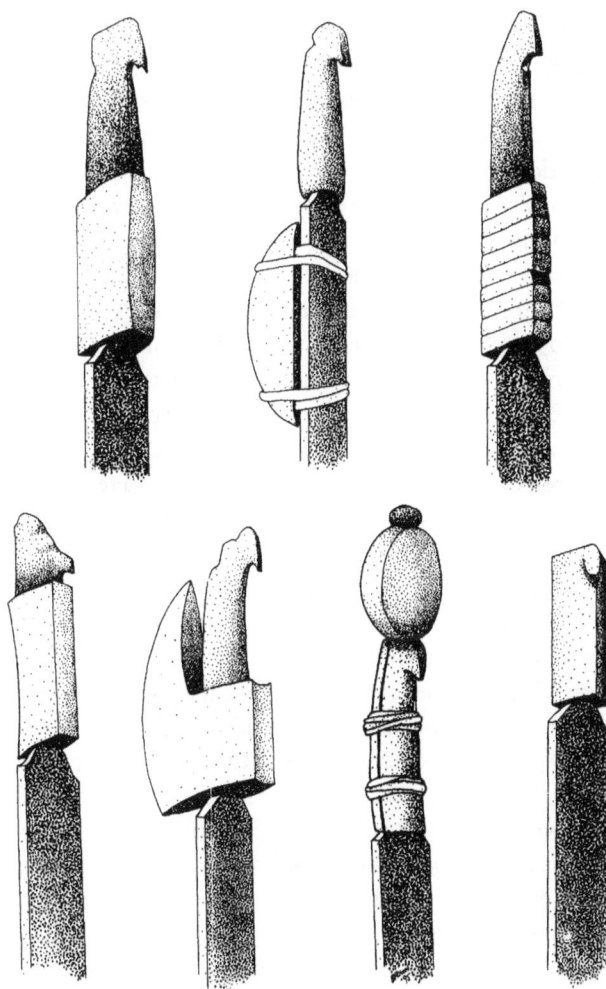

Fig. 4-1.   Examples of atlatls fitted with weights and long antler hooks (*top row*), and evolved forms (*bottom row*) with innovations believed by Webb to improve efficiency of momentum transfer (after Webb 1957:54, 58).

tations of the mechanics of spear throwing. In their recent study of preindustrial technology, Cotterell and Kamminga (1990:168) acknowledge that a spear-thrower lessens the amount of strength and skill needed to cast a spear, but they argue that "its mass should be as small as possible, consistent with the need to maintain its stiffness so that little energy is lost in bending the spearthrower." This conclusion contradicts Webb's inferences about increased mechanical efficiency, leaving one to ponder the true significance of atlatl weights. In the words of Cotterell and Kamminga (1990:168–169), "whatever purpose the [atlatl weight] served it had nothing to do with mechanical *advantage*" (emphasis mine).

The extraneousness of atlatl weights in spearthrower technology did not escape Webb's attention, for he recognized that they were more than simply mechanical devices (Webb 1957:51). Indeed, because many atlatl weights are elaborate in form (fig. 4-2) and represent sizable time and energy investments, there is a tendency to regard them as ceremonial or nonutilitarian (Fowler 1957; Knoblock 1954; Miles 1986). The term *bannerstone* is frequently invoked to convey this extraordinary sense of function. In its original, two-word usage during the early twentieth century, *banner stone* was the preferred term for winged varieties of perforated polished stone objects (e.g., Claflin 1931:28–29; Knoblock 1939). The term was preceded by all sorts of nomenclature of uncertainty and mystery. C. C. Jones (1873) and A. E. Douglass (1882) referred to the items as "ceremonial axes," and W. H. Holmes (1992 [1897]) called them "winged ceremonial stones." Each term was meant to connote a sense of adornment and distinction, a banner of prestige: "We are under the impression that most of them were carried as matters of ceremony, ornament, or distinction; and it may be that the American war-chief suspended from his belt one of these delicate implements, and regarded it with emotions akin to those which possessed the breast of the Scandinavian warrior as he cherished and displayed his *victory-stone*" (Jones 1873:284–285; italics original).

Although he acknowledged nonutilitarian uses for atlatl weights, Webb obviously had little regard for this line of thinking. In the last section of his 1957 treatise he admonished proponents of the bannerstone theory (individuals he referred to as "antiquarians" and "collectors") by noting that "no ethnologist, scientist, trader, or historian, or for that matter any Indian, has ever seen or reported a stone so used" (Webb 1957:70). Webb's insistence in this regard is easy to appreciate. He had to counter the claim made by C. B. Moore that antler hooks and drilled stones found in Indian Knoll burials were net-making tools, not atlatl parts (Moore 1916), an erroneous conclusion that denied the very existence of atlatl technology among Green River Archaic inhabitants. Webb had firsthand experience with removing atlatl parts from Archaic period graves in the Green River valley, where contexts provided proof that drilled prismoidal stones, composite drilled shell, and even stone bars were situated between the hook and handle ends of spearthrowers (Webb 1946:159–168; Webb and Haag 1939:50, 55). As we have already seen, Webb later went on to develop a functional explanation for changes in atlatl weights through time, one accommodating even the elaborate winged

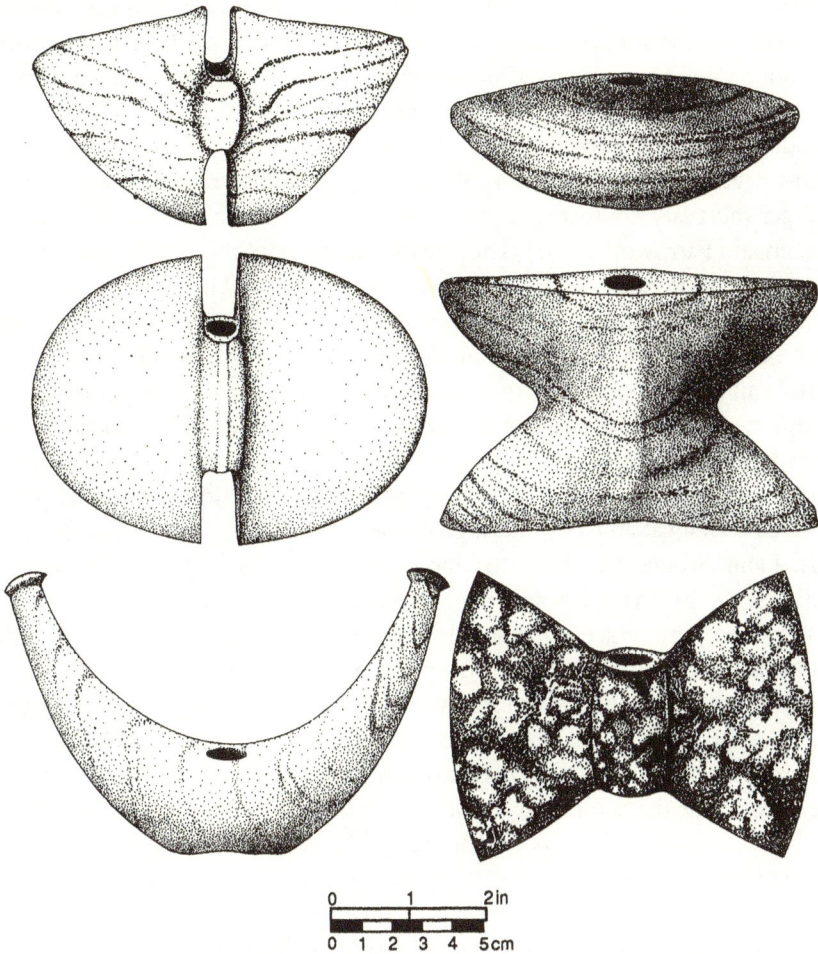

Fig. 4-2.   Examples of elaborate bannerstones.

varieties that, in his mind, were designed to bring more of the stone's mass toward the point of oscillation.

Aside from his interest in atlatl design and function, Webb had an acute appreciation for the importance of atlatls in Archaic mortuary ceremonialism. Forty-four of the 275 burials with grave goods excavated by Webb at Indian Knoll included atlatl parts, 25 of which were bannerstones (Webb 1946:320). An even higher proportion was observed in the earlier excavations by Moore (1916), and more than half of the bannerstones from the nearby Barrett site came from burials (unpublished data collected by author at Museum of Anthropology, University of Kentucky, Lexington). In these and other Green River site contexts, Webb observed that entire atlatls were interred with individuals, often after being broken. Significantly, women and children were as likely as men to have associated atlatl parts, so a simple connection between division of labor and grave goods does not appear plausible (see Claassen, this volume, for a more detailed discussion of division of labor and funerary objects).

Additional evidence for mortuary uses of bannerstones is found in the lower Illinois River valley. A sizable assemblage from the Bullseye site includes several in direct mortuary context, and the remainder are believed to be from graves (Hassen and Farnsworth 1987). The remarkable aspect of this find is that bannerstones are rare in habitation sites in the area, unlike the Green River sites and other Southeast locations, where broken specimens are commonly found among other household refuse. Thus, Bullseye and at least two other nearby sites (Hassen and Farnsworth 1987:19) may represent a distinct mortuary program in floodplains involving atlatl parts and other polished stone artifacts such as axes.

In contrast to those of the Green and lower Illinois river valleys, Archaic shell-midden burials in the middle Tennessee, Savannah, and St. John's river valleys do not often contain atlatl parts, although bannerstones are not uncommon in these areas. Bannerstones are altogether inconspicuous items in some areas of the Southeast and Midwest, a point I return to shortly.

On balance, the evidence for burials at Green River shell middens leaves little doubt that weights were used on spearthrowers. Whether these particular spearthrowers were ever used to throw spears is unknown. Webb acknowledged (1957:36), and many archaeologists today would agree, that all-wood atlatls were also probably used throughout prehistory in the Southeast. It is likewise reasonable to conclude that simple, cylindrical stone weights as well as bars were commonly used on spearthrowers, as attested by the large number of broken specimens in midden deposits across the region. The purpose of more elaborate stone items, such as the winged bannerstones, remains a mystery. Accepting Cotterell and Kamminga's (1990) calculations, we must conclude that Webb's model for changes in bannerstone form does not represent a developmental sequence of increased spearthrowing efficiency. It is noteworthy that virtually all of the examples of weights on atlatls from Green River burials are cylindrical or prismoidal varieties, so the evidence linking winged bannerstones to atlatls is slim. Expressly social or ceremonial uses of the elaborate forms are thus plausible.

The craft and sometimes the size of certain winged bannerstone forms are indeed impressive, and it hard to escape the conclusion that more went into the design and execution of some items than function alone might dictate. The elaborate crescent-shaped forms from the Ferry site (Fowler 1957), for instance, draw attention to the considerable effort devoted to selecting raw material with aesthetic properties such as banding, the careful pecking to produce such intricate shapes, the painstaking and precise drilling, and the degree of polishing required to achieve a smooth, uniform texture. In other cases, bannerstones have exaggerated size. Unfinished examples from the middle Savannah River valley, for instance, weigh several pounds and presumably were not intended for use on a throwing stick (e.g., Claflin 1931: Plate 46; 38ED31, unpublished data collected by author at South Carolina Institute of Archaeology and Anthropology, Columbia).

Such elaborate and exaggerated forms conjure up Malinowski's concept of "technical hypertrophy." In theorizing about objects involved in Kula exchange among the Trobriand Islanders, Malinowski suggested that value was based on labor investment, "not rarity within utility" (1961:173): "An article is valued where the workman, having found specially fine or sportive material, has been induced to spend a disproportionate amount of labour on it. By doing so, he creates an object which is kind of an economic monstrosity, too good, too big, too frail, or too overcharged with ornament to be used, yet just because of that, highly valued" (1961:173). Through comparison with ordinary forms, hypertrophic bannerstones may have allowed for distinctions among individuals, potentially contributing to status differentiation (see Clark and Parry 1990:293–297). At the same time, the circulation and ceremonial destruction of such goods may have been effective in the reproduction of egalitarian relations. Some evidence for ceremonial destruction of atlatls has already been noted; evidence for exchange is limited because of difficulties with sourcing igneous and metamorphic materials. However, exchange can be inferred in several cases. The banded slate materials used for some of the bannerstones found at the Bullseye and Ferry sites are purportedly from upper Great Lakes sources (Fowler 1957; Hassen and Farnsworth 1987). To the far southeast, bannerstones cached at Tomoko Mounds in Florida (Douglass 1882; Piatek 1994; Russo, this volume) were made from soapstone and greenstone sources at least 300 km distant.

Another line of evidence for regional exchange or interaction comes from distributional data on bannerstones. At an early stage in accumulating these data, I have already observed that the widespread distribution of bannerstones in the Southeast is punctuated by nodes spaced at intervals of about 200–300 km (fig. 4-3). Abundant evidence for bannerstone manufacture is found at nodes within source areas. My preliminary work also suggests that each of the source nodes has high proportions of one or two "styles" of bannerstones that are not found in comparable proportions elsewhere, although there is a great deal of morphological variation across the region (e.g., Kwas 1981:149). The nonsource nodes, such as east Florida, contain less morphological variability than source area nodes, suggesting more restricted networks of interaction and exchange.

Nodes of bannerstones that exist at the regional scale seem to mirror peaks in the distribution of people, as Anderson's data (this volume) show. If so, production and exchange of bannerstones may have been central to social mechanisms of integration, including marriage, initiation, and alliance formation. The trade fair model proposed by Jackson (1991) to explain Poverty Point exchange may be useful here (cf. Gibson, this volume), but it is also possible that the nodal properties of bannerstone distributions emerged from social interactions with no known ethnographic analog. However, in contemplating alternative functions of atlatls and the significance of regional distributions, we may do well to consider possible symbolic continuities and reinterpretations among recent Native American cultures. Robert Hall (1977) once suggested that atlatls survived in the United States as ceremonial emblems long after bow and arrow technology was introduced. Arguably having been re-created in other material forms—such as the atlatl-pipe, arrow-pipe, and the calumet—the symbolism of atlatls may be historically linked to ritual that sanctified membership or leadership in clans, lineages, or other corporate groups. In this regard, bannerstones may embody some of our best evidence for prehistoric social organization.

Grooved Axes

Judging from the degree of wear typical of their cutting edges, grooved axes apparently served important utilitarian purposes in the everyday lives of Archaic people. As woodworking tools, grooved axes were preceded by the Dalton adze (Morse and Goodyear 1973), which Gaertner (1990) has determined was used to shape charred wood, perhaps for making dugout canoes; by chipped and polished adzes and celts of the Early Archaic period (Anderson and Hanson 1988:275; Broyles 1971; Chapman 1985b:147); and by a variety of chipped stone axes, such as the Guilford axe (Coe 1964:113). The innovation of grooving first appears in the Middle Archaic of the Midwest by 7000 B.P. (Brown and Vierra 1983:183; Fowler 1959:36). These early examples are full-grooved varieties, which were followed,

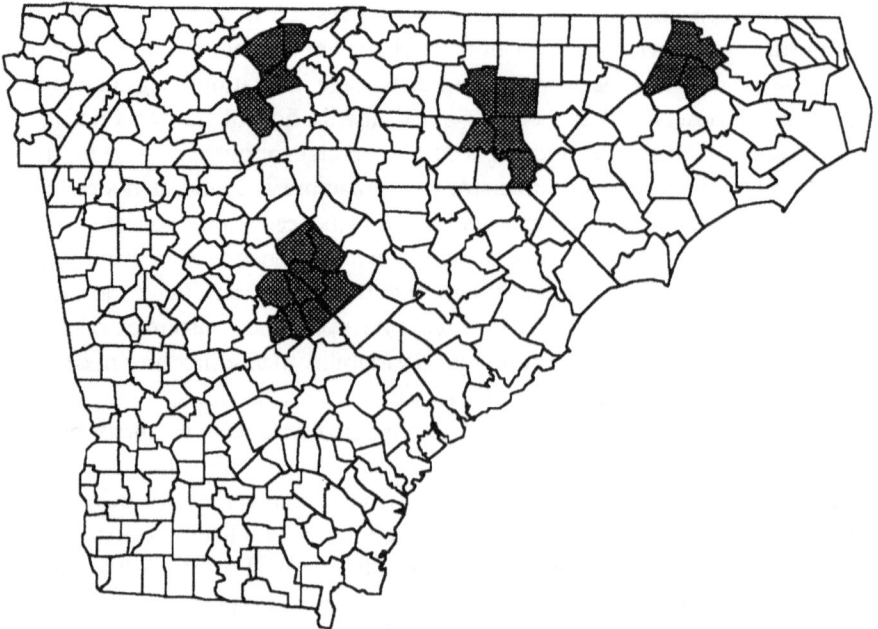

Fig. 4-3.   Major concentrations of bannerstones in the South Atlantic Slope.

though not replaced, by three-quarter-grooved varieties sometime after 6000 B.P. (fig. 4-4). Grooved axes continued to be used well into the Woodland period (Griffin 1952b:356, 1955), so they are not as chronologically sensitive as other artifact classes. Parenthetically, the seeming attenuation of grooved axe technology may be partly attributable to Woodland period scavenging of Archaic refuse. By way of analogy, the Waorani Indians of Amazonia collect the stone axes left behind by their ancient predecessors, relating to anthropologists that the items were left for their use by ancestral spirits (Nova film, *Nomads of the Rainforest*).

Beyond the obvious notion that axes were used for chopping, functional variation in axes is not self-evident. In his seminal work on use-wear, for instance, Semenov (1964:129) notes that the shape of chopping tools is insufficient to

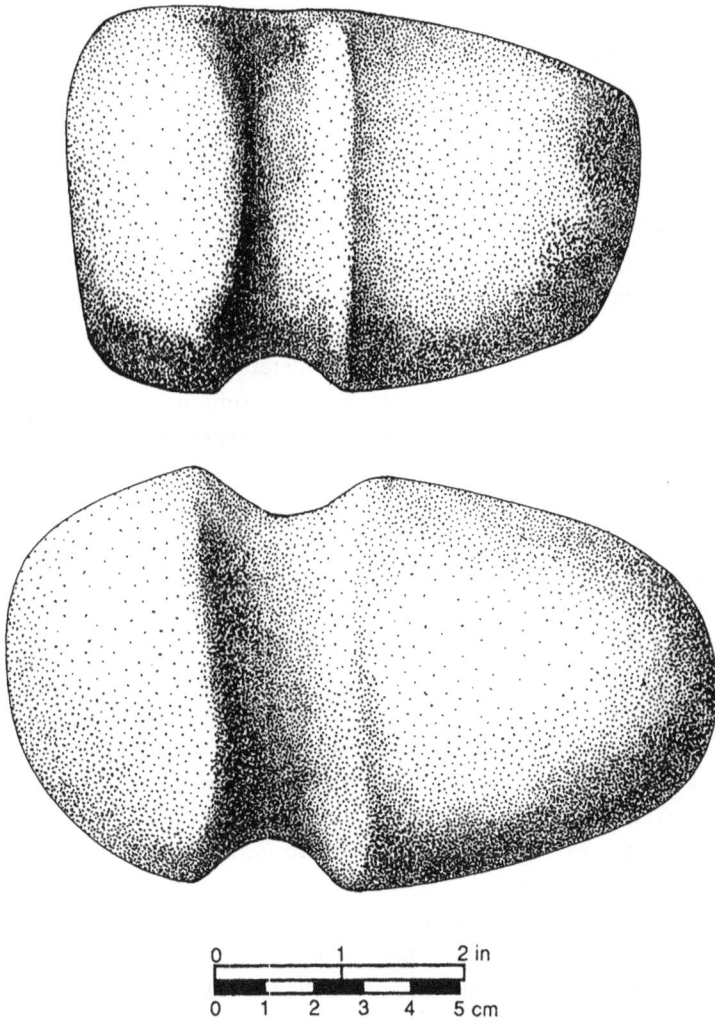

Fig. 4-4. Examples of three-quarter-grooved (*top*) and full-grooved (*bottom*) axes.

determine function, as only microscopic striations and polish can discriminate between adze and axe chopping or among the various materials on which implements were used. Axe chopping (i.e., oblique, curved trajectory of implement hafted with edge parallel to long handle) of wood produces on both faces striations oriented diagonally. The angle of chopping is affected by both the angle of the cutting edge and the overall weight of the axe. Obtuse-angled tools with thick cross sections would be effective only with angled blows, which, if not alleviated by repeated thinning of the blade, would result in lopsided wear (Semenov 1964:130). As resharpening progressed and mass decreased, the effective scale of wood chopping would decrease. It follows that axes may have undergone considerable change in function and manner of use through their use-lives.

I am aware of no detailed studies of use-wear on Archaic period axes from the Southeast. There is little in the professional literature on Archaic axe technology. This lack of attention arises partly from the fact that few archaeologists encounter axes in their excavations; indeed, the vast majority of axes are in the hands of private collectors (e.g., Hannant 1955). However, many large collections are available for professional examination, and these certainly lend themselves to analysis of function. For example, among three-quarter-grooved axes from the Barnes Collection in eastern Tennessee (housed at the Frank H. McClung Museum, University of Tennessee), there are three general size classes: small axes about 3 cm thick at the haft end, medium axes about 4.5 cm thick, and large axes about 6 cm thick. I have yet to compare these various size classes for differences in edge damage, though even a casual inspection reveals considerable variation in dulling, edge spalling, degree of resharpening, and butt-end battering. If variation in size, edge angle, and use-wear relate to function, as one would expect, then a variety of functions is evident in this sample of 195 axes.

Chronological factors in the design and use of axes may also come into play, but here the utility of collector data falls short. Instead, we need well-provenienced collections to examine temporal trends in axe technology, and there are few such collections. The little information I have been able to amass thus far suggests that there are appreciable synchronic differences in axe technology across the Southeast. For example, the seven full-grooved axes in a sample from the Butterfield site in the Green River valley average 3.4 cm thick and 6.3 cm wide (unpublished data collected by author at Museum of Anthropology, University of Kentucky, Lexington), whereas the roughly contemporaneous Penitentiary Branch site in the upper Cumberland valley had a sample of seven full-grooved axes averaging 5.5 cm thick and 10.8 cm wide (Cridlebaugh 1986). Variation within these samples is minor.

Besides size differences, variation exists in the quality of grooved axe technology across the region. The generally small axes of Green River valley shell-midden sites are relatively simple tools made from locally available cobbles, exhibiting a minimal amount of pecking and polishing to achieve desired haft and blade shapes. In contrast, most of the axes in the Barnes Collection from east Tennessee are elaborate in design and required large amounts of time and labor to shape the blade and haft elements. Noting also that some Middle and Late Archaic populations in the Southeast seemed to have lacked grooved axes altogether, one is struck by the considerable diversity evident across the region.

Assuming that all Southeast populations in stone-rich areas had knowledge of grooved axe technology, can we understand variation in its use (presence/absence, infrequent/abundant, simple/elaborate) in economic terms alone? To address this question I draw from a model proposed by Hayden (1989). Contemplating the costs of making and using tools, Hayden suggests that as conservation of raw materials becomes increasingly important under conditions of limited mobility, reduction and resharpening techniques that limit the amount of waste are adopted despite the higher energy costs involved. He relates this principle to woodworking technology by linking woodcutting requirements to levels of residential stability and economic intensity. Hayden cites the trend from chipped Dalton adzes to chipped/ground Kirk adzes to Middle/Late Archaic fully ground axes as an example of increased use efficiency, hence increased economic intensity.

Whereas the overall trend identified by Hayden is hard to deny, variation in grooved axe technology during the Middle and Late Archaic periods cannot be so readily interpreted. Extending his model to variation in economic intensity across the Archaic Southeast, we would expect the most elaborate expressions of grooved axe technology in the Shell Mound Archaic and Midden Mound contexts of redundant land use, subsistence intensification, and other elements of increased complexity. This is clearly not the case. Instead, grooved axe technology is most abundant and elaborate among the seasonally mobile populations of the Ridge and Valley and Piedmont provinces, populations that seemingly lacked the trappings of complexity found among their Green and Tennessee river counterparts. A simple economic model will not suffice to explain these differences, and once again other factors must be considered.

Patterns in the distribution of axes of equivalent function may provide an important means to delimit some of the social elements contributing to technological variation. At a macroscale, for instance, three-quarter-grooved axes occur in significant numbers in only two areas of the Southeast: the inner Piedmont of Georgia-Carolina and adjacent portions of the Appalachians, and the northwest periphery in eastern Missouri and southern Illinois. At a finer scale, variations in design may be important in recognizing cultural boundaries and interaction among populations. The Barnes Collection includes grooved axes from nearly every county in eastern Tennessee. Three-quarter-grooved axes are concentrated in the counties bordering the upper Tennessee River (fig. 4-5). Peculiar to these forms are longitudinal slots on the ungrooved edge, presumably for haft wedges. Another peculiar type with a wider distribution is a full-grooved axe with a constricted butt end (i.e., ball peen). Yet another with very limited distribution has a fully grooved offset haft element.

Other lines of data suggest that axes were not filling the same social or ceremonial uses as bannerstones. Axes are not often included in the graves of Shell Mound Archaic sites. The Bullseye site in Illinois may represent the only incidence of numerous axe offerings, but this is not conclusive. Likewise, the distribution of grooved axes outside source areas is limited. Finds in the South Atlantic Coastal Plain and peninsular Florida are exceedingly rare, and those in the Gulf Coastal Plain may be related exclusively to Poverty Point exchange. Still, the importance of axe exchange in reproducing social relations within source areas should not be overlooked. Like bannerstones, axes often embody a large amount of labor, and exaggerated or hypertrophic forms have been observed in the Midwest and Midsouth. There are thus some parallels between the two. The contrasts between bannerstones and axes in terms of contexts of use and regional distributions suggest that they were circulated at different scales and perhaps under different mechanisms, and this indeed seems a promising avenue for research. In contemplating future research directions, the extensive work on Neolithic axe production and exchange in Europe (e.g., Bradley and Edmonds 1993) may provide a useful point of entry.

Durable and Heat-Resistant Containers

Whereas Bruce Smith (1986) downplays the revolutionary aspects of many Middle Archaic innovations, he describes the innovation of stone vessels, followed shortly by early ceramic vessels, as a "container revolution." The purported value of stone and ceramic containers is that they provided durability and heat-resistance that enabled more efficient food processing, particularly sustained boiling.

Stone boiling with baskets, skin bags, and clay-lined pits served needs for moist cooking for millennia before durable vessels appeared, but it had several disadvantages, not the least of which was the rapid attrition of cooking stones from cycles of heating and rapid cooling. A unique innovation to alleviate this problem was the perforated soapstone cooking slab (Sassaman 1993a:115–119; fig. 4-6), introduced in the Savannah River area no later than 5000 B.P. and used well into the fourth millennium after fiber-tempered pottery of the Stallings series and sand-tempered pottery of the Thom's Creek series were locally adopted.

Elsewhere (Sassaman 1993a, 1995b), I have argued that soapstone cooking slabs were exchanged in the Savannah River valley and that variation in the form, function, and distribution of early pottery can be attributed to differential access to soapstone. Innovations to improve the thermal efficiency of pottery were first developed in nonsource areas, but the tradition of stone boiling, using pottery, persisted for several centuries in source areas.

Soapstone vessels were not made or used in the Savannah River valley before pottery was widely adopted, that is, before 3500 B.P. This is not the case elsewhere.

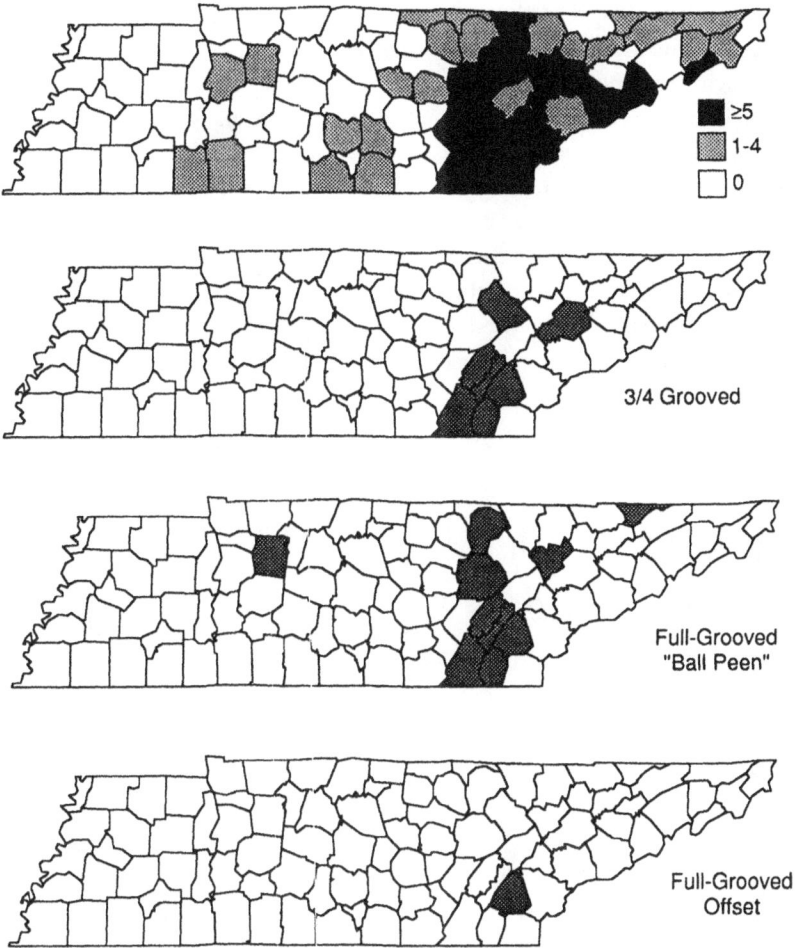

Fig. 4-5. County distribution of grooved axes in the Barnes Collection, Frank H. McClung Museum, University of Tennessee (*n* = 195).

Soapstone vessels were being used as early as 4000 B.P. in source areas to the north and west of the Savannah River valley. A considerable degree of morphological variation is seen among these early vessels, but the incidence of soot on exterior surfaces shows that they were usually employed in direct-heat cooking.

Early ceramic vessel technology occurred in at least two areas of the Southeast outside the Stallings area: peninsular Florida, heartland of Orange fiber-tempered pottery, and the Midsouth, where Wheeler pottery was made (fig. 4-7). Each of these technologies involved the use of fiber as a tempering agent. Lacking absolute dates, early investigators assumed that early pottery traditions were contemporaneous, having spread through contact (Sears and Griffin 1950). Later, when dates became available to suggest that Stallings pottery predated Orange pottery, which predated Wheeler pottery, more detailed models of diffusion appeared in the literature (e.g., Bullen 1974; Jenkins et al. 1986; Walthall and Jenkins 1976). Alternative models based on the economic contexts of early pottery use were also proposed (e.g., Goodyear 1988; Peterson 1980; Stoltman 1972). My own explanation, as noted above, emphasizes the apparent lag in adopting pottery and innovations to improve its thermal properties. All of the various models depend greatly on detailed data on the spatial and temporal distributions of pottery, little of which has been amassed. Moreover, since collection of such data for the Savannah River valley, new evidence has emerged that potentially alters details

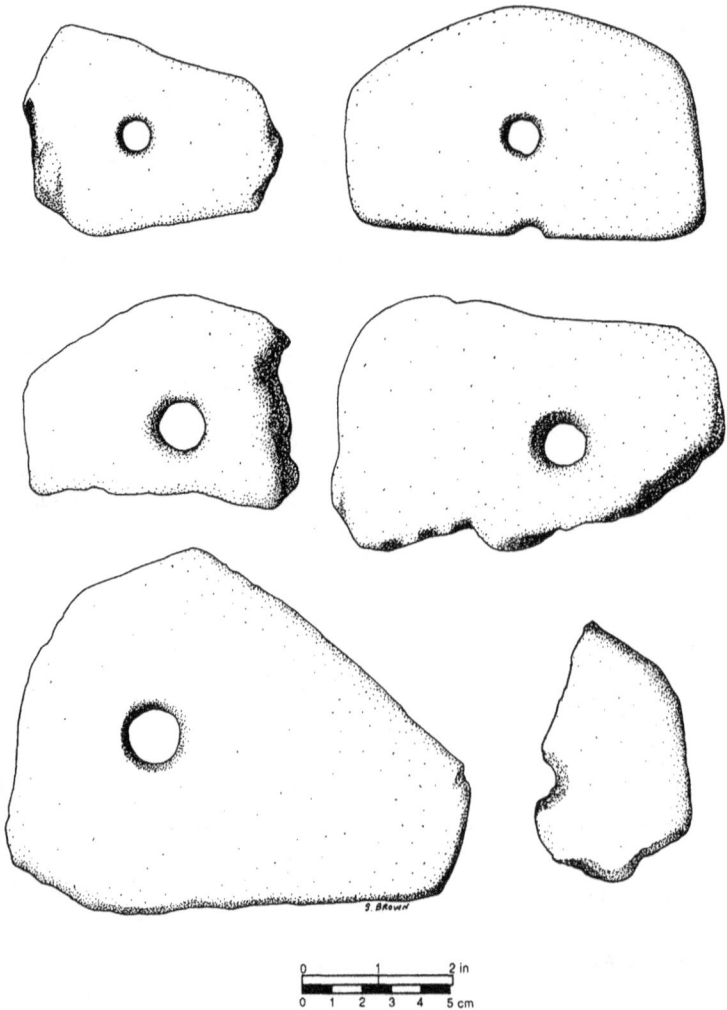

Fig. 4-6.   Examples of perforated soapstone cooking stones, Savannah River valley.

of the local sequence (e.g., Elliott et al. 1994), and it is becoming increasingly apparent that the time-space dimensions of pottery elsewhere are expanding (e.g., Gibson, this volume; Milanich 1994; Russo et al. 1992; Stowe 1991).

When and where pottery was first used, how and why it spread, and variation in the rates of adoption are all questions yet to be resolved. Nonetheless, it is clear that the routine use of durable, heat-resistant vessels from about 5000 to 3500 B.P. was limited to a small fraction of the Southeast. The only locations producing an abundance of early pottery are sites of the Stallings, Thom's Creek, and Orange traditions of the South Atlantic Slope. Any one of a number of fourth-millennium Stallings sites contains more pottery than all Poverty Point sites combined. Conversely, one pit at Poverty Point (Webb 1944) contained more soapstone vessel fragments than the documented inventory from the entire Savannah River valley. There remain vast stretches of the Southeast where neither vessel technology was important, and other areas that entailed the use of both.

Regional variation in the use of stone vessels cannot be reduced to stone accessibility. Soapstone sherds are not found far from source areas before 3500 B.P., but afterward the picture changes when soapstone vessels where imported into nonsource areas. The distribution of soapstone vessels in nonsource areas is far from continuous, as there is a distinctive nodal quality to the pattern (fig. 4-8). Nodes on the Gulf Coast have been linked to Poverty Point exchange (Bruseth 1991; Thomas and Campbell 1991), which purportedly involved the importation of soapstone from source areas in northwest Georgia or eastern Alabama (Smith 1991). The Atlantic coastal and peninsular Florida nodes lack direct traces of Poverty Point exchange, suggesting instead some direct contact with populations in upriver source areas. Distribution of soapstone sherds in North Carolina exemplifies this sort of pattern (fig. 4-9), as do the South Carolina and Georgia distributions. Still, the overall nodal pattern is pervasive across the region, not unlike that of bannerstone distribution cited earlier, and underscores the possibility that the integration of diverse and widely distributed populations was served through the production and exchange of labor-intensive goods. That involving soapstone vessels exceeded any other form of exchange in its pervasiveness, geographical scale, and regularity. I suggest that this signifies not so much an increase in the number of people brought into contact but rather a reduction in the flexibility and diversity of contacts, perhaps a greater level of control over interaction. It was not until this kind of interaction, including Poverty Point exchange, dissolved in the early third millennium that the innovation of durable vessels, in the form of ceramic vessels, had the economic impact insinuated by the phrase "container revolution."

In developing better information to compare the alternative use of stone and ceramic vessels, it is imperative that more data be collected on vessel function and chronology. Perhaps the most important aspect of my research on Stallings fiber-tempered pottery was evidence showing that some pots were used as containers for stone boiling, and were thus incorporated into traditional cooking

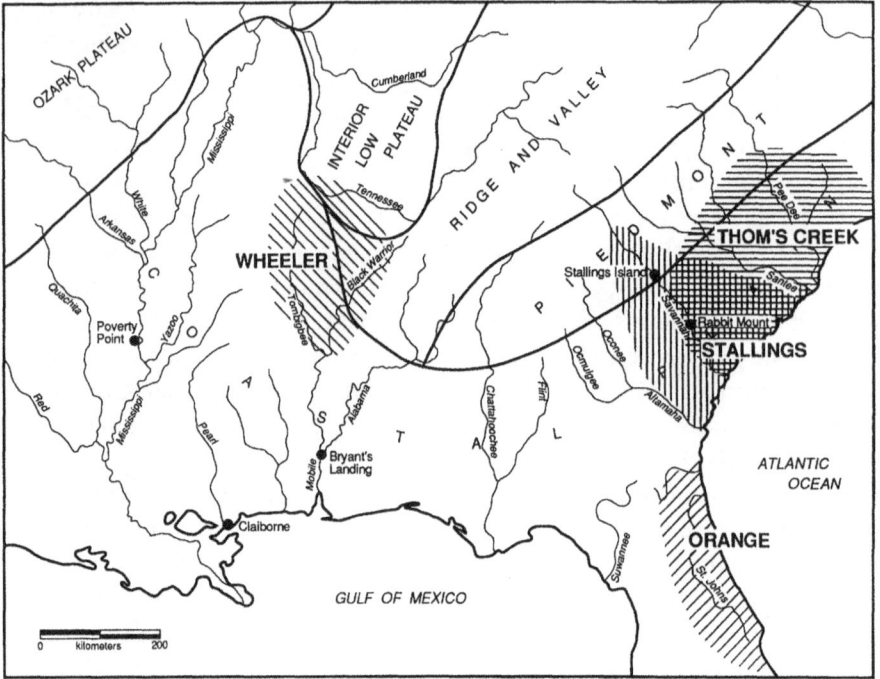

Fig. 4-7. Locations of major Late Archaic pottery traditions in the Southeast (after Sassaman 1993a:17).

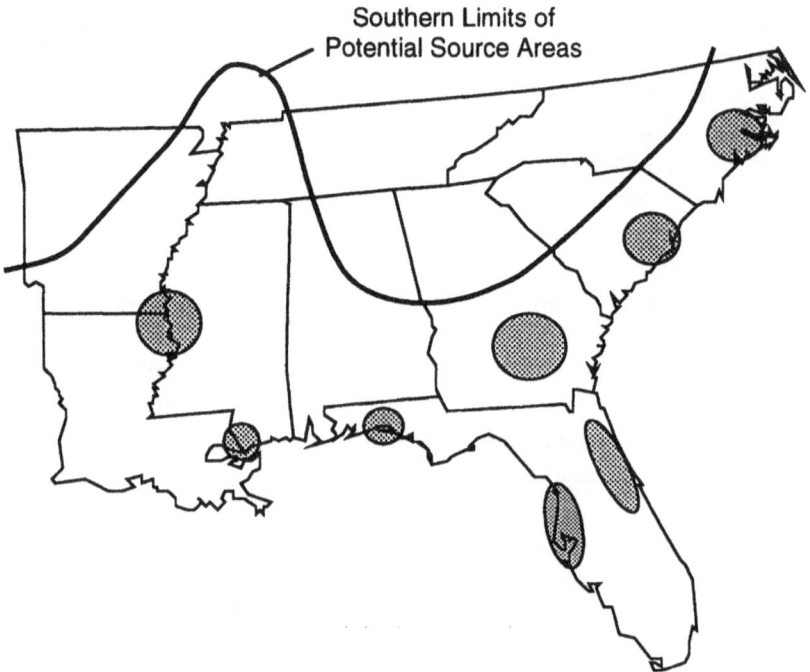

Fig. 4-8. Nodes of soapstone vessels outside source areas.

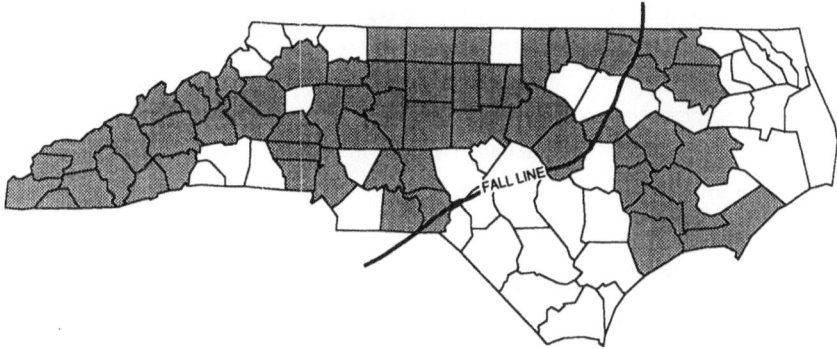

Fig. 4-9.   County distribution of soapstone vessel sherds in collections at Laboratories of Anthropology, University of North Carolina, Chapel Hill, 1993. (Counties with two or more sites are represented.)

methods, while others were developed for use directly over fire. Putting this into the context of traditional soapstone cooking stone technology, I argued that individuals standing to lose the ability to appropriate the labor of others through alliances built upon soapstone exchange were resistant to innovations (direct-heat cooking with ceramic vessels) that could potentially undermine the value of soapstone. I extrapolated from my Savannah River case study to explore the possibility that Poverty Point trade in soapstone vessels was threatened by a similar contradiction between tradition and innovation (Sassaman 1993a, 1995b). I would not have been able to build my case for the Savannah River valley without detailed technofunctional and chronological data, and no doubt the plausibility of my regional extrapolation will live or die on the derivation of similar data.

Conclusion

Innovations cannot be understood in microeconomic terms alone. The social relationships Middle and Late Archaic people had at a variety of scales were preconditions for the demand for and spread of innovations. I fully endorse Barbara Bender's (1985) position that the impetus for innovation in the Archaic was alliance formation. Social relations of obligation and reciprocity ensured long-term economic security in ways that no technological innovation, no matter how efficient, could do. The high labor expenditures involved in making fancy bannerstones, axes, and stone vessels were cost-deficient if examined within the isolated confines of the domestic mode of production. However, when these labor expenditures are projected to a regional scale of analysis, there emerges a network of exchange patterns involving labor-expensive goods that helped to underwrite alliances ensuring cooperation, reducing land-use redundancy, and alleviating the potential for conflict. I suggest then that many of the conspicuous innovations of the mid-Holocene helped to reproduce the regional distribution of labor, and this indeed was a precondition for the economic success of each constituent household. I further suggest that established patterns of production and exchange sometimes imposed constraints on the adoption of innovations, even if innovations stood to increase the efficiency with which individuals could perform certain tasks.

Acknowledgments

Access to the collections of the Frank H. McClung Museum, University of Tennessee, was graciously provided by Jeff Chapman. Collections at the Museum of Anthropology, University of Kentucky, were kindly made available by Mary L. Powell. I am grateful to Steve Davis for making available collections of the Research Laboratories of Anthropology, University of North Carolina, and to Sharon Pekrul, curator of the South Carolina Institute of Archaeology and Anthropology, for access to the Wiles collection.

5

Middle and Late Archaic Architecture

KENNETH E. SASSAMAN
AND R. JERALD LEDBETTER

A synthesis of architectural patterns for the Middle and Late Archaic periods would seem a short presentation given the limited amount of direct evidence for structures. As with most things old, the general lack of evidence is partly to blame on poor preservation. Another factor is the presumed ephemeral nature of Archaic architecture. Judging from early descriptions of Archaic lifeways, one would conclude that early structures are archaeologically invisible. Consider, for example, some of the speculation about Archaic structures by contributors to James Griffin's (1952a) *Archaeology of Eastern United States:* "crude temporary shelters" (DeJarnette 1952:274); "flimsy little shelters made of small poles and boughs" (Jennings 1952:258); "no evidence that they possessed permanent dwellings" (Caldwell 1952:314); "no evidence for the use of any type of shelters or the existence of any organized communities" (Coe 1952:305). Built largely upon negative evidence, these presumptions about Archaic shelters were both product of and precedent for the received wisdom about Archaic lifeways in general: that groups were small, mobile, nonagricultural, and technologically unsophisticated. Some archaeological research in the Southeast has since confirmed the use of simple, temporary structures at Archaic sites, lending support to these early characterizations of the Archaic lifestyle. However, other recent work has documented the existence of permanent architecture dating to at least the seventh millennium before present. Combined with other evidence for intensive site use, these new data have contributed to a revised outlook on Archaic lifestyles, one that recognizes a great deal of variation in Archaic period settlement mobility, coresident group structure, and sociopolitical organization. Architecture is an important entry point into such issues and sufficient data are now available for the mid-Holocene to offer some tentative conclusions about the significance of architectural variation. In this chapter we review the data to date, draw parallels and contrasts whenever possible, and offer some suggestions for improving efforts to locate and interpret evidence for Archaic period architecture.

The Evidence for Middle and Late Archaic Architecture

How one chooses to define permanent architecture is inextricably linked to how one defines sedentism. As a relative rather than absolute condition, sedentism is a condition somehow less mobile than another (Kelly 1992:49). The same might be said of architecture. Knowing what we do about the architecture of sedentary agricultural populations in the Southeast, we might equate substantial postholes, prepared floors, and plastered walls with a high level of permanence. Lesser states of permanence would thus be manifested in architecture lacking these features. This appears a defensible proposition, but when applied to the Archaic period we find that measures of architectural permanence do not always agree with other data classes indicative of sedentism. Part of the incongruity can be attributed to the difference between actual mobility and anticipated mobility. Architecture, like other aspects of site structure, is more sensitive to measures of anticipated mobility or permanence than to actual mobility (Kent 1991). Also contributing to the lack of congruence are scalar differences in mobility among hunter-gatherers. A camp that is occupied continuously over a long period may be simultaneously occupied by long-term residents, newcomers, and short-term visitors. The use of existing structures and domestic space will depend on the social relationships of newcomers and visitors to residents. Similarly, continuity of structure use will depend on continuity in the composition of and social relationships that exist among a coresident population. A camp that is occupied each winter for twenty years by members of the same population may involve structures designed to last no more than one or two seasons due to continuous change in interpersonal relations that affect coresident composition, household size, interhousehold patterns of sharing and cooperation, and the like. Architectural variation, like sedentism, must therefore be viewed as a multidimensional continuum that includes individual mobility, group moves, and territorial shifts (Kelly 1983, 1992), and we must allow a certain degree of independence between structure design and mobility to examine these various scales of inquiry.

Having noted the difficulty in drawing connections between architectural permanence and settlement permanence among hunter-gatherers, we cannot deny that substantial architecture (structures with large wall posts, prepared floors, and other indications of a large labor investment) signifies a level of settlement permanence that belies the notion of mobility and flux archaeologists have come to associate with prehistoric hunter-gatherers. Indeed, these features are anomalous to the received wisdom, and are among some of the more conspicuous sources of data that have caused archaeologists to reevaluate simplistic notions of hunter-gatherer organization (e.g., Price and Brown 1985a).

Structure Platforms

Central to this revised thinking has been the evidence for permanent structures at the Koster site in the lower Illinois River valley. Horizon 8C at Koster contained Middle Archaic deposits dating from 7300 to 6850 B.P. that included an undetermined number of house platforms dug into the slope of a deeply buried occupation surface (Brown and Vierra 1983:184). Rectangular structures measuring about 4.5 × 5.0 meters in plan were delineated by series of deep postholes (fig. 5-1). Each structure contained an interior hearth and large amounts of occupational debris. Brown and Vierra (1983:184) note that "these structures are not lightly built shelters but represent a substantial investment in permanent shelter."

The subsequent Helton phase (5800–4900 B.P.) is represented at Koster by four components. Those located in Horizons 6A and 6B include evidence for three house platforms similar to those of Horizon 8C. The placement of hearths and other features were likewise similar to the earlier structures, but the postholes of the Helton structures were situated within wall trenches with sloping sides. Other Helton phase occupations at Koster lacked evidence for structures, as did the subsequent Late Archaic occupations. Brown and Vierra (1983) suggest that the relative degree of settlement permanence evident during the Middle Archaic period was made possible by the growth of productive slack-water environments of the lower Illinois River floodplain after 7000 B.P.

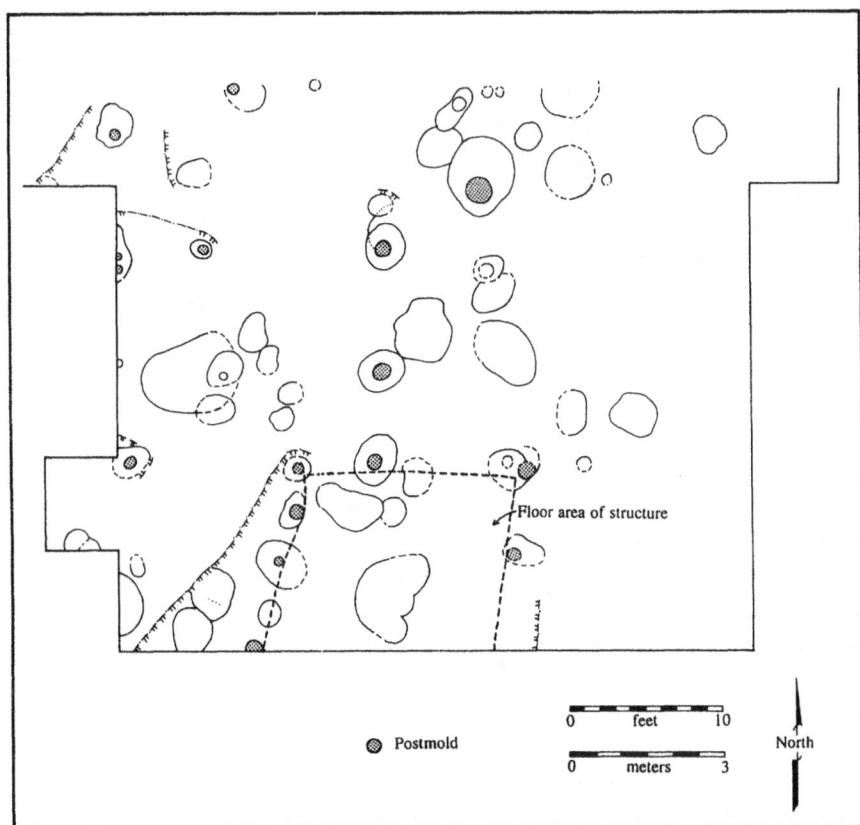

Fig. 5-1.   Planview of Horizon 8C in southeast corner of Koster block, showing postholes (stippled) and floor of well-preserved structure (after Brown and Vierra 1983:184).

Other Middle Archaic sites located in river floodplains in the Midwest and Mid-south reflect intensive occupations aimed at exploiting the resources of shoals and backwater sloughs. These include the early shell-mound sites along the Tennessee and Green rivers (e.g., Lewis and Lewis 1961; Webb 1946; Webb and DeJarnette 1942) and the so-called midden mounds along the Tombigbee River and Yellow Creek (Bense 1987a; Ensor and Studer 1983; Otinger et al. 1982; Rafferty et al. 1980). Modern investigations of these sites often conclude that occupations were focused on dry-season exploitation of backwater and riverine resources. Seasonal flooding probably precluded year-round occupation in many locations, so a pattern of seasonal dispersal into upland or interriverine areas may have characterized Middle Archaic settlement throughout the region. However, as Bruce Smith indicates (1986:25), the lowland sites reflect an increase in the duration and reuse of dry-season camps at locations that offered relatively well drained soils adjacent to productive shoals or oxbow lakes.

The evidence for architecture at some of the sites supports Smith's proposition. Recent excavations at midden mounds along the Tombigbee River have yielded evidence for clay floors dating primarily to the Sykes–White Springs and Benton phases (ca. 6300–5000 B.P.). A Benton component floor at the East Aberdeen site measuring about four meters in diameter was delineated by an arc of 17 postholes (Rafferty et al. 1980). Similar clay floors at the Poplar and Walnut sites lacked postholes but were apparently maintained for long-term and/or repeated use (Ensor and Studer 1983). Clay floors of uncertain cultural affiliation have been observed at Perry (Webb and DeJarnette 1942:61), Mulberry Creek (Webb and DeJarnette 1942:238), Eva (Lewis and Lewis 1961:15), Indian Knoll (Webb 1946:129), Robinson (Morse 1967), and other shell-midden sites in the Midsouth. Often superimposed over layers of shell, these floors include postholes, hearths, pits, food remains, and human interments. As part of the Shell Mound Archaic, the occupations of these sites spanned the Late Archaic period as well as the late Middle Archaic.

Well-documented examples of prepared clay floors dating to the Late Archaic period are found in the report of the Riverton Culture by Winters (1969). At least ten such features were located at the Riverton site along the Wabash River (fig. 5-2). These consisted of platforms of yellow clay 4–6 inches thick placed directly over midden deposits. They were generally rectangular in shape, averaging about 4.5 × 3.0 m in plan. Only a few postholes were associated with these features, suggesting to Winters that the postholes "could have served no function beyond anchors for a lean-to and/or storage facilities" (1969:98). Alignments of postholes at the nearby Robeson Hills site indicate the use of small enclosed structures about the same size as the Riverton clay floors. Also documented at Robeson Hills were arcuate arrangements of postholes with projected diameters of about 3–10 m (Winters 1969:92). Given this evidence for fully enclosed architecture, Winters concludes that the clay platforms at Riverton supported insubstantial structures used during the warm seasons, whereas Robeson Hills represented a

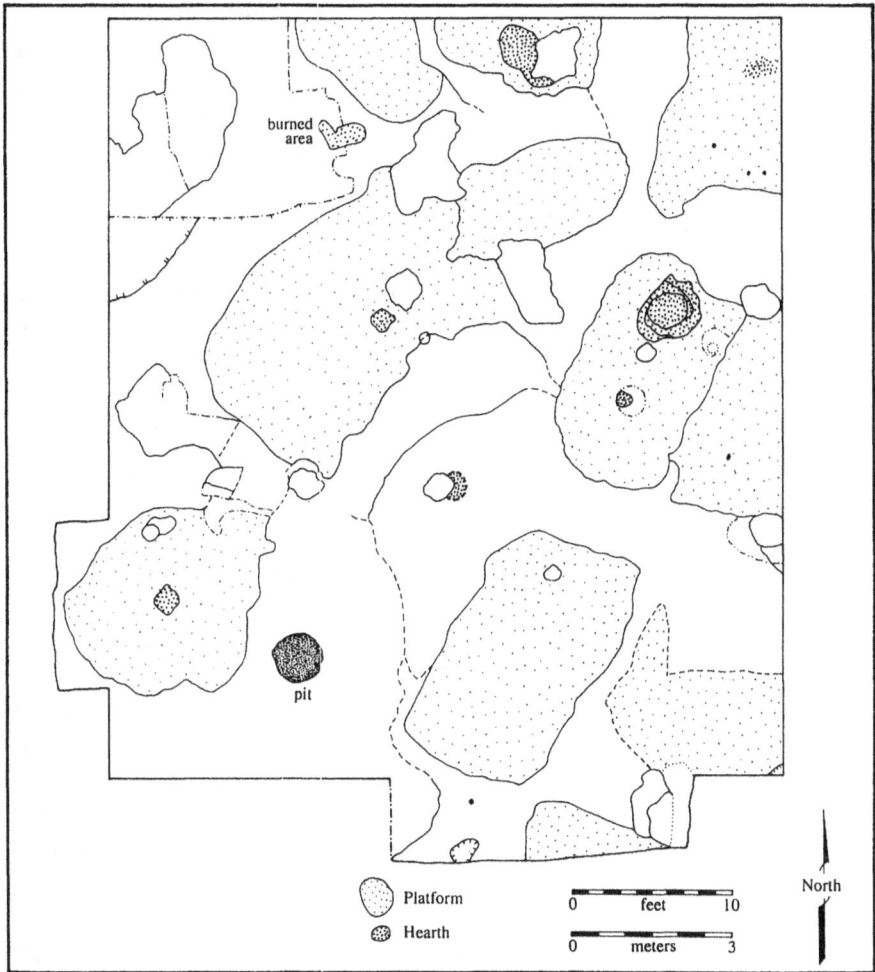

Fig. 5-2. Planview of Area X, phase 2, Riverton site (11CW170), showing several clay house platforms (after Winters 1969:96).

winter occupation that required protection from the elements. This conclusion is supported with other lines of evidence, yet it is interesting to note that all of the clay platforms at Riverton contained one hearth or more.

From this review, it is apparent that prepared clay surfaces are not uncommon in shell-mound sites and other locations of midden accumulation in the lower Midwest and Midsouth. East of the Appalachian Summit, however, clay surfaces have not been routinely observed at sites with thick midden deposits. For instance, the only examples from the middle Savannah River valley are from the poorly documented Lake Spring site and from a shell-midden site recently tested by Sassaman (1995c). The brief report of testing at Lake Spring by Miller lacks information concerning clay floors or structures (Miller 1949). Recently, however, Elliott (1993) has reviewed field notes and records from the excavations by Caldwell, who found at least two fired areas "with clear evidence of postholes indicating that some type of semi-permanent shelters had been used" (Caldwell field notes quoted in Elliott 1993:72). Direct traces of habitation structures have not been observed at the better-documented Stallings Island site. Pits and hearths concentrated in the center of the mound may mark the locations of structures, but lacking any better evidence, Claflin concluded that shelters were only temporary and insubstantial (1931:12).

Recent work at the small Mims Point site near Stallings Island is helping to fill the information gap about structures left by the Lake Spring and Stallings Island expeditions (Sassaman 1993c). After three seasons of excavation, at least three structures have been observed, two of which are marked by a series of shallow postholes. Features associated with one of these structures and with a third lacking posthole evidence include hearths, storage pits, and refuse-filled pits. No prepared floors were observed, though we note that plowing and looting at this shallow midden site may have destroyed traces of occupational surfaces. Despite the damage, enough evidence has been collected to infer a semicircular community pattern of structures surrounding a communal space of about 200 square meters.

Structures at Shell Rings and Mound Sites

Shell rings on the coasts of Georgia and South Carolina represent a different site type than the riverine shell mounds. The work of Trinkley (1980, 1985) at the Lighthouse Point and Stratton Place shell rings confirmed the suspicions of Waring and Larson (1968) that the rings formed through accretion of household refuse. Postholes were abundant at the base of the ring midden, but, unfortunately, no structure outlines were discerned. Still, the pattern of roasting pits, hearths, and refuse disposal documented by Trinkley conclusively showed that rings were habitation sites. His work also confirmed that ring interiors are generally free of occupational debris. Trinkley suggests that interiors were used for communal purposes that did not involve the accumulation of food remains or abundant artifacts. Mims Point may represent a parallel community pattern for freshwater shell-midden sites.

Large, ringlike accumulations of shell are also found along the Gulf Coast. Crescent or horseshoe-shaped middens along the Gulf Coast in Mississippi and Florida bear some affiliation with the Poverty Point culture of Louisiana (cf. Gibson, this volume). Included are sites of the Elliott's Point complex at Choctawhatchee Bay (Thomas and Campbell 1991) and the Cedarland and Claiborne sites at the mouth of the Pearl River (Bruseth 1991). The latter sites were apparently occupied during the fourth millennium, before Poverty Point florescence. Unlike the Georgia-Carolina shell rings, the Cedarland (semicircular) ring encloses a rich habitation midden; Claiborne, on the other hand, conforms to the Atlantic coastal pattern. Credible evidence for habitation structures is not apparent in the literature for any of these Gulf Coast sites (cf. Greenwell 1984), though the accumulation of midden deposits is certainly testimony to intensive occupations. It is noteworthy that the shapes of the Gulf Coast rings mimic the Poverty Point plan of concentric earthworks. Postholes have been recorded at the type site (Byrd 1986), but patterns to particular structures have remained elusive (the purported first structure at Poverty Point was reported in 1992 by Greene and Becton). At the Jaketown site, a single oval house pattern only about three meters in size remains the only unequivocal structure of Poverty Point culture (Ford et al. 1955).

Large shell mounds, shell rings, and the earthen mounds of Poverty Point affiliation are not the only, nor the earliest, accumulations attributed to Archaic period populations. Recent work in Florida and Louisiana is documenting the construction of earthworks as early as the Middle Archaic period (Russo 1994a, this volume). Many such sites show evidence for occupation, including unequivocal traces of habitation structures. The Horr's Island site in southwest Florida is a good example. Extensive excavations by Russo have documented over 600 postholes representing small circular houses dating to the late fifth millennium (Russo 1991). Mound A at Horr's Island is a tall conical mound consisting of alternating layers of shell and sand. Russo argues that the mound was deliberately constructed for ceremonial purposes, perhaps as a mortuary mound. His seasonality studies of the faunal assemblage document year-round occupation at the site. Together with evidence for multiseasonal use at other coastal sites in Florida (e.g., Russo et al. 1992; Russo, this volume), the Horr's Island data suggest that Late Archaic coastal settlements were relatively permanent.

An even earlier example of structures at Archaic mound sites is the Monte Sano site in Baton Rouge, Louisiana (Haag 1992; R. Saunders 1994). Salvaged by Haag in 1967, the site contained two mounds, the larger of which covered a posthole pattern representing a structure approximately 10 × 10 m in plan. These were located below an old humus layer upon which was constructed a small, truncated pyramidal mound that apparently served as a pyre for cremation. Though not aligned with the structure, the mound did overlap it considerably. Charcoal and bone from one of two small domes atop the truncated mound returned an (uncorrected) radiocarbon date of 6220±140 B.P. (Gibson and Shenkel 1989). Mound B showed no evidence for a submound structure, but Haag observed blotches of white material similar to what Ford observed in Mound B at Poverty Point (R. Saunders 1994). Although bone was not found, the white stains may represent human cremations.

A mortuary function for Archaic mounds is certainly plausible given the eventual popularity of mortuary mounds in the Woodland period. The origins of mortuary mounding may in fact lie in the Shell Mound Archaic culture of the Midsouth. Claassen (1991a, 1991b, 1992, this volume) has indicated that although riverine shell-mound sites attest to intensive habitation by Archaic groups, the density of human interments at many of these sites shows that mortuary functions were more than incidental. Her argument is not yet fully supported on empirical grounds (see Hensley 1991, 1994 for a review of relevant data from Green River sites). Unlike the earthen and shell mounds such as Mound A at Horr's Island, the riverine shell middens accumulated largely through routine refuse disposal. This does not, however, dismiss the possibility that some layers within middens were added in the context of mortuary feasting or other ceremonies for the dead. Also, the possibility of structures associated with mortuary ceremonies cannot be dismissed out of hand.

Other Direct Evidence for Structures

To this point in our review most of the examples of permanent architecture have come from large riverine or coastal sites with thick accumulations of organic refuse, features, and artifacts. Lesser examples of riverine and coastal sites with evidence for structures are found throughout the Southeast, though these are largely limited to the Late Archaic period. Among these are the Lovers Lane site in the middle Savannah River valley, where Elliott found posthole evidence for at least five structures (fig. 5-3), the best of which, Structure 1, was subrectangular and measured 6 × 7 m in plan (Elliott et al. 1994). Another of the structures was demarcated by two linear, parallel lines of posts, spaced about 8 m apart. Elliott suggests that the 8 × 8 m structure had two open sides and, judging from an abundance of fired clay, may have been mud-covered. A similar sort of structure may have been used at Sara's Ridge in South Carolina (fig. 5-4), where Wood and colleagues found an incomplete pattern of postholes within a Late Archaic midden rich in hearths and hearth-related debris (Wood et al. 1986). Other large and presumably enclosed structures demarcated by postholes have been reported from the Tarver site in central Georgia (Ledbetter et al. 1994; fig. 5-5) and the Grayson site in northeast Kentucky (Ledbetter and O'Steen 1991; fig. 5-6). The Grayson structure, dated to about 3550 B.P., was interpreted as a cold-weather structure based on the presence of an interior hearth.

A combination of enclosed and open architecture was found by Bentz (1988a, 1988b) at the Bailey site (40GL26) in Giles County, Tennessee (fig. 5-7). An enclosed, circular structure measuring 10.5 × 8.9 m contained a central hearth and three adjacent storage pits. A second interior hearth was positioned next to the south wall behind a partition. Three open, rectangular structures measured 4.1–7.0 m long and 2.6–4.0 m wide. Each contained one or more shallow, interior hearths, and two included storage pits. Bentz speculates that open structures were the warm-weather dwellings of single families and that the enclosed structure was used by multiple families during seasons of cold weather.

Small, open dwellings may have been relatively common during the Late Archaic period in Tennessee. Arcuate arrangements of postholes, such as those found at Banks I (Faulkner and McCollough 1974) and the Higgs site (McCollough and Faulkner 1973), bound areas of burned clay and charcoal reminiscent of the Shell Mound Archaic sites (fig. 5-8). In their discussion of the evidence, Faulkner and McCollough (1974:204–211) describe such structures as simple,

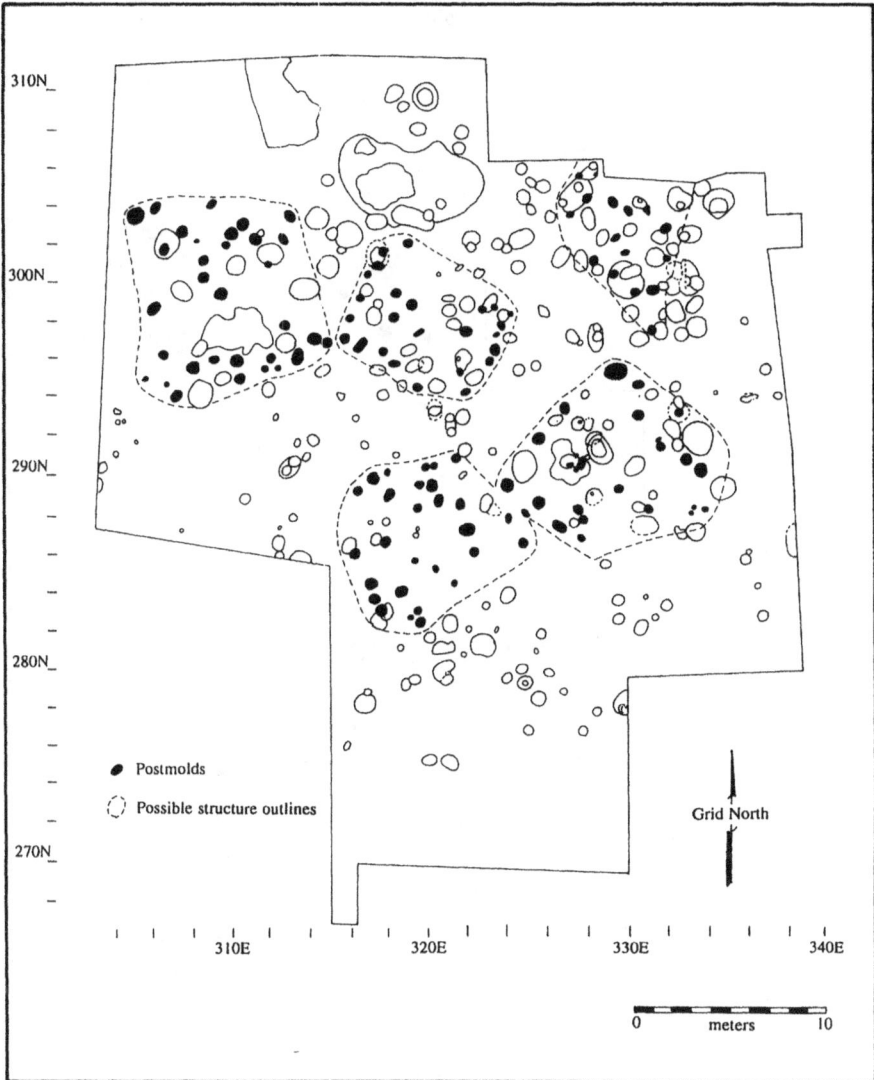

Fig. 5-3.   Planview of features in Block B of Lovers Lane site (9RI86), with outlines of five possible structures (after Elliott et al. 1994:331).

impermanent windbreaks and cabanas composed of vertical posts interlaced with branches or cane. They further speculate that the partially roofed cabana variety served the need for protection from sun and rain, but like the simpler windbreaks, it was not designed for long-term or repeated use. They argue that simple structures such as these were used during the warm season.

The relationship between seasonality and architectural design is not so clear. With the exception of coastal sites in Florida, few, if any, of the sites discussed thus far were occupied throughout the year. Indeed, late winter and spring

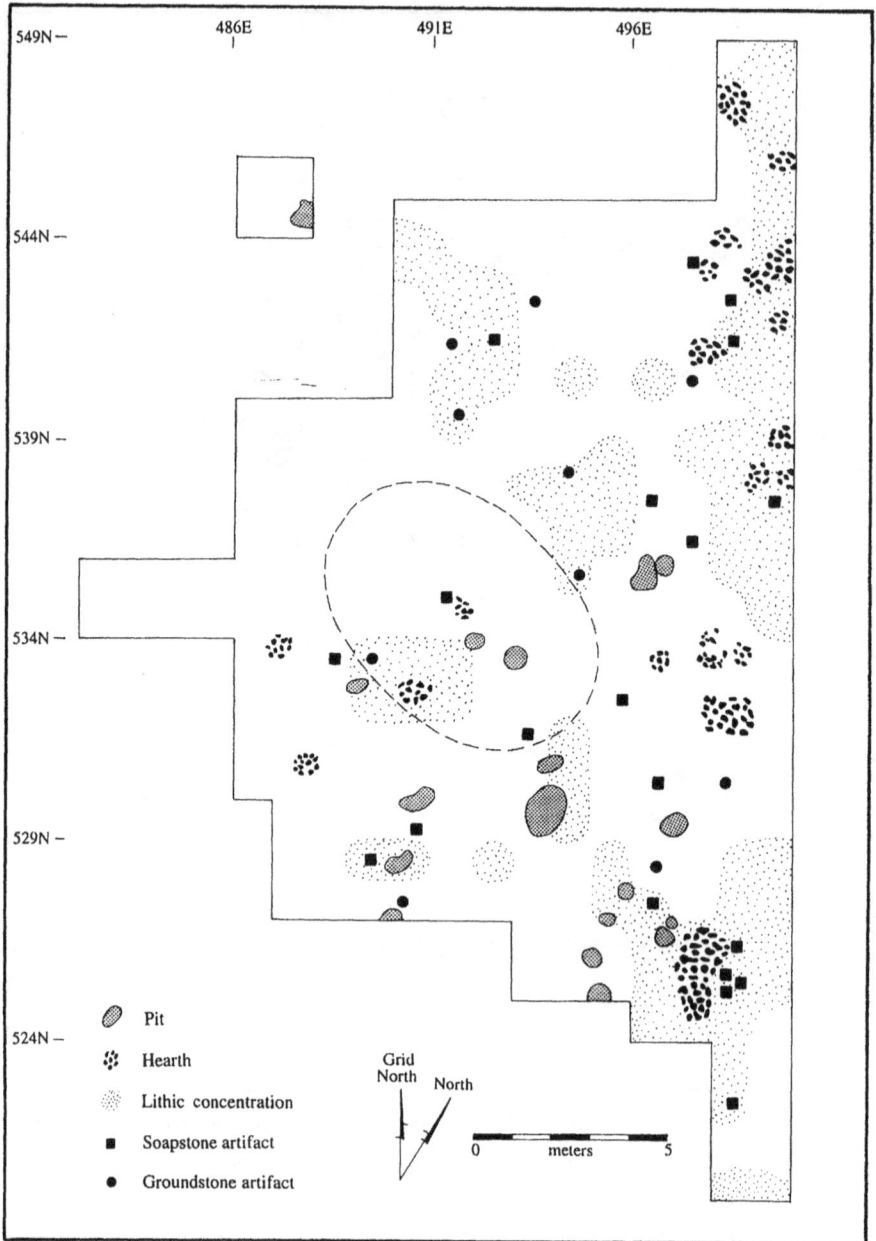

Fig. 5-4. Composite plan of Excavation Unit 2, Sara's Ridge (38AN29), showing location of possible shelter (after Wood et al. 1986:161).

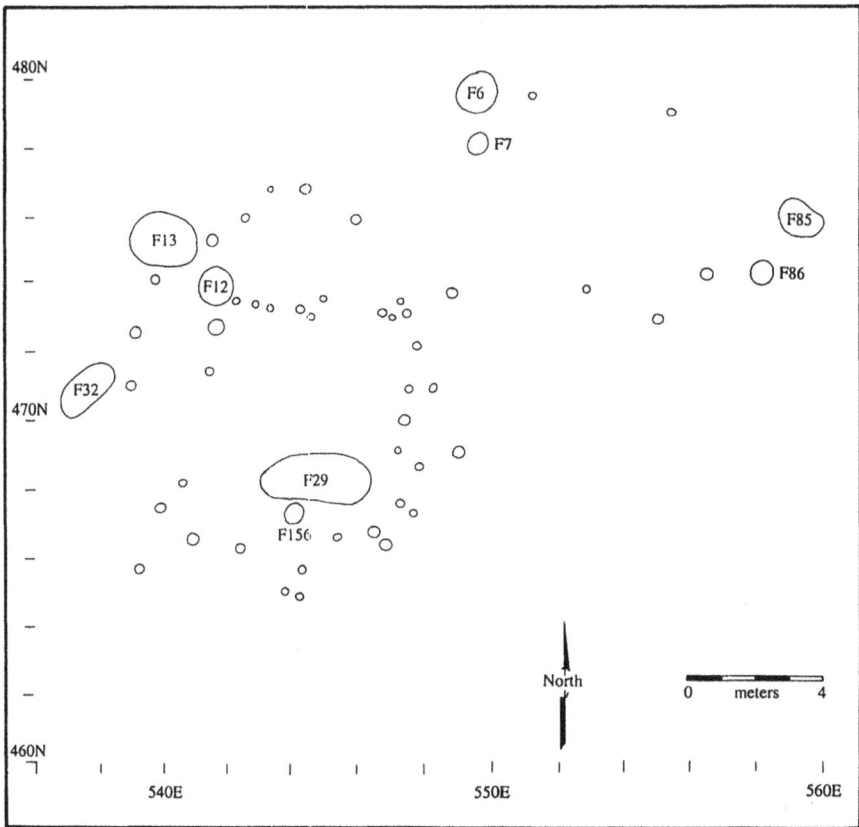

Fig. 5-5.   Posthole pattern to structure in Block A of the Tarver site (9JO6) (after Ledbetter et al. 1994).

flooding would have precluded year-round occupation of floodplain sites. Models of Middle and Late Archaic settlement usually feature a pattern of seasonal transhumance in which groups move into upland or riverine areas during the cool and wet months (e.g., Alexander et al. 1983; O'Hear 1978; Sassaman et al. 1990). Because of the limited data from upland sites, it is not always possible to discern settlement relocation from settlement dispersal. The latter implies that groups divided into small coresident groups while occupying upland sites. The small dwellings at Bailey and Banks I might exemplify small coresident group occupations, but they have designs suggestive of warm-weather use and are found in riverine and upland settings alike. Similarly, large structures vary from fully enclosed to partially open, and are found across a variety of landforms. It is apparent that the discovery of any patterning between architectural design and season of use will require much more analysis.

One area that especially requires more research is upland site use. Compared to bottomland sites, upland sites have received little attention. They are not

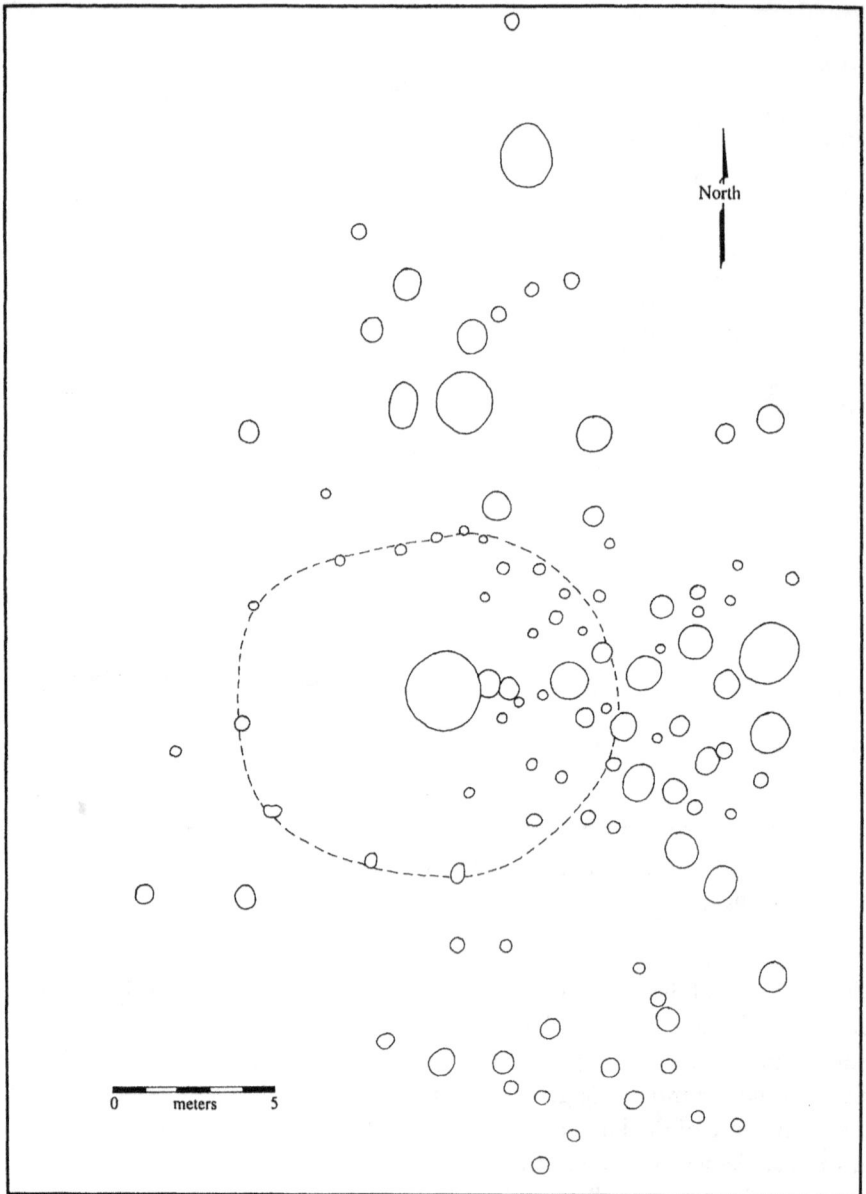

Fig. 5-6.   Posthole pattern to Structure 3 at Grayson site (15CR73) (after Ledbetter and O'Steen 1991:240).

often well preserved, lacking organic traces of structures and other features. Also, there is a persistent bias about upland sites that can be traced to the investigative emphasis on shell middens and presumptions about settlement permanence. Recent models of Archaic settlement generally incorporate seasonal dispersal into upland zones, but there is little hard data on group size, duration of

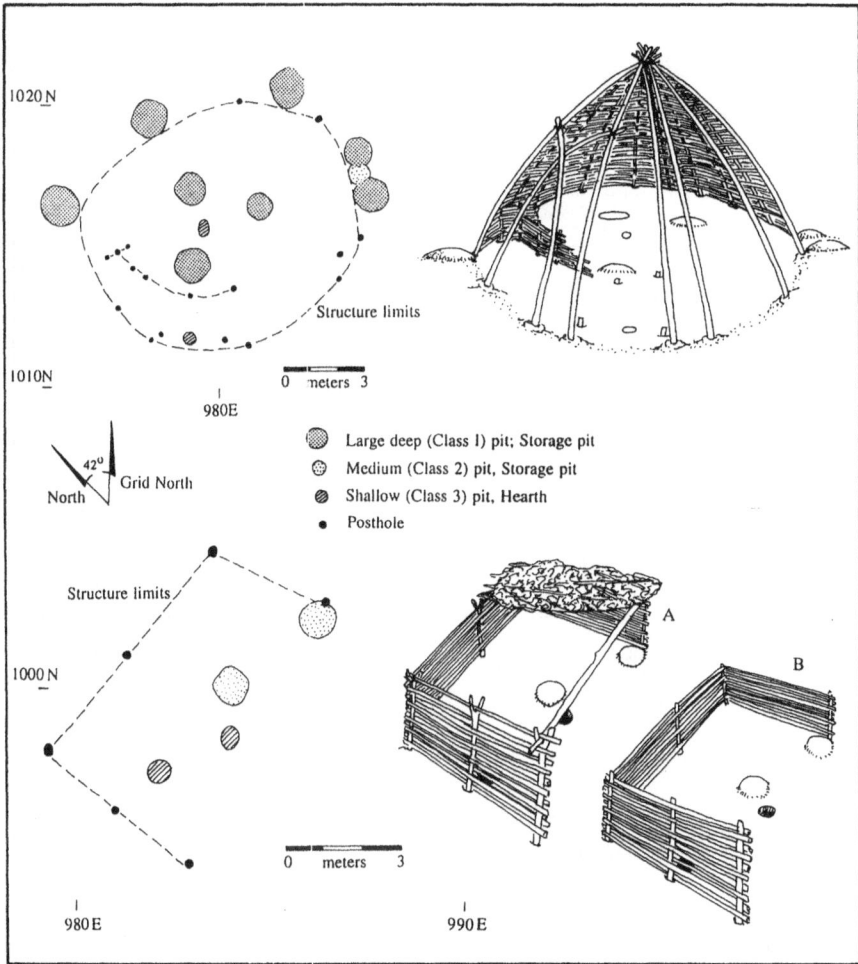

Fig. 5-7. Planviews and artist's reconstruction of large, closed circular structure (*top*) and small, open rectangular structure (*bottom*) at Bailey site (40GL26) (after Bentz 1988b:57, 59, 61, 63).

occupations, and patterns of reuse. And even though models of upland cold-weather settlement imply the use of enclosed architecture, few would argue that upland sites entailed the level of occupational redundancy that warranted permanent structures. Combined with the poor preservation regime of most upland locations, these sorts of arguments may help to account for the dearth of data on upland structures.

A major exception to this general rule is the recent discovery of a pithouse in Warren County, Georgia. At Mill Branch site 9WR4 in 1990, Ledbetter (1991, 1995) uncovered a large midden-filled pit with numerous flaked and ground stone artifacts. The fill was removed to reveal a flat-bottomed feature approximately 4 × 5 meters in plan (fig. 5-9). The maximum depth of the floor below the graded

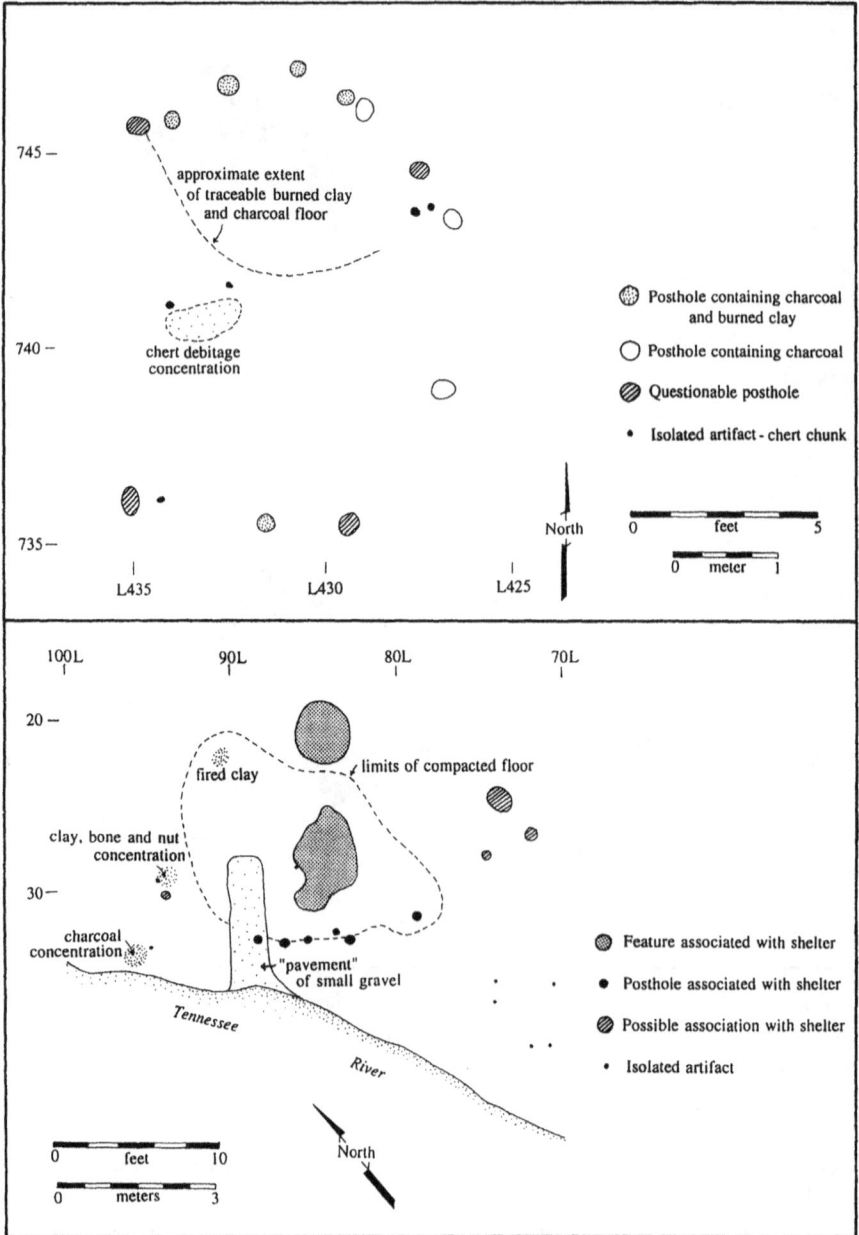

Fig. 5-8.   Planviews of Structure I area: (*top*) Banks I site (40CF34) (after Faulkner and McCullough 1974:244), and (*bottom*) Stratum IV, Higgs site (40LO45) (after McCullough and Faulkner 1973: fig. 9).

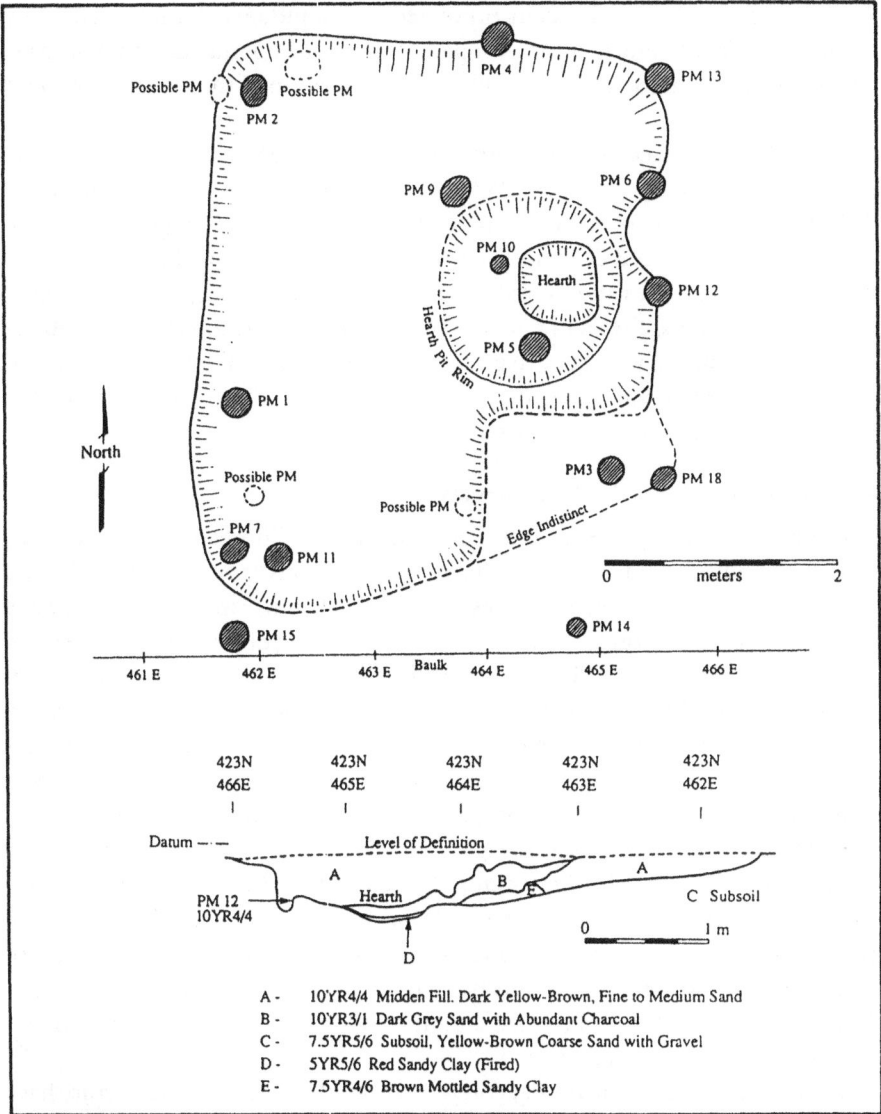

Fig. 5-9.   Planview (*top*) and profile (*bottom*) of Late Archaic pithouse at the Mill Branch site (9WR4) (after Ledbetter 1991:199–200; 1995: 194–195).

surface was 25 cm, but an interior pit containing a hearth extended well below the floor. Along the interior edge of the large pit was a series of postholes. Ledbetter's observations of the distribution of artifacts within the feature suggest that it became filled through use as a structure, not from secondary deposition. Based on a clear concentration of artifacts around the hearth and against the interior edge of the walls, and in view of the large accumulation of ash and charcoal around the hearth, it appears that the pithouse was occupied repeatedly or for a long period.

The more than 7,000 artifacts incorporated in the pithouse fill included many Savannah River Stemmed points, winged bannerstone fragments, and soapstone cooking stones. Radiocarbon dates place the occupation of the pithouse at about 3850 B.P.

Alleged Late Archaic pithouses have been reported from the Cherry (Lewis and Kneberg 1947) and Spring Creek (Peterson 1973) sites in Tennessee, and from the F. L. Brinkley Midden (22TS729) in northeast Mississippi (Otinger et al. 1982). The latter site produced evidence for several "large basin shaped features" interpreted as fall-winter earth-covered structures, though investigators found little evidence for internal fires and few postholes for superstructural supports. Alternatively, noncultural processes (e.g., uprooted trees) may account for these features. Given the unequivocal evidence for a pithouse at Mill Branch, however, the Brinkley Midden evidence is somewhat strengthened.

Indirect Evidence for Upland Structures

Direct evidence for upland structures remains elusive. Efforts to recognize structures from indirect evidence such as feature distributions or artifact patterning are beginning to fill this gap. Examples include the Iddins site in east Tennessee (Chapman 1981), Falcon Field in west-central Georgia (Elliott 1989), Shakey Pot in northeast Georgia (Ledbetter, unpublished data), and 38AK157 in western South Carolina (Sassaman 1993b, 1993d). Ethnoarchaeological data on hunter-gatherer site structure have been used to build inferences about artifact and feature patterns associated with huts (Kimball 1981; Sassaman 1993b, 1993d). Important too have been studies that relate indirect evidence for structures to unequivocal traces such as posthole patterns. The Grayson site mentioned earlier is a good case in point. Ledbetter and O'Steen (1991) identified a 9-m-diameter Late Archaic structure and analyzed artifact distributions to establish patterns of refuse discard, tool manufacture, and hearth-related activities. In the absence of postholes, such patterns can be effectively used to infer the location of structures. Importantly, upland sites of limited duration and reuse contain the level of clarity necessary to make such inferences.

To summarize, the available data on Middle and Late Archaic architecture have grown considerably in the last decade, but there is yet little direct evidence and few attempts to seek indirect evidence compared to the number of sites investigated. Most sites with organic preservation produce postholes, but these are not often in patterns that can be interpreted as structures (e.g., Black Earth site in Illinois [Jefferies and Butler 1982]). In many cases the level of settlement intensity and site reoccupation is so great as to preclude clarity in feature recognition. In other cases, absolutely no evidence for in-the-ground architecture is found despite other lines of data that suggest relatively intensive occupations (e.g., Koster Horizon 8B; Brown and Vierra 1983:185). Pithouses reflect another type of substantial architecture, but only one good example has thus far been documented. Otherwise, architectural evidence and indirect evidence reflect the use of impermanent or simple structures indicative perhaps of short-term occupation. In short, a variety of structures is apparent in the relatively small sample available. Explanations for this variation undoubtedly involve numerous factors, including but not limited to seasonality, latitude, group size, and site function.

Community Patterns

Our knowledge of community patterning is dependent on the recognition of individual structures and unequivocal evidence for contemporaneity among them. Never has the excavation of an Archaic site with multiple structures been large enough and thorough enough to document a complete picture of community organization. Efforts to collect such data are often hampered by sample constraints and the analytical noise created by reoccupation and postdepositional disturbances. We are thus left to speculate on variables such as coresident group size, interhousehold spacing, and the geometry of structure placement. Inspiration for this often comes from generalizations about ethnographic hunter-gatherers, namely that they lived in groups of 25–50 people, organized their huts in circular or semicircular fashion, and maintained communal space in the area bounded by huts (e.g., Yellen 1977). Many of these notions are conveyed through artists' impressions of Archaic camp life, which also include interpretations of the shapes and coverings of dwellings. Virtually all of these cases involve assumptions about contemporaneity and spacing that cannot be addressed with archaeological data alone. Footnotes or captions associated with the artistic renderings usually provide disclaimers about accuracy and detail.

Archaeologists are rightfully cautious about their interpretations of community patterns. Even when the outlines of structures are clearly delineated and there is no overlap among adjacent structures, contemporaneity is not easy to establish. Order to the arrangements of nonoverlapping structures may, however, provide a powerful basis for inferring contemporaneity. The arrangement of house platforms at the Riverton site is a case in point (Winters 1969:98). Such inferences can be strengthened by ethnographic data on community patterning that relate interhousehold spacing to social distance (Whitelaw 1989) and anticipated mobility (Kent 1991). The close spacing of small, adjacent structures at sites in the middle Savannah River valley, for instance, may represent the sorts of short-term occupations of kin-related households seen among the San, Efe, and other African hunter-gatherer bands (Sassaman 1993b, 1993d). In contrast, a greater degree of spacing among large structures (e.g., Ledbetter et al. 1994) may reflect greater interhousehold social distance and longer site occupations, such as those of the Alyawara (O'Connell 1987).

Another entry point into community patterning is the analysis of household spacing and geometry at shell rings and mound sites. The symmetry of shell-ring occupations suggests to Trinkley (1985) that Late Archaic societies of the South Carolina coast were egalitarian. That some occupants of shell-ring sites may have been situated outside of rings suggests instead some form of social differentiation (Simpkins and McMichael 1976). The same might be said of Poverty Point, where concentric mounds supporting domestic structures may signify social ranking.

Examples of isolated structures at Archaic habitation sites in the Southeast are not common, but this may be partly attributable to biases against small site investigations. The Mill Branch pithouse described earlier is a good example of an isolated structure, one that could not have housed more than a few adults. Unless one is willing to interpret the structure as a specialized, short-term occupation (e.g., hunting stand), it may be difficult to explain this example with popular models about hunter-gatherer settlement organization. Because interhousehold sharing is fundamental to the hunter-gatherer models we use to interpret Archaic prehistory, an isolated household seems enigmatic. However, put into a regional context, this structure may reflect the wide spacing of households dispersed into the uplands after seasons of large-scale integration, communal labor obligations, and pressures to conform. The site unit of analysis used by archaeologists, particularly in the context of cultural resource management, is not conducive to such interpretation inasmuch as wide household spacing would produce an archaeological record of separate sites.

The significance of community pattern data to studies of regional settlement organization cannot be exaggerated. For instance, social relations at the regional scale may be manifested in the structure of large aggregate camps. Among the Hidatsa, the living arrangements of visitors depend on the type of alliance between host and guest. In merger relationships, guests share the domestic space of their hosts, whereas in symbiotic relationships, visitors camp apart from their guests (Bowers 1965, cited in Albers 1993:117). As Albers (1993:117) indicates, the former arrangement reflects cooperation and the possibility of shared use of labor and resources; the latter arrangement conveys a measure of social distance whereby individuals do not have rights to appropriate one another's property and services freely. Community data such as these can thus help us to recognize and interpret the social changes associated with increased residential permanence and economic intensification witnessed in certain riverine and coastal settings.

All of the foregoing discussion begs for more detailed work on community patterning. Now that the search for structures is becoming routine, we must endeavor to collect data on communities, and this must be framed in regional terms so that variation in community structure can be understood as a reflection of the regional distribution of people. Obviously, more large-scale excavations are required, but also important are methods for documenting contemporaneity, including painstaking work such as flake refitting, and creative efforts to bring ethnographic observations to bear on archaeological data.

Explaining Architectural Variation

The range of architectural variation now evident in the archaeological record of the Middle and Late Archaic periods provides a prime research opportunity for exploring a variety of organizational variables. A thorough examination of these prospects is beyond the scope of this paper, but in this final section we delimit a series of relevant issues that we hope will guide future research.

Presence or Absence of Structures

The presence of structures at a site is usually taken as an indication of some type of habitation. As the review here shows, a range of structure types was used by Middle and Late Archaic peoples, and the degree of permanence to structures may provide some measure of settlement duration, at least anticipated duration. The type of habitation in question is another issue altogether (see below), but suffice it to say that efforts to construct any sort of structure to protect individuals from wind, precipitation, solar radiation, and the like imply at least overnight occupation. A human-made structure is, of course, unnecessary when natural features such as rock shelters are available, and under favorable weather conditions a structure may be unnecessary even for long-term stays, unless privacy and other cultural values come into play.

Whereas structures do imply some type of habitation, lack of evidence for structures does not necessarily imply a nonhabitation function. Ephemeral structures are not expected to leave direct traces of use, even under good preservation conditions. Moreover, most locations in the Southeast will lack direct evidence for structures even when substantial architecture was used. Methods for inferring the presence of structures from indirect evidence must be exhausted before interpretations of site function are reached. All too often the lack of features and a limited assemblage of flakes and cracked rock is equated with a specialized, limited-use, nondomestic function. The ethnoarchaeological literature of mobile, small-scale hunter-gatherer societies (e.g., Yellen 1977) shows that short-term occupations involving temporary structures leave little evidence of an archaeologically visible nature. It behooves us to examine more seriously small, ephemeral sites for indirect traces of structures and domestic functions if we are to ever reach a complete picture of regional organization and integration.

Permanent vs. Temporary Structures

The issue of structure permanence raised at the outset of this chapter cannot be resolved with a simple typology. Like mobility, structure permanence is a relative term. Some of the features of Archaic structures imply a considerable level of settlement permanence. These include prepared clay floors, substantial posts, and daub. It is not at all clear whether such architecture represents anticipated settlement permanence, reoccupation, or something altogether different. Likewise, the absence of these features may reflect the short-term use of particular structures, but it does not necessarily say anything about settlement permanence at particular locations. The lack of concordance among features indicative of substantial architecture embodies these ambiguities. Many of the prepared clay floors of Middle and Late Archaic structures lack postholes, whereas structures with sizable postholes lack evidence for intensive use. These and other ambiguities cannot be resolved with structural evidence alone. Because the design of structures is in part a reflection of anticipated mobility, the actual duration of occupations will have to come from other lines of evidence, such as refuse disposal patterns, subsistence remains, and tool replacement. Once better data are available on duration of occupancy, we suspect that factors such as seasonality and coresident group size will account in large measure for variation in structure permanence, or, more precisely, for the elaborateness of structures.

Structure Size

Structure size, like structure permanence, is affected by a variety of factors. If we could assume that all structures served the same function (i.e., domestic habitation), then structure size might be directly correlated with group size. Of course, group size will reflect function because hunter-gatherer organization is generally flexible to meet changes in ecological, social, and economic conditions. In this respect, the variation apparent in structure size during the Middle and Late Archaic periods reflects a variety of social arrangements. Structures on the order of 4–6 m in maximum dimension appear to represent the minimal social and economic unit of coresidency, that is, a nuclear family. Structures nine or more meters in maximum dimension have been interpreted as multifamily dwellings (e.g., Bentz 1988a, 1988b). This implies that nuclear families comprised the minimal units even during periods of coresidency under a single roof. Obviously this should be considered problematical, not inevitable, because there is nothing inherent about a nuclear family arrangement. Multifamily coresidency with periods of household dispersal is certainly a plausible scenario. But what determines whether households reside under a single roof or under separate roofs when occupying the same site? Even this question presupposes things about households that we have not even begun to address. This line of inquiry will depend very much on the mounting evidence for structures and how variation among them relates to functional differences within regional settlement and social systems.

Functional Variation

The general category of "domestic structure" encompasses a considerable deal of functional variation. Seasonality is an especially important variable because it subsumes some of the variables already discussed. For instance, the dichotomy between summer and winter houses described by Faulkner (1977) may be paralleled in the Middle and Late Archaic data, though there is apparently less regularity to the patterns of use in these early periods. Open, temporary structures would seem to provide sufficient architecture during warm-weather months, whereas fully enclosed dwellings would be required for cold-weather months. The extent to which group size varies seasonally is not readily apparent from this dichotomy. Both large and small open structures are documented in the Late Archaic period; interior hearths are also found in both cases, and whereas warm-climate groups such as the San do not set fires inside huts (Yellen 1977), Efe bands of the Congo employ interior hearths because of frequent rain (Fischer and Strickland 1991). Hearths for heating purposes are expected of cold-season structures in the Southeast, particularly in the higher elevations of the Interior Low Plateau, Ridge and Valley, and upper Piedmont provinces. Winter structures or "hot houses" used during the Middle Woodland in central Tennessee included twin earth ovens (Faulkner 1977). Described as "domestic hot houses" by Faulkner, such structures were built at permanent settlements where groups had come to depend on food production. He hypothesizes that a precedent for winter houses existed in the Late Archaic and Early Woodland periods when groups dispersed into upland winter hunting camps. Because these were seasonal sites, winter structures were impermanent. They would nonetheless contain evidence for internal heating, such as earth ovens, hearths, and ash accumulations. The Mill Branch pithouse is a good example. We add, however, that during the mid-Holocene winters were likely milder than today, so the use of a "hot house" may have been highly situational.

Ultimately, arguments about seasonal variation in architectural design must be bolstered with independent data. Subsistence data are implicated here, yet these will not usually be available and rarely are they conclusive with respect to seasonality. Again a regional perspective allowing for intersite comparisons and model building will have to be coupled with empirical data from particular sites to build strong inferences about season of use.

Other functions for structures should not be dismissed. The ceremonial functions of southeastern "hot houses" in late prehistory may have their seeds in the Late Archaic period (cf. Faulkner 1977). Mortuary structures are likely to occur at early mound sites. Other curative and magical activities may have been set apart from domestic dwellings in special structures, and we should not be surprised to find evidence for menstrual huts (Galloway 1991).

Conclusion

None of our expectations about architectural variation run counter to current notions of hunter-gatherer society in that our modern view of hunter-gatherers allows for a wide range of organizational diversity. Despite prior characterizations of Archaic structures as crude and flimsy, it is now obvious that Middle and Late Archaic structures included substantial and elaborate architecture as well as the ephemeral hut. We have yet to document the full range of architectural variation that existed, so our explanations will remain tentative. However, we advocate an aggressive program of research on the data currently available and suggest that such data, when combined with other lines of evidence and ethnographic insights, will form some of the best material available on regional social organization and integration.

Section III

Subsistence and Health

Syntheses of mid-Holocene subsistence and health begin in chapter 6 with a summary of paleoethnobotanical evidence by Kristen J. Gremillion. She starts by questioning the perceived stability in mid-Holocene plant use, rightfully noting that observed continuity in the exploitation of hickory nuts, for example, may have entailed modifications in technology, in mobility patterns, and in storage that cannot be reflected in floral data alone. Other chapters in this volume tend to support this notion. From evidence for human modification of local environments, or lack thereof, Gremillion suggests that responses to the Climatic Optimum varied across the region. Some variability in foraging patterns through time and across space is observed, although hickory consistently is the dominant component of Middle and Late Archaic mast assemblages, with the possible exception of assemblages from coastal sites—locations woefully underrepresented in the regional database. The record for early domesticates in the Southeast is especially varied. Unlike the Midwest, where plant domestication appears to have begun in lowland habitats, early native seed domesticates in the Southeast are found at mountainous locales like the Ozarks and Kentucky. Evidence for mid-Holocene domestication elsewhere is limited, underscoring the divergence of historical and environmental developments across the region. It also brings to the fore biases of differential preservation and recovery, topics Gremillion addresses in her recommendations for future research.

Faunal exploitation is of the subject of chapter 7 by Bonnie W. Styles and Walter E. Klippel. Increases in the use of aquatic resources and white-tailed deer are documented for the Midsouth in an analysis of fauna from several sites in Tennessee and Alabama. Although Styles and Klippel note that variation among these assemblages is explained by changes and differences in local resource availability, the Midsouth trends duplicate evidence from the lower Midwest, pointing to a paneastern pattern of subsistence, at least with regard to mammal exploitation. Because aquatic resources had more restricted distributions, intensified use of fish, turtles, and shellfish signify more stringent site-selection parameters and pressures to reoccupy. This is perhaps nowhere more apparent than in the record of coastal subsistence, which Styles and Klippel do not address but which is a secondary theme of chapter 10 by Michael Russo. Heavy reliance on shellfish and fish in coastal Florida, for instance, is coupled with independent evidence for year-round occupation. Use of aquatic resources at sites described by Styles and Klippel may form a Midsouth parallel, although evidence to support this is yet to be developed. One might further consider that although heavy reliance on white-tailed deer was paneastern in at least noncoastal settings, strategies of deer hunting likely varied with differences in group size, settlement permanence, and the like. If evidence for technological organization and innovations is any indication, deer hunting and aquatic resource use intensified simultaneously at sites in the Midsouth.

Maria O. Smith introduces data on biocultural adaptations in her treatment of trauma and occupational stress in chapter 8. Far from the idyllic and peaceful picture of Rousseau's Noble Savage, certain hunter-gatherer populations appear to have been embroiled in considerable interpersonal strife. Incidences of violent trauma covary with independent evidence for economic and social intensification, although preservational and interanalyst biases are legion in the regional data, as Smith repeatedly warns. Nevertheless, reexamination of extant skeletal populations, coupled with an increased appreciation for hunter-gatherer complexity, allows Smith to sketch a fairly detailed picture of strife, work load, and occupational stress, at least for the Midsouth. Intersite differences in the incidence of deliberate trauma suggest that there were important differences in the degree to which violence could be alleviated or avoided as well as caused. Certain work- and subsistence-related pathologies also reflect intersite variation that may implicate differences in gender relations, labor organization, and prestige. Ultimately it will be important to relate occupational stresses to evidence for violence; toward this end Smith provides many good recommendations for future research.

6

The Paleoethnobotanical Record for the Mid-Holocene Southeast

KRISTEN J. GREMILLION

The mid-Holocene has for the most part held little attraction for the paleoethnobotanist. Except for the transition to the late Holocene, when the first domesticates appear in the archaeological record, the mid-Holocene gives the impression of being an undifferentiated and monotonous continuation of the nut harvesting and limited environmental disturbance that characterized the early Holocene. In fact, particularly in the Southeast (where post-Pleistocene changes in the composition and distribution of forest communities were in many cases less dramatic than they were to the west and north), the stretch of time from the earliest well-documented human occupations to the initiation of food production appears to have been characterized by remarkable stability (or at least persistence) in the use of plant foods. Of course, late Pleistocene/early Holocene archaeobotanical assemblages are comparatively few in number, but a strong argument for subsistence continuity can be made on the basis of foraging theory and environmental data in conjunction with the limited archaeological database (Meltzer 1988; Meltzer and Smith 1986; Smith 1986).

However, this apparent stability should not discourage researchers from viewing the mid-Holocene Southeast as a worthy focus of paleoethnobotanical inquiry. If long-term continuity of plant use in the Southeast during most of the Archaic period turns out to be more apparent than real, paleoethnobotanical evidence will be central to research agendas that emphasize subsistence change. This outcome seems likely in light of the scarcity of high-quality paleoethnobotanical data sets from relevant archaeological contexts; those that do exist represent a sample of limited size and from scattered localities. Thus, inferences about continuity may simply reflect the inability of the limited database to provide adequate tests of hypotheses about subsistence change. The transformation of such inferences into assumptions may further reinforce our ignorance by discouraging the formulation of alternative hypotheses. Furthermore, stability in material evidence of behavior may mask adaptation to changing environments (Winterhalder 1980).

For example, local continuity in the subsistence importance of hickory nuts over several millennia probably entailed modifications of mobility patterns, storage, and processing technology that represent responses to changes in abundance and distribution of these resources. In such a case, what has really changed is not the set of resources used or their approximate relative contributions but the specific behaviors involved in their procurement. The observation that this kind of subsistence change may not be equally well reflected by all portions of the material record stands as a compelling argument for integration of paleoethnobotanical, faunal, spatial, and artifactual data sets.

Even if continuity is neither the product of limited data nor an adaptive response disguised as stasis, it nonetheless requires explanation. Stability is not to be taken for granted; it has causes, just as change does. Evolutionary biologists sometimes identify as *stabilizing selection* situations in which there is a single adaptive optimum for a given population so that the average phenotype is favored while extreme ones are eliminated (Mayr 1970:175). This process dominates in relatively constant environments that favor the same range of phenotypic states over at least several generations. Selection operating on cultural variation may likewise account for the persistence of low-level environmental disturbance and management and the dietary dominance of particular plant foods throughout much of the mid-Holocene. Thus, stability cannot simply be written off as a case of cultural inertia but must be evaluated in terms of the costs and benefits of different subsistence behaviors in a given environment.

Whether or not mid-Holocene stability in plant use is more apparent than real, then, a great deal of work awaits the archaeologist or paleoethnobotanist concerned with this period in southeastern prehistory. Broad generalizations about change and continuity over such a large region obscure important variation, both spatial and temporal. What is perceived as long-term stasis for the Southeast as a whole may mask considerable local variation in environment and responses to it. Likewise, chronological summaries will not capture all of the fluctuations in resource use within temporal analytic units that underlie any given directional trend.

The purpose of this chapter is, first, to summarize the most important archaeobotanical evidence for mid-Holocene plant use and discuss its significance for various models of subsistence change. Second, I identify important research issues that require continued acquisition of paleoethnobotanical data in order to be satisfactorily addressed. Finally, I offer some guidelines for ensuring that this research agenda can take full advantage of the research potential of paleoethnobotany. At times, I discuss sites and localities that lie outside the boundaries of the Southeast as it has been defined for this volume, but within the Southeast as most broadly defined in treatments of regional prehistory (Smith 1986:fig. 1.1). Locations referred to in this chapter are indicated on figure 6-1. Unless otherwise noted, all radiocarbon ages are uncalibrated.

Research Issues for Mid-Holocene Paleoethnobotany in the Southeast

Three basic areas of research can be identified that have contributed significantly to present knowledge as well as holding considerable promise for future investigation of mid-Holocene plant use. The first centers around environmental change and the development of anthropogenic ecosystems. Human modification of the environment, which greatly intensifies after the initiation of food production, may in fact have predated and in some respects precipitated that important transition. The role of climatic change in this trend is central to models such as Bruce Smith's "floodplain weed" theory of plant domestication (Smith 1987, 1992). Whether this theory is applicable to the Southeast hinges in part upon the regional effects of the Hypsithermal climatic interval, evidence for which therefore deserves close scrutiny. A second research area, the foraging adaptations of the mid-Holocene as viewed in both synchronic and diachronic perspectives, serves as a framework for documenting regional variability in plant use and paves the way for testing explanatory models. These adaptations set important precedents for and con-

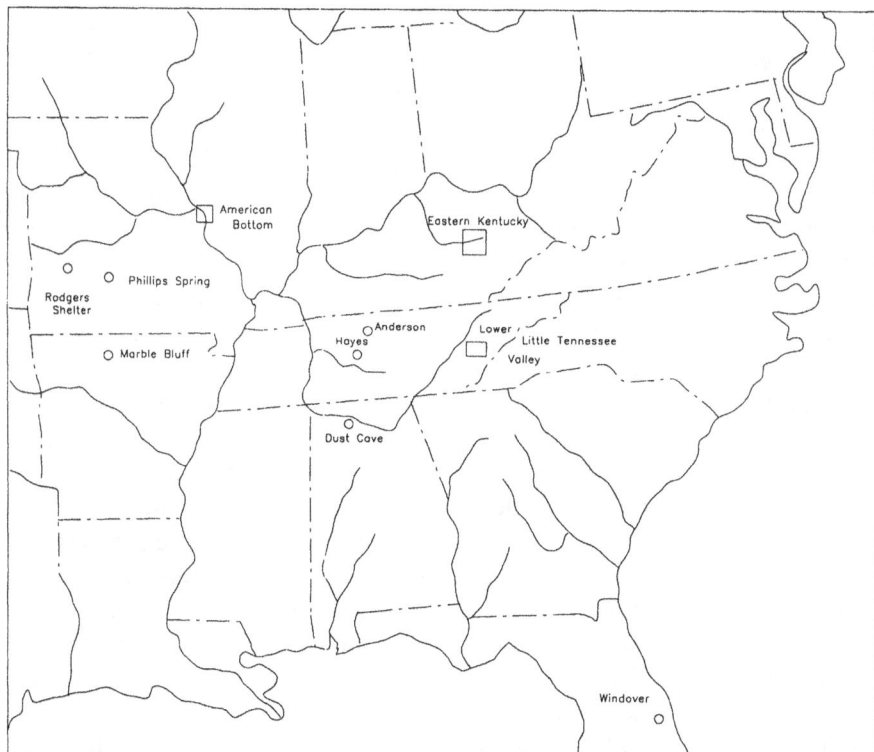

Fig. 6-1. Locations of selected southeastern sites and archaeological localities that have produced mid-Holocene paleoethnobotanical data.

straints upon the subject of a third research focus, the development of food production at the transition to the late Holocene.

Environmental Change and Anthropogenic Ecosystems

Bruce Smith (1987, 1992) has proposed a model of initial plant domestication in the major river drainages of the Midwest that is both theoretically sound and has so far stood up well to empirical tests. Following Anderson (1952), Smith identifies various human behaviors that improve the habitat and reproductive potential of weedy annuals growing in floodplain areas in the Midwest. He argues that the creation of extensive slow-moving aquatic habitats beginning around 6500 B.P. during the Hypsithermal climatic episode (ca. 8000 to 5000 B.P.) attracted human foragers to bottomland settlements. The repeated occupation of favored locations resulted in ongoing disturbance of existing vegetation, creating favorable environments for several weedy species including chenopod or lambsquarters (*Chenopodium berlandieri*), sumpweed or marshelder (*Iva annua*), and sunflower (*Helianthus annuus*). These prolific seed producers soon became preferred and ultimately managed resources, setting the stage for developed gardening economies. The plausibility of this scenario is supported by archaeological evidence from central and southern Illinois of intensified bottomland settlement and harvesting of wild precursors of weedy domesticates during the Middle and Late Archaic (Asch and Asch 1985; Brown and Vierra 1983).

Because this model has high potential for identifying important processes involved in initial plant domestication, its applicability to the Southeast deserves evaluation. Although its impact was felt more keenly farther west, the Hypsithermal climatic interval produced changes in the distribution and abundance of plant species in the Southeast that would have had repercussions for human foraging. For example, at Anderson Pond in central Tennessee, mid-Holocene forest composition reflects more xeric conditions, with oak, hickory, and ash as dominants (Delcourt 1979:277). Similar changes occurred between 7300 and 3900 B.P. at Jackson Pond in central Kentucky, where oaks, hickories, and chestnut replaced mesic taxa in upland forests (Wilkins et al. 1991:236). The pattern of river aggradation and stabilization that is correlated with intensified human occupation of floodplains and creation of shell and midden mounds can also be observed in the Southeast, at least west of the Appalachians. Evidence exists too for sedentary settlements including features such as prepared clay floors, extensive burial areas, and repeated occupation of locations in proximity to aquatic resources (Smith 1986:21–22; 25–27). On the western margins of the Southeast, mast resources were negatively impacted by the Hypsithermal. At Rodgers Shelter in west-central Missouri, for example, the shifting prairie-forest ecotone resulted in declining availability of oak and hickory in upland habitats between 8000 and 5000 B.P. (McMillan 1976:228).

Whether such environmental changes resulted in increased anthropogenic disturbance, thereby setting up conditions favoring plant domestication, remains to be seen. However, in at least one southeastern drainage, that of the Little Tennessee River in the Ridge and Valley province of eastern Tennessee, environmental and archaeological evidence has been collected that allows some tentative conclusions about relationships between climatic change, sedentism, and food production. Unfortunately, there is no pollen record from the Middle Archaic occupations of the drainage (Delcourt et al. 1986). However, there is some evidence that mid-Holocene aggradation of the river's first terrace was accompanied by increased exploitation of bottomland tree taxa for firewood (Chapman et al. 1982). Although aquatic resources were utilized during the Middle Archaic at sites such as Icehouse Bottom, repeated occupation of floodplain localities is not indicated (Chapman 1977, 1985b:148–149). Earliest evidence of gardening in the lower Little Tennessee valley is associated with Late Archaic deposits (Chapman and Shea 1981; Delcourt et al. 1986).

The lower Little Tennessee valley sequence represents one of the most complete combined paleoenvironmental and archaeological records for the interior Southeast. Unfortunately, there is a gap in that record during the critical 6500–4500 B.P. interval, during which the greatest effects of the Hypsithermal would have been felt. In order to evaluate Smith's floodplain weed model in the Southeast, such high-quality data sets must continue to be collected and supplemented. Problems of preservation may impede progress in this regard, given the likelihood of site destruction due to erosion (Chapman 1985b:149), but interpolation using data from preceding and later periods may offer a reasonable alternative. At present, Smith's model holds some promise for explaining initial plant domestication in interior southeastern drainages, but it is probably less applicable (at least without appropriate adjustments) to regions minimally affected by the Hypsithermal, such as the Gulf and Atlantic coastal plain and the Piedmont uplands. Interestingly, it is in these latter settings that evidence of food production prior to the ca. 1000 B.P. rise of maize agriculture is limited primarily to seeds of container crops such as bottle gourd and *Cucurbita* (Byrd 1976; Smith 1986:38).

Foraging Adaptations

Considerable geographic variability in foraging patterns is evident across the Southeast during the mid-Holocene, corresponding in some measure to contrasting environments of coastal plain, piedmont, and mountain regions. Temporal variability in the distribution of plant resources is also quite evident at this scale of analysis, with pine forests expanding in the coastal plain but not west of the Appalachians as the Hypsithermal drew to a close (Delcourt 1979:277). Climate consequently had different subsistence consequences for foraging populations across the Southeast. For this reason, it is for the most part possible to identify only the most general trends in plant use during the mid-Holocene.

At first glance, a good candidate for such a trend would seem to be the growing emphasis upon plant (as opposed to animal) food resources during the Middle Archaic. It has been argued that the specialized nature of hunting during the late

Pleistocene and early Holocene has been exaggerated for the Southeast, where deciduous forests of one type or another (rather than tundra and its associated megafauna) were established by ca. 10,000 B.P. or even earlier (Meltzer and Smith 1986:11). Instead, a relatively broad resource base including numerous plant taxa is indicated. Similarly, continuity with earlier adaptations characterized the mid-Holocene, with no evidence of expansion of the plant component of the diet (Smith 1986:10–11; 21). In fact, although the assumptions of a clear break with earlier plant use patterns and of ever-increasing adaptation are unwarranted, for the most part the evidence needed to determine the relative importance of plant and animal foods or to identify regional trends is simply not available.

Better opportunities exist to evaluate the relative subsistence importance of different plant resources during the mid-Holocene. Clearly the primary source of carbohydrates and vegetable fats (and probably a large portion of the calories) for many southeastern populations was mast (here including hickory nuts, walnuts, hazelnuts, chestnuts, and beechnuts as well as acorns). Of these, hickory (*Carya* sp.) is the most abundant nutshell type in Middle and Late Archaic archaeobotanical assemblages, although some samples and deposits deviate from this norm. This is certainly true of Kirk Stemmed/Stanly, Morrow Mountain, Savannah River, and Iddins collections from the Lower Little Tennessee River valley, where hickory makes up more than 50 percent of nutshell from four sites (Chapman and Shea 1981). Even more pronounced is the quantitative dominance of hickory shell throughout deposits at the Hayes site in middle Tennessee (Crites 1987). The same pattern is reflected in data from Dust Cave on the Tennessee River in northern Alabama, where hickory nuts appear to have been the principal mast resource throughout the Archaic occupation of the site (Gardner 1994). Thick-shelled hickory similarly dominates nutshell assemblages in the American Bottom during the Late Archaic (Johannessen 1984). Nut use at Rodgers Shelter in the lower Pomme de Terre valley of west-central Missouri during the mid-Holocene appears also to have been dominated by hickory, but evidence is based upon waterscreened samples and thus may be biased against thinner-shelled, more fragile nut types such as acorn (Parmalee et al. 1976). All in all, however, a strong case can be made for the subsistence importance of hickory throughout the Southeast during the mid-Holocene.

Although the subsistence centrality of hickory is seldom contested, its importance relative to that of acorn has been a subject of some controversy. One stimulus for this debate was the recognition that equivalent quantities of hickory and acorn shell represent different quantities of edible product, with acorn having a higher meat-to-shell ratio (Lopinot 1983). The fact that acorn shell breaks up more easily than hickory shell also contributes to a strong bias in the archaeological record of mast exploitation, rendering direct comparison of nutshell quantities (particularly those based on weight rather than fragments) unreliable for inferring subsistence importance. This bias prompted Yarnell and Black (1985:97) to argue that acorn, rather than hickory, was "the most important plant food in the Southeast until Mississippian times when it was replaced in this position by corn." They cite adjusted ratios of acorn to hickory created by multiplying acorn shell quantities by a factor of 50; this ratio is greater than one for all components included in their study and for all periods except the Late Archaic (Yarnell and Black 1985:98). Whether or not this interpretation is accurate, application of this correction factor to combined totals from many sites obscures interassemblage and interdeposit variability and may be inaccurate by several levels of magnitude, depending on the nut-to-shell ratios characterizing local populations. Certainly acorn was more important during the mid-Holocene than its quantities appear to indicate, but the question of its dietary importance relative to that of hickory remains unresolved.

Even if subsistence importance of these two key resources cannot be directly assessed using paleoethnobotanical data, trends in their utilization can be identified by comparing the representation of each taxon along a temporal scale. Yarnell and Black (1985:97) note that percentages of hickory shell in the Archaic and Woodland Southeast are variable, being highest in the terminal Archaic. Overall, there does not seem to be much temporal fluctuation in the importance of hickory based upon the total regional database; however, local sequences sometimes reveal trends in mast exploitation. For example, although hickory dominates Archaic nutshell assemblages at Dust Cave, it becomes more abundant (measured as numbers of fragments per 10 kg fill) in the Late Archaic Seven Mile Island levels than during the earlier Big Sandy occupation of the site (in which deposits were incidentally devoid of acorn shell) (Gardner 1994). In the lower Little Tennessee River valley, total percentages of hickory shell change little between the Early and Middle Archaic but are rather low for two Late Archaic components. For the same sites, acorn shell exceeds 10 percent of nutshell in six out of nine Early Archaic assemblages as compared to one out of six for the Middle Archaic and zero out of two for the Late Archaic (Chapman and Shea 1981).

Other sources of mast, such as butternut *(Juglans cinerea)* and walnut *(Juglans nigra)* and to a lesser extent hazelnut *(Corylus americana)*, beechnut *(Fagus* sp.), and chestnut *(Castanea dentata)*, were also used during the mid-Holocene. In comparison to hickory and acorn, walnut exhibits a clearer temporal pattern of occurrence during the Archaic sequence for the Southeast (Yarnell and Black 1985:97). In the lower Little Tennessee, walnut increases greatly in percentage during the Middle and Late Archaic (Chapman and Shea 1981) and throughout the Southeast becomes increasingly visible archaeologically beginning in the Middle Archaic (Yarnell and Black 1985:97). Percentages of walnut and butternut are relatively high during the Late Archaic at the Cloudsplitter shelter in eastern Kentucky, although Cowan et al. (1981:70) caution that overall differences between nutshell densities of Late Archaic and later periods are not statistically significant.

It is apparent that the use of mast resources in mid-Holocene subsistence varied considerably both geographically and temporally. At this point, perhaps the most valid generalization that can be drawn regarding this topic is that hickory was a key resource throughout the interior Southeast during the mid-Holocene. Acorn, and less frequently walnut, were in some situations of equal or greater importance but do not show as consistent a pattern of archaeological occurrence across time and space. The importance of acorn is almost always greater than relative raw nut-shell quantities seem to indicate, but even taking this potential bias into account it is not possible to make a convincing case for acorn consistently exceeding hickory in subsistence importance during the mid-Holocene.

So far, discussion has focused upon interior southeastern sites located in areas where deciduous forests were the dominant mature vegetation type, although grasslands were more common farther east than they are today. Less is known about plant use in coastal regions where wetlands, pine woods, and aquatic habitats make up a large portion of the local landscape and hardwood stands are restricted to well-drained soils (Vankat 1973:148). Unusually well preserved plant remains from waterlogged deposits at the Middle Archaic Windover site (ca. 8000 to 7000 B.P.) provide one of the few sources of evidence for mid-Holocene plant use in a coastal area (Newsom 1988). At Windover, samples associated with human burials (some of which appear to represent abdominal contents) varied in botanical composition but considered together contained numerous types of fleshy fruit seeds, including grape (*Vitis* sp.), hackberry (*Celtis* sp.), persimmon (*Diospyros virginiana*), and maypops (*Passiflora incarnata*). Hickory nutshell was not found in association with human remains, but hickory was frequent and live oak present in general site deposits. The difference between the evidence from carbonized assemblages from the southeastern interior (which suggests high dietary importance for mast) and that of human remains from Windover reflects local resource availability as well as the influence of differential preservation and depositional context. Coastal Floridians of the mid-Holocene probably utilized a different set of resources than that reflected in archaeobotanical assemblages from interior and more northerly sites due to differences in frequency and abundance of tree taxa. In addition, acorn and hickory may have been used to some extent at Windover despite their absence from abdominal contents. The likelihood of at least seasonal or occasional use of hickory and acorn by coastal populations is supported by data from fourth millennium B.P. shell middens on the South Carolina coast (Trinkley 1976).

Given the great variety of mast exploitation patterns in the mid-Holocene Southeast, it is difficult to assess the impact of the Hypsithermal on plant use. Gardner (1996) suggests that the warming trend of the Hypsithermal may have increased the abundance of xeric taxa such as most oaks and hickories and perhaps reduced the frequency of mast failure. Enrichment of the environment in this way permitted specialization on highly ranked resources (such as hickory) by reducing the costs that would have been incurred by rejecting less preferred foods in a resource-poor environment. However, there is little archaeobotanical support for increased importance of hickory in the Southeast during the mid-Holocene, although trends in acorn use are less clear. Subsistence continuity of this kind can perhaps be explained as a result of stabilizing selection in a relatively constant environment; however, if a similar mix of plant resources persisted despite environmental fluctuations, complex adjustments in other aspects of subsistence behavior may be implicated.

Besides nuts, other plant food remains from mid-Holocene sites in the Southeast are relatively rare and generally of limited quantity. Most of the seeds identified represent wild sources of fleshy fruits, grains, or greens, with some significant exceptions occurring at the mid to late Holocene transition (see Initial Plant Domestication, below). Although seeds of weedy annuals that occupy disturbed habitats are relatively meager in quantity during the mid-Holocene as compared to later periods (Yarnell and Black 1985), evidence of anthropogenic disturbance of vegetational communities in the lower Little Tennessee valley occurs as early as 6000 B.P. in the form of increasing representation of disturbance-favoring taxa in wood charcoal assemblages (Delcourt et al. 1986). More extensive land clearance awaited the further development and expansion of agricultural ecosystems in the Southeast. While mid-Holocene foragers did not live in a closed-canopy forest unmodified by human activity, their impact on existing vegetation was probably quite limited (with the possible exception of fire management; Hammett 1992).

Initial Plant Domestication

During approximately the last decade, the *terminus post quem* for initial plant domestication in the Southeast has been revised backward on several occasions. At present, it appears that morphological change related to domestication predates 4000 B.P. (Crites 1993), which implies that harvesting and replanting of seed is of somewhat greater antiquity. It is clear that several native seed crops were brought under domestication before 3500 B.P. in the Eastern Woodlands; most of the evidence for this development comes from sites in the Midwest (especially west-central and southern Illinois) and adjacent parts of the Southeast (notably central and eastern Tennessee and eastern Kentucky). A more controversial issue has been the cultigen status and geographic origin of cucurbits (*Cucurbita pepo*, gourd/squash, and *Lagenaria siceraria*, bottle gourd) dating to the mid-Holocene. Once accepted as solid evidence of contact with Mesoamerica, occurrences of *C. pepo* in mid-Holocene contexts are now believed to represent a hard-shelled native gourd that existed as a "camp-following" weed of human settlements for centuries before human manipulation resulted in morphological changes to fruits and seeds (Cowan and Smith 1993; Smith et al. 1992). Mid-Holocene bottle gourd also occurs in contexts that predate dietary dependence on domesticated plants (Doran et al. 1990).

Systems of food production did not develop at the same pace throughout the Southeast, however. Although problems of differential preservation complicate the reconstruction of intraregional patterns in the timing of initial plant domestication, it seems clear that groups in the Piedmont and Atlantic and Gulf coastal plains were only minimally involved with agriculture until the expansion of maize-based economies after ca. 1000 B.P. There is also variability in the environmental settings associated with the earliest domesticates, which include those dominated by riverine as well as upland vegetation and landforms. On a more restricted spatial scale, early crop remains have been found at both rock shelters and terrace or floodplain localities. At present it seems highly unlikely that there was a single "hearth" for plant domestication in the East, although its impact occurred earlier and was more pronounced in some southeastern regions than in others (see also Fritz 1990).

Mid-Holocene cucurbits and the independent domestication controversy. For many years, it was widely assumed by archaeologists working in the Southeast that prehistoric agriculture in the region had external roots. Maize, beans, and squash, economically central crops of the historic period in the Eastern Woodlands, were known to have considerable antiquity in Mesoamerica. Although in subsequent years the origins and domesticate status of maize and common bean have not been questioned, that of *Cucurbita* has undergone close scrutiny. The possibility of native domesticates preceding these crops was recognized by some, but their temporal priority over cucurbits at sites such as Newt Kash in eastern Kentucky could not be demonstrated (Gremillion 1993a, 1996; Jones 1936). The discovery of mid-Holocene cucurbit remains (ca. 4000 B.P.) from Phillips Spring, Missouri, and Carlston Annis and Bowles in central Kentucky was consequently greeted with great excitement by the archaeological community because they seemed to indicate the priority of Mesoamerican-derived crops (and, by implication, an external stimulus for the adoption of agriculture) (Chomko and Crawford 1978; Kay et al. 1980). By the time cucurbit rind from Napoleon Hollow and Koster in Illinois had been accelerator dated at ca. 7000 B.P. (Asch and Asch 1985; Conard et al. 1983), doubts had arisen as to both the cultigen status and the Mesoamerican origin of such materials. For example, King (1985) showed that the thickness of mid-Holocene rinds fell within the range of free-living *Cucurbita* gourds. Comparison of isozymes within and between populations of *C. pepo* (Decker 1988; Decker-Walters et al. 1993) and investigations into the ecology of free-living *Cucurbita* (Cowan and Smith 1993; Smith et al. 1992) added further support to the "indigenous gourd hypothesis."

Finds of *Cucurbita* from the Southeast to date indicate initial domestication sometime before 3000 B.P., with most examples being thin-shelled and indistinguishable from the free-living forms of *C. pepo*. For example, *Cucurbita* rinds from Hayes and Anderson in central Tennessee (Crites 1987, 1991) ranging in age from ca. 4500 to 7000 B.P. are similarly quite thin. The size of the Anderson site *Cucurbita* seed also is consistent with the interpretation that this material represents a nondomesticated (but possibly commensal) taxon. Archaic material from the lower Little Tennessee sites is limited to small fragments (Chapman and Shea 1981; King 1985). Cowan (1996) used a large collection of material from eastern

Kentucky to identify several stages in the utilization and domestication of *Cucurbita*. Based on changes in morphology, this plant was initially a source of seeds and a container crop, with fleshy-fruited forms developing only during the Woodland period. Increases in rind thickness over maxima for free-living populations are clearly evident by 3000 B.P. at the Cold Oak shelter (Gremillion 1993b), and possibly are represented in earlier Archaic assemblages from Cloudsplitter (Cowan 1996).

The domesticate status, source, and initial introduction of bottle gourd to the Southeast have also been reevaluated in recent years. Found alongside *Cucurbita* remains from Phillips Spring, bottle gourd rind and seeds added support to the notion of Archaic adoption of Mesoamerican crops in the East (Kay et al. 1980). However, Heiser (1985:67) does not reject the possibility that bottle gourd, although of African origin, might have been dispersed by ocean currents to the New World and migrated as a "camp follower" for millennia before becoming a crop. The discovery of a nearly intact bottle gourd fruit in association with a Windover human burial directly dated to ca. 7000 B.P. (Doran et al. 1990) documents the association of this useful container plant with mid-Holocene human foragers.

Native seed crops in the Southeast.   Like cucurbits, native seed crops such as sunflower, sumpweed, and chenopod make their earliest appearance in the Southeast west of the Appalachians and north of the Fall Line. Two regions producing such material, the Ozark uplands and the Red River Gorge area of eastern Kentucky, owe much of the quality and quantity of their contribution to the database to the arid and protected environments of dry rockshelters that were occupied by prehistoric people. A third area, central Tennessee, has produced carbonized evidence of mid-Holocene seed crops.

Dry rock shelters have produced the most useful assemblages from the standpoint of tracking morphological change and the development of plant management techniques. The "bluff shelters" of the Ozark uplands of northwestern Arkansas and southeastern Missouri have produced evidence of late mid-Holocene (ca. 3000 B.P.) domestication and storage in the form of a cache containing seeds of domesticated goosefoot, sunflower, sumpweed, and *Cucurbita* seeds from Marble Bluff (Fritz 1996). Far to the east, on the Cumberland Plateau of eastern Kentucky, a similar record of early domestication has emerged along with the acquisition of additional radiocarbon dates on key finds. At the Cold Oak shelter, terminal Archaic occupations (ca. 3000 B.P.) are associated with small quantities of seeds of goosefoot, sumpweed, and sunflower in addition to *Cucurbita* and crop plants such as maygrass, although large quantities of these seed types in storage contexts postdate ca. 2600 B.P. (Gremillion 1993b). Domesticated chenopod from the Newt Kash and Cloudsplitter shelters have been dated at ca. 3500 B.P. (Smith and Cowan 1987). Further support for dietary importance of cultigens in Late Archaic diets in eastern Kentucky is provided by human paleofeces from Hooton Hollow and Newt Kash containing various combinations of sunflower, sumpweed, and chenopod and directly dated by the AMS method to ca. 3000 B.P. (Gremillion 1995).

Archaeological investigations in central and eastern Tennessee have to date produced the bulk of carbonized archaeobotanical evidence for mid-Holocene seed crop domestication. Pre–4000 B.P. sunflower from the Hayes site (Crites 1993) revises the long-standing *terminus post quem* for domestication of this taxon, previously set at ca. 2900 B.P. (or, by implication, somewhat earlier) by material from the Higgs site on the Tennessee River (Brewer 1973). Although too small to represent a domesticated population, achenes of sumpweed from Hayes that appear to be of similar age (Crites 1991:73) are of interest because they indicate harvest or perhaps initial domestication of this taxon. Early use of maygrass, suspected of being a crop plant in later periods based on its occurrence at archaeological sites outside its present natural range and on its association with known domesticates, is indicated at the Hayes site in deposits that appear to be between ca. 6000 and 4000 years in age (Crites 1991:79). Maygrass was also recovered from Late Archaic samples at Bacon Bend in the lower Little Tennessee valley (Chapman and Shea 1981; Delcourt et al. 1986).

This record of early domesticates in the Southeast raises some important questions about the selective value of agricultural production in different environmental settings as well as about the mechanisms by which crops and associated cultural information were transmitted. Some of the earliest evidence for plant domestication in the Southeast comes not from lowland areas with broad floodplains and limited relief (such as the valleys of the Mississippi and its major tributaries), as Smith's floodplain weed model predicts, but from rugged, mountainous landscapes where rivers run along narrow, incised channels. Such localities would appear to be suboptimal for floodplain farming, although cultivation of hillsides would have had some advantages, including increased exposure to sunlight and avoidance of temperature inversions in deep valleys (Ison 1991). It seems at present that both upland and lowland regions served as "hearths" for domestication but with different processes and causes characterizing each (Fritz 1990:414–415; Watson 1985:146). There is no reason *not* to assume that the earliest farming was roughly contemporaneous in both types of settings, since the contribution of upland-dominated regions (such as the Cumberland Plateau of eastern Kentucky) to the record of early farming reflects to some degree the exceptional preservation of organic remains in rockshelters.

In any case, the floodplain weed theory requires some modification to be made applicable to initial domestication of local populations in regions lacking large expanses of bottomland. Perhaps, as Gardner (1996) suggests (following Munson 1986), a useful model to test is one in which climatic change at the end of the mid-Holocene simultaneously reduced predictability of mast yields and caused oaks and hickories to retreat in upland slopes and ridgetops. Attempts to increase the yield of mast trees in these settings could have produced the same type of anthropogenic disturbance in xeric uplands that improved habitats for weedy annuals in the larger floodplains of the Midwest. A similar pathway for domestication of the starchy and oily seed crops might have ensued, given the local availability of wild plant populations. Alternatively, domesticates may have been introduced through exchange.

In many respects, the absence of early food production from many south-eastern regions is as interesting and as worthy of explanation as is its occurrence in others. Little can be said about such matters for the Piedmont and Coastal Plain, except that regular (if geographically patchy) and systematic analysis of flotation samples has yet to produce a record of mid-Holocene plant domestication. Although some of the native domesticates were utilized in areas such as west-central Alabama in later times (Caddell 1982; Scarry 1986), there does not seem to have been an agricultural tradition of the same scale and degree of economic importance as that practiced to the north and west until the rapid rise of maize-based systems after ca. 1000 B.P. A high degree of investment in agricultural production does not seem to have developed over most of the Southeast until that time for reasons probably related to the relative costs and benefits associated with foraging and food production in different types of habitats. Particularly for coastal areas, in Archaic times a great discrepancy in the relative costs and benefits of farming and fishing-gathering-hunting might be expected to have kept the use of domesticates at low levels and low frequencies in human populations. In addition, historical factors including the distribution of various plant taxa, frequency and periodicity of environmental disturbance, and the character of exchange networks were important determinants of the patterns that emerged during the mid-Holocene and later.

Future Research

There is still a great deal that we do not know about mid-Holocene plant use in the Southeast, though we have a good foundation with which to begin formulating models and hypotheses for future testing. In order to advance knowledge in the three critical areas of investigation defined above (environmental change and anthropogenesis, foraging patterns, and initial food production), concerted efforts of archaeologists and archaeobotanical specialists alike are necessary. The most critical need is for continued (in some areas) and improved (in others) procedures for collecting the relevant archaeobotanical data. Second, but of equal importance for building and interpreting a regional database, is the systematic gathering of archaeobotanical and archaeological data from sites that crosscut environmental boundaries at various scales of analysis, at the same time taking into account both cyclical and unpredictable periodicity in environmental parameters and their effects upon subsistence behavior. Third, more syntheses are needed that marshal a wide range of types of data (archaeobotanical, palynological, archaeological, faunal, geological) to assist in the documentation and explanation of mid-Holocene plant use.

Data Collection and Analysis

All too often, analysis of plant remains is the first item on the budget of a Cultural Resource Management project to be deleted when costs run high or is contingent upon having funds left over after the "real archaeology" is done. The tendency of some archaeologists to underbudget for paleoethnobotanical research reinforces the perception that such expenditures provide little return, since the limited nature of results is often a function of limited investment in collection and analysis. In other cases, results are less rewarding even given an adequate sample, but absence of plant remains of certain types (if less entertaining for the analyst) is potentially of great significance in understanding regional patterns. Fortunately, the tendency to disregard, underfund, or ritualize archaeobotanical analysis is diminishing greatly in the Southeast, although these factors vary from firm to firm and from laboratory to laboratory.

Now that flotation recovery has become routine on archaeological projects in the region, how can we ensure the maximization of the potential of the archaeobotanical database for contributing to our knowledge of mid-Holocene plant use? First, soil samples of adequate quantity must be taken, and they should be either of standard size or of known volumes. Ten liters is *not* too much; it is a good standard size to begin with and can be modified as more is learned about the site and its deposits. Recording of soil volumes is crucial to documenting the density of plant remains in different deposits and adjusting for differential sample size when making quantitative comparisons. Second, an adequate quantity of samples must be taken to increase the probability of recovering rare items (such as seeds of domesticates that might have been of only minor economic importance) and to sample adequately different contexts within each site. It is impossible to say what percentage of total excavated sediments should be treated in this way, but flotation of 50 to 100 percent of the fill from each feature is feasible for many projects. In addition, general excavation levels, lenses, and "off-site" deposits should be sampled. I cannot overstress the importance of obtaining such high-quality, high-volume archaeobotanical collections from mid-Holocene sites. In most cases, interpretations of subsistence change from this period will depend heavily upon comparison of quantified data from habitation residues. Cases in which a single seed is a matter of great significance are likely to be rarer as earlier periods are approached, and there will probably not be well-preserved collections of crop seeds to distract analysts from the task of sorting and quantifying nutshell and wood. But in order to identify what may be quite subtle shifts in the use of mast resources and other wild foods, good sampling and accurate, reliable quantification are crucial. In addition, in contexts that allow it, environmental data (especially in the form of pollen) should be collected wherever conditions are such that good preservation can be expected. As many sources of evidence as possible should be enlisted to reconstruct mid-Holocene environmental variability, since such conditions affect the fitness value of different subsistence behaviors.

Regional Sampling Strategies

Seasonal patterns of movement between bluffs or ridgetops and lower slopes, ter-races, and floodplains provided both opportunities for and constraints upon pro-duction and collection of plant foods. In order to identify causal relationships between land use and food acquisition, we need to understand what role each type of locality played in annual subsistence and how those roles changed over time and varied across space. For example, storage of plant foods (including domesti-cates) became important in the Early Woodland in the Red River Gorge and is associated with increased utilization of rock shelters (Cowan 1985). Perhaps, as Wills (1992) suggests for the Mogollon highlands, agriculture initially served simply as a source of storable food that enabled extended occupation of environ-mental zones containing abundant resources of temporally limited availability. To evaluate models such as this one, we need to know more about intra-annual move-ment and site function for specific localities. In addition, thorough sampling will limit the tendency to base interpretations about an entire cultural period upon a data set that may reflect a single season's or single year's activity. This caveat is par-ticularly important since year-to-year and seasonal variability can have important consequences for subsistence decision making (Winterhalder 1980). Thus it is important whenever possible to take into account the full range of variation of any environmental or cultural parameter.

Synthesis

Archaeobotanists too often work in isolation, with little knowledge of the site or region they are investigating. This situation is changing with the tendency of pa-leoethnobotanists to be "real" archaeologists involved in doing their own field-work, and with growing sensitivity in the archaeological community as a whole to the potential and difficulties of paleoethnobotanical research. In most cases, that potential can be maximized only by integrating various archaeological data sets. Studies of site distribution alone will not give us the answers we need about mid-Holocene subsistence, and interpretations of archaeobotanical data will always be somewhat flawed without some understanding of how prehistoric people inter-acted with the landscape in which they lived. Ideally, faunal data must be consid-ered to avoid the false impression that plant harvesting and management took place free of contingency upon other subsistence activities. Geological expertise is crucial for understanding deposition patterns in stratigraphically complex sites and for accurately determining the context of plant remains. The conditions for this ideal scenario, of course, will not always be met, even given the most extrav-agant budgets. However, it is a worthy goal to work toward.

Finally, our chances of coming up with answers to the important questions about mid-Holocene plant use will be greatly enhanced by a program of model development and hypothesis testing. Only by this means can we direct our limited resources toward the most important questions and expect to develop useful answers. Focusing in this way advances knowledge, whether in a small way or a major one. Darwinian approaches to change, particularly but not exclusively the theory of natural selection, offer some potentially powerful tools for archaeobotanical research. These approaches can be tailored to take into account the unique features of cultural transmission of information (Boyd and Richerson 1985). Although Darwinian approaches to subsistence change hold much potential, more important than adherence to any particular theory is the recognition that theory is a key component of understanding prehistory. Such understanding has never been simply the product of accumulated facts, and the best paleoethnobotanical research recognizes this.

7

Mid-Holocene Faunal Exploitation in the Southeastern United States

BONNIE W. STYLES AND WALTER E. KLIPPEL

The early to mid-Holocene transition in the southeastern United States was marked by changes in climate, vegetation, (Delcourt and Delcourt 1979, 1981, 1983; Watts 1980, Watts et al., this volume), geomorphology (e.g., Brackenridge 1984), resource distributions, and human adaptations, including subsistence patterns. In a discussion of early to mid-Holocene subsistence shifts, Bruce Smith (1986:21) writes: "While it is often difficult to determine accurately either the intensity or the direction of these subsistence changes, they do not reflect a uniform pansoutheastern convergence on a single, ultimate adaptive solution. Rather they suggest a variety of local adjustments—some major, some minor—to alternations in the habitat and changes in the potential resources of the catchment areas of different populations." He suggests (1986: 21–22) that the only significant shift in the range of fauna exploited was the "dramatic increase in the utilization of riverine aquatic species, which became a major component in the diet of middle Holocene populations situated along major southeastern river valleys."

Quantitative comparisons of faunal remains from a series of southeastern archaeological sites serve to document changes in early and mid-Holocene faunal assemblages. These data support the premise that at a local scale, environment is important in configuring the focus and mix of subsistence pursuits. Nevertheless, this chapter documents that on a regional scale the evolution of subsistence patterns in the Midsouth was similar to that described for the Mississippi and Illinois river valleys of the Midwest (Styles 1993; Styles et al. 1983). At the regional scale—and perhaps beyond—there is an evolutionary trend to a greater use of aquatic resources and an increased emphasis on white-tailed deer (when compared with other mammals) as one moves from the early to the mid-Holocene. The patterns we describe do not encompass coastal subsistence practices, which apparently involved an even greater reliance on aquatic resources and less dependence on white-tailed deer (Russo, this volume).

Methods

We restrict this study to sites from southern Illinois and the Ohio River drainage southward and from the Mississippi River eastward. We include only sites for which settlement function was reported and from which vertebrate fauna have been recovered through at least quarter-inch (0.64 cm) mesh screens; were well preserved; and have been systematically identified, tabulated, and reported—a process that resulted in a small sample of sites, all in the Midsouth. The subsistence analysis is based on 15 components from six sites (fig. 7-1): Modoc Rock Shelter and the Black Earth site in southern Illinois, the Austin and Hayes sites in Tennessee, and Russell Cave and the Stanfield-Worley site in Alabama. Cheek Bend Cave in Tennessee is included because its rich paleontological deposits provide evidence for local environmental changes. Smith Bottom Cave in northwestern Alabama contains a rich faunal assemblage including Early through Late Archaic strata (Parmalee 1993; Snyder and Parmalee 1991) but is not used for quantitative comparisons due to stratigraphic problems. The Eva site (Lewis and Lewis 1961), which also yielded well-preserved early and mid-Holocene faunal assemblages, is omitted from quantitative comparisons because of obvious biases against the recovery and identification of small animals.

Vertebrate faunal taxa are initially divided into eight categories based on economic importance and gross habitat preference (e.g., Styles 1994): fish, aquatic turtles, terrestrial turtles, water birds (i.e., waterfowl and other birds associated with aquatic habitats), other birds, white-tailed deer, other terrestrial mammals, and semi-aquatic mammals. The category of other terrestrial mammals includes primarily small and medium-sized mammals like squirrels, raccoon, cottontail rabbit, canids, and small rodents. For specific analyses of mammalian composition, squirrels are included as a separate category.

Quantitative summaries use the number of identified specimens (NISP). Although comparisons based on NISP suffer from differences between taxa, such as in the numbers of elements that can be identified and in the density and fracturing of bone, these data are not biased by differences in how the faunal remains are grouped for calculations of minimum numbers of individuals (MNI). Given that the goal of this analysis is to examine broad changes in the proportional representation of faunal taxa, the use of NISP is appropriate (see Grayson 1984:64). Besides, MNI data were not available for all assemblages under consideration (i.e., Stanfield-Worley and Russell Cave). Our review of evidence for early to mid-Holocene changes in environment and faunal exploitation is organized by sites in the sections that follow.

Modoc Rock Shelter

Modoc Rock Shelter, situated in the Mississippi River Valley of southern Illinois (fig. 7-1) occurs in an optimal setting for the exploitation of aquatic resources. Data are summarized for grouped Early Archaic/early Holocene strata (ca.

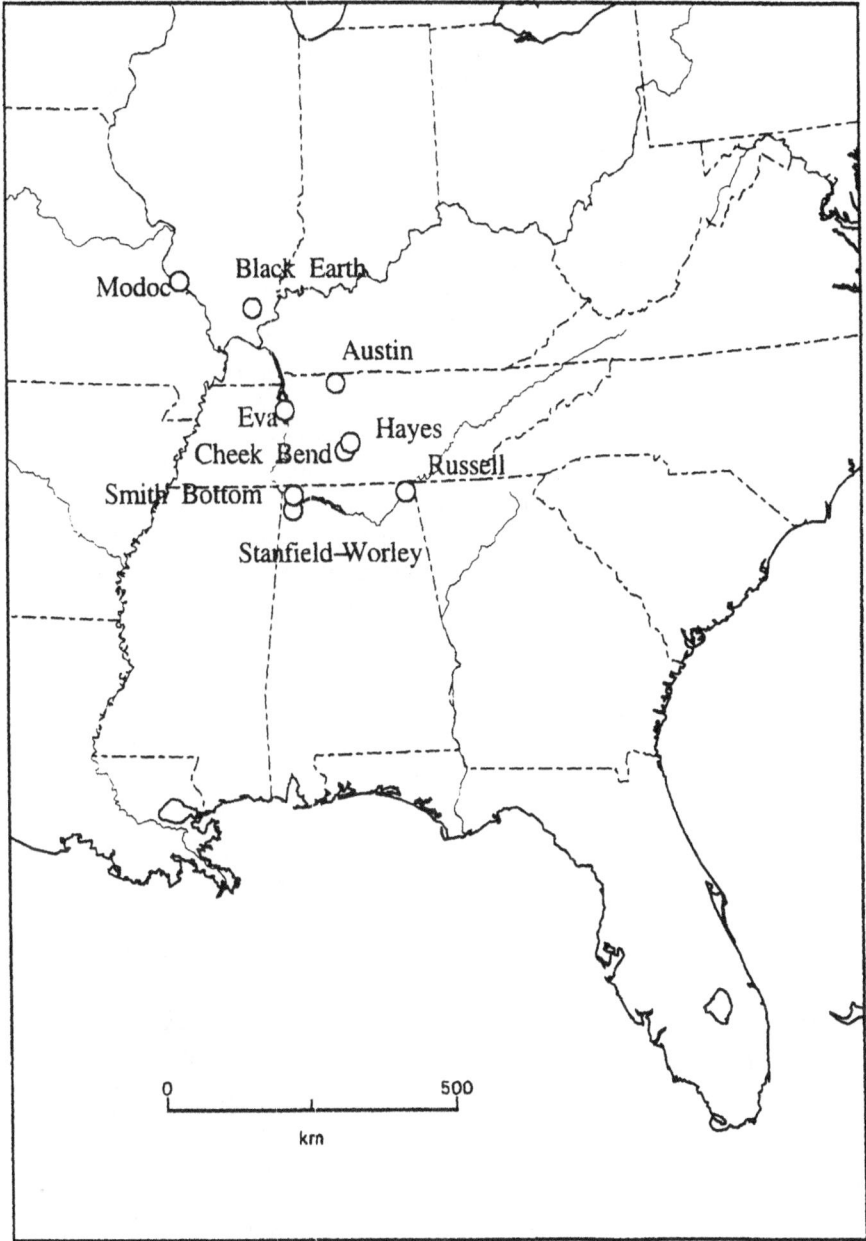

Fig. 7-1.   Locations of archaeological and paleontological sites in the study area.

8500–8200 B.P.) and three series of Middle Archaic/mid-Holocene strata (early Middle Archaic [8000–7200 B.P.], middle Middle Archaic [6800–6200 B.P.], and late Middle Archaic [5600–5200 B.P.]). There are obvious shifts in faunal composition from the early to mid-Holocene (fig. 7-2). Strata dating to the mid-Holocene show a greater proportional representation of white-tailed deer and fish. The increase in fish corresponds with geologic (Hajic 1991) and faunal evidence for development of backwater lake habitat and with a general trend toward longer-term base camp occupations (Styles and White 1991). A sudden and dramatic increase in bowfin (*Amia calva*), a species characteristic of quiet water habitats (P. Smith 1979:23), may herald the presence of productive, shallow-backwater habitats by 8000 B.P. (Styles and White 1991). Aquatic habitats were thus enhanced as floodplains evolved, especially with the development of backwaters in major river valleys of the mid-Holocene (Styles 1986). These floodplain developments were prerequisite for shifts in subsistence and settlement strategies that led to floodplain-focal economies in some areas in the midwestern United States.

Changes in mammalian taxa (fig. 7-3) reflect a clear decline in the representation of squirrels and other terrestrial mammals and an increase in the representation of white-tailed deer in the mid-Holocene. An abundance of squirrels, particularly gray squirrels (*Sciurus carolinensis*), in early Holocene sites in the lower Illinois River valley has been attributed to opportunistic exploitation of locally abundant small mammals at mobile residential camps (Neusius 1982). McMillan and Klippel (1981) link the high frequency of gray squirrels in deposits at Graham Cave in central Missouri with greater availability of this species in early Holocene forests. Clinally, gray squirrels at Graham Cave were smaller in size (Purdue 1980), which suggests a moister, perhaps cooler environment during the early Holocene (Graham and Mead 1987:390). Styles et al. (1983) and Styles and White (1991) argue that Early Archaic subsistence and settlement strategies at short-term residential camps at Modoc Rock Shelter may have targeted these arboreal rodents. Styles and White (1991), like McMillan and Klippel (1981), argue that environmental differences played a role. In Illinois, the gray squirrel is associated with extensive, mature, closed forest settings (Hoffmeister 1989:166–167). In fact, numbers and proportions of gray squirrels relative to fox squirrels have historically declined in Illinois forests with lumbering and the overall reduction of forest habitat (Hoffmeister 1989:167). Thus, gray squirrels may have been more abundant in early Holocene forests than in more open mid-Holocene forests, and, as will be argued below, white-tailed deer may have been less abundant in the early Holocene than in the mid-Holocene.

Some researchers (e.g., Neusius 1982) have noted that a greater focus on white-tailed deer during the Middle Archaic parallels the establishment of base camps with logistical mobility strategies for the exploitation of deer and other resources. Changes in subsistence-settlement systems are ultimately linked to (1) "increased patchiness in resource distributions in response to drier climate," which "would have differentially affected the cost curves for procurement strategies," and (2) the

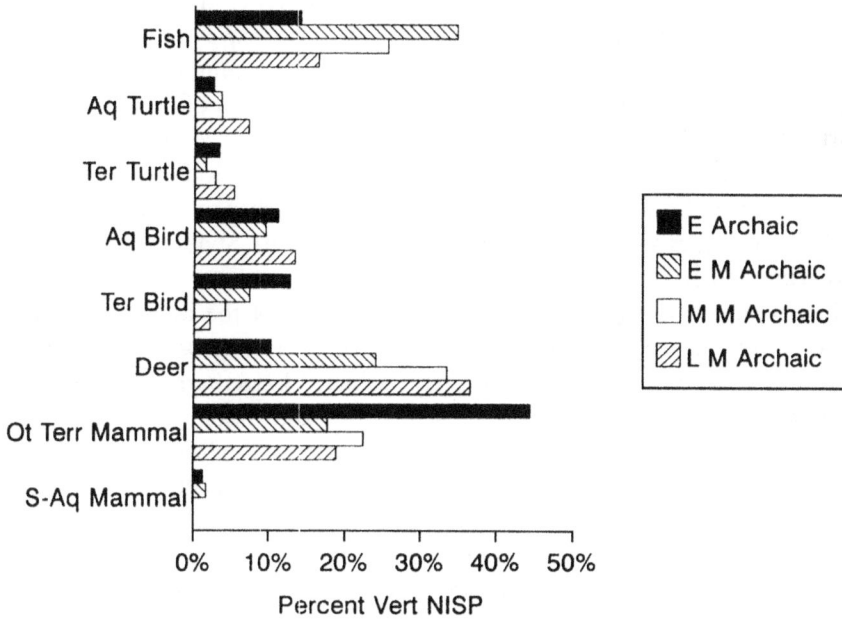

Fig. 7-2. Proportional representation of fauna in Early and Middle Archaic strata at Modoc Rock Shelter (Aq = Aquatic, Ter = Terrestrial, Ot = Other, S-Aq = Semi-aquatic, E = Early, M = Middle, L = Late, NISP = number of identified specimens).

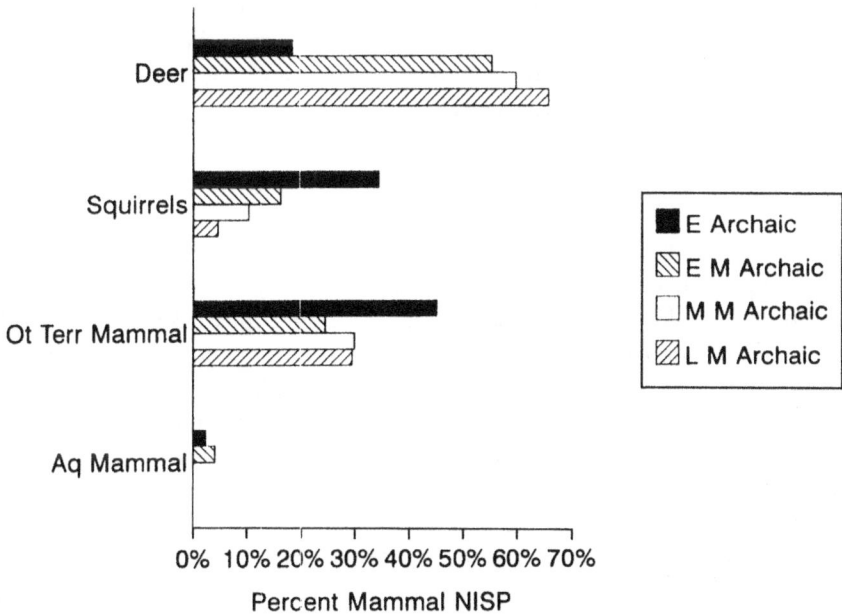

Fig. 7-3. Proportional representation of mammals in Early and Middle Archaic strata at Modoc Rock Shelter (Ot = Other, Terr = Terrestrial, Aq = Aquatic, E = Early, M = Middle, L = Late, NISP = number of identified specimens).

raising of "output requirements" due to the concentration of populations in major river valleys (Neusius 1982:316). Others have related the greater focus on deer in some regions, such as the areas around Graham Cave in central Missouri and Modoc Rock Shelter in southern Illinois, to an opening of the forest that expanded optimal deer habitat and thus led to an expansion of deer populations during the mid-Holocene (McMillan and Klippel 1981; Styles and White 1991; Styles et al. 1983). The increased use of white-tailed deer at Modoc is attributed to the combined effects of opening of the forest and a change in settlement and mobility strategies to longer-term base camp occupations (Styles et al. 1983; Styles and White 1991).

Improvements in aquatic habitats and an opening of the forest in the mid-Holocene provided the opportunity for increased use of fish and white-tailed deer in Middle Archaic economies and ultimately facilitated longer-term occupations in some areas. Changes in subsistence, settlement, and mobility strategies contributed to even more intensive use of faunal resources. Environmental and subsistence changes are discernible through changes in the proportional representation of taxa, rather than in gross presence or absence of species.

There is some evidence for minor changes in species distributions and in body sizes of animals at Modoc Rock Shelter. Three species of mammals (i.e., spotted skunk, pocket gopher, and hispid cotton rat) show minor northward or eastward range extensions during the mid-Holocene (Styles et al. 1983). Changes in species composition and clinal variation in size of gastropods support claims for cooler and moister early Holocene environments and drier mid-Holocene settings (Theler and Baerreis 1981, 1991). In addition, mid-Holocene deer at Modoc are 20 percent smaller than Woodland and Mississippian deer from the same region; the size reduction is related to nutritional deficits in summer forage based on more xeric conditions in the mid-Holocene (Purdue 1991).

Black Earth Site

The Black Earth site, situated on the South Fork of the Saline River in southern Illinois (fig. 7-1), along the edge of a shallow lake, yielded abundant faunal remains from midden and feature deposits (Breitburg 1982). Although aquatic resources would have been available near the site, the area would not have been as lucrative for waterfowl and fish as the Mississippi River Valley. The thick midden was arbitrarily divided into four late Middle Archaic strata, which we have numbered arbitrarily from 1 to 4, from oldest to youngest. They range in age from 5640 to 4860 B.P. and reflect long-term base camp occupations. The composition of the fauna in the four strata is remarkably similar (fig. 7-4). Fish and waterfowl are more sparsely represented than in mid-Holocene strata from Modoc Rock Shelter. However, remains of small fish are relatively abundant in fine-screened column samples (Oetelaar 1982); they are probably underestimated in the screened faunal data presented here. The Black Earth assemblage clearly shows the dominance of white-tailed deer. The composition of the mammalian taxa reveals a low frequency of squirrels and other terrestrial mammals and a high representation of deer (fig. 7-5) when compared to the Early Archaic strata at Modoc and other early Holocene sites.

Stanfield-Worley Bluff Shelter

The Stanfield-Worley Bluff Shelter, situated in the valley of Henson's Creek, about seven miles from the Tennessee River in northwestern Alabama (fig. 7-1), offers the earliest archaeofaunal record, with radiocarbon dates of 9600 and 8920 B.P. The Dalton Zone appears to have been associated primarily with hunting camps (DeJarnette et al. 1962:87). The composition of the faunal assemblage (fig. 7-6) indicates a reliance on terrestrial resources, especially deer and other terrestrial mammals. Only five fish bones were recovered. Deer dominate the mammalian assemblage, but as noted for Early Archaic strata at Modoc Rock Shelter, squirrels are notably abundant (fig. 7-7). Parmalee (1962:112) argues that the abundance of gray squirrel indicates "a formerly heavily timbered region with an ample undercover of brush." The porcupine is the only species in the assemblage that occurs outside its modern range (Parmalee 1962, 1963). Guilday et al. (1977, 1978) note that the porcupine prehistorically occupied diverse areas—as it does today—and thus is not a good indicator species for climatic change.

Russell Cave

Russell Cave, situated three miles up a steep-sided valley, is about seven miles from the Tennessee River valley in northeastern Alabama (fig. 7-1). Proximal water bodies include Dry Creek, an intermittent stream, and Widows Creek about 1.5 miles down the valley from the cave. Weigel, Holman, and Paloumpis (1974) analyzed the vertebrate faunal remains from the well-preserved early and mid-Holocene layers. The Early Archaic layer (G) yielded dates of 8500–7600 B.P. The Middle Archaic layer (F) dates between 6300 and 6000 B.P. The Early and Middle Archaic occupations have been interpreted as seasonal but not specialized. Griffin (1974:111–112) proposed that they represent a series of winter camps. The descriptions of settlement function are similar to those noted for the early Holocene residential camps at Modoc Rock Shelter. The mid-Holocene layer (fig. 7-8) shows a greater representation of white-tailed deer and fish and lesser representation of other terrestrial mammals when compared to the early Holocene layer. Squirrels are more abundant than deer in the early Holocene mammalian assemblage (fig. 7-9). The pattern is reversed for the mid-Holocene assemblage. Porcupine occurs in the early and mid-Holocene assemblages and one bone from an extinct peccary occurs in the early Holocene assemblage. As noted above, porcupine had such a broad distribution in the Pleistocene and Holocene that its occurrence here may be of little environmental significance

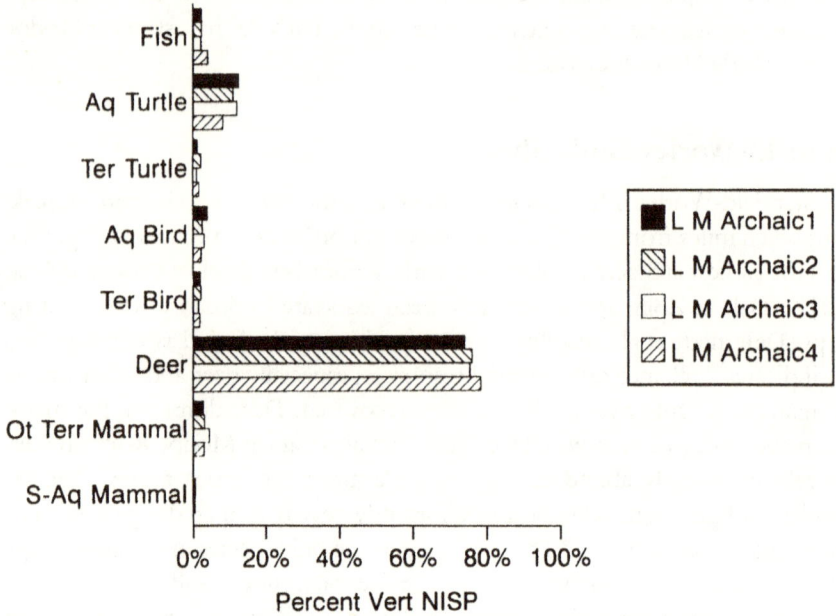

Fig. 7-4. Proportional representation of fauna in Middle Archaic strata at the Black Earth site (Aq = Aquatic, Ter = Terrestrial, Ot = Other, S-Aq = Semi-aquatic, L = Late, M = Middle, NISP = number of identified specimens).

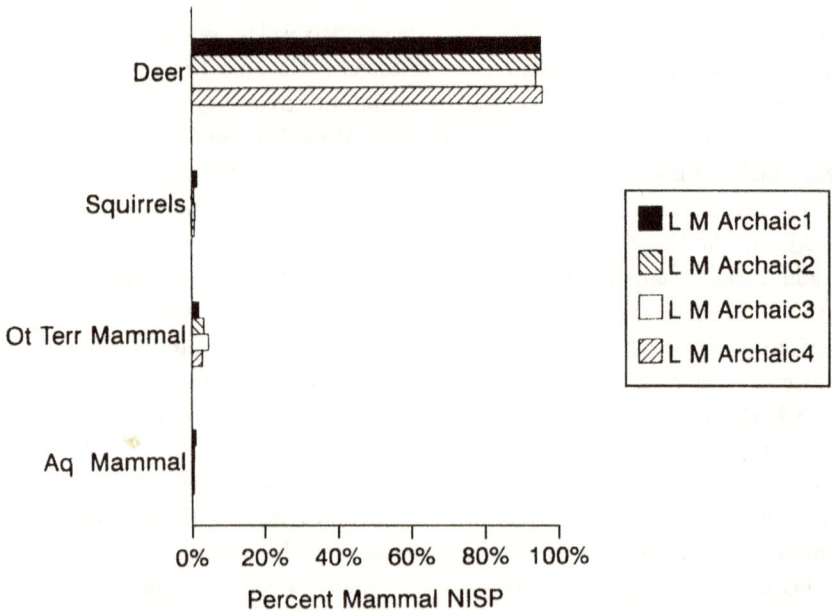

Fig. 7-5. Proportional representation of mammals in Middle Archaic strata at the Black Earth site (Ot = Other, Terr = Terrestrial, Aq = Aquatic, L = Late, M = Middle, NISP = number of identified specimens).

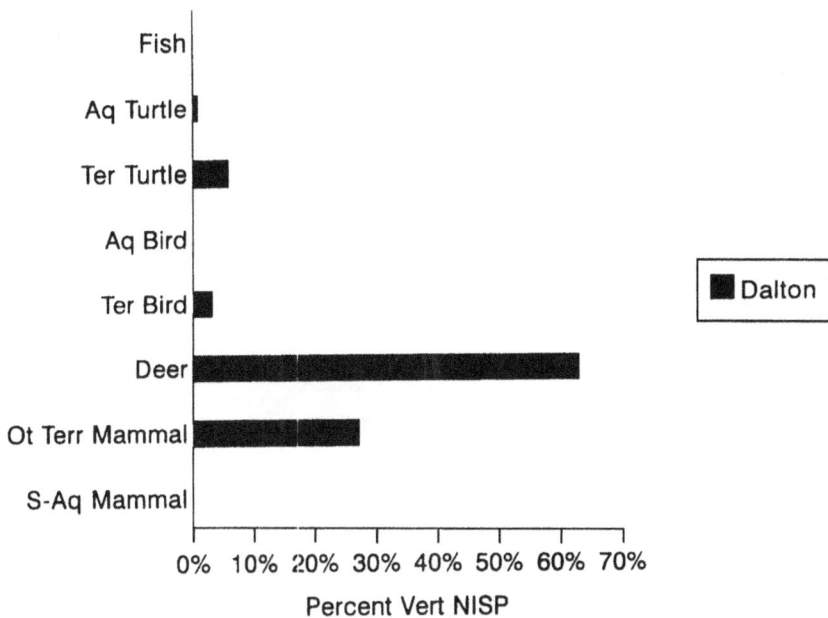

Fig. 7-6. Proportional representation of fauna in the Dalton component at the Stanfield-Worley site (Aq = Aquatic, Ter = Terrestrial, Ot = Other, S-Aq = Semi-aquatic, NISP = number of identified specimens).

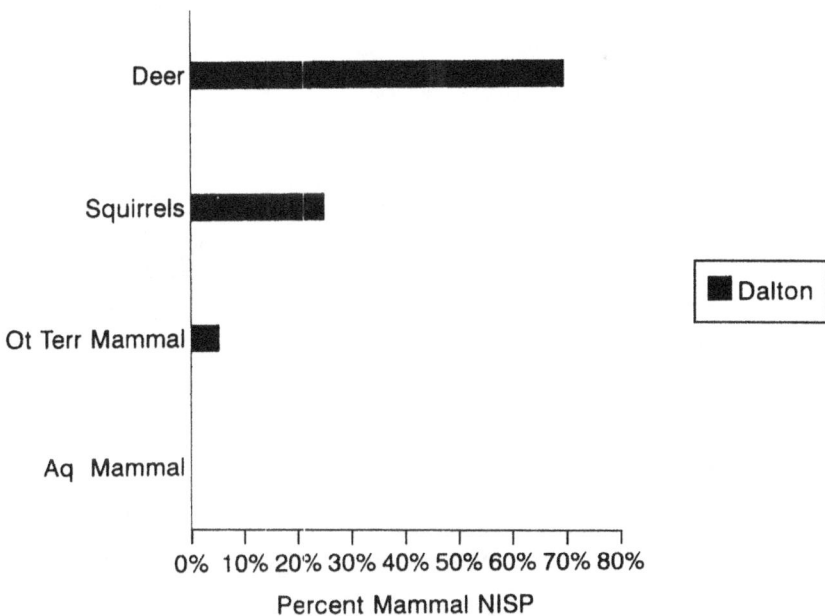

Fig. 7-7. Proportional representation of mammals in the Dalton component at the Stanfield-Worley site (Ot = Other, Terr = Terrestrial, Aq = Aquatic, NISP = number of identified specimens).

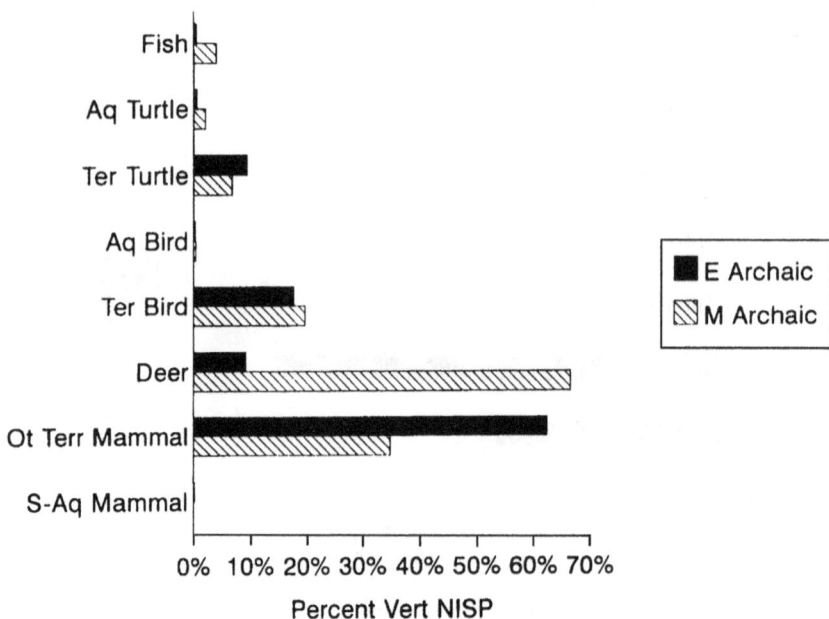

Fig. 7-8. Proportional representation of fauna in Early and Middle Archaic strata at Russell Cave (Aq = Aquatic, Ter = Terrestrial, Ot = Other, S-Aq = Semi-aquatic, E = Early, M = Middle, NISP = number of identified specimens).

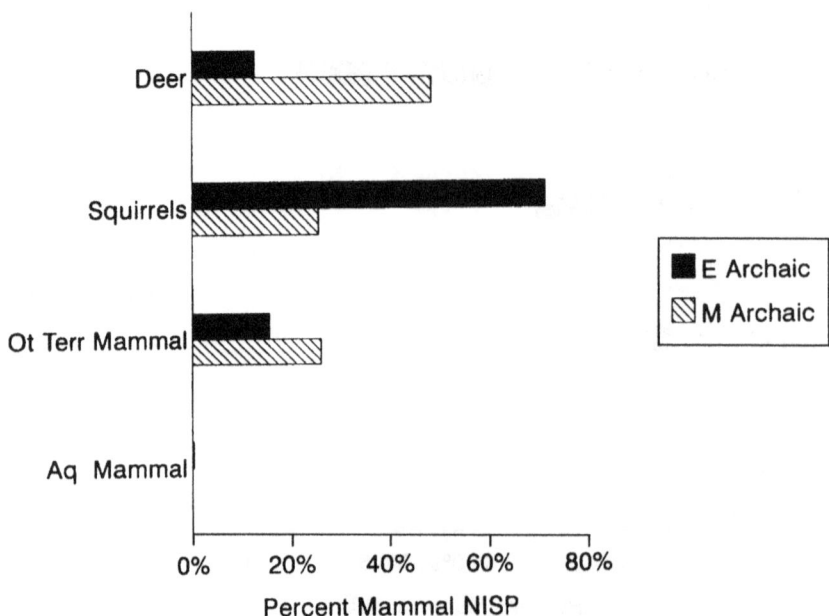

Fig. 7-9. Proportional representation of mammals in Early and Middle Archaic strata at Russell Cave (Ot = Other, Ter = Terrestrial, Aq = Aquatic, E = Early, M = Middle, NISP = number of identified specimens).

(Graham and Mead 1987:390). The extinct peccary, originally interpreted as a potential relict occurrence of this late Pleistocene woodland species in the Holocene (Weigel et al. 1974:82), has been argued by Graham and Mead (1987:387) to be evidence for "redeposition from the remnant Pleistocene strata."

Austin Site

The Austin site, situated along a tributary of the Cumberland River in north-central Tennessee (fig. 7-1), yielded two faunal assemblages attributed to Middle Archaic base camps. Barker and Breitburg (1992) reported the two assemblages: the older (Stratum III) yielded dates of 6630 and 6220 B.P., and the younger (Stratum II) yielded dates of 6250 and 6010 B.P. but constituted a small sample. Although some minor differences in the two strata are noted (fig. 7-10), the assemblages are dominated by terrestrial taxa, especially deer and other terrestrial mammals. The larger of the two samples shows that white-tailed deer, squirrels, and other terrestrial mammals, especially cottontail rabbits, are relatively abundant (fig. 7-11). As noted, the opening of mid-Holocene forests may have favored forest-edge species like deer and, in this case, rabbits. The squirrel assemblage, although dominated by gray squirrels, did include 35 bones from fox squirrels.

Hayes Site

The Hayes site, located at the confluence of Caney Creek and the Duck River in central Tennessee (fig. 7-1), yielded two late Middle Archaic faunal assemblages that have been analyzed by Morey (1988). The older stratum (Composite Stratum IV) yielded a small sample that has been dated between 5870 and 5430 B.P. According to analyses by Carr (1991), the debris associated with this stratum reflects a mobile foraging strategy. Mortality profiles suggest that deer, which dominate the faunal assemblage, may have been procured in the fall (Beauchamp 1993:71). The younger stratum (Composite Stratum III) dates to 5600 B.P. Analyses of debris suggest a strategy that incorporated less mobility with logistical hunting and collecting of important resources (Carr 1991). A shell midden, primarily composed of gastropods, is associated with this stratum. Based on Hofman's (1984) model of the seasonal round, the gastropods may reflect spring collecting activities. Deer were apparently procured during the fall and winter, based on mortality profiles (Beauchamp 1993:71).

As noted for other mid-Holocene assemblages, deer are abundant in both Middle Archaic components at the Hayes site (fig. 7-12). Fish and aquatic turtles are more abundant than noted for early Holocene sites outside major river valleys. Deer clearly dominate the mammalian assemblage; squirrels are sparsely represented (fig. 7-13). The most dramatic increase in aquatic resources occurs in the late Middle Archaic component (Composite Stratum III), dated to 5600 B.P.,

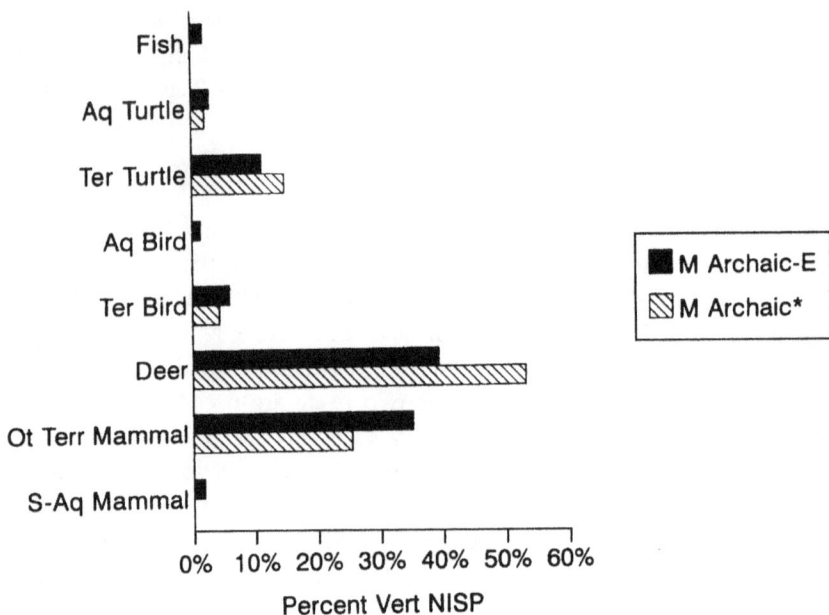

Fig. 7-10. Proportional representation of fauna in Middle Archaic strata at the Austin site (Aq = Aquatic, Ter = Terrestrial, Ot = Other, S-Aq = Semi-aquatic, M = Middle, E = Earlier, * = small sample, NISP = number of identified specimens).

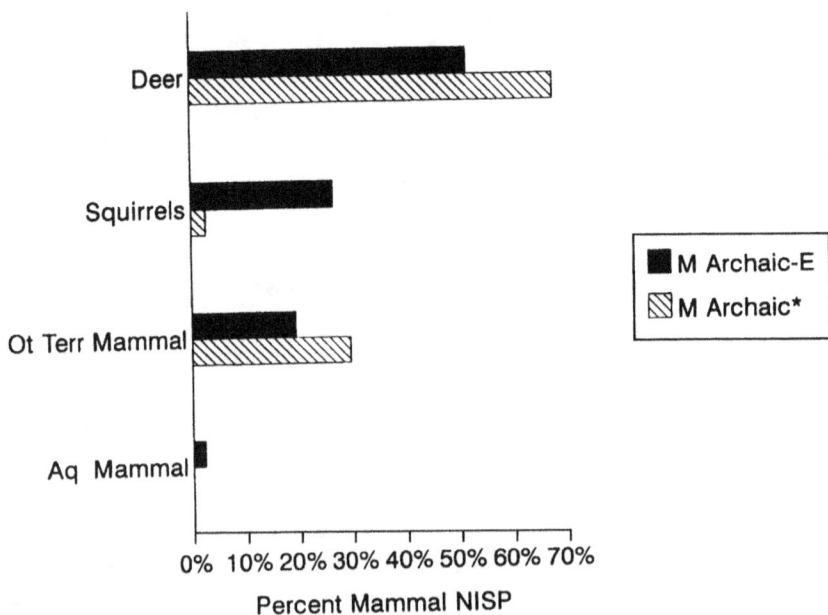

Fig. 7-11. Proportional representation of mammals in Middle Archaic strata at the Austin site (Ot = Other, Terr = Terrestrial, Aq = Aquatic, M = Middle, E = Earlier, * = small sample, NISP = number of identified specimens).

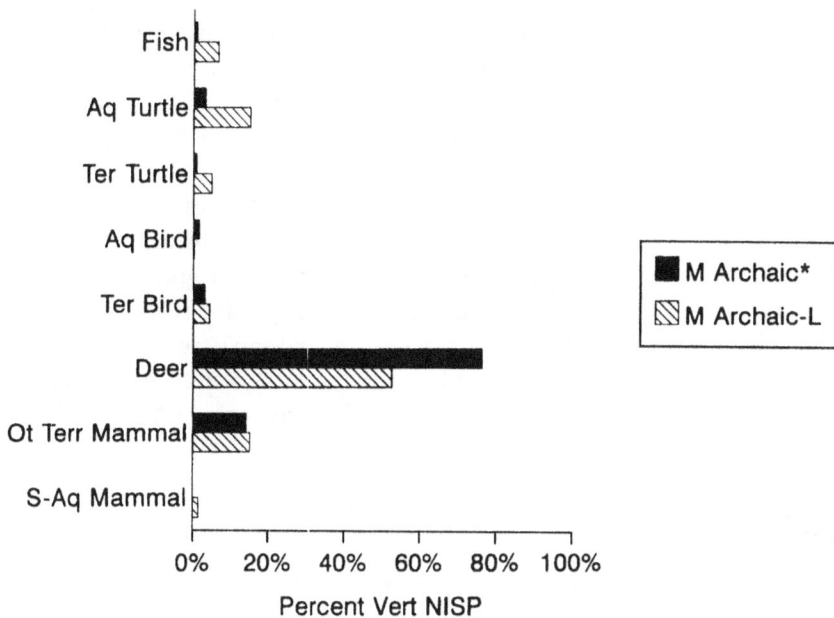

Fig. 7-12. Proportional representation of fauna in Middle Archaic strata at the Hayes site (Aq = aquatic, Ter = Terrestrial, Ot = Other, S-Aq = Semi-aquatic, M = Middle, L = Later, * = small sample, NISP = number of identified specimens).

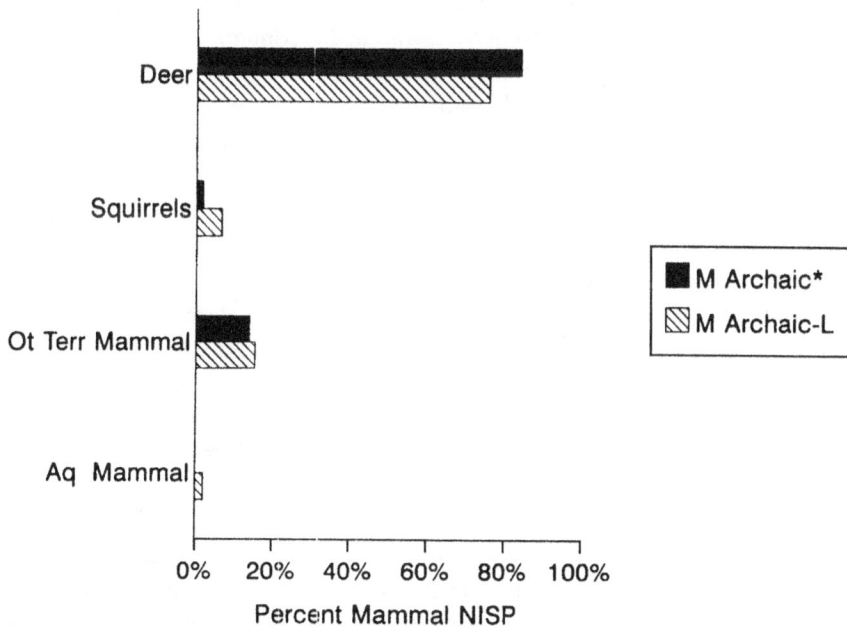

Fig. 7-13. Proportional representation of mammals in Middle Archaic strata at the Hayes site (Ot = Other, Terr = Terrestrial, Aq = Aquatic, M = Middle, L = Later, * = small sample, NISP = number of identified specimens).

when the midden that is filled with aquatic gastropods formed. Klippel and Morey (1986:800) believe that there is "strong evidence that Middle Archaic hunter-gatherers were collecting freshwater gastropods in considerable quantities and were using them as a food resource." They further suggest that these gastropods offered important sources of vitamins and minerals to the mid-Holocene occupants.

Brackenridge (1984) argues for the stabilization of the Duck River floodplain around 7200 B.P. and a concomitant enhancement of shoal habitats. According to Hofman (1984:172–173) shell-midden sites served as foci for group aggregation and as bases for logistical hunting and collecting of first-line resources, such as white-tailed deer. Hofman (1984) suggests that mid-Holocene environmental changes and population growth contributed to the changes in economic and settlement strategies. Middle Archaic groups in this region became less mobile and "resource utilization became more intensive and localized" (Hofman 1984:174).

Cheek Bend Cave

Cheek Bend Cave, located high on a bluff face of the Duck River (fig. 7-1), yielded early and mid-Holocene faunal assemblages, which have been attributed primarily to natural accumulations from owl pellets. This cave provides an important environmental record for the region of central Tennessee near the Hayes site (Klippel and Parmalee 1982a). Shrew (soricid) and mole (talpid) remains provide the most striking evidence for environmental change (Klippel and Parmalee 1982b). Early Holocene Stratum IV contained greater frequencies of short-tailed shrew (*Blarina brevicauda*), which prefers mesic, deciduous forest. Mid-Holocene Stratum V, which dates to about 7500 B.P., contains greater frequencies of least shrew (*Cryptotis parva*). This species inhabits drier open grasslands and forest glade environments. According to Klippel and Parmalee (1982b:455–456), a reduction in summer precipitation or increased summer heat "would diminish preferred habitat for *Blarina* but produce more extensive openings (glades) in the upland areas where soils are exceptionally thin. More drought-tolerant vegetation . . . . would predominate under these conditions and produce a more preferred habitat for *Cryptotis*."

The mole data reflect environmental changes at the Pleistocene-Holocene transition. In early Holocene Stratum IV, the star-nosed mole (*Condylura cristata*), a species with a current distribution to the north and east of Tennessee, disappears from the record and the eastern mole (*Scalopus aquaticus*), a species characteristic of temperate forests throughout the eastern United States, dominates. Klippel and Parmalee (1982a) note the correspondence of their interpretations of the Cheek Bend data—for a cool, mesic early Holocene and a dry and/or hot mid-Holocene—with reconstructions based on pollen data from Anderson and Mingo Ponds in middle Tennessee (Delcourt 1979).

Correspondence Analysis

In order further to evaluate patterns in the data, we employ a correspondence analysis or reciprocal averaging technique. Correspondence analysis is an ordination technique that shows the structure of the data, both cases and variables, in two-dimensional space (Gauch 1982). The cases are the early Holocene and mid-Holocene archaeological components from the sites and the variables are the percentages of fauna in the major taxonomic categories. Correspondence analysis shows how the faunal categories vary based on the sites (fig. 7-14). Fish and birds associated with aquatic habitats load high on the first and second axes. A series of terrestrial resources—birds, turtles, and other terrestrial mammals—load high on the first axis but not on the second. Deer and aquatic turtles load negatively on the first axis. Semi-aquatic mammals are not grouped with any other category and were not abundant in any of these assemblages.

The site components from the various regions (fig. 7-15) show some temporal clustering and also reflect the differing geographic contexts. Two of the three early Holocene sites (prefix E), Modoc and Russell Cave, load relatively high on axis 1. The placement of the early Holocene component at Russell Cave reflects the extremely high abundance of other terrestrial mammals—62 percent of the faunal NISP, combined with a very low representation of white-tailed deer—only 9 percent of the bones. In fact, there were more bones from terrestrial birds and turtles than from deer in this assemblage. The Early Archaic at Modoc also shows relatively high percentages of other terrestrial mammals and other terrestrial birds, and a low representation of white-tailed deer—only 10 percent of the bones; but it shows a higher representation of fish and aquatic birds than do the other early Holocene sites. The early Holocene deposit at Stanfield-Worley shows a much higher representation of white-tailed deer—63 percent of the NISP—than do the early Holocene components at Modoc Rock Shelter and Russell Cave. Although Stanfield-Worley was excavated earlier than the faunal remains reported here for Modoc and Russell Cave, quarter-inch mesh was employed at all three sites. Thus, the variation should not be attributed to differences in recovery techniques. At any rate, all of these early Holocene components show relatively high proportions of gray squirrels, which in figure 7-15 are included in the category of other terrestrial mammals, when compared to younger sites.

The Middle Archaic components (fig. 7-15, prefix M) show clustering that reflects geographic contexts. All of the Modoc components, including the Early Archaic component, occur in the upper right-hand quadrant, reflecting the relatively high use and abundance of fish and waterfowl in the Mississippi Valley. The mid-Holocene component at Russell Cave groups roughly with the Middle Archaic components from the Austin site—with all showing relatively strong emphases on terrestrial resources. The earlier Middle Archaic component from Austin yielded a larger sample that was very similar to Russell Cave

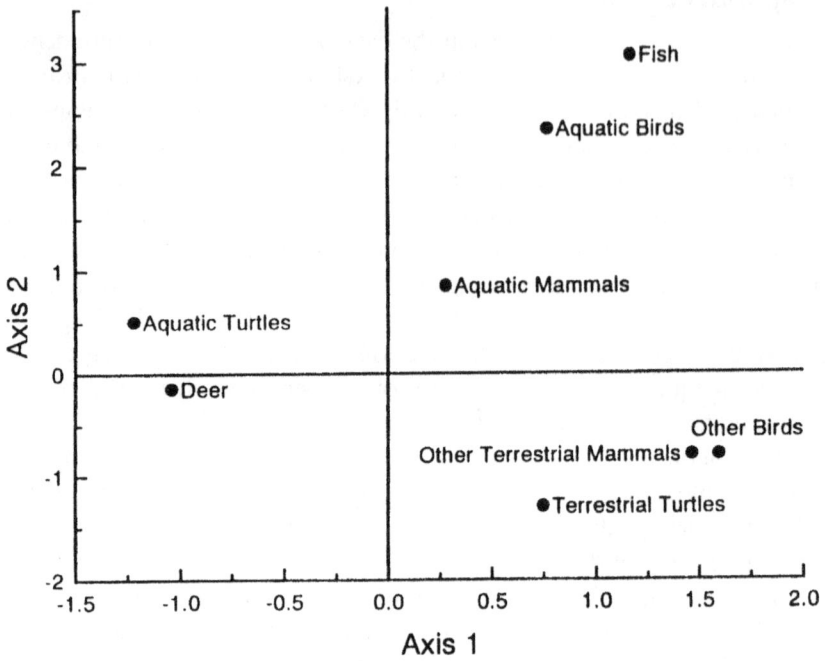

Fig. 7-14. Correspondence analysis of faunal categories based on sites.

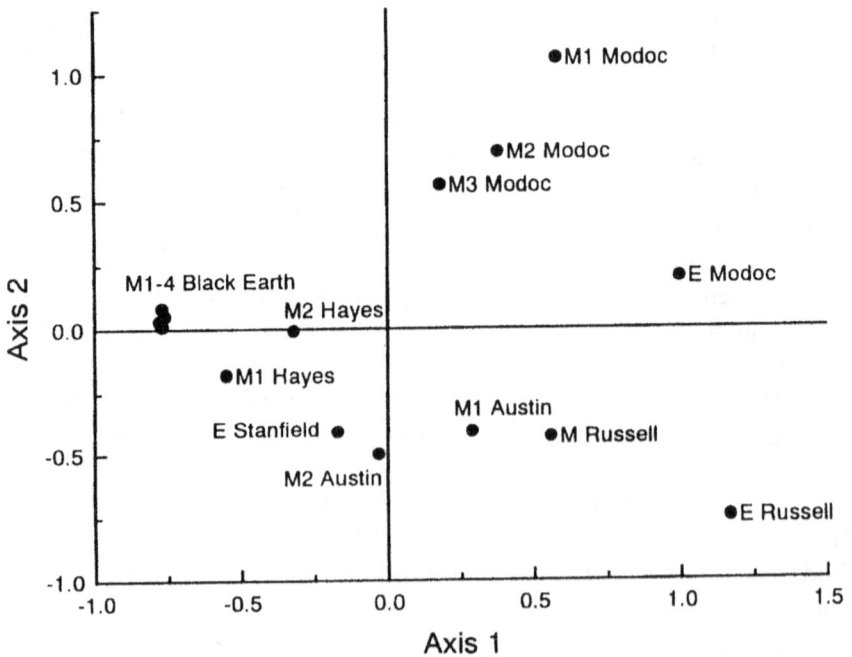

Fig. 7-15. Correspondence analysis of sites based on faunal categories (E = Early Archaic, M = Middle Archaic, 1–4 = Order of components from oldest to youngest).

in overall faunal composition: deer and other terrestrial mammals dominate. Mid-Holocene components from the arbitrarily divided middens at the Black Earth site are remarkably similar to one another and group most closely with the Middle Archaic components at the Hayes site. Black Earth and Hayes show high representation of white-tailed deer and relatively high representation of aquatic turtles, rather than fish or waterfowl.

Conclusions

The variation in assemblages across sites is best explained by changes and differences in local resource availability and attendant subsistence strategies. As indicated at the outset, because of local differences the mid-Holocene did not lead to one uniform faunal exploitation strategy. Further examination of Holocene temporal shifts in the Midsouth requires examination of additional sites from within smaller geographic regions, ones characterized by at least grossly similar access to resources. For example, the trends noted for the early and mid-Holocene at Modoc Rock Shelter are best interpreted within longer-term trends recorded for the resource-rich lower Illinois and central Mississippi river valleys (Styles 1993). The declining representation of squirrels from the early to mid-Holocene (fig. 7-16) is even more dramatic given the dearth of squirrel remains in faunal assemblages throughout the remainder of prehistory. The increasing focus on white-

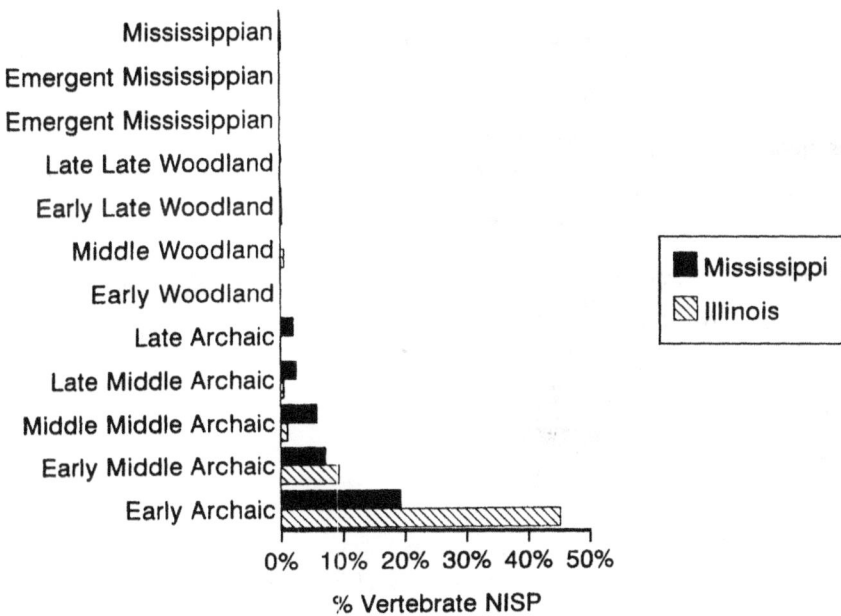

Fig. 7-16. Proportion of squirrel (*Sciuridae*) remains in vertebrate faunal assemblages from the lower Illinois and central Mississippi river valleys (NISP = number of identified specimens).

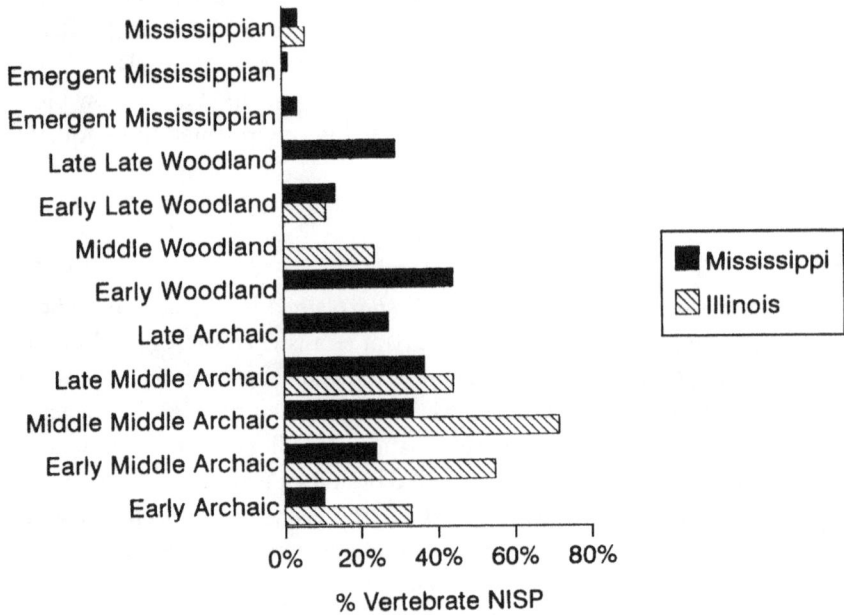

Fig. 7-17. Proportion of white-tailed deer remains in vertebrate faunal assemblages from the lower Illinois and central Mississippi river valleys (NISP = number of identified specimens).

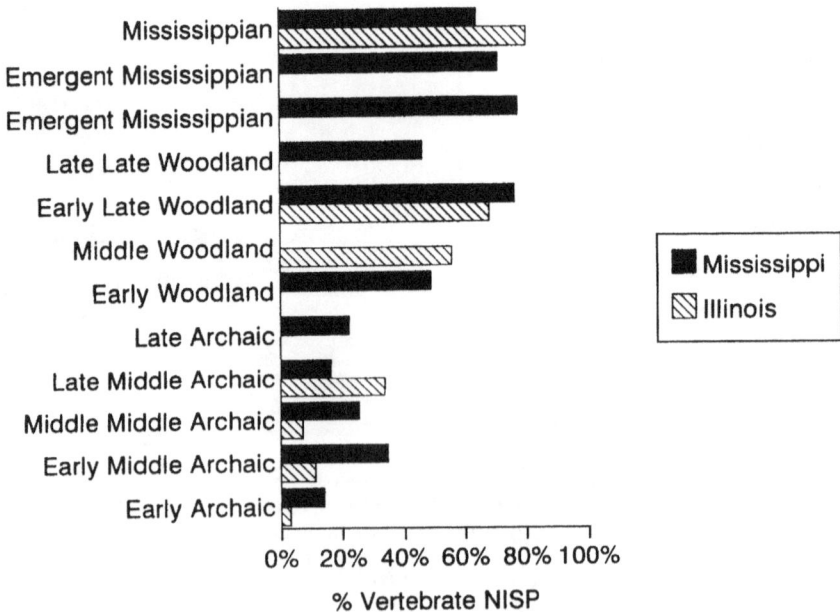

Fig. 7-18. Proportion of fish remains in vertebrate faunal assemblages from the lower Illinois and central Mississippi river valleys (NISP = number of identified specimens).

tailed deer, which started in the Middle Archaic, was followed by a decline in late prehistory (fig. 7-17). Increased use of fish in the Middle Archaic is only part of a continuum of growing use throughout prehistory (fig. 7-18).

The early and mid-Holocene data for the Midsouth show similar temporal trends, especially where mammals are concerned. Proportions of squirrels clearly decline as those of deer increase. As might be expected, the use of fish and water-fowl at most of the sites in our study appears lower than at Modoc Rock Shelter and other sites in major river valleys. This is not surprising given differences in the environmental settings and resource availability for these sites. Greater use of aquatic resources at mid-Holocene sites is demonstrated, however, by slightly higher proportions of fish at some sites (such as Russell Cave, Hayes, and Black Earth); by increases in use of aquatic mollusks at Hayes and other shell-midden sites in the Midsouth (e.g., Dye 1993); and by relatively high use of aquatic turtles at Hayes and Black Earth. These patterns again reflect variation in local resource availability, but in general, regionally specific mid-Holocene river stabilization would have improved aquatic habitats for a variety of resources. Overall, when local patterns based on resource availability are eliminated, there is a broad pan-regional pattern of increased use of white-tailed deer and aquatic resources by aboriginal populations in the Midsouth and Midwest as subsistence-settlement systems evolved in a dynamic postglacial landscape.

Acknowledgments

The authors thank Ken Sassaman and David Anderson for inviting us to partici-pate in the symposium at the 1993 Southeastern Archaeological Conference. A version of this chapter was presented in their symposium on the mid-Holocene in the southeastern United States. Our work benefited greatly from a critical but constructive review by Bruce McMillan. Eric Grimm, associate curator of botany at the Illinois State Museum, introduced the senior author to correspondence analysis and assisted with the analyses and with production of figures 7-14 and 7-15. Other figures were generated on Harvard Graphics.

8

Biocultural Inquiry into Archaic Period Populations of the Southeast

Trauma and Occupational Stress

MARIA O. SMITH

The benefit of the biocultural approach, now almost 20 years old, is that osteo-logical data were transformed from an appendixed list of measurements and cra-nial typology to culturally meaningful information (see Smith 1993a). However, this recent adoption means bioarchaeological analysis is spotty and often focused on large cemetery samples. Therefore a review of bioarchaeological inquiry of Middle and Late Archaic period human remains from the Southeast may be less a summation of information than a matter of presenting points of departure for future research. This may be a surprising statement considering that data on abrupt trauma (broken bones) or arthritic changes would be expected to be long-standing baseline information in osteological inquiry. But most Archaic period human skeletal remains were recovered during the huge salvage operations undertaken in the 1930s and 1940s when the prevailing paradigm was typology. The emphasis was on craniometrics; analysis of trauma, with few exceptions, was restricted to descriptions of specific cases. This analytic approach yielded data but little meaningful information about Archaic populations. As a result, until the ini-tiation of biocultural inquiry, the most anyone could say about Archaic popula-tions was that they were robust and had high levels of dental attrition, few caries, and long heads.

Besides the recent shift in the analytical paradigm, there are two other reasons why recent Archaic period research is uneven in the Southeast. First, much cur-rent information on Archaic period trauma, as well as other health status infor-mation, derives from the larger osteological collections, which are differentially located in the Midsouth (Kentucky, west Tennessee, northern Alabama). With few exceptions, little is known of Archaic samples south of the Fall Line. Poor preservation accounts for this dearth of skeletal material in South Carolina and Georgia. Archaic period osteological data in South Carolina are restricted to the small samples of 10 individuals from Daws Island (Michie 1974; Rathbun 1993; Rathbun et al. 1980) and three individuals from Mims Point (Rathbun et al. 1992; Sassaman 1993c:108–116). In Georgia, the scant osteological remains include 18 interments at Lake Spring (Elliott 1993; Miller 1949) and 84 individuals from Stallings Island Mound where the Archaic burials apparently cannot be reliably discriminated from later Mississippian interments (Claflin 1931:44; Sassaman 1993c:114).

   Although recently recovered human remains from Archaic period wet sites in Florida such as Warm Mineral Springs (Haeussler et al. 1990; Royal and Clark 1960), Windover Pond (Dickel and Doran 1989; Doran et al. 1986) and Little Salt Springs (Clausen et al. 1979:612) are noteworthy for preservation (e.g., brain tissue) or antiquity, they belie the fact that little baseline information on Gulf Coast Archaic populations exists. However, there are coastal Louisiana sites like Cowpen Slough and late Tchefuncte culture interments (Collins 1941; Mires 1991) as well as Florida Archaic sites such as Republic Groves (Saunders 1972), Bay West (Beriault et al. 1981:50), Tick Island (Bullen 1962; A. Bullen 1972), and Gauthier (Carr and Jones 1981; Winland et al. 1993) that are potentially fundamentally informative, and this information needs to be synthesized and disseminated. One reason for this call for a broader information base is that recent research seems to challenge the presumptive homogeneity among Archaic hunter-gatherers in the frequency and pattern of certain pathological conditions. This variation may reflect interobserver differences, but it may also be true that in the ecologically and socially variable Southeast, local modifications of subsistence behavior could result in interarea differences of certain activity-related pathological conditions. More research is needed to identify or verify interarea differences.

   The second reason for the uneven analysis is that Archaic skeletal populations have often served as the contrast for directed examinations of the pathological change concomitant with the adoption or intensification of agriculture. The sample most often used as the generic hunter-gatherer comparison is Indian Knoll, by far the most widely utilized Archaic sample in the eastern United States. Whereas information about Archaic samples was generated by these studies, only sporadic discussion was devoted to explaining the hunter-gatherer pattern(s). Therefore, we are only at the threshhold of a broad understanding of Archaic period populations.

   It is ironic that the adoption of the first biologically meaningful analytical paradigm, the biocultural approach, is concomitant with efforts to initiate repatriation of osteological collections. Hopefully this review of Archaic period literature will underscore the need for continued research.

Defining Trauma and Occupational Stress

The common denominator of the pathologies and remodeling patterns discussed here is physical activity. Labor-intensive or repetitive tasks can alter normal bone structure (cortical remodeling) or can factor in pathological changes. These pathologies include fractures, lesions (e.g., enthesopathies, Schmorl's nodes, etc.), or degenerative changes such as arthritis and osteophytosis. Since many of these pathologies appear to be differentially distributed among subsistence strategies or are linked to particular repetitive movements, they offer potential windows into the lifestyle of prehistoric populations. Although there is a wide range of these stress-related pathologies, only a small spectrum has been identified in mid-Holocene archaeological populations in the Southeast. For this review, these pathologies have been defined and classified into three areas. *Accidental trauma* is abrupt injury and is identifiable in the osteoarchaeological record by the fracture callous or improper healing. *Deliberate trauma* includes warfare-related perimortem violent injury such as inflicted projectile points, scalping, and trophy-taking dismemberment; it also includes nonlethal interpersonal violence such as forearm or "parry" fractures. *Progressive degenerative joint changes* can occur from labor-intensive repetitive tasks that initiate degenerative or destructive changes on bone. Although not a pathological change, bone remodeling in response to intensive physical activity is also considered.

Accidental Trauma

Accidental trauma seems to lend itself more readily to case descriptions (e.g., Funkhouser 1939:124–125; Snow 1948; Stewart 1974), but bioarchaeological inquiry is more revealing of lifestyle and health status information. However, interobserver variability in reporting the pattern and frequency of accidental trauma makes it difficult to detect subsistence or interarea patterns, a theme that runs through much of the literature review that follows.

It is often noted that hunting and gathering put people at higher risk for accidental trauma than do other subsistence strategies. Presumably the greater mobility of hunter-gatherers increases the likelihood of tripping or falling. Although some directed research has been undertaken to assess the pattern and frequency of accidental trauma throughout antiquity (Angel 1974; Wells 1964), a short table constructed by Steinbock (1976:23) of postcranial fractures over time and subsistence strategy change is the information most often cited. It suggests a linear trend of decreasing frequency from the Archaic period (ranging from 9 to 11%) to the Mississippian (<5%). However, the frequencies for postcranial trauma cited in Steinbock's table include individuals with cranial trauma (e.g., Morse site and Dickson Mounds) and individuals with multiple fractures (e.g., Robinson, Morse, and Klunk sites). For example, burial C36-5 from the Klunk site in Illinois had four rib fractures (left side, ribs 8–11). This presumably single traumatic event was recorded as four "cases" and constituted 20 percent of the fractures observed for the site. Therefore a reassessment of the trauma data was undertaken for the above-mentioned sites and compared to other Archaic period sites from the Southeast. Because individual bone counts are not often published, the percentages were recalculated to reflect the proportion of individuals in an archaeological population exhibiting trauma (table 8-1). There remain, however, interobserver differences in the set or subset of the skeleton examined (postcranial, appendicular, or total skeleton).

Although a number of individual sites mirror the temporal trend of frequency reduction, the broader picture revealed by a larger sample size and the adjusted frequencies (table 8-1) does not support such a trend. However, it remains to be tested whether intersite variability (temporally and spatially) is spurious or affected by local conditions (e.g., terrain) which may factor independently or synergistically with subsistence to affect the likelihood of accidential injury. Clearly, a broader database is needed.

A single study by Donisi (1982) in the Southeast examined the pattern of appendicular fractures between subsistence strategies (hunter-gatherer vs. agriculturalist) within the same geographic area. His overview of the northern Alabama Archaic data (divided into an eastern and a western sample) is complemented by unpublished trauma data I collected for five Kentucky Lake sites and one at Cordell Hull reservoir, here referred to collectively as Tennessee. Of seven paired bones examined (clavicle, humerus, radius, ulna, femur, tibia, fibula) in samples from western northern Alabama (Pickwick Basin), the subsistence contrast revealed that only Mississippian period female humeri are statistically significant. In eastern northern Alabama (Wheeler and Guntersville basins), Archaic male humeri and female forearms (radius and/or ulna) are more frequently broken. In Tennessee, Archaic female humeri, radii, and ulnae and male femora are more frequently broken. Apparently arm and leg frequencies will reveal subsistence differences but, perhaps predictably, not all reservoir areas yield higher frequencies or patterns in traumatic injury to individual bones for the Archaic sample.

Collapsing the data for the three geographic areas into Archaic and Mississippian samples by gender, it was determined that the ankle (fibula) in males and forearms in females are more frequently broken in the Archaic (table 8-2). Other Archaic sites also have exhibited a high proportion of forearm fractures (irrespective of gender). For example, forearm fractures account for 58 percent of all postcranial trauma at Indian Knoll (Stewart 1974), 45 percent at the Perry site in the Pickwick Basin (Donisi 1982), 50 percent in the sample from Wheeler and Guntersville basins (Donisi 1982), and 40 percent at Robinson in middle Tennessee (Morse 1969). Only 24 percent of the sample from the Mississippian Dallas site of Toqua in east Tennessee (Parham 1982), 28 percent of the Wheeler and Guntersville basin Mississippian sample (Donisi 1982), and 12.5 percent at Dickson Mounds (Morse 1969) are forearm fractures. Not unexpectedly, data exist that confound simple subsistence contrasts. Forty-one percent of the postcranial

Table 8-1.   Frequency of postcranial fractures

Population	# individuals with fractures/# individuals	%	Reference
Archaic			
Daw's Island, SC	5/10	50.0	Rathbun et al. 1980
Modoc Rock Shelter, IL	8/28	28.0	Neumann 1967
Carrier Mills, IL	23/153	15.0	Bassett 1982
Eva, TN	16/110	14.5	Smith n.d.
Flint River, AL	12/97	12.4	Donisi 1982
Indian Knoll, KY	57/521	10.7	Snow 1948
Kentucky Lake, TN	24/286	8.3	Smith n.d.
Pickwick Basin, AL	33/399	8.3	Donisi 1982
Morse, IL	4/62	6.4	Morse 1969
Robinson, TN	3/51	5.8	Morse 1969
Elizabeth, IL[a]	2/47	4.3	Frankenberg et al. 1988
Woodland			
Elizabeth, IL[a]	15/99	14.0	Frankenberg et al. 1988
Steuben, IL	3/54	5.5	Morse 1969
Tolliferro, VA	2/37	5.4	Hoyme and Bass 1962
Klunk, IL	11/395	2.8	Morse 1969
Mississippian			
Guntersville/Wheeler Basins, AL	13/149	8.7	Donisi 1982
Pickwick Basin, AL	8/104	7.7	Donisi 1982
Dallas, TN	5/108	4.6	Smith n.d.
Clarksville, VA	3/77	3.9	Hoyme and Bass 1962
Fains Island, TN	5/170	3.0	Smith n.d.
Dickson Mounds, IL	9/331	2.7	Morse 1969
Toqua, TN	3/117	2.5	Smith n.d.

a. Reflects trauma plus arthritis of traumatic origin.

trauma in the Mississippian sample from Pickwick Basin consists of forearm fractures (Donisi 1982).

While many forearm fractures (fig. 8-1) are attributable to falls braced by an outstretched arm, some of these midshaft or "parry" fractures of the radius and/or ulna have been interpreted as the result of interpersonal violence (Angel 1974; Salib 1967; Wells 1964). Higher parry fracture frequencies have been observed in females in several Archaic period samples in the Southeast (Wheeler, Pickwick, and Kentucky Lake), which may indicate female-directed interpersonal violence (Donisi 1982; see Ortner and Putschar 1985). However, my recent analyses of Tennessee Archaic and Mississippian data indicate that in the absence of corroborative injuries (to the head or face), there is no evidence to suggest anything but an accidental etiology (Smith 1990; 1993b). Using corroborative cranio-facial trauma data, female-directed violence has, however, been identified osteoarchaeologically

Table 8-2. Differences in the location of postcranial trauma between Archaic
and Mississippian samples from northern Alabama and western Tennessee
(Donisi 1982; Smith, unpublished data)

Sex	Bone	Archaic cases/N	Mississippian cases/N
Male	clavicle	2/578	2/738
	humerus	9/651	5/804
	ulna	9/631	13/793
	radius	6/647	6/789
	femur	6/650	5/842
	tibia	3/528	6/855
	fibula	7/597	3/818[b]
Female	clavicle	1/562	3/684
	humerus	2/606	7/759
	ulna	17/614	5/739[a]
	radius	6/610	2/756[b]
	femur	1/631	1/790
	tibia	1/624	2/782
	fibula	1/586	3/744

a. X^2 significant at .05 level.
b. X^2 significant at .1 level

in later horizons in the Northern Plains, the Southwest, and Midwest (Martin and
Akins 1994; Martin et al. 1993; Shermis 1982–84; Wilkenson and Van Wagenen
1993). It has yet to be unequivocally identified in any archaeological horizon in the
Southeast.

Accepting that parry fractures are accidental injuries, their frequencies might be
attributed to risk factors associated with gender-specific tasks, or it may be that
the generally more gracile females were more vulnerable to fractures. Interarea
differences may offer some insight (table 8-3). For Archaic males, the ankle or
upper arm frequencies vary among the three reservoirs, but no pattern emerges.
Females seem to exhibit a patterned interarea difference in the frequency of
forearm and ankle fractures. This may suggest regional differences in the terrain
(likelihood of falling) or differences in division of labor. The "pattern" may also
prove to be spurious. Clearly subsistence or geographical generalizations concerning the predisposition of certain bones to traumatic injury are premature.
Continued, comprehensive, and standardized analyses are needed.

Spondylolysis

Spondylolysis is a probable fatigue fracture of the lumbar neural arch, which
occurs between the superior and inferior articular facets (fig. 8-2). Usually, the
entire posterior lamina becomes detached from the vertebral body. The incidence
of spondylolysis in clinical Euro-American samples ranges between 5 and 7

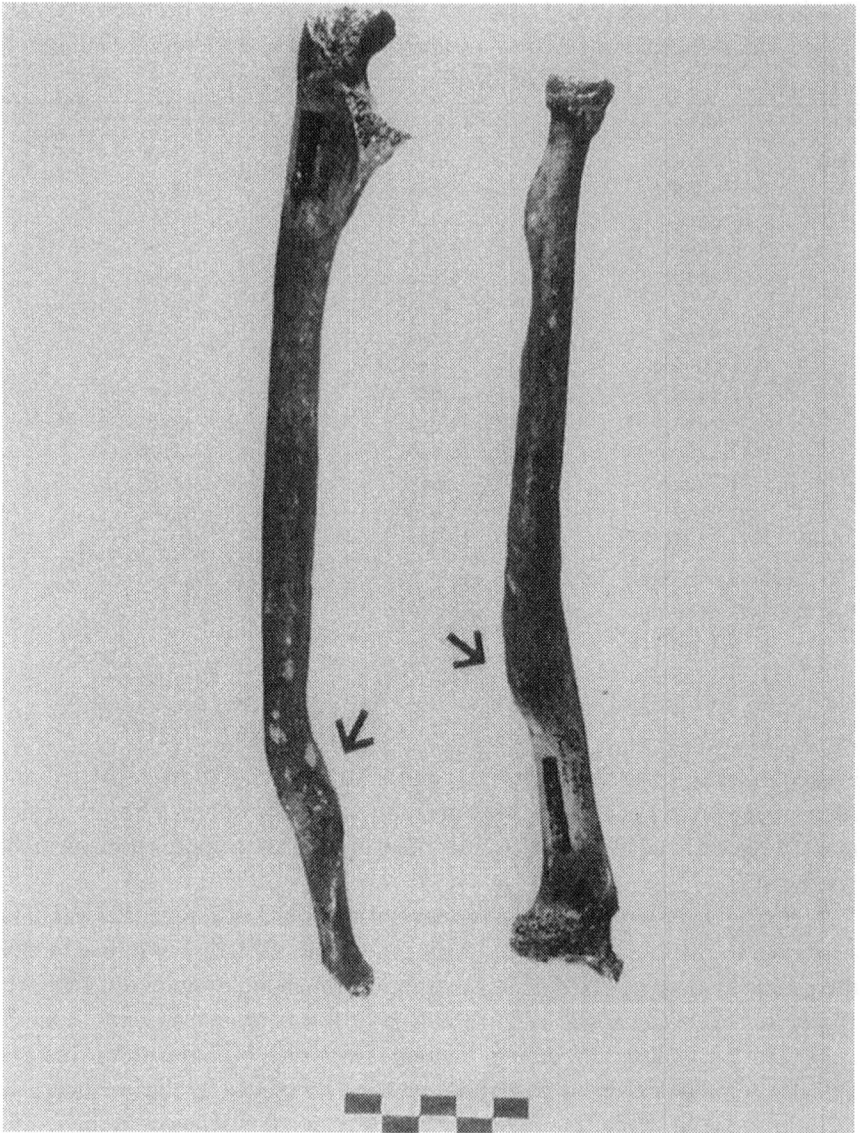

Fig. 8-1.   Forearm fractures on a left ulna and radius from the Tennessee valley.

percent but varies interethnically (Frederickson et al. 1984; Roche and Rowe 1952). For example, occurrence is 7–10 percent among adult Japanese (Hoshina 1980) and 2–3 percent among African Americans (Frederickson et al. 1984; Roche and Rowe 1952).

Spondylolysis has been associated with high levels of physical activity in modern samples. It can occur at frequencies as high as 21 percent among athletes (Hoshina 1980; Jackson et al. 1976; McCarroll et al. 1986). Not unexpectedly, it is

Table 8-3. Interregional differences in postcranial trauma among Archaic
period populations (Donisi 1982; Smith, unpublished data)

Sex	Bone	P/W	X^2 tests (.05) T/P	T/W
Male	clavicle	—	—	W
	humerus	P	—	—
	ulna	—	—	—
	radius	—	—	—
	femur	—	—	—
	tibia	—	—	—
	fibula	—	P	—
Female	clavicle	—	—	—
	humerus	—	—	—
	ulna	—	T	T
	radius	W	—	—
	femur	—	—	—
	tibia	W	—	—
	fibula	W	—	—

Note: Comparisons of Archaic period samples from Pickwick Basin (P), Wheeler/Guntersville basins
(W), and west Tennessee (T). Letters indicate sample with higher frequency in a statistically significant test.

extremely common (as much as 40%) among certain Inuit whose posture habits
include kayaking and working sitting straight-legged for hours (Lester and
Shapiro 1968; Lundy 1981; Merbs 1983; Stewart 1931, 1953).

Seventeen percent of the sample at Indian Knoll exhibit spondylolysis (Snow
1948), which is much higher than any clinical samples and similar to the frequency
in athletes. Bridges (1989a, 1989b) undertook a comprehensive comparative
examination of spondylolysis for the Archaic and Mississippian samples in the
Pickwick Basin, Alabama. She observed Archaic period frequencies to be similar
between the genders, 17 percent for males and 20 percent for females, but found
only one case in the Mississippian period sample. Gender differences do occur
and are manifested by earlier onset among males (third decade of life), while
spondylolysis is present only in mature females (40+ years). This may be related
to gender-specific activities, or as Bridges speculates, it is possibly related to
osteoporotic weakening predisposing older women to spondylolysis. Association
with progressive degenerative joint disease (DJD) is weak, although osteoarthritis in the lower lumbars is possibly related. Bridges surmises that spondylolysis, being a trauma, is not simply associated with amount of activity but rather
reflects specific activities involving twisting or bending of the lumbar spine to
cause trauma. While it appears that a subsistence difference occurs, and that
spondylolysis may be related to subsistence-specific activities, it is not possible to
identify these activities.

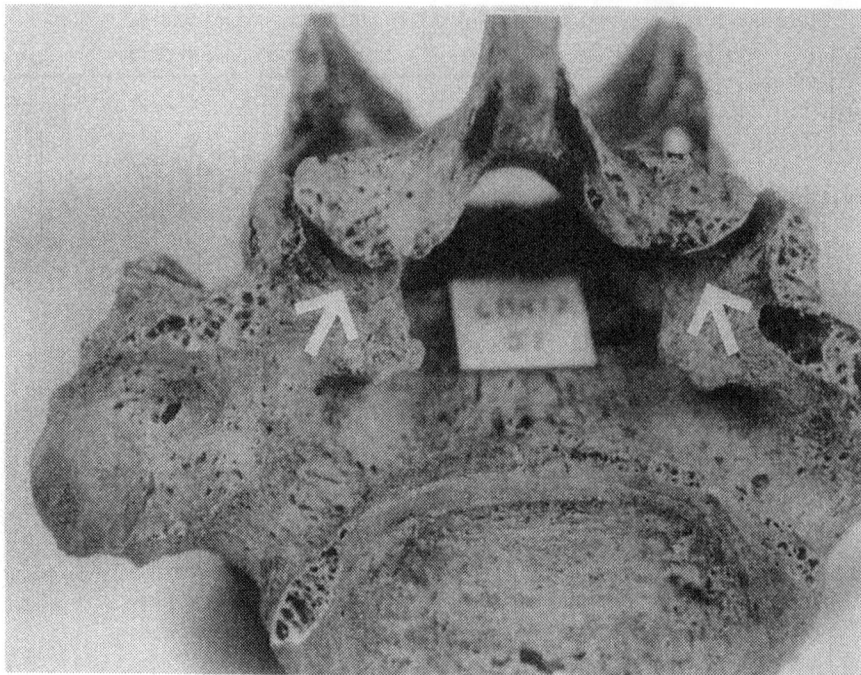

Fig. 8-2.   Separate neural arch (spondylolysis) in a fifth lumbar vertebra from the Eva site, western Tennessee valley.

Deliberate Trauma

Although there is no consensus concerning the causes of social complexity, certain theories, particularly materialistic/ecological models (Begler 1978; Cashdan 1980; Ferguson 1990; see Haas 1990 for discussion) stress the catalytic role of warfare in social change. Focused attention on patterns and frequency of warfare-related peri-mortem violence in prehistoric intensive hunter-gatherers could potentially con-tribute information pertinent to the genesis of social complexity. According to Price and Brown (1985b:12), "evidence of violent death appears dramatically among the skeletal remains of more complex foragers." This was defined and, for many years, exemplified by Indian Knoll, the traditional definitive Archaic site for the eastern United States. According to Webb (1946:204), 23 individuals or 4.4 per-cent (23/521) of the Indian Knoll skeletal population died violently and 25 individ-uals or 4.8 percent (25/521) were dismembered, implying violence. These percent-ages are based on my calculation of the number of measurable individuals. Webb never provided the frequency data, underscoring the paradigm difference between typology and biocultural inquiry. However, the first figure is inflated because it included cases where projectile points were found in the body cavity and not inflicted. Snow (1948:523) reported that the cutmarks he observed suggested dismemberment as a mortuary alternative rather than perimortem violence.

Therefore, warfare indications based on published data from Indian Knoll are equivocal at best.

Until recently, most directed osteoarchaeological examination of warfare-related violent trauma has been for later prehistoric periods. These have been restricted to single sites noteworthy for the high frequency of violent trauma or massacre episodes, including the massacre at Hopi in Arizona (Turner and Morris 1970), the Crow Creek massacre (Willey 1990) and the Larson site in South Dakota (Owsley et al. 1977), and the Norris farms Oneota site in Illinois (Milner et al. 1991). They provide important definitive information of the kinds of trauma associated with warfare but as yet little can be concluded about intersite variability, endemicity, or temporal change. Directed examination of Archaic period warfare is recent (M. Smith 1992, 1993b, 1993c, 1993d, n.d.) and provides a point of departure for future work. In conjunction with miscellaneous information gleaned from site reports, a picture is beginning to emerge.

Scalping and dismemberment trophy taking were identified initially at the Kentucky Lake reservoir (M. Smith 1992, 1993b, 1993c, 1995, n.d.) and more recently at the Cordell Hull reservoir (Smith 1993c). Instances include scalping (three Kentucky Lake sites) (fig. 8-3), decapitation (at Robinson site at the Cordell Hull reservoir), and certainly arm (Big Sandy site at Kentucky Lake, Robinson site) and possibly leg (Eva site, Kentucky Lake) dismemberment. Although the situation at Indian Knoll is far from clear, I suspect that possibly burial 537, a headless and limbless torso with an inflicted projectile point described by both Webb (1946:153) and Snow (1948:529), may be evidence of trophy taking.

At Kentucky Lake, only males exhibit perimortem violence, with the exception of a possible massacre episode at the Cherry site where a young adult female and several juveniles join a young adult male with an inflicted point in a mass grave. Unfortunately, a later storage pit bisected the interment and removed the torsos of the adults and any corroborating information.

Human bone grave inclusions occuring in Hopewell contexts have been irresolutely interpreted as trophy items (Seeman 1988) or "memento mori" (Fenton 1991). In the Southeast (including Tennessee), Archaic period grave inclusions consisting of modified human remains (including human crania) are described in site reports but have been routinely overlooked in interpretations of grave inclusions (table 8-4). I have observed (Smith 1993c) that Archaic period grave inclusions do not consist of elements of the postcranial axial or trunk skeleton (i.e., vertebrae, ribs, etc.) but rather long bone and cranial items like the presumptive trophy elements removed from the west Tennessee human remains and the late prehistoric massacre episodes mentioned earlier. Because mortuary activity at both the Kentucky Lake and Cordell Hull reservoirs does not include defleshing or dismemberment, the grave inclusions from Ledbetter Landing and Robinson are best interpreted as trophy items.

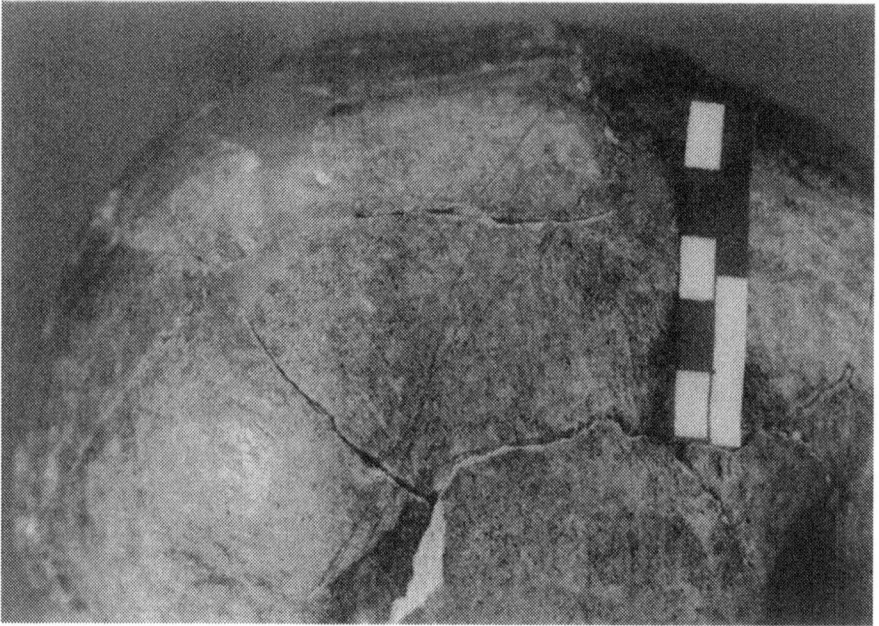

Fig. 8-3.   Cut marks on a presumptive scalping victim from the Eva site, western Tennessee valley.

There appears to be intersite variability in the frequency of warfare-related trauma. The Cherry site at the Kentucky Lake reservoir accounts for 25 percent of all of the trauma identified for seven sites. Over 10 percent of the Cherry sample died violently as opposed to 1.2 percent for the other six sites combined (Eva, Ledbetter Landing, Oak View Landing, Big Sandy, Kays Landing, McDaniel). If the probable massacre event at Cherry is included, the frequency jumps to a dramatic 20.4 percent. The Cherry site lies on an upland tributary stream, in contrast to the other six sites, which are along the main channel. The remoteness of the Cherry site may have rendered it more vulnerable to raiding or, another possibility, it may have occupied a territorial frontier that was disputed in times of ecological stress (M. Smith 1992, 1993b).

Clearly, patterns of perimortem violence identified in later prehistoric horizons have considerable antiquity. If scalping and cranium and limb removal are interpreted as trophy-taking activities, then these may have provided an avenue of prestige enchancement that could have contributed to increased social complexity.

Progressive Degenerative Joint Changes

Activity patterns that are strenuous or excessive may result in remodeling of and/or injury to the skeleton such as progressive degenerative joint diseases. Considered in this review are arthritis, osteochondrosis, and vertebral osteophytosis. Although dental attrition short of pulp exposure is not an injury, it is considered

Table 8-4.   Presumptive trophy items in Archaic period graves (modified after
Morse 1967)

Site name, state	Modified bone	Reference
Mulberry Creek, AL	skull cap	Webb and DeJarnette 1942
	2 carved fibulae	Webb 1946
Bluff Creek, AL	radius awl/pin	Webb and DeJarnette 1942
	4 fibulae awl/pins	
	131 grooved teeth	
Flint River, AL	2 skull gorgets	Webb and DeJarnette 1948b
Long Branch, AL	"artifacts made from	Webb and DeJarnette 1942
	human bone"	
Robinson, TN	cut femur shaft	Morse 1967
Ledbetter Landing, TN	2 cut and polished	Smith 1993b
	femoral shafts	
Indian Knoll, KY	cut femur shaft	Webb 1946
	fibula awl	
	tibia/femur pins	
	cut shaft sections	
Carlston Annis, KY	skull cup fragment	Webb 1950a
	incised ulna	
	cut tibial shaft segment	
	1 femur shaft	
	3 split femur shafts	
	3 cut fibulae segments	
Read, KY	fibula awl	Webb 1950b
Sloan, AR	1 cut femur shaft	Morse 1977

here because it is the progressive erosion of tooth structure as a response to excessive mastication or dietary grit, and it is a factor in arthritis of the temporo-
mandibular joint.

Osteochondrosis.   According to Schmorl and Junghans (1971), as the intervertebral disk ages, dehydration and wear occur. This leads to a condition known
as osteochondrosis, or degenerative disk disease, which may be identified on
vertebrae as a half-moon or sickle-shaped sequestrum on the intervertebral
surface (fig. 8-4). Degenerative disk disease is a combination of disk destruction
and secondary involvement of the vertebral plates.

    In a comparison of prehistoric Native American material reflecting three dif-
ferent subsistence strategies, Kelley (1982) observes that the hunter-gatherer
sample (Indian Knoll) has a much higher frequency of osteochondrosis than do
the horticultural and agricultural samples. Indian Knoll had a frequency of 14
percent, in contrast with 0.6 percent for horticultural Mobridge (South Dakota)
and 2.4 percent for agriculturalist Grasshopper Pueblo (Arizona). Kelley also
notes the early onset of osteochondrosis at Indian Knoll, occurring in the second
and third decades of life. As osteochondrosis is a degenerative disease process, he

postulates that this early onset is due to a harsh lifestyle. No other sites in the Southeast have been examined for degenerative disk disease.

Arthritis.   Arthritis is a generic term that includes the degenerative processes of osteoarthritis and osteophytosis and inflammatory processes such as rheumatoid arthritis, ankylosing spondylitis, and gout. With the exception of gout, the etiology of arthritis is not well understood and is likely multifactorial. The degenerative processes are progressive and therefore age related, but they are frequently linked to intensive and/or repetitive activity. The principal focus of this review is these degenerative processes. Key osteoarchaeological studies (particularly on Arctic peoples) have linked heightened activity levels with increased frequency, severity, and particular patterns of osteoarthritis (e.g., Angel 1966; Angel et al. 1987; Jurmain 1977, 1991; Kelley and Angel 1987; Merbs 1983; Stewart 1947, 1958). However, clinical examination of laborers (e.g., miners, lumberjacks) suggests that labor-intensive activity is not strictly isomorphic with arthritis (Anderson 1974; Anderson and Duthis 1963; Lindberg and Danielson

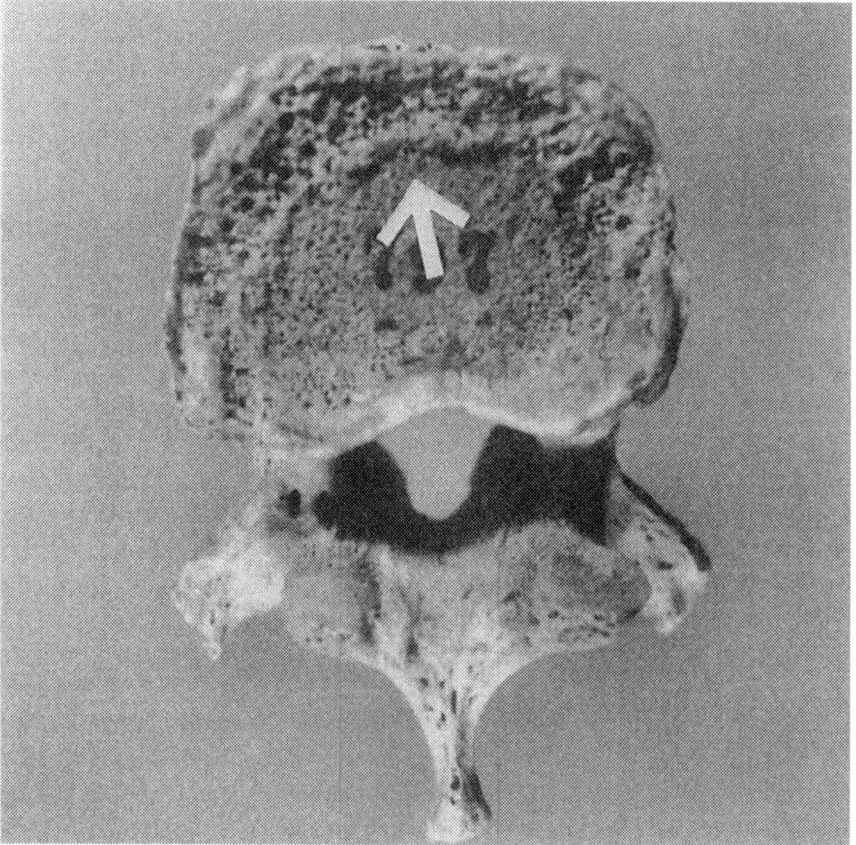

Fig. 8-4.   Inferior view of an eleventh thoracic vertebra with a crescentic lesion indicative of intervertebral osteochondrosis.

1984; Lockshin et al. 1969; Sairanen et al. 1981). Therefore, modulating factors may be involved, which may include predisposition, initiation by traumatic injury, and whether performance of activities was ergonomically correct. In spite of this cautionary note, much can be learned about lifestyle patterns from degenerative joint disease, and bioarchaeological inquiry is still at the threshold of basic information.

By far the most common pathology encountered in prehistoric skeletal samples is osteoarthritis, which is so ubiquitous that it is often ignored. Quantification problems (scoring standards, controlling for age, statistical procedures) hamper interobserver comparability (see Rogers et al. 1985; Rogers 1966; and Waldron and Rogers 1991, for a discussion of the problem). For example, the frequency of osteoarthritis at Indian Knoll has been reported as 39, 60, and 72 percent (Cassidy 1984; Kelley 1980; Snow 1948). Variation in scoring, determination of the threshold of involvement, and controlling for age, among other things, account for much interobserver difference. Current discussion, therefore, must avoid using subjective data (frequencies and severity) and limit discussion to pattern(s) of joint involvement, gender differences, and side asymmetry.

Osteoarthritis (OA) of the synovial joints may be identified by characteristic bony changes of lipping (peripheral osteophytosis), porosity on joint surfaces, and ultimately eburnation and grooving as joint cartilage is eroded away and bone-on-bone rubbing is initiated (Ortner and Putschar 1985; Steinbock 1976) (fig. 8-5). Degenerative arthritic changes in the cartilagenous (intervertebral) joints of the vertebral column consist of progressive lipping at the margins of the superior and inferior surfaces of vertebral bodies (fig. 8-6). This vertebral osteophytosis (OP) can culminate in fusion of the vertebra (Ortner and Putschar 1985; Steinbock 1976).

Mindful of the inability to compare frequency data directly (interobserver variability), a quick review of the literature will nevertheless be illuminating. In her seminal review of arthritis in the Americas, Bridges (1992) observes much temporal and interregional variability. In coastal Georgia (C. S. Larsen 1982, 1984; Ruff 1987a; Ruff et al. 1984), a reduction in the frequency of individuals with OA occurs in agriculturalists when compared with a composite pre-agriculturalist (but not Archaic) sample. This would anticipate a trend of reduction in arthritis in the Southeast over time, but other data suggest that the scenario is far more complex. For example, the Elizabeth site (Illinois) Archaic horizon exhibits less OA than the combined (Middle and Late) Woodland sample (Frankenberg et al. 1988). In contrast to the Georgia coast, and illustrating inter-area variability, an increase in the frequency of OA was observed at Dickson Mounds in Illinois (Lallo 1973) and in the lower Illinois River valley (Pickering 1979) with agricultural intensification. Indian Knoll has often been used as a representative hunter-gatherer sample in subsistence strategy contrasts. Comparisons with Indian Knoll reviewed here also affirm interarea variability. Kelley (1980) examined osteoarthritis at Indian Knoll and contrasted the pattern with

that in human remains from Mobridge in South Dakota (Arikara horticultur-
alist) and from Grasshopper Pueblo. The highest frequency for appendicular OA
occured at Mobridge, but most axial (vertebral) OA occured at Indian Knoll.
The lowest frequencies were observed among the pueblo agriculturalists.

A comparison of Indian Knoll with nearby Hardin Village (Cassidy 1984)
revealed no significant differences in frequency in the vertebra, but earlier onset
occurred in the agriculturalists. Complicating the interarea differences, Indian
Knoll, in comparison to the Averbuch site (middle Tennessee), had higher frequencies in all the appendicular joints (knee, hip, shoulder, elbow; Pierce 1987).
Clearly, there is no obvious agriculturalist pattern or temporal trend from earlier
horizons. Northern Alabama hunter-gatherer and agriculturalist comparisons
(controlling for age) yielded no differences in arthritis frequencies, with the single
exception of less cervical OP in older agricultural males (Bridges 1991a, 1991b;
Dobbs 1988). Underscoring the interpretive complexities of osteoarthritis data,
this contrasts with other evidence that suggests that the agriculturalist sample
experienced more cortical remodeling, reflecting a more labor-intensive economy
(Bridges 1990, 1991a; see section below on cortical remodeling).

In the absence of direct comparability between Archaic samples from the
Southeast for certain arthritis data, there appears to be the potential of interarea
variability among southeastern hunter-gatherers of the mid-Holocene. This variability may be the consequences of interarea differences in resource procurement
or processing habits or in traumatic injuries leading to joint destruction. More
research is clearly needed.

Contrasting Archaic period males and females may reveal patterns in the division of labor. According to Bridges (1992), gender differences, when they occur,
are most common in agricultural samples (higher frequency in males), but again
there is much regional variation. In Archaic samples from northern Alabama,
none of the major appendicular joints (shoulder, elbow, wrist, hip, knee, ankle)
nor the combined vertebral segments (cervical, thoracic, lumbar) show significant sexual dimorphism (Bridges 1991b, 1992). Archaic samples from the lower
Illinois River valley also exhibit no gender differences (Pickering 1979, 1984). At
Indian Knoll, when individual joints are considered, males exhibit the greater frequency of appendicular arthritis (shoulder, hip, knee). But when a composite
arthritis score is used, Indian Knoll males maintain the higher frequencies, but the
differences are not statistically significant (Cassidy 1984; Pierce 1987). At Chiggerville, the differences appear to be that females experienced a wider range of
affected joints, with males having more arthritis in the shoulder (Sullivan 1977).

In vertebral osteophytosis (OP), as a consequence of bipedalism, osteophytic
remodeling occurs principally along the maximum curvatures of the spine, usually at C4–C6, T7–T11, L3–L4 (Kilgore 1984; Merbs 1983; Nathan 1962). With a
few exceptions (e.g., Koniag Eskimos, Sadlermiut, California hunter-gatherers),
the greatest osteophytic remodeling occurs in the lumbar vertebrae (Gunness-
Hey 1980; Stewart 1947; Walker and Hollimon 1989). But considerable popula-

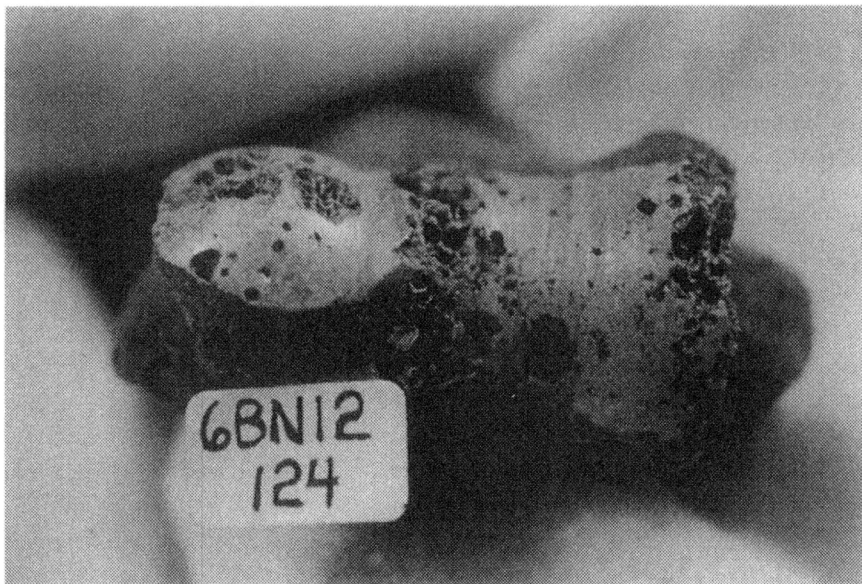

Fig. 8-5.   Osteoarthritis on a distal humerus from the Eva site illustrating porosity, eburnation, and parallel grooving.

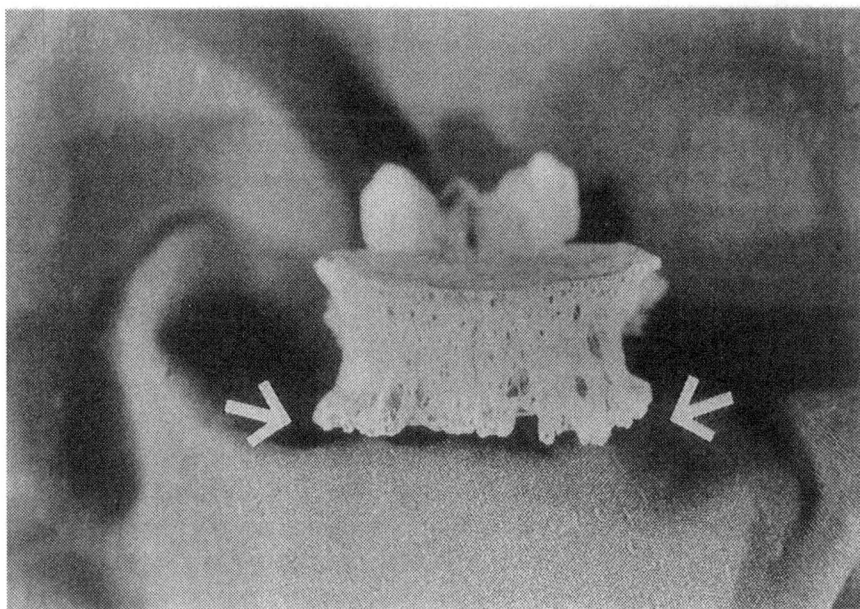

Fig. 8-6.   Proliferative remodeling of vertebral osteophytosis.

tion variability occurs over which is next highest, the cervical or thoracic region. Bridges argues (1994) that there does appear to be a geographic pattern. In western North America and other parts of the world, thoracic osteophytosis is next highest, if not highest (e.g., Gunness-Hey 1980; Jurmain 1990; Merbs 1983; Stewart 1947; Walker and Hollimon 1989). But the pattern is different in eastern North America. Irrespective of subsistence economy, the cervical vertebrae are the second highest area of osteophytic remodeling (Anderson 1974; Clabeaux 1976; C. S. Larsen 1982; Pickering 1979; Webb and Snow 1974). As if to underscore the contrast with the western United States, the Southeast includes some extremely low frequencies of thoracic involvement (Bridges 1994). Bridges suggests a neck-straining activity that all populations might share. Based on Merbs's (1983) suggestion, she hypothesizes that there was widespread use of the tumpline.

   In an attempt to discern osteological correlates of weapon use, that is, spear vs. bow, Bridges (1990) contrasted Pickwick Basin (Alabama) Archaic and Mississippian degenerative joint disease in the shoulder and elbow. She found a lack of correlation between hunting technology and arthritic changes in the shoulder and elbow ("atlatl elbow"). The degenerative changes presumably associated with atlatl use have multiple causes and are not gender specific. The study did reveal that the highest frequency and marked right-side assymetry occurred in Archaic females. She hypothesizes that for Archaic females, repetitive one-handed tasks, such as the use of the mortar (pounding) rather than the metate (grinding), were responsible for the pattern of shoulder-and elbow-joint degeneration (Bridges 1992).

Rheumatoid arthritis.   Ankylosing spondylitis (AS) and rheumatoid arthritis (RA) are inflammatory joint diseases that are independent of physical activity. There is only one reported case of AS or "bamboo spine" in the Archaic (Modoc Rock Shelter [Neumann 1967]). In contrast, Rothschild (Rothschild et al. 1988; Woods and Rothschild 1988) found several cases of a polyarticular resorptive arthritis, which resembles RA, in precolumbian sites in the eastern United States. The earliest data derive from Archaic period sites in the Midsouth (middle and western Tennessee River valley). Significantly, several researchers have hypothesized that RA is of recent origin in Europe (Bourke 1967; Rothschild et al. 1988; Short 1974). Rothschild hypothesized that RA is a New World infectious disease that originated in the Southeast, was contained within the western and middle Tennessee River valley until Woodland times, and then spread rapidly throughout North America. Presumably it reached Europe after 1492. There are problems with this model, which include the pattern of dispersion (late rapid spread) and the unknown etiology of rheumatoid arthritis. It is not certain that the erosive peripheral polyarthritis that has been identified is indeed the precursor of rheumatoid arthritis. Apparently several infective diseases, such as erysipelothrix, cause or mimic rheumatoid symptoms (Hudson et al. 1975), as does a current health problem, tick-borne Lyme disease.

I should add that the observed confinement of this polyarthritis in the Archaic period to the Tennessee valley may be an artifact of the available osteological data. As mentioned, the greatest concentration of large and fairly well preserved Archaic skeletal remains is in the Midsouth. With few exceptions (such as its demonstrable absence in the lower Illinois River valley), the spatial distribution of RA-like cases outside the region is unknown. Clearly, on a number of fronts, more research needs to be undertaken.

Dental Attrition

Mindful that a number of variables factor into dental attrition, the principal variable that affects rate of wear appears to be the physical consistency, including abrasive contaminants, of food (Goldstein 1948; Smith 1972). Although methods of quantification vary from study to study, there is a consistent pattern of higher attrition rates among hunter-gatherers. This is also true in west Tennessee in Archaic samples from the Kentucky Lake reservoir (Smith 1982). This pattern is attributed to a shift in food preparation techniques with the adoption of agriculture. Besides rate of wear, relative anterior to posterior wear varies between populations (Brothwell 1972; Merbs 1968). Based on ethnographic analogy (usually involving Aborigines or Bushmen), it has been suggested that hunter-gatherers use their anterior teeth more extensively than do food producers. This pattern has been observed in some skeletal samples (Anderson 1965; Molnar 1971a, 1971b) and interethnically using skeletal samples with Inuit as hunter-gatherer models (Hinton 1981). However, a study of anterior to posterior wear in Archaic samples from the Kentucky Lake reservoir showed that the tooth-wear pattern resembled that of agriculturalists (Smith 1982). Clearly not all patterns based on marginal peoples apply to populations occupying more complex habitats. There also appear to be interpopulational differences in the form of anterior tooth wear (Gould 1968; Molnar 1968). Hunter-gatherers exhibit rounded incisor wear while agriculturalists exhibit cupped wear (Hinton 1981). This pattern was verified among the Archaic samples of Kentucky Lake reservoir with the addition of lingual wear on the maxillary incisors of the agriculturalists. This lingual wear did not occur in the Archaic sample (Smith 1982). Other published reports of this pattern of attrition are restricted to prehistoric Latin America—Archaic Brazil and pre-Conquest Panama (Irish and Turner 1987; Turner and Machado 1983), hunter-gatherer populations from the Texas coast (Comuzzie and Steele 1988), and cases from agriculturalists in the Old World (Turner et al. 1991). Although the etiology of lingual wear is unknown, and such wear may possibly be caused by a variety of agents, Irish and Turner (1987) speculate that consumption of an abrasive cariogenic carbohydrate, specifically manioc, may be a factor in its occurrence in Latin America (but see Robb et al. [1991] and Turner et al. [1991] for further discussion). Whether this lingual wear in Tennessee agriculturalists is a reflection of maize consumption, culinary preparation, or culturally specific masticatory behavior is open to speculation. An explanation for the appearance of this particular lingual wear in coastal Texas hunter-gatherers and its absence in west Tennessee hunter-gatherers requires further analysis.

Mechanical Stress and Cortical Remodeling

Sustained intensive physical activity alters the structure of long bone shafts. Bone material is deposited or redistributed, according to Wolff's Law, to counteract strain that results from the regular performance of labor-intensive activities. Bioarchaeologically, this means that if subsistence strategies differ in the kinds and intensities of manual labor, there should be measurable differences in the dimension and shape of the long bone diaphyses and their cross sections. It is often argued that prehistoric agriculturalists, in contrast to hunter-gatherers, were engaged in more labor-intensive activities tied to food production and should demonstrate commensurate cortical remodeling. An examination of femoral midshaft diameters, robusticity, and sexual dimorphism in Archaic and Mississippian samples from Tennessee by Boyd and Boyd (1989) revealed no significant differences between the subsistence strategies. There was also no pattern of femoral length reduction (Boyd and Boyd 1989). In contrast, with the transition to agriculture Georgia coast pre-agriculturalists exhibited a decrease in workload, reflected in a reduction in femur length and in sexual dimorphism (C. S. Larsen 1982; Ruff 1987b; Ruff et al. 1984). A third pattern, observed by Bridges (1985, 1989b, 1991a), is an increase in labor-intensive activities in northern Alabama samples. Results such as these have suggested interregional variability in the degree of agricultural labor intensity. However, this conclusion presumes interregional homogeneity of hunter-gatherer labor intensity. Since bioarchaeological inquiry has long been focused on the transition to agriculture, it is not surprising that interarea differences are seen to emerge with food production. Confirmation or reevaluation of hunter-gatherer homogeneity would provide a clearer picture of these interregional differences spatially as well as temporally.

Bridges, in several publications (1985, 1989b, 1991a), reports gender differences within and between Archaic and Mississippian samples from the Pickwick reservoir. In the male samples, there is little difference in the upper arm between the subsistence strategies, but Mississippian males are more robust in the proximal lower extremity. Subsistence-related causes for this are unknown. Archaic females experienced less cortical remodeling of the femur and the upper arms than did their Mississippian counterparts. What this means with respect to activity levels is that the Mississippian sample specific to the Pickwick basin had a more demanding lifestyle than did Archaic intensive hunter-gatherers, and the Mississippian sample reflects gender-specific activity patterns. With respect to patterns of activity, Archaic females lack the bilateral symmetry of upper-arm remodeling that has been associated with pounding or grinding of corn. This is certainly not unexpected, based on the Archaic female asymmetry of degenerative joint disease of the arm reported above.

Conclusion

Since the adoption of the biocultural approach, the principal research focus of human skeletal analysis has been the biological consequences of adoption and intensification of agriculture. Examination of the association between food production and poor nutritional status revealed a pattern of comparatively better health status in hunter-gatherers (Cohen and Armelagos 1985). This pattern conformed to a perception of hunter-gatherer homogeneity that derived, in part, from early efforts to identify and define the hunter-gatherer subsistence strategy (Lee and DeVore 1968). Presumption of homogeneity may also have fostered the frequent use of a small number of larger Archaic samples (especially Indian Knoll) to obtain the definitive biological pattern for hunter-gatherers in the Southeast. Avoidance of redundancy and lack of personnel and financial resources resulted in the comparative neglect of other Archaic period osteological collections in the Southeast. Recent appreciation for the variability and complexity of hunter-gatherer societies (e.g., Price and Brown 1985a) may provide the theoretical framework for future Archaic period bioarchaeology in the Southeast. Specifically, the ecological diversity of this region might predict patterned interarea differences in labor intensity among hunter-gatherers. This could be detected as interpopulational patterns in activity-related pathologies. Regional differences in labor investment have already emerged for agricultural samples in the Southeast, as defined by cortical bone apposition or remodeling in long bones (Boyd and Boyd 1989; Bridges 1990, 1991a; Ruff 1987a, 1987b; Ruff et al. 1984). This review of Archaic period bioarchaeology suggests that the pattern and frequency of certain pathologies, such as accidental and deliberate trauma, and progressive changes, such as lingual surface maxillary incisor wear, already imply interarea patterns. This means that local conditions such as the availability, procurement ease, and/or the processing of subsistence resources are perhaps indicators as sensitive as the subsistence strategy for detecting basic lifestyle information such as division of labor, labor intensity, and behavioral practices (e.g., posture, atlatl elbow). Such sources of information need to be explored.

Pathologies such as spondylolysis and osteochondrosis occur at higher frequencies in Archaic hunter-gatherer samples than in Mississippian agriculturist samples. They may yet demonstrate interarea variation or at least provide informative baseline data for assessing other activity-related conditions (as independent variables or synergistic factors) that do vary from population to population. More complex disease processes such as osteoarthritis would be more difficult to address. The association between pathological condition and physical activity is not isomorphic, and interobserver differences in quantification and method of analysis certainly confound intersite comparisons. However, recent efforts to standardize quantification for arthritis and other pathologies will positively impact bioarchaeological analysis (Bridges 1993; Danforth et al. 1993; Ruff and Leo 1986). In the meantime, identification of local patterns and temporal trends is necessary fundamental information for Archaic period populations. This is especially true for collections that are understudied.

Clearly interarea differences introduce complexity in hunter-gatherer biology, but they also increase our repertoire of informative variables to help us understand prehistoric food procurement strategies beyond the thumbnail sketch. This argues for the integral role biological data can play in anthropological problem solving. Repatriation of human remains at this juncture would leave us with either a naive understanding of mid-Holocene lifestyles or no record at all.

Acknowledgments

I wish to thank Ken Sassaman and Pat Bridges for their comments on earlier drafts of this chapter. As always, I wish to thank Jeff Chapman and the staff at the Frank H. McClung Museum in Knoxville, Tennessee, for access to the anthropological collections.

SECTION IV

REGIONAL SETTLEMENT VARIATION

The "big picture" of Archaic period settlement is the subject of chapter 9 by David G. Anderson. Drawing from site file data from ten contiguous states in the Southeast, Anderson examines the regional distribution of Early, Middle, and Late Archaic sites to make inferences about settlement organization, mobility, and territoriality and how these may have changed through time. For mid-Holocene populations various settlement strategies are inferred, among them mobile foraging in the South Appalachian Piedmont; infrequent or focused use of Coastal Plain and Mississippi Delta locales; logistic-based coastal adaptations in peninsular Florida; and complex, river-based settlement of major Midsouth drainage basins. Anderson reviews extant interpretations for these varied patterns, including the possibility that divergent settlement strategies resulted from interaction among groups. He rightfully acknowledges that research emphases to date have been subregional or local in scope, owing in large measure to the structure of federally mandated work. Whereas this has led to a considerable amount of detailed information about local settlement, lack of comparative analyses hinders our ability to reveal regional patterns of broader anthropological interest. Anderson calls for continued efforts to examine regionwide patterns, offering recommendations for improving comparability and utility of site file data.

Knowledge about coastal settlement in the mid-Holocene has been stymied by lack of evidence. That very lack of archaeological data, combined with information on the dynamics of sea level rise, has led some to speculate that sustained coastal settlement was not possible until after 4200 B.P. Alternatively, if coastal settlement did take place during the mid-Holocene, transgressions in sea level destroyed the evidence. In chapter 10 Michael Russo renders these excuses untenable. Russo reviews the accumulating body of evidence for mid-Holocene coastal sites in locations spanning nearly the entire southeastern coastline. These include sites such as Horr's Island in southwest Florida that lie on Pleistocene landforms next to embayments. Russo's important work at Horr's Island builds on the growing evidence for year-round occupation of coastal sites in Florida. As Russo convincingly argues, coastal environments were indeed productive during the mid-Holocene, fully capable of supporting sizable, sedentary groups. If these same conditions apply to the Carolina-Georgia coastline, the dearth of Middle Archaic Coastal Plain sites noted by Anderson (chapter 9) may be deceiving. As Russo states, now that evidence for mid-Holocene coastal settlement exists, we need to search actively for additional sites in places too long ignored.

Further consideration of inundated mid-Holocene sites is provided in chapter 11 by Dennis B. Blanton. Introducing evidence collected by "watermen" of the Chesapeake Bay of Virginia, Blanton argues that models of Middle and Late Archaic settlement in the area have suffered from a nonrepresentative sample of site types. His sample of inundated sites has produced numerous grooved axes, adzes, and hafted bifaces, items dating primarily to the Late Archaic period and indicative of intensive occupation. The sites are located on the upper edges of submerged terraces, locations mirroring the terrestrial terraces that are noted in settlement models as locations of Archaic base camps. Blanton thus argues that prevailing models can be extrapolated to offshore contexts. This provides an effective means of predicting the locations of sites from submerged topography, as well as an opportunity to expand the database on riverine base camps in near-shore environments. It is important to note that Blanton's evidence differs from that presented by Russo (chapter 10) in that Blanton is identifying submerged sites with terrestrial counterparts (i.e., seasonal riverine base camps), whereas Russo is identifying site types with no terrestrial counterpart (i.e., permanent coastal base camps). These data sets are not contradictory; rather, they reflect different contexts for buried and submerged sites, as well as distinct settlement systems. Blanton's review of the potential for contexts similar to those found in the Chesapeake will help guide research to determine how far southward the seasonal mobility model applies.

9

Approaches to Modeling Regional Settlement in the Archaic Period Southeast

DAVID G. ANDERSON

In an attempt to examine Archaic settlement at a large scale, in late 1993 I contacted the site file curators in the ten states comprising the lower Southeast. As of March 31, 1994, a total of 179,944 archaeological sites had been recorded in these states, and for each of them it was possible to obtain information on the number with Early, Middle, and Late Archaic components present, reflecting occupations during the intervals from approximately 10,000 to 8000, 8000 to 5000, and 5000 to 3000 B.P. (table 9-1). A total of 32,428 sites with Archaic components (18.0 percent of the site total) have been recorded in the lower Southeast, ranging from lows of 1,206 and 1,241 sites in Florida and Louisiana, respectively, to highs of 5,161 and 5,931 sites in South Carolina and North Carolina.

Examining the raw data state by state, two major patterns are evident: first, a marked increase in the number of sites occurs over time, and second, this increase is not uniform across the region. With regard to the first observation, for the Southeast as a whole an increase in the total number of sites occurs over the course of the Archaic, from 7,081 (4.1 percent) in the Early Archaic to 10,423 (5.8 percent) in the Middle Archaic to 14,924 (8.3 percent) in the Late Archaic (table 9-1). An increase of some kind is as expected, since most researchers believe regional populations grew appreciably during the Archaic. Because it is not possible at present to control for the kinds of assemblages reflected by the raw data— components can range from isolated artifacts to dense middens, and component identifications are rarely comparable from state to state—it is not entirely clear that population increase is the actual message being conveyed by these numbers. Furthermore, the three subperiods are not equal in extent but differ by as much as a thousand years. Standardizing for time and taking the Early Archaic as a base value of 1.00, the proportional occurrence of sites in the Early, Middle, and Late Archaic subperiods is actually 1.00 to 0.98 to 2.11. Thus, the standardized data indicate that a slight *decrease* in site incidence occurred from the Early to Middle Archaic, followed by a *dramatic increase* from the Middle to Late Archaic. This

Table 9-1.   Early, Middle, and Late Archaic sites in the southeastern
United States: summary data by state

State		Total sites	Early Archaic	Middle Archaic	Late Archaic	Archaic total
Alabama	n	15,700	818	757	1,207	2,782
	%	100.0	5.2	4.8	7.7	17.7
Arkansas	n	27,581	501	386	1,574	2,461
	%	100.0	1.8	1.4	5.7	8.9
Florida	n	17,131	233	284	689	1,206
	%	100.0	1.4	1.7	4.0	7.0
Georgia	n	23,597	851	1,585	1,657	4,093
	%	100.0	3.6	6.7	7.0	17.4
Kentucky	n	16,775	553	347	1,046	1,946
	%	100.0	3.3	2.1	6.2	11.6
Louisiana[a]	n	8,574	—	1,104	137	1,241
	%	100.0	—	12.9	1.6	14.5
Mississippi	n	14,645	711	862	1,834	3,407
	%	100.0	4.9	5.9	12.5	23.3
North Carolina	n	25,919	1,259	2,262	2,410	5,931
	%	100.0	4.9	8.7	9.3	22.9
South Carolina	n	16,769	911	1,890	2,360	5,161
	%	100.0	5.4	11.3	14.1	30.8
Tennessee	n	13,253	1,244	946	2,010	4,200
	%	100.0	9.4	7.1	15.2	31.7
Total[b]	n	179,944	7,081	10,423	14,924	32,428
	%	100.0	4.1	5.8	8.3	18.0

a. Louisiana Middle Archaic mapping data employ the total Mesoindian values (generalized Archaic excluding Poverty Point, n = 1,104 sites). Late Archaic figures reflect identified Poverty Point sites only.
b. Early Archaic figures calculated minus Louisiana data.

suggests that regional population levels may have more or less stabilized fairly early (i.e., in the Early Archaic) and then remained uniform (or even dropped slightly) through the mid-Holocene, with marked growth only coming at the end of the Archaic.

The individual state data in table 9-1 also indicate that Archaic sites are not distributed evenly or change consistently over the region from one period to the next. That is, some areas appear to have been clearly favored over others at different times during the Archaic. Except in Georgia and the Carolinas, for example, there is little evidence for growth in the number of sites between the Early and Middle Archaic periods. In several states, in fact, a significant decrease in the number of sites actually occurs (e.g., Alabama, Arkansas, Kentucky, and Tennessee). Between the Middle and Late Archaic periods, in contrast, in every state except Louisiana, where Archaic data are not well documented by subperiod, the numbers of Late Archaic sites are typically much higher than the number of sites present during preceding periods.

As we shall see, when the data are examined in greater detail, some of the trends that appear on first inspection to reflect population growth or decline are more likely tied to changes in mobility and technological organization or to broad, environmentally influenced patterns of population relocation or consolidation. As we shall also see, some of these trends are shaped by survey and recording biases in the site file data from across the region. In spite of these concerns, at least some of the patterns identified here are believed to be sufficiently robust as to offer important insights about the Archaic occupation of the Southeast. Furthermore, while the analysis indicates that care must be taken in the use of existing site file data, it also indicates ways by which its value can be strengthened.

Examining Regional Site Distributions by Period

The regional site file records were used to generate distributional maps on the occurrence of sites with Early, Middle, and Late Archaic components present, as a percentage of all sites recorded by county or parish, within each state and collectively over the region (figs. 9-1–9-3). The standardization procedure employed—presenting the occurrence of sites with Archaic components as a percentage of all sites (prehistoric and historic) recorded in a county or parish—was intended to control at least partially for differing levels of survey intensity.

Examining the regional maps, considerable differences are evident in the incidence of sites with Archaic components. Arkansas, Florida, and Kentucky, for example, have a low incidence of sites during one or more Archaic subperiods, whereas sites are common in every subperiod in Mississippi, North Carolina, South Carolina, and Tennessee. While some of these patterns can be attributed to differences in the cultural systems in various parts of the region, in some areas the picture is more ambiguous or major sources of bias can be identified. Differential survey intensity is perhaps the most serious problem researchers have in interpreting component incidence from site file data. That is, a high incidence of Archaic sites may occur in some counties simply because extensive professional or avocational survey has taken place there. In areas where large numbers of sites are repeatedly and intensively examined, as for example along reservoir and river shorelines, ephemeral Archaic components are likely to be recognized, whereas these would probably be missed by more cursory examinations.

Another problem lies in the recognition and classification of Archaic components, which is not standardized or equivalent from state to state. In Louisiana, for example, a generalized "Mesoindian" category is used to encompass all pre–Poverty Point Archaic period components in the site files, while Late Archaic sites are typically only those yielding Poverty Point diagnostics (i.e., baked clay objects, lapidary items). This appears to have led to an unusually large number of sites being considered potentially mid-Holocene in age. In producing the Middle Archaic map (fig. 9-2), consequently, the numbers of Mesoindian sites per parish from Louisiana were examined as is and then divided by two, in an effort to see if

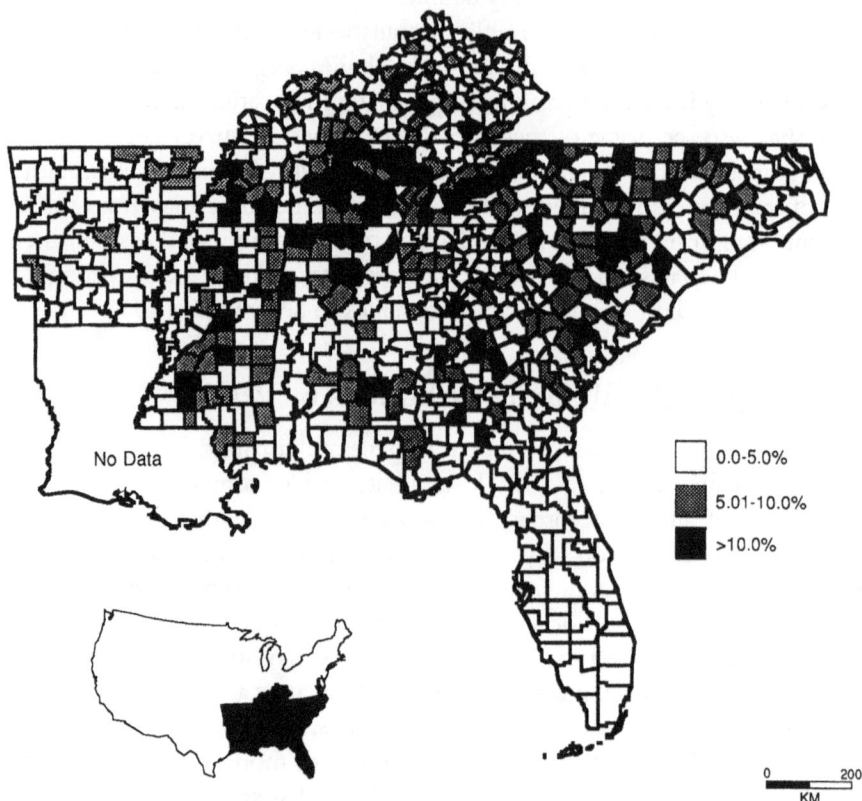

Fig. 9-1.   Incidence of Early Archaic components in the southeastern United States.

any major changes in distributional patterning occurred. None were evident and, hence, the figure is based on the total sample. Given these caveats about the problems with the data, interpretation of mapped distributions must obviously proceed cautiously. In spite of these limitations, however, I believe these first regional views of the southeastern Archaic are remarkably informative.

Early Archaic Sites: General Observations

Early Archaic sites (n = 7,081) are widely but unevenly distributed over the regional landscape. Early Archaic sites are common (i.e., more than 10 percent of the sites in any given county) over large areas in western, central, and eastern Tennessee, northern Alabama and Mississippi, central Georgia, and eastern South Carolina (fig. 9-1). In addition, several minor concentrations encompassing one or two counties occur in eastern Kentucky and along and near the Fall Line across the Atlantic and Gulf coastal plains. There is some tendency for these concentrations, and counties with lesser but still appreciable incidence of

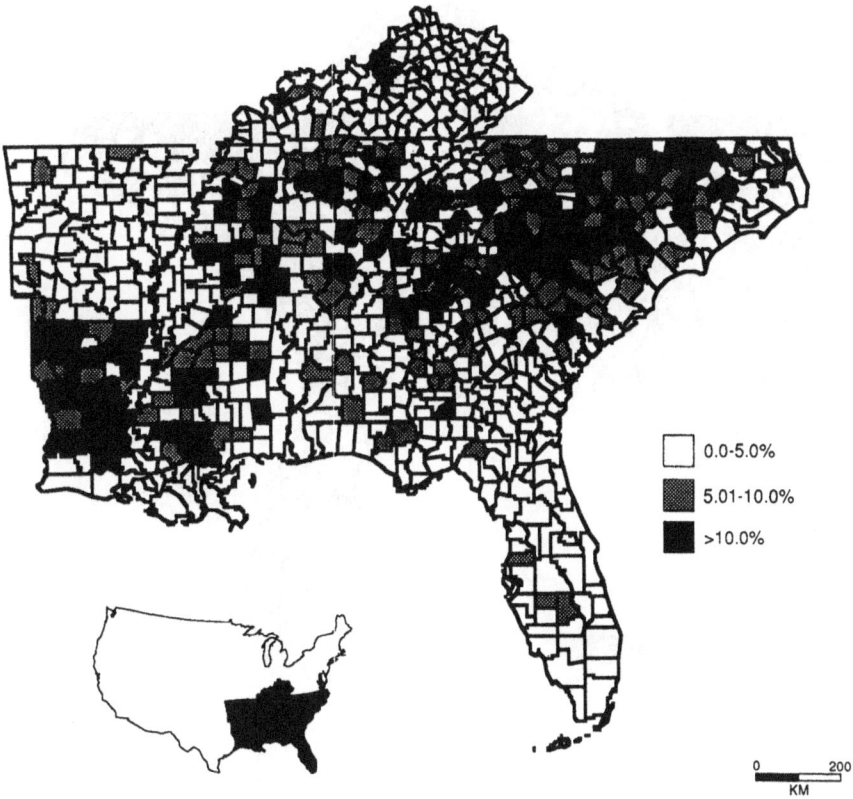

Fig. 9-2.   Incidence of Middle Archaic components in the southeastern United States.

sites of this period, to occur along or near major river systems, such as the Cumberland, Duck, Tennessee, Little Tennessee, Pearl, Yazoo, upper Alabama, upper
Tombigbee, Chattahoochee, Ocmulgee, Savannah, Pee Dee, Neuse, and
Roanoke. Some concentrations also correspond to the locations of major lithic
raw material source areas, for example, those in western South Carolina, the
southern Piedmont of North Carolina, in south Georgia, and along a number of
the major drainages of the interior Midsouth, indicating that quarries were
important foci for these populations (e.g., Daniel 1994; Gardner 1983, 1989).
These distributions offer some support to riverine-oriented settlement models
advanced for the period, with at least some of the observed concentrations
reflecting areas where aggregation loci, seasonal camps, or quarries were likely
located (e.g., Anderson and Hanson 1988; Kimball 1981, 1992; Morse and Morse
1983). Populations moving over large areas, primarily along river drainages (albeit
with some cross-drainage movement likely in some areas), and employing a mixture of logistical and residential mobility strategies, are inferred during this

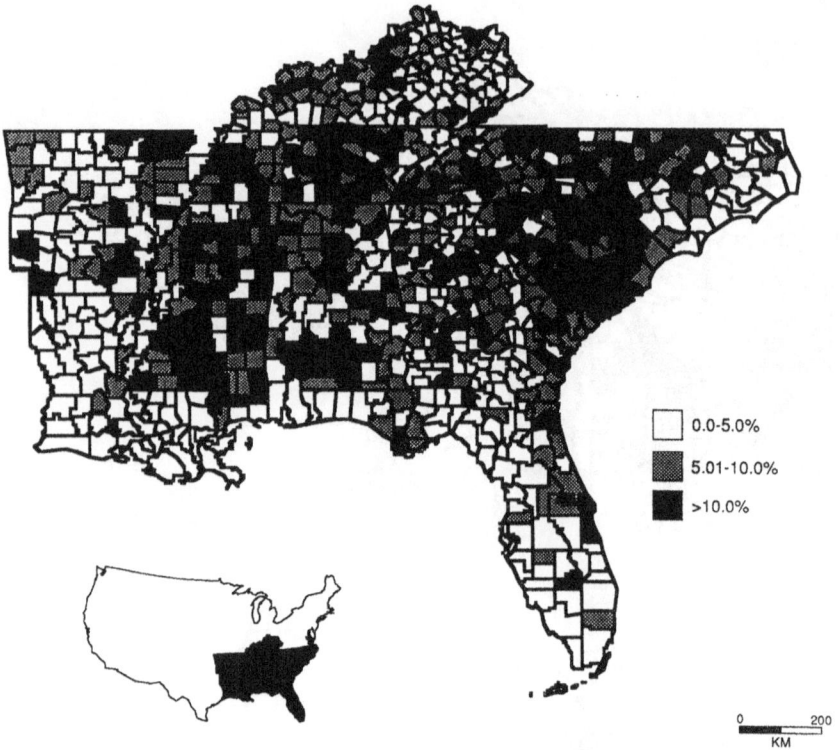

Fig. 9-3.   Incidence of Late Archaic components in the southeastern United States.

period. Particularly large population concentrations may have been present along the Tennessee, Cumberland, Pearl, and Pee Dee river systems, areas that may represent the centers of macroband systems.

Few Early Archaic sites are evident along the modern-day coast of North Carolina, in the lower Coastal Plain of Georgia, over much of the Florida peninsula, in parts of southern Alabama, and in southeastern Arkansas and extreme western Mississippi (no data are available from Louisiana for this time level). The effect of lowered sea level, which during the Early Archaic was 10–20 m below present level, is unclear but may have rendered some parts of the lower Coastal Plain less attractive to early populations. Moderate occupation or use of the interior of the Atlantic and Gulf coastal plains is indicated over much of the region, however, and use of (modern) coastal areas is evident in some areas, notably in southwestern South Carolina, the western Florida panhandle, and southern Mississippi. Given the inferred presence of a mixed hardwood-pine forest across much of the southeastern Coastal Plain during the Early Archaic period (Delcourt and Delcourt 1987; Watts et al., this volume), conditions favorable for hunting and gathering populations were likely present in both riverine and interriverine settings, which may help to explain the numbers of sites present. The dense Early Archaic site concentrations evident at and just below the Fall Line in the inner Coastal Plain across much of the region support observations that this is where extended (seasonal) occupation sites or multiband aggregation loci may have been located during this period (Anderson and Hanson 1988).

The data from the extreme lower Southeast, where (except for certain areas) few sites are found, suggests that climatic or biotic conditions here may have resembled more closely conditions inferred for the subsequent Middle Archaic era, when pine forests spread over much of the Coastal Plain. That is, while a mixed hardwood-pine forest may have been present, it may have been dominated by species that made the area comparatively unattractive for extensive settlement or use. The interior of peninsular Florida, as was the case during the preceding Paleoindian era, may have been too xeric to support large populations, which are for the most part found only in the karst-rich northwest and along the major rivers of the central panhandle (Dunbar 1991). The absence of early components in the counties on either side of the Mississippi Valley, an area that likely offered rich resources to early populations, may reflect depositional conditions; that is, the early occupations in these areas may have been either deeply buried or else scoured away. Why the coastal area of North Carolina is comparatively unoccupied is unclear, although moderate use of areas farther into the Coastal Plain is indicated; coastal/marine resources may not have been of much interest to groups ranging in this part of the region, or, again, the lowered sea levels may have made this area comparatively unattractive. The low incidence of Early Archaic occupations in Arkansas is somewhat unusual, given the numerous Dalton finds reported from across the state, although a decline in post-Dalton settlement has been suggested in northeast Arkansas (Morse 1975; Morse and Morse 1983). As the actual numbers of Early Archaic components in Arkansas are not substantially less than in several other southeastern states, the patterning may be masked by the vast numbers of subsequent (ceramic prehistoric and historic) sites that have been recorded in this state. As elsewhere in the region, where present, Early Archaic sites in Arkansas tend to occur either near major drainages (i.e., the Red, Arkansas, St. Francis), or in resource-rich areas like northeastern part of the state away from the Mississippi River.

Middle Archaic Sites: General Observations

Examining the regional distributions of Middle Archaic sites (n = 10,423), it is immediately evident that dense concentrations of sites occur throughout the Piedmont of North Carolina, South Carolina, and (to lesser extent) Georgia (fig. 9-2), a distribution that apparently represents the remains of Morrow Mountain projectile point–using populations. In recent years a number of researchers have argued that this area was occupied by highly mobile foraging groups using an expedient lithic technology characterized by the frequent manufacture and discard of diagnostic Morrow Mountain projectile points (Blanton and Sassaman

1989; Claggett and Cable 1982; Sassaman 1983, 1991). These artifacts are so ubiquitous that they are jokingly thought to occur on every hilltop in the Carolina Piedmont. The site concentrations in Georgia and the Carolinas are thus unlikely to represent the presence of dense populations but instead reflect the remains of small, organizationally uncomplicated groups ranging widely over the landscape. This distribution does not extend past the Appalachian summit nor west of the Georgia Piedmont, and is in fact largely confined to the South Atlantic Slope, only minimally extending into areas drained by rivers flowing into the Gulf of Mexico.

In the interior Midsouth of Kentucky and Tennessee, and in northern Georgia, Alabama, and Mississippi, in contrast, areas where large numbers of Middle Archaic sites occur appear to be somewhat more restricted. Furthermore, these concentrations, unlike those of the preceding Early Archaic and subsequent Late Archaic periods, are localized and rarely extend over more than a few counties. Such concentrations are found along the major drainages, including along the Tennessee, Cumberland, and Duck rivers, with lesser concentrations along the Green River and in the upper reaches of the major Gulf-trending drainages like the Chattahoochee, Coosa/Alabama, and Tombigbee. Some of these concentrations occur in areas where extensive shell- and earth-midden deposits have been found, such as along the Green and Tennessee rivers. Generations of researchers have argued that Middle Archaic populations in these drainages occupied comparatively restricted riverine environments, at least for part of the year (Hensley 1991, 1994; Marquardt and Watson 1983). Settlement concentrations along some of the other major drainages of the Midsouth, in contrast, such as along the Duck and Cumberland rivers (where dense shell middens are less common), may reflect cultural systems evincing greater seasonal mobility and a less pronounced riverine focus to their annual ranges. The lesser yet still widespread Middle Archaic site incidence over much of the remainder of the Midsouth away from these concentrations, in turn, may reflect the (seasonally exploited?) foraging ranges of these groups, with obvious voids possibly indicating boundaries between cultural or adaptational systems.

The organizational complexity of middle Holocene populations in the Midsouth area is assumed by most researchers to have been appreciably greater than in other parts of the region (i.e., than in the South Appalachian area, for example). Evidence for group participation in long-distance exchange, indications for at least occasional if not endemic warfare, and mortuary data suggesting the emergence of appreciable differences in individual achieved status are all apparent (see chapters by Claassen, Jefferies, and Smith, this volume). Given this, the major site concentrations in the Midsouth may represent the maintained territorial centers of individual groups. Interestingly, between at least some major site concentrations there are noticeable voids or areas of low site incidence that may represent buffer zones.

The Coastal Plain across much of the region from southeastern Mississippi to

North Carolina is characterized by low site incidence, somewhat of a reversal of the pattern noted in the Early Archaic. The mid-Holocene warming trend and concomitant widespread emergence of pine forests in the Coastal Plain beginning about 8000 years ago is thought to have made this physiographic province less attractive for settlement than during the previous Early Archaic period, when a mix of hardwoods and softwoods are thought to have been present. These environmental changes are thought to have prompted a relocation of populations into the interior and to have led to appreciable changes in adaptation in different parts of the region (Anderson 1991a; Sassaman 1995a, 1996). Appreciable numbers of Middle Archaic sites are present in the counties and parishes on either side of the Lower Mississippi Valley, however, as well as along the lower reaches of some larger drainages and in portions of Florida, suggesting that the Coastal Plain was not completely abandoned.

The major site concentrations observed in Louisiana appear to represent a combination of factors and may not give an accurate picture of Middle Archaic population distributions. As noted above, the state site files employ a Mesoindian category encompassing all post–San Patrice (i.e., late Paleoindian), pre–Poverty Point (i.e., terminal Late Archaic) assemblages. This overly broad temporal grouping is a reflection of the difficulties local researchers have had recognizing Early, Middle, and Late Archaic diagnostics and hence components. Even if the incidence of Mesoindian sites is divided in half in an attempt to portray the occurrence of Middle Archaic sites more accurately, however, large numbers are still present over much of the northern two-thirds of the state. The concentrations to the east of the Mississippi River occur in an area where a number of early mound complexes have recently been reported (R. Saunders 1994, J. Saunders et al. 1994; see also chapters by Gibson and Russo, this volume), while the concentrations to the west along the upper Red River and over much of the interior uplands (away from major drainages) may, in the absence of other evidence for cultural complexity, be the by-product of a highly mobile foraging adaptation similar to that noted in the South Appalachian area. The low incidence of sites in the counties and parishes immediately along the Mississippi River and along the coast, in contrast, may reflect low populations or, alternatively, a masking of the original mid-Holocene archaeological record by erosional and depositional factors associated with the movements of the Mississippi.

Late Archaic Sites: General Observations

Late Archaic sites (n = 14,924) occur widely over the Southeast (fig. 9-3). Moderate to extensive use of almost every part of the region is indicated, suggesting that considerable landscape filling had occurred. The sole exception to this patterning, the Louisiana data, consists primarily of sites with diagnostic Poverty Point artifacts, and hence significantly underrepresents the actual numbers of Late Archaic components present, particularly in the western part of the state.

When compared with earlier Archaic periods, the regional data in all likelihood reflect much higher population levels and possibly the use of a broader array of resources. For the first time sites occur with appreciable incidence in coastal areas, particularly along the Atlantic seaboard and in peninsular Florida. This patterning is unquestionably due, in part, to the increased use of shellfish and other marine resources that occurs at this time. Although the onset of shellfish utilization begins well back in the Middle Archaic in the Midsouth, and in some coastal areas by the late Middle Archaic (see Russo, this volume), widespread use of this type of resource appears to date to the Late Archaic.

Dense concentrations of components occur at a number of locations that closely correspond to well-documented Late Archaic cultures and (where these cultures did not span the entire period) their probable immediate predecessors or descendants (e.g., Bruseth 1991; Gibson 1991, this volume; Marquardt and Watson 1983; Morse and Morse 1983; Phillips 1970; Russo, this volume; Sassaman 1993a). Particularly evident are the Stallings Island/Thom's Creek cultures from the southern Coastal Plain of South Carolina and the northern Georgia coast on up the Savannah River; the Orange cultures in the vicinity of the St. Johns River of northeastern Florida; the Indian Knoll/Green River cultures of western Kentucky; and the Poverty Point culture of northeast Louisiana and the corresponding Jaketown phase in the Yazoo Basin of west-central Mississippi. Less well defined are concentrations that may include the Norwood culture and Elliott's Point complex in the northwestern Florida Panhandle; the Cedarland/Claiborne occupations in southern Mississippi; the Catahoula phase in southeastern Louisiana ; the O'Bryan Ridge phase of northeast Arkansas; and the Wheeler culture of north-central Alabama. In addition, several concentrations that may represent more or less discrete cultures are evident in portions of Tennessee and North Carolina, northeastern South Carolina, in southern Alabama, and in north-central Kentucky.

As during the preceding Middle Archaic period, areas between dense concentrations may reflect buffer zones or hunting territories between prehistoric societies. The fact that Late Archaic components occur in so many areas and with such high incidence, however, makes defining possible core areas, boundaries, or the extent of such (admittedly hypothetical) societies difficult. Different organizational systems were operating in different parts of the region, furthermore, necessitating care when interpreting specific concentrations. Sites of the Stallings culture area in southeastern South Carolina, for example, are appreciably different in character from presumably contemporaneous sites just a few hundred kilometers away in the northeastern part of the state and in adjoining North Carolina, where pottery is rare or absent, shell middens are absent in the interior, and use of coastal areas appears greatly reduced. Greater residential mobility, less investment in fixed territories (as evidenced by an absence of mounding behavior), and possibly a lower level of organizational complexity may be indicated.

Observations State by State

Alabama

Traversing the regional settlement data state by state alphabetically, the Alabama site files yielded information on 2,782 components, data provided by Eugene Futato of the Office of Archaeological Research at Moundville. Early Archaic sites are most common along and near the Tennessee River in the northern part of the state, where dense Paleoindian assemblages are documented from earlier periods (Anderson 1990, 1991b; Futato 1996). Appreciable use of the southeastern Coastal Plain is indicated, although little evidence for early settlement is indicated along the lower Tombigbee drainage or in the vicinity of Mobile Bay. Middle Archaic sites in Alabama are along the major drainages of the interior, which from the north to south include the Tennessee, Cahaba/Coosa, Tallapoosa, Tombigbee, and Alabama. Some of these concentrations reflect the extensive examination of river and reservoir shorelines, or areas such as Cedar and Little Bear creeks where major Cultural Resource Management projects have occurred. In general the site distribution suggests that occupations in the Coastal Plain were relatively uncommon and focused along rivers, while those in the interior Piedmont were more widespread. Major concentrations along and near the Tennessee River likely represent sites left by the groups creating the major shell middens that have been found in this area. Late Archaic components are widespread, although again little evidence exists for use of the coast. Unusually dense concentrations of components are evident in the southern and eastern Coastal Plain, indicating renewed use of this area. As during earlier periods, substantial occupation occurred in the northern part of the state, in the Piedmont and particularly along and near the Tennessee River valley.

Arkansas

In Arkansas, data on 2,461 Archaic components were provided by Lela Donat of the Arkansas Archeological Survey. Many of the Early Archaic components that are present occur along or just to the east of the Ozark escarpment in a band from northeast to southwest over the state, with fairly dense concentrations in northeast Arkansas and in the central and southwestern part of the state near the Arkansas and Red rivers. These distributions are comparable to those observed for earlier Dalton populations in the state (Morse 1996) and may reflect a continuation, in attenuated form, of the same general kind of adaptation. Sites dating to the Middle Archaic are rare, which contrasts sharply with data from areas immediately to the south in Louisiana, where large numbers of sites of this period are noted. Such apparent settlement differences delimited by state lines not following physiographic divides likely reflect classificatory problems, with Arkansas researchers being perhaps too conservative and Louisiana researchers too generous in assigning sites to the Middle Archaic period.

Middle Archaic site concentrations in Arkansas appear to fall along larger drainages, including the White, Arkansas, Little Saline, L'Anguille, St. Francis, and Red rivers, areas that have also seen extensive survey. Morse and Morse (1983) have argued that major population shifts from the Mississippi Valley lowlands into the Ozark uplands and along larger streams occurred during the Hypsithermal interval, a settlement shift brought about by the replacement of mixed oak forests in lowland areas by prairies. The low incidence of Middle Archaic sites in northeast Arkansas, an area rich in sites during most prehistoric periods, would appear to support this inference. Late Archaic components occur widely over much of the state, with an incidence several times that noted during the two previous periods. Major concentrations are evident in a number of areas, including in northeast Arkansas along and between the White, Cache, L'Anguille, and St. Francis rivers; in southeast Arkansas along and between the Ouachita and Saline rivers and Bayou Bartholomew; and in the southeastern part of the state near the Red and Little rivers. In addition, appreciable occupations are indicated along the upper course of the Arkansas and in the Ozark escarpment.

Florida

Data on a total of 1,206 Archaic components are recorded in the state site files and were provided by Steve Amis, Scott Edwards, and Marion Smith of the Bureau of Archaeological Research. Early Archaic components are uncommon compared with their incidence elsewhere in the region and are largely restricted to the northwestern part of the peninsula between the Suwannee and Withlacoochee rivers and to the central panhandle in the vicinity of the Apalachicola and Ochlockonee rivers. These are essentially the same areas as were occupied by earlier Paleoindian populations, in karst-rich or well-watered areas, suggesting that xeric conditions brought about (in part) by lowered sea levels may have precluded much use of other areas.

Major Middle Archaic site concentrations are observed in similar areas in the northern part of the state along the Choctawhatchee, Apalachicola, Aucilla, Withlacoochee, and upper Suwannee rivers as well as along the coast, in the karstic uplands to the east of Tampa Bay, and along portions of the St. Johns River. Milanich and Fairbanks (1980) have argued that Hypsithermal warming and drying trends would have concentrated peoples in areas where both water and hardwoods were readily available, including in the central Highlands and the Tallahassee Red Hills. As Russo and others (1992; Russo, this volume) have recently documented, however, toward the end of this period, year-round utilization of coastal shellfish began in earnest. While riverine adaptations are clearly indicated in portions of Florida during the Middle Archaic, there is little evidence except around Tampa and along the St. Johns that coastal adaptations were particularly common or widespread. The kinds of Archaic remains present in offshore waters, of course, remain to be fully explored (Dunbar et al. 1992). Unfortunately, the identification of Middle Archaic components in the state is at times ambiguous, since heat treating (in the absence of any other diagnostics) is sometimes used to infer the presence of components of this age.

Late Archaic components have a much higher incidence than earlier Archaic occupations and occur more widely over the state. Substantial population increase is indicated, as is the first intensive use of a number of new areas and resources. For the first time large numbers of components are evident around the major lakes in the interior of southern and central peninsular Florida, for example, and large numbers of sites occur along much of the coast. The concentration in northeastern Florida, along the St. Johns River, is where the Orange culture was located, and those in the Panhandle around Apalachicola and Pensacola bays, represent, in part, Norwood and Elliott's Point complex occupations. The appreciable increase in the use of the coast reflects the rise in importance of shellfish and other marine resources, at least when compared with earlier periods (Russo et al. 1992; Russo, this volume).

Georgia

A total of 4,093 Archaic components is currently recorded in the Georgia site files, data provided by Thomas Foster and Mark Williams. Early Archaic sites are fairly widely distributed over the northern and eastern part of the state, throughout much of the Savannah River basin, in the upper Piedmont, and in the Ridge and Valley province. Concentrations are also evident at and below the Fall Line along the Chattahoochee, Flint, Ocmulgee, and Oconee rivers, and in the vicinity of major chert quarries in the central Coastal Plain near Albany along the Flint and in eastern Georgia along Brier Creek and the Savannah River. Away from the Flint, Ocmulgee, and Savannah rivers there is little evidence for much use of the lower Coastal Plain. Riverine-focused, logistically organized settlements with base camps and aggregation loci in the Fall Line/inner Coastal Plain area, coupled with wider-ranging foraging behavior in the Piedmont, are inferred at this time in the Savannah River basin (Anderson and Hanson 1988), and similar strategies may be evident over much of the remainder of the state.

Middle Archaic sites in Georgia are fairly common and tend to be situated in the Piedmont along the upper reaches of the Chattahoochee, Oconee, and Savannah rivers. Lesser concentrations occur in the Ridge and Valley province along the upper Coosa, Tennessee, and Chickamauga rivers, and in the lower Coastal Plain along the Chattahoochee, Flint, and Savannah rivers. As during the Early Archaic period, use of the Coastal Plain appears directed to lithic source areas and major waterways; settlement, although poorly documented, seems to have decreased appreciably, as the remainder of this physiographic province is almost completely devoid of sites. This may reflect the spread of pine forests and xeric conditions during the Hypsithermal. Foraging adaptations like those observed and inferred in the Carolina Piedmont may be present over much of northern Georgia, although riverine-centered systems may have existed along the Tennessee River.

Late Archaic sites are fairly widespread over all but the extreme southern part of the state in the Coastal Plain. A number of small but dense concentrations of components are evident in several of the counties along the Fall Line, suggesting that this area was a focus for settlement during this period. Similar concentrations are evident in the central Piedmont and, together with the centers from the Fall Line, may reflect the centers of differing (seasonal?) occupations or perhaps even discrete cultures (e.g., Sassaman et al. 1988). Use of and probable movement over appreciable portions of the Piedmont, Ridge and Valley, and Blue Ridge provinces is indicated, although the mobility strategies employed are poorly documented. Data from the upper Savannah River suggests logistically organized, riverine-centered adaptations, perhaps coupled with a high degree of movement away from rivers and by greater use of the interriverine zone (Anderson and Joseph 1988; Goodyear et al. 1979). Finally, the dense concentrations along much of the coast and up the Savannah and Ogeechee rivers reflect the southern and western margins of the Stallings Island culture area. Williams (1994) has recently presented a GIS analysis of site data from Georgia for all periods of human occupation, based on data compiled a few months before the present study; his analysis, accordingly, is in close agreement with that presented here and should be examined by readers interested in seeing the Georgia data in greater detail.

Kentucky

A total of 1,946 Archaic components are recorded in the site files, data provided by R. Berle Clay, Kentucky state archaeologist. Early Archaic sites are fairly common and occur in low to moderate incidence over much of the state, with a few small concentrations evident along major drainages like the Green, Salt, Cumberland, and Ohio rivers. Whether these reflect territorial cores or, more likely, slightly more favored areas is unknown. Site density appears to be appreciably lower in the mountainous extreme eastern part of the state. If riverine-centered, logistically organized adaptations are present, as is sometimes inferred for the Early Archaic in and near the Ohio River valley, routine use of interriverine areas or lesser streams is suggested by the distributional evidence.

Unlike areas to the south in the Appalachian Summit and the trans-Mississippi South, Middle Archaic components occur in comparatively few areas, and in pronounced concentrations, including along the Green River, along the Ohio River just south of the Kentucky River, and at the mouths of the Cumberland and Tennessee rivers. Some of these concentrations are clearly tied to riverine-focused cultures, such as those producing the major shell middens of the Green River. Interestingly, major distributional voids also occur in the state, including along the Ohio River opposite the mouths of the Great Miami and Wabash rivers, and between the major Green and Kentucky river concentrations. These may reflect buffers or territorial boundaries between societies of the period, which from other evidence (i.e., for trade and conflict) were likely in fairly intense competition with one another (see chapters by Claassen, Jefferies, and Smith, this volume).

Late Archaic components exhibit a similar distribution to that noted during the preceding period, although more and larger concentrations are evident. Sites occur somewhat more widely over the landscape, however, with the result that few true empty areas or possible buffer zones are evident. A number of processes may be at work, including greater cooperative or competitive interaction between groups, resulting in more activity and components in intervening areas; greater permeability of social boundaries, fostering increased movement of individuals and groups over the landscape; or an increase in range mobility to encompass larger areas. Given evidence for at least some weapons trauma (Smith, this volume), it is possible that areas between groups were increasingly the scene of conflict. It is possible, therefore, that during this period or perhaps slightly earlier, the pattern of low intensity warfare that characterizes the contact-era Southeast may have been initiated.

Louisiana

A total of 1,104 Mesoindian and 137 Poverty Point sites are recorded in Louisiana, data provided by Michael Russo from the state site files. No Early or Late Archaic sites are present that are explicitly recorded as such, although many components assigned the Mesoindian classification unquestionably fall within these periods. The overly general approach to classification is because the identification and dating of Archaic diagnostics have remained controversial in the state down through the years. Major Mesoindian site concentrations are evident over much of the uplands in the western part of the state, including along and away from the upper and lower Red and central Sabine rivers. The large numbers of components in this area may reflect the remains of a foraging adaptational strategy similar to that observed in the South Atlantic Slope; sites and assemblages examined in this area appear to be fairly uncomplicated, suggesting brief use by mobile, loosely organized groups.

Another major concentration of Mesoindian sites is evident in eastern Louisiana, along and between the Amite and Pearl rivers. An early appearance for mound-based ceremonialism is indicated in this area, suggesting that it was an early focus for settlement (R. Saunders 1994). The minimal evidence for Mesoindian/Middle Archaic occupations along the coast may reflect subsidence and site discovery procedures or biases; or alternatively it may be part of an apparent pan-regional pattern of general avoidance of the lower Coastal Plain. The absence of components in the parishes along the Mississippi River, in contrast, appears to reflect channel scouring and depositional effects. For the Late Archaic period only Poverty Point components are mapped, since these are all that are recorded apart from the Mesoindian category. Major concentrations of Poverty Point period sites occur where they are expected in Louisiana, in the northeastern part of the state around the type site, with lesser concentrations further to the south and east (e.g., Byrd 1991).

Mississippi

Archaic components are fairly common in Mississippi, with 3,407 recorded to date in the state site files, data provided by Keith Baca, Patricia Galloway, and Sam McGahey of the Department of Archives and History. Early Archaic sites occur widely over the eastern two-thirds of the state but are decidedly uncommon in the western part near the Mississippi River and in the Delta, where they may have been deeply buried. Concentrations are evident in the southern, central, and northern parts of the state, in the vicinity of the lower Pearl and Amite, the Big Black and upper Pearl/Yockanookany, and the Tallahatchie and Yalobusha rivers, respectively. These concentrations may represent territorial centers or possibly favored areas occupied seasonally (or longer). Galloway (1994) has recently presented a detailed analysis of site data from Mississippi for all periods of prehistoric and historic American Indian occupation, based on data compiled a few months before the present study. Her figures and analysis mirror those presented here and should be examined by readers interested in seeing the Mississippi data in greater detail.

The occurrence of large numbers of Middle Archaic sites in many parts of Mississippi is like the pattern inferred over much of Louisiana. Similar cultural systems, perhaps characterized primarily by foraging adaptations, may have made use of the uplands away from both sides of the Mississippi River. Large numbers of Middle Archaic sites are also found along the upper Tombigbee drainage and Yellow Creeks in the northern part of the state, as well as along the Big Black, upper Pascagoula, and Pearl rivers to the south in the Coastal Plain. Some of these concentrations appear to reflect survey intensity as well as the existence of local universities employing archaeologists. The almost complete absence of sites in the Mississippi Delta, however, is similar to the pattern observed in both Arkansas and Louisiana. A combination of mechanisms is likely operating, including both depositional and erosional forces. It is also possible that these lowland areas, as Morse and Morse (1983) have suggested for northeast Arkansas, were largely abandoned in favor of the adjoining uplands during the middle Holocene.

Late Archaic components are so common over much of Mississippi that resolving and then interpreting concentrations within the general distribution is difficult. Some of the components in the south-central and northern parts of the state, particularly those in the alluvial lowlands, are unquestionably associated with the Poverty Point culture, while those further to the east are probably more closely affiliated with societies in the Tombigbee and Pascagoula/Chickasawhay drainages.

North Carolina

Archaic components in North Carolina are extremely common, as they are across the South Atlantic Slope in the Carolinas and in portions of the Midsouth. In total 5,931 components from this period, the largest tally from the region, have been documented in the state site files, data provided by Almeta Rowland of the North Carolina Archaeology Branch. Early Archaic sites are common from the inner Coastal Plain through the Piedmont and into the Blue Ridge. The high occurrence of components along major river systems like the Catawba, Pee Dee/Yadkin, Neuse, Haw, Deep, and Roanoke suggests riverine-oriented annual ranges like those posited for the Savannah drainage to the south, with dense concentrations perhaps reflecting seasonal camps or aggregation areas (Anderson and Hanson 1988). Extensive use of the Pee Dee/Yadkin is indicated; if an Early Archaic society was centered on this drainage (e.g., Daniel 1994), appreciable use of the inner Coastal Plain is supported by the South Carolina data (see below).

Middle Archaic sites occur in large numbers across much of the Piedmont landscape and into the adjoining Coastal Plain and Blue Ridge provinces. These distributions have been interpreted as the remains of highly mobile, open, and egalitarian foraging populations (Blanton and Sassaman 1989; Sassaman 1983, 1991). Some tendency toward major riverine areas is suggested by the occurrence of the densest concentrations along the Yadkin, Catawba, Broad, Dan, Haw, Roanoke, Little Tennessee, and French Broad rivers, although these are merely peaks in an otherwise extensive and dense distribution. Only the lower Coastal Plain appears relatively unoccupied or unutilized; areas in this province where sites are found are along major drainages like the Cape Fear and Black rivers or near major features like Great Dismal Swamp. Late Archaic components are widely distributed over North Carolina, in a pattern similar to that noted for the preceding Middle Archaic period. There is little evidence for much use of the lower Coastal Plain or immediate coastal areas, something that is atypical when compared with Late Archaic distributions over the rest of the region. As during earlier periods, appreciable use of the major river systems of the inner Coastal Plain and Piedmont is indicated.

South Carolina

Archaic site incidence is also high in South Carolina, where 5,161 components have been recorded, the second highest total for the region. Because the state site files are not computerized, primary data on component incidence had to be compiled by hand, something that had fortunately been accomplished as part of the development of historic context studies (Anderson and Sassaman 1992:333; Sassaman and Anderson 1994:101–102). Save for the northeastern area of the lower Coastal Plain, Early Archaic use is evident in all of the major physiographic regions, with a particularly dense concentration in the northeastern part of the state, in the inner Coastal Plain in the vicinity of the Wateree and Pee Dee rivers. Seasonal base camps are predicted in the inner Coastal Plain at this time (Anderson and Hanson 1988), although Daniel (1994) has argued that they may alternatively occur around lower Piedmont quarry sources; the North and South

Carolina data, taken together, suggest that both strategies may have been used. Lesser concentrations of Early Archaic components are found in the central Coastal Plain along the Savannah, Santee, and Pee Dee rivers, perhaps also reflecting base camp locations. The concentration along the lower Savannah occurs in the vicinity of the Allendale chert quarries and may additionally represent quarrying behavior.

Middle Archaic components are common across the state although, as in North Carolina, dense concentrations are present in the Piedmont and an appreciably lower incidence is evident in the Coastal Plain, particularly near modern coastal areas. This may correspond to a general relocation of population out of the Coastal Plain and into the Piedmont at this time, something equated with the spread of pine forests across the region (Anderson 1991a, Sassaman 1995a; Watts et al., this volume). South Carolina analyses, in fact, have formed much of the basis for the foraging-based characterizations of Middle Archaic settlement in this part of the region (e.g., Sassaman 1983). A minor concentration along the lower Savannah River may reflect quarrying behavior at the Allendale chert quarries.

Late Archaic components occur widely over the state, and the intensive reoccupation and use of the Coastal Plain following the inferred Middle Archaic "retrenchment" is clearly indicated. A pronounced concentration of Late Archaic materials is evident in the southern and central Coastal Plain, extending into the central Piedmont between the Savannah and Santee rivers, an area corresponding to the heartland of the Stallings Island and Thom's Creek cultures. A second concentration in the northeastern Coastal Plain and Piedmont, between the Little Pee Dee and Catawba rivers, is not currently associated with a readily recognizable Late Archaic culture. Nonetheless, the data appear to point to such an entity, albeit one in which pottery played a minimal role. Analyses of Archaic settlement in South Carolina have been recently prepared that examine component as well as diagnostic artifact distributions during these periods in great detail (Anderson et al. 1992; Sassaman and Anderson 1994:99–132) and, like the Mississippi and Georgia statewide studies noted earlier, help illustrate the potential of large-scale, statewide distributional analyses.

Tennessee

Archaic sites are common in Tennessee, with 4,200 recorded in the state site files, data provided by Suzanne Hoyal and Kevin Smith of the Tennessee Division of Archaeology. Early, Middle, and Late Archaic sites occur widely, with concentrations in the eastern, central, and western parts of the state that appear to represent a combination of survey coverage and actual past settlement patterning. Some site concentrations, such as those along the Duck, Tennessee, and upper Cumberland rivers, for example, appear to reflect in part reservoir impoundments where extensive survey work by professionals and avocationals has occurred. Early Archaic settlement is particularly pronounced in and near the major river systems traversing the state, including the Cumberland and Duck rivers in the central area, and the Tennessee River and its tributaries in both the east and west. Appreciable use of riverine and interriverine (or smaller stream) zones is indicated by the distributions.

Middle Archaic populations appear to have made extensive use of riverine environments as well as of portions of the intervening uplands. While major concentrations are present, they are somewhat smaller than during earlier and later periods, suggesting that mid-Holocene populations over much of state may have been less riverine-focused and more geographically mobile than the societies to the north and south, along the Green and Tennessee rivers in Kentucky and Alabama. Late Archaic components, in contrast, occur so widely and with such incidence that, as is the case in several other southeastern states, accurately resolving and interpreting concentration boundaries is difficult. Unusually large numbers of sites are present in the central part of the state, along and between the Cumberland and Tennessee rivers, but what is represented by this is unclear. For the state as a whole, appreciable population increase, coupled with the use of most major physiographic areas, would appear indicated.

The Value of Regional Settlement Mapping

These analyses, besides the light they help shed on past human behavior, also have important implications for how we collect and classify data over the region. How components are classified, that is, assigned to particular periods, needs to be carefully considered and in some states rendered somewhat more precise than is done at present, if possible. The use of the Mesoindian designation in the Lower Mississippi Valley for post-Paleoindian, pre–Poverty Point components, for example, appears far too coarse grained to be of much utility. Site forms all too typically appear to be filled out (and then forgotten) early in the research process; all of us need to make an effort to upgrade the component information in our state site files. Mechanisms need to be developed, in fact, for the regular submission of data to the site files from large synthesis projects as well as from focused research studies. State and regional maps, here presented using county-level summary data, will undoubtedly shortly be produced using site point (i.e., UTM) data, and will be explored in detail with GIS-based analyses. In some states within the region, notably Arkansas and Georgia, this capability already exists (e.g., Morse 1996; Williams 1994), while in others it is under development. Until every state computerizes site files at some basic level, regional-scale analyses will continue to prove difficult. These problems, fortunately, are all resolvable. In the years to come the production and refinement of maps like this will occur for all the major periods of southeastern prehistory, a process that will likely continue to prove highly informative (Anderson and Horak 1995).

Conclusions

As this study has demonstrated, several differing patterns of large-scale land use are evident over each of the major Archaic periods in the Southeast. For the Middle Archaic period alone these include (1) South Appalachian Piedmont foragers of low social complexity and high (albeit geographically restricted) mobility; (2) a pattern of infrequent or focused use of the Coastal Plain from North Carolina to Alabama; (3) possible logistically based coastal adaptations in Florida coupled with (seasonal?) foraging in interior areas; (4) complex, riverine-focused occupations along some of the major river drainages of the Midsouth, possibly with territorial buffers as well as less complex systems in intervening areas; (5) foraging adaptations in the interior uplands of Mississippi and Louisiana; and (6) minimal use of the Mississippi Delta lowlands. Similar variability is evident during the Early and Late Archaic periods, demonstrating that regional adaptations were anything but homogeneous.

The varying levels of social complexity observed over the Archaic Southeast were, I believe, related to regional physiography, resource structure, and intensity of intergroup interaction. Areas rich in resources where interaction potential was greatest, such as in the major river drainages of the Midsouth, for example, were the areas that over time tended to have the densest site concentrations and, in many cases, among the highest levels of sociopolitical complexity. In contrast, in marginal zones or areas poor in resources, where interaction potential would have been lower, less complex cultural systems are evident, particularly in the Early and Middle Archaic. The Southeast during the Archaic period, much as during later periods, was a varied cultural landscape characterized by a range of adaptations. To understand occupations in any one area, we must have an appreciation for the larger regional picture. While exploring the Archaic societies of the Southeast will occupy archaeologists for many years to come, the present analysis suggests one way that we can begin to recognize the cultural variability that existed within the region.

Acknowledgments

County-level site data used to produce the maps presented here were provided by the following individuals, by state: Eugene Futato (Alabama); Lela Donat (Arkansas); Steve Amis, Scott Edwards, and Marion Smith (Florida); Thomas Foster and Mark Williams (Georgia); R. Berle Clay (Kentucky); Michael Russo (Louisiana); Keith Baca, Patricia Galloway, and Sam McGahey (Mississippi); Almeta Rowland (North Carolina); and Suzanne Hoyal and Kevin Smith (Tennessee). Interpretations of the maps were suggested by all of the above, plus Keith Derting, Mark Mathis, Ken Sassaman, and Bob Thorne. Their help is greatly appreciated.

10

Southeastern Mid-Holocene Coastal Settlements

MICHAEL RUSSO

Until recently, shell rings and middens in Georgia, South Carolina, and northeast Florida ca. 4200–3800 B.P. have been identified as sites of the earliest coastal cultures in the Southeast. These sites contain evidence of some of the earliest pottery in North America and are thought to have been occupied by Late Archaic peoples who moved to the coast from interior river valleys. The limited occurrence of such sites, combined with the lack of evidence for earlier coastal sites, has prompted suggestions that mid- to late Holocene coastal environments were not fully developed. Cultures could not adapt effectively to coastal resources until sea level stabilized sufficiently to allow for estuarine development (DePratter and Howard 1980; Miller 1991; Widmer 1988).

The normative model suggests that five to six thousand years ago, marine waters along southeastern coastlines lay 3 to 7 m below present-day levels, and up to 20 miles seaward from their present locations. Sea level was rising rapidly and coasts are presumed to have lacked the rich estuarine fauna necessary to support large-scale human exploitation. Sea level had yet to rise to the point where it breached Pleistocene formations behind which the present-day marsh/lagoon systems could develop. In addition, the rapidly transgressing sea prevented establishment of estuarine vegetation, and rainfall was insufficient to supply the fresh water necessary for the development of coastal estuaries (Brooks et al. 1989; DePratter 1979; Widmer 1988:187).

Recent archaeological investigations and reconsiderations of theories about the pace and timing of early coastal occupations are altering our views of how and when southeastern coasts were initially settled. Contrary to expectations, some of the late Holocene cultures producing fiber-tempered pottery appear to have been long-established, permanent, and complex societies, not incipient cultures adapting to a new and rapidly changing environment. Pre–4200 B.P. preceramic mid to late Holocene coastal occupations have been identified, suggesting that coasts were productive and capable of supporting human occupation earlier than was previously thought. In fact, mid-Holocene coastal cultures were widespread along the Gulf and Atlantic coasts and represent some of the most permanent, sedentary societies of the time.

Mid- to Late Holocene Coastal Environment and Human Settlement

The general theory that sea level during the mid-Holocene rose rapidly then gradually slowed during the late Holocene is factually based and widely accepted across the Southeast (Brooks et al. 1989; Fairbridge 1961; Scholl et al. 1967; Upchurch et al. 1992), albeit with significant qualifications as to the timing, rate, and frequency of rebounding. Equating this Fairbridgian view of sea level rise to the relative productivity of mid- to late Holocene estuaries, however, has been a far more speculative endeavor. Evidence of limited mid-Holocene productivity is largely based on the absence of archaeological data (i.e., shell middens) rather than on any in situ natural biological data. The absence of shell middens in South Carolina prior to 4200 B.P., for instance, has been used to support the idea of an "unstable" coastal environment prior to the late Holocene (Brooks et al. 1989:96). A similar argument has been advanced for southwest Florida, where documented shell middens did not predate 5000 B.P., and there were few shell middens dating to between 5000 and 2700 B.P. (Widmer 1988). However, because any mid-Holocene coastal formations and attendant archaeological sites are presumed to lie beneath a risen sea, such negative evidence is not altogether compelling proof that estuaries were not productive and were not being exploited by human populations.

Ideally, the best evidence for determining the productivity of mid-Holocene estuaries should come from the sedimentological and biological record of the estuaries themselves, the same sources used to determine sea level curves. Problems associated with such studies, however, make assessments difficult. For one, most of the mid-Holocene record lies offshore, where the actions of waves and storms have served to remove deposits. As a result, late Holocene deposits may lie directly on sculpted Pleistocene bedrock without intervening early or mid-Holocene sedimentary records. Further, if estuarine sediments are identified, the inability to distinguish depositional sequences such as salt-marsh vs. riverine estuaries (Frey and Howard 1986) precludes the ability to estimate resource potential for humans. In the Southeast, models of estuarine structures are still inadequately developed, and techniques to define and determine the kinds, let alone the productivity, of ancient estuaries are wanting. Because of these problems, and a general lack of interest in estuarine productivity by sea level modelers, nowhere has independent, nonarchaeological evidence been used to corroborate the hypothesis of depauperate mid-Holocene coastal estuaries. Archaeologists interested in questions concerning coastal productivity have, perforce, extrapolated from sea level studies not specifically designed to measure productivity: that is, the absence of mid-Holocene shell middens on present-day landforms has been most frequently used to determined that coastal settlement was limited, if not unknown, during the mid-Holocene (DePratter 1979; Miller 1991; Widmer 1988).

However, abundant evidence for mid-Holocene estuaries exists beneath coastal waters. Evidence includes 8000-year-old oyster deposits off the coast of North Carolina (Merrill et al. 1965); 7000–9000-year-old rangia clam and oyster deposits up to 33 m below the marsh and lake water of the Ponchartrain Basin; brackish-water peat deposits dating to 10,000 B.P. along the coasts of Louisiana and Texas (Gagliano et al. 1982:9); mangrove forest peats 6000 to 8000 years old along the southwest Florida coast and the Florida Keys (Parkinson 1987:53, 139; Widmer 1988:163, 311); and estuarine shellfish dating between 5000 and 7000 B.P. on Sanibel Island, Florida (Stapor et al. 1988, 1991).

It is clear that despite a rapidly transgressing sea, early and mid-Holocene estuaries were widespread along the southeastern coasts. The rapidity of sea level rise as an obstacle to panregional estuarine development is questionable. Indeed, even faster marine transgressions (and regressions) occurred during the late Holocene, yet estuaries flourished (e.g., Brooks et al. 1989). Although sea level rise obviously affected coastal development, it apparently did not preclude the development of estuaries across the entire Southeast. Sufficient freshwater flow, barrier island embayments, riverine deltas, and sea level stability allowed for the establishment of productive estuaries at numerous locations. Archaeological research is beginning to demonstrate that mid-Holocene coastal environments were more than sufficient to support diverse social formations, including relatively sedentary, complex societies (fig. 10-1).

Mid- to Late Holocene Coastal Archaeological Sites

Texas

Two of the earliest mid-Holocene coastal sites in the United States lie outside the boundaries of the Southeast proper but serve as examples of the character and location that mid-Holocene archaeological evidence may take. Along the banks of the Nueces River, at Corpus Christi Bay, and at nearby estuaries, eleven shell middens predating the earliest fiber-tempered Atlantic Coast sites (table 10-1) have been identified (Cox 1994; Prewitt and Paine 1987; Ricklis 1988; Ricklis and Cox 1991; Ricklis and Gunter 1986). A number of the sites today lie above the banks of the Nueces River, inland from coastal waters. After the Pleistocene, the Nueces River lay in a deeply entrenched valley allowing estuaries to develop farther upriver under a lower mid-Holocene sea than is possible with the infilled river basin and higher seas of today. The various middens consist of a variety of shellfish including oyster, scallop, quahog, and two rangia species, and vary in size from 300 to 2000 m^2. Middens are typically less than one meter deep, contain variably dense deposits of estuarine shellfish and fish remains, and are situated on top of Pleistocene clay formations with no intervening Holocene soils. Archaic

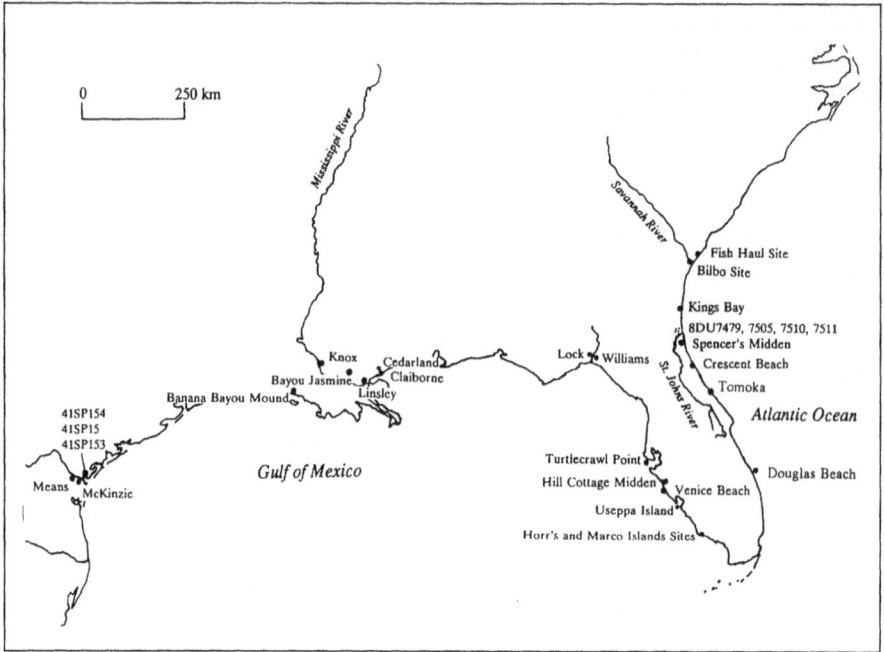

Fig. 10-1.   Mid-Holocene preceramic Archaic coastal sites and other sites discussed in
chapter.

points, other lithic tools, and a wide variety of worked shell artifacts that include
sunray venus knives, quahog anvils, and conch adzes, celts, and columella tools
have been recovered.

Based on calibrated radiocarbon assays, 41SP153 and 41SP136 date between
6800 and 7200 B.P. while six other sites predate 5000 B.P. (Cox 1994:223). Two of
these, the Means site, 41NU184, and the McKinzie site, 41NU221, have yielded
rangia shell mid-Holocene radiocarbon dates. The Means site yielded postmolds
of a circular structure 3.8 m in diameter with associated hearths, pits, and shell
deposits older than 5000 B.P. (Ricklis 1988; Ricklis and Gunter 1986). The authors
note that the substantial structure is the earliest evidence that Archaic hunter-
gatherers in the region were not as mobile as was previously thought.

Ricklis and Cox (1991; Cox 1994) hypothesize that Archaic coastal habitation in
Texas was not continuous from the mid-Holocene on, but rather, was limited to
stillstands that occurred between 8000 and 7200 B.P., from 6000 to 4500 B.P., and
again at 3000 to 2000 B.P. Using the absence of coastal archaeological sites
between these periods as evidence of rapidly rising sea levels, they suggest that at
such times the "rates of sedimentation in the coastal estuaries might not have been
great enough to create the broad, shallow bay systems which are optimal for the
development of extensive shellfish beds, and for effective human access to those
resources" (Ricklis and Cox 1991:27). By the Late Archaic (ca. 2000 B.P. in Texas),

the development of estuarine productivity obtained its modern-day richness, allowing semisedentary occupation of the coast throughout the year. Ricklis (1988:65) suggests that at least the fall/winter occupational pattern identified along the coast at this time may have extended back to the mid-Holocene, as evidenced by seasonality patterns at the McKinzie site. Consequently, as with the normative models of the Southeast, the earliest coastal settlements in Texas are considered seasonal occupations of interior hunter-gatherers.

Louisiana

Because of the extreme subsidence that has occurred at the mouth of the Mississippi River, the coastal archaeological record of the mid-Holocene is not nearly as rich in Louisiana as it is in Texas. Relative sea level rise has been measured in Louisiana to exceed 1.5 m over the last century, compared to less than 20 cm along parts of the Florida Gulf Coast and 85 cm in coastal Texas (Penland et al. 1989). This pan-Gulf disparity in relative sea level rise is a multimillennial phenomenon that has had a tremendous impact on the coastal archaeological record, submerging most mid-Holocene sites near the Mississippi, while allowing a few favorably located in Florida and Texas to survive.

The earliest widely recognized coastal occupation in the Mississippi Delta region dates to the Late Archaic period. Two coastal sites—Linsley, 16OR40, and the multicomponent Bayou Jasmine, 16SJB2—consist of fresh to brackish water shellfish species (mostly rangia with some oyster) and earth midden yielding baked clay objects, bone tools (including fish hooks), and great quantities of vertebrate remains indicative of brackish to freshwater marsh environments (Coastal Environments, Inc. 1977:261; Duhe 1976; Gagliano 1963; Gagliano and Saucier 1963). Both sites are deeply buried beneath coastal marsh on relict river levees. The Linsley site lies under 2.5 m of peat, 3 to 4 m below mean sea level. The Poverty Point component at the Bayou Jasmine site extends to nearly 6 m below mean sea level (Coastal Environments, Inc. 1977:261; Gagliano and Saucier 1963).

Although both sites are thought to lie upon levees no older than 4000 years, there is the possibility that pre–Poverty Point deposits, some older than 4000 years, may lie below the Poverty Point middens. At Bayou Jasmine, Neuman (1975) notes that excavations had to cease at 2.8 m below surface within a Tchefuncte component, without reaching the Poverty Point levels identified by the presence of baked clay objects and other artifacts within the dredge spoil. Because the site extends nearly 6 m below the marsh surface, and because baked clay objects can predate Poverty Point (e.g., Saunders et al. 1994; see chaps. 14 and 15, this volume), a Middle Archaic occupation cannot be ruled out.

At Linsley a radiocarbon determination of 4440 ± 140 B.P. came from the Rangia midden lying on top of a relict levee and beneath a Poverty Point earth midden (table 10-1). This date was dismissed as "inconsistent" (Gagliano and Saucier 1963:326) because peat taken more than 3 m below the rangia midden dated only to 4040 ± 140 B.P. Upon closer examination, however, the date may

Table 10-1. Radiocarbon dates from mid-Holocene and other southeastern preceramic Archaic coastal middens

Provenience	Lab no.	Sample	Uncorr. C14 years B.P.	Corr. C14 years B.P.	C14 years B.C.	Calibrated date, 2 sigma	Reference
Florida Gulf							
Horr's Island							
Test 9, Village midden Stratum H	UM 1926	oyster	3895±75	4295[1]	2345	4599 (4409) 4209	McMichael 1982; Russo 1991
Test 9, Village midden Stratum B	UM 1927	oyster	3895±85	4295[1]	2345	4629 (4409) 4159	McMichael 1982; Russo 1991
Test 9, Village midden Stratum A	UM 1928	whelk	4120±85	4520[1]	2570	4869 (4784, 4745, 4729) 4449	McMichael 1982; Russo 1991
Test 9, Village midden Stratum D	UM 1929	quahog	4080±80	4480[1]	2530	4849 (4646) 4419	McMichael 1982; Russo 1991
Test 9, Village midden Stratum C	UM 1930	oyster	3975±85	4375[1]	2425	4799 (4511) 4289	McMichael 1982; Russo 1991
Test 9, Village midden Stratum J	UM 1931	whelk	3890±80	4290[1]	2340	4609 (4406) 4169	McMichael 1982; Russo 1991
Test 7, Village midden Stratum B	Beta 1273	oyster	3615±75	4015[1]	2065	4239 (3999) 3819	McMichael 1982; Russo 1991
Test 7, Village midden Stratum D	Beta 1274	oyster	4100±110	4500[1]	2550	4949 (4702) 4399	McMichael 1982; Russo 1991
Test 7, Village midden Stratum D	Beta 1275	oyster	3885±100	4285[1]	2335	4687 (4403) 4099	McMichael 1982; Russo 1991
Test II, Village midden Stratum D	Beta 1276	oyster	4070±80	4470[1]	2320	4839 (4629) 4419	McMichael 1982; Russo 1991
Test II, Village midden Stratum B	Beta 1277	oyster	4260±90	4660[1]	2710	5109 (4844) 4639	McMichael 1982; Russo 1991
Test II, Village midden Stratum A	Beta 1278	oyster	3790±85	4190[1]	2240	4499 (4270) 4019	McMichael 1982; Russo 1991
8CR205, FS363, midden	Beta 40275	oyster	3600±70	3990[3]	2040	4199 (3975) 3809	Russo 1991
Useppa Island							
"clam shell touching Burial 1"	Beta 14152	quahog	4130±80	4530[1]	2580	4879 (4797) 4509	Marquardt 1992b:11**
"clam shell just below Burial 1"	Beta 14142	quahog	4090±70	4490[1]	2540	4849 (4702) 4479	Marquardt 1992b:11**
Test 2, shell midden with Busycon	UM-1836	"shell"	4935±100	5335[1]	3385	5929 (5711) 5479	Milanich et al. 1984:270
Hill Cottage Midden							
below fiber-tempered pottery, 8' bs	G-599	Busycon	4050±125	4450[1]	2500	4899 (4614) 4299	Bullen and Bullen 1976:13
below fiber-tempered pottery, 11' bs	G-600	Busycon	4100±125	4500[1]	2550	4989 (4771, 4756, 4713) 4379	Bullen and Bullen 1976:13
Turtlecrawl Point							
oyster/quahog dredge spoil	—	Busycon tool	4460±130	4860[1]	2910	5469 (5217) 4829	Goodyear et al. 1993:5
oyster/quahog dredge spoil	—	Busycon tool	4675±120	5075[1]	3125	5689 (5441) 5099	Goodyear et al. 1993:5
Williams Site							
fire pit in oyster shell	FSU-146	charred wood	5460±510	—	3510	7419 (6292) 4994	Phelps 1967:41

Florida Atlantic

Rollin's Bird Sanctuary							
120 cmbs	Beta 45925	oyster	3730±60	4150[2]	2200	4399 (4230) 4059	Russo 1992a:110
Oxeye Islands							
80 cmbs	Beta 47531	oyster	3990±70	4370[3]	2420	4789 (4515) 4349	Russo 1992a:110
McGundo Midden							
190 cmbs	Beta 45924	oyster	4210±70	4630[2]	2680	5019 (4843) 4699	Russo 1992a:110
Pepper Island							
30 cmbs	Beta 47533	oyster	4500±70	4870[3]	2920	5329 (5227) 4959	Russo 1992a:110
Spencer's Midden							
180 cmbs	Beta 50153	oyster	5210±80	5570[3]	3620	6169 (5944) 5759	Russo 1992a:110
Crescent Beach Site							
150 cmbs	—	quahog	3840±80	4240[1]	2290	4549 (4375) 4119	Bond 1992:152–153
Douglas Beach Site							
salvage feature	I-13, 8410	wood stake	4630±100	—	2680	5589 (5320) 4990	Murphy 1990:27*
South Carolina/Georgia							
Kings Bay, 9CAM167							
hearth	UM-1432	wood	5000±180	—	3050	6189 (5734) 5319	Calvert et al. 1979:109
Bilbo Site							
Zone 3 oyster/mussel	O-1046	charcoal	5500±115	—	3550	6607 (6302) 5991	Williams 1968:330*
Fish Haul Site							
hearth or tree hole	Beta 16925	charcoal	6060±110	—	4110	7189 (6941, 6928, 6895) 6676	Trinkley 1986:141*
Louisiana							
Knox Site							
rangia midden	—	rangia	5464±135	5864[1]	3914	6609 (6287) 5959	Gagliano 1963:114
Linsley Site							
rangia midden	—	rangia	4440±140	4840[1]	2890	5469 (5124) 4809	Coastal Environments, Inc. 1977:262*

Note: All calibrations determined using University of Washington Quaternary Isotope Lab Radiocarbon Calibration Program 1987, Rev. 2.0 (Stuiver and Reimer 1986). Prior to calibration, 400 years ([1]) or 420 years ([2]) as described in Russo 1993 were added to uncorrected B.P. dates to correct for 13C/12C fractionation on all shell samples unless otherwise noted.

[3]Correction performed by radiocarbon lab.

*Archaeologist questions context or whether date reflects period of site occupation.

**Calibrated dates presented herein differ from original citations.

not be out of stratigraphic position—three Poverty Point midden dates above it are younger, averaging 3690 B.P. In actuality, the 4440 B.P. date may be even older. If shell corrections are similar to those for other brackish water shells from the Gulf waters (cf. Ricklis and Gunter 1986:26; Russo 1991:424), the corrected and calibrated date is 5124 B.P.

Whether the date of 5124 or 4440 is accepted, the "Poverty Point" dates obtained above it are nearly a thousand years older than those attributed to the main occupation of the Poverty Point site itself. This suggests that delta coastal sites yielding baked clay objects arose out of a Middle Archaic tradition, rather than the Late Archaic/Poverty Point tradition. The early dates on rangia shell minimally testify to the presence of a productive estuary during the mid- to late Holocene.

One other mid-Holocene coastal site, the Knox site, 16EBR4 (Gagliano 1963:114), has been identified near Baton Rouge, Louisiana. Situated along the Mississippi River, the site is remarkable not only for its early age but also for its distance from the present-day coast, 140 miles from the mouth of the Mississippi and 40 miles from the nearest coastal marsh. This site has not been intensively studied, but it has produced an uncorrected and uncalibrated radiocarbon date obtained from rangia shell of 5464 ± 135 B.P. (Gagliano 1963:114). At this time the main channel of the Mississippi River lay 40 miles west. The great distance of the site from the present-day coast suggests that when the site was occupied, coastal embayment extended farther upstream along the modern channel than is possible today against the massive flow.

Along this western, former mid-Holocene Mississippi River channel, other early sites have been recorded within the coastal zone. The Avery Island Pleistocene salt dome rises 50 m above surrounding coastal marsh and represents one of the few elevated landforms in the area. From a filled, freshwater pond on the island, deeply buried bipolar lithic tools were recovered and associated with extinct Pleistocene fauna in strata that dated between 10,000 and 8000 B.P. (Gagliano 1967:100). Elsewhere on the island, preserved basket fragments have been radiocarbon dated to 4260 B.P. (uncorrected and uncalibrated; Gagliano 1967:34, 43, 99), while charcoal from a small earthen mound, the Banana Bayou Mound (16IB24), yielded a calibrated radiocarbon date with a two-sigma range between 5899 and 4529 B.P. (table 10-1; Gagliano 1967:18). A faunal midden next to the site, which may represent an associated living area, was revealed by dredging operations to lie beneath at least a meter of marsh sediment (Brown and Lambert-Brown 1978). A wide variety of stemmed and fluted points found across the island confirm the initial occupation sequence of the island during the early to mid-Holocene (Gagliano 1967).

Although it is clear that Avery Island was occupied during the mid-Holocene, based solely on archaeological data, it is not altogether clear that the island was situated within a coastal environment throughout the period. The dredged fauna from near Banana Bayou were identified only to the class level (fish and shellfish), so it is unclear whether the marsh from which they were obtained was freshwater or brackish. Between 8500 and 6000 years ago, the main channel of the Mississippi shifted from the west side of the salt dome to the east, leaving the former island surrounded by dry, parklike prairie but with both fresh and saltwater marsh only a few miles away (Coastal Environments, Inc. 1977:325; Gagliano 1967:101). Significantly, however, a hearth consisting of ash and brackish-water rangia was identified (Gagliano 1970a:10), indicating that nearby coastal environments existed and were exploited by Paleoindian and Early Archaic cultures living on the island from 12,000 to 8500 years ago (Coastal Environments, Inc. 1977:320).

Mississippi and Alabama

The earliest coastal sites in Mississippi are the Cedarland, 22HC30, and Claiborne, 22HC35, sites located on the edge of a Pleistocene terrace east of the mouth of the Pearl River. The two sites are both arcuate shell middens, with Cedarland consisting primarily of oyster and Claiborne, lying only 50 m south, containing mostly rangia. The sites have been classified as Late Archaic and Poverty Point, respectively, based largely on the presence of fiber-tempered pottery, soapstone, and baked clay objects as well as a wider range of trade items and effigy beads at Claiborne (Bruseth 1991). Despite these differences, similarities in lithic points at the sites indicate that the two were closely related in time, and the sites have been presented as a case study for the transition from coastal Archaic to Poverty Point (Bruseth 1991; Coastal Environments, Inc. 1977:259; Gagliano and Webb 1970). Ironically, the lone radiocarbon date of 3190 B.P. from Cedarland (the "Late Archaic" site) is younger than three of the four dates from Claiborne (the "Poverty Point" site), which range between 4000 and 3100 B.P. (Bruseth 1991:15).

No mid-Holocene sites are found along the central Gulf Coast east of the Mississippi River. Eleuterius and Otvos (1979) suggest by 4000–3500 years ago, rising sea levels would have covered (and likely eroded) most earlier coastal sites in Mississippi. The result is that most coastal marsh sites are of more recent ceramic-producing eras. Preceramic sites consisting of rangia and oyster, however, have been identified in the Mississippi Sound marsh, and shell from the surface of these middens has yielded dates between 2500 and 3000 B.P. Because a number of these sites extend more than 3 m below the surface of the marsh (Eleuterius and Otvos 1979), there is the possibility that mid-Holocene deposits may eventually be identified.

In Alabama a similar situation exists. A number of shell middens have been identified in the coastal marsh, but few have been examined below marsh levels. Stowe (1991) has noted that the earliest of these coastal sites date to the Gulf Formational stage, ca. 3200–2700 B.P. at Coon Neck, View Point, and Bryant's Landing. All these sites contain rangia shell and fiber-tempered pottery in their lowest levels up to a meter below sea level, but no preceramic components have yet been identified.

Northwest Florida

In northwest Florida, more than 30 coastal sites dating 4000 to 2400 B.P. have been identified as the Elliott's Point complex (e.g., Thomas and Campbell 1991; White and Estabrook 1994). Unlike the Alabama sites, those in Florida are linked to the Poverty Point sphere of influence, based primarily on the presence of baked clay objects and microliths found within the rangia and oyster shell middens. A number of these sites are large (over 100 m in length), and like the Claiborne and Cedarland Poverty Point Period sites, they are arcuate in shape (Thomas and Campbell 1991). As elsewhere in the northern Gulf, however, few preceramic coastal occupations have been identified.

Although submerged mid-Holocene sites are well known and postulated both inshore and at considerable distances offshore, these are usually either noncoastal sites or are shell sites that may or may not be archaeological (Anuskiewicz 1988; Dunbar 1988; Faught 1988; Stright 1988). Onshore, at least two sites in the Florida panhandle have been identified as mid-Holocene deposits. The Lock site, 8JE57, is a multicomponent oyster shell midden located on the edge of salt-marsh at the mouth of the Aucilla River. The lower levels lie below deposits containing fiber-tempered ceramics. Based on their stratigraphic position, Smith (1968:115) estimated a minimum date for an oyster feature at 5000 B.P. In support of this claim, he cites Phelps (1967) as having obtained a date of 5460 ± 510 (table 10.1) on charred wood from the nearby Williams site, 8TA32. The wood came from a context in association with oyster shell and stemmed Archaic points.

The South Carolina–Georgia Coast

At least 70 early fiber- and sand-tempered ceramic period coastal sites have been identified in South Carolina and Georgia, generally dating between 4200 and 3000 years B.P. Because no earlier preceramic coastal sites have been identified, these are thought by some to represent the earliest occupations as well as the earliest ceramic-producing sites on the southeastern coast (Sassaman 1993a:44). However, a number of aceramic estuarine shell deposits have been identified below strata containing fiber-tempered wares. Few investigations of these aceramic deposits have produced radiocarbon dates older than 5000 years, and none has unequivocally been accepted as containing preceramic cultural components.

One site, Bilbo, 9CH4, has produced a surprisingly early preceramic date. The site is a small shell midden situated in a former tidal marsh near Savannah. Beneath 1.5 m of mixed fresh- and saltwater shellfish midden containing sand-tempered and fiber-tempered pottery, a dense deposit of oyster shell up to 50 cm thick yielded a bone awl, a perforated soapstone slab, a perforated conch shell, and a baked clay ball/cylinder (Waring 1968:155, 182). When first reporting in an unpublished draft in 1940, Waring was careful to point out that the "deposit does not necessarily represent pre-pottery levels," but more likely was a "special activity" area, "not comparable at all to the type of habitation refuse which made up the later levels." Later archaeologists concurred, noting that if the lower oyster stratum was indeed a preceramic deposit, "it would be the only one known from the coast" (DePratter 1976:101).

Of course, the fact that a site may be the "only" preceramic coastal site does not preclude it from being a real preceramic coastal site. Unfortunately, the publication of the site report more than 25 years after it was investigated has not helped to resolve the problem of site interpretation. Material was not submitted for radiocarbon dating for 17 years, excavation profiles have been lost, proveniences of radiocarbon samples could not be matched precisely to known strata, and possible mix-ups of dated material may have occurred (Williams 1968:330). The oldest date of 5500 ± 115 B.P. (calibrated between 6607 and 5991 B.P.; table 10-1) was obtained from charcoal from 60 to 70 cm (2.0 to 2.5 feet) below ground surface. It seems to have been taken from ceramic period deposits, rather than the possible preceramic level, while deeper material produced younger dates. Haag (Williams 1968:330) suggested that the unexpectedly old date may have resulted from the use of ancient logs by the inhabitants for firewood.

Another mid-Holocene date has been obtained from South Carolina at the Fish Haul site, 38BU805, a Stallings period assemblage of shell features and hearths. In one hearth containing numerous Stallings sherds, however, a charcoal sample yielded a radiocarbon date of 6060 ± 110 B.P. (calibrated between 7189 and 6676 B.P.; table 10-1). As with the Bilbo radiocarbon assay, the early date has not been accepted as dating the hearth, and the pitlike feature was subsequently interpreted to contain the remains of an old stump that must have contaminated the charcoal sample (Trinkley 1986:141). At King's Bay in Georgia, a date of 5000 ± 180 B.P. (calibrated between 6189 and 5319 B.P.; table 10-1) was obtained from carbonized wood from a hearth at 9CAM167 associated with fiber-tempered sherds. Unfortunately, another date of 4260 ± 100 B.P. was obtained from the same feature, confounding clear interpretation (Calvert et al. 1979:109; Sassaman 1993a:242–243).

Despite the absence of confirmed coastal mid- to late Holocene preceramic occupations, the South Carolina–Georgia coast continues to produce some of the more extensive studies and liveliest debates on the causes and consequences of initial coastal occupations in the Southeast. Settlement is thought to have started with the movement of interior Savannah River groups to the coast to take advantage of the burgeoning estuarine resources brought about by a stabilized sea level. Initially visiting the coast in seasonal forays, populations permanently occupied the coast by 4200 B.P. (Sassaman 1993a). Concomitant with this settling down was a relatively complex coastal settlement pattern with extensive sheet middens largely made up of great quantities of shell (mostly oyster) representing base camps; unusual "shell rings" representing either sacred sites (Marrinan 1975:95; Michie 1979) or communal habitation centers (Trinkley 1979); and nonshell, inland-from-the-shore sites representing seasonal hunting camps (Sassaman 1993a). A number of archaeologists suggest that the coastal site complexes represent permanent, year-round settlement (DePratter 1979; Trinkley 1980) with a degree of sedentism found nowhere else in the interior Southeast at the time.

Peninsular Florida–Northeast

From the St. Johns River south to just beyond Cape Canaveral, fiber-tempered ceramic coastal sites have had a long history of archaeological investigations in Florida. Extensive sheet and mounded shell middens are found on barrier and marsh islands as well as the mainland coast (Bullen and Bullen 1961; Goggin 1952; Rouse 1951; Russo 1988a, 1988b). The almost exclusive use of the small coquina clam, a beach resource, at some of these middens prompted speculation that the coastal estuaries were not developed when the coasts were initially occupied (Goggin 1948; Miller 1991; Rouse 1951; Thanz 1977) and that permanent coastal settlement was not possible for the early ceramic-producing cultures. In this view, coastal sites were seen as the winter seasonal occupations of interior groups that settled along the St. Johns River, which paralleled the coast 10 to 20 miles inland. Not nearly enough subsistence and settlement studies were ever undertaken to support this hypothesis, and more recent research suggests that both the interior St. Johns River sites and the coastal sites (e.g., Tomoka Stone) were occupied throughout the year, indicating that separate sedentary populations existed within the interior and along the coast (Russo and Ste. Claire 1992; Russo et al. 1992).

Most recently, north of the St. Johns River, extensive fiber-tempered era settlements ca. 4200–3700 B.P. have been identified on Fort George Island and neighboring barrier and marsh islands. Sites include expansive sheet middens, mounded shell middens, cemeteries, isolated hunting stations, shellfish processing sites, and at least one shell ring (Dickinson and Wayne 1987; Russo 1992a; Russo et al. 1993). At 3 m in height and 250 m in diameter, the Rollins Bird Sanctuary ring is the largest shell ring in the Southeast. It differs from the numerous shell rings in Georgia and South Carolina in that coquina shell is a significant component, besides oyster. This and the seasonal analyses of other faunal data indicate that marine as well as estuarine resources supported the Florida populations throughout the annual cycle (Russo 1992a; Russo et al. 1993).

The identification of large-scale, ceramic period coastal settlement as early as 4200 B.P. sets the stage for the search for possible coastal precursors. Although identification of aceramic components beneath shell midden strata bearing fiber-tempered ceramics had occurred early in the archaeological history of east Florida (Nelson 1918), a preceramic stage had never gained widespread acceptance and had rarely been incorporated within coastal chronologies (Goggin 1952; Milanich and Fairbanks 1980). Recent surveys at the mouth of the St. Johns River, however, have revealed both terrestrial and inundated sites dating to the preceramic Archaic (Russo 1992a; Russo et al. 1993). Four sites on the northern side of the river in the Timucuan Ecological and Historic Preserve have returned surprisingly early corrected and calibrated radiocarbon ages (table 10-1) obtained from oyster shell middens. These include Oxeye Islands, 8DU7479 (4789–4349 B.P.); Pepper Island, 8DU7505 (5329–4959 B.P.); McGundo Midden, 8DU7511 (5019–4699 B.P.); and an eastern, nonshell ring section of Rollins Bird Sanctuary, 8DU7510 (4399–4059 B.P.). Based on the presence of aceramic strata below ceramic-bearing strata, 12 other coastal shell middens within the Timucuan Preserve contain preceramic components.

Located on Fort George Island, McGundo Midden and the eastern, nonshell ring component of Rollins Bird Sanctuary are large mounded oyster middens that have been extensively mined for their shell. At one time they were enormous features, and shell stood over 10 m high (Dickinson and Wayne 1987:6.33). Today most of the shell has been removed and McGundo Midden is all but destroyed, with only a small portion of preceramic and fiber-tempered ceramic components left. The preceramic component of Rollins Bird Sanctuary is still impressively extensive, if no longer towering. Along the eastern side of the site, shell deposits up to 3 m deep and a mile in extent remain and are observable eroding out of the bluff shore of Fort George Island.

The other preceramic sites are small (less than 3 m) to large (greater than 100 m) intertidal marsh islands lying wholly or partially submerged beneath high tide. These intertidal shell deposits extend from 20 cm to over a meter in depth and are composed predominantly of oyster shell with variable amounts of small fish remains. The Oxeye Islands site is almost totally submerged at high tide save for ten small features, the only visible portions of shell midden otherwise buried beneath a meter of marsh sediment. This buried site is likely part of the larger, adjacent Dead Cedar Islands site, 8DU7478, a large mounded shell midden that extends a meter and a half above the high tide mark. There, surface collections and three subsurface tests produced one fiber-tempered ceramic near the surface, fragments of fired clay objects (cooking balls?), and a faunal assemblage dominated by oyster. A single test in the low-lying Oxeye Islands revealed a much wider variety of shellfish, fish, and charcoal. The two sites form an arcuate shell midden more than 100 m in length and may represent a living area (Oxeye Islands) and disposal area (Dead Cedar Islands) of a single site (Russo et al. 1993). On the northern edge and separate from the main mounded shell midden at Dead Cedar is a small shell ring (20 m) that, based on its shape (and if interpretations of other shell rings containing fiber-tempered ceramics is correct), may have sacred or communal significance. Although work is preliminary, with a date 600 years earlier than that of the Rollins Bird Sanctuary shell ring, the sites may represent a preceramic Archaic precursor to the fiber-tempered ceramic period settlement pattern of shell rings associated with shell-midden villages.

Surprisingly early as the preceramic sites in the Timucuan Preserve are, an even earlier site lies on the barrier island south of the mouth of the St. Johns River. At the city of Atlantic Beach, the oldest date yet found from a coastal Atlantic midden (corrected 5570 ± 80 B.P.; calibrated to 6169–5759 B.P.) was obtained from Spencer's Midden, 8DU5626. The site consists of an arcuate oyster/coquina shell midden over a meter deep and 50 m in length surrounding a former freshwater pond. Two Archaic stemmed points were recovered by the property owner while excavating her driveway for improvements. No other artifacts were recovered despite extensive testing (Russo 1992a; Russo et al. 1993).

Subsistence and seasonality analyses of the zooarchaeological remains from Spencer's Midden and the other preceramic sites in the region indicate multiple seasonal occupation with emphasis on the collection of oyster, coquina, and small estuarine fish such as herring, pinfish, croaker, and catfish (Russo et al. 1993). Contrary to the idea that coquina are strictly a winter resource, the coquina from Spencer's Midden were collected in the summer. Small estuarine fishes were caught from spring through fall, and oysters were collected during the winter.

These data suggest that the coast was occupied by preceramic Archaic peoples throughout the annual cycle in a pattern similar to that suggested for the fiber-tempered ceramic period (Russo 1992a; Russo and Ste. Claire 1992). Larger sites probably served as permanent or semipermanent villages. The unknown subsurface extent of the smaller marsh island sites precludes determination of their possible functions in the larger settlement system. They may once have been larger than their present surface expressions indicate and have functioned as permanent settlements. Or they may represent smaller procurement stations. Irrespective of function, year-round occupation of the coast is indicated for the preceramic Archaic both by the size and distribution of sites and by seasonal determinations of their subsistence remains.

Between the St. Johns River and Cape Canaveral, preceramic sites and site components have been identified over the years (Goggin 1952:41; Miller and Griffin 1978:52–54; Nelson 1918; Rouse 1951:151, 219; Russo 1988a:62), although they have not been widely accepted as evidence of preceramic coastal occupations. More recently at Guana River State Park, four shell sites (8SJ33, 50, 2463 and 2554), the latter a large shell ring, have been identified as containing possible preceramic Archaic components (DAHRM 1985; Newman and Weisman 1992; Weisman, personal communication 1995). A few miles south at Crescent Beach, a preceramic component has been identified in the lower levels of a large mounded coquina midden containing ceramics, 8SJ43 (Bond 1988, 1992). It has produced a corrected radiocarbon age of 4240 ± 80 B.P. (calibrated between 4549 and 4119 B.P.; table 10-1).

The most surprising new evidence of significant preceramic occupation comes from the Tomoka Mound Complex, 8VO81, at the Tomoka State Park near Daytona. There, up to nine shell/sand conical mounds have been identified and have stood as a conundrum since 1881 when Douglass (1882) recovered eight bannerstones from Mound Six, the largest of the mounds at 3 m in height. Because they believed that Archaic people did not construct ceremonial mounds, archaeologists have subsequently been puzzled by the bannerstones (Archaic artifacts) and the cultural assignment of the site has languished (Goggin 1952:53; Piatek 1994). Most recently, Piatek (1994) has identified the site as a preceramic village/ceremonial mound complex, based on the absence of ceramics in the village and in Mound Six and on a corrected date of 4460 ± 70 B.P. (calibrated between 4829 and 4419 B.P.; see table 14-1) from the submound midden beneath the mound. In the upper strata of Mound Six, later people producing fiber-tempered ceramics placed disarticulated burials, one of which yielded an age of 2880 ± 55 B.P. (calibrated between 3209 and 2859 B.P.; table 14-1). The dates from Mound Six establish the Tomoka Mound Complex as the earliest use of burial mounds on the East Coast (see chap. 14). Combined with the data presented above, a strong case can be made for continuity of settlement, subsistence, and belief systems between the preceramic and the ceramic Archaic in eastern coastal Florida.

South Florida and the Peninsular Florida Gulf Coast

South of Cape Canaveral, only one Atlantic Coast preceramic site is known, a submerged midden 3 m beneath the ocean offshore of St. Lucie County. The Douglas Beach site, 16SL17, has revealed a wide variety of both saltwater fish and turtles and terrestrial and freshwater vertebrates (Murphy 1990). A corrected and calibrated radiocarbon date on a wood stake ranged between 5589 and 4990 B.P. (table 10-1), but whether the site is "coastal" is unclear.

On the Gulf side of the Florida peninsula, from the Big Bend to the Ten Thousand Islands, shell middens bearing fiber-tempered pottery are not uncommon and are occasionally large (Bullen and Bullen 1976; Widmer 1974). Most of the larger sites are found between Tampa Bay and Charlotte Harbor, with areas to the north and south characterized by smaller shell-midden sites or wave-washed deposits. Surprisingly, the Florida Gulf Coast sites bearing fiber-tempered ceramics have received relatively little extraregional attention (e.g., Sassaman 1993a; Smith 1986), perhaps because so few have been intensively investigated. Although fewer sites are known than on the Atlantic Coast, sufficient numbers have been investigated to establish that a substantial ceramic Archaic coastal culture with a well-developed tool technology existed along the peninsular Gulf Coast some 4000 years ago (e.g., Bullen and Bullen 1976; Bullen et al. 1978; Marquardt 1992b; Milanich 1994; Widmer 1988).

As elsewhere in the Southeast, earlier mid-Holocene sites are presumed to have been submerged or destroyed by rising sea levels. Yet, supporting evidence for preceramic Archaic sites is abundant. Archaic stemmed points of the mid-Holocene have been recovered from dredged oyster and other shell deposits, indicating use of the coastal environment from the Early to Middle Archaic. The best investigated site of this sort is Turtlecrawl Point, 8PI881, identified in a dredge spoil pile on the shore of Tampa Bay (Goodyear et al. 1993). A stratum of sand and quahogs was brought up from 1–2 m below the surface of the bay and yielded 12 Early Archaic Bolen points, 11 Middle Archaic points, and numerous unifacial tools (all of local chert abundant around Tampa Bay). These artifacts clearly indicated a mid-Holocene occupation, but it was not clear whether the occupation was coastal until analyses of the quahogs revealed them to have come from midden rather than natural deposits. Uncorrected and uncalibrated radiocarbon ages on three of five individual shells were 3425, 3080, and 2850 B.P., while two "columella cutting-edged tools" yielded dates of 4460 ± 130 and 4675 ± 120 B.P. Corrected and calibrated between 5469 and 4829 B.P. and 5689 and 5099, respectively (table 10-1; Goodyear et al. 1993), the ages of these tools place them in the mid-Holocene.

Numerous other dredged sites have been identified in and around Tampa Bay, but the association between artifacts (which include Paleoindian and Archaic) and shell midden has not been as strongly established (e.g., Lazarus 1965; Warren 1972; Warren et al. 1967). One site, Venice Beach, 8SO26, lies beneath 5.5 m of Gulf water, 100 m offshore from a submerged, ceramic period shell midden (Ruppe 1980; Stright 1988:397). Found there are Middle Archaic lithic points and pollen indicating a predominance of oak and pine. Whether the site is "coastal" is unclear.

On land, in situ coastal mid-Holocene sites have rarely been identified. Bullen and Bullen (1976) published the lone report on a preceramic shell midden identified prior to the 1980s. The Hill Cottage Midden (part of 8SO2) on Little Sarasota Bay was viewed primarily as a large mounded fiber-tempered Late Archaic component, however, and the preceramic component below the ceramic strata was only briefly mentioned. Five stratigraphically sequential dates were obtained from the shells within the midden (Bullen and Bullen 1976:13). Correcting and calibrating these dates (table 10-1) suggests that ceramics were first introduced around 4000 B.P. and that preceramic occupations occurred sometime between 4299 and 4989 B.P. Significantly, the Bullens noted that because the earliest date did not come from the bottom of the midden, earlier occupations were likely.

Because the Bullens' description of the preceramic component at Hill Cottage midden was so understated, terrestrial mid-Holocene deposits remained in the eyes of most archaeologists little more than a possibility, until the discovery at Useppa Island of an "Archaic period shell columella tool manufacturing camp," 8LL51, on the summit of a large Pleistocene sand dune island in Charlotte Harbor (Milanich et al. 1984:271). Due, in part, to disturbance, the overall extent of the site was unknown, but subsurface testing revealed dense deposits of quahog, conch, oyster, and saltwater fish remains. The large amount of conch debitage and columella tools indicated to the investigators that the occupants used the site as a camp to manufacture shell tools. At the time, investigators thought the shell was being reduced "presumably for use as tools elsewhere" (Milanich et. al 1984:271). Two strikingly early uncorrected dates of 4935 ± 100 and 5625 ± 100 B.P. were obtained (calibrated between 5929 and 5479 B.P. and 6689 and 6259 B.P., respectively; table 10-1). Because mid-Holocene peoples were thought to be hunter-gatherers of interior zones, the site was interpreted to represent a temporary camp with a specific purpose—the manufacture of shell tools for use elsewhere, presumably the interior of Florida where mid-Holocene groups were known to exist.

Recently, the site has been reinvestigated, and Torrence (1992) has identified multiseasonal use of the site based on analysis of the faunal remains. In addition, extensive excavations have revealed hearths, posts, and activity areas indicating multipurpose and daily maintenance uses of the site. Different intrasite locales were used for different aspects of tool manufacture, and all stages of manufacture and use of the columella tools are represented at the site. Combined with the abundant and varied subsistence remains, these data indicate that the site did not function solely as a station for the manufacture and subsequent removal of shell tools. Nearby, Marquardt (1992b:11) has obtained other early dates from a burial investigated at an oyster shell midden. The burial lay below a stratum with fiber-tempered pottery, and shell above and below it dated (corrected and calibrated) to 4500 and 4900 B.P., respectively (table 10.1; Marquardt 1992b:11, 27). Together, the data from Useppa indicate that the island was occupied periodically throughout the mid- to late Holocene interface. In light of models that place the coast tens of miles west of Useppa Island during the mid-Holocene (Widmer 1988:205), it is somewhat surprising to find that mid-Holocene sea level had actually risen and flooded Charlotte Harbor, providing a productive estuary for human exploitation. Although the coast may, indeed, have lain farther west, apparently deep Pleistocene river entrenchment allowed the sea to invade upstream sufficiently to create the Charlotte Harbor embayment.

Eighty miles south of Useppa, another embayment occurred during the mid-Holocene near Marco and Horr's islands. On these islands are a series of oyster shell middens that lacked ceramics (8CR107, 109, 110, 114, 116, 119, 149, 150, and 151) (Cockrell 1970; McMichael 1982; Widmer 1974, 1988). The middens lay atop a Pleistocene parabolic dune formation reaching up to 12 m above mean sea level, making them, along with Useppa Island, the highest natural features along an otherwise low-lying, mangrove-dominated southwestern Florida coast. Along with the aceramic middens, Cockrell (1970) and Widmer (1974) identified a series of late Archaic sites bearing fiber-tempered ceramics located on the high dune ridges surrounding Barfield Bay across from Horr's Island. Some of the ceramic-bearing middens had aceramic components at their lower levels. Both the aceramic and ceramic-bearing sites were circular to semicircular, varied in size from 12 m in diameter to 45 m, and were usually relatively shallow, less than a meter in depth. Because of these similarities and based on radiocarbon dates ranging between 3400 and 3060 B.P. from one of the sites, all sites were assigned to the fiber-tempered ceramic-producing Late Archaic cultures or were not classified as to culture or period (Widmer 1974:23, 27, 37, 42, 47, 48, 50).

I have detailed elsewhere (Russo 1991:244–249) that some of these sites may actually date to the mid-Holocene or at least may be preceramic. Undeniably, the presence of fiber-tempered period peoples on and around Marco Island is well established. However, even earlier occupations may have occurred. The limited surveys on Marco Island, however, have not recovered enough data from definable contexts to determine if the aceramic middens represent Late Archaic (fiber-tempered ceramic era) or Middle Archaic (preceramic) sites (Cockrell 1970; Widmer 1974; cf. Griffin 1988:132). Subsequently, Widmer has recognized the likelihood that some of the Marco Island sites may be Middle Archaic (Widmer 1988:65). In fact, at 8CR112, Widmer (1974) obtained a mid-Holocene date, uncorrected and uncalibrated, of 4965 ± 100 B.P. Although this was initially hailed as one of the oldest dates in the New World for the occurrence of ceramics (Widmer 1974:32), in view of the questionable stratigraphy (Griffin 1988:132), the date's true significance may be its association with a mid-Holocene oyster midden, making it, at the time of its discovery, one of the oldest dates from any coastal context in the Southeast.

Across the bay on Horr's Island, McMichael (1982) recognized the true age of early settlement in the area at a large preceramic Archaic site. He obtained from shell a series of (uncorrected) radiocarbon dates that consistently placed the site between 4000 and 4500 B.P. Combined with more recent dates from the site (Russo 1991) obtained from shell, charcoal, and human bone, once corrected and calibrated, most of the thirty dates from Horr's Island fall between 4600 and 5200 B.P. (tables 10.1 and 14.1). Two calibrated ages predating the main occupation of the site come from a deeply buried 7000-year-old oyster midden (table 14.1). The remarkably early dates from well-studied contexts, combined with the large size and complexity of the site, make Horr's Island the best evidence that by the mid- to late Holocene, coastal estuaries were productive and were being intensively exploited.

On the western arm of Horr's Island lies the largest midden, the village site 8CR209 (fig. 10-2). It consists of extensive shell deposits up to 5 m deep, the bulk of which are made up of oyster. These deposits lie on top of dune crests and slope down into and beneath the mangrove swamps that bound the island. Over a million faunal specimens have been identified and seasons of capture determined for the most important species. These analyses established that year-round collection of a variety of saltwater shellfish and small estuarine fishes characterized the settlement and subsistence strategies of the Archaic inhabitants (Russo 1991).

The village site is demarcated by a high, arcuate shell ridge encircling a nearly level, dense midden area 300 m in length. Situated at the western, open end of the arc is the most dramatic feature of the site, Mound A (8CR208), a 6-m-tall ceremonial mound. West of it lies Mound B, 1.5 m tall (8CR206). Another possible ceremonial mound, Mound C (8CR207), 2 m in height, lies between them, while Mound D (8CR211), 4 m tall, lies 500 m to the east. Mounds A, B, and D are all purposefully constructed mounds made up of alternating strata of sand and shell, while Mound C consists solely of shell. All the mounds have yielded corrected and calibrated dates indicating construction during the mid- to late Holocene between 4600 and 5200 B.P. (table 14.1; see chap. 14, this volume, for a more complete description).

The village containing mounds A, B, and C and the shell ridge is abutted on its east and west sides by shallower, but equally dense, shell midden for 200 to 300 m.

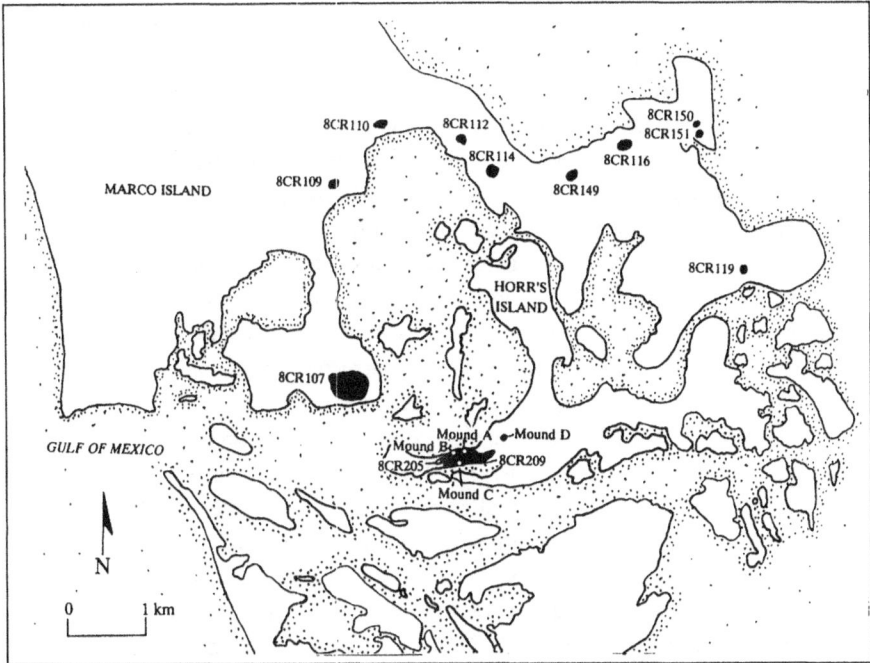

Fig. 10-2. Preceramic and possible preceramic Archaic sites on Horr's and Marco islands discussed in chapter.

Together, these dense middens extend unbroken for nearly a kilometer west to east and a quarter-kilometer north to south, well into and beneath the mangrove swamp on the southern shore. Within portions of the shell ridge and within the central village area, successive living floors, organically stained to a gray-black color, accumulated up to 4 m in depth. Throughout the village were numerous postmolds representing the remains of small, lightweight structures around 3 m in diameter (Russo 1991, 1994a). Associated with these structures were hearths and pits which frequently overlapped one another. Combined with the evidence for intensive marine resource exploitation and a diverse technology consisting largely of shell tools, the Horr's Island village assemblage attests to year-round occupation by at least one large Late Archaic group.

Discussion

More than 75 years ago, Nelson (1918) recognized that aceramic components lay beneath the earliest ceramic-bearing shell middens at Florida coastal sites. Practical and theoretical impediments have since conspired to conceal that record from view. Inundated sites, overlying deposits, and the scarcity of temporally diagnostic artifacts have discouraged investigations of preceramic sites and fostered a dependance on radiocarbon dates to determine cultural affiliation.

Because theoretical models of mid-Holocene coastal occupations are wanting, southeastern archaeologists have generally been reluctant to accept radiocarbon dates that appear "too old" for coastal sites and have offered instead ad hoc explanations to account for the unexpectedly old dates. In addition, because radiocarbon dates from marine shell have generally not been adjusted and calibrated, mid-Holocene sites have gone unrecognized. On the average, radiocarbon dates uncorrected for 13C on marine shell from southern Gulf and Atlantic waters are 400 years too young (Ricklis and Cox 1991; Russo 1991:424; Stuiver and Reimer 1986; Stuiver et al. 1986:982). Corrected but uncalibrated shell dates may be an additional 400 years too young. Because most absolute coastal chronologies are based on dates derived from charcoal or uncorrected and uncalibrated shell, the real antiquity of coastal occupations has been obscured.

The identification of preceramic sites above mean sea level has revealed that some of the mid-Holocene and early late Holocene coastal zones remain intact on present-day shores and even further inland from present-day beach fronts (Gagliano 1963: 111, 114; Ricklis and Gunter 1986; Russo 1991; Russo et al. 1993). Deep Pleistocene scouring encouraged coastal embayment of river valleys far upstream as sea level rose during the mid-Holocene, and the locations of these preceramic sites likely represent the innermost extent of mid-Holocene embayments. As such, they represent but a fraction of mid-Holocene coastal settlements.

Mid-Holocene deposits of high salinity marine shellfish (coquina), moderate salinity estuarine shellfish (oyster, scallop), and fresh to brackish water shellfish (rangia) have been identified across the Gulf and Atlantic shores. These data challenge models positing that stable, productive coastal environments could not develop under the rapidly rising sea levels of the mid-Holocene and ancillary arguments that rainfall was too limited, that embayments were too saline, and that productive coastal environments were too impermanent to allow for the occupation of coastal zones. The same shellfish species most abundant in the late Holocene middens are also most abundant in the mid-Holocene deposits. A continuity in the coastal resources that humans could and did exploit began at least in the early Holocene (e.g., Avery Island, Louisiana) and is found throughout the Southeast during the mid- and late Holocene.

As such, it may be ill conceived to think of the "stabilization" of coastal environments and a concomitant increase in productivity sometime after 5000 B.P. as the cause for the "initial" coastal occupations in the late Holocene. At many coastal locations what was likely "stabilized" with a slowing of sea level rise was not sufficient estuarine productivity for human exploitation (estuarine productivity had been exploited for thousands of years by the late Holocene), but rather it was the landforms on which people settled. The reduced rate of sea level rise allowed the deposition of shell refuse at human habitation sites to outpace the sites' inundation. This resulted in more frequent occupations of particular sites and a concomitant increase in their archaeological visibility.

During the mid-Holocene, however, the relatively rapid rise of sea level, although not enough to preclude coastal exploitation by people, likely affected the kinds of settlement and societies that occurred in specific topographic settings. Poorly drained soils in low-lying areas probably precluded extensive and prolonged settlement, which in turn inhibited territorial behavior and societal closure. In fortuitously elevated locales, other social formations may have resulted. It is probably no coincidence that the largest and most complex preceramic Archaic settlement is found on Horr's Island, situated on a rare topographically high Pleistocene dune. This geological feature allowed a permanence of settlement otherwise difficult to attain in the low-lying mangrove swamps. With long-term settlement possible, the trappings of social complexity—year-round habitation, large villages, ceremonial mounds, and the complex social integration necessary to construct these—not usually associated with preceramic Archaic peoples could and did arise.

All coastal preceramic Archaic Florida sites for which seasonality analyses have been undertaken reflect multiseasonal and year-round settlement. This is a settlement pattern markedly distinct from that typically associated with most contemporary interior Archaic peoples, where seasonal transhumance from summer-fall, low-water base camps to upland winter-spring, short-term wet-season camps was necessitated by seasonal flooding of river valleys (Smith 1986). Such movements did not occur on the Florida coasts. In peninsular Florida, coastal flooding is rare (usually hurricane related) at any specific locale and is not seasonally predictable. (The wet and dry seasons that have been suggested to drive the seasonal transhumant pattern of the interior, in fact, are exactly the reverse on the peninsular Florida coasts, which have a summer wet season and a winter dry season.) Consequently, the generally climatically benign and bountiful coasts demanded no regular movement by most coastal populations to escape seasonal floods.

Although interior southeastern mid-Holocene groups are thought to have depended seasonally on deer and nuts obtained from uplands (Smith 1986), it is debatable whether such resources would have been sufficient to draw coastal populations in Florida to the interior uplands. On peninsular Florida coasts, fish and shellfish resources are abundant and present throughout the year (deer and nuts were also available, but were used in relatively limited amounts). "Upland interior" sites are distant from the coast, and unproductive piney flatwoods as well as interior and riverine cultural groups stood in the way of any coastal population seeking to migrate in search of upland subsistence resources. Down-the-line trade undoubtedly occurred between coastal and interior groups, as reflected in the minor presence of chipped stone found at coastal preceramic sites, but with well-developed shell-tool technologies, a material demand for connections with interior groups did not arise.

Lacking the need and opportunity to migrate great distances for interior subsistence and lithic resources, coastal populations developed a sedentism based on logistical foraging of the immediate estuarine environments. At Horr's Island, a permanent residential village was surrounded by smaller camps and collection stations. A similar pattern may have occurred in the St. Johns River estuaries, where both large and small preceramic sites have been recorded. Less is known about the regional settlement patterns at Charlotte Harbor and Tomoka State Park. Although the particular nature of the sedentism may vary among coastal sites (and this remains to be tested), they do have in common a multiseasonal or year-round exploitation of estuarine resources. Particular embayments were occupied by some, if not all, of the population throughout the year. This is a settlement strategy distinct from contemporary interior groups, which are most often seen as having been seasonally transhumant or semisedentary.

Southeastern archaeologists have placed great significance on sedentism in modeling the rise of social complexity in prehistoric cultures. Increasing sedentism has been seen as the catalyst impelling Archaic and Woodland peoples to develop new, socially integrative solutions to problems arising from increased population and demands on limited resources. Ultimately, sedentism, facilitated by the adoption of agriculture, is seen as giving rise to the most complex of southeastern social formations, the Mississippian chiefdom. This path of sedentism under the southeastern model is unilineal, evolving from the egalitarian, nomadic Archaic to the seasonally dispersed, hierarchically achieved statuses of the Woodland, to the sedentary, hereditary Mississippian chiefdoms.

Of course, researchers have not had the benefit, until recently, of knowledge of early populations inhabiting the mid-Holocene coasts. The archaeology of these peoples demonstrates that nonagriculturally based infrastructures gave rise to sedentary and socially complex communities long before the late Holocene. The coastal sedentism was not progressive (at least not in the staged progressions hypothesized for the interior Southeast), and did not lead to the development of hereditary chiefdoms. The level of social complexity under which the mid-Holocene coastal groups operated, however, has yet to be determined (see chap. 14 of this volume for a discussion of Horr's Island). Minimally, we know that year-round occupation of the coast did allow the development of social formations sufficiently integrated to construct large-scale public works of sizes not again achieved in most of the Southeast until the Woodland period.

Under current models, the sedentism and social complexity attained by the Florida mid-Holocene coastal cultures may seem out of time and place. But it should not. Largely isolated from each other, interior and coastal populations followed separate histories. If we can accept social history as a prime mover of cultural evolution, then we should expect socially distinctive, contemporary cultures to have arisen in the Southeast during the Archaic. There is nothing about the mid-Holocene environments or climate that precludes the development of sedentary, complex societies alongside seminomadic, egalitarian hunter-gatherers.

Acknowledgments

Appreciation goes out to David Phelps, Mark Mathis Reed Stowe, Joe Giliberti, Joe Saunders, Ken Sassaman, Michael Trinkley, Dennis Blanton, Gerald Ferguson, Stan Bond, Richard Weinstein, Al Goodyear, Randolph Widmer, Janice Campbell, Corbett Torrence, and Robert Ricklis, who provided me with information as well as little known and unpublished site data including radiocarbon dates from their research. Special thanks go to the Bennie Keel of the Southeast Archeological Center; Kathleen Deagan of the Florida Museum of Natural History, William Marquardt of the Institute of Archaeology and Paleoenvironmental Studies at the University of Florida; and Key Marco Developments, who supported the investigations at the Timucuan Ecological and Historic Preserve and Horr's Island.

11

Accounting for Submerged Mid-Holocene Archaeological Sites in the Southeast

A Case Study from the Chesapeake Bay Estuary, Virginia

DENNIS B. BLANTON

Studies addressing the issue of submerged sites in the southeastern and middle Atlantic and regions of North America have traditionally focused on late Pleistocene "early man" sites. Further, this research has tended to consider either the expansive offshore areas of the continental shelf in the Atlantic and Gulf of Mexico (Dunbar et al. 1992; Edwards and Merrill 1977; Emery and Edwards 1966; Faught 1988; Gagliano et al. 1982; Hoyt et al.1990; Pearson et al. 1986; Stright 1990), or the highly restricted environs of sinkholes (Cockrell and Murphy 1978). The work of Gagliano (1970b), Kraft (1977), Kraft and John (1978) and DePratter and Howard (1977, 1980, 1981) in the 1970s extended consideration of inundated sites to include near shore environments and has since been complemented by analogous research elsewhere (Brooks et al. 1986; Dunbar et al. 1992; Gagliano et al. 1982; Goodyear et al. 1993; Johnson and Stright 1992).

My concern in this chapter is the submerged Holocene record of the southeastern United States, especially as it exists in the major embayments or estuaries of the region. The meager results of archaeological searches on the continental shelf, and greatly improved knowledge of shoreline processes (Waters 1992), have given cause to consider the potential of more sheltered waters, not to mention that by the mid-Holocene all of the continental shelf was effectively submerged and, thus, unavailable for habitation.

I introduce new information from the Chesapeake Bay in Virginia to demonstrate the potential for submerged sites in near shore areas of the Atlantic Coast.

My ultimate aim is to demonstrate how data on submerged sites can be incorporated in regional-scale studies to revise current coastal settlement models.

The Conventional Model of Chesapeake Area Estuarine Adaptation

Sea level fluctuation is the principal agent of natural change in coastal regions of the southeastern United States, and since the onset of the Holocene there has been a net rise in the base level. Along with the more obvious result of transgression or submergence, a rise in sea level also means that shorelines eroded, stream gradients dropped, and floral and faunal communities shifted. This is no less true of the Chesapeake Bay, which owes its very existence to sea level rise. In spite of the popular and scientific attention this premier estuary receives, long-term sea level data are scarce, so extrapolations must be made from the results of studies in adjacent areas. The basic trends described for the Chesapeake appear to be generally true of the greater Southeast (Brooks et al. 1986; Coastal Environments, Inc. 1977; Colquhoun and Brooks 1986; DePratter and Howard 1981).

After the continental glacier began to retreat about 15,000 B.P., sea level rose at the rapid rates of more than 100 cm/century to no less than 30 cm/century until 6000–5000 B.P. It was during this span that humans first settled the area and the ancient Susquehanna River valley was flooded to form approximately 80 percent of the modern Chesapeake Bay (Brush 1986). Sea level was then within 7–8 m of the modern level and subsequently rose at the slower average rate of 20 cm/century, eventually creating what we would all recognize as the modern bay. Even further slowing is documented after 2000 B.P., when the average rate of rise was about 15 cm/century. This approximate rate persisted until about 400 B.P., when it increased to nearly equal late Pleistocene/early Holocene rates (Finkelstein and Hardaway 1988; Hicks and Crosby 1974; Kraft 1985:114).

The segment of the Chesapeake area curve bracketing the mid-Holocene appears to be representative of the greater Southeast in character, but less so in absolute terms owing to local variation (fig. 11-1). Between 8000 and 6000 B.P. sea level was still rising rapidly as it had since the end of the Pleistocene, but during the sixth millennium B.P. the rate decreased nearly 50 percent, signaling a period of greater stability in the region's coastal areas. After 5000 B.P. the net eustatic effect was an overall rise in sea level, but most curves indicate that this was punctuated with a series of oscillations (Finkelstein and Ferland 1987; Kraft 1977; Newman and Munsart 1968). The precise timing and amplitude of these ups and downs are variable from one section of coastline to another, due to the combined effects of local subsidence, rebound, sediment load, and shore morphology (Colquhoun et al. 1980).

Many who have considered the archaeological potential of the continental shelf express only limited optimism for the discovery of intact sites there. An appreciation of the dynamic nature of shorelines has led them to acknowledge the

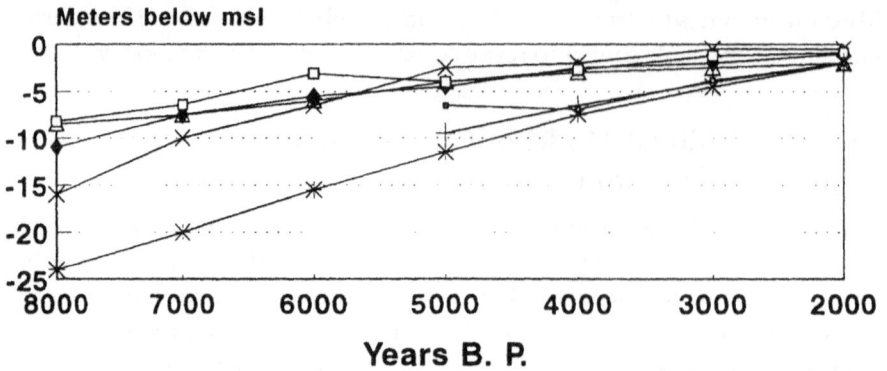

Fig. 11-1.   Representative mid-Holocene sea level curves for the southeastern United States (*Sources:* VA-a, Newman and Munsart 1968; VA-b, Van de Plassche 1990; DE, Belknap and Kraft 1977; SC, Colquhoun and Brooks 1987; Gulf, Curray 1965; S. FL, Lidz and Shin 1991; NC, Heron et al. 1984).

damaging effect of erosion on most if not all submerged sites (Belknap and Kraft 1981, 1985; Stright 1990), outside of restricted settings such as alluviated, relict channels (Pearson et al. 1986; Stright 1986). William Haag observed these processes in coastal North Carolina four decades ago and came to much the same conclusion, but he proposed that sheltered estuaries probably hold greater potential for preserved sites (Haag 1975). This would be particularly true for the mid-Holocene since most of the offshore shelf areas were already inundated. The greatest potential for Holocene sites in the coastal strand is where shorelines are prograding, or building. Sites in these settings remain above water and exemplify one of the effects of local oscillations. These conditions are well illustrated in the work of DePratter and Howard (1977, 1981) on the Georgia coast.

A working knowledge of this information is necessary for developing realistic archaeological models. It allows us to predict better what the environment was like and where possible site locations might be at given times. Using the sea level curves as a guide, inundated versus exposed landforms can be identified for given intervals, as can potential resource-rich estuarine and open-water areas.

Most overviews of Chesapeake area archaeology account for the effects of sea level fluctuation only in general terms, and they tend to be strongly reliant upon physical and natural science data in the absence of archaeological information. Regional models, for instance, acknowledge the 6000–5000 B.P. slowing of sea level rise by stating that the modern bay environment was effectively in place beginning then (Custer 1986; Potter 1993). That change is perceived to be very significant in the sense that stabilization of the estuarine environment after 5000 B.P. created conditions favorable for more intensive exploitation of coastal resources, especially shellfish. The implication in these cases—that after this time, sea level rise had nominal effects—is contrary to geological data.

Lacking firm information on submerged sites, archaeologists have been left with the options of either ignoring them altogether or qualifying their models to accomodate negative evidence. The latest summaries (Custer 1986; Potter 1993; Waselkov 1982) agree on several points, however. One is that the Chesapeake Bay basin before 5000 B.P. would not have been unique among other major stream valleys. It was the creation of the modern estuary after 5000 B.P. that ostensibly distinguished the area as a resource-rich zone. Shell middens all postdate this transition and their appearance is taken to signify the point when estuarine resources first figured significantly into subsistence schedules and settlement organization. This new facet of local economies is believed to have been gradually refined by the subsequent Woodland period to the point that some groups were targeting specific shellfish species. So, beginning in the Late Archaic period, the resources of the Chesapeake estuary became an important cornerstone in the subsistence of local groups, persisting even as prominent supplements to horticultural economies of the Late Woodland (Custer 1986; Kraft et al. 1978; Potter 1993). As Russo (chap. 10, this volume) shows, these inferences recur in models of coastal settlement.

Pioneering work on the topic was conducted by John Kraft (1977, 1985) and his colleagues (Kraft and John 1978; Kraft et al. 1974, 1978) for the mid-Atlantic. Their work is most notable for lucid discussion of the implications of sea level changes on human settlement in and around Delaware Bay. Intensive coring in the vicinity of the Island Field site and Cape Henlopen served to demonstrate the considerable scope of changes to the coastline and in human settlement (Kraft 1985; Kraft et al. 1978), even after the slowing in sea level rise about 5000 B.P.

A more recent statement of the local effects of sea level change on prehistoric settlement is found in an article by Klein and Klatka (1991). In their discussion of Late Archaic settlement in Virginia, they express strong reservations about the utility of current models for coastal settings: "The archaeological remnants indicative of the use of the saline portions of the rivers draining onto the Chesapeake Bay prior to the Late Archaic may be submerged, buried beneath deposited sediments, destroyed by wave action, or located in modern environments that do not reflect the distributions of resources in earlier Holocene environments" (Klein and Klatka 1991:165). Without honest appraisals such as theirs, modeling estuarine adaptations is simplified through allusions to missing information or an incomplete record.

Also, the effects of sea level rise have not been an exclusively coastal phenomenon. Implicit in any consideration of the issue is the effect it has on interior streams that feed the estuaries, specifically how stream gradients are reduced as base level rises (see Schuldenrein, this volume, for more detailed discussion). This is recognized with increasing frequency at archaeological sites in fluvial Coastal Plain settings in Virginia (Blanton et al. 1994; Jones and Blanton 1993) and elsewhere (e.g., Brooks and Sassaman 1990; Gagliano 1984).

The current scheme for early and mid-Holocene settlement in the Chesapeake region is necessarily general. When they are attempted, syntheses of regional data tend to contrast conditions before and after 6000–5000 B.P. when sea level stabilized. The post–5000 B.P. emphasis on riverine and estuarine resources is evident in shell middens or other rich sites, when prior to this period such sites are altogether lacking in the coastal record. For obvious reasons, possible submerged sites are seldom accounted for and their omission is what keeps the models general in scope.

Across the Southeast the situation is much the same, again due to a lack of solid evidence. A recent inventory of known submerged sites in the United States (Stright 1990) includes only 10 in the coastal waters of the Southeast (fig. 11-2, table 11-1). Two features of this sample are worthy of note: at least seven of the sites occur in embayments or other sheltered waters, and the same proportion have mid-Holocene as opposed to earlier or later components.

New Information from the Chesapeake Area

New information on submerged sites comes from an unusual source: Chesapeake Bay "watermen." Watermen are the storied fishermen of the bay and they wrest a living from it by crabbing, oystering, and clamming. Since early 1991 I have been fortunate to interview several watermen who have recovered prehistoric artifacts from the bay bottom by "tonging" for clams. Using mechanical patent tongs, clams and debris are grubbed from the bottom sediments and hoisted to the decks of boats for sorting. In this process artifacts are often collected and saved with the clams. This technique is unsophisticated but, in much the same way as shovel testing on land, provides an unprecedented glimpse at the archaeological resources in submerged areas.

Eight watermen have assisted thus far by sharing their own finds and reporting word of others. In this way 18 "sites" or find areas are confirmed and several others reported (fig. 11-3). What is significant about these reports is that the kinds of artifacts and the locations of their discovery are showing consistent patterns.

The Material Record

What the watermen tend to notice and bring home are complete flaked stone points or axes and ground stone axes and adzes. These artifacts are readily dated and therefore provide a firm basis for reconstructing settlement trends.

Late Archaic artifacts dominate the assemblages from submerged contexts, with components represented at 78 percent of reported sites (table 11-2). Savannah

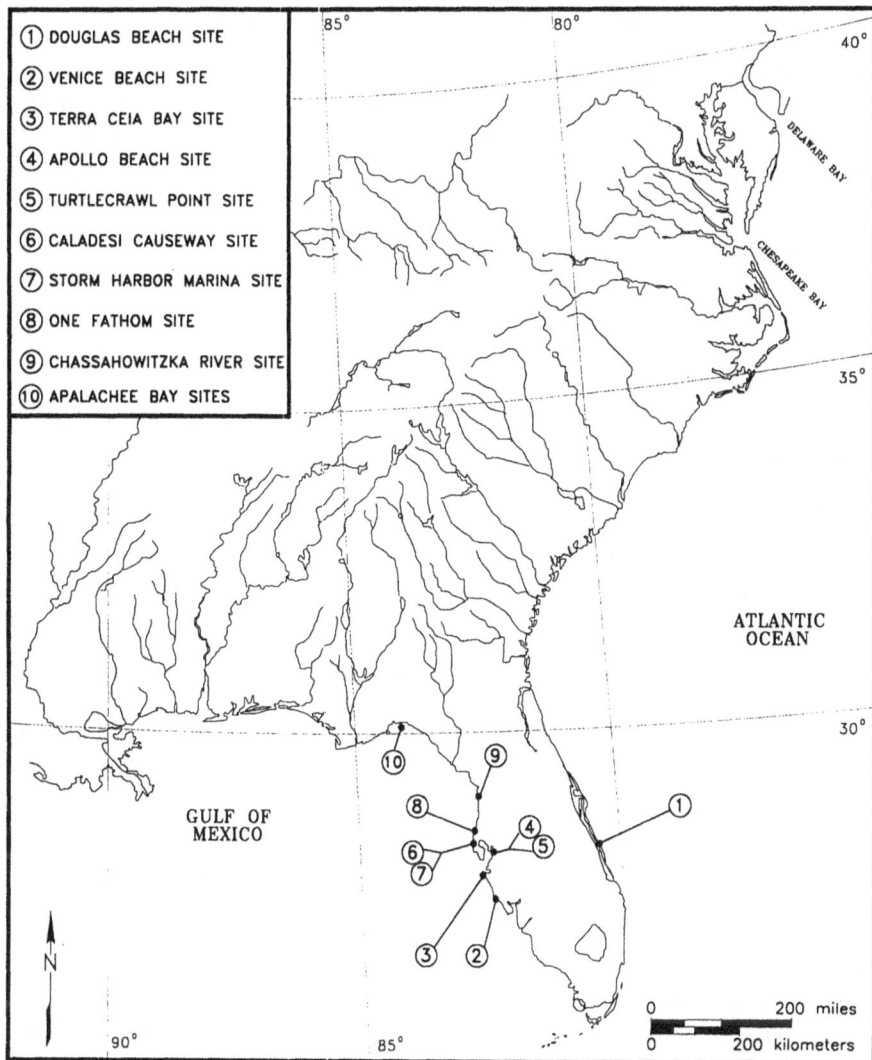

Fig. 11-2.   Reported submerged sites in the southeastern United States (after Stright 1990).

River, Susquehanna, and other "broadspear" hafted bifaces have been recovered at eight of these sites. Found just as often, probably due to their size, are ground stone axes. No less than 14 grooved axes are documented from eight different sites. Ground stone adzes or gouges are documented from two sites.

Only four areas have yielded earlier artifacts. From one came the only Paleo-indian artifact seen, but more typical are occasional Early and Middle Archaic hafted bifaces. The earlier projectile points include Clovis, Palmer/Kirk, Morrow Mountain, Brewerton, and Halifax types. Flaked and notched (Guilford) axes

Table 11-1. Inventory of known submerged sites in coastal waters
of the Southeast (after Stright 1990:441)

Site	Body of water	Components	Depth below mean sea level (m)
Douglas Beach	Atlantic Ocean	Middle Archaic –Woodland	3–12
Venice Beach	Gulf of Mexico	Middle Archaic; Woodland	2.2–3
Terra Ceia Bay	Terra Ceia Bay	Dalton; Woodland	?
Apollo Beach	Tampa Bay	Late Archaic –Woodland	1–5.5
Turtlecrawl Point	Tampa Bay	Early–Late Archaic	1–3
Caladesi Causeway	St. Joseph's Sound	Paleoindian –Archaic	0–5.5
Storm Harbor Marina	—	Early–Late Archaic	0–5.5
One Fathom	Gulf of Mexico	Late Archaic –Woodland	2
Chassahowitzka River	Chassahowitzka River	Middle–Late Archaic	0.5–2.5
Apalachee Bay	Apalachee Bay	Middle Archaic	0–2.5

from three sites are believed to date from the end of the Middle Archaic, associated with the Brewerton/Halifax components (McLearen 1991: 99).

Even less frequently, the watermen recover Early and Middle Woodland artifacts, including ceramic sherds. Such material is confirmed from only two locations, but reports from other sites have been received.

Locational Patterns

Just as the ages of the artifacts tend to be consistent, so do the locations where they are found. Nearly all of the offshore sites are situated at the upper edge of submerged terraces (table 11-2, fig. 11-4). Twelve are specifically recorded from terrace edge locations while one is from a secondary channel margin, another is from a submerged knoll, and two are from offshore "flats." The watermen, in fact, use the term *edges* and remember them since a knowledge of bottom topography is important in their search for clams. The depth of the terrace edges supporting sites is fairly consistent as well; most sites have been recorded between 5.5 and 8.5 m below mean sea level.

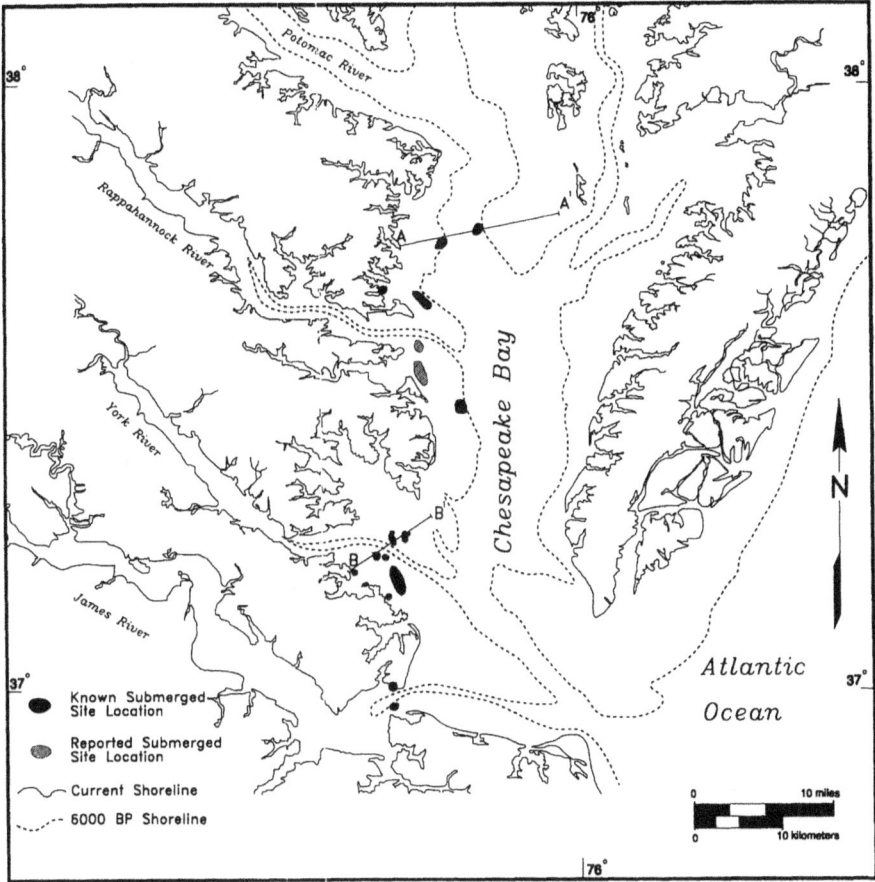

Fig. 11-3.   Locations of known and reported Chesapeake Bay submerged sites.

A group of sites on York Spit serves as an example. The spit represents a now submerged extension of a Quaternary terrace, bounded on the south by the York River channel. Its surface gradually slopes from west to east with depths ranging, respectively, from 1 to 6 m. At the channel is an abrupt slope that plunges to over 10 m; the opposite margin slopes more gently. A shallow channel about 2 m deep is cut into the spit near its western end. Three sites have been located at the edges of this submerged landform (fig. 11-4b). One is at the crest of the steep slope at the river channel (5.5 m below msl), one is at the edge of the swash channel (2 m below msl), and the other is at an edge on the more gentle northeastern slope (5.5 m below msl). A fourth site is reported on an isolated knoll adjacent to the spit, also 5.5 m below msl.

The documented site locations correspond closely to terraces that should have been dry at the time of occupation, based on the associated artifact types. Put another way, the artifacts seldom occur in areas that the sea level curves indicate

Table 11-2.   Summary of submerged prehistoric sites

Site	Components	Average depth (m)	Distance offshore (km)	Artifacts	Location
Moore/Wilmer	Middle and Late Archaic	8.5	7.8	Flaked & grooved axes	Terrace edge
Daniels	Late Archaic?	18.0	12.3	Ground stone adze	Terrace slope
Croxton	Late Archaic	18.0	11.3	Grooved axe, stemmed hafted biface	Terrace slope?
Moore 1	Late Archaic	2.0	0.3	Savannah River hafted biface	Terrace edge
Brown	Early–Late Archaic	8.0	2.9	Hafted bifaces, other bifaces	Terrace edge
Setterholm 1	Late Archaic	2.0	3.1	Flaked & grooved axes	Shallow channel
Setterholm 2	Late Archaic	5.5	5.1	Grooved axe, hafted bifaces	Terrace edge
Setterholm 3	Late Archaic	5.5	5.7	Hafted biface	Knoll
Setterholm 4	—	5.5	4.0	?	Terrace edge
Holloway 1	Late Archaic	6.0	5.0	Grooved axe	Terrace edge
Holloway 2	Late Archaic	8.0	5.0	Grooved axe, bannerstone?	Terrace edge
Holloway 3	Paleoindian–Late Archaic	6.0	5.0	Fluted point, Kirk, Savannah River, grooved axes, gouge, celt	Terrace edge
Holloway 4	Early–Middle Archaic	2.5	0.5	Flaked axe, Kirk, Palmer points	Terrace edge
Holloway 5	Early Woodland	1.5	0.5	Perkiomen point	Terrace edge
Holloway 6	Late Archaic	0.5	0.2	Savannah River	Flat
Wilmer	Late Archaic	2.5	0.5	Hafted biface, other biface	Flat?
Moore 2	Late Archaic	12.0	0.8	Grooved axe	Terrace edge
West	Late Archaic	8.0	4.8	Grooved axes, bifaces	Terrace edge

would have been submerged at their time of manufacture and use. The many
Late Archaic sites at or just above the ±8–9-m shoreline are suggestive of stability in the estuary environment and possibly of more intensive use of the area.

An adze and one axe are from deeper than predicted water on terrace slopes
(see fig. 11.4). These exceptions confirm that at least some sites have been eroded
and material displaced. In their descriptions, watermen describe some of the find
spots as "rock piles" or places with stony bottoms. More than likely this signifies

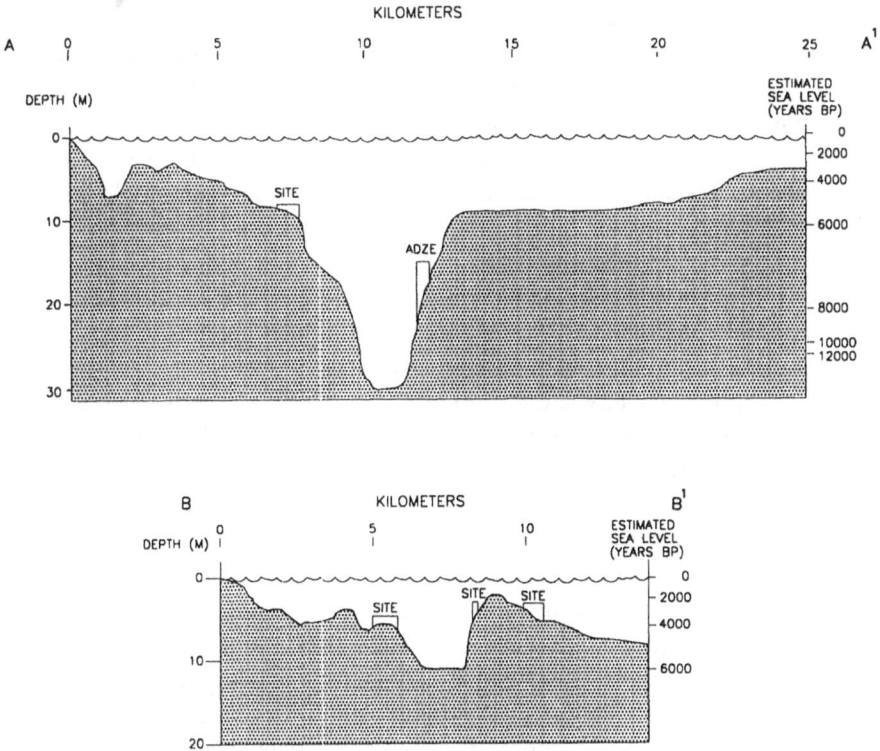

Fig. 11-4.   Chesapeake Bay submerged site locations in cross section.

that the artifacts are occurring in lag or palimpsest deposits redeposited on an erosional, ravinement surface (Belknap and Kraft 1985; Swift et al. 1972). On the other hand, sites have been described from areas with muddy or peaty bottoms where tree stumps are encountered. These latter reports offer more encouragement than typical results from the continental shelf. Even the redeposited material can potentially be invaluable, as I argue below.

Refining the Chesapeake Estuary Model

The new information on submerged sites corroborates the dating of major events in the development of the Chesapeake Bay. The recovery of Late Archaic artifacts more often than material from other periods is tempting to interpret as evidence for the intensification of settlement about 5000 B.P. This corresponds, of course, to the interval immediately following the slowing of sea level rise, when sea level is estimated to have been about 7–8 m below what it is today. With rare exceptions, all of the submerged Late Archaic components are on landforms above the estimated level of the bay at that time, usually 1–2 m above it. There is, therefore, a comfortable concordance of geological and archaeological measures of sea level fluctuation.

The occurence of components which both pre- and postdate the Late Archaic on some submerged sites potentially is very telling. In the simplest terms, these components demonstrate the utilization of now submerged areas for probably all of the time that they were available for human settlement, both before and after the 6000–5000 B.P. slowing. The scope of settlement is open to question, however, until a larger sample is obtained. Assuming that the present sample is representative, intensive use is indicated only for the Late Archaic.

A simple review of submerged site locations yields few surprises, in the sense that most would be predictable following general terrestrial models. Bathymetric charts show that the sites are typically located along the margins of submerged terraces adjacent to relict stream channels. These are precisely the places that are viewed as high-probability site locations in the still-dry uplands. As might be expected, the basic tenets of terrestrially based predictive models can, therefore, be extended to now submerged landscapes.

The context of some of the submerged sites can be questioned since artifacts are sometimes recovered from reworked deposits. The degree of displacement from original deposits in these cases is unknown, however. More than likely the "rock pile" deposits are somewhat lower than the original context but probably not more than about a meter. This is not unexpected given the generally low relief of the area, which insures that most ravinement surfaces will be a minimal distance below the original level. Lateral transport is more difficult to gauge, but at present it is believed that the artifact concentrations approximate original site locations.

The substantive contribution of this work, beyond mere confirmation of the existence of submerged sites, is a more accurate portrayal of prehistoric settlement in the outer Coastal Plain. By considering what lies beneath the bay and viewing the entire area as an integrated whole, site data that for so long were intuitively known to exist underwater can now be incorporated into model building.

Both the kinds of artifacts recovered by the watermen and the method they have used to recover them speak volumes about the likely nature of the sites. The numerous, large ground and flaked stone axes are generally regarded as items characteristic of intensively occupied sites. This is also true of the very large hafted bifaces. The chances of recovering these and other artifacts with clam tongs would seem remote except on rich sites. This is even more strongly indicated when different watermen independently recover the same kinds of the artifacts from an area. All of this gives the impression that most of the submerged sites documented thus far are extensive, high-density loci.

Just as rich sites seem to dominate the record from offshore, smaller sites dominate the terrestrial record near the coast. Indeed, sites such as White Oak Point (44WM119; Waselkov 1982) are dry land exceptions. Early and mid-Holocene sites considered to be "base camps" are rarely recorded in the terrestrial portions of the outer Coastal Plain, a fact that has naturally acted to limit accurate model building for the area. Taken together, however, data from these adjoining areas can be combined to generate realistic models. Proposed refinements are:

(1) Coastal Plain groups of the mid-Holocene followed a seasonal round within territories that encompassed both now submerged and terrestrial areas.

(2) Virtually all current models imply the presence of "base camps," "aggregation sites," or "macro social unit" sites but documented examples are scarce on dry land. Many of the recorded submerged sites appear to be suitable candidates for the base camps that would have been established within group ranges.

(3) Most typical of the dry land record are small sites labeled camps, extractive sites, or micro social unit habitations. Under a revised scenario the plethora of small sites dotting the present shorelines and interior stream margins would indeed be described as more temporary extractive sites, which at the time would have been in more interior settings. However, they would also be more explicitly linked to the potential base camps now offshore.

A temporal dimension should be built into these revisions as well, recognizing the required shift of entire settlement systems away from the transgressive shoreline. Indeed, the early and mid-Holocene record is scant and underwhelming when only now dry areas are considered. The submerged site data, however, establish that extensive and rich sites are present offshore. Eventually it might be feasible to construct for the early Holocene a version of the drainage-based model proposed by Anderson and Hanson (1988) that unifies all of the site information. As the submerged sites are plotted and evaluated as to function, their distribution relative to natural features such as drainage systems and physiography can serve to delimit prospective group ranges or territories.

Implications of the Chesapeake Results for the Greater Southeast

The Chesapeake case suggests that regionwide attention to the Holocene site potential of submerged areas is in order, and that the traditional fixation on Paleoindian sites must be overcome. In fact, the documented searches for such early sites usually turn up Holocene sites, if anything (Dunbar et al. 1992). Stright's (1990) summary of documented submerged sites nationwide reveals that 70 percent of such sites in the Southeast have Middle to Late Archaic components (table 11-1); this climbs to over 80 percent if all eastern sites are considered. Further, the search for sites will probably be most productive in more sheltered embayments or estuaries rather than on the offshore shelf. This study alone cannot answer all of the questions that arise, but it can provoke similar work elsewhere that will bring us closer.

Submerged Holocene Site Potential of the Greater Southeast

It is clear that no single model such as that emerging for the Chesapeake will suffice for the region as a whole. Indeed, data summarized by Russo (chap. 10, this volume) reflect greater levels of residential stability at Gulf coastal sites than predicted for the Cheasapeake region. Discovery and interpretation of submerged sites is predicated on the construction of models that take into account physiographic, marine, and cultural factors unique to different sections of the region. To the extent that high-potential locations for sites have been identified in the Chesapeake Bay, the potential of other submerged areas in the region can be identified on a limited basis.

The key features of the Chesapeake area that appear to account for numbers of submerged sites are the shallowness of the embayment and the many flooded stream channels that drained the area. In turn, the discernible, relict channel systems and the landforms they help to create are the primary aid in defining potential site locations. More area is submerged on low-relief surfaces per unit of sea level rise than on high-relief surfaces. Therefore, the density of submerged archaeological sites will likely be greater in shallow bodies of water that characterize this area and other portions of the southeastern Coastal Plain. The underwater fluvial landscape essentially is the submerged extension of adjacent dry land, from which topographic or hydrologic predictors can be applied in the underwater context.

Estuaries across the Southeast are relatively shallow. Consequently, the southeastern region almost certainly has the greatest potential for submerged sites within estuarine waters nationwide. Compared to the north Atlantic region, for example, estuaries of the Southeast average less than half the depth but cover more than three times the area (NOAA 1990). All of them cover fluvial landscapes, too, but distinct, relict channel systems which so readily define many high-potential site locations are not always evident. This appears to reflect the natural characteristics of an area and may not be a prerequisite for high site potential.

Pertinent statistics are summarized in table 11-3 for selected embayments along the southeastern coast from Virginia to Alabama (fig. 11-5). Of the 10 examples considered, five can be rated as having a high site potential under the Chesapeake Bay model. These areas include Port Royal and St. Helena sounds and Charleston Harbor in South Carolina and Apalachee Bay in Florida, where distinct channels and other bottom features exist to define high-probability areas. Indeed, previous work in Apalachee Bay has confirmed the presence of sites (Dunbar et al. 1992).

That the other embayments are not so highly rated reflects their more subdued bottom features. Estuaries such as the Albermarle/Pamlico Sound in North Carolina and the Gulf of Mexico estuaries of Charlotte Harbor and Tampa Bay, Florida, and Mobile Bay, Alabama, are not marked by distinct channels or "edge" features. It is risky though to describe them as having a lower site potential. Instead, lower ratings indicate that potential site locations cannot always be readily identified using the Chesapeake model. The report by Goodyear et al. (1980) of a submerged site in Tampa Bay bears out this caution. In some of these cases relict channels are obscured by sedimentation but can be identified through remote sensing so that prospective site locations can be delimited.

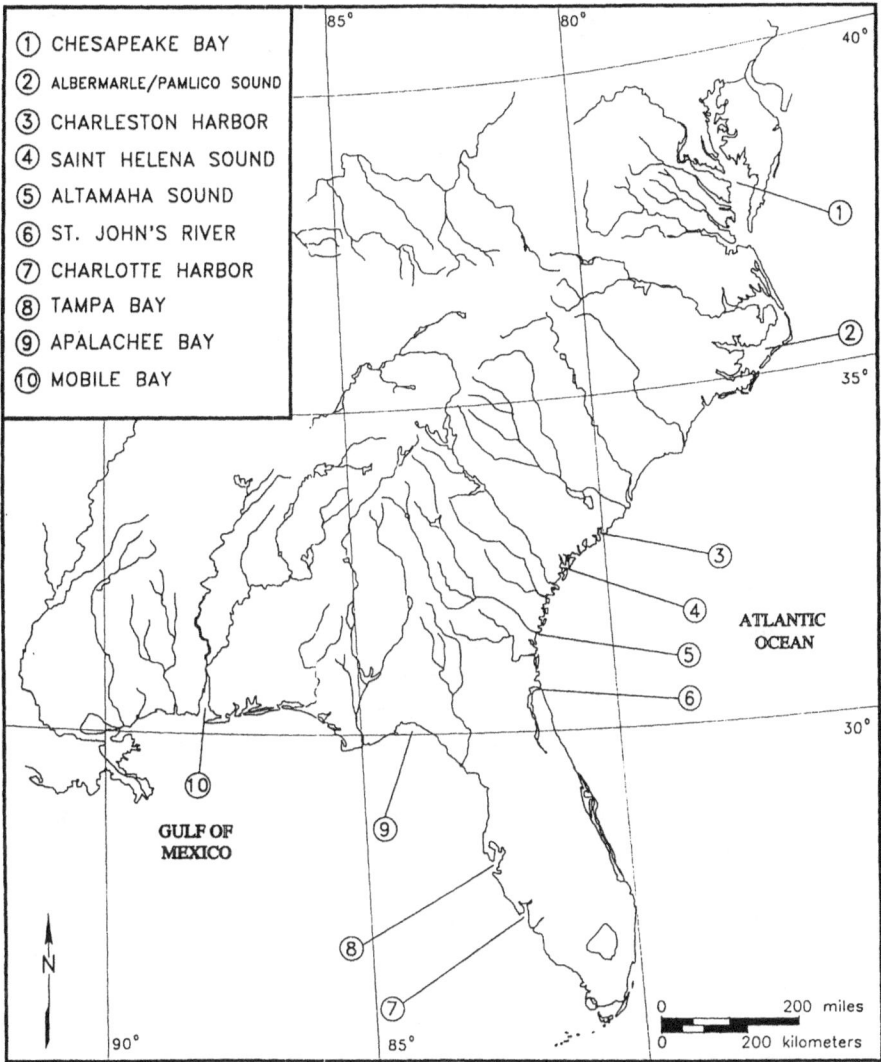

Fig. 11-5. Representative embayments/estuaries of the southeastern United States.

The St. Johns River, Florida, represents another situation. This waterway differs in its narrow course from most of the others considered. In this situation the channel dominates the bottom with only very restricted bottom areas flanking it. Furthermore, the St. Johns has been heavily dredged to maintain channels, thus compromising site potential further. These conditions exist to a lesser degree in Charleston Harbor. Dredged channels are prominent there but broader bottom expanses lie adjacent to them.

This review serves to highlight the overall potential of southeastern estuaries for submerged sites and to establish that no one model can be applied to assess

Table 11-3.   Description of selected southeastern embayments

Embayment	Surface area (km²)	Average depth(m)	Extant channels	Other topography	Previous research
Chesapeake Bay, VA	9,958	7	Distinct	Spits; edges	Blanton, this volume
Albemarle/Pamlico Sound	7,667	4	Rare and limited	Shoals and edges	Haag 1975
Charleston Harbor, SC	96	5	Distinct	Edges and banks	None
St. Helena Sound, SC	221	4	Distinct	Edges and banks	?
Altamaha Sound, GA	39	3	Distinct	Edges and banks	?
St. Johns River, FL	671	4	Distinct	Edges	?
Charlotte Harbor, FL	809	2	None evident	Rare; occa- sional reefs	?
Tampa Bay, FL	900	4	Rare and limited	Occasional shoals, edges	Goodyear et al. 1993
Apalachee Bay, FL	413	3	Limited	Edges	Dunbar et al. 1992
Mobile Bay, AL	1,063	3	Rare and limited	Spits and edges	?

them all. These estuaries share a common broad geography, but the variation among them requires different considerations beyond those now defined for Chesapeake Bay. At the very least, embayments with distinct bottom features must be evaluated and examined differently from those lacking such features. In at least some areas, these two general categories are probably indicative of the adjacent Coastal Plain terrain. When this is the case, the physiographic elements of existing, terrestrial site models may be extended into offshore areas to predict higher probability areas. For example, prevailing settlement models for the Chesapeake area can be extended offshore into the Chesapeake Bay, just as the models relevant to southern peninsular Florida, for example, should be applied in predicting site locations in Charlotte Harbor or Tampa Bay. The success of Dunbar and his colleagues in Apalachee Bay attests to the merits of this approach (Dunbar et al. 1992), where they targeted submerged outcrops of chert and sub- merged sinkholes or springs that are unique to that area.

Future Directions

The sheltered coastal waters of the Southeast have exceptional potential for ancient, submerged sites. Evidence to support this claim is only beginning to emerge, and so the challenge for the future is actively to collect more information from underwater contexts across the region. The initial step in this effort is to extend terrestrial settlement models offshore and define locations under these schemes that should support sites. This process requires detailed bathymetric charts and benefits further from a local sea level curve.

The costs of and logistical requirements for actually testing the models reach far beyond those of dry sites. This is particularly the case for controlled excavation, but even simple dives to sites usually must be brief and visibility is often limited. Where divers have succeeded is naturally where visibility is best. Dive surveys are usually among the least efficient means of inventorying sites and should be reserved for later stages of site evaluation. The exception will be in clearer waters such as in the Gulf of Mexico where Dunbar et al. (1992) have conducted surveys by towing divers.

Remote sensing techniques may be the most attractive alternative to dives, and will be most effective in refining predictions of site locations and reconstructing their settings (Stright 1990). Side-scan sonar surveys have the capability of documenting bottom conditions, especially areas of significant relief and exposed outcrops. In this way the associations between sites and landform features such as terrace edges and stream channels can be better documented. Because side-scan sonar images depict current conditions only, sub-bottom profiling can reveal obscured features of the former land surface now masked by sediments. With this equipment, filled channels and sloughs or hidden topography can be detected; this technique has allowed mapping of the early Susquehanna River channels beneath the bay (Colman et al. 1990). Large targets hidden beneath sediment, such as shell middens, outcrops of knappable stone, or high-potential topographic features, are detected best with seismic surveys (Stright 1990:462).

Remote sampling techniques can be designed to complement the remote sensing data. These represent means to recover limited bottom samples with devices operated from surface vessels. With coring devices, samples of sediment and organic deposits may be recovered for dating and other analyses. Modified patent tongs like those used by Chesapeake clammers, or modified dredge rigs, might also be considered for recovering artifact samples, especially when the survey design calls for "prospecting."

There is further the crucial question of site integrity, and pioneers in this realm of study have acknowledged that problem from the beginning (DePratter and Howard 1977; Edwards and Emery 1977, Edwards and Merrill 1977). The crux of the matter is simple: erosion occurs at every shoreline and at the leading edge of any marine regression or transgression is a shoreline; therefore, every submerged site has been subjected to erosion to some degree and the effect of it on the archaeological deposits must be taken into account. The Southeast can boast one of the original systematic studies designed to address this issue by Gagliano and colleagues in the Gulf of Mexico (Dunbar et al. 1992; Gagliano 1984; Stright 1990), and similar efforts in the neighboring Middle Atlantic are relevant as well (Belknap and Kraft 1985; Hoyt et al. 1990). The superb review of the contributions of these and other studies in Waters' (1992) recent text makes clear the myriad factors that dictate the severity of erosion. Suffice it to say that the general consensus is that well-preserved deposits are unlikely to exist except in the exceptional cases where either (1) relatively sudden in-place drowning occurs or (2) sites were blanketed by sediments prior to submergence.

The experiences in the Chesapeake compared with efforts elsewhere to identify drowned sites suggest that local conditions will play a considerable role in the level of success. In summarizing the findings of many studies, Waters (1992:278) lists pertinent local conditions as the rate of sea level rise, topography, wave energy, nature of the sediment matrix, degree of subsidence, tidal range, and depostitional patterns. The effects of local conditions in the Chesapeake area are being sought through observation at the current shoreline. It stands to reason that processes observable today at the shoreline are similar to those along earlier shorelines. Current observations, then, offer some measure of how the now sub-merged deposits might have been transformed and what we might expect from them. The two major processes noted thus far are erosion and the activities of organisms.

That erosion occurs is beyond question, but the degree to which it affects sites appears to vary. Two principal factors dictating the degree of these effects are shoreline morphology and wave energy. Erosion at high bluffs is most damaging. Wave action undercuts the base of these exposures, leading to collapse of the upper deposits where most archaeological material is present. The effect on lower-lying shores is less damaging, and offers some promise for feature preser-vation on submerged sites. In these situations, the shore advances rapidly and ero-sion removes the deposits only to the depth at which equilibrium is reached to create a ravinement surface. This level is sometimes above the basal depth of cul-tural features, as demonstrated on eroded prehistoric and colonial sites in the area. Low tide exposures of such surfaces have revealed remnants of pit features, graves, cellars, and wells. Therefore, deep features may be truncated but not nec-essarily lost completely.

The significance of wave energy is obvious. Where shorelines are exposed to a long fetch, wave action is most severe and so are the negative effects of erosion. These conditions are typical of open bay and ocean shore settings. Lower-energy environments in sheltered coves and along smaller streams offer the greatest potential for less-eroded deposits. By nature, wave energy and its effects are char-acteristically more subdued in more sheltered areas and so, too, is the negative effect on shorelines.

Organisms that inhabit shoreline and intertidal zones probably have an effect that is underestimated. The activities of fiddler crabs (*Uca* sp.) serve to make the point. These small creatures forage in the intertidal zone, especially in marshes, and inhabit burrows made in marsh deposits. Their burrows commonly extend 50 cm below the marsh surface and literally riddle the underlying sediments. The burrowing appears to rework marsh deposits thoroughly, including any cultural strata that may be preserved beneath them. To gauge the potential of sites, a great deal more attention must be paid in the future to this kind of natural transforma-tion of the record.

Finally, there are cultural impacts to consider, the most obvious of which is the very source of the Chesapeake data. As they tong for clams, the watermen are constantly tilling the bottom. This process undoubtedly approximates the effects of plowing on terrestrial sites, and I have accepted that there must be a "tong zone" at the upper portion of these sites. There are other methods of clamming, crabbing, and fishing that also disrupt bottom deposits, including dredging and trawling. Even greater threats exist as channels are dredged for shipping. Maintenance of existing channels poses some threat but opening of new channels will clearly be of the greatest concern. Boat wakes, too, exacerbate erosion on many shorelines.

In the end, this emerges as a good news–bad news tale. The good news is that the coastal waters of the southeastern United States, especially in more sheltered embayments, are not only rich in submerged archaeological resources but may be among the richest anywhere. The bad news is that they remain virtually unknown and cannot be effectively accounted for in current models. The submerged nature of these sites is an obstacle that must be overcome. Tedious and costly effort will be necessary to identify and evaluate them, paying special attention to their integrity. The state of preservation can also be expected to vary in different areas according to local conditions. By acknowledging the contribution that nonprofessionals can make in locating sites, and by following up with well-designed data recovery efforts, we can open many new doors in our quest to incorporate these sites into our models. There are precious few frontiers left in the field and this is one that demands our attention.

Acknowledgments

My greatest debt is to the Chesapeake watermen who have not only tolerated my queries but patiently responded to them. Without these men there would be little to say. John Roberts is responsible for preparing the figures, and I thank the rest of the William and Mary Center for Archaeological Research staff for their vital but often less obvious contributions. Comments by Carl Hobbs and Melanie Stright on earlier drafts improved this chapter considerably. Any errors or omissions are solely the responsibility of the author.

SECTION V

REGIONAL INTEGRATION AND ORGANIZATION

Long-distance exchange networks of the Poverty Point, Hopewell, and Mississippian societies of the Southeast have attracted worldwide archaeological attention. In chapter 12 Richard W. Jefferies summarizes new data on the existence of long-distance exchange networks that predate the more widely known examples by as much as 3000 years. Assemblages from sites in the lower Ohio/central Mississippi, middle Tennessee/upper Tombigbee, Savannah, and St. Johns river valleys contain items made from exotic raw materials and/or involving considerable investments of artistic energy. Bone pins of the lower Midwest and exaggerated bifaces from sites of the Midsouth exemplify the elaborate forms of craft production associated with exchange networks. Jefferies suggests that exchange in bone pins was one of the means by which increasingly stationary and circumscribed groups compensated for reduced daily contact among themselves, thereby maintaining social buffers to risk. Biface exchange in the Benton phase of the Midsouth may have had similar functions, but in this case mortuary contexts suggest that sacred significance was attached to long-distance contacts. The variety of media, scales of exchange, and contexts for exchanged goods across the region indicate that mechanisms of interaction likely varied. Despite mechanistic differences, Jefferies suggests that evidence for exchange coincides with increased risks associated with environmental unpredictability, and that participating groups would have been distributed over sufficiently diverse habitats to avoid similar shortfalls or risks. Given the evidence for strife described by Smith (chapter 8), it would be reasonable to include social and political risks in the environmental parameters cited by Jefferies.

Social organization and interaction among people of the Shell Mound Archaic is the subject of chapter 13 by Cheryl P. Claassen. Building on her revisionist perspectives of Archaic prehistory, Claassen argues that shell mounds were more than simply the refuse piles of concentrated and relatively stationary people—they were special places of the social and ritual landscape where, among other things, the dead were interred. Reviewing historical data on the availability of freshwater shellfish, Claassen convincingly argues that shell mounds do not coincide with the local availability of productive shellfish beds, hence environmental explanations of shellfish use and site selection can be dismissed. The use of shell, Claassen argues, was social. To examine the social circumstances surrounding shellfishing and shell mounding, she reviews efforts to reconstruct social organization from analyses of gender, exchange, and mortuary treatment. Each of these areas of inquiry has been undertheorized and difficult to support with data, although what is available reveals considerable variation in scale, content, and function. This is exemplified in Claassen's careful analysis of Shell Mound Archaic beads, which suggests distinct zones for beads in the region, some possibly corresponding with those for other material expressions of identity, such as carved bone pins. But despite this divergence, the participants, sharing burial ceremonialism involving shell mounding, formed an interlocking network, with, as Claassen puts it, "negotiations that blended and distinguished elements in each society." Of course, many of these same elements surfaced later in the Adena and Hopewell societies of the Woodland period, underscoring the cyclic nature of many of the social and ritual phenomena of eastern U.S. prehistory while also reminding us that Woodland developments have deep historical roots in the Archaic.

Reviewing sites of ceremonial mounds from across the lower Southeast in chapter 14, Michael Russo argues that intentional mounding of earth and shell was widespread in the Middle and Late Archaic periods. He addresses the difficult issue of distinguishing between mounded earth and midden accumulations. Biased by preconceptions about the limits to Archaic culture, early investigators dismissed the lack of sherds and early radiocarbon dates from mound excavations as aberrant. While the bias persists today, recent fieldwork at sites in Louisiana by Joe Saunders and others and Russo's own work in Florida are providing conclusive evidence for intentional mounding. Knowledge of the functions of Archaic mounds remains elusive. Russo suggests that an economy based on intensive use of aquatic resources underwrote the settlement stability and social complexity necessary to support mound construction. Long-distance exchange was possibly also involved, though the evidence is scant. In comparing contexts of mound building, Russo considers the Florida cases to be isolated and short-lived. Those of Louisiana, on the other hand, suggest historical continuity with the famed Poverty Point mounds of the terminal Archaic. How all of this relates to the Shell Mound Archaic is another issue altogether. Irrespective of the historical relationships and scalar dimensions among these similar developments, each embodies a variety of social, political, and ideological issues heretofore unappreciated.

Scale and complexity are concepts that are hard to ignore in investigating the Poverty Point phenomenon. With its elaborate mounds, diverse assemblages of exotic material culture, and air of mystery, the Poverty Point site in northeast Louisiana has long represented the culmination of Archaic cultural complexity, at once a burst of creative success and an aberration seemingly without precedent or parallel. In the early 1970s, Jon Gibson (1974) declared Poverty Point the "first North American chiefdom." Now, after more than 20 years of analysis and debate, Gibson, in the closing chapter to this volume, downgrades the scale and complexity of Poverty Point. In his review of radiocarbon dates, Gibson argues that Poverty Point was short-lived, lasting only a few centuries and not the 1500 years originally implicated. Geographically, Poverty Point–like items are distributed across a broad stretch of the lower Southeast, but Gibson argues that these superficial similarities do not constitute a large-scale cultural tradition. The importation of raw materials and finished goods into northeast Louisiana from points hundreds of miles away is undeniable, although Gibson considers this to be the coincident result of a strategic location in the Mississippi River Valley and a lack of local stone. Acknowledging that exchange may have something to do with how locals gained prestige, Gibson nevertheless views participants in Poverty Point exchange as coming from socially and politically independent cultures. While one could argue that prestige enhancement through exchange links all people into networks of social and political obligation, Gibson's downscaling of the Poverty Point phenomenon goes to show that interpretations of social complexity among Archaic societies will remain a topic of debate for many years to come.

12

The Emergence of Long-Distance Exchange Networks in the Southeastern United States

RICHARD W. JEFFERIES

North American archaeologists have long been interested in identifying and explaining the physical and social factors associated with the development of regional-scale exchange networks. Although researchers have usually focused their attention on more complex Woodland and Mississippian exchange systems (Brose and Greber 1979; Caldwell and Hall 1964; Hall 1991; Winters 1981), examples of Late Archaic regional exchange involving a variety of materials and dating to between 5000 and 3000 B.P. have been documented in the southeastern United States. Of particular note is the development of the Poverty Point trade network (ca. 3700–2700 B.P.) in the Lower Mississippi River Valley. The inhabitants of the Poverty Point site, along with numerous smaller contemporary settlements, participated in the exchange of a wide variety of exotic raw materials, including argillite, slate, fluorite, magnetite, hematite, copper, galena, red jasper, quartzite, and steatite, as well as items manufactured from these materials. The sources of some of these materials lay as far as 1000 km away from Poverty Point itself (Neuman 1984:102). Gibson (1980) has suggested that the Poverty Point site served as a gateway community, acting as a depot for nonlocal lithic materials being imported from northern source areas and dispersed to other Poverty Point groups living to the south. Involvement of some Poverty Point groups in this interaction and exchange may eventually have led to the development of more complex forms of social organization, some individuals developing their marketing and economic abilities as a result of their proximity to primary trade routes (Gibson 1980:343; but see Gibson [this volume] for an alternative view).

In contrast, Jackson (1991) has proposed that the Poverty Point site was the scene of a series of Late Archaic "trade fairs." According to this model, Late Archaic groups from throughout the Lower Mississippi River Valley traveled to Poverty Point on a regular basis to exchange goods and information and to conduct other kinds of socially integrating activities. Although trade fairs probably started as a way of reducing subsistence risks through the establishment of intergroup alliances, opportunities for increasing individual status and prestige also existed, leading to a higher degree of social differentiation among group members.

Further to the north along the Green River of Kentucky, copper and marine shell artifacts found at shell-midden sites like Indian Knoll and Carlston Annis reflect the involvement of other Late Archaic groups in long-distance exchange networks (Goad 1980; Marquardt and Watson 1983:334; Winters 1968). While the presence of exotic materials at these sites clearly indicates that these Green River Late Archaic hunter-gatherer groups participated in long-distance exchange, the factors responsible for the development of exchange networks and the exact role these groups played in the regional distribution of the copper and shell remain unclear (Marquardt and Watson 1983).

Additional evidence of Late Archaic regional exchange has been documented in the Great Lakes area among archaeological manifestations traditionally labeled "Old Copper," "Glacial Kame," and "Red Ocher" (Stoltman 1986). Archaeological data from a number of sites in southeastern Ontario, Illinois, Michigan, Indiana, and Wisconsin suggest that Late Archaic groups obtained high-quality cherts from contemporary hunter-gatherer groups living to the south in southern Illinois and southern Indiana. Marine shell artifacts found in the northern portion of the midcontinent were also obtained through contact with more southern groups (Stoltman 1986).

The preceding examples indicate that regional interaction and exchange systems were operating in the Southeast and adjacent areas by at least 4500 B.P. In general, with the exception of a few anomalies like Poverty Point, most examples of Late Archaic economic transactions have been characterized as innumerable, multidirectional, down-the-line exchanges of information and materials between nearby as well as distant trading partners (Smith 1986:30).

Over the past 15 years, archaeological investigations conducted at several sites in the Southeast and Midwest have yielded new data that push back the development of regional-scale exchange networks to the late Middle Archaic period (ca. 6000–5000 B.P.). This chapter investigates the development of exchange networks by southeastern and midwestern late Middle Archaic groups as a means for coping with increasing stress associated with mid-Holocene environmental degradation, decreased group mobility, and the emergence of more bounded (restricted) local group territories.

Hunter-Gatherer Social Networks

Prehistoric hunter-gatherer exchange networks represent the archaeologically visible aspects of broader social networks that involved far more than the simple exchange of exotic or nonlocal materials. Ethnographic and ethnohistoric data indicate that in addition to serving as a mechanism for obtaining nonlocal resources, these networks also provided a variety of risk-averting mechanisms that could be operationalized in times of economic or social stress. Wiessner (1982) suggests that because of the uncertainty of resource availability among hunter-gatherers, strategies for averting risk could have a dramatic impact on social organization. One of the most common risk-averting mechanisms used by hunter-gatherers is the sharing or pooling of resources. She views risk sharing as a social method of "insurance" that combines the principles of risk transfer with those of storage and storage of obligations. Wiessner (1982:173) maintains that in pooling, "risk is distributed over a broad segment of the population, so that loss is made more predictable and shared by those in the pool." Relatively small everyday losses, represented by gifts and assistance, are substituted for larger, more unpredictable losses, such as prolonged periods of poor hunting or widespread sickness within the group (Wiessner 1982:173).

Activities based on the concept of risk sharing include feasting, exchange, and gift giving (Brown 1985:206; Wiessner 1982). Risk sharing can be organized locally through widespread sharing between individually chosen partners, or it can be centralized through a central person for redistribution. Wiessner (1982:172) suggests that individually organized risk sharing is associated with what Binford (1980) termed a "foraging" strategy used by relatively mobile hunter-gatherers. This often takes the form of trading partnerships between individuals living in nearby and distant groups. Centralized pooling is more commonly associated with a "collector" strategy used by more sedentary groups.

Braun and Plog (1982:504–506) suggest that nonhierarchical regional networks represent lines for the transmission of information and materials among participating individuals and groups. The relative strength of these relationships reflects the social distances among network participants, with the level of regional integration rising as social and environmental risks increase. Interaction within these networks involves communication through at least two archaeologically visible phenomena: goods exchanged as tokens of social obligations and style reflected in domestic items (Braun and Plog 1982:509). These authors (1982:512) suggest that greater social interaction should be accompanied by increasing stylistic similarities between localities and that this increase should be accompanied by growth in the quantity of exchange goods.

Although Braun and Plog's research does not apply specifically to hunter-gatherers, studies by Wiessner (1982, 1983), Sampson (1988), Gilman (1984), and others suggest that these same characteristics can be used as measures of hunter-gatherer social interaction. In terms of exchange and stylistic variation, Wiessner (1982:175) predicts that the distribution of exchange goods should not decrease in proportion to distance since members of the risk-pooling network must integrate themselves with distant groups that have access to complementary resources. Likewise, stylistic variation among interacting groups will be minimal, since an attempt will be made to blend the individual into the greater population, not to emphasize differences between individuals.

Based on the previous discussion, several predictions can be made concerning the development of hunter-gatherer exchange networks. First, evidence of social integration and exchange will increase as the risks associated with environmental unpredictability and stress rise. Second, greater social integration will be reflected by increased evidence for exchange and more stylistic similarity of certain items among interacting groups. Third, groups participating in a risk-reducing network will be distributed over sufficiently diverse habitats to avoid the same shortfall impacting all network participants. Fourth, the geographical extent of the network will be reflected by the distribution of stylistically similar artifacts.

The Emergence of Late Middle Archaic Exchange Networks

Research conducted in various parts of the Southeast and its borderlands has yielded information suggesting that regional-scale interaction networks were developing in several areas by 6000 B.P. Examples discussed here come from the lower Ohio–central Mississippi River valleys, the middle Tennessee–upper Tombigbee valleys, the Savannah River valley, and the St. Johns River valley (fig. 12-1).

Lower Ohio–Central Mississippi River Valleys

This area includes portions of the lower Illinois, central Mississippi, and lower Ohio river valleys (fig. 12-1). By 6000 B.P., an assortment of aquatic and wetland habitats (i.e., backwater lakes, swamps, sloughs) was developing along these riverine corridors, creating important sources of food for mid-Holocene hunter-gatherers (Brown 1985:210). The mid-Holocene coincides with the Hypsithermal interval (Deevey and Flint 1957), a climatic episode characterized by slightly drier and warmer conditions that reached its maximum about 7000 B.P. (King and Allen 1977:319–322). These climatic changes may have contributed toward making locations adjacent to wet areas preferred site settings since these "strategic" positions provided immediate access to abundant, reliable, and diverse food resources (Brown and Vierra 1983:170). Early Middle Archaic (ca. 8000–6500 B.P.) sites generally reflect short-term occupations in a variety of environmental settings, conforming to Early Archaic settlement patterns documented in many areas. Early Middle Archaic settlement-subsistence was apparently based on the scheduled exploitation of seasonally available resources through frequent residential moves (Brown and Vierra 1983:190).

There appears to have been a reorganization of settlement-subsistence strategies in some parts of the region following 6500 B.P., reflected by longer occupations at sites located near food-rich wet areas (Brown 1985; Brown and Vierra 1983:190; Jefferies 1983). Brown (1985:215) maintains that "base camps," characterized by thick midden deposits, multiseasonal occupations, substantial structures, burials, and high levels of artifact and feature diversity, reflect the transition from a residential to a logistical mobility strategy. These data suggest that by the sixth millennium, hunter-gatherer groups associated with the Helton phase in Missouri and Illinois (Cook 1976), the Carrier Mills area of southeastern Illinois (Jefferies 1982b; Jefferies and Butler 1982), the French Lick phase in southern

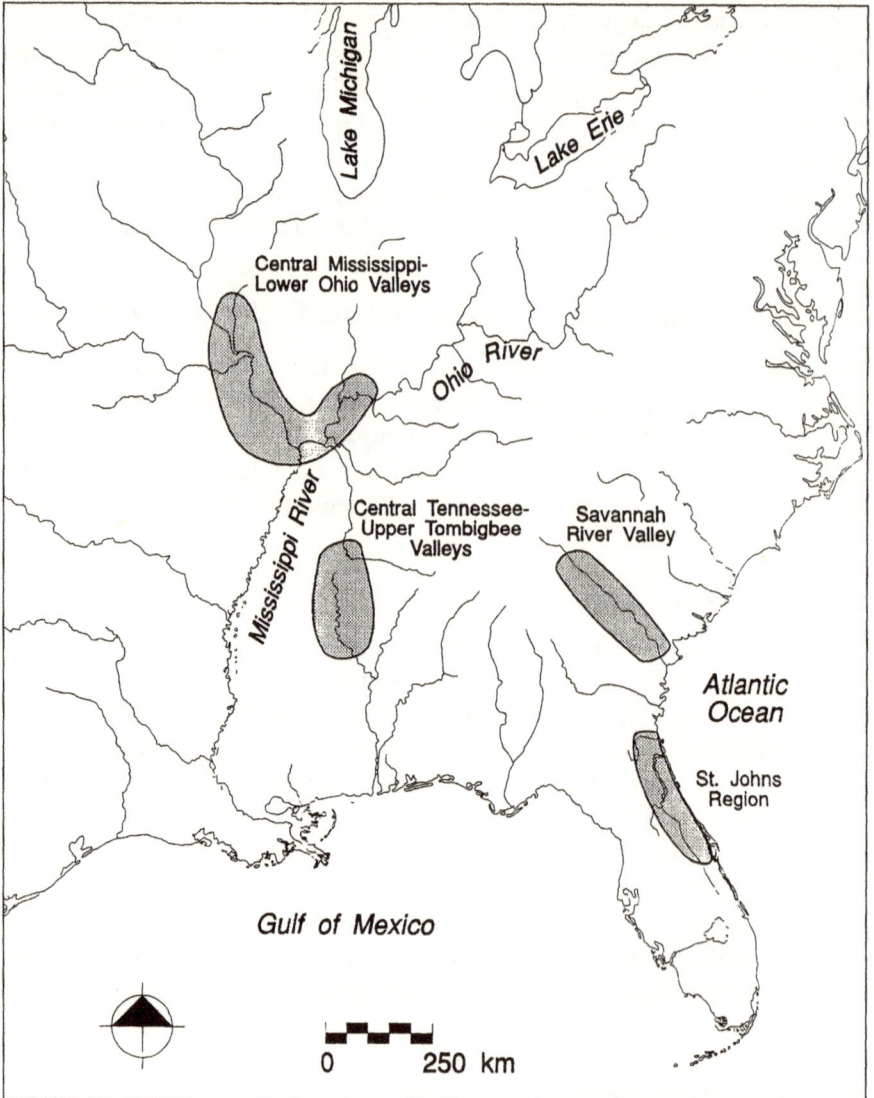

Fig. 12-1.   Geographic distribution of Middle Archaic interaction networks discussed in chapter.

Indiana (Munson and Cook 1980), and the Old Clarkesville phase in Kentucky (Bader 1992; Granger 1988) were becoming increasingly sedentary and more socially complex. Radiocarbon dates associated with late Middle Archaic components at these sites generally range from 6000 to 5000 B.P.

Brown (1985:219–223) suggests several possible explanations for increased sedentism, including Hypsithermal environmental degradation, population pressure, the increased resource potential of major river valleys, and social risk factors. He maintains that social risk factors best explain this change, since the attractiveness of the resource-rich areas encouraged sedentism, thereby lowering the potential for intergroup conflict. Increased sedentism can be attributed to efforts of hunter-gatherer groups to maintain intergroup spacing when a sufficiently rich resource base made this possible (Brown 1985:224). Intergroup spacing would have resulted in the establishment of boundaries separating one group's territory from that of a neighboring group. As noted by Brose (1979:6), stylistic boundary markers tend to develop among structurally similar ethnic populations living in a single cultural-ecological system. The development of these boundaries contributes toward increased ecological stability providing unambiguous access to important resources, thereby insulating other aspects of the culture from confrontation and change (Barth 1969, cited in Brose 1979:6). On the negative side, increased sedentism and the development of group territories could lead to a decrease in intergroup contact and reduced information flow and interaction once maintained through more regular intergroup contact.

The loss of risk-averting regular face-to-face interaction could have been compensated for by increased intergroup cooperation and the elaboration of intergroup social networks. As suggested by Brose (1979) and others (Brown 1985; Marquardt 1985), the flow of social and environmental information may have been maintained by individuals establishing ties, perhaps as trading partners, with members of distant groups. This practice would be reflected archaeologically by evidence of intergroup exchange.

Although limited in quantity, evidence of late Middle Archaic intergroup exchange exists in the lower Ohio–central Mississippi river valley region (Jefferies 1995). First, artifacts made from exotic raw materials (copper and certain types of nonlocal lithic material) occur in archaeological contexts for the first time (Brown and Vierra 1983:185). The presence of these items indicates that regional Middle Archaic groups participated in an exchange network that extended from the Great Lakes to the Gulf or south Atlantic coasts.

Unfortunately, the presence of these nonlocal items provides few clues about the nature of interaction among participating groups or about the extent and scale of the social networks in which they participated. These issues can be better addressed using a second source of evidence, consisting of distinctively carved and engraved bone pins (fig. 12-2) that occur at a number of late Middle Archaic sites within this region (Breitburg 1982:fig. 255; Cook 1976:fig. 21; Jefferies 1995; Stafford and Anslinger 1988). Not surprisingly, not all pin styles occur at all sites. Instead, interacting groups shared a wide variety of shapes and designs that occur in varying frequencies at some late Middle Archaic sites in the region.

Although the presence of similar pin styles throughout this area suggests regional-scale interaction, the exact form of this interaction is unclear. It is possible that the diversity of pins found at some sites reflects the actual exchange of pins between members of local groups or the movement of people who wore the pins from one group to another. It is also possible that each group produced a variety of pin forms, reflecting the flow of information among these groups concerning preferred ways of making and decorating bone pins (Jefferies 1995).

Nevertheless, I suggest that the distribution of these stylistically similar pins defines a socially bounded area extending over several hundred kilometers of the midcontinent, within which groups of increasingly sedentary hunter-gatherers interacted and exchanged information that facilitated their survival. Bone pins may represent symbols used by individuals to signal their affiliation with the regional group, reflecting an increased level of interaction and social circumscription among late Middle Archaic hunter-gatherers in the midcontinent. Exchange may have been much more restricted or of a different nature with groups living outside the area defined by the distribution of pins (Jefferies 1995).

Middle Tennessee–Upper Tombigbee River Valleys

Evidence of a second possible mid-Holocene regional-scale exchange network has been documented along an approximately 200-km section of the middle Tennessee and upper Tombigbee river drainages of northern Alabama and Mississippi (Johnson and Brookes 1989) (fig. 12-1). The definition of this network, termed the "Benton Interaction Sphere," is based on the distribution of caches of oversize and regular Benton points, Cache Blades, and Turkey Tail–like points (fig. 12-3). Benton projectile points have been dated from roughly 5600 to 5000 B.P., making the emergence of the Benton Interaction Sphere contemporary with similar developments in the midcontinent.

As in the lower Ohio–central Mississippi river valleys, the development of the Benton social network is associated with a marked environmental change and a shift in settlement strategies (Johnson and Brookes 1989). Pollen data from the

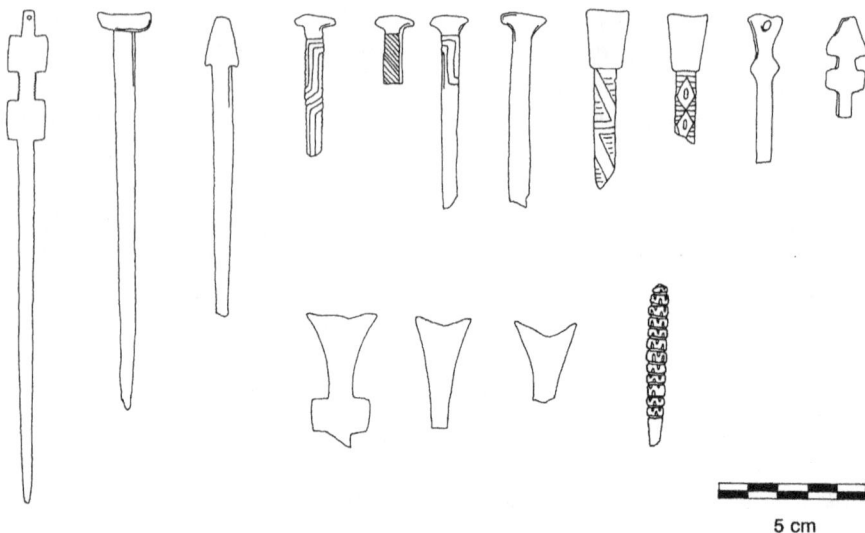

5 cm

Fig. 12-2.   Examples of late Middle Archaic carved and engraved bone pins from the Black Earth site.

central Tombigbee valley indicate that mid-Holocene climatic conditions warmed increasingly, and possibly became drier, with maximum xeric conditions reached between 6500 and 5000 B.P. (Muto and Gunn 1985, cited in Bense 1987b:30). Although slightly later in timing, these events closely parallel the climatic impact of the Hypsithermal recorded for the lower Ohio–central Mississippi river valleys. Archaeological data suggest a major reorganization of the settlement pattern during this time, going from one characterized by "a series of relatively homogeneous small encampments at many locations to large base

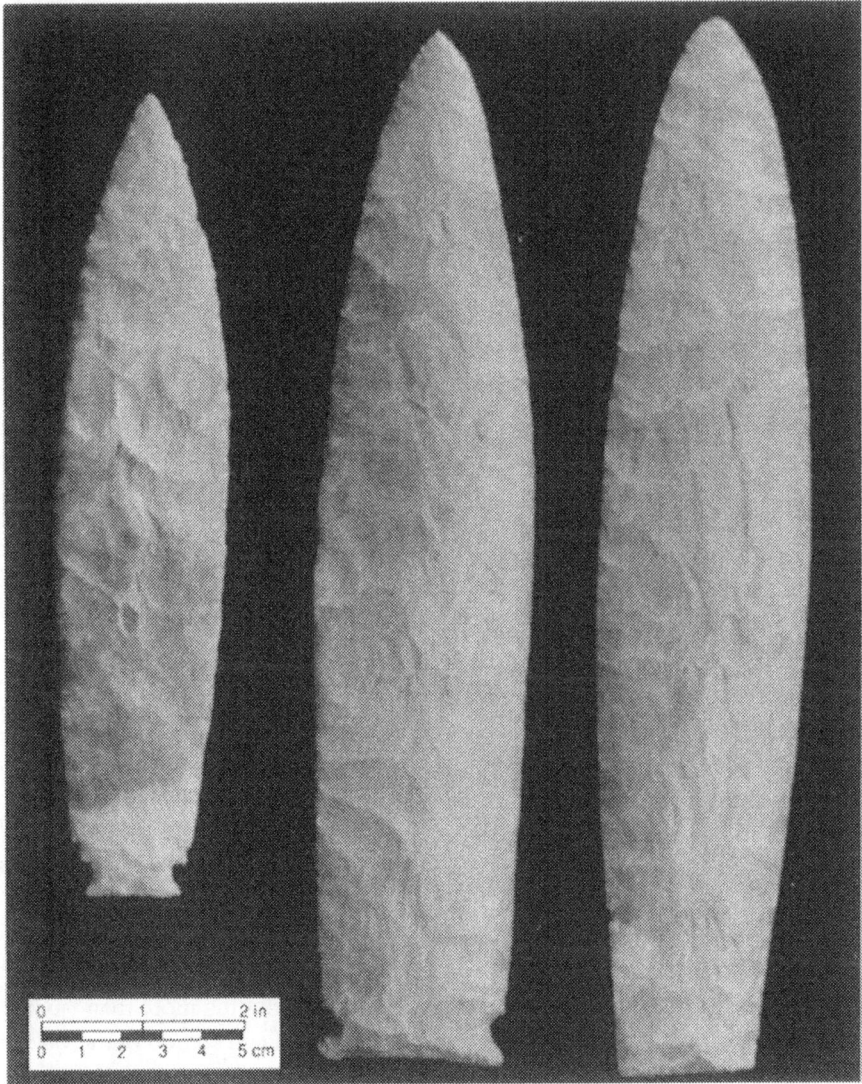

Fig. 12-3. Oversize Benton bifaces and cache blades from the central Tennessee-Tombigbee valleys (Laboratory of Archaeology, University of Mississippi).

camps with small satellite camps" (Bense 1987c:14). Base camps were located on or overlooking floodplains, with smaller sites situated in surrounding floodplain and upland habitats. Many Benton base camps are characterized by intensive midden accumulation, an increase in site features, possible structural remains, and burials. Chronological data from a number of these sites indicate that base camps became focal points of activity early in the Middle Archaic, but the most intensive use of these sites was by late Middle Archaic Benton culture groups some 5600 to 5000 years ago (Bense 1987c:14–15).

The similar distribution of utilitarian Benton points and elaborate bifaces suggests that caches represent sacred markers defining the extent of a secular exchange network. Caches found with burials may identify individuals who actively participated in long-distance exchange (Johnson and Brookes 1989:142). Interestingly, the Benton exchange network did not include nonlocal exotic materials like copper and marine shell, nor did it continue to evolve into apparently more complex forms of social interaction as exhibited during the Late Archaic at Poverty Point and along the Green River of Kentucky (Johnson and Brookes 1989:144).

The Benton Interaction Sphere appears to have developed in response to increasing risk associated with rising population density, decreasing mobility, and an unstable resource base (Johnson and Brookes 1989:144). The coincidence of Benton base camps, biface caches, and Benton points made of nonlocal Fort Payne chert appears to reflect increased sedentism, the formation of regional territories, and the growing need to establish regional social networks to maintain intergroup affiliations. These developments, while differing in material expression, appear to parallel adaptive strategies for dealing with increased environmental and social risk adopted by other late Middle Archaic groups living hundreds of kilometers to the north.

Savannah River Valley

The evolution of regional-scale late Middle Archaic social networks has also been documented along the Savannah River valley (fig. 12-1). Analysis of lithic procurement strategies suggests a reduction in territorial range through time, accompanied by economic intensification involving technological and social changes. This trend toward the increased circumscription of band territories appears to have led to the development of Late Archaic social networks involving the exchange of ceramic vessel technology and soapstone (Sassaman et al. 1988:91).

The development of Middle Archaic band territories is reflected by a greater emphasis on local lithic resources and decreased group mobility. These data suggest that the Savannah River valley was occupied by two geographically distinct bands during the Middle Archaic, the range of each including more than 150 km of the valley. One of these bands occupied the Coastal Plain section of the valley, the other, the Piedmont section (Sassaman et al. 1988:fig. 4).

Bifaces collected from Savannah River Middle Archaic sites, as well as from caches and isolated finds, conform in both age and morphology to Benton points from the Tennessee-Tombigbee region. The production-distribution system described for Savannah River bifaces parallels that recorded by Johnson and Brookes (1989), including the use of nonlocal lithic material for the manufacture of oversized Benton-like bifaces. Local Savannah River valley lithic resources were too small to produce the desired oversized bifaces, so groups obtained larger specimens of nonlocal rhyolite from as far away as the Morrow Mountain region of Piedmont North Carolina (Goodyear et al. 1990:5), a distance of approximately 175 km.

Sassaman (1994b) suggests that the production of Benton-like points must be examined from the perspective of social reproduction and the need to maintain conditions necessary for labor. Social reproduction is expressed through ritual and tribute but also through less formal means such as food and information sharing and gift giving. Production of large numbers of these Benton-like bifaces can be viewed as a social activity directed toward debt fulfillment or the anticipation of exchange opportunities, not solely as a subsistence activity (Sassaman 1994b). The exchange of bifaces may represent one of many options for establishing and maintaining alliances with other individuals and groups by establishing cooperative labor ventures, economic buffers, and conflict avoidance. Sassaman (1994b) also interprets the distribution of Benton-like bifaces as reflecting an increase in social boundedness of hunter-gatherer groups, closely paralleling the explanation offered by Johnson and Brookes (1989:143) for the Benton Interaction Sphere.

St. Johns River Valley

Possible evidence for another late Middle Archaic regional-scale social network comes from the St. Johns River valley in northeast Florida (fig. 12-1). Radiocarbon dates from the Tick Island site indicate that between 5500 and 5000 B.P., hunter-gatherer groups associated with Mount Taylor culture were becoming increasingly sedentary and spending more of their annual cycle collecting shellfish from the rivers. The Tick Island excavations also disclosed 175 flexed burials that had been interred in several distinct mortuary episodes, possibly related to the use of a charnel house. Radiocarbon dates associated with these burials ranged from 5500 to 5000 B.P. (Milanich 1994:82–83; Milanich and Fairbanks 1980:147–152).

Evidence supporting the involvement of Mount Taylor groups in regional-scale social interaction consists of a variety of artifacts made from nonlocal lithic materials, particularly atlatl weights (fig. 12-4) of stone originating far to the north in South Carolina, Georgia, and Tennessee (Milanich and Fairbanks 1980:151; Piatek 1994:111–112). For example, excavations conducted in the early 1880s at the Tomoka Mounds in Volusia County by A. E. Douglass (1882) yielded seven atlatl weights made of steatite (1), diabase (2), ferruginous stone (1), fine limestone (1), and greenstone (2). A greenstone pendant made from a broken "bannerstone" was also found (Piatek 1994:111).

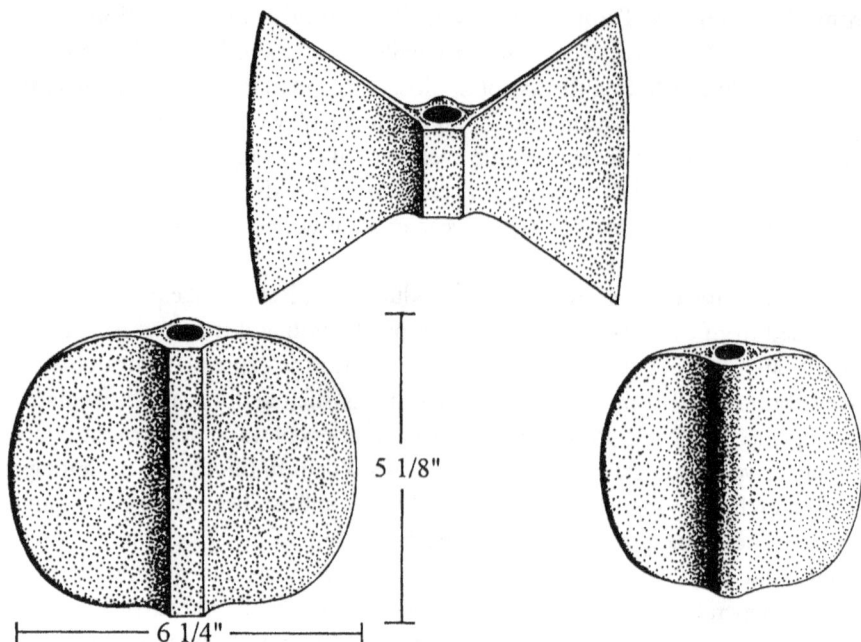

Fig. 12-4.   Atlatl weights from the Tomoka Mounds, Volusia County, Florida (from Piatek 1994).

The size and depth of the Tomoka Mound Complex suggest that the site represents a relatively large and permanent village. A single calibrated radiocarbon date from the base of one of the mounds indicates that mound construction was under way by 4629 B.P. Collectively, data from Tomoka and other Mount Taylor sites indicate that inhabitants were well adapted to the environs of coastal east Florida and were sufficiently settled and organized to construct complex mortuary facilities (Piatek 1994:117).

Again, the coincidence of the development of regional-scale social or exchange networks and the establishment of a more sedentary way of life is striking. Obviously, much more research will be needed before the nature of interaction between Mount Taylor groups and other late Middle Archaic groups living in the surrounding regions is understood.

Summary and Conclusions

Data from several areas of the Southeast and Midwest suggest that regional-scale social/exchange networks were starting to develop by about 6000 B.P. The emergence of these networks may reflect similar responses by regionally distinct late Middle Archaic groups to increasing social and environmental risk associated with increased sedentism and the breakdown of traditional communication and interaction mechanisms used by more mobile hunter-gatherer groups. Several researchers have suggested that exchange networks represent risk-averting mechanisms that compensated for the loss of information and materials formerly obtained through more direct intergroup contact. Increased social interaction among groups participating in these exchange networks is reflected archaeologically by the distribution of certain kinds of artifacts and raw materials and by a greater similarity of artifact styles within the region inhabited by those groups.

In order to assure that risk-averting mechanisms were sufficient to meet the needs of local groups, networks included groups that were distributed over a sufficient space to reduce the chances of the same risks or threats impacting all groups. Examples discussed here extended over hundreds of kilometers of prime riverine habitats containing abundant and diverse subsistence resources.

A trading partner who directly participated in intergroup exchange would have had access to exotic materials, esoteric knowledge, and practical information not generally available to other group members. As suggested by Marquardt (1985), such an individual could conceivably use this knowledge to benefit the whole group, thereby increasing his or her prestige and status. Differentiation of these individuals might eventually lead to the emergence of more formalized leadership positions and the development of more complex expressions of sociopolitical organization. Late Archaic Green River burials containing copper and marine shell may reflect the existence of these new leadership positions some 500 to 1000 years later.

Late Middle Archaic groups inhabiting parts of the Southeast and Midwest where no evidence of regional-scale interaction has been found may have developed other kinds of risk-averting mechanisms to cope with increased levels of social and environmental stress. Alternatively, this lack of evidence may reflect areas where less complex groups of hunter-gatherers lived and where increased levels of risk had not yet developed. The co-occurrence of hunter-gatherer groups having strikingly different levels of social complexity has led Sassaman (1995a) to suggest that these less sedentary, apparently less complex groups may be explained as the historical consequence of their splitting from more complex groups of sedentary hunter-gatherers. These less complex groups appear to have maintained highly mobile lifestyles and open social interactions as a way of resisting domination by neighboring groups.

Future research should focus on further clarifying those environmental and social factors contributing to the development of mid-Holocene social networks and on improving our understanding of the scale, direction, and mechanics of interaction among participating regional groups. Efforts should also be made to identify those factors contributing to the existence of apparently less complex mid-Holocene societies that also inhabited the midwestern and southeastern United States.

Acknowledgments

This chapter represents a continuation of research started in 1992 on the development of mid-Holocene social networks. Portions of the information here are also included in a paper presented at the 1992 Southeastern Archaeological Conference in Little Rock, Arkansas, and later published (Jefferies 1995). Figure 12-1 was drafted by John Scarry, Department of Anthropology, University of North Carolina. Figure 12-3 courtesy Jay K. Johnson; figure 12-4 reprinted courtesy Southeastern Archaeological Conference. The assistance of Kenneth E. Sassaman (SCIAA) and Mary Lucas Powell (University of Kentucky) is gratefully acknowledged, as is the help of several anonymous reviewers.

13

A Consideration of the Social Organization of the Shell Mound Archaic

CHERYL P. CLAASSEN

The Shell Mound Archaic (SMA), known so vividly from excavations of deep shell mounds on the Tennessee and Green rivers, has been explained to the satisfaction of many as a reflection of human response to environmental stimuli. Riverine conditions favored shellfish proliferation, attracting human predators, and then waned, losing their attention. Howard Winters's (1968) assertion that the SMA was also a social phenomenon was a significant break with previous research and a stimulus for succeeding work on social exchange and differentiation. Perhaps because of the invigoration Winters's work brought to the study of this prehistoric culture, Middle and Late Archaic intensification of shellfishing and burial ceremonialism attracted the full firepower of environmental determinists. Seventeen years later Bender (1985) found it necessary to remind those of us studying the Archaic that ecological constraints are reflected in social imperatives, that all labor is socially construed, and that adaptation is about social reproduction. The environmental determinists demonstrated a co-occurrence of environmental stimuli and cultural activity that is of interest, but the environmental changes of the Altithermal impacted the entire eastern United States. It is because Archaic shell and dirt mounds occur in so few places that environmental stimuli are insufficient to explain the cultural phenomenon known as the SMA. Social factors must have weighed heavily in the locus and evolution of this culture and those with which it interacted. In this chapter, after defining the SMA, I will take stock of recent thinking and data relevant to the social organization involved, highlighting issues of site function, gender, and exchange. Given that sample sizes for many of these topics are woefully small, this review provides less in the way of statements of fact than in the way of stimulus for future research. I draw heavily on recent research projects, new compilations of previously gathered data, and the presentation of new data on beads.

Defining the Shell Mound Archaic

Discussing the Shell Mound Archaic requires deciding just which regional manifestations of the eastern United States 8000 to 2000 years ago are to be included and excluded. All involved would agree that the label refers to the sites clustered on the Green River in Kentucky and on the Tennessee River of Tennessee and Alabama. A number of researchers have placed the shell mounds and rings of the Savannah River, the South Carolina and Georgia coasts (Crusoe and DePratter 1976; Fairbanks 1942), the hilltop middens in West Virginia (Mayer-Oakes 1955), and the mounds on the St. Johns River into this cultural manifestation.

One is hard pressed to find stated criteria for defining the SMA other than the presence of mounded shell, in a pile or in a ring. Morse (1967) seems to define the phenomenon by its settlement pattern—winter camps established in the anticipation of deer yarding—a strategy that he says neighboring groups lacked. He states that using the criterion of shell mounds to define the culture is invalid (1967:246). In the Savannah River valley and along the adjacent coastline and in the St. Johns River valley, the presence of fiber-tempered pottery or a site type with much shell in the matrix qualifies a site for inclusion. Rolingson (1967:3) explicitly excluded sites on the Atlantic Slope.

Several years ago I utilized the criteria of human burial in mounded shell with few indications of features (Claassen 1991a), including only the cluster of sites on the Tennessee and Green rivers and in the Nashville basin. Work since 1986 has reminded us, however, of the variation in a number of elements in the sites within the Green River valley alone—in burial location, in shell presence or absence and density, in dog burials, etc.—which means that heretofore excluded sites might well be included when they fall within the range of variation seen at Green River valley sites. Given the mounting evidence for widespread mound construction during the Late Archaic, not all of which seems to contain burials, I wonder now if the great heaps of shell elsewhere in the East should not also be added to future considerations of the SMA. I would draw attention particularly to the deep blufftop shell accumulations found on the eastern bank of the Hudson River and the Archaic mounds on the coasts of Florida. Table 13-1 gives a partial list of the sites assigned to the SMA by their reporters or by Morse (1967).

The problem of definition is not only one of geography but also one of time. Sites assigned to the SMA have components radiocarbon dated from 7180 to 2400 B.P. Chronological control of these sites is perhaps the least well developed of any manifestation in the eastern United States, forcing a reliance on the criterion of shell mounding. It is currently impossible to say which of all of these sites were occupied earliest. Viewing table 13-2, one can see that radiocarbon dates greater than 6000 B.P. have been returned on samples from Eva (Eva component), Anderson, and Ervin, on three different rivers—the Tennessee, Harpeth, and Duck, respectively. (The early dates on Kirkland are viewed by Haskins [1992] as erroneous.) From 6000 to 5000 B.P., intensive shellfishing occurred on

Table 13-1. Freshwater shell-bearing mound sites of the Middle and Late Archaic periods

West Tennessee	Duck, Harpeth, Cumberland	Central Tennessee	Savannah, Ogechee	St. Johns
Big Sandy	Anderson	Perry	Rabbit Mount	Bluffton
Eva	Ervin	Vaughn	Stallings Island	Black Hammock
Kay's Landing	Hayes	Bluff Creek	Bilbo	Hontoon Island
Ledbetter	Penitentiary Branch	Ct 17	Fennel Hill	King Philiptown
	Robinson	Ct 19	Midden Point	Mt. Royal
	40SM1	Ct 24	Lake Spring	Mt. Taylor
	40SM8	Georgetown	Chew Mill	Orange
	40SM10	Li 36	Strange	Possum Bluff
	40JK10	Long Branch		Rock Island
		Lu 86		Tick Island
		Town Creek		
		Ma 4		
		Mulberry Creek		
		O'Neal		
		Smithsonia		
		Union Hollow		

Upper Ohio	Middle Ohio	Wabash	Green
Brenneman	Crib	Riverton	Carlston Annis
East Steubenville	Cut-off	Robeson Hills	Butterfield
Globe Hill	McCain		Jimtown
New Cumberland	Swan Island		DeWeese
	Clarksville		Chiggerville
	Reid		Indian Knoll
	Ferry Landing		Read
	Miller		16HE637
	Kyang		16HE638
			Wilson-Seymour
			Hollins
			Ebelhar
			Taylor
			Bowles
			Jackson Bluff

Table 13-2. Radiocarbon dates for freshwater shell-bearing sites

Site	Depth	Date B.P.	Date B.C.	Sample #	Reference
Eva, TN	St. IV	7150±500	—	M 357	Lewis and Lewis 1961
Anderson, TN	—	7180±230	—	URC 1941	Dowd 1989
	—	6720±220	—	GX 8215	Dowd 1989
	—	6700±150	—	URC 1940	Dowd 1989
	—	6490±205	—	GX 8365	Dowd 1989
	—	5680±200	—	Gx 9900	Dowd 1989
Kirkland, KY	—	7320±80	6127	ISGS 2299	Haskins 1992
	—	6600±80	5493	ISGS 2298	Haskins 1992
	Bu 40	5650±80	5680	Beta 82081	Claassen
	—	4240±150	2892	ISGS 2306	Haskins 1992
	—	3990±160	2544	ISGS 2304	Haskins 1992
	—	3830±80	2299	ISGS 2297	Haskins 1992
Ervin, TN	base plowzone	6645±185	—	GX 9082	Hall et al. 1985
	—	6160±175	—	GX 9954	Hall et al. 1985
	—	6115±205	—	GX 8918	Hall et al. 1985
	—	5765±200	—	GX 8917	Hall et al. 1985
Vaughn, MS	—	6010±95	4660	UGa 689	Atkinson 1974
	—	—	3800	UGa 688	Atkinson 1974
Hayes, TN	St. IV2	5870±165	—	GX 9081	Hall et al. 1985
	—	5245±230	—	GX 9315	Hall et al. 1985
	St. II	4270±155	—	GX 9080	Hall et al. 1985
Miller, IN	6–15″	5220	4040–4060	M 2389-2391	Janzen 1977
Reid, IN	Zone 3	5480±90	4400	UGa 309	Janzen 1977
	Zone 3	4555±70	3350–3370	UGa 267	Janzen 1977
Tick Island, FL	—	5450	—	M 1268	Bullen 1972
	—	5320	—	M 1265	Bullen 1972
	—	5030	—	M 1264	Bullen 1972
Carlston Annis, KY	—	5730±640	—	UA AMS	Watson 1985
	L 19	5350±80	—	WIS 1302	Marquardt and Watson 1983
	—	5149±300	—	C 116	Winters 1974
	L 9	5030±85	—	UGa 3393	Marquardt and Watson 1983
	—	4900±250	—	C 251	Winters 1974
	L 13	4760±90	—	WIS 1301	Marquardt and Watson 1983
	L 15	4670±85	—	UGa 3391	Marquardt and Watson 1983
	L 7	4655±540	—	UGa 3395	Marquardt and Watson 1983
	L 12	4500±60	—	UCLA 2117I	Marquardt and Watson 1983
	L 20	4350±85	—	UGa 3390	Marquardt and Watson 1983
	—	4333±450	3025	C 739	Winters 1974
	—	4289±300	2970	C 738	Winters 1974
	L 10	4250±80	2924	UCLA 1845A	Marquardt and Watson 1983
	L 8	4040±180	2655	UCLA 1845B	Marquardt and Watson 1983
	L 5	3330±80	—	UCLA 2117B	Marquardt and Watson 1983
	L 15	2515±80	—	UCLA 2117D	Marquardt and Watson 1983
Indian Knoll, KY	12″	5302±300	4160	C 254	Winters 1974
	12″	4282±250	2962	C 740	Winters 1974
	53″	3963±350	2558	C 741	Winters 1974

Table 13-2—*Continued*

Site	Depth	Date B.P.	Date B.C.	Sample #	Reference
Perry, AL	3.5–4.0′	4764±250	—	C 756-755	Lewis and Kneberg 1959
Stallings Island, GA	70″	4700±150	—	M 1279	Sassaman 1993a
	70″	4450±150	—	M 1277	Sassaman 1993a
	30″	3730±150	—	M 1278	Sassaman 1993a
Rabbit Mount, SC	L. B2	4450±135	—	GXO 343	Sassaman 1993a
	L. B2	4465±95	—	GXO 345	Sassaman 1993a
Kay's Landing, TN	St. V; 96″	4750±500	—	M 108	Lewis and Kneberg 1959
	St. II	4050±300	—	M 109	Lewis and Kneberg 1959
	St. II	3580±300	—	M 356	Lewis and Kneberg 1959
Old Clarksville, IN	—	4460±180	3210	M 2308	Janzen 1977
	—	4460±180	3210	M 2309	Janzen 1977
	—	4180±180	2920	M 2307	Janzen 1977
East Steubenville, WV	—	4220±500	2830	M 229	Murphy 1977
Globe Hill, WV	—	4120±220	2610	CWR 184	Murphy 1977
Bilbo, GA	5.5–6′	4125±115	—	O 1047	Sassaman 1993a
	5.5–6′	3820±125	—	M 1111	Sassaman 1993a
	3–3.5′	3700±125	—	M 1109	Sassaman 1993a
	5.5–6′	3730±125	—	M 1112	Sassaman 1993a
Bowles, KY	—	4060±220	—	UA AMS	Watson 1985
	L 11	3440±80	—	UCLA 2117G	Marquardt and Watson 1983
	—	2420±200	—	UCLA 2117F	Marquardt and Watson 1983
	—	1820±300	—	UCLA 2117E	Marquardt and Watson 1983
Penitentiary Branch, TN	—	3600±195	2071	GX 8582	Cridlebaugh 1986
	—	3375±345	1777	UGa 1626	Cridlebaugh 1986
	—	3185±165	1528	UGa 1628	Cridlebaugh 1986
	—	3050±140	1357	UGa 1627	Cridlebaugh 1986
	—	2975±145	1261	GX 8584	Cridlebaugh 1986
	—	2370±205	503	GX 8583	Cridlebaugh 1986
Read, KY	—	3470±200	1771	ISGS 2245	Haskins 1992
	—	3400±100	1712	ISGS 2246	Haskins 1992
	—	3350±70	1658	ISGS 2249	Haskins 1992
Robeson, IL	—	3490±200	—	M 1288	Winters 1969
	—	3440±200	—	M 1289	Winters 1969
Swan Island, IL	60″	3450±125	—	I 1461	Winters 1969
	30–36″	3450±120	—	I 1462	Winters 1969
Riverton, IL	36–42″	3460±250	—	M 1285	Winters 1969
	84–123″	3320±140	—	I 1463	Winters 1969
	60–66″	3200±200	—	M 1286	Winters 1969
	78–84″	3270±250	—	M 1287	Winters 1969
	18–24″	3110±200	—	M 1284	Winters 1969
Robinson, TN	—	3200±160	—	M 1797	Morse 1967
	—	3230±160	—	M 1800	Morse 1967
	—	2970±150	—	M 1798	Morse 1967
	—	2970±150	—	M 1799	Morse 1967
	—	2830±130	—	M 1802	Morse 1967
	—	2630±130	—	M 1805	Morse 1967
	—	2530±150	—	M 1801	Morse 1967
	—	2450±140	—	M 1803	Morse 1967
	—	2410±200	—	M 1806	Morse 1967
Walker, TN	—	2915±80	—	?	Dye 1980

the Ohio River at Miller and Reid, the Green at Read, at the Vaughn site in Mississippi, and on the St. Johns River at Tick Island. Midway through this millennium, accumulations ceased on the Duck and Harpeth rivers in the Nashville basin. From 5000 to 4500 B.P., intensive harvesting of freshwater shellfish took place in the Pickwick basin (Perry) and on the Savannah River (Rabbit Mount). Late in the millennium, freshwater shellfishing was possibly under way on the upper Ohio River (the dates from East Steubenville and Globe Hill should be redone), while intensive shellfishing ceased at the sites in the fall of the Ohio River region (Janzen 1977). The phenomenon spread to the Wabash River some 3400 years ago. The latest deposits now known are those at the Robinson site on the Cumberland and at the Walker site, 2500 to 3000 B.P. The Robinson and Walker communities most certainly had neighbors in the Pickwick and Wheeler basins and on the Savannah and St. Johns rivers, however.

Inception of the Shell Mound Archaic

An understanding of what has traditionally been called the SMA, and more specifically of the social organization that maintained it, is framed by our understanding of its inception. Scholars have been nearly unanimous in their depiction of the events leading up to the Late Archaic florescence of the SMA. First, environmental conditions in the mid-Holocene made riverine shellfish available in abundance to the opportunistic Middle Archaic human predator; shellfish were added to a broadening predation pattern made necessary by shrinking human territories; the resource proved so reliable and bountiful that social complexity increased and was focused in areas of abundant shellfish. Recently, it has been argued that the resource was suitably abundant in only a few areas and thus became a contested resource for which ownership markers—shell piles—were needed (Hofman 1985:198; Walthall 1980:66; see also Charles and Buikstra 1983:177). Where these shell mounds were located was dictated by the environment, while their contents reflected both environmental strictures and social negotiations.

Upon closer scrutiny, however, the role of the environment in this scenario fades. The Mississippi and St. Lawrence river systems have the richest freshwater molluscan fauna in the world. In fact, eastern North America has roughly one half of all species of freshwater bivalves in the world (Stansbery 1970:9). Historic records of musseling activity for the freshwater shell-button industry indicate that nearly every river in the Mississippi Valley watershed yielded bivalves in quantity suitable for commercial exploitation for many decades. These records, presented in detail elsewhere (Claassen 1994), will be sampled now to impress upon the reader the abundance of the resource.

From 1891 until 1950, 108 rivers were harvested repeatedly for the freshwater shell-button industry and a number of them have provided the total shell inventory for the Japanese cultured pearl industry since 1955. The Illinois River has produced commercially viable quantities of shell almost every year since 1907 and quantities remain high: 1159 tons sold in 1965 and 204 tons sold in 1986. In the Kampsville area, 150 boats got daily yields of 700 pounds of shell per musseler in 1912. In the first three months of that shelling season, 1000 tons of shells were sold from Hardin. Two years earlier a buyer received 122 tons at Gafton. In the Valley City area in 1910, 40 boats dredged 200 tons of shell, while 17 tons had been shipped from there by July of 1912.

The largest and best mussel beds in the Cumberland River are located between Nashville and Dover (an area with no recorded prehistoric shell-bearing sites). The Meeks Spring bar had been worked for 10 years by 1913, yielding over 600 tons of shells in that period. Eighty-eight tons awaited sale on Gower's Island in 1913. Two buyers working the Cumberland River from Nashville to Paducah bought 2283 tons of shell in 1907, 1900 tons in 1908, 1600 tons in 1909, and 1125 tons in 1910. There were several other buyers operating in the area as well.

The Mississippi River dividing Iowa and Illinois has been musseled without interruption since 1891. When state record keeping began in 1974, 735 tons of shell were sold; in 1986 the figure was 2916 tons. After two years of heavy shelling in the Fox River (Illinois) at the Five Island bed, the average annual haul was 10–12 tons per sheller.

There were, then, at least one hundred rivers (in addition to streams and lakes) that could have yielded shellfish in rewarding quantities for the Archaic human predator, from South Dakota and Minnesota through Oklahoma to Alabama and central Ohio. Quantities harvested varied over time not due to abundance but due to market issues. Most of the extremely productive rivers for the historic industries—the Black, White, St. Francis, Neosho, Des Moines, Illinois, Fox, Mississippi, Muskingham—lack Archaic sites with freshwater shell in any quantity. Only in Alabama, on the Tennessee River, does the prehistoric level of exploitation foreshadow the historic level of shellfishing. Nor am I the first to make this observation. "The concentration of Archaic shell midden sites in the Green River drainage is most remarkable, given the fact that mussel beds were common in streams throughout Kentucky" (Hockensmith et al. 1983). Kneberg (1952:92) observed that shell mounds were not found upriver from Chattanooga, even though "shoals where clams might be secured are present." The same can be said of streams in the Piedmont of South Carolina.

This abundance of shellfish is not a historic phenomenon. Conditions for shellfish reproduction have steadily deteriorated during this century. Dozens of species are now extinct. Dams have raised silt loads to intolerable levels in many streams; heat and chemical discharges have killed molluscan communities. Instead, this richness and abundance of the molluscan fauna have been characteristic of the Mississippi River watershed throughout the time humans have occupied the continent. Malacologists retrodict this abundance of shells into the Pleistocene (e.g., La Rocque 1966:15; Stansbery 1970:9). In northern Ohio, the Wisconsin ice sheets withdrew, leaving "a vast forested area dotted with lakes and streams that supported, among other forms of life, an abundant molluscan fauna almost identical in composition with the living molluscan fauna of northern lakes" (La Rocque 1966:15). "The conditions for speciation of stream dwelling animals has [*sic*] been nearly ideal in eastern North America for many million years. . . . Although the prehistoric North American Indians utilized prodigious quantities of these mollusks their harvests apparently had little effect on the survival of these species. A comparison of the shells recovered from prehistoric mounds and midden heaps with pioneer lists reveals that the species composition of our streams had not changed appreciably for at least six to eight thousand years" (Stansbery 1970:9).

The implication of this incongruity between the locations of prehistoric shell-bearing sites and historic musseling endeavors is that social considerations of 8000 to 2000 years ago overrode environmental considerations to determine where these sites were founded and where they persisted. The environmental determinism argument cites environmental changes that impacted the entire eastern United States. It is because Archaic shell-dirt mounds occur in so few places that neither optimal foraging theory nor environmental change can explain either their advent or demise. Instead, sites attributable to the SMA constitute a landscape shaped by social concerns.

Social Organization

The Shell Mound Archaic is to be understood principally as a social phenomenon, so much so that even site location and matrix were expressions of cultural concerns. What some of these social concerns might have been is the focus of the second half of this paper. I will address the topics of site function, gender, and exchange for areas where my predecessors have applied the concept of the Shell Mound Archaic.

Site Function

Funkhouser and Webb judged the shell mounds of Kentucky to be villages lived in continuously over many years (although speculating on seasonal occupation in the same volume [1932:425]). By the end of the WPA era, opinion held that these sites were permanent villages. Janzen (1977) claimed that shell sites in the Falls of the Ohio River area represented permanent occupations, as did Trinkley (1979) for the shell rings of South Carolina and Mayer-Oakes (1955:19) for the hilltop middens of West Virginia.

Rolingson (1967) concluded that the occupations were discontinuous and primarily seasonal. Concluding that there had been a summer-fall occupation of Green River valley and western Tennessee River valley shell-bearing sites were Marquardt and Watson (1983), Claassen (1986), and Hofman (1986c). Arguing for winter occupation for the large Midsouth mounds was Morse (1967). Thanz (1977:16) made the same claim for the Orange period coastal shell mounds in Florida (cf. Russo, chap. 10, this volume).

Considering the activities implicated by the various artifact classes at different Green River shell mounds, Winters (1974) proposed that these locations should not be considered a single site type. Instead of all shell mounds being villages or settlements, Winters found that some were more appropriately considered transient camps, hunting camps, and base camps. Russo (1991:490) sees the numerous St. Johns River sites as the result of residential mobility with few logistical hunting or fishing camps in the site sample. Michie (1979) believed that the irregular shell matrix sites on the South Carolina coast were extractive camps and that the shell rings were base camps. Hofman (1985, 1986c) defined the function of aggregation camp for Ervin and for the contemporaneous activities at Eva, both in Tennessee. Aggregation camps were places of predictable abundant resources, where dispersed families came together for a season of ritual including burial of cremated, bundled, and flesh bodies. Hensley (1991:91) redefined six of the Green River shell mounds as aggregation sites—Carlston Annis, Indian Knoll, Barrett, Butterfield, Chiggerville, and Read—and equivocated on such an assignment for the shell-free Kirkland and Ward sites. The shell-mound sites of Jimstown Hill, Baker, and Jackson were not seen as aggregation sites because of their low density of cultural materials and few burials. The burial program at these three sites was thought to equate to that of a family burial plot rather than the "tribal" burial grounds at aggregation locations. Hofman (1986c) also equated the smaller burial populations in contemporaneous winter rock shelter sites of the Midwest to family burial areas.

For over a decade now, evidence of Middle and Late Archaic intentional mound building in the eastern United States has been accumulating (see Russo, chap. 14, this volume, for a detailed discussion of Archaic mounds). The rock and earth mortuary mound at the Hobart Bride site (Kay 1983:51) and others in the Nebo Hill phase of the lower Missouri valley (Reid 1983), and similar mounds in the late Helton-Titterington phases of Illinois (Fortier 1983) were erected 5000 to 4000 years ago. Recent research in Louisiana and Arkansas has sustained the Archaic age assignment of the Monte Sano site (Haag 1992), the LSU campus site (Neuman and Homburg 1992), Stelly and Courtableau mounds (Fogelman 1992), four complexes in northeastern Louisiana (Saunders et al. 1994), and the Lake Enterprise mound (Jackson and Jeter 1994). Russo (1991, chap. 14, this volume) has argued the Archaic age and intentional construction of the Horr's Island shell mounds 5000 years ago and the case has been made for the Tomoka mounds on the northeast Florida coast (Piatek 1994).

As evidence mounts for the construction of burial and ceremonial mounds before 4000 years ago in the Southeast, it is appropriate that we reconsider the interpretation of the Archaic shell mounds as simply villages where people lived and were buried among their garbage, and entertain the hypothesis that these mounds were actually ceremonial mounds similar to later Woodland period mounds. There are some data in the site reports suggesting that this idea is worth pursuing and was present in the 1930s and 1940s.

The Vaughn mound is a shell-bearing Archaic site located on the Tombigbee River in Mississippi near Columbus. Its earliest inhabitants some 6500 years ago "initiated construction of the mound by erecting low, primary earthen mounds over the flexed or semiflexed corpses of their dead. . . . These low earthen mounds, comprised of fill containing occupational and midden debris, seem to have grown by accretion until perhaps the entire basal one half of the mound consisted solely of smaller, contiguous burial mounds" (Atkinson 1974). Shellfish were moderate in quantity within Zone 1 but more prevalent in Zones 2 and 3. The abundance of shell, the mounding of shell, and flexed burials with few grave goods in the shell-dirt mound led to an assignment of this mound to the Shell Mound Archaic. The constituent mounds were said to be of reused village refuse.

At site Li 36 in the Wheeler basin (Tennessee River), Webb observed that after the burial stratum, the site was abandoned as a dwelling place but continued to be used "as a kitchen midden and as a burial ground. This would account for the midden layer above the hearths as well as the burials and the fact that no other hearths, post holes, or signs of occupancy were found" (Webb 1939:79).

At the Long Branch site (Lu 67) in the Pickwick basin, the basal layer was composed of clean shell with no soil and showed no evidence of occupation (Webb and DeJarnette 1942:180). At Lu 59 (Pickwick), the basal deposit was a compact shell layer containing only two knives. The O'Neal site in the same basin had layers of clean shell alternating with other types of layers. Several burials had been surrounded with clean shell and the pits sealed with a layer of clean shell (Webb and DeJarnette 1942:134).

A formal burial area in the Orange site on the St. Johns River was dug by C. B. Moore (Milanich and Fairbanks 1980:151). Russo (1994a) has recently discussed the Tick Island site as an Archaic ceremonial mound. The oldest documented use of shell in South Carolina is at Mims Point, where it occurs in a mortuary context (Sassaman 1993c). The basal stratum at Bilbo and at a number of the shell rings is clean shell (Kenneth Sassaman, personal communication, 1994).

In 1928, Funkhouser and Webb puzzled over the reason behind the mounds, wondering if the human burials were intrusive or the reason the mounds were constructed. The thought that these sites were not habitation areas must have annoyed Webb for in several publications can be found a sentence that reassures the reader that these loci surely were villages. There is also the indirect evidence that these were sacred mounds provided by the later use of the mounds for burial and for sites of earthen and sand burial mounds. For instance, the center of the McKelvey Mound in Pickwick basin was directly over "a considerable shell heap," which itself contained sherds, bones, burials, and occasional artifacts. Copena burial mounds were often erected atop the Archaic mounds. Woodland and Mississippian peoples continued to utilize these mounds as burial loci, further suggesting that the places had accumulated considerable "power" and were part of a symbolic landscape.

At Horr's Island, Russo (1991) found that nearly 2000 years of shell accumulation had been under way before the mounds were constructed 5000 years ago and that intrusive burials appeared 1000 years later. He argues that most of the mound accumulated gradually through the primary deposition of shell debris generated by on-mound ritual activities rather than by permanent occupation. The completed mound afforded too little space to be the site of any more than one common-sized house, if there were any there at all. The numerous mounds at the site were thought to have been constructed/renewed gradually so that no permanently supported leadership was necessary.

I do not wish to speculate on whether all shell-mound aggregation sites were initiated as burial mounds or if some later ones were while older ones came to assume that function as they accrued spiritual power through the earlier burials in them. It does seem necessary to this hypothesis to specify that at the time burial activities ceased at these locations, at least some of them were functioning solely as burial mounds. (Since I first proposed that the shell mounds were ceremonial mounds [Claassen 1988], several individuals have reevaluated this idea [Claassen 1992; Hensley 1991; Watson 1992].)

While not shell mounds, the shell-bearing sites at Globe Hill, East Steubenville, Brenneman, and New Cumberland Heights on the upper Ohio River in West Virginia have locations that suggest a ceremonial purpose. All are located on the tops of bluffs overlooking the river, not on the floodplain where shell-free Archaic sites have been identified. Globe Hill is a shell midden on top of a high hill, 140 feet above the Ohio River. The East Steubenville shell midden is located on a bluff more than 100 feet above the present level of the river, with a trail to the site that is quite precipitous. The one human body in the shell deposit had a spear lodged in a vertebra (Mayer-Oakes 1955:132). The Banneman site is likewise situated 140 feet above the Ohio River. The New Cumberland Heights shell midden is 310 feet above present river level (Mayer-Oakes 1955:130).

Having a similar location to the West Virginia sites is Robeson Hills on the Wabash in Illinois. This shell-bearing site is 100 feet above the river. "Flanking the site on the west and south are deep ravines containing intermittent streams, while the Wabash River flows close to the foot of the bluff on the east side, thus the site occupies an isolated promontory" (Winters 1969:13). Such too are the locations of a dozen more Middle and Late Archaic sites with large quantities of shell in the Hudson River valley of New York. Sites such as the 7000-year-old Dogan Point, with oyster shell deposits four feet thick in some areas, sat more than 10 feet above and 600 feet east of the Hudson River at the time of occupation.

The sites of Globe Hill, Banneman, East Steubenville, New Cumberland Heights (all in West Virginia), and Robeson Hills (Illinois) have in common with Archaic burial sites and mounds from the Midwest their hilltop location. Especially pertinent to the case being made here for a ceremonial function to these sites is an observation made by Brown referring to the Archaic midwestern mounds: "I find it revealing that these mounds resemble later and larger mounds more for their hilltop locations and the compactness of interment in a single disposal facility than in their 'moundedness.' It suggests that the actual size of the fill placed on top of these facilities was unimportant in the beginning and only took on the 'Woodland sized' dimensions much later and as a by-product of other factors" (Brown 1983:9).

It is the burial practices of the Green River and Tennessee River sites in addition to the height or depth of shell mounding that lie at the heart of the concept of the SMA. With the exception of shell, these burial practices are not unique. Many Archaic cultures in the eastern United States buried humans flexed in round pits; buried dogs; used red ochre; and included atlatl parts, copper objects, and marine shell beads in the graves. Twenty-five years ago, Rolingson (1967) recognized in the Green River an undefined burial complex, which we have yet to define.

Burial mounds or not, several archaeologists have identified formal cemeteries at SMA sites: at Butterfield where 90 burials were concentrated (Rolingson 1967:337), at Barrett (Hensley 1991), at Robinson (Morse 1967), at Tick Island (Milanich and Fairbanks 1980:151), and at Vaughn (Atkinson 1974). Variation has been observed in the placement of burials. At Indian Knoll 55 percent of the burials are placed in the hardpan below the shell, while at Carlston Annis only 16 percent are so located. Eighty-two percent of the bodies were among the shells at Carlston Annis but only 42 percent are there at Read and slightly more at Butterfield. Comparable data from mounds in other regions are lacking (Hensley 1991). There is also variation in how the bodies were treated at the time of interment, suggesting to some researchers social ranking in the population (Rothschild 1979; Winters 1968).

The presence of formal cemeteries has been interpreted to indicate competition over scarce resources and a need to claim and visibly mark territories and resources. Shellfish have been proposed as the contested resource in the SMA area (Walthall 1980), but such an expectation is predicated on the notion that shellfish were a limited, even point-specific, resource. If the only origin of cemeteries lies in competition, perhaps it is not a discrete resource but access to mates or a territory of sufficient size that is being marked, as discussed in the next section.

Gender

Some researchers have proposed that competition over alliances was a driving social issue in the Archaic of the midcontinent (Bender 1985; Sassaman 1995a). Sassaman (1995a) suggests that the most stable of alliances were those made through marriage and that the most productive of marriages were polygynous. The frequent incidence of traumatic deaths and parry fractures in SMA populations are attributed by Sassaman to conflict over mates. Restrictions on potential spouses would not be expected in kin-based societies but would occur in sociopolitical organizations with clans or moieties. Sassaman sees these extralineage groupings beginning by Middle Archaic times and characterizing the members of the SMA. He suspects that they were never uniformly adopted because of the labor demands, and ultimately proved too laborious for many of the Archaic societies of the Southeast.

Nurit Goldman-Finn (personal communication, 1993), Sassaman (1993a), and

I (Claassen 1991a) have raised the point that previous archaeologists have ignored the impact of new technology and different social practices on labor organization in the Middle and Late Archaic. Technological innovations appear to have impacted women's lives the most, if we follow through on the stereotypes. The SMA was the cultural context for a burgeoning plant-processing technology, for the adoption of cultigens (Watson and Kennedy 1991), for intensive shellfishing (Claassen 1991a), and for pottery adoption (Sassaman 1993a). For men we have imputed the new endeavors of copper and shell ornament manufacture (with minor labor requirements), the maintenance of trade relationships (Sassaman 1993a), and atlatl technology. I would add the construction and maintenance of mounds to the workloads of both sexes. How were these new activities accommodated by our SMA actors? Did they incorporate previously unproductive community members? Did they substitute new tasks for old ones? Did they divide labor more strictly?

Rather than being a cooperative enterprise, division of labor is a symptom of competition and arises, I believe, as a means of minimizing or reducing competition by dividing up the environment to assure that there is something for everyone. It is analogous to speciation in acultural life forms. Dividing labor so that subsets of individuals now sought reserved resources and were restricted from others was a plausible way of minimizing competition within and between communities.

Opportunistic laboring, when whoever is at hand performs the activity regardless of age, gender, status, etc., would probably be accompanied by shared tools and facilities in shared camps, keeping the numbers of tools (and sites) low. An important ramification of a stricter division of labor where people responded by pooling into many smaller social units would be the creation of many more tools, for each unit would need a complete inventory of tools for the labors it performed, often at a distance from other social units to minimize competition. This redundancy of residential units and sites would account for the increased numbers of subsistence-related tools in the Middle and Late Archaic remarked upon by many authors. The year-round community life of the late Pleistocene/early Holocene may have been replaced by the short-term aggregation site of the Middle and Late Archaic.

Division of labor was of interest to Dan Morse (1967) also. Morse equates pestles, mullers, hammerstones, hearths, bone tubes (menstrual drinking straws, he posits), and broken atlatls (1967:291) with women generally and observed that dog burials at Barrett, terrapin carapaces at Carlston Annis, and bone needles at Eva were usually associated with females. Men were associated with functional atlatls and axes generally; with whistles and rattles at Barrett; and with medicine bags, fishhooks, and the one plummet at Indian Knoll. Morse interpreted the presence of "women's objects" as evidence for kin group occupation (1967:251). More men were often present among the burials because every effort would be made to return the body of a man to the village (Morse 1967:294).

Winters had a different list of male- and female-associated objects from Indian Knoll (1968:205–208). Female-linked grave goods were domestic equipment (e.g., nutting stones), certain ornaments (e.g., bone beads), and gravers. Most pestles were observed with women. "Definitely linked male grave goods were axes, cannon bone awls, fishhooks, groundhog incisors, antler drifts, flakers, antler chisels, and animal bones and jaws of several species." More men were buried with dogs, more women with red ochre. Men and women equally often received grave goods, flutes, atlatls, and turtle-shell rattles. (Kelley's [n.d.] reassessment of Indian Knoll sex did not result in any modifications to these gendered associations. What the age and sex changes do invalidate are the discussion by Morse of the age-at-death differences between males and females.)

What bead data I have been able to generate or appropriate (table 13-3) indicate that most patterns in gender associations at the site level may not be patterns at a regional scale. Women are said to have received less marine shell than did men, particularly fewer disk beads (Winters 1968:198). While both statements are true at Indian Knoll, viewing either the number of beads or the number of burials, and at Perry, neither statement is true at Chiggerville, Barrett, Robinson, Kay's Landing, or Cherry (although skeletal analyses are adequate at only Indian Knoll, Cherry, and Chiggerville).

At Robinson, Morse anticipated that there would be gendered work areas: "Clusters of tools and debris associated with artifact manufacturing parallel each other and indicate the shifting position of the men's working area through successive occupations at the site. The 14 pestles which should reflect the women's working areas are distributed in the site slightly differently, but not enough are present to definitely define these areas. Unexpectedly, the distribution of cataloged faunal remains does not parallel the pestle distribution; but, perhaps the men were cracking the bones for marrow and bone splinters" (Morse 1967:304). To explain the increase in pestles from lower to upper levels, he offered that the excavations had not been extensive enough to include the women's areas of the earlier components (Morse 1967:237).

Gender interactions have been invoked to explain several events at the close of the SMA era. Of particular interest are the adoption of pottery first by SMA peoples and the cessation of mounding shell.

Numerous authors have assumed a ceremonial function for the shell rings on the southeastern Atlantic Coast while denying any intentionality to the height or depth of shell mounding achieved at Stallings Island and elsewhere in the Midsouth. I have argued for intentional mounding motivated by symbolism attached to shell and mounds (Claassen 1988, 1991a, 1991b, 1992). Accepting this argument, Sassaman has reasoned that shell-ring and shell-mound construction on the Savannah River and adjacent coastline "required material provisioning that put demands on individual labor," which stimulated technological change, specifically the adoption of direct-heat cooking via ceramic containers. Assuming that women had leadership roles in these rituals and in their communities "then

Table 13-3. Shell Mound Archaic bead distribution by age and sex

Site	Shell							Bone	Stone				Copper	Other Shell	Dog	Ochre	Burials w/beads
	L	Ma	O	D	d	t	b		E	Cr	Co	Gen					
Indian Knoll F	1,065	—	—	—	749	38	—	—	—	1	1	2	—	3	3	8	18
Indian Knoll M	1,880	4	—	—	1,253	2	—	—	—	—	3	3	—	13	3	5	23
Indian Knoll S	3,606	101	37	—	2,014	23	4	—	—	439	7	14	—	18	4	19	58
Chiggerville F	272	—	—	—	288	—	—	—	—	—	—	—	—	2	—	—	5
Chiggerville M	—	—	—	—	252	9	—	—	—	—	—	—	—	1	1	1	4
Chiggerville S	501	—	—	—	332	—	—	—	—	—	—	—	—	3	2	4	10
Barrett F	1,186	—	—	—	15	—	—	1	—	—	1	—	—	2	1	1	10
Barrett M	73	—	—	—	369	5	—	3	—	—	—	1	—	18	1	1	16
Barrett S	461	—	—	—	644	38	2	3	—	—	—	7	1	2	—	2	18
Cherry F	—	—	—	—	2	—	—	—	—	1	—	—	—	—	—	—	1
Cherry M	—	—	—	—	—	—	—	—	—	—	—	—	—	—	2	—	—
Cherry S	159	—	—	—	5	—	—	—	—	—	—	1	—	1	1	—	3
Kay's Landing F	—	—	—	—	—	—	—	—	—	—	—	—	—	—	—	—	—
Kay's Landing M	—	—	—	—	—	—	—	—	—	—	—	—	—	—	—	—	—
Kay's Landing S	442	—	—	—	—	—	—	—	—	—	—	3	—	—	—	—	—
Perry F	167	—	—	—	—	12	—	—	—	—	—	2	—	—	—	—	—
Perry M	896	—	—	—	592	85	15	—	—	7	—	33	—	—	—	—	—
Perry S	—	406	—	117	343	54	—	—	1	1	—	15	—	—	—	—	—
Robinson F	—	—	—	—	20	—	—	—	—	—	—	—	—	—	—	—	—
Robinson M	—	—	—	—	—	—	—	—	—	—	—	—	—	1	1	2	—
Robinson S	—	—	—	—	—	—	—	—	—	—	—	—	—	1	—	—	—

Note: All beads are counts of beads while the remaining categories are counts of burials. F = female; M = male; S = subadult; L = Leptoxis; Ma = Marginella; O = Olivella; D = Dentalia; d = disk; t = tube; b = barrel; E = effigy; Cr = crinoid; Co = coal; Gen = general women would probably be the first to develop new technology (pottery) and to accelerate the adoption of innovations that enhanced their social position" (Sassaman 1993a:217). The combined circumstances of decreased soapstone for indirect cooking and intensified ritual/communal labor requirements paved the way for a rapid rate of adoption of ceramic cooking on the lower Coastal Plain.

Such was not the case in the Stallings Island area upriver, the heart of the soapstone export area. Here, Sassaman argues, men invested in the soapstone trade and deriving status from that activity blocked the adoption of a cooking method that circumvented soapstone slab cooking. Only when the soapstone trade dissolved did ceramic vessel direct-heat cooking spread into the Piedmont and elsewhere.

The uneven appearance of fiber-tempered pottery in the various regions of the SMA relates to the role of women in subsistence and in interregional exchange, according to Sassaman (1992c):

> Where women gained greater control over the subsistence economy through shellfishing and occupied a peripheral position in interregional exchange, innovations in pottery were quickly adopted for use [St. Johns, coastal Southeast]. Where women experienced similar economic constraints but were situated within the sphere of exchange, innovations were adopted but used in modified ways to accommodate both traditional and novel gender relations in society. . . .
>
> At the pan-southeastern level, the resistance to pottery innovations was even more severe, and pottery was not widely adopted until interregional exchange networks collapsed. To the extent that the use of pottery enabled women to appropriate surplus labor for other ends, the adoption of pottery may have itself undermined male-dominated exchange and prestige systems. I suspect that if we looked at the geographical peripheries of river-based Late Archaic settlement systems, that is, at upland locations that were used on a seasonal basis, we would find that women were developing pottery and other innovations that were otherwise absent during periods of social aggregation and ritual. (Sassaman 1992c:74)

Both Sassaman and I see women's subsistence activities as a route to prestige in their communities, prestige which the addition of shellfishing enhanced (see Claassen 1991a for support of this link between shellfish and prestige). It is clear from the burial data that the supposed ritual paraphernalia was deposited with women in quantities equal to or greater than with men. Leadership roles for women in community rituals and spiritual life seem beyond question. In the Savannah River region, the shaman-potter would have been a potent voice for technological change. I have documented elsewhere the symbolism of shell in

Maya and Aztec societies (Claassen 1988, 1991a, 1991b), which was one of death, completion, South, and fertility. Prentice (1986) argues that with the advent of horticulture there was an influx of new perceptions and symbols of fertility, life, death, growth, and earth. The shaman-gardeners would have been at the forefront of the movement to replace the old symbolism with the new.

Before leaving the topic of gender in the SMA, I want to comment on the notion of egalitarianism, so commonly and thoughtlessly applied to most hunter-gatherer groups. We readily admit that social distinctions are made in these societies along gender and age lines, so where is the equality implied? If adults and children are not equal and women and men are not equal, who is? In use by archaeologists, the concept systematically ignores gender and age inequities, casting them as unimportant. We should abandon use of the term, replacing it with one more in keeping with our perception of gender and age inequities, or cease to insist that egalitarian societies must discriminate along age and gender lines.

Exchange and Social Status

Competition and differences in grave goods are elements in a ranked society. The variation in grave goods in the sites of the Green and Tennessee rivers and Nashville basin has captured the attention of archaeologists since the second decade of the twentieth century and provided the impetus for several studies focusing on the importance of social variables in the SMA (Goad 1980; Hofman 1986c; Rothschild 1975, 1979; Winters 1968, 1969, 1974). Findings that few people were interred with goods, that subadults are often more richly endowed than adults, that different body preparation was used, that different burial attitudes are evident, that copper and shell goods originated great distances away, and that quantities of things fluctuate tremendously between graves, have led Winter (1968) and Rothschild (1979) into a search for quantifiable social rankings and Goad (1980), Marquardt (1985:81), and Sassaman (1993a) to assume an exchange network that rewarded participants with enhanced social status.

That most burials lacked grave goods is the case at all SMA sites, inside and outside the Green River valley, for which data are available (percentages in Claassen 1992; Winters 1968). As for those burials that did have goods, few patterns have been discovered.

Magennis (1977:82–84) found a random distribution of artifact classes by age at the late Cherry site but did find that no grave goods were accorded individuals less than 20 years old in the late Eva III sample. At both sites males had more than 60 percent of the utilitarian objects but females and males received equal proportions of the ceremonial and ornamental items. No females at either site were buried with marine shell or copper; subadults received 75 percent of the exotic artifacts.

Rothschild (1979) sought to discriminate statistically the assumed differences in gender and age at Indian Knoll through type of grave goods. She found that sex was a discriminating trait but age at death was not (1979:671), when viewing graves with multiple artifact types. However, when considering specific tech-nomic artifact types (e.g., shell disk beads), age was a discriminating trait but sex was not (Rothschild 1975). She suggested that there were at least two types of status governing the grave goods associations at Indian Knoll, one involving the variety of objects included, the other determining the type of object included. Life at Indian Knoll had not been egalitarian, she concluded.

The important point raised by Hofman's (1986c) evaluation of burial programs at SMA sites is that sex, age, and a ranked social status are not the only factors con-ditioning the burial program for these hunter-gatherers. At least the differences in occurrence of primary and secondary burials might be explainable by the mobility of a group having preferred burial at a place away from the locus of a death. Quan-titative differences in age and sex distributions of secondary burials result from logistical versus residential mobility, the former resulting in more male burials at the camp site (Hofman 1986c). The archaeological literature on mortuary prac-tices is full of subtle differences in burial practices that caution against any simple equation of quantity, quality, and variety in grave goods with social rank differ-ences in life. As yet, no SMA site project has demonstrated social ranking in life and no project will be able to until chronological control has been established within and between sites.

Marine shell and copper were considered by Morse (1967) and Winters (1968) to be key elements for understanding burial variation at Indian Knoll and Carl-ston Annis. Ornamental items fabricated from *Busycon* sp., *Marginella* sp., *Oli-vella* sp., *Dentalia* sp., and *Fasciolaria* sp. are with very few exceptions (< 5%) found in burial context, not in the general midden at SMA sites. The same can be said for copper. These observations led Winters (1968:182) to conclude that objects of these materials were precious to SMA people, who attached less value to antler, bone, and stone items, which were often found in midden context. Win-ters (1968:182) also noted that "with the exception of atlatl weights there was no diversion of imported marine shell for the manufacture of utilitarian artifacts" in the Green River valley. For this reason, Winters considered shell beads to be more than mere bangles on the clothing of the deceased (1968:185).

I have reexamined the collections of beads from the Kentucky SMA sites of Indian Knoll, Chiggerville, Barrett, Read, Butterfield, Carlston Annis, and Ward; the western Tennessee sites of Ledbetter, Cherry, Oak View, Kay's Landing, Eva, McDaniel, Frazier, Young's Landing, Danville Ferry, Big Landing, West Cuba, Bridges, and Bn 13; and the Alabama sites of Perry, Lu 5, and Ct 17, and the South Carolina site of Lake Spring. Only six of the Tennessee sites had shell beads (table 13-4). My counts of beads differ from those previously published for Indian Knoll and Chiggerville, provide the first quantifications for the Tennessee River sites, and are complemented by age and sex information at seven sites. It will now be possible to revise the shell analysis that Winters (1968) offered and the quantifica-tion for which he called. For instance, Winters (1968:169) noticed that all

Table 13-4. Bead types at selected Shell Mound Archaic sites

Site	Conch	Marginella	Olivella	Leptoxis	Dentalia	Coal	Copper	Crinoid	Stone	Bone
Globe Hill	—	—	—	—	—	—	—	—	—	x
East Steubenville	—	—	—	—	—	—	—	—	—	x
Riverton	—	—	—	—	—	—	—	—	—	13+
Robeson	—	—	—	—	—	—	—	—	—	3
Swan Island	25	—	—	—	—	—	—	1	—	—
Indian Knoll	4,119	105	37	6,551	—	16	x	440	24	x
Carlston Annis	5,567	3,575	483	—	—	2	1	26	34	7
Chiggerville	910	—	—	1,008	—	—	—	—	—	—
Read	x	—	—	—	—	x	—	—	x	x
Barrett	1,073	—	—	1,720	—	1	1	—	8	7
Butterfield	—	—	—	—	—	1	1	1	—	—
Ward	222	—	—	x	—	2	—	—	—	—
Ervin	6	—	—	125	—	—	—	—	—	1
West Cuba	—	—	—	100	—	—	—	—	—	—
Eva	—	—	—	—	—	—	4	6	—	4
Danville	11	—	—	—	—	—	—	—	—	—
Anderson	1,013	—	—	—	—	27	—	—	8	27
Robinson	20	—	—	—	—	—	—	—	—	—
Cherry	7	—	—	159	—	—	—	1	1	—
Kay's Landing	—	—	—	442	—	—	—	—	3	—
Oak View	—	—	—	—	—	—	72	—	—	—
Ledbetter	1,096	6	193	10	—	—	2	1	1	—
Lu 5	—	—	—	114	—	—	—	—	—	—
Ct 17	—	—	—	—	769	—	—	—	—	—
Perry	1,101	406	—	1,063	117	—	—	8	51	—
Long Branch	x	—	—	x	x	—	—	—	x	x
Whitesburg	1,160	—	—	—	—	—	—	—	3	—
Stallings Island	2,000	—	x	—	—	—	—	—	x	x
Lake Spring	113	—	—	—	—	—	—	—	—	—

associations of *Marginella* and *Olivella* beads from Indian Knoll and Carlston Annis were with subadults. However, the reexamination of beads at Indian Knoll located a total of four *Marginella* beads in the grave of a 30-year-old man, and 101 with a child. All other beads identified as *Marginella* in the text were actually misidentified *Leptoxis* shells, a local freshwater snail. One adult skeleton at Ledbetter had the only *Marginella* beads and one of the *Olivella* beads.

Previously proffered explanations for how copper and marine shell reached the Green River valley are (1) through direct ties to a redistributive center (Winters 1968:216–219), (2) down-the-line transfer with Green River valley sites at the interface of a southern shell network and a northern copper network (Goad 1980:11), and (3) males journeying out to meet trading partners (Marquardt 1985:80). Sassaman (1993a) has posited the later explanation for the Savannah River soapstone trade through the Gulf Coastal Plain. Traders would have been of higher social standing than nontraders because of the information they possessed and because of their control over the valuable goods they handled.

Quantification is necessary to evaluate the claims for trade and the mechanisms for movement of exotics. In table 13-4 it is obvious that in a sample of 29 SMA sites, the quantity of *Marginella* and *Olivella* snails derived from the sea coast is miniscule. Both species are available close in to shore at the Atlantic or Gulf coasts. *Dentalia* or tusk shell, however, which is present in several of the northern Alabama sites, is not as conveniently situated. There are numerous species of *Dentalia* that are found on the Pacific Northwest Coast, in the West Indies, and in fossil beds in South Dakota. At least some of the Perry site *Dentalia* beads are the West Indies species. While the distance involved is much greater than to the Gulf Coast and is therefore strongly suggestive of trade, the quantity of material again is quite small.

Winters (1968:279) argues that the whole *Busycon* shell was imported because whole shells with columella removed are an occasional grave good, because of the different gorget shapes, and because stages of bead manufacture were preserved in Burial 610 at Indian Knoll. The uniformity in diameter and thickness of shell beads given the same field specimen number in the Kentucky sites (less common in the Perry site collection) does suggest that multiple beads were cut at once and that in many cases entire strands spent their use-lives together. The numbers of cut conch shell beads, whole shells, and other conch shell items are large enough to support trade but not to distinguish the type of movement nor to require trade.

Most intriguing about the tabulation of bead types presented in table 13-4 is the geographical sorting of several types of beads. Cannel coal beads are found only in the region of cannel coal deposits, the Green River. There it is common to encounter field specimen sets with many cut conch beads, one or two stone beads, and one coal bead (fig. 13-1). This same fashion is found at the Anderson site, in the Nashville basin adjacent to the Green River valley, suggesting that it had greater affinity with the Green River valley sites than with Eva, its standard of comparison (Dowd 1989), where conch and coal beads are absent.

The majority of the western Tennessee sites lacked shell beads, while those having some had only small quantities of any type of bead and little variety in beads. Most striking about the bead distribution in those sites is the rarity of *Leptoxis* (*Anculosa*) beads. The Tennessee and Alabama rivers may well be the place of origin of this genus; it is abundant there today. *Leptoxis* beads usually occur in large quantities when they occur, sometimes with adult burials but usually with preadults (table 13-3). It would seem that the dress and shroud of western Tennessee folks rarely included beads (a total of 10 burials in 13 sites) and that when they did, the beads were not of precious materials. For five sites (Danville Ferry, Bridges, West Cuba, Oak View, and Kay's Landing), it is curious that only one burial at each has any beads. By contrast, 10 burials at Ledbetter and four at Cherry include beads.

In the Pickwick and Wheeler basins bead use is more common, although quantification is not systematically offered in the reports. Bead variety is greater than that found downstream in Tennessee and more like that in the Green River valley. Only here is *Dentalia* shell used as beads (fig. 13-2). The greater use of stone beads in this region and the presence of a stone effigy bead at Perry probably signify their proximity to the stone bead province of the Poverty Point culture (fig. 13-3). In the West Virginia shell-matrix sites of Globe Hill and East Steubenville and at Robeson and Riverton in Illinois, the only bead type found was the bone bead. Beads have been reported from Stallings Island, Lake Spring, and several of the shell rings, and in the St. Johns valley, although none was recovered from Rabbit Mount or Hontoon Island.

There is ample documentary evidence of the gifting of beads so we need not require that every bead at a site be manufactured there or that the culture involved necessarily embraced the symbolism implied by beads gifted to its members.

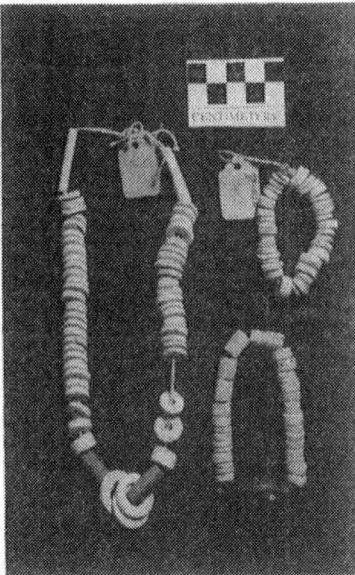

Fig. 13-1. Bead necklaces from Indian Knoll (Green River, Kentucky). A cannel coal bead is evident in the lower right necklace.

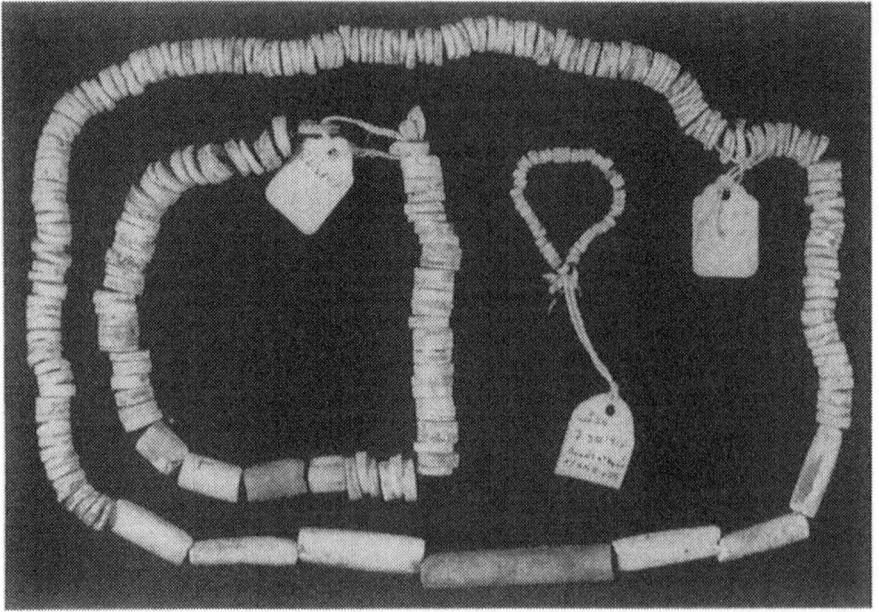

Fig. 13-2. Necklace of dentalia segments from the Perry site (Tennessee River, Alabama).

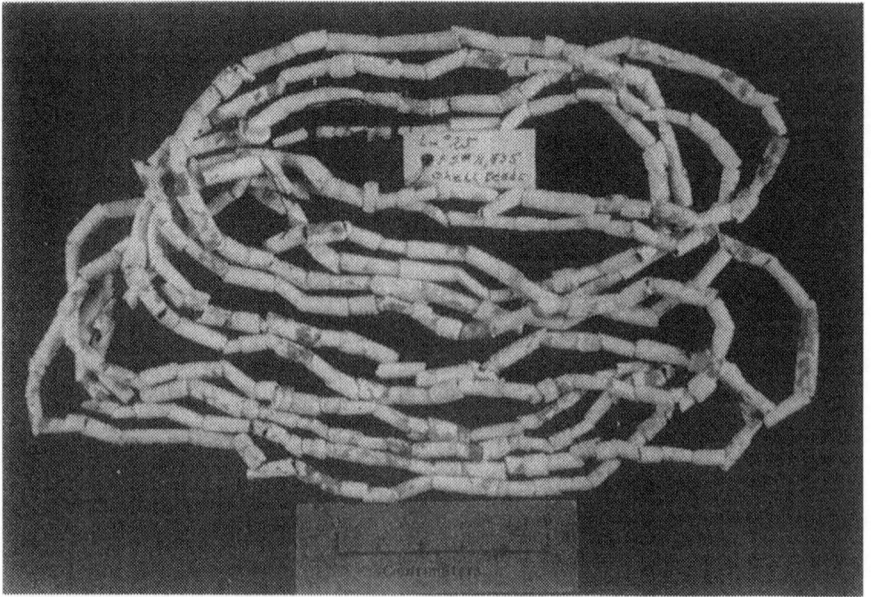

Fig. 13-3. Three necklaces from the Perry site. The larger two necklaces are composed primarily of cut marine shell beads and secondarily of stone.

However, the peoples of West Virginia and western Tennessee seem rarely to have had the kind of contact with the inhabitants of the Green or middle Tennessee rivers that resulted in bead exchange.

Marquardt and Watson (1983:334) noted that the actual quantity of copper in SMA burials is not large. If the main cycling mechanisms for copper and marine shell were redistributive centers or trade fairs, it would seem that there would be a greater use and distribution of these objects and less variety in fashion as people from different regions interacted.

Trade fairs seem less likely as the means of shell or bead exchange than does down-the-line transfer. Down-the-line transfer of shell or beads or the use of trading partners would bring fewer people together and thus impact fashion less. (By fashion I do mean appearance but do not mean to imply that beads and pendants were simply decorative.) It would seem, however, that down-the-line trade did not include the Georgia–South Carolina sites or Alabama sites. The Savannah River sites, those closest to the ocean, have only a few freshwater shell beads. If marine shells passed through their hands, they did not linger there in any form. The sites on the central Tennessee River in Alabama are the only ones to have West Indian *Dentalia* shells (with one possible exception at Indian Knoll, Moore's [1916] Burial 82). Furthermore, these sites occasionally contain shells from the Pacific Ocean (*Haliotis* or abalone, giant clam or *Tridacna* sp. seen by the author in the Smithsonian collections), indicating that their sources of shell were independent of those used by other SMA provinces. The lack of coal beads on the Tennessee River, the lack of virtually any beads in the Illinois and West Virginia sites, and the popularity of crinoid beads on the central Tennessee River further suggest bead fashion provinces and nonshared bead sources.

Within the various provinces with beads, bead variety and quantity, and the number of burials with beads, may constitute a hierarchical measure of site and personnel. The phenomenon being ranked is probably the expression of particular religious beliefs and occupation. It seems that the activities with which beads were associated went on more often at Perry in Alabama, at Ledbetter in western Tennessee, and at Carlston Annis and Indian Knoll in Kentucky than elsewhere in their respective river basins and provinces.

Conclusion

There are, of course, other objects made of other foreign materials that have not been examined here. From the perspective of marine shell and copper, however, there are not enough objects to require extensive or even regular trading. The bead data suggest different bead provinces within the SMA—east of the Appalachians, central Tennessee River, western Tennessee, Green River–Nashville basin, Ohio River. (The distribution of engraved bone pin styles corresponds with some of these boundaries—see Jefferies, this volume.)

The ideas validated in this paper emphasize social concerns as central to the

SMA societies and should, therefore, be of greatest interest to archaeologists in explaining the culture and the differences between sites. The mound-building phenomenon means that social life in the Midcontinent and southern Atlantic Slope was much more complex than we have been willing to recognize. These cultures, sharing burial ceremonialism, were not isolated creative flashes in the struggle for harmony with nature but constituted an interlocking social world vibrant with negotiations that blended and distinguished elements of each society. These hypotheses mean that the Woodland period traits of mound building and pottery use have an unappreciated developmental history, which is reflected in the time of adoption of both traits and in location of mound use in the later period. These hypotheses mean that the Archaic as a stage in the prehistory of the eastern United States needs to be reconceptualized significantly. Historic period beliefs and societies may have Archaic or even Paleoindian antecedents. As a stage, the Archaic is almost meaningless, as is any Archaic-Woodland boundary. As a consequence, the Woodland stage needs to be reexamined.

This summary has presented ideas and data for just a few aspects of Middle and Late Archaic social organization. Such an endeavor is constrained by several types of handicaps, principally missing information on (1) internal site chronology, (2) skeletal populations, and (3) site formation processes. Together, they make investigation at the regional level treacherous and comments tenuous. As frustrating as the data are for the sites in the Green River valley, our understanding of the other regions of shell mounding is even poorer.

For too long we have relied for data on the published reports of excavations conducted in the 1930s and 1940s. The tasks are clearly delineated if we are to improve our understanding of the activities of riverine and coastal dwellers of this era: we must have new excavations focusing on site formation processes, new site reports, revised site reports, reanalysis of material categories, an extensive dating program, many more reports on the recovered skeletal materials, and clear statements of what are the archaeological markers of note.

14

Southeastern Archaic Mounds

MICHAEL RUSSO

The initiation of ceremonial and burial-mound construction in the eastern United States has long been thought to date to the Woodland period (e.g., Davis 1984:321–322; Smith 1986:42, 45; Steponaitis 1986; Walthall 1980:2, 104–109). With the possible exception of the mounds at Poverty Point, no ceremonial mounds have been universally accepted as dating earlier than 2500 B.P. A few earlier Archaic cemeteries and rock cairns have been identified in the Midwest as Archaic "mounds" (Brown 1983:9; Charles and Buikstra 1983:133; Kay 1983:51; Phillips 1983:1; Reid 1983:22), although they are not usually viewed as intentionally constructed ceremonial features. Other midwestern mounds with multiple components cannot be attributed with certainty to the Archaic period (Charles and Buikstra 1983:133; Reid 1983:22). Such features are frequently described as "low" (Brown 1983:9; e.g., 20 and 75 cm above the surrounding surface [Charles and Buikstra 1983:133]), and they "resemble later and larger mounds more for their hilltop locations and the compactness of interment in a single disposal facility than in their 'moundedness'" (Brown 1983:9). Brown (1983:9) suggests that these areas were more cemeteries than mounds during the Archaic: "the actual size of the fill placed on top of these facilities was unimportant in the beginning and only took on the 'Woodland-sized' dimensions much later and as a by-product of other factors." A number of the "mounds" are actually referred to as cemeteries, knolls, or "small earth works," and there is some confusion as to whether the Midwest mounds are actually ceremonial constructions, incidental, natural, or cultural features associated with cemeteries, or even related to the Archaic. Whatever they are, there is wide agreement that these features arose in direct response to the regionalism brought about by increasing populations, which resulted in the need for symbolic markers of territory, lineage, and status (Brown 1983:9; Charles and Buikstra 1983:133; Claassen, this volume).

A bias against Archaic mounds has persisted because a Woodland origin for mound construction seemed to fit neatly with other developments of the Woodland period, such as pottery, agriculture, and sedentism (Gibson 1994a; Smith 1986; Steponaitis 1986; Willey and Phillips 1958). Whatever the cause and function of the early Woodland mounds, their construction made sense because the Woodland was a time when cultures were seen as in transition from nomadic Archaic peoples to settled agriculturalists. The general consensus was that mound construction was not possible without the more complex level of social and labor organization brought about by the increased populations and sedentism characteristic of the formative Woodland cultures and believed to be lacking in Archaic cultures.

Defining Ceremonial Mounds

Ceremonial mounds are tumuli that may contain human burials, ceremonial objects, tombs, earthen platforms, and structures, reflecting construction episodes and shapes indicating that mound construction was intentional and purposeful for activities unrelated to or beyond the simple disposal of refuse and other mundane activities. Ceremonial mounds in the Southeast include earthen burial mounds, temple mounds, and effigy mounds.

Ceremonial mounds are distinguished from mounded middens, which are usually seen as the incidental accumulations of midden refuse that may include earth, shell, animal bone, and other cultural material associated with daily maintenance activities. As such, mounded middens may include features such as postmolds of domestic structures, hearths, tools associated with food preparation, and storage pits. When these daily maintenance remains are removed by occupants of a site and discarded in a particular locale, another kind of mounded midden may result, containing the remains of the incidentally accumulated midden but representing a secondary, rather than a primary, mounded midden.

Distinguishing ceremonial mounds from mounded middens becomes difficult when characteristic traits of each are found, or are lacking, in a mounded feature. When burials are placed in mounded middens, when shell or earth middens are mined and used to construct ceremonial mounds, when the shape of the mound is obfuscated by disturbance or erosion, or when no diagnostically ceremonial objects are recovered, the classification of the feature may prove difficult (e.g., Claassen, this volume; McMichael 1982; Piatek 1994; Russo 1991).

On this point, Claassen (this volume) suggests that a number of preceramic Archaic mounded shell middens in the Midsouth were actually built as ceremonial mounds, or at least were used as such at some time in their existence. Proving the latter is a relatively easy task if distinctive ceremonial features are found within the midden. But proving the former, that is, that ceremonial or symbolic intent was behind the initial construction of mounded middens, is more difficult (e.g., Russo 1991:380–387), even when burials and other ceremonial objects are found within them.

Archaeologists have known about burials in mounded shell middens for over a century, yet few have posited that the Archaic occupants of the sites were anything but semisedentary, egalitarian hunter-gatherers. This is because for most archaeologists, what ultimately distinguishes ceremonial mound construction from mundane, accretionary mounding of shell refuse in middens is not the fill material, nor the presence or absence of symbolic intention by the features' creators. Rather, it is the kinds of social formations thought necessary to construct the architectural tumuli. Large-scale public constructions such as ceremonial mounds are seen as correlates of particular, hierarchically ranked social formations traditionally viewed as having been absent from Archaic societies. Consequently, mounded Archaic features have most often been interpreted to have resulted either from routine trash disposal activities of egalitarian cultures (Archaic shell middens) or to have been built by more recent, socially ranked cultures. Because of this theoretical baggage, archaeologists have found it difficult to classify any clearly ceremonial, mounded feature as an Archaic period construction.

Early Recognition Of Archaic Ceremonial Mounds

Despite the conceptual bias against Archaic mound construction, a few investigators have explored the possibility. The earliest was Gagliano (1963). Perhaps because Gagliano's principal training was in geology, he was open-minded about the possibility of Archaic ceremonial mounds. More than 30 years ago he defined the pre–Poverty Point, Archaic Amite River phase, centered in southeastern Louisiana and characterized by earth-midden sites located near stream valley margins. These sites yielded stemmed points as their most common artifacts, traits not unlike other Archaic phases found throughout the Southeast. However, one unusual aspect of the phase was the inclusion of small conical earthen mounds, often occurring in groups near or adjacent to Archaic quarry and habitation sites. Because no mounds were actually investigated, and because the paper was published in a state journal, the concept did not gain southeastern regionwide discussion or acceptance.

When surprisingly early radiocarbon dates from Amite River phase and other Louisiana mounds began to trickle in (table 14-1; fig. 14-1), first from the Banana Bayou Mound (Gagliano 1967) and later from the Hornsby (Manuel 1979), Monte Sano Bayou (Haag 1992), and the LSU Campus Mounds (Homburg 1992; Neuman 1992) sites, the possibility of an unusually early mound-building culture gained some support. Unfortunately, investigations undertaken prior to 1988 of Archaic mounds were conducted under emergency mitigation projects (Haag 1992), by volunteer societies (Manuel 1979), or as master's thesis projects (Homburg 1992:36) and went unpublished or were published outside major southeastern journals (e.g., Gibson 1968; for an exception see Brown 1980). Consequently, widespread recognition of the mounds continued to be frustrated. Prior to the 1990s, no effective, sustained effort was being conducted toward confirming the antiquity, understanding the development, or informing the greater southeastern archaeological community of the existence of Archaic mounds.

:

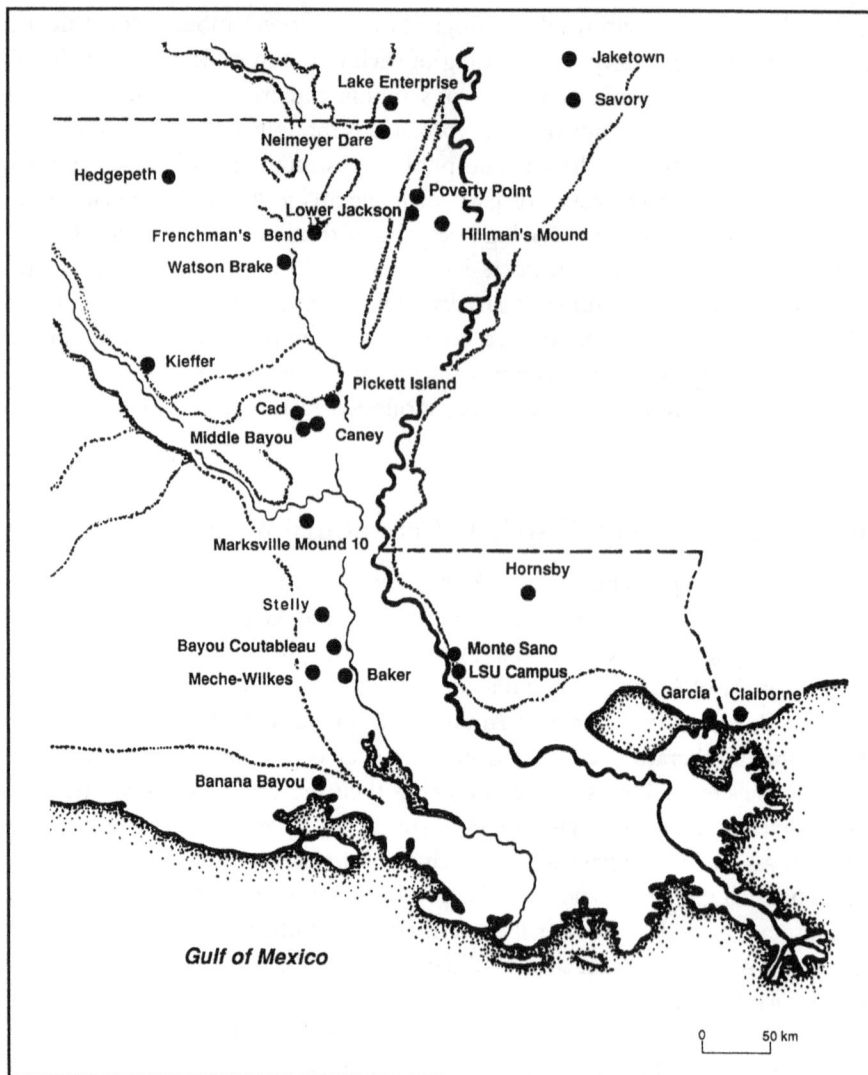

Fig. 14-1. Some confirmed and suspected Lower Mississippi Valley preceramic Archaic and Poverty Point mound sites.

Because of prevailing theory, the limited Archaic mound data seemed suspect even to those who had obtained it. For example, Gagliano (1967:18) noted that he was not sure of the validity of the date obtained from the Banana Bayou Mound. Haag (personal communication, 1992) did not publish an early date from the Monte Sano Bayou Mound excavated in 1967, in part because the radiocarbon date seemed too old. Notes of caution were also attached to the few articles that recognized the work on Archaic mounds (Gibson and Shenkel 1989:12; Shenkel 1984:65). Justification for the caution probably was best exemplified at the 1984 Mid-South Archaeological Conference, when Jon Gibson and Richard Shenkel

Table 14-1. Radiocarbon dates for southeastern Archaic ceremonial mounds

Provenience	Lab no.	Sample	Uncorr. C14 years B.P.	Corr. C14 years B.P.	C14 years B.C.	Calibrated date, 2 sigma	Reference
Horr's Island							
FS501, Mound A Zone 5: 10YR 6/4	Beta 35345	charcoal	4360±170	4760	2810	5909 (5564, 5528, 5476) 4989	Russo 1991
FS507, Mound A Zone 10: 10YR 4/1	Beta 35346	charcoal	3870±60	4270	2320	4982 (4858) 4618	Russo 1991
FS243, Mound A hearth	Beta 36466	charcoal	3740±60	4140	2190	4859 (4814, 4759, 4696, 4674, 4646, 4623, 4617) 4454	Russo 1991
FS462, Mound A Zone 3: 10YR7/1	Beta 36467	charcoal	3860±80	4260	2310	5026 (4852) 4567	Russo 1991
Stratum A, Md. A: dense oyster (top)	UM 1923	cockle	4335±70	4735	2785	5229 (4963) 4819	McMichael 1982*; Russo 1991
Stratum B, Mound A: 10YR 5/3	UM 1924	oyster	4025±75	4425	2475	4819 (4557) 4389	McMichael 1982*; Russo 1991
Stratum A, Md. A: dense oyster (bottom)	UM 1925	oyster	4055±75	4455	2505	4829 (4608) 4409	McMichael 1982*; Russo 1991
FS464, Mound A Zone 1, intrusive burial	Beta 35344	human bone	3420±100	—	1470	3969 (3689) 3459	Russo 1991*
FS533, Mound B: burial	Beta 35347	human bone	4030±230	—	2080	5251 (4525, 4480, 4459) 3869	Russo 1991
FS369, Mound B: 10YR5/3	Beta 40276	charcoal	5670±90	6070	4120	7179 (6945, 6913, 6897) 6729	Russo 1991
Stratum C, Mound B: dense oyster (top)	UM 1919	quahog	4215±75	4615	2665	4989 (4830) 4609	McMichael 1982*; Russo 1991
Stratum C, Md. B: dense oyster (bottom)	UM 1920	oyster	6330±85	6730	4780	7639 (7230) 7069	Russo 1991
Stratum A, Mound B: 10YR 3/1	UM 1921	oyster	4245±85	4645	2695	5059 (4845) 4629	McMichael 1982*; Russo 1991
Stratum A, Md. C: dense oyster (bottom)	UM 1918	whelk	4060±105	4860	2910	5429 (5204, 5167, 5138) 4849	McMichael 1982*; Russo 1991
Stratum A, Md. C: dense oyster (top)	UM 1922	conch	4470±75	4870	2920	5329 (5217) 4919	McMichael 1982*; Russo 1991
FS587, Mound D Zone 8: 10YR 8/6	Beta 35348	charcoal	4450±190	—	2500	5589 (5045, 5002, 4997) 4539	Russo 1991
Tick Island							
scattered in burial fill	M 1264	charcoal	5450±300	—	3500	6889 (6289) 5589	Jahn and Bullen 1978:22
scattered in burial fill	M 1265	charcoal	5320±200	—	3370	6603 (6174, 6145, 6104) 5650	Jahn and Bullen 1978:22
scattered in burial fill	M 1268	charcoal	5450±180	—	3500	6669 (6289) 5773	Jahn and Bullen 1978:22
associated with burial	M 1270	marine shell	5030±20	5430	3480	5885 (5833, 5782, 5778) 5729	Jahn and Bullen 1978:22

(*continued*)

Table 14-1—Continued

Provenience	Lab no.	Sample	Uncorr. C14 years B.P.	Corr. C14 years B.P.	C14 years B.C.	Calibrated date, 2 sigma	Reference
Tomoka Mounds							
intrusive burial in Mound 6	Beta 55287	human bone	2880±55	—	930	3209 (2993) 2859	Piatek 1994*
coquina midden at base of Mound 6	Beta 54622	coquina	4060±70	4460	2510	4829 (4614) 4419	Piatek 1992a:333, 1994
Monte Sano							
cremation on primary mound	GX 1011	charcoal/bone	6220±140	6220	4270	7424 (7174) 6754	Gibson and Shenkel 1989
Banana Bayou							
"top of primary mound"	O 1846	charcoal	4560±260	—	2610	5899 (5293) 4529	Gibson and Shenkel 1989
"primary mound on top of a low platform"	TI, I-II 981	charcoal	420±75	—	AD 1530	619 (507) 300	Brown 1991*
Hornsby Mound							
scattered in Mound B fill	UGa 5336	charcoal	2455±150	—	505	2859 (2702, 2653, 2482) 2139	Gibson and Shenkel 1989*
scattered in Mound B fill	RL 1270	charcoal	2930±180	—	980	3548 (3103, 3096, 3080) 2739	Manuel 1983
Mound B earth oven in mound	RL 1029	charcoal	4464±210	—	2514	5639 (5206, 5197, 5049) 4529	Manuel 1979, 1983
Stelly Mounds							
hearth within Mound B fill	Beta 55925	charcoal	4720±190	—	2770	5909 (5459, 5345, 5337) 4869	Russo 1992
charred post in Mound C	Beta 63982	charcoal	5290±70	5260	3310	6276 (6159) 5778	Russo 1993
Hedgepeth Mounds							
Mound A 2Ab horizon	Beta 47621	humates	5710±110	—	3760	6840 (6526, 6502, 6496) 6299	Saunders et al. 1994*
Mound A, surface of stage I within mound	Beta 52776	humates	6550±100	—	4600	7589 (7431) 7193	Saunders et al. 1994*
Mound A, hearth in paleosol beneath mound	Beta 47622	charcoal	4270±100	4270	2320	5240 (4888) 4539	Saunders et al. 1994

Frenchman's Bend

hearth in Mound C, feature 1	Beta 5358	charcoal	5580±140	5530	3580	6669 (6309) 5958	Saunders et al. 1994
hearth in Mound A	Beta 6145I	charcoal	4170±130		2220	5040 (4821, 4753, 4725, 4666, 4653) 4409	Saunders et al. 1994*
Mound A Stage II	Beta 66635	charcoal	4790±170	4780	2830	5919 (5571, 5521, 5484) 4994	Saunders et al. 1994
Md. C submound hearth	Beta 5359	charcoal	5740±232	5720	3770	7159 (6602, 6597, 6530) 5989	Saunders 1992, Saunders et al. 1994
LSU Campus Mounds							
near base of Mound A	GX 8777	soil	5345±235	—	3395	6669 (6181, 6139, 6114) 5639	Homburg 1992; Neuman 1992*
Mound A "near base of mound"	GX 8778	soil	4840±180	—	2890	5949 (5591) 5049	Homburg 1992; Neuman 1992*
Mound A "near base of mound"	GX 8776	soil	4840±185	—	2560	5639 (5267, 5180, 5108, 5088) 4616	Homburg 1992; Neuman 1992*
Poverty Point							
Mound B base, B sample	Schatzman	charcoal	2339±200	—	389	2847 (2349) 1891	Gibson 1987a*
Mound B base, A sample	Schatzman	charcoal	2685±210	—	735	3359 (2779) 2329	Gibson 1987a*
Mound B base	L-272	charcoal	2700±100	—	750	3137 (2837, 2834, 2781) 2543	Gibson 1987a*
Mound B base	M-403	charcoal	2850±250	—	900	3636 (2996, 2993, 2962) 2349	Gibson 1987a*
Mound B base	O-66	charcoal	3150±120	—	1200	3570 (3383) 3004	Gibson 1987a*

Note: Radiocarbon ages from Archaic mounds and associated features in the Southeast. All calibrations determined using University of Washington Quaternary Isotope Lab Radiocarbon Calibration Program 1987, Rev. 2.0 (Stuiver and Reimer 1986). Prior to calibration, 400 years were added to uncorrected B.P. dates to correct for $^{13}C/^{12}C$ fractionation on all shell samples. All Horr's Island proveniences are from Russo 1991.

*Archaeologist questions context or whether date reflects period of mound construction.

(1989) summarized the case for Archaic mounds in Louisiana to a larger regional audience. Gibson (personal communication, 1994) recalls that audience members seriously doubted the veracity of the data and radiocarbon dates, and they suggested that mounds predating Adena/Hopewell manifestations were an unlikely possibility.

One of the problems with identifying these Archaic mounds investigated early was that there was little in them—no definitive burials, few temporally diagnostic artifacts, and little datable material from contexts that could not be questioned. It was unlikely that the archaeological community could (or should) be convinced that Archaic mounds were real until and unless definitive evidence was mustered. By the early 1990s a number of researchers were actively investigating Archaic mounds in Florida and Louisiana and began producing evidence that supported the early claims. A summary follows of these sites and of the best studied of the sites recognized early.

Monte Sano

The Monte Sano (16EBR17) site was originally investigated by James Ford, William Haag, and others and presented in a series of oral papers (e.g., Haag 1992). The mound site was destroyed in 1967, but the information obtained by Haag has recently been summarized by Rebecca Saunders (1994).

The site originally consisted of two mounds, A and B, measuring over 4 and 1.5 m in height (fig. 14-2). Mound A contained within its center what has been described as a pyramidal or platform mound that measured approximately 0.5 m high and lay atop a humic stratum. Beneath the pyramidal mound were the post-molds of a structure measuring 10.5 × 10.5 m, while atop the pyramidal mound were two domed crematory piles. Charcoal from the cremation produced a radio-carbon age of 6220 ± 140 B.P. (table 14-1). Bone in the cremation has not yet been confirmed to be human, although some of it is definitely that of a large mammal (R. Saunders 1994). The entire surface of the pyramidal mound had been burned. Few diagnostic artifacts were recovered, and all were from the upper levels of the mound. These included two tubular beads and one red jasper cicada or owl bead, which is typically associated with the Poverty Point period.

At Mound B, a single stage of construction was identified along with indirect evidence of more cremations (R. Saunders 1994). No recognizable bone was obtained from these "cremations," and no radiocarbon dates were obtained that would help establish the period of mound construction. Both mounds were subsequently destroyed and only small amounts of data are available for determining their time of construction: the radiocarbon date, the beads, and the absence of ceramics. These indicate that both mounds were preceramic Archaic. It may be important to note, however, that a nearby midden contained dart points, for which ages of use range from the Archaic to the Marksville period. The midden also contained Marksville pottery but its possible association with the mounds is unclear.

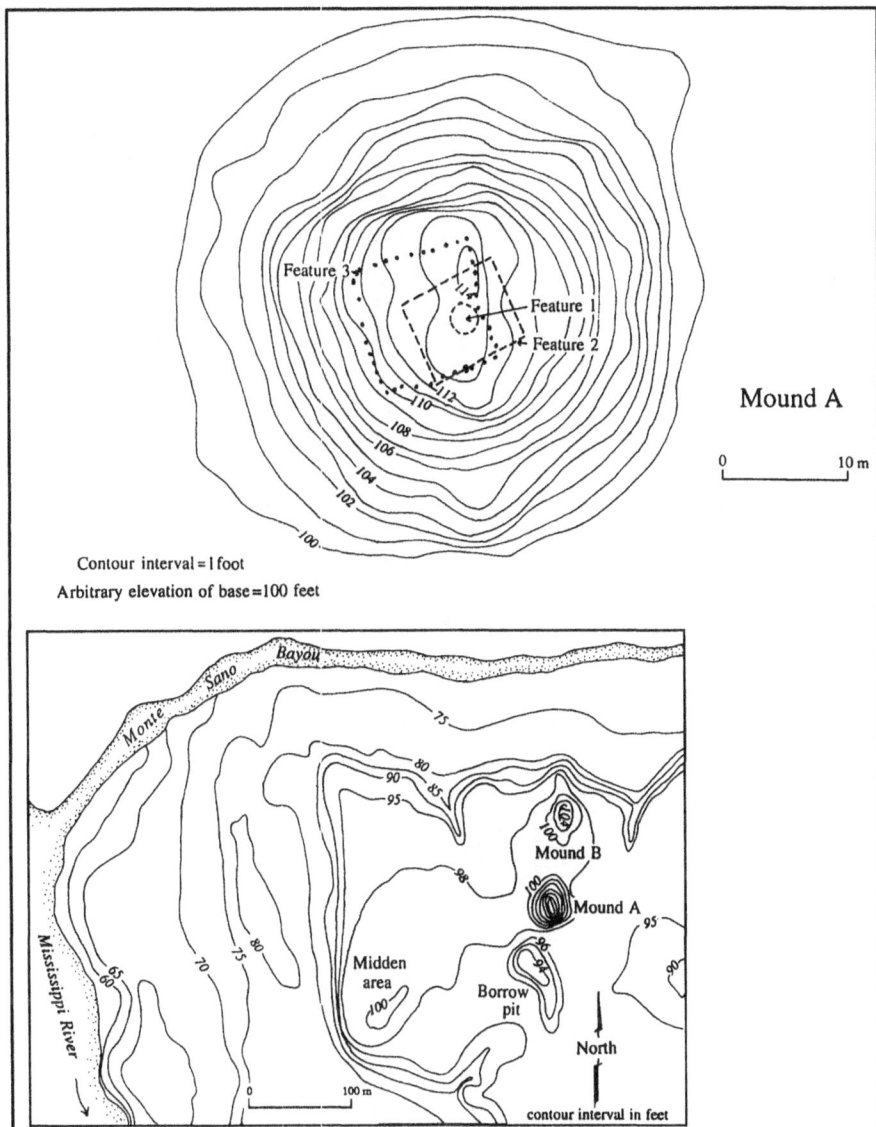

Fig. 14-2.   Monte Sano site (16EBR17): (*bottom*) Mounds A and B and (*top*) detail of Mound A topography and features (after R. Saunders [1994], and with permission of William G. Haag).

Hornsby Mounds

The Hornsby Site (16SH21) was investigated in 1967 by the Baton Rouge Junior Archaeological Society (R. Saunders 1994) and further investigated in 1978 by the Delta Chapter of the Louisiana Archaeological Society. Full reports of this work have never been published, although a draft of the 1978 effort is available (Manuel 1983; cf. R. Saunders 1994). Two earthen mounds were present at the site. Mound

A was reported to be nearly 4 m high, while Mound B was 1.7 m. By the time the Delta Chapter began their investigations, Mound A had been destroyed, and sub-surface work was limited to Mound B (fig. 14-3). These investigations yielded no ceramics from the mound, and only Archaic diagnostic artifacts were recovered, including baked clay (Poverty Point) objects and a wide variety of lithic points. Charcoal from a hearth within the mound yielded a radiocarbon date of 4464 ± 210 B.P. Scattered charcoal from mound fill, however, yielded a much more recent date of 2930 ± 180 B.P. The stratigraphic relation of this date to the hearth is not entirely clear (Manuel 1983).

Rebecca Saunders (1994) suggests that another possible Archaic mound exists across the stream from the Hornsby site and that Mound B is also surrounded by a lithic scatter containing Archaic points. Interpretations of the mounds at

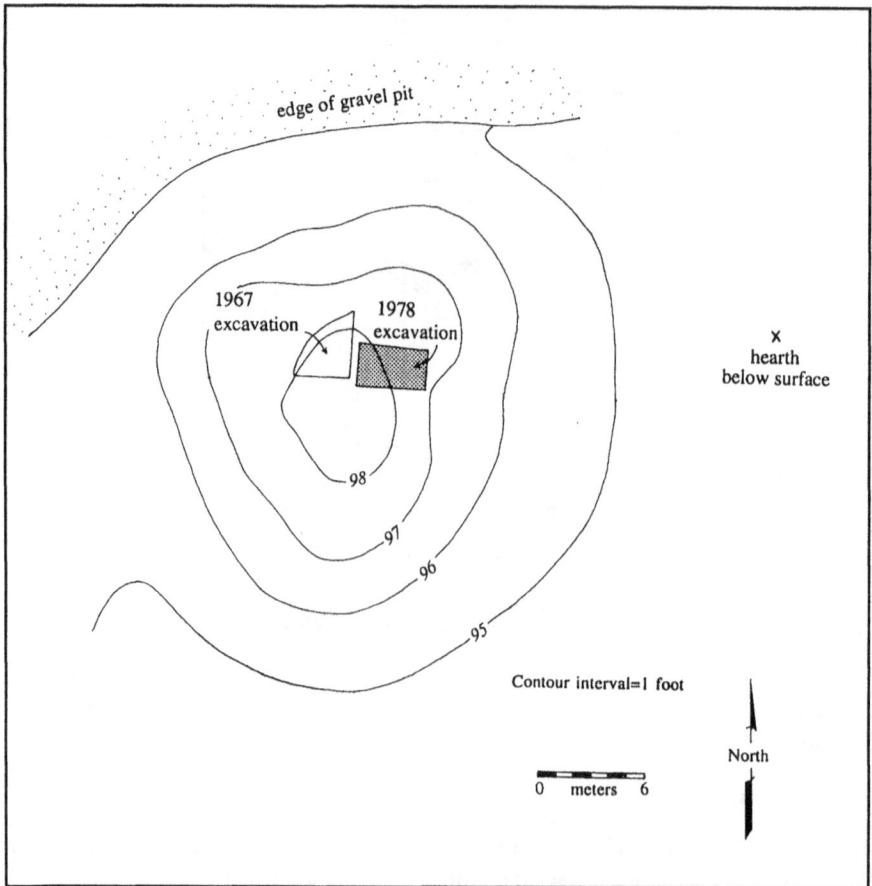

Fig. 14-3.   Hornsby Mound B (16SH21) (after Delta Chapter of the Louisiana Archae-ological Society, in Manuel 1983).

Hornsby are limited, but all conclude that at least Mound B dates from the Middle to Late Archaic period (Manuel 1983; R. Saunders 1994).

LSU Campus Mounds (16EBR6)

Two mounds over 5 m tall are located on the campus of Louisiana State University (fig. 14-4). Radiocarbon dates from soil humates taken from the interface between the original ground surface and the base of the mound yielded three dates ranging from 4510 to 5345 B.P. (table 14-1). Although ceramics were recovered from the A horizon at the base of the mound, Homburg (1992) suggests that these are not related to the initial period of mound construction, which he estimates at around 5000 B.P. The presence of the ceramics, combined with a reliance on soil humate dates from questionable contexts, however, have been enough to

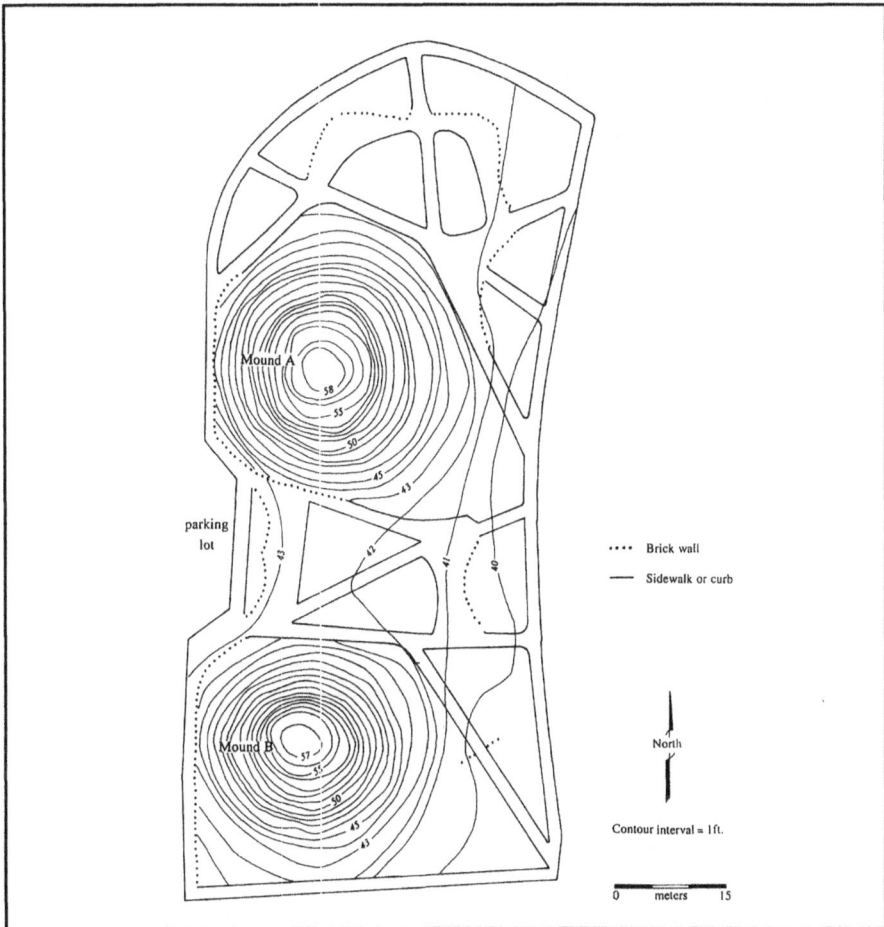

Fig. 14-4.   LSU Campus Mounds (16EBR6) (Homburg 1992).

create a debate as to whether or not the mounds are of Archaic period construction (Homburg 1993; Jones 1993; Neuman 1993).

Banana Bayou Mound (16IB24)

The 2-m-tall Banana Bayou Mound (fig. 14-5) is located on the edge of a large coastal salt dome, Avery Island, in southwestern Louisiana. In his investigations, Gagliano (1963, 1967) noted two stages of construction in the mound profile. Initially a small primary mound was placed on top of a ground surface that had sustained a fire. In turn, a fire had been placed on top of the primary mound before the second and final stage of mound fill capped the construction. The primary mound fill contained baked clay objects, and charcoal from the top of the primary mound yielded a radiocarbon date of 4560 ± 260 B.P. (table 14-1).

Although Gagliano associated the mound with an Archaic period of construction, based mainly on the radiocarbon date, later investigations by Brown and

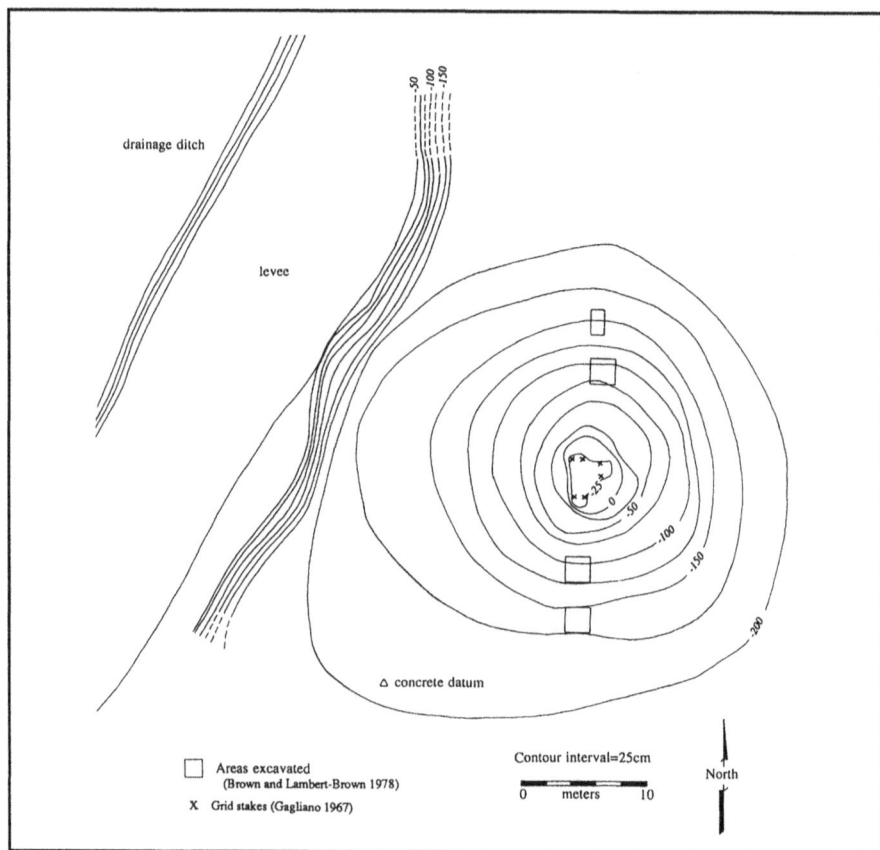

Fig. 14-5. Banana Bayou Mound (16IB24) (after Brown and Lambert-Brown 1978).

Lambert-Brown (1978) produced a more recent age on charcoal from the primary mound (420 ± 75 B.P.), complicating the interpretations. The very recent date has subsequently been dismissed by Brown, however (R. Saunders 1994), who additionally recovered more baked clay objects and Archaic points from the mound. Pottery obtained from the upper levels of the mound suggests that the second stage of the mound may have been constructed more recently than the Archaic period (Brown 1980), but an accurate understanding of the mound chronology has yet to be reached.

Recent Investigations of Preceramic Archaic Ceremonial Mounds

Until recently, the four mound groups discussed above—Banana Bayou, Monte Sano, Hornsby, and LSU Campus mounds—formed the primary evidence for Archaic period mound-building cultures in the Southeast. As shown, contexts of radiocarbon samples have been questioned; ceramics found in or near the upper levels of the mounds preclude conclusive attribution to the Archaic; and mounds have been destroyed, preventing further investigation. Recently, a number of other mounds in Louisiana and Florida have been radiocarbon dated to between 4200 and 5700 B.P. These findings provide credence to the earlier investigations and provide further data that mound construction was a common and widespread phenomenon during the Middle and Late Archaic periods.

Florida

Horr's Island Archaic (8CR205–209, 211).   Horr's Island is the most intensively studied of all the Archaic mound groups. Three sand/shell mounds and a possible fourth shell mound (figs. 14-6, 14-7) were originally identified by McMichael (1982) as protohistoric ceremonial constructions associated with a large coastal Archaic habitation site (8CR209). McMichael obtained Archaic period radiocarbon dates from three of the mounds and did not find a single ceramic sherd or other diagnostic prehistoric artifact in any of the mounds. He acknowledged that although the mounds lay within the boundaries of the largest coastal Archaic site in the Southeast, he assumed that the mounds had to date to the protohistoric period, in part because Archaic peoples were thought to have been incapable of attaining the complex level of social and labor organization necessary for large-scale mound constructions. The Archaic period radiocarbon dates from the mounds were consequently explained as the result of later protohistoric groups, who were known mound builders, using shell midden from the Archaic village as mound fill to build the ceremonial tumuli.

More recent investigations of the Horr's Island Archaic mounds have demonstrated that all were constructed during the Middle to Late Archaic (Russo 1991; table 14-1). At Mound A, construction stages are clearly indicated by alternating

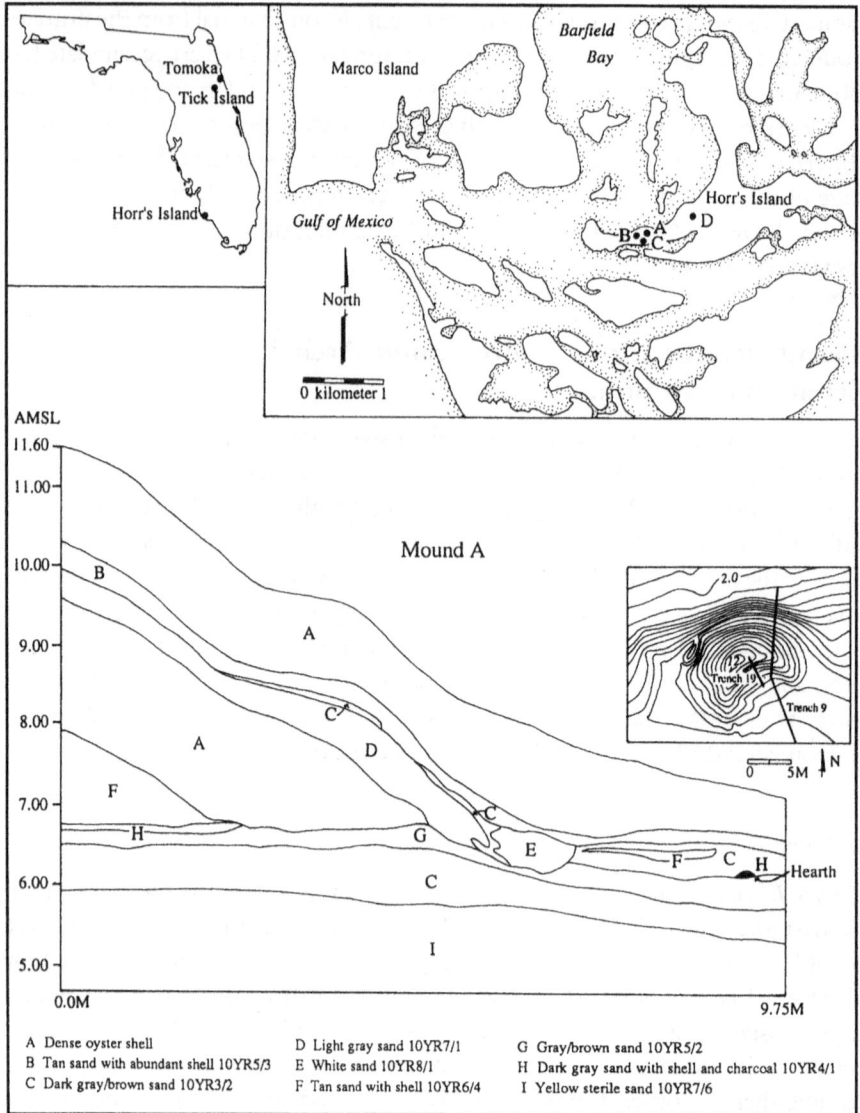

Fig. 14-6.   Contour map and east wall profile of Trench 19, Mound A, Horr's Island.

strata of shell and sand. A central sand mound was initially constructed and capped with shell. Consecutive episodes of sand and shell capping continued until a final shell cap made the mound over 6 m in height above the surrounding village. As do the other mounds and village, Mound A rests on a dune and its summit rises more than 12 m above the embayed Gulf waters at its base. An intrusive burial into the final shell cap was radiocarbon dated and secures the construction of the mound as predating 3420 ± 100 years B.P. Seven other dates obtained from both shell and charcoal from various stages of construction place

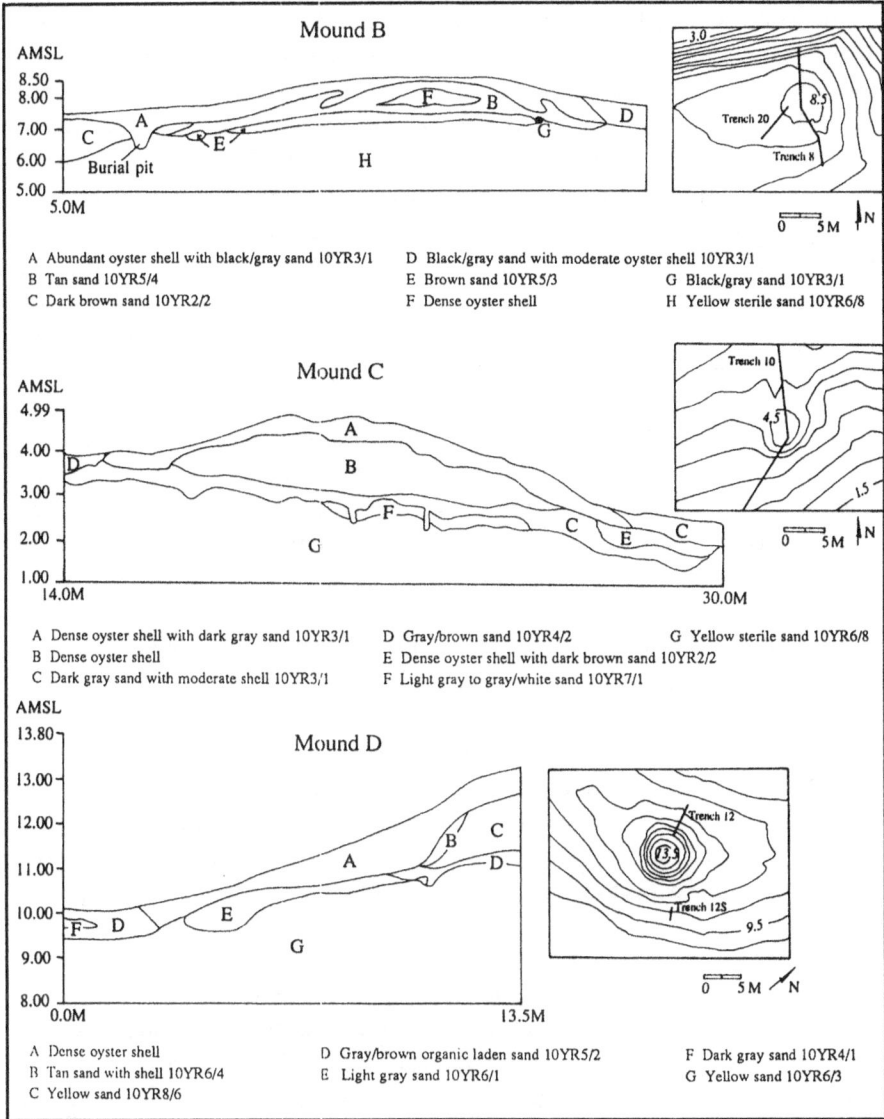

Mound B

A Abundant oyster shell with black/gray sand 10YR3/1
B Tan sand 10YR5/4
C Dark brown sand 10YR2/2
D Black/gray sand with moderate oyster shell 10YR3/1
E Brown sand 10YR5/3
F Dense oyster shell
G Black/gray sand 10YR3/1
H Yellow sterile sand 10YR6/8

Mound C

A Dense oyster shell with dark gray sand 10YR3/1
B Dense oyster shell
C Dark gray sand with moderate shell 10YR3/1
D Gray/brown sand 10YR4/2
E Dense oyster shell with dark brown sand 10YR2/2
F Light gray to gray/white sand 10YR7/1
G Yellow sterile sand 10YR6/8

Mound D

A Dense oyster shell
B Tan sand with shell 10YR6/4
C Yellow sand 10YR8/6
D Gray/brown organic laden sand 10YR5/2
E Light gray sand 10YR6/1
F Dark gray sand 10YR4/1
G Yellow sand 10YR6/3

Fig. 14-7.   Contour map and west wall profile of Trench 8, Mound B (*top*); east wall profile of Trench 10, Mound C (*center*); and east wall profile of Trench 12, Mound D (*bottom*), Horr's Island.

the dates of construction between 4400 and 5900 B.P. (uncorrected and uncalibrated, between 4200 and 4800 B.P. [table 14-1]).

One hundred meters west of Mound A is Mound B, a 1.5-m-tall earthen and shell mound. An intrusive burial radiocarbon date calibrated to a range between 3869 and 5251 B.P. (4030 ± 230 B.P.; table 14-1) dates when all stages of mound construction had to have been completed and indicates that all stages of mound construction occurred during the Archaic. The lowest levels of the mound may actually represent a premound shell midden. One radiocarbon date on shell from the lower levels (uncalibrated at 6730 ± 85 B.P.) and one on charcoal (uncalibrated at 6070 ± 90 B.P.) represent the two earliest ages obtained from a coastal site in the Southeast. A date on quahog shell (uncalibrated at 4615 ± 75 B.P.) from the uppermost construction stage indicates when mound construction ended.

Southeast of Mound B lies Mound C, a 3-m-high conical shell mound. At first, the absence of earthen strata within the mound appeared to preclude any possible ceremonial function—it may simply have been a mounded refuse midden (Russo 1991). But considering its proximity to the other mounds, its possible ceremonial significance should not be summarily dismissed. Two uncorrected and uncalibrated radiocarbon dates (4870 ± 75 and 4860 ± 105 B.P., table 14-1) on shell from the upper and lower levels of the mound indicate a short period of construction.

Three hundred meters east of the Archaic village, Mound D sits atop the tallest dune on the island. It is an earthen and shell mound that rises 4 m above the dune and consists of a central sand mound capped with oyster shell. Scattered charcoal within the sand mound yielded an uncalibrated radiocarbon date of 4450 ± 190 B.P. (table 14-1).

None of the Horr's Island mounds contained ceramics or any other indication of more recent construction. Occasional shell tools, typical of the tools commonly found in the associated Archaic village, were the only diagnostic artifacts recovered from any of the mounds. (Mound A may have been mined for shell earlier in this century and its southeastern side disturbed. Hrdlicka [1922:22–23] claims to have recovered two highly polished bannerstones, typically identified as Archaic artifacts, from the mound.) Shell tools are not exclusively limited to Archaic contexts, however, and it is the radiocarbon dates that provide the definitive ages for the mounds.

Tomoka Mounds (8VO81). The Horr's Island mounds are not the only Archaic mounds in Florida. On the east coast near Daytona, Piatek (1992a, 1994) has identified one mound in the Tomoka State Park as an Archaic period construction. The Tomoka site consists of nine mounds surrounded by a village midden on the mainland side of the Halifax River, a coastal lagoon (fig. 14-8). The deposits in both the mounds and midden consist predominantly of coquina, a small beach clam, and oyster, an estuarine species indicating that both estuaries and beach environments were exploitable and being exploited at the time of mound and village occupation.

Piatek conducted limited testing at Mound 6, the largest of the mounds at 3 m in height, and in the village midden surrounding the mound. A radiocarbon date on an intrusive burial in the upper levels of the mound indicates that final mound construction occurred sometime before 2880 ± 55 B.P. (calibrated between 3209 and 2859 B.P.; table 14-1), while another date from the base of the mound indicates that initial mound construction occurred around or after 4460 ± 70 B.P. (calibrated between 4829 and 4419 B.P.; table 14-1). The latter date predates the known time that ceramics were first produced in the region by at least 100 and perhaps as long as 500 years.

No tests recovered any ceramics despite the fact that a number of ceramic period sites surround the mounds (Piatek 1992b; Russo and Ste. Claire 1992). No diagnostic artifacts, in fact, were recovered by Piatek from either the mound or village; only cut deer bone, a drilled shark's tooth, and a small number of shell tool fragments, including a *Busycon* columella, were recovered from the village (Piatek 1992a, 1994). Because other researchers failed to locate ceramics in the mounds, and in light of the fact that Douglass (1882) recovered eight Archaic

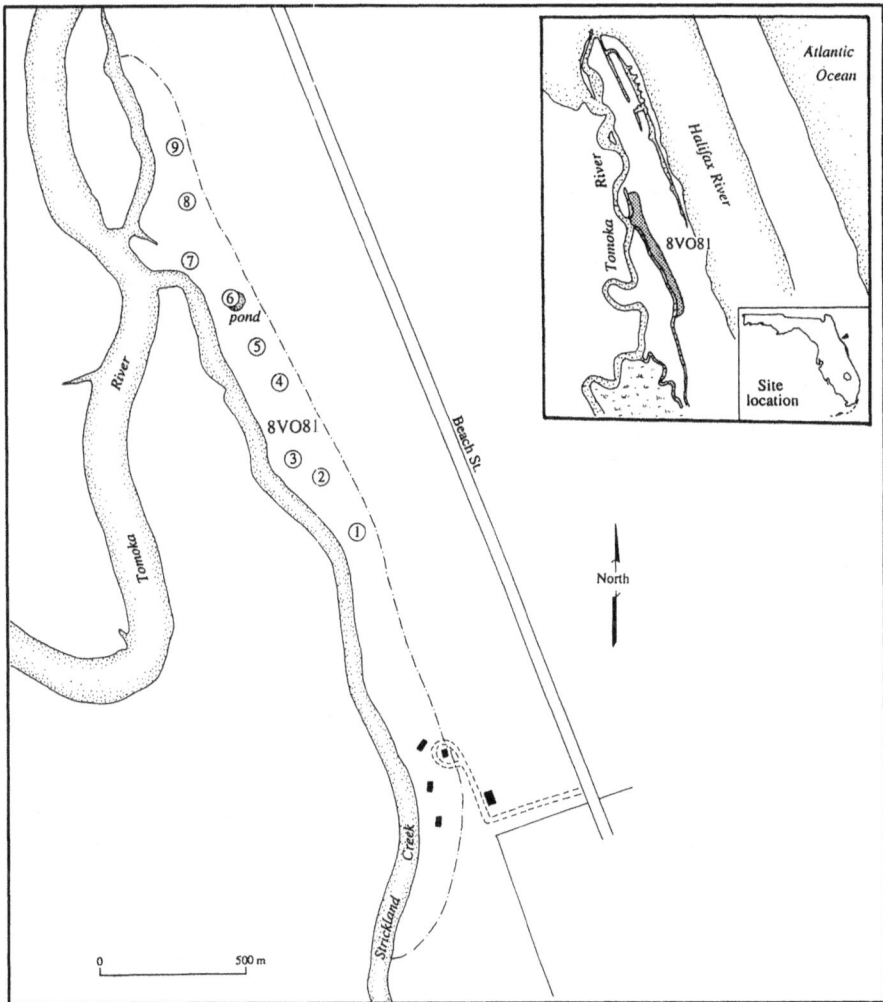

Fig. 14-8. Tomoka Mound Complex (8VO81) (after Piatek 1994).

bannerstones from Mound 6, Piatek (1992a:334) tentatively suggests that the entire mound complex may date to the preceramic Archaic.

Tick Island (8VO24).   At least one other possible Archaic mound may be found in Florida at Tick Island on the freshwater St. Johns River. In 1961 Bullen investigated an extensive Middle Archaic "cemetery" containing over 175 burials (Jahn and Bullen 1978:20). Excavations were conducted under salvage conditions, and the final report was written posthumously (Jahn and Bullen 1978). Because of this, the mounding aspect of the cemetery has gone unrecognized (Russo 1994a).

By the time Bullen arrived at the site, mining operations had removed from the 6-m-tall mound most of the shell strata, which had lain atop a lower stratum of sand. The meager data indicate that the removed shell dated to the ceramic Late Archaic and more recent prehistoric periods. But the burials in the lower sand stratum dated to the Middle Archaic, as evidenced by numerous stemmed (Archaic) lithic points. In addition, dates yielded by charcoal—assumed to have been introduced by charnel activity (Jahn and Bullen 1978:21)—scattered in the fill of three individual burials and by a marine shell associated with one burial are 5450 ± 300, 5320 ± 200, 5450 ± 180, and 5430 ± 20 B.P., respectively (table 14-1).

Conflicting data are presented by Jahn and Bullen (1978) as to whether the sand stratum in which the burials occurred was a cemetery or a sand burial mound (Russo 1994a). However, it is clear from Bullen's discussion that he struggled with reconciling the possible association of a sand burial mound, a decidedly late pre-historic phenomenon in his view, with a Middle Archaic burial site. Because of this, he determined that the site was a cemetery rather than a mound, despite phys-ical description of the mounding of sand (Jahn and Bullen 1978; Russo 1994a). Because the site has since been destroyed, the question of whether the site repre-sented a ceremonial mound may never be satisfactorily answered. Given Bullen's description and the fact that other Archaic mounds in Florida are now being rec-ognized, the idea that Tick Island may have contained a preceramic Archaic mound appears more probable then when it was investigated in 1961. Piatek (1994:112) points out other likely Archaic mounds in the area (Russo 1994b:92).

Louisiana

Initially linked to the Amite River phase of southeastern Louisiana by Gagliano (1963), Haag (1992) and Manuel (1983), Archaic mound construction has more recently been identified in northeast Louisiana by Joe Saunders and colleagues. Archaic mounds have also been identified in south-central Louisiana (Fogleman 1992; Russo 1992b). These discoveries are confirming mid-Holocene mound con-struction by providing the sound empirical evidence that was often lacking or ambiguous in the pioneering work of earlier Louisiana investigations. Stemmed dart points and baked clay objects have been recovered in and around the mounds, but radiocarbon dates are providing the most definitive evidence for the

Archaic periods of construction. Saunders et al. (1994) have also demonstrated how characteristics of soil formation in mound fill of these ancient architectural features may ultimately be used to identify them.

Frenchman's Bend (16OU259). Saunders, Allen, and Saucier (1994) have identified Frenchman's Bend as a five-mound complex (fig. 14-9) located near Monroe in northeastern Louisiana. Mound A, the largest of the mounds, stood 4 to 5 meters in height before it was bisected by looters with a bulldozer. Charcoal from midden that was used as fill in the lower levels yielded a radiocarbon age of 4780 ± 170 B.P., while charcoal from a hearth above it produced a date of 4170 ± 130 B.P. (uncalibrated; Saunders et al. 1994; table 14-1). A baked clay "block" was recovered from the secondarily deposited midden. Clay blocks have been found at a number of Archaic Louisiana mounds and they may be diagnostic of the period (Gibson, this volume; Saunders et al. 1994).

A test unit into the 1.6-m-tall Mound C produced two uncalibrated radio-carbon dates on charcoal from hearths within and below the mound. These dates are 5530 ± 140 and 5720 ± 232 B.P., respectively (Saunders et al. 1994; table 14-1). From the mound a clay block and a stemmed dart point were recovered. From surrounding surfaces other Archaic artifacts were recovered, including dart points, a bannerstone, a jasper bead blank, grinding stones, and 163 clay blocks (Saunders et al. 1994).

Hedgepeth (16LI7). The Hedgepeth Mounds (fig. 14-10) are situated 35 miles west of Frenchman's Bend. First identified by Joe Saunders (1992) as a possible Archaic mound site, Hedgepeth has since yielded considerable evidence to support that hypothesis (J. Saunders 1994; Saunders and Allen 1994; Saunders et al. 1994). The site consists of Mound A at 6 m in height and Mound B at over 1 m. Bulk carbon samples from the surface of Stage I mound construction yielded a date of 6550 ± 100 B.P. and from the 2Ab horizon below the mound, 5710 ± 110 B.P. Charcoal from a hearth just below the mound yielded a date of 4270 ± 100 (all dates uncalibrated; table 14-1). No diagnostic artifacts were found in the mound investigations, although a ground stone adze was recovered from a looter's trench. Beneath the mound were found two Archaic points, along with numerous chipped stone and fire-cracked rock fragments. In total, more than 1300 artifacts were recovered from the A horizon on which Mound A lies. All the diagnostic artifacts date to the Archaic, while none of the them are post-Archaic (Saunders and Allen 1994). From five backhoe trenches placed around the mound, two clay blocks and an amorphous clay ball were also recovered (Saunders et al. 1994).

Stelly Mounds (16SL1). The Stelly Mounds (fig. 14-11) lie in south-central Louisiana but are in many ways similar to the mounds being investigated in northeast Louisiana. The complex consists of three mounds, with Mounds C and

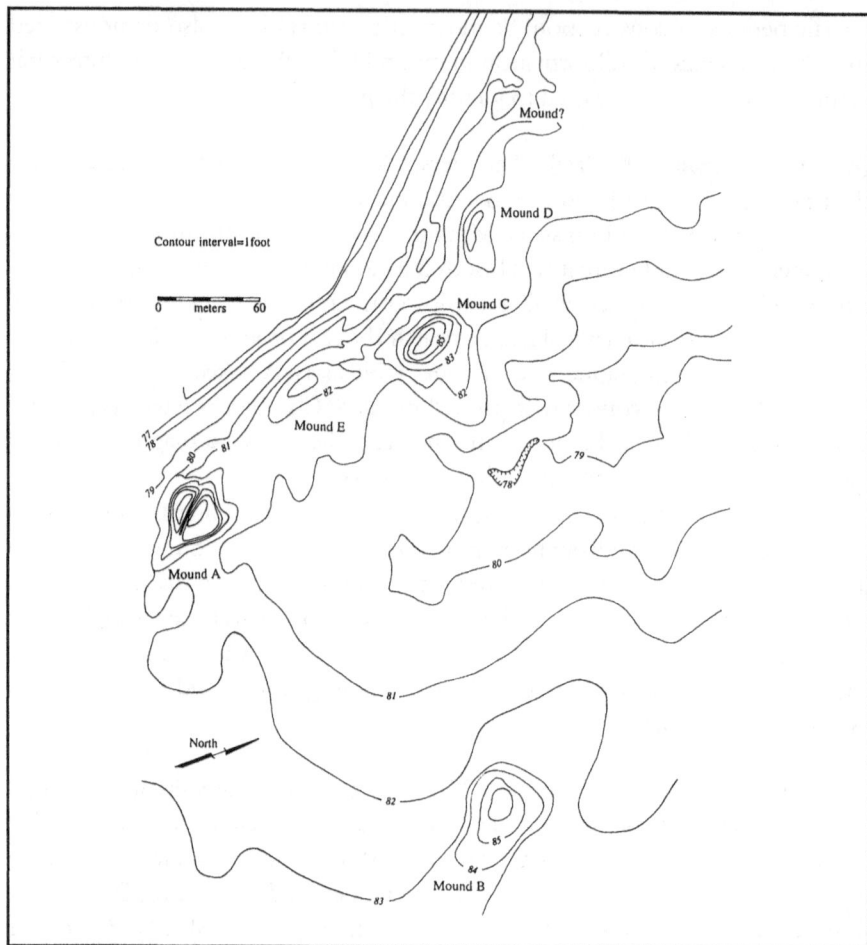

Fig. 14-9.   Mounds at Frenchman's Bend site (16OU259) (after Saunders 1992).

B each over 4.5 m in height. Mound A is smaller at 1.5 m, but all mounds were likely taller prior to modern disturbance (Russo 1992b, 1993). No archaeological investigations have been conducted at Mound A, although when a house was constructed on the mound in the 1970s, a cache of large "potato-shaped" baked clay objects was uncovered (Fogelman, personal communication).

In 1992–1993, I tested mounds C and B (Russo 1992b, 1993). The profile of Mound C showed that construction was initiated with the leveling of the ground, upon which a fire and post were burned prior to mound fill deposition. The charred post yielded a radiocarbon date of 5260 ± 70 B.P. Within the mound fill at Mound B, charcoal from a hearth produced a date of 4720 ± 190 B.P. (both dates uncalibrated; table 14-1). The only temporally diagnostic Archaic artifacts from either mound were a Jaketown perforator recovered below the hearth in Mound B and two red jasper beads from a disturbed context in the upper levels of

Mound C (Russo 1992b, 1993). Although the beads are not exclusive to the Archaic, they are commonly found in Archaic contexts. In addition to these, over 100 Archaic points, numerous baked clay objects (including two block fragments), and ground stone tools have been recovered from the surface of the mounds and of a ridge connecting mounds A and B (Russo 1992b).

Watson Brake (16OU175).   Perhaps the most spectacular Archaic mound site in Louisiana is Watson Brake (fig. 14-12). It consists of 10 (possibly 11) mounds connected by a ridge that surrounds a central "plaza" (J. Saunders 1994; Saunders et al. 1994). The circular complex is more than 300 m wide, with the tallest mound (Mound A) over 7 m in height. Surface collections have produced Archaic projectile points, spherical clay balls, soapstone fragments, and baked clay blocks. An auger test placed in the ridge fill between Mounds A and B has produced fragments of clay blocks along with fire-cracked rock, flakes, and other

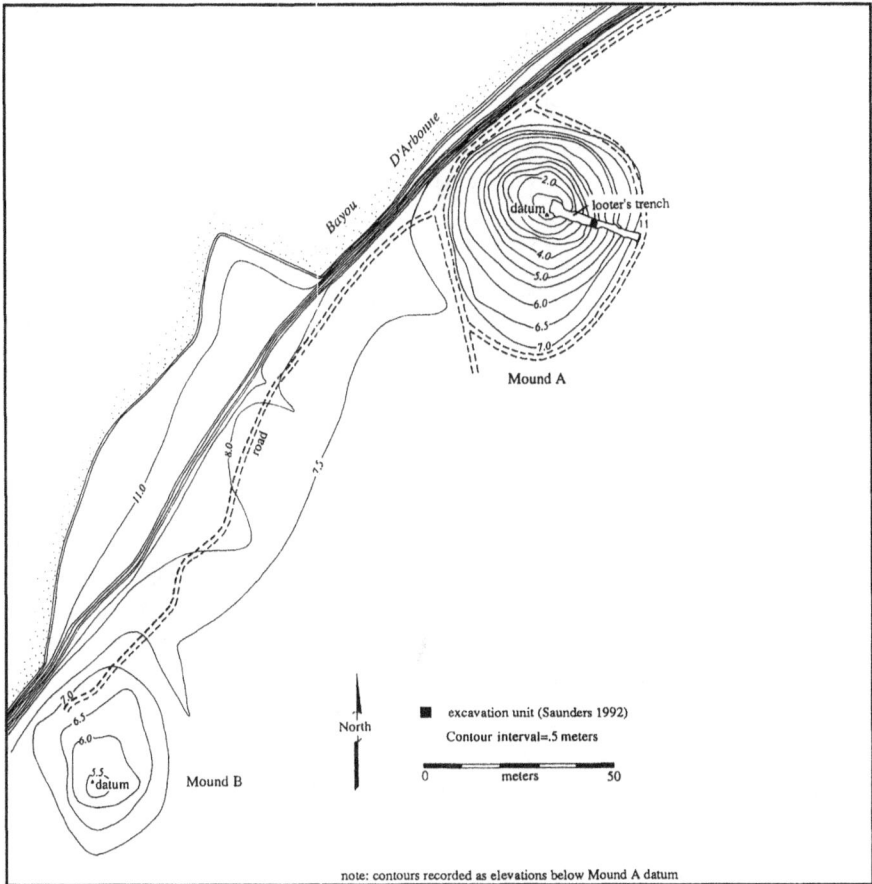

Fig. 14-10.   Hedgepeth Mounds (16LI7) (after Saunders and Allen 1994).

baked clay fragments (Saunders et al. 1994). Soil probes into Mound A indicate weathering similar to that found at Hedgepeth and Frenchman's Bend, evidence of an Archaic age for the mound.

Most recently, six calibrated radiocarbon dates have been reported from the ridge and Mound B contexts ranging between 5250 and 5850 B.P., with another at around 4150 B.P. (J. Saunders 1994:58). Excavations revealed that alternating midden and mound fill strata underlie the ridge and mound. Joe Saunders (1994:58) concludes that "parts of the ridges are purposefully constructed, while other parts were accumulations of burned-rock middens." The creators of the complex were apparently living on the ridges, as evidenced by in situ midden, as well as intentionally mounding them. Saunders links the complex to that of nearby Frenchman's Bend through similarities in dates and artifacts, which consist mostly of fire-cracked rock and baked clay objects as well as chipped stone tools. The diversity of clay objects is greater at Watson Brake, consisting of

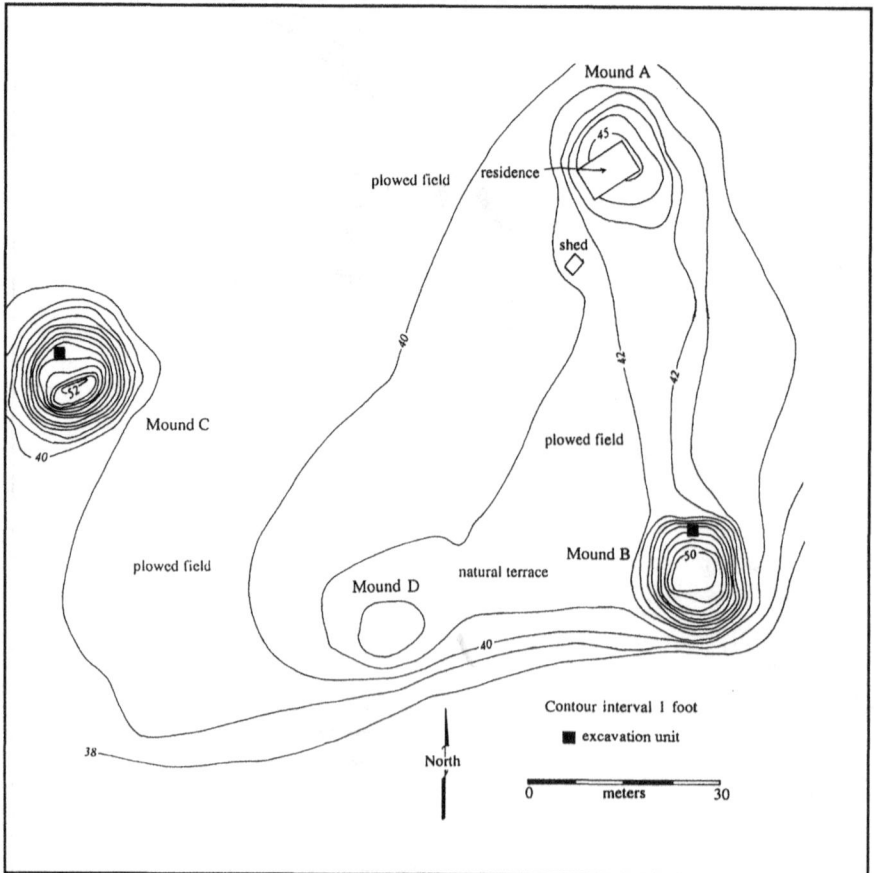

Fig. 14-11.   Stelly Mounds (16SL1) (with permission of James Fogelman; after Jones and Shuman 1991).

spheres, blocks, and tabular forms. Saunders (1994) suggests that the blocks may have been used in heat treating chert.

Implications of Mid-Holocene Mound Sites

The sites discussed above provide the best evidence of Archaic mounds but certainly not the only evidence. At least 60 mound groups in the Southeast (Russo 1994b) are suspected or have been demonstrated to date to the Middle and Late Archaic (including Poverty Point–related mounds). Most are in Louisiana, but they also occur in Florida, Mississippi, and Arkansas (e.g., Gibson 1994a, this volume; Jackson and Jeter 1994; Piatek 1994; Russo 1994a; R. Saunders 1994;

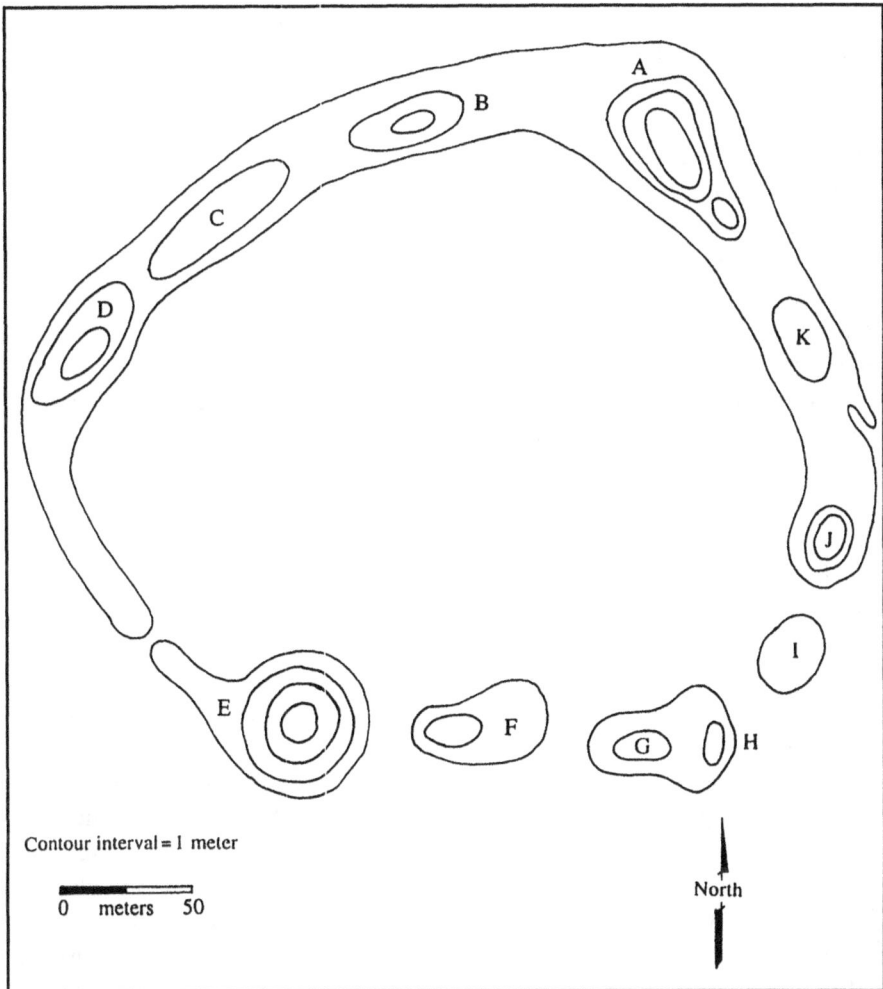

Fig. 14-12. Watson Brake (16OU175) (after Louisiana Archaeological Society 1983 in Jones 1983).

Saunders et al. 1994). The majority of suspected Archaic mound sites are not yet dated by absolute techniques. Undoubtedly, some will turn out not to be Archaic constructions. (Some of the original Amite phase mounds described by Gagliano [1963] have subsequently yielded evidence of ceramic period construction [Jones and Shuman 1988:27; R. Saunders 1994; Servello 1984].) Nonetheless, as has been demonstrated, much of the current data placing ceremonial mound construction within the realm of the Archaic is unequivocal.

Southeastern cultures are traditionally viewed as having been incapable of achieving permanency of settlement until domesticated plant production provided a stable and storable food supply during the Woodland period. Despite incipient domestication of native plants (Gremillion, this volume), no evidence has yet been identified to suggest that horticulture was sufficiently developed anywhere in the Southeast during the mid-Holocene to support large, permanently settled populations. Based on the seasonally dispersed resources typically associated with mid-Holocene subsistence economies, general synthetic perspectives on mid-Holocene social formations preclude the possibility that populations could obtain the size and complexity to support monumental construction of the larger mound complexes in Louisiana and Florida. It should, thus, not be unexpected that horticulture and other "increments" of the evolution toward the sedentary, complex social formations associated with the Woodland mound-building cultures—such as pottery production, long-term storage, substantial housing, and even mortuary ceremonialism—are absent at all or most of the mid-Holocene mound sites. Traditional markers of progressive evolution, of the slow and incremental move toward sedentism and hierarchical social development, stand silent in attempts to understand the precocious mound-building cultures of the mid-Holocene.

Gibson (this volume) has rightly pointed out that broad syntheses "are not meant to substitute for detailed regional and local syntheses, which rarely fit the broad picture perfectly." The general southeastern model of seminomadic, seasonally foraging mid-Holocene cultures seems so far removed from the implied social and economic systems behind the large-scale public works described above that if evidence for the mound-building cultures does not enlighten us as to a more variable depiction of mid-Holocene cultures, it does enlighten as to the poor foundation on which our current models of the period are built. Prior to the investigations of the Archaic mounds in Louisiana, local models of the preceramic Archaic were largely based on general southeastern models. No significant excavations had been conducted on nonmound preceramic Archaic sites (Neuman 1984:82), and the collective mound investigations in both Louisiana and Florida, although few and recent, represent one of the best studied aspects of the local preceramic Archaic cultures. How atypical Archaic mounds really are in Louisiana and Florida, thus, remains an open question until local settlement patterns are better investigated.

What can we say about Archaic mound builders? The scale of mound construction at the more extensive sites such as Watson Brake and Horr's Island is sufficiently large to suggest that settlement was relatively permanent. Supporting this conclusion are seasonality data from Horr's Island, where mound and village subsistence remains consist largely of marine fish and shellfish (Russo 1991; chap. 10, this volume).

No evidence has yet been recovered from other Archaic mounds indicating that they are associated with peoples who gardened, who occupied large, permanent villages, or who traded extensively with far-off cultures. A few exotic lithics have been identified from Frenchman's Bend (Saunders et al. 1994), Hornsby Mound (Manuel 1983:36), Stelly Mounds (Fogleman 1992), and other Louisiana mounds, but not in large enough quantities to indicate that the mound builders were involved in extensive trade networks. A few exotic bannerstones have been found at Tomoka (Douglass 1882) and Horr's Island (Hrdlicka 1922), but aside from these, virtually all artifacts found in Florida Archaic mounds were made from locally available resources. There is no evidence that the various mound-building societies in Louisiana and Florida were in direct contact.

Although extensive lithic scatters have been collected from the surfaces of some Lower Mississippi Valley mound sites (e.g., Hornsby, Frenchman's Bend), associated habitation sites have not been securely identified at Louisiana mound sites (although the evidence from Watson Brake is mounting), and what subsistence systems supported the mound-builder societies needs further investigation. Watson Brake and three other Louisiana sites have produced faunal assemblages from midden contexts. Watson Brake has yielded a small faunal assemblage dominated by freshwater fish (J. Saunders 1994:58). A short list of the Banana Bayou fauna identifies mostly turtle and fish (presumably freshwater), shellfish, and deer (Brown and Lambert-Brown 1978). The midden at Frenchman's Bend consists primarily of freshwater mussel and fish with deer included. A faunal assemblage from Stelly Mound C consists primarily of freshwater fish.

Whether these fauna represent daily maintenance refuse of the mound builders is unclear. The Banana Bayou fauna was identified some distance from the mound site (Brown and Lambert-Brown 1978). The Frenchman's Bend fauna was part of the fill at Mound A and may predate the mound (Joe Saunders, personal communication). And the relation of the Stelly Mounds fauna to the mound builders is unclear. No extensive faunal analyses have been done on any of these assemblages. Although we know that the mound builders in Louisiana did not rely on horticulture to support the large-scale work, in the absence of detailed studies, we cannot say for certain whether they relied principally on aquatic resources. All of the confirmed Louisiana mound sites are located next to what were streams, marshes, and swamps during the mid-Holocene, and Gibson (this volume) believes that locations along these "ecological seams" provided "abundant and practically inexhaustible food resources" conducive to "logistical

based sedentism." Aquatic resources certainly supported large, resident populations of mound builders in Florida, and a reliance on aquatic resources in combination with forest fauna and plants remains the most likely resource base in
Louisiana. It is far from clear, however, whether all Louisiana mound sites represent aspects of sedentary settlement systems.

Whatever fired the economic engines behind Archaic mound building, the
question also arises of what extinguished them. The mounds at Horr's Island
stand alone in southwest Florida during the preceramic Archaic—ceremonial
mounds are found nowhere else in the region at the time. The southwest Florida
Archaic mound construction phenomenon seems to have begun and ended at
Horr's Island. Not until nearly 2000 years later were ceremonial mounds again
constructed in the region. If the known archaeological record is accurate, the
remarkable social phenomenon of ceremonial mounding ended within a few
hundred years after it began at this single locale. Certain Horr's Island Archaic traditions persisted after the demise of mound building (e.g., shell tool tradition),
indicating some cultural continuity. Yet the initial ceramic cultures that developed from the mound builders were smaller in size and more simply organized
(Russo 1991; Widmer 1974, 1988:65).

A similar precociousness can be seen in the eastern Florida Archaic mounds.
Prior to the identification of the Tomoka mounds as Archaic, the earliest mounds
along the southeastern Atlantic coast were thought to be the simple and rather
small sand burial mounds of the Refuge-Deptford phase (Early Woodland) in
Georgia (Thomas and Larsen 1979). These mounds fit cleanly into the progressive
scheme for the evolution of complex societies. The idea that mounds started out
rather small and "evolved" into larger and more complex structures with the
adoption of agriculture and the evolution of increasingly complex societies provided the neat incremental trajectory predicted by normative models of Southeastern cultural evolution. The mounds at Tomoka (if they all turn out to be
Archaic), in contrast, are earlier, larger, more numerous, and, if Mound 6 can
serve as a measure, more complicated in structure than the subsequent Refuge-
Deptford mound sites that would appear nearly 2000 years later (Thomas and
Larsen 1979:142–143).

Because the Archaic mounds of east Florida are isolated in character (Russo
1994b:93–94), time, and place from the next earliest mound-building traditions,
it is not likely that the idea for the earliest Refuge-Deptford mounds arose from
earlier shell and sand mounds of Florida. Along with that from Horr's Island, the
data from east Florida (including a possible distinct and even earlier mounding
tradition along the St. Johns River [Russo 1994a]) indicate that all Archaic
mound-building cultures in Florida were short-lived, dead-end traditions.

The Archaic mound-building cultures in the Lower Mississippi Valley present
a somewhat different picture. If the greater numbers of mounds (Russo 1994b) in
Louisiana are real, they do not seem to have been as temporally isolated as in

Florida. Similarities in artifacts, which include baked clay items, chipped stone points, "clinkers" (pumice-like artifacts), stone beads, and a few exotic lithics, connect the mid-Holocene mound-building tradition to later Poverty Point mound-building traditions. Gibson (1994a) has noted that the arcuate layout of mound groups such as at Watson Brake and Caney mounds anticipates the semi-circular ridges at Poverty Point. While all connections of the early mounds to the later Poverty Point traditions are arguable at this point, they do point out that early mound construction had a more persistent Archaic tradition in the Mississippi Valley than in Florida.

The argument as to whether the Archaic mound-building tradition continued after Poverty Point remains open to debate. Some have implied (Griffin 1979:270–271; Shenkel 1984:64) that mound-building traditions in Louisiana may have ended with the demise of Poverty Point, only to be reintroduced later during Marksville times. They suggest that few, if any, definitive mounds were constructed during the Tchula period sandwiched between Poverty Point and Marksville times. In point of fact, with the recent identification of the numerous early mounds, preceramic Archaic mounds far outnumber all known and suspected Poverty Point (Gibson 1994a, this volume; Russo 1994b) and Tchefuncte mounds combined. If mound construction had not ceased by the Tchula period, it apparently had been in a long decline, and the rise of a separate and distinct Marksville mounding tradition seems to have gotten its impetus, if not its pedigree, from the midwestern Hopewell phenomenon (Shenkel 1984:64; Toth 1979).

It seems, then, there is the possibility that none of the earliest mound-building traditions survived beyond the Archaic. Does this mean that something about Archaic cultures was inimical to sustaining labor-intensive community endeavors as complex as mound construction? Does it mean that a nonhorticultural resource base is incapable of supporting complex social formations for extended periods? Probably not. The evidence actually indicates that the Mississippi Valley Archaic mound tradition, extending from the Middle Archaic to Poverty Point traditions, lasted longer than any later southeastern mound-building traditions dependent on horticulture or intensive agricultural production.

The location of nearly all Lower Mississippi and Florida Archaic mound sites next to major rivers, swamps, marshes, and estuaries suggests that aquatic resources were important to early mound builders. Once the technology was established and the need perceived to settle and devote most of the societies' subsistence energies to the exploitation of aquatic resources, the abundance of those resources allowed for surplus time and energies to be devoted to nonsubsistence-related tasks, much in the same way that agriculture would support Mississippi monumental constructions. Certainly, the exploitation of aquatic resources is not a sufficient cause for mound construction—other aquatic-dependant cultures along Southeast coasts and rivers did not adopt a mound-building tradition. But in the absence of intensive horticulture, only those Archaic societies who relied on aquatic resources (with terrestrial plants and animals necessary as secondary resources) could sustain and provide the population base, labor, and surplus time to develop the larger of the mound constructions.

As are all public works, symbolic and ceremonial mound traditions are initiated to fill some perceived cultural or social need. Unfortunately, so little work has been undertaken at Archaic mounds that assessment of the historic circumstances that compelled ceremonial constructions has not yet been broached. Most investigations have been restricted to determining the age and content of mounds. To date, the limited data suggest that all Archaic mounds were distinctly different from Woodland and Mississippian mounds that followed. With the possible exception of Monte Sano, none has so far revealed any evidence of hierarchical social ranking in terms of differential burials or structures placed within or on top of the mounds. This would seem to suggest that all members of the societies had equal access to resources, be they foodstuffs, living quarters, tools, or exotic trade items. This perceived egalitarian character of the mound builders may, of course, be an artifact of inadequate investigations. But it is of anthropological significance that North America's earliest mound traditions may have had little functional similarity with later traditions.

Throughout this chapter I have suggested that archaeologists have traditionally viewed large-scale mound-building societies as being "hierarchically ranked." In order to build monumental architecture, some degree of social ranking is required in which leaders or classes of people can compel or persuade others to do their bidding. However, simple or complex chiefdoms or big men societies typically attributable to Woodland and Mississippi mound-building societies need not persevere as our only models of ranked societies capable of mound construction. Some Archaic mounds are sufficiently small to have been built by few people in less than a year. The social formations necessary to achieve this accomplishment could be impermanent and apolitical—one or more people directed a large project agreed upon by the group. Social ranking in such cases may be heterarchical rather than hierarchical (e.g., Crumley 1979)—achieved by group consensus for project specific needs (Russo 1991). Depending on historical circumstances, permanent social ranking may or may not arise out of these temporary formations.

That the mounds are small and simple, however, does not necessarily mean that the societies building them were also small and simply organized. That is only one possibility. The simpler mound sites may, of course, be part of a larger complex of societies integrated in hierarchically ranked formations. Building larger sites such as Watson Brake and Poverty Point may have taken a number of affinally or politically related societies representing complex, regional social alliances that persisted for generations. Based on the size of the larger mound sites, the ranking in these societies was likely hierarchical and permanent. Based on the absence of evidence for high status individuals, the ranking was most likely achieved by consensus. Entrepreneurial or political self-interests, the primary motivators of the chiefs and big men attributed to later mound-building cultures, seem to have been absent or downplayed in Archaic mound-building societies. Such unusual social formations should give southeastern archaeologists pause because they challenge normative models of the causes and archaeological correlates of hierarchical social ranking. However, because no adequate investigation of the interior of Archaic mounds has been accomplished, only further research can answer the question of whether Archaic mounds and mound-building societies were distinctly different from the mound-building societies that followed them.

Acknowledgments

Thanks go to William Marquardt of the Institute of Archaeology and Paleoenvironmental Studies at the University of Florida and to Key Marco Developments, who funded the investigations at Horr's Island. Joe Saunders and his colleagues generously kept me abreast of their ongoing work on Archaic mounds in north Louisiana. Thanks too to Ken Sassaman, the South Carolina Institute of Archaeology and Anthropology, and the South Carolina Department of Archives and History for their support of graphics production.

Much appreciation goes out to Thomas Johnson and Jon Gibson, who funded the radiocarbon dates from Stelly Mounds. Jon also provided access to his works in progress. He, Arville Touchet, Thurman Allen, and Becky Saunders volunteered their time and efforts in investigating the Stelly Mounds. The investigations there were undertaken on a shoestring budget and could not have succeeded without the scores of volunteers who suffered through long, hot, and frequently unproductive days. In particular, University of Southwestern Louisiana Anthropology Club members Lynn Shreve, Denise Decuir, Phyllis Lear, and Elaine Lear were of great help. Jim Fogelman was instrumental in providing the impetus for the investigations as well as the bulk of the volunteer crew. Eddy Ray Stelly was most gracious in allowing us access to the site and enduring the concomitant intrusion into his daily life.

15

Poverty Point and Greater Southeastern Prehistory

The Culture That Did Not Fit

JON L. GIBSON

Syntheses of southeastern prehistory depict broad cultural patterns and sweeping historical trends. That is the nature of syntheses. Older syntheses emphasize culture history—culture origin and change (Ford 1969; Ford and Willey 1941; Griffin 1946, 1952a, 1967; Sears 1962; Spaulding 1955; Willey and Phillips 1958). Newer ones integrate culture-historical and cultural-adaptational paradigms (Johnson 1993c) and, for the Archaic period Southeast, are concerned with developments, such as expanding sedentism, intensifying economic use of starchy seeds and aquatic resources, burgeoning interregional exchange, and growing dependence on containers, especially those of stone and pottery (Jeter et al. 1989; Smith 1986:18–32; Steponaitis 1986:373–374).

As useful as these syntheses are for revealing salient patterns and trends across the entire Southeast, they are not meant to substitute for detailed regional and local syntheses, which rarely fit the broad picture perfectly and sometimes deviate significantly from it. The Lower Mississippi Valley is one of those regions, which just does not fit very well, especially in terms of timing, and the Poverty Point site and culture are reasons for this deviation. "For a number of years after Moore's [1913] report appeared, archaeologists working in the South were fully cognizant of the unusual nature of this site [Poverty Point] and of the artifacts found there. Although the locality was visited a number of times, no one was prepared to undertake additional work. Other problems more readily solvable were too numerous for much time to be spent on a unique culture that did not fit into the gradually clarifying outline of Southeastern prehistory" (Ford and Webb 1956:14).

Four decades after James Ford and Clarence Webb penned those words, archaeologists are still grappling with the Poverty Point problem. How close they are to making Poverty Point fit the clarifying outline of southeastern prehistory is the matter I take up in the following pages. My examination focuses on three interwoven processes—mound building, pottery making, and long-distance exchange. Independently, all three processes had precedents in the Holocene Southeast, but they were integrated in Poverty Point culture. Poverty Point culture upped the scale of mound building and exchange above anything previously seen in the Southeast. We are only beginning to define enabling contexts and to see how everything was put together, but one thing is clear: Poverty Point culture, as a relatively uniform way of life or intensive interaction system, has little meaning beyond a 30-km radius of the Poverty Point site and none outside the Lower Mississippi Valley.

The Poverty Point Site

The Poverty Point site is located in northeastern Louisiana on the eastern escarpment of Maçon Ridge, some 25 km west of the Mississippi River and about 330 km inland from the Gulf of Mexico (fig. 15-1). It is the largest and most unusual of the Poverty Point cultural sites because of its monumental earth architecture (fig. 15-2). The central part of the site covers more than 200 ha and the entire site area, counting all outlying mounds and occupational areas, spreads over more than three square kilometers. There are six mounds—three small platforms, one large conical mound, and two massive structures thought to be shaped like birds (Ford and Webb 1956:33). One of the platforms appears to have been surmounted by a small dome (Gibson 1986:217, fig. 6). The conical mound stands 7.5 m high and is 55 m in diameter (Ford and Webb 1956:33–34). The charred end of a human femur and a few other unidentified burned bones were found in an ash bed underneath the mound (Ford and Webb 1956:35). The smaller bird mound is 15.5 m high and measures 121 by 170 m in basal dimensions (Ford and Webb 1956:18, fig. 4). And the larger bird mound towers over 21 m high, has a wing spread of 194 m, and stretches 216 m from head to tail (Ford and Webb 1956:14–16, fig. 3). The two bird mounds have volumes of nearly 100,000 and 180,000 steres and the large conical one nearly 5000 cubic meters (Shenkel 1986:table 1).

A series of six concentric elliptical ridges surrounds an open area of some 15 ha (Ford and Webb 1956:16-17, fig. 2). These artificial ridges range from about one and a half to less than a meter high at present and were probably never much higher. Their height is visually exaggerated because they are separated by swales, where fill dirt was borrowed. The inner ring is about 600 m in long diameter and the outer one nearly 1200 m. Around a third of a million steres of fill was used to build the ridges (Gibson 1987a:16). If all the dirt that went into the six mounds, six ridges, and preconstruction land leveling is added together, it amounts to somewhere between two-thirds and three-quarters of a million steres.

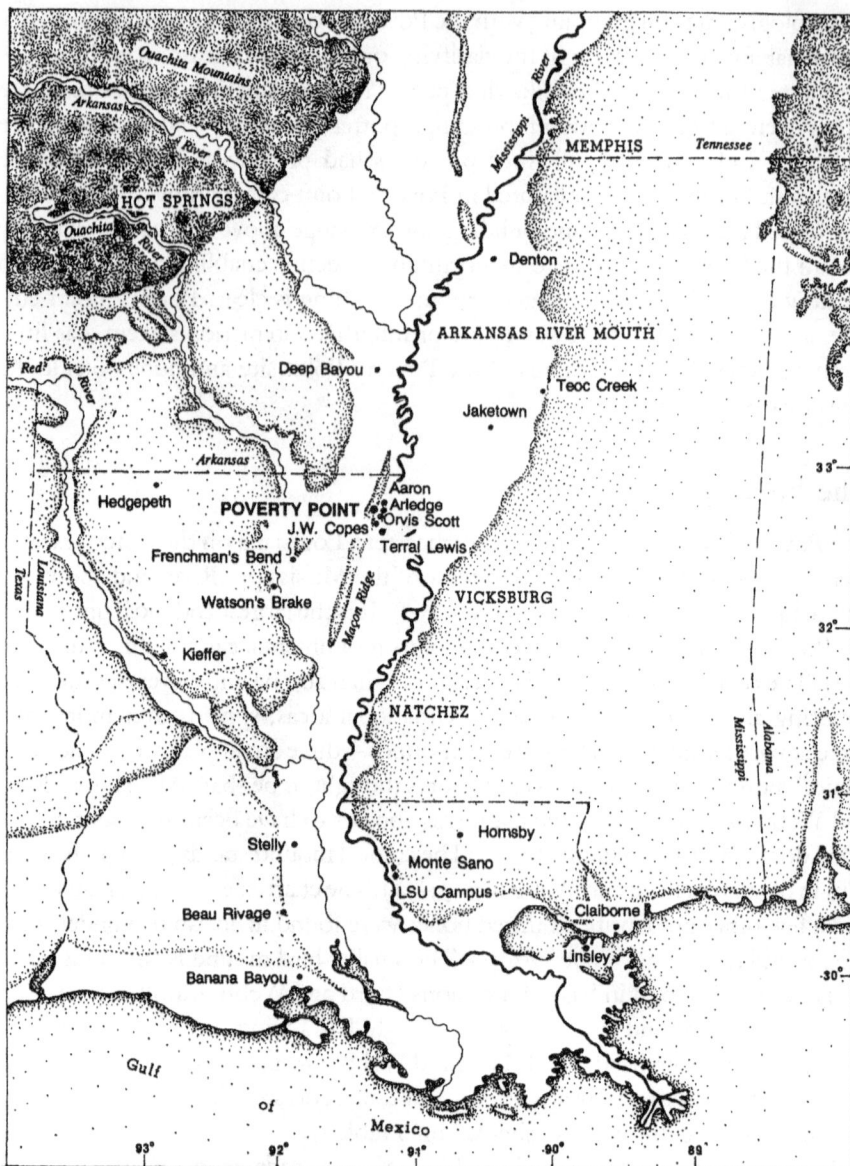

Fig. 15-1.   Poverty Point and Archaic mound sites in the Lower Mississippi Valley.

The ridged arrangement is crescent-shaped, and the open side is delineated by a steep bluff (fig. 15-2). Five aisles radiate through the ridged figure, one more than Ford and Webb (1956:16, fig. 2) realized. The aisles are actually aligned gaps through the ridges, which run through the midpoints and convergence planes of the long and short radians of the six elliptical ridges (Gibson 1986:229). They look like spokes of a giant wheel.

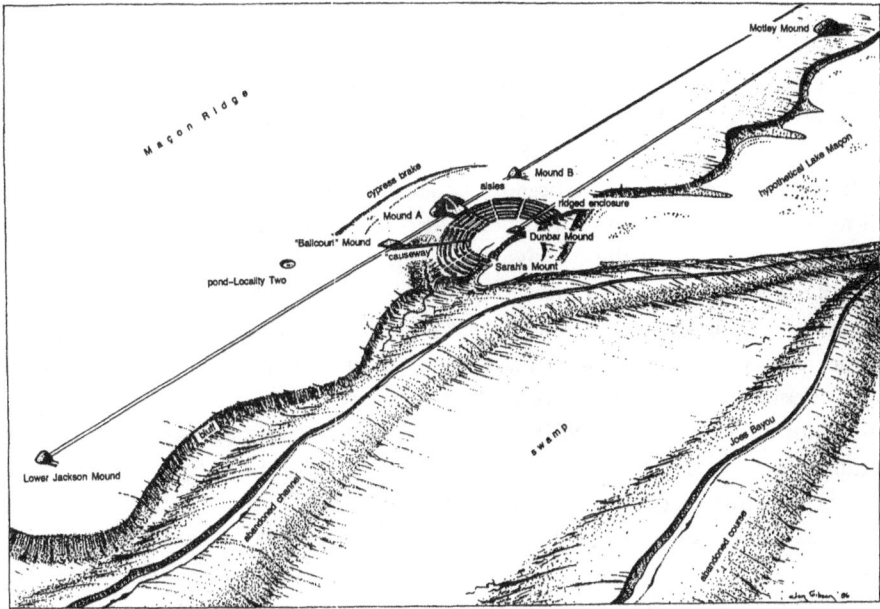

Fig. 15-2.   Earthworks and landscape at the Poverty Point site (drawing by Jon Gibson).

Some archaeologists view the Poverty Point site as a large permanent village with the rings serving as raised foundations for houses (Ford and Webb 1956:128–129; Gibson 1974; Haag 1961:322; Webb 1982:19). Others envision it as a figment of typology (a misassociation of artifacts from successive occupations, which just happen to occur on the same spot [Spaulding 1955:19]); a vacant ceremonial center (Phillips 1970:872; Willey 1957:198–199); a ceremonial center with a small resident population and a large periodically influxing one (Brain 1971:47, 51); or as a trade fair meeting ground (Gagliano 1967:21; Jackson 1991; Winters 1968:218–219). Sociopolitically, Poverty Point is interpreted variously as the seat of a class-structured society subjugated by a mighty Hopewellian empire (Ford and Webb 1956:129); as a complex society that coalesced under religiopolitical stimulation from the Olmec area of the Mexican Gulf Coast (Ford 1969:191); as a pristine chiefdom with strong leaders and wide hegemony (Gibson 1973, 1974; Webb 1982:71); and as a intersocietal institution, a trade fair, and not an integrated society at all (Jackson 1991:266–271).

Despite appearances, these interpretations really have a common theme—they all portray Poverty Point as a unique cultural phenomenon—and they express that uniqueness under the paradigms and terminologies that prevailed during their day. I do not think we have yet said what Poverty Point was sociopolitically, but when we do, it will be because we have calculated how the salient factors of large, sedentary, well-fed hunter-gatherer populations, strong though perhaps temporary or situational leadership, inspirational religion, and long-distance exchange all came to be integrated. I believe the unapproached scale of Poverty Point reflects the shortfall of local rock resources (real or presumed) and the magnitude of the effort needed to overcome it (Gibson 1994a).

In my view, the Poverty Point site and culture could not have developed anywhere but where they did because other stone-impoverished regions in the Southeast were not as impoverished and did not bear a similar strategic locational relationship to the Mississippi River, which linked the major resource supply zones. Other rock-impoverished places did not offer the absolute abundance of wild foods and the established pattern of logistical foraging. People in other places did not have the organizational and mound-building experience. And people of other places were content to use locally available stone, shell, bone, or antler to make their durable equipment and were not as motivated to import the exotic raw materials. In my opinion, it was the unique combination of these factors that enabled the development of the Poverty Point site and culture, and it was the vision and actions of inspirational leaders that brought it all together.

All of these conditions except intensive interregional exchange existed in northeastern Louisiana before Poverty Point culture emerged. Middle and Late Archaic mound sites in the region produce only a few exotic materials. Benton exchange did not reach into the Poverty Point region (Johnson 1994; Johnson and Brookes 1988). Local resources underpinned early mound building, and the simple fact that mounds were built before Poverty Point indicates that the enabling labor and organizational capabilities were present too. Although our evidence is primarily circumstantial, we can make a strong argument that logistical patterns of fishing-hunting-gathering were already established in some localities (Ramenofsky 1986).

The one ingredient that is missing in Late (terminal) Archaic culture in northeastern Louisiana is intensive long-distance exchange. Before the onset of the Poverty Point period (ca. 3300 B.P.), foreign exchange materials are limited to small amounts of novaculite and an occasional quartz crystal (Ouachita Mountain sources; Gibson 1994b). The quantity of these materials nowhere approaches the quantity found on later Poverty Point components, although it does pick up on sites closer to the central Arkansas sources in the Ouachitas. However, the earliest occupation levels at the Poverty Point site are laden with imported exotic lithics. Exotics occur over the entire occupational area; they are plentiful; and they are varied, not just novaculite and crystals but practically every kind of foreign rock that ever made its way to Poverty Point seems to be present. Thus, from the beginning, vibrant long-distance exchange was a fact of life at the Poverty Point site. Whatever else may have been involved, long-distance exchange was undoubtedly a major, perhaps the primary, factor in the unprecedented growth spurt of the Poverty Point site and in its expanded local and far-reaching interactions.

The Geographic and Chronological
Position of Poverty Point Culture

Around the Poverty Point site at distances up to 30 km are dozens of small sites with similar assemblages and artifact types. They comprise the Poverty Point phase (Phillips 1970:872). Up to 300 km farther afield in southeastern Arkansas, western Mississippi, and southern Louisiana are sites assigned to other phases of Poverty Point culture (Phillips 1970:869–876; Webb 1968, 1982:5–9). They generally resemble Poverty Point phase components in terms of assemblage composition but differ in typological detail. Still other sites that Webb (1968: table 1) identifies as possible Poverty Point and Poverty Point-related extend as far upvalley as southeastern Missouri and as far eastward as the Atlantic Coast of Georgia, Florida, and South Carolina, more than 1200 km distant. Their identification is based primarily on the *occurrence* of baked earth cooking objects and not on assemblage composition or artifact type similarities.

I maintain that the term *Poverty Point culture,* as a maximum (taxonomic) unit reflecting a major segment of culture history (Willey and Phillips 1958:48), has no sociocultural or even practical utility outside the Lower Mississippi Valley core area. The sweeping geographic scope of the present examination allows me to embolden some of those faint cultural taxonomic lines and erase others.

The Poverty Point site and culture pattern highlight the terminal Archaic or middle Gulf Formational stage in the Lower Mississippi Valley (Ford and Webb 1956; Walthall and Jenkins 1976; cf. Ford 1969). Critical examination of more than four dozen radiocarbon dates (Gibson 1992a, 1994a), coupled with refined cultural taxonomy, indicates that the pattern formed during the last half of the fourth millennium B.P. The Poverty Point site and other dated components, such as Terral Lewis (Gregory 1991; Gregory et al. 1970) and J. W. Copes (Jackson 1986:308–310), located on Joes Bayou within 30 km of the Poverty Point site, and Teoc Creek (Connaway et al. 1977:106–108, table 9), located on the Yalobusha River in western Mississippi some 160 km northeast of Poverty Point, coexisted between about 3300 and 3050 B.P. (uncalibrated ages; Gibson 1992a, 1994c).

The late dates from the Jaketown site on Wasp Lake near the Yazoo River in western Mississippi, about 90 km northeast of Poverty Point, were obtained during the early days of radiocarbon dating and are questionable (Ford 1969:30; Ford and Webb 1956: table 9). A more recent thermoluminescence (TL) date, 3030 ± 110 B.P. (OxTL 143d; average of assays of four baked earth balls), indicates that Jaketown too was occupied during the general 250-year span (Huxtable et al. 1972: table 2). On the other hand, radiocarbon dates from the Linsley site, located near New Orleans in the neck of land separating Lake Pontchartrain and Lake Borgne, about 285 km southeast of Poverty Point, are from one to four centuries earlier than the indicated span (Gagliano and Saucier 1963:326). These dates were taken on spoil bank materials dredged from two to four meters deep

(Gagliano and Saucier 1963:321), and we do not know their exact contexts or associations. I also have reservations about classifying Linsley as a Poverty Point site in light of the apparent absence of exotic lithic (exchange) materials and the typologically distinctive assemblage. However, even if my reservations are unfounded and Linsley deserves its Poverty Point identity, adding its dates would only lengthen the indicated span by a couple of centuries (or less, considering the standard deviations).

The main point of all this is that the Poverty Point period represents a shorter span and incorporates fewer sites than we thought just a few years ago when we were envisioning Poverty Point culture lasting 1500 years, covering much of the Lower and Middle Mississippi Valley, and having strong influences that reached from the Great Lakes to the Atlantic Coast. Although not all archaeologists will agree, the short chronology and geographical narrowing are, in my opinion, more in line with historical and organizational dimensions of Poverty Point culture than is the broader version, which roughly corresponds to the geographic distribution of small, hand-molded earthen cooking objects (Poverty Point objects) and not to a sociopolitically integrated group.

Mound Building

Long regarded as the earliest and largest pre-Hopewellian earthworks in America north of Mexico, the Poverty Point complex can now claim the distinction only of being the largest of the earliest, and even that distinction is diminishing as other large Archaic earthworks come to light (see Russo, chap. 14, this volume, for detailed treatment of pre–Poverty Point mounds). Strong evidence is emerging of Archaic mound building in the Lower Mississippi Valley and Florida as early as 6220 B.P. (Brown and Lambert-Brown 1978; Coastal Environments, Inc. 1977; Gagliano 1963, 1967; Gibson 1994c; Gibson and Shenkel 1989; Haag 1992; Homburg 1992; Manuel 1979; Neuman 1992; Piatek 1994; Russo 1991, 1994a, 1994b, this volume; R. Saunders 1994; Saunders and Allen 1994; Saunders et al. 1994). If Claassen's (1991a, this volume) suggestion that some mounded Archaic shell middens are really intentionally built is accepted, then early mound building is more widespread than imagined. I also suspect early earth mounds will begin to show up in other parts of the Southeast when open-minded investigators begin to excavate mounds assumed to be of Early or Middle Woodland origin and shed their reluctance to call Archaic mounded-earth "middens" mounds.

The question is no longer whether mounds were built during the Archaic period but how widespread mound building was during that time. The issue I examine here is what Archaic mound building has to do with Poverty Point. In order to pursue this, I must first point out the cultural contexts of Archaic mounds, reminding myself all the while that generalizing from the little data in hand may not be warranted. I view the location of Archaic mounds along strong ecological seams, particularly river valley walls, a sand cay, and a coastal spit, as evidence for settlement stability and arguably for logistically based sedentism (Gibson 1994a). For the Lower Mississippi Valley, the argument is based strictly on ecological possibilism—the abundant and practically inexhaustible food resources of warm climate floodplains and adjoining upland forests, coupled with exploitational facility promoted by living on the edge. Ecological edges have the greatest biomass and widest species diversity in this riparian cornucopia, and exploitation costs are simplified. We have little hard data on Lower Mississippi subsistence, pro or con. On the other hand, sedentism is directly revealed by the Florida subsistence data (Russo 1991).

A single function for Archaic mounds is not clearly indicated. In fact, nothing about mound function is very clear. Of the 18 confirmed and suspected Archaic and Poverty Point mounds in Louisiana that have been tested, only three (Poverty Point Mound B, Monte Sano, and Kieffer) have produced a few bone fragments, all burned; however, except for bone from Mound B at Poverty Point (Ford and Webb 1956:35), none has been positively confirmed as human (Coastal Environments, Inc. 1977:243; Gibson 1968:14–15; Haag 1992; R. Saunders 1994). Two of the Florida mound sites (Horr's Island and Tomoka) produced a few burials (or rather, human bones), but in neither case can these be certainly attributed to the mound builders (Piatek 1994; Russo 1994a). However, not all of the mounds in these multiple-mound groups seem to have been so used, so other reasons must have underpinned construction too. Tick Island, on the other hand, has numerous flexed burials, but contextual details are ambiguous (Jahn and Bullen 1978; Russo 1994a). There is some question as to whether they were interred in a deliberately constructed mound, although Russo (1994a), who has studied the situation, thinks they were. All in all, we cannot make a strong case for Archaic mounds having been built primarily to bury people.

Artifacts are not much help in determining function either. Few artifacts are recovered from mound fill, and those that are seem to be mainly domestic refuse (Gibson 1994a). Only three of the tested Lower Mississippi mounds produced ornaments, and two of these, Monte Sano and Kieffer, also yielded bones, presumably human. Only the Kieffer Mound, however, had stone beads and burned bones in direct association (Gibson 1968). One of the Tomoka mounds contained several bannerstones, although they were apparently not directly placed with human bones (Piatek 1994). Russo (1994a) reports no ceremonial artifacts with the burials or elsewhere at Horr's Island.

The current evidence from Archaic mounds in Louisiana and Florida is insufficient to determine what they were used for, but they differ so much that I am inclined to think they had many purposes. They do, however, have one thing in common—conspicuous elevation. In an earlier paper, I speculate that this might be the key to their construction, a practical way of objectifying the traditional southeastern cosmological separation of the Upper and Lower Worlds, of raising ritual and ritual leaders above the ordinary plane of existence and validating their specialness (Gibson 1994c; Knight 1989; Lankford 1992). If this idea has merit, then Archaic mounds may have been used for all rituals requiring segregation of functionaries from the masses. Social and religious distancing could also have been crucial to establishing group identity and relationships with other groups. Mounds, by commemorating the mythical place of origin (Blitz 1993:33–35; Gibson 1992b; Swanton 1931:5–37) and being the seat of the most important village and pantribal ceremonies and other civic activities (DuPratz 1774; Swanton 1911), act to remind neighbors and strangers alike of a group's rights to the land and of its resolve to protect those rights. They serve as a sort of no trespassing sign with implied threat of sanction, and they do not need to have burials in them to do that.

Merely being older does not mean that Archaic mounds have any necessary relevance to the development of Poverty Point. What ties Archaic mound building directly to Poverty Point is the presence of an apparent Archaic mound, the Lower Jackson Mound, just south of the Poverty Point ridged enclosure (Gibson 1986:209, 1989:67–74). For a while, this mound was considered to be a Poverty Point construction because Poverty Point artifacts were found around it, and much to-do was made about the fact that a straight line running north from it intersected three mounds up at the Poverty Point site, including the large bird mound (Gibson 1986:209; Webb 1970).

We now know that the Poverty Point artifacts came from a small, isolated exposure located about a hundred meters or so northwest of the mound and were mixed together with the materials surface collected from immediately around the mound (Dennis LaBatt, personal communication, 1989). The Lower Jackson artifacts include cuboidal baked clay objects and Evans (double-notched) points, and these two types are diagnostic of the northeastern Louisiana Late Archaic mound-building era. So, we realize that there is a pre–Poverty Point Archaic mound literally within sight of the main earthworks, a mound that may have even been used as a marker for later architectural alignments. This means that the know-how and concerted action essential to mound building existed at the Poverty Point site long before the massive rings and mounds were ever raised.

Mound building is not a Poverty Point innovation, nor is it responsible for Poverty Point. It is a consequence of the social conditions that prevailed in certain Lower Mississippi and Floridian localities, and those conditions seem to have been a long time in the making.

Early Pottery

The question of whether pottery is an integral part of the Poverty Point assemblage has been discussed for years (Ford 1969:180–182; Ford et al. 1955:62; Ford and Webb 1956:105; Jenkins et al. 1986; Phillips 1970:529–532; Webb 1968:309–310, 1982:40–42; Williams and Brain 1983:354–356). This discussion was prolonged because pottery was rare, stratigraphic data were correspondingly few, and archaeological lore in the Mississippi Valley held pottery to be a Woodland trait, despite its early appearance along the southern Atlantic Coast (Bullen and Stoltman 1972; Claflin 1931; Fairbanks 1942; Ferguson 1951; Flannery 1943; Goggin 1952; Griffin 1943, 1945, 1952b; Jahn and Bullen 1978; Sassaman 1993a; Sears and Griffin 1950). However, archaeologists got around the sticky issue of the early Atlantic Coast pottery by attributing it to the Formative instead of the Archaic stage. By definition, the Formative was more progressive than the Archaic (Willey and Phillips 1958), and Ford's (1969) grand vision of sweeping diffusionary influences from South America and Mexico explained why it was more progressive. Everything fit nicely.

It has taken more than three decades to build a consensus, but most investigators today concede that pottery was made during the Poverty Point period (Ford 1969:180–182; Webb 1968:309–310, 1982:40–42). Although the stratigraphic evidence was available all along (Ford et al. 1955; Ford and Webb 1956:105–106; Webb 1968:309), normative historical reconstructions depicting Poverty Point as a Late Archaic preceramic culture sidetracked and slowed general acceptance of the idea (Ford et al. 1955:62; Phillips 1970:876). The growing weight of empirical evidence at Poverty Point and other nearby sites (Ford and Webb 1956:105–106; Webb et al. 1970), coupled with clarification of the chronological position of early ceramics across the Southeast (Sassaman 1993a: appendix), tipped the balance in favor of the idea (Jenkins et al. 1986; Sassaman 1993a; Webb et al. 1970; Webb 1982:40).

Poverty Point pottery is the oldest known in the Lower Mississippi Valley, and it seems to be as early at the Poverty Point site as anywhere. Although the Teoc Creek site produces radiocarbon dates that exceed the average for the construction period at the Poverty Point site (Connaway et al. 1977:106–108, table 9), they are not any older than the range of dates on the preconstruction occupation at Poverty Point. By a similar token, the Jaketown site, also in the Yazoo basin, produces the latest dates (Ford 1969:30; Ford and Webb 1956:123–124, table 9), but these dates obtained in the 1950s may not be dependable because they were obtained by dry carbon and by CO_2 techniques (Ford and Webb 1956:117). A TL date of 3030 ± 110 B.P. puts Jaketown squarely within the occupational span of the Poverty Point site (Huxtable et al. 1972: table 2).

Pottery from the Poverty Point site can be separated into five main fabric classes: grog-tempered, fiber-tempered, sand-tempered, clay grit-tempered, and untempered (or löessial) (Webb et al. 1970). The hard, thin-walled, grog-tempered material is Baytown ware. It postdates the Poverty Point occupation by more than 1500 years and thus will not be further considered here. The other four classes are early and occur in undisturbed Poverty Point deposits. They are classified as Wheeler (fiber-tempered), Alexander (sand-tempered), Tchefuncte (clay grit-tempered), and untempered (sometimes called Poverty Point) series (Webb 1982:40–42; Webb et al. 1970).

The Wheeler series includes plain, punctated, simple-stamped, finger-fluted, and fabric-impressed types; the Alexander series, plain and pinched types; the

Tchefuncte series, plain, rocker-stamped, incised, pinched, simple-stamped, and drag-and-jab types; and the untempered (Poverty Point) series, plain, incised, pinched, and rocker-stamped types.

The decorations on clay grit-tempered (Tchefuncte) and untempered ceramics are indistinguishable. The difference lies in the fabric; untempered pottery is made from löess (silty clay loam, probably derived from the B and upper C soil horizons underfoot), while clay grit-tempered pottery is made from gritty löess (silt loam taken from the A and E horizons), alluvium, or any soil to which aplastics were added—or perhaps from all three. The fabrics intergrade considerably, making consistent visual sorting practically impossible.

The long-held suspicion that the untempered pottery is earlier than clay grit-tempered pottery is not borne out by relative stratigraphy. Even though decorated fractions of the two fabric classes are typologically conflated, the plain clay grit-tempered ware is stratigraphically lower than any other and therefore must be regarded as the oldest. That the oldest material is also plain may be nothing more than a sampling quirk, although plain-to-decorated evolutionary trends have been noted elsewhere in the Southeast (Bullen 1961, 1972; Stoltman 1966, 1972).

The main historical question is this: Does the ceramic succession at the Poverty Point site fit this general southeastern sequence? The answer is that it does not. The main reason it does not seems to be that Poverty Point is not one of the earliest centers of pottery making. These are all on the south Atlantic Coast. Poverty Point is later and began to assimilate pottery influences from the east only after independently beginning to make ceramics.

To show how it does not fit, I adopt an indicator developed by Ford et al. (1955:107) in analyzing the Jaketown stratigraphy—mean vertical position (MVP). This statistic is derived by adding up the numbers of the arbitrary levels in which each relevant artifact occurs and dividing the results by the total occurrences. Because levels are counted from top to bottom, larger MVPs mean that the types in question are deeper *and presumably older* than those with smaller MVPs. The possibility of stratigraphic reversals in basket-loaded soils does not appear to upturn the MVPs because similar results obtain in test units placed outside the rings.

MVPs of the various fabric classes are fiber-tempered, 2.6; sand-tempered, 3.5; clay grit-tempered, 3.6; untempered, 3.6; unspecified (but not fiber- or sand-tempered), 6.0 (Gibson 1987b: tables 3–36, 1989:A1–A22, 1990:A1–A13, 1993a: A1–A13). If the clay grit-tempered, untempered, and unspecified (but not fiber- or sand-tempered) categories are combined, then this enlarged class of Tchefuncte pottery has the lowest MVP of all potteries, 4.4, lower even than fiber-tempered, which is supposed to be the earliest southeastern ceramic.

This raises an interesting point. Fiber-tempered pottery does not appear to be the earliest pottery at the Poverty Point site. The earliest ceramic is either tempered with clay grit or is not tempered at all, which, incidentally, may be saying the same thing. The most unsettling thing about the clay grit-tempered and untempered pottery is that decorations on both wares are typologically identifiable as Tchefuncte (Ford and Quimby 1945). Except for sherds with löessial (untempered) paste, I cannot separate sherds with Tchefuncte decorations at the Poverty Point site from later Tchula period Tchefuncte materials elsewhere in middle and coastal Louisiana. We hold Tchefuncte decorations to be diagnostic of the Tchula period, ca. 500–100 B.C., and finding them on pottery at Poverty Point, which dates 500 to 800 years earlier, compromises cultural taxonomy and points out one of its great shortcomings.

I skirt the problem by informally calling the Poverty Point material "Old Floyd" Tchefuncte, even though this "solution" still leaves us in a bind when it comes to classifying early clay grit-tempered/untempered Tchefuncte pottery from undated contexts elsewhere. Poverty Point components are now being and will continue to be misclassified as Tchefuncte, meaning Tchula period occupations. Our methods are creating history where there is none; we have a problem with current pottery classification and are going to have to face up to it at some point. For now, I heuristically divide the indivisible and refer to the earliest pottery at Poverty Point as "Old Floyd" Tchefuncte.

The MVPs are interesting, not only in terms of their implications for pottery succession at Poverty Point but for their possible bearing on historical and functional relationships of pottery and soapstone vessels (Jenkins et al. 1986; Sassaman 1993a). Jenkins et al. (1986:548–551) propose that fiber-tempered pottery and soapstone moved into the Mississippi Valley together from western Georgia and eastern Alabama, via the Chattahoochee River, Gulf of Mexico, and Mississippi River, as a consequence of the extensive exchange network focused on the Poverty Point site (Ford and Webb 1956:126–127; Gibson 1994c, 1994d). Sassaman (1993a:36–37), on the other hand, argues that soapstone and ceramic containers were functional competitors and would thus have made incompatible trade items. He maintains that traders, who promoted soapstone exchange, would have discouraged the spread of pottery because it would have undermined the need for soapstone and consequently their own roles, with a loss of all rights and privileges (and statuses) pertaining thereunto.

The MVPs of soapstone and fiber-tempered pottery at the Poverty Point site are similar, soapstone 3.1 and Wheeler pottery 2.6. While this does not necessarily mean that Jenkins et al. (1986) are right and Sassaman (1993a) is wrong, it does suggest that the circumstances under which fiber-tempered pottery appeared at Poverty Point existed when soapstone vessels were brought in (cf. Sassaman 1993a:222–225). We do not yet have a coherent model to explain their common occurrence, but we cannot deny their nearly simultaneous appearance.

Even if soapstone and fiber-tempered vessels were functional competitors, they were not exchange competitors because fiber-tempered pots were homemade. Other forces and factors besides trade personages and intergroup alliances were at work. Formal or informal trade arrangements are a seedbed for social interaction and communication, which carry beyond exchange transactions, and if the process and actual trade events could be dissected analytically, I suspect we would find many, many messages being sent and the information being differentially assimilated or ignored by various divisions within trading groups.

Having "Old Floyd" Tchefuncte, an apparently indigenous ware, as the earliest pottery at the Poverty Point site calls into question interpretations about the functional contexts of ceramic diffusion, which are all predicated on having fiber-tempered precedents. Poverty Point was already making its own brand of clay containers before fiber-tempered and stone vessels appeared, and this had to alter the circumstances under which fiber-tempered and soapstone containers were assimilated. Wheeler ceramics and soapstone pots may still have been competing for a place in Poverty Point kitchens, but neither was able to gain much ground against "Old Floyd" Tchefuncte pottery. After the cessation of Poverty Point exchange and the abandonment of the Poverty Point site, the pottery made in the southern Lower Mississippi Valley would all bear Tchefuncte decoration.

The fact that Tchefuncte wares won out and Wheeler pottery and soapstone did not may have something to do with ease of replaceability. "Old Floyd" Tchefuncte pottery was made at Poverty Point from löess underfoot and alluvium from the bayou bank alongside. Soapstone in the form of finished vessels was hauled in from a long way off. We have not found any bowl blanks or unfinished vessels, like those that litter quarry sites on Soapstone Ridge in Georgia (Dickens and Carnes 1983) and in western Alabama (Mosley 1958), and although some small pieces of soapstone cannot be confirmed as sherds, they probably are, or they may just be lagniappe for making small ornaments. Some of the Georgia, Alabama, and Carolina groups working the quarries were probably making fiber-tempered pottery (DeJarnette 1952:275; Jenkins et al. 1986:548–549; Walthall 1980:89). Even if they were not, soapstone vessels passed through fiber-tempered pottery country en route to Poverty Point, thereby giving fiber-tempered vessels or information about them a chance to piggyback, to infiltrate exchange dealings.

The crux of the replaceability matter is cost. Whether by land or water, it is a long way from the soapstone quarries in the Piedmont to the swamps of the Lower Mississippi Valley. Many intersocietal connections were required to maintain supply. When those costs got too high or the intersocietal supply chain became undone, soapstone exchange stopped, and with it went the lore and perhaps the allure of fiber tempering. Under this view, it is not necessary for actual vessels to have been brought from Alabama, Georgia, Tennessee, or the Carolinas in order for fiber-tempered pottery to disappear at practically the same time as soapstone; fiber-tempered pots could have been (and probably were) made at the Poverty Point site and nevertheless given up when the foreign spark presumably behind both soapstone importation and Wheeler style ideas was snuffed out, and a single bad link in the exchange chain could have been sufficient to extinguish it. The "Old Floyd" Tchefuncte pottery would have been left to take up the slack.

It would be helpful if we knew how long all this took. Because these patterns are inferred from the composite stratigraphy of the artificial rings at Poverty Point, we might not be looking at a long time. Although we are not sure how long it took to build Poverty Point's rings, current indications are that it did not take long, perhaps less than a couple of centuries, perhaps much less (Gibson 1992a). The only part of the site where both preconstruction occupational and constructional levels have been dated is the west sector of the ridged enclosure. Radiocarbon dates on the old buried ground surface average 3229 ± 53 B.P.; those from the building levels immediately above average 3047 ± 33 B.P. (weighted averages but uncalibrated dates, Stuiver and Reimer 1986)(Gibson 1993a:63–66). It is tempting to see this apparent 180-year span as the time when pottery making and soapstone exchange began, flourished, and stopped. However, we are uncertain at the moment just how close these dates come to revealing the full occupational span. Preconstruction occupational levels in the north sector, for example, average 3288 ± 44 (weighted averages but uncalibrated dates), or about 60 years older than in the west, but without dates from any other sections of the earthworks proper, we do not know if construction continued elsewhere after the western rings were completed and, if it did, for how long (Gibson 1992a). In any event, average old ground dates everywhere on the site are within two standard deviations of each other and thus may not really be different.

Long-Distance Exchange

Much of what Poverty Point is all about has to do with exchange, long-distance exchange. Although eastern North America had seen earlier exchange networks (Jefferies, this volume), e.g., Red Ochre (Brose 1979, 1994), Green River (Goad 1980; Marquardt 1985; Winters 1968; Wright and Zeder 1977), and Benton (Johnson 1994; Johnson and Brookes 1988), it had not seen anything like that of Poverty Point. Large volumes of rocks gravitated toward the Poverty Point site from various parts of the Southeast and Midwest: novaculite, magnetite, hematite, crystal quartz, and other materials from the Ouachita Mountains in central and western Arkansas; Crescent Hills chert and galena from the Ozark Rim in eastern Missouri; Mill Creek and Dongola/Cobden cherts and flourite from the Shawnee Hills in southern Illinois; Wyandotte and Harrodsburg flints from the Knobs region of northern Kentucky–southern Indiana; Fort Payne, Dover, Camden, and Pickwick cherts, phyllite, and schist from along the Tennessee River from its confluence with the Ohio to the Ridge and Valley province near the common corner of Alabama, Georgia, and Tennessee; Tallahatta quartzite from western Alabama; soapstone and greenstone from the Piedmont sections of Georgia, Alabama, and South Carolina; copper from the Great Lakes; galena from the common corner of Iowa, Wisconsin, and Illinois (Conn 1973; Ford and Webb 1956:125, fig. 45; Gibson 1994c; Jeter and Futato 1994; Jeter and Jackson 1994; Lasley 1983; Lehmann 1982:16; Smith 1976; Walthall et al. 1982). There is even a little obsidian from out West somewhere (Richard Hughes, personal communication, 1989). Most of these sources, especially those of chert/flint, are merely presumed at the moment, but sources for soapstone, galena, copper, hematite, and magnetite have all been confirmed by chemical identification (Lasley 1983; Anthony Simon, personal communication, 1984; Smith 1976: tables 1–2; Walthall et al. 1982).

Several things stand out about Poverty Point exchange (Gibson 1994d). One, volume was heavy; tons and tons of rocks were imported, especially to the Poverty Point site. Two, partially or wholly fabricated rather than plain raw materials seem to have been traded. Three, exchange materials were largely, if not entirely, consumed by the domestic sector. And four, nothing of identifiable Poverty Point origin seems to have reached the lands where the lithic materials originated.

The enormous scale of domestic consumption stands in sharp contrast to both earlier Archaic and later Hopewellian exchange systems, which seem to have focused on ritual consumption of exotics (Brose 1979, 1994; Gibson 1994d; Jefferies 1979; Johnson 1994; Smith 1979; Walthall 1979). It looks to me now as if Poverty Point exchange, at least on the local and perhaps on the regional level, may have supplied everybody, regardless of social standing; at any rate I recognize no evidence of ceremonially restricted access to exotic materials, which might suggest at least situational, if not permanent, social discrimination. Two decades ago, I thought the western ring segments at Poverty Point might have been a ritzy neighborhood. The area was close to the big mound, and analysis of surface collections disclosed a disproportionate number of jasper beads, zoomorphic pendants, and stone pipes (Gibson 1973, 1974:102). However, my recent excavations in the western rings do not support that interpretation, or at least they do not produce a lot of status objects/icons in the fill dirt (Gibson 1993a). Maybe the western rings did not become a socially prominent or sacred precinct until after construction was concluded. I no longer see persuasive evidence for directional trade, wherein exchange intensity among places varies according to their importance (cf. Brasher 1973; Lehmann 1982; Walthall et al. 1982), although I once did (Gibson 1979, 1980). Recent, more comprehensive information and quantitative analyses dismiss that hypothesis (Gibson 1994b, 1994d; Gibson and Griffing 1994). Johnson (1980) arrived at this conclusion a decade ago, but few of us believed him. While the Poverty Point site stands out above all others, none of the others in the exchange orbit do for reasons other than size, and I do not think that size alone is sufficient reason to proclaim them commercially more important (cf. Gibson 1980).

However, I do not see Poverty Point exchange as being ad hoc or informal either. The Poverty Point site rules that out; nothing about Poverty Point is ad hoc. It was *the* trade center, the primary destination for incoming exotic materials. Even if it served as the scene of an annual institutionalized trade fair, where peoples from near and far met to swap goods (Jackson 1991), it was more, much more.

There is too much material at Poverty Point for it to have been solely a periodic meeting place. Fairgoers would undoubtedly have carried their goods back home when they left. I imagine that well over 95 percent of the absolute volume of exotic lithic resources present on Poverty Point components throughout the entire Lower Mississippi region occurs at the Poverty Point site. Besides, what would people from the Lower Mississippi Valley have been swapping with each other? Bowfin for crappie, raccoon for alligator meat, venison haunch for backstrap, a brown chert pebble for a yellow one? Doubtful. From the Gulf to the mouth of the Arkansas River, sites all seem to wind up with the same kinds of lithic materials, some more and some less, but all the same nonetheless.

In addition, if Poverty Point had been a fairground, what or who persuaded people who saw each other only occasionally to work together to build such massive earthworks? Who took charge? No, the people who built the Poverty Point mounds and ridges did so because they shared a dream. They wanted to work, they did not have to be coerced, they could not be. Familial and ethnic pride and social identity resound from every grain of basket-loaded earth. Whatever else the Poverty Point site (and phase) may represent, I am convinced it has a sociocultural nucleus, a community weld, a singular spirit.

A recent analysis of local exchange, exchange that transpired within 30 km of the Poverty Point site (the geographic extent of the Poverty Point phase), reveals that the volume of specific exotic exchange materials getting out into the hinterland varies independently of distance (Gibson and Griffing 1994). In other words, how far a site is from the Poverty Point site does not seem to matter in determining how much foreign rock it has. This finding, however, does not necessarily make Poverty Point exchange directional. What seems to be more important than distance, at least in some cases, is the nature of the toolkit on each site.

Take the case of Poverty Point phase sites, such as Aaron, Arledge, Terral Lewis, and Orvis Scott, located in the Tensas swamp east of the Poverty Point site less than 30 km away. These sites have relatively large numbers of chipped hoes — large bifacial foliates often bearing sickle sheen on bits and obverse faces — and they also have a high percentage of northern gray flint, especially the Dover variety (Gibson 1993b; Gibson and Griffing 1994; Gregory 1991). Why? Because hoes are primarily made of northern gray flint. They required constant resharpening and that, coupled with their size, produced abundant debitage. Even after they were resharpened so much that they could not be used as hoes any more, they were laterally recycled into cores and other artifacts, producing even more debitage (Jackson 1986). Large quantities of northern gray flint correlate with hoes and hoeing and not particularly well with distance. Other materials show similar trends: lots of plummets mean abundant hard hematite and magnetite, lots of pseudocelts mean abundant greenstone, lots of gorgets mean abundant limonite, and so on. There is a pervasive functional undercurrent to the distribution of exotic exchange materials among Poverty Point phase components, and this goes hand in glove with the apparently open availability of trade materials and the primarily commonplace and utilitarian uses to which they were put.

Despite the overall domestic and egalitarian aura that envelops Poverty Point exchange, I have no doubt that the people who oversaw its operation gained and maintained prestige and power. I see nothing temporary or situational about this, although I suspect that the leaders of the Poverty Point site were probably the major benefactors. Poverty Point does not have to have been a chiefdom to have supported a small, prestigious group of people, a group whose status and power remained constant and did not wax and wane with every exchange and building episode (cf. Gibson 1974). I am not sure we want to call this a ranked society, if by that we evoke the stereotypical, ethnographic model of a chiefdom with all the trimmings. It matters little what we label the society, as long as we recognize the potential social inequalities that inhere.

In my opinion, two things make Poverty Point exchange functionally and historically unique in the Southeast—its purpose and its magnitude (Gibson 1994a). Although the Lower Mississippi Valley is an exceptionally rich environment biotically, it is rock-poor. There are a few local resources and for most of the region's history, these resources satisfied needs; but not for Poverty Point. Providing domestic hardware materials for large numbers of relatively sedentary people was an enormous job, requiring stupendous effort, coordination, and integrative skill. Why such a large area came to be involved in the exchange network is not known, although most of the materials, especially the most bulky and distant, originated at points on or near the Mississippi River and its tributaries, *upstream* from Poverty Point. River transport probably eased what would otherwise have posed formidable acquisition problems, even if materials had been passed hand-to-hand. However, that the rocks were there and that logistics were favorable do not tell us why exchange started or how it worked. Those answers lie in the social aspect of Poverty Point culture, in its peoples and their interactions among themselves and with others.

Other southeastern exchange systems do not seem to have focused on general domestic supply as at Poverty Point but were more sectarian. I say this despite being unable to separate ritual from residence at the Poverty Point site. Everything about the site may be ceremonial, as some have argued, but if this was the case, then much of the ceremony was devoted to feeding and otherwise maintaining the people who lived and gathered there. The push and coordination of the exchange effort emanated from or focused on the Poverty Point site. Transportational logistics, historical circumstances, and substantial populations all converged there. The Poverty Point site was unique in the Archaic Southeast.

Conclusions

The Poverty Point site was a special place, home for a sizable group and seat of ritual and sponsor of long-distance exchange. Unique as it was, it is still a perfectly logical consequence of (1) logistical fishing-hunting-gathering by relatively large populations in a bountiful and self-renewing riparian environment lacking in one major resource, hard rock; (2) a concerted and successful effort to supply that missing resource by means of long-distance exchange; and (3) a long mound-building tradition, which passed on the technical know-how, the labor organizational and managerial capabilities, and the spiritual inspiration and motivation that made a people want to work, even without threat of reprisal.

The Poverty Point site had a profound effect on its immediate countryside. Many of the small nearby sites were probably created by families and unisexual work teams from Poverty Point who were engaged in some temporary exploitive activity. Others were more or less permanent places of abode, which depended on Poverty Point for their supply of lithic resources and which drew on it for identity and possibly even help during hard times. But beyond this familiar 30-km circle, I suspect Poverty Point's influence was largely exchange-related and had little or no socioculturally integrative significance. River-connected sites, such as Jaketown, Claiborne, Deep Bayou, and Beau Rivage, and others to a lesser extent, participated in Poverty Point exchange and were close enough to pick up more than vague rumors about the place with giant rings and big bird mounds and thereby to assimilate selected functional and stylistic ideas. The interconnected sites mark the widest realm of Poverty Point culture; beyond them—outside the Lower Mississippi Valley—Poverty Point culture has no taxonomic utility.

Poverty Point culture does not span the greater Southeast; there is no areawide Poverty Point–related culture nor any closely similar Archaic culture. There are many socially and politically independent cultures, some of which participated in an exchange network focused on the Poverty Point site. Exactly how each local culture participated is not known, although some look more like suppliers and others like consumers of stone materials. Establishing mutual-aid consortia sounds like a perfectly good explanation for intercultural exchange (see Jefferies, this volume), but I think the reasons why the Poverty Point site and its 60-km-wide sphere of intensive interaction became the focus of exchange and the scene of massive earthwork contruction go beyond practical and worldly explanations. Poverty Point owes its unique character to its leaders and to the spirits and forces that controlled their lives.

REFERENCES CITED

Ahler, S. A.

1971   *Projectile Point Form and Function at Rodgers Shelter, Missouri*. Research Series 8. Columbia: Missouri Archaeological Society.

1981   *Microwear Analysis and Evaluation of the Chipped Stone Tool Classification System for the University of West Florida Archaic Midden Mound Project*. Department of Anthropology, University of North Dakota, Grand Forks. Submitted to the Office of Cultural and Archaeological Research, University of West Florida, Pensacola.

Ahler, S. A., and R. B. McMillan

1976   Material Culture at Rodgers Shelter: A Reflection of Past Human Activities. In *Prehistoric Man and His Environments: A Case Study in the Ozark Highlands,* ed. W. R. Wood and R. B. McMillan, pp. 163–99. New York: Academic Press.

Albers, Patricia C.

1993   Symbiosis, Merger, and War: Contrasting Forms of Intertribal Relationship among Historic Plains Indians. In *The Political Economy of North American Indians,* ed. J. C. Moore, pp. 94–132. Norman: University of Oklahoma Press.

Alexander, L. S., C. Davis, D. Lenhardt, and R. Skrivan

1983   Archaeological Excavations at 22TS954, Tishomingo County, Mississippi. Paper presented at the annual meeting of the Society for American Archaeology, Pittsburgh.

Amick, D. S.

1984   Designing and Testing a Model of Raw Material Variability for the Central Duck River Basin, Tennessee. In *Prehistoric Chert Exploitation: Studies from the Midcontinent,* ed. B. Butler and E. May, pp. 167–84. Occasional Paper 2. Carbondale: Center for Archaeological Investigations, Southern Illinois University.

1985a   Late Archaic Fort Payne Biface Manufacture at the Topsy Site (40WY204), Buffalo River Basin, Tennessee. *Southeastern Archaeology* 4:134–51.

1985b   Buried Late Holocene Terrace Site Testing in the Central Duck River Basin. In *Exploring Tennessee Prehistory: A Dedication to Alfred K. Guthe,* ed. T. Whyte, C. Boyd, and B. Riggs, pp. 23–38. Report of Investigations 42. Knoxville: Department of Anthropology, University of Tennessee.

1986   Excavations at the Fattybread Branch Site (40MU408): Late Archaic Floodplain Adaptations. In *Cultural Adaptations in the Shelby Bend Archaeological District,* ed. D. Amick, J. Herbert, and M. Fogarty, pp. 290–416. Report submitted to the Southeast Archeological Center, National Park Service, Tallahassee. Contract CX-5000-4-0624.

1987   *Lithic Raw Material Variability in the Central Duck River Basin: Reflections of Middle and Late Archaic Organizational Strategies*. Report of Investigations 46. Knoxville: Department of Anthropology, University of Tennessee. Publications in Anthropology 50. Norris: Tennessee Valley Authority.

1994   Technological Organization and the Structure of Inference in Lithic Analysis: An Examination of Folsom Hunting Behavior in the American Southwest. In *The Organization of Prehistoric North American Chipped Stone Tool Technologies,* ed. P. Carr, pp. 9–34. Archaeological Series 7. Ann Arbor: International Monographs in Prehistory.

Anderson, David G.

1990   The Paleoindian Colonization of Eastern North America: A View from the Southeastern United States. In *Early Paleoindian Economies of Eastern North America,* ed. K. B. Tankersley and B. L. Isaac, pp. 163–216. Research in Economic Anthropology, supplement 5. Greenwich, Conn.: JAI Press.

1991a The Bifurcate Tradition in the South Atlantic Region. *Journal of Middle Atlantic Archaeology* 7:91–106.

1991b Examining Prehistoric Settlement Distribution in Eastern North America. *Archaeology of Eastern North America* 19:1–22.

Anderson, David G., and Glen T. Hanson

1988   Early Archaic Settlement in the Southeastern United States: A Case Study from the Savannah River Basin. *American Antiquity* 53:262–86.

Anderson, David G., and J. W. Joseph

1988   *Prehistory and History along the Upper Savannah River: Technical Synthesis of Cultural Resource Investigations.* Russell Papers 1988. Atlanta: Interagency Archeological Services Division, National Park Service.

Anderson, David G., and Kenneth E. Sassaman

1992   Managing Paleoindian and Early Archaic Cultural Resources in South Carolina. In Anderson, Sassaman, and Judge, eds., q.v., pp. 331–58.

Anderson, David G., and Joseph Schuldenrein

1983   Early Archaic Settlement on the Southeastern Atlantic Slope: A View from the Rucker's Bottom Site, Elbert County, Georgia. *North American Archaeologist* 4:177–210.

Anderson, David G., and Joseph Schuldenrein (assemblers)

1985   *Prehistoric Human Ecology along the Upper Savannah River: Excavations at the Rucker's Bottom, Abbeville and Bullard Site Groups.* Russell Papers 1985. Atlanta: Interagency Archeological Services Division, National Park Service.

Anderson, David G., and Virginia Horak (editors)

1995   *Archaeological Site File Management: A Southeastern Perspective.* Readings in Archeological Resource Protection 3. Atlanta: Interagency Archeological Service Division, National Park Service.

Anderson, David G., Kenneth E. Sassaman, and Christopher Judge (editors)

1992   *Paleoindian and Early Archaic Period Research in the Lower Southeast: A South Carolina Perspective.* Columbia: Council of South Carolina Professional Archaeologists.

Anderson, Edgar

1952   *Plants, Man, and Life.* Berkeley: University of California Press.

Anderson, J. A. D.

1974   Occupation as a Modifying Factor in the Diagnosis and Treatment of Rheumatic Diseases. *Current Medical Research and Opinion* 2(9):521–528.

Anderson, J. A. D., and J. J. R. Duthis
  1963   Rheumatic Complaints in Dockyard Workers. *Annals of the Rheumatic Diseases* 22:401–9.
Anderson, J. E.
  1965   Human Skeletons of Tehuacan. *Science* 148:496–97.
Andrefsky, W., Jr.
  1994   Raw-Material Availability and the Organization of Technology. *American Antiquity* 59:21–34.
Angel, J. Lawrence
  1966   Early Skeletons from Tranquility, California. *Smithsonian Contributions to Anthropology* 2:1–19.
  1974   Patterns of Fractures from Neolithic to Modern Times. *Anthropologiai Kozlemanyek* 18:9–18.
Angel, J. Lawrence, J. O. Kelley, M. Parrington, and S. Pinter
  1987   Life Stresses of the Free Black Community as Represented by the First Baptist Church, Philadelphia, 1823–1841. *American Journal of Physical Anthropology* 74:213–29.
Anuskiewicz, Richard J.
  1988   Preliminary Archaeological Investigations at Bay Hole Spring. *Proceedings: Eighth Annual Gulf of Mexico Information Transfer Meeting*, December 1987:416–18. New Orleans: Mineral Management Service.
Asch, David L., and Nancy B. Asch
  1985   Prehistoric Plant Cultivation in West-Central Illinois. In *Prehistoric Food Production in North America*, ed. R. I. Ford, pp. 149–204. Anthropological Papers 75. Ann Arbor: Museum of Anthropology, University of Michigan.
Atkinson, James R.
  1974   Appendix A: Test Excavations at the Vaughn Mound Site. In *Archeological Survey and Test Excavations in the Upper-Central Tombigbee River Valley*, compiled by Marc Rucker. Report submitted to the Southeast Archeological Center, National Park Service. Contract CX-5000-3-1589.
Autin, Whitney J.
  1993   Influences of Relative Sea-Level Rise and Mississippi River Delta Plain Evolution on the Holocene Middle Amite River, Southeastern Louisiana. *Quaternary Research* 39:68–74.
Bader, Anne Tobee
  1992   *An Analysis of Bone and Antler Tool Use Patterns from the Kentucky Air National Guard Site*. M.A. thesis, University of Kentucky, Lexington.
Bamforth, D. B.
  1985   The Technological Organization of Paleo-Indian Small-Group Bison Hunting on the Llano Estacado. *Plains Anthropologist* 30:243–58.
  1986   Technological Efficiency and Tool Curation. *American Antiquity* 51:38–50.
  1991   Technological Organization and Hunter-Gatherer Land Use: A California Example. *American Antiquity* 56:216–34.
Barker, Gary, and Emanuel Breitburg
  1992   Archaic Occupations at the Austin Site (40Rb82). Paper presented at the annual meeting of SEAC, Little Rock.

Barth, Fredrik

  1969   *Ethnic Groups and Boundaries.* Boston: Little, Brown.

Bassett, Everett J.

  1982   Osteological Analysis of Carrier Mills Burials. In Jefferies and Butler, eds., q.v.,
         pp. 1027–1114.

Beauchamp, Renee

  1993   *White-tailed Deer Crown Height Measurements and Mortality Profiles from the
         Hayes Site, Middle Tennessee.* M.A. thesis, University of Tennessee, Knoxville.

Begler, E.

  1978   Sex, Status and Authority in Egalitarian Society. *American Anthropologist*
         80:571–88.

Belknap, Daniel F., and John C. Kraft

  1981   Preservation Potential of Transgressive Coastal Lithosomes on the U.S. Conti-
         nental Shelf. *Marine Geology* 42:429–42.

  1985   Influence of Antecedent Geology on Stratigraphic Preservation Potential and
         Evolution of Delaware's Barrier Systems. In *Barrier Islands,* ed. G. F. Oertel and
         S. P. Leatherman, pp. 235–62. Special issue of *Marine Geology,* vol. 63.

Bender, Barbara

  1985   Emergent Tribal Formations in the American Midcontinent. *American Antiquity*
         50:52–62.

Bense, Judith A.

  1987b   Research Design. In Bense, ed., q.v., pp. 21–32.

  1987c   The Setting. In Bense, ed., q.v., pp. 5–20.

Bense, Judith A. (editor)

  1987a   *The Midden Mound Project: Final Report.* Report of Investigations 6. Pensacola:
          Office of Cultural and Archaeological Research, University of West Florida.

Bentz, Charles, Jr.

  1988a   The Late Archaic Occupation of the Bailey Site (40GL26), Giles County, Ten-
          nessee. *Tennessee Anthropological Association Newsletter* 13(5):1–20.

Bentz, Charles, Jr. (editor)

  1988b   *The Bailey Site: Late Archaic, Late Woodland, and Historic Settlement and Subsis-
          tence in the Lower Elk River Drainage of Tennessee.* Report submitted to Tennessee
          Department of Transportation, Project 28004-0241-94. Knoxville: Department
          of Anthropology, University of Tennessee.

Bergman, C. A., and J. F. Doershuk

  1992   How the Data Come Together: Refitting in Lithic Analysis. *Journal of Middle
         Atlantic Archaeology* 8:139–60.

Beriault, John, Robert Carr, Jerry Stipp, Richard Johnson, and Jack Meeder

  1981   The Archaeological Salvage of the Bay West Site, Collier County, Florida.
         Florida Anthropologist 20:39–58.

Binford, L. R.

  1980   Willow Smoke and Dogs' Tails: Hunter-Gatherer Settlement Systems and
         Archaeological Site Formation. *American Antiquity* 45:4–28.

  1983a   *Working at Archaeology.* New York: Academic Press.

  1983b   *In Pursuit of the Past.* New York: Thames and Hudson.

Binford, L. R., and J. F. O'Connell

  1984   An Alywara Day: The Stone Quarry. *Journal of Anthropological Research*
         40:406–32.

Birkeland, Peter W.

1984   *Soils and Geomorphology*. New York: Oxford University Press.

Blanton, Dennis B.

1985   Lithic Raw Material Procurement and Use During the Morrow Mountain Phase in South Carolina. In *Lithic Resource Procurement: Proceedings from the Second Conference on Prehistoric Chert Exploitation*, ed. S. C. Vehik, pp. 115–32. Occasional Paper 4. Carbondale: Center for Archaeological Investigations, Southern Illinois University.

1994   Building Better Models Using Depositional Histories from Sandy Sites: A Case Study in the Virginia Coastal Plain. Paper presented at the annual meeting of SEAC, Lexington.

Blanton, Dennis B., and Kenneth E. Sassaman

1989   Pattern and Process in the Middle Archaic Period of South Carolina. In *Studies in South Carolina Archaeology: Essays in Honor of Robert L. Stephenson*, ed. A. C. Goodyear III and G. T. Hanson, pp. 53–72. Anthropological Studies 9. Columbia: Institute of Archaeology and Anthropology, University of South Carolina.

Blanton, Dennis B., Joe B. Jones, and Joseph Schuldenrein, III

1994   *Phase III Archaeological Data Recovery for Mitigation of Adverse Effects to Site 44HN202 Associated with the VNG Mechanicsville to Kingsmill Lateral Pipeline, Hanover County, Virginia*. Prepared for Virginia Natural Gas, Inc., Norfolk. Williamsburg: Center for Archaeological Research, Department of Anthropology, College of William and Mary.

Blanton, Dennis B., William Childress, Jonathan Danz, Leslie Mitchell, Joseph Schuldenrein, and Jesse Zinn

1994   *Archaeological Assessment of Sites 44PY7, 44PY43, and 44PY152 at Leesville Lake, Pittsylvania County, Virginia*. Submitted to the Virginia Department of Historic Resources, Richmond. Williamsburg: Center for Archaeological Research, Department of Anthropology, College of William and Mary.

Bleed, P.

1986   The Optimal Design of Hunting Weapons: Maintainability or Reliability. *American Antiquity* 51:737–47.

Blitz, John H.

1993   Locust Beads and Archaic Mounds. *Mississippi Archaeology* 28(1):20–43.

Bloom, A. L.

1983   Sea Level and Coastal Changes. In Wright, ed., q.v., pp. 42–51.

Bond, Stanley O., Jr.

1988   Preliminary Report: Archaeological Excavations at 8SJ43, the Crescent Beach Site, St. Johns County, Florida. Report on file at the Historic St. Augustine Preservation Board.

1992   Archaeological Excavations at 8SJ43, the Crescent Beach Site, St. Johns County, Florida. *Florida Anthropologist* 45:148–61.

Bourke, J. B.

1967   A Review of the Paleopathology of the Arthritic Diseases. In *Diseases in Antiquity*, ed. D. R. Brothwell and A. T. Sandison, pp. 352–70. Springfield, Ill.: C. C. Thomas.

Bousman, C. B.
  1993   Hunter-Gather Adaptations, Economic Risk and Tool Design. *Lithic Technology* 18:59–86.
Boyd, Donna C., and C. Clifford Boyd
  1989   A Comparison of Tennessee Archaic and Mississippian Femoral Lengths and Midshaft Diameters: Subsistence Change and Postcranial Variability. *Southeastern Archaeology* 8:107–16.
Boyd, Robert, and Peter J. Richerson
  1985   *Culture and the Evolutionary Process.* Chicago: University of Chicago Press.
Brackenridge, G. R.
  1984   Alluvial Stratigraphy and Radiocarbon Dating along the Duck River, Tennessee: Implications Regarding Floodplain Origin. *Geological Society of America Bulletin* 95:9–25.
Bradley, Richard, and Mark Edmonds
  1993   *Interpreting the Axe Trade: Production and Exchange in Neolithic Britain.* Cambridge: Cambridge University Press.
Brain, Jeffrey P.
  1971   The Lower Mississippi Valley in North American Prehistory. MS on file, Arkansas Archeological Survey, Fayetteville.
Braley, Chad, and Robert Benson
  1994   The Sandhills Revisited: Early and Middle Holocene Settlement Patterns along the Atlantic and Gulf Slopes. Paper presented at the annual meeting of SEAC, Lexington.
Braley, Chad, and Joseph Schuldenrein
  1993   *An Intensive Cultural Resources Survey and Site Testing on Fort Bragg's Sicily Drop Zone, Hoke County, North Carolina.* Submitted to U.S. Army Corps of Engineers, Savannah District Headquarters. Athens, Ga.: Southeastern Archeological Services.
Brasher, Ted J.
  1973   *An Investigation of Some Central Functions of Poverty Point.* M.A. thesis, Northwestern State University, Natchitoches.
Braun, David P., and Stephen Plog
  1982   Evolution of "Tribal" Social Networks: Theory and Prehistoric North American Evidence. *American Antiquity* 47:504–25.
Breitburg, Emanuel
  1982   Analysis of Area A Fauna. In Jefferies and Butler, eds., q.v., pp. 863–952.
Brewer, Andrea J.
  1973   Analysis of Floral Remains from the Higgs Site (40LO45). In McCollough and Faulkner, eds., q.v., pp. 141–44.
Bridges, Patricia S.
  1985   *Changes in Long Bone Structure with the Transition to Agriculture: Implications for Prehistoric Activities.* Ph.D. dissertation, University of Michigan. Ann Arbor: University Microfilms.
  1989a   Changes in Activities with the Shift to Agriculture in the Southeastern United States. *Current Anthropology* 30:385–93.
  1989b   Spondylolysis and Its Relationship to Degenerative Joint Disease in the Prehis-

toric Southeastern United States. *American Journal of Physical Anthropology* 79:321–29.

1990   Osteological Correlates of Weapon Use. In *A Life in Science: Papers in Honor of J. Lawrence Angel,* ed. J. Buikstra, pp. 87–98. Scientific Papers 6. Kampsville, Ill.: Center for American Archaeology.

1991a   Skeletal Evidence of Changes in Subsistence Activities Between the Archaic and Missisippian Time Periods in Northwestern Alabama. In *What Mean These Bones?* ed. M. L. Powell, P. S. Bridges, and A. M. W. Mires, pp. 89–101. Tuscaloosa: University of Alabama Press.

1991b   Degenerative Joint Disease in Hunter-Gatherers and Agriculturalists from the Southeastern United States. *American Journal of Physical Anthropology* 85:379–91

1992   Prehistoric Arthritis in the Americas. *Annual Review of Anthropology* 21:67–91.

1993   The Effect of Variation in Methodology on the Outcome of Osteoarthritic Studies. *International Journal of Osteoarchaeology* 3:289–95.

1994   Vertebral Arthritis and Physical Activities in the Prehistoric Southeastern United States. *American Journal of Physical Anthropology* 93:83–94.

Britsch, L. D. and L. M. Smith

1989   Geomorphic Investigation of the Terrebonne Marsh, Louisiana: Foundation for Cultural Resource Surveys. *Geoarchaeology* 4:229–50.

Brooks, Mark J., and Kenneth E. Sassaman

1990   Point Bar Geoarchaeology in the Upper Coastal Plain of the Savannah River Valley, South Carolina: A Case Study. In *Archaeological Geology of North America,* ed. N. P. Lasca and J. E. Donahue, pp. 183–97. Centennial Special Volume 4. Boulder, Colo.: Geological Society of America.

Brooks, Mark J., Peter A. Stone, Donald J. Colquhoun, and Janice G. Brown

1989   Sea Level Change, Estuarine Development and Temporal Variability in Woodland Period Subsistence-Settlement Patterning on the Lower Coastal Plain of South Carolina. In *Studies in South Carolina Archaeology: Essays in Honor of Robert L. Stephenson,* ed. A. C. Goodyear III and G. T. Hanson, pp. 91–100. Anthropological Studies 9. Columbia: Institute of Archaeology and Anthropology, University of South Carolina.

Brooks, Mark J., Peter A. Stone, Donald J. Colquhoun, Janice G. Brown, and Kathy B. Steele

1986   Geoarchaeological Research in the Coastal Plain Portion of the Savannah River Valley. *Geoarchaeology* 1:293–307.

Brose, David S.

1979   A Speculative Model of the Role of Exchange in the Prehistory of the Eastern Woodlands. In Brose and Greber, eds., q.v., pp. 3–8.

1994   Trade and Exchange in the Midwestern U.S. In *Prehistoric Exchange Systems in North America,* vol. 2, ed. T. G. Baugh and J. E. Ericson, pp. 215–40. New York: Plenum Press.

Brose, David S., and N'omi Greber (editors)

1979   *Hopewell Archaeology: The Chillicothe Conference.* Kent, Ohio: Kent State University Press.

Brothwell, D. R.

1972   Paleodemography and Earlier British Populations. *World Archaeology* 4:75–86.

Brown, Ian W.

1980   Archaeological Investigations on Avery Island, Louisiana, 1977–78. *Southeastern Archaeological Conference Bulletin* 22:110–18.

1991   Letter on file at the Regional Archaeological Program, Department of Geosciences, Northeast Louisiana University, Monroe.

Brown, Ian W., and Nancy Lambert-Brown

1978   *Lower Mississippi Survey, Petite Anse Project, Research Notes Number 5.* Cambridge: Peabody Museum, Harvard University.

Brown, James A.

1983   Summary. In Phillips and Brown, eds., q.v., pp. 5–10.

1985   Long-Term Trends to Sedentism and the Emergence of Complexity in the American Midwest. In Price and Brown, eds., q.v., pp. 201–31.

Brown, James A., and Robert K. Vierra

1983   What Happened in the Middle Archaic? Introduction to an Ecological Approach to Koster Site Archaeology. In Phillips and Brown, eds., q.v., pp. 165–95.

Brown, J. G., and A. D. Cohen

1985   Palynologic and Petrographic Analyses of Peat Deposits, Little Salt Spring. *National Geographic Research* 1:21–31.

Broyles, Bettye

1971   *Second Preliminary Report: The St. Albans Site, Kanawha Valley, West Virginia.* Report of Archaeological Investigations 3. Morgantown: West Virginia Geological and Economic Survey.

Bruseth, James E.

1991   Poverty Point Development as Seen at the Cedarland and Claiborne Sites, Southern Mississippi. In Byrd, ed., q.v., pp. 7–25.

Brush, Grace

1986   Geology and Paleoecology of Chesapeake Estuaries. *Journal of the Washington Academy of Sciences* 76:146–60.

Bullen, Adelaide K.

1972   Paleoepidemiology and Distribution of Prehistoric Treponemiasis (Syphilis) in Florida. *Florida Anthropologist* 25:133–74.

Bullen, Ripley P.

1961   Radiocarbon Dates for Southeastern Fiber-Tempered Pottery. *American Antiquity* 27:104–6.

1962   Indian Burials at Tick Island. Philadelphia: *American Philosophical Society Yearbook,* 1961, pp. 477–80.

1972   The Orange Period of Peninsular Florida. In Bullen and Stoltman, eds., q.v., pp. 9–33.

1974   The Origins of the Gulf Tradition as Seen from Florida. *Florida Anthropologist* 27:77–88.

Bullen, Ripley P., and Adelaide K. Bullen

1961   The Summer Haven Site, St. Johns County, Florida. *Florida Anthropologist* 14:1–15.

1976   *The Palmer Site.* Florida Anthropological Society Publications 8. Gainesville: Florida Anthropological Society.

Bullen, Ripley P., Walter Askew, Lee M. Feder, and Richard McDonnell
  1978   *The Canton Street Site, St. Petersburg, Florida.* Florida Anthropological Society Publications 9. Gainesville.
Bullen, Ripley P., and James B. Stoltman (editors)
  1972   *Fiber-Tempered Pottery in Southeastern United States and Northern Colombia: Its Origins, Context, and Significance.* Florida Anthropological Society Publications 6. Gainesville: Florida Anthropological Society.
Bunting, B. T.
  1967   *The Geography of Soil.* Chicago: Aldine.
Buol, Stanley W., Frank D. Hole, and Ralph J. McCracken
  1988   *Soil Genesis and Classification.* 3d ed. Ames: Iowa State University Press.
Butzer, Karl W.
  1980   Holocene Alluvial Sequences: Problems, Dating, Correlation. In *Timescales in Geomorphology,* ed. R. A. Cullingford, D. A. Davidson, and J. Lewis, pp. 131–42. London: John Wiley and Sons.
Byrd, Kathleen Mary
  1976   Tchefuncte Subsistence: Information Obtained from the Excavation of the Morton Shell Mound, Iberia Parish, Louisiana. *Southeastern Archaeological Conference Bulletin* 19:70–75.
Byrd, Kathleen M. (editor)
  1986   Recent Research at the Poverty Point Site. *Louisiana Archaeology* 13.
  1991   *The Poverty Point Culture: Local Manifestations, Subsistence Practices, and Trade Networks.* Geoscience and Man 29. Baton Rouge: Louisiana State University.
Cable, J. S.
  1982a Organizational Variability in Piedmont Hunter-Gatherer Lithic Assemblages. In Claggett and Cable, q.v., pp. 637–88.
  1982b Technological Aspects of the Assemblages. In Claggett and Cable, q.v., pp. 267–89.
  1992   Haw River Revisited: Implications for Modeling Terminal Late Glacial and Early Holocene Hunter-Gatherer Settlement Systems in South Carolina. In Anderson, Sassaman, and Judge, eds., q.v., pp. 96–142.
Caddell, Gloria
  1982   *Plant Resources, Archaeological Plant Remains and Prehistoric Plant-Use Patterns in the Central Tombigbee River Valley.* Bulletin of the Alabama Museum of Natural History 7. Tuscaloosa: University of Alabama.
Caldwell, Joseph R.
  1952   The Archaeology of Eastern Georgia and South Carolina. In *Archaeology of Eastern United States,* ed. J. B. Griffin, pp. 312–21. Chicago: University of Chicago Press.
  1958   *Trend and Tradition in the Prehistory of the Eastern United States.* Scientific Papers 10. Springfield: Illinois State Museum. Memoir 88. Menasha, Wis.: American Anthropological Association.
Caldwell, Joseph R., and Robert L. Hall (editors)
  1964   *Hopewellian Studies.* Scientific Papers 12. Springfield: Illinois State Museum.
Calvert, P. M., D. S. Introne, and J. J. Stipp
  1979   University of Miami Radiocarbon Dates XIV. *Radiocarbon* 21:107–12.

Camilli, E. L., and J. I. Ebert
    1992   Artifact Reuse and Recycling in Continuous Surface Distributions and Implica-
            tions for Interpreting Land Use Patterns. In *Time, Space, and Archaeological
            Landscapes,* ed. J. Rossignol and L. Wandsnider, pp. 113–36. New York: Plenum
            Press.
Canouts, V., and A. C. Goodyear
    1985   Lithic Scatters in the South Carolina Piedmont. In *Structure and Process in South-
            eastern Archaeology,* ed. R. S. Dickens and H. T. Ward, pp. 180–94. Tuscaloosa:
            University of Alabama Press.
Carr, P. J.
    1991   *Organization of Technology and Lithic Analysis: Prehistoric Hunter-Gatherer Occu-
            pation of the Hayes Site (40ML139).* M.A. thesis, University of Tennessee,
            Knoxville.
    1994a   The Organization of Technology: Impact and Potential. In *The Organization of
            Prehistoric North American Chipped Stone Tool Technologies,* ed. P. Carr, pp. 1–8.
            Archaeological Series 7. Ann Arbor: International Monographs in Prehistory.
    1994b   Technological Organization and Prehistoric Hunter-Gatherer Mobility: Exami-
            nation of the Hayes Site. In *The Organization of Prehistoric North American
            Chipped Stone Tool Technologies,* ed. P. Carr, pp. 35–44. Archaeological Series 7.
            Ann Arbor: International Monographs in Prehistory.
Carr, P. J., and W. E. Klippel
    1993   Foragers and Collectors as Two Extremes: What Lies Between the Continuum?
            Paper presented at the annual meeting of the Society for American Antiquity, St.
            Louis.
Carr, Robert S., and B. Calvin Jones
    1981   Interview with Calvin Jones, Part II: Excavations of an Archaic Cemetery in
            Cocoa Beach, Florida. *Florida Anthropologist* 34:81–89.
Cashdan, Elizabeth A.
    1980   Egalitarianism among Hunters and Gatherers. *American Anthropologist*
            82:116–20.
Cassidy, C. M.
    1984   Skeletal Evidence for Prehistoric Subsistence Adaptation in the Central Ohio
            Valley. In Cohen and Armelagos, eds., q.v., pp. 307–45.
Chapman, Jefferson
    1976   The Archaic Period in the Lower Little Tennessee River Valley: The Radio-
            carbon Dates. *Tennessee Anthropologist* 1(1):1–12.
    1977   *Archaic Period Research in the Lower Little Tennessee River Valley—1975, Icehouse
            Bottom, Harrison Branch, Thirty Acre Island, Calloway Island.* Report of Investiga-
            tions 18. Knoxville: Department of Anthropology, University of Tennessee.
    1981   *The Bacon Bend and Iddins Sites: The Late Archaic Period in the Lower Little Ten-
            nessee River Valley.* Report of Investigations 31. Knoxville: Department of
            Anthropology, University of Tennessee.
    1985a   *Tellico Archaeology.* Report of Investigations 43. Knoxville: Department of
            Anthropology, University of Tennessee.
    1985b   Archaeology and the Archaic Period in the Southern Ridge-and-Valley Province.
            In *Structure and Process in Southeastern Archaeology,* ed. R. S. Dickens and H. T.
            Ward, pp. 137–53. Tuscaloosa: University of Alabama Press.

Chapman, Jefferson, and Andrea B. Shea
  1981   The Archaeobotanical Record: Early Archaic Period to Contact in the Lower
         Little Tennessee River Valley. *Tennessee Anthropologist* 6:61–84.
Chapman, Jefferson, Paul A. Delcourt, Patricia A. Cridlebaugh, Andrea B. Shea, and
    Hazel R. Delcourt
  1982   Man-Land Interaction: 10,000 Years of American Indian Impact on Native
         Ecosystems in the Lower Little Tennessee River Valley. *Southeastern Archaeology*
         2:115–21.
Charles, Douglas, and Jane Buikstra
  1983   Archaic Mortuary Sites in the Central Mississippi Drainage: Distribution, Struc-
         ture, and Behavioral Implications. In Phillips and Brown, eds., q.v., pp. 117–46.
Chatters, J. C.
  1987   Hunter-Gatherer Adaptations and Assemblage Structure. *Journal of Anthropolog-
         ical Archaeology* 6:336–75.
Chomko, Stephen A., and Gary W. Crawford
  1978   Plant Husbandry in Prehistoric Eastern North America: New Evidence for Its
         Development. *American Antiquity* 43:405–8.
Christenson, A. L.
  1977   Some Trends in Biface Technology in Central Illinois. *Plains Anthropologist*
         22:282–90.
Claassen, Cheryl P.
  1986   Seasonality of Carlston Annis and DeWeese Mounds, Ky. In *Archaeology of the
         Middle Green River,* ed. W. H. Marquardt and P. J. Watson (in preparation).
  1988   New Hypotheses for the Demise of the Shell Mound Archaic. Paper presented at
         the annual meeting of SEAC, New Orleans.
  1991a Gender, Shellfishing, and the Shell Mound Archaic. In *Engendering Archaeology:
         Women and Prehistory,* ed. J. M. Gero and M. W. Conkey, pp. 276–300. Oxford:
         Basil Blackwell.
  1991b New Hypotheses for the Demise of the Shell Mound Archaic. In *The Archaic
         Period in the Mid-South,* ed. C. McNutt, pp. 66–72. Archaeological Report 24.
         Jackson: Mississippi Department of Archives and History.
  1992   Shell Mounds as Burial Mounds: A Revision of the Shell Mound Archaic. In
         Current Archaeological Research in Kentucky, vol. 2, ed. D. Pollack and A. G. Hen-
         derson, pp. 1–12. Frankfort: Kentucky Heritage Council.
  1994   Washboards, Pigtoes, and Muckets: Historic Musseling in the Mississippi
         Watershed. *Historical Archaeology* 28:1–145.
Clabeaux, M. S.
  1976   Health and Disease in the Population of an Iroquois Ossuary. *Yearbook of Physical
         Anthropology* 20:359–70.
Claflin, William H., Jr.
  1931   *The Stalling's Island Mound, Columbia County, Georgia.* Papers, vol. 14, no. 1.
         Cambridge: Peabody Museum of American Archaeology and Ethnology, Har-
         vard University.
Claggett, Stephen R., and John S. Cable (assemblers)
  1982   *The Haw River Sites: Archaeological Investigations at Two Stratified Sites in the
         North Carolina Piedmont.* Report 2386. Commonweath Associates, Jackson,
         Mich. Prepared for the U.S. Army Corps of Engineers, Wilmington District.

Clark, J. S.
  1988   Stratigraphic Charcoal Analyses on Petrographic Thin Sections: Application to
          Fire History in Northwestern Minnesota. *Quaternary Research* 30:81–91.
Clark, John E., and William J. Parry
  1990   Craft Specialization and Cultural Complexity. *Research in Economic Anthropology*
          12:289–346.
Clausen, C. J., A. D. Cohen, C. Emiliani, J. A. Holman, and J. J. Stipp
  1979   Little Salt Spring, Florida: A Unique Underwater Site. *Science* 203:609–14.
Coastal Environments, Inc.
  1977   *Cultural Resources Evaluation of the North Gulf of Mexico Continental Shelf,* vol. 1.
          Submitted by Coastal Environments, Inc., to Interagency Archeological Ser-
          vices, Office of Historic Preservation, National Park Service, U.S. Department of
          the Interior, Washington.
Cockrell, Wilburn A.
  1970   *Glades I and Pre-Glades Settlement and Subsistence Patterns on Marco Island (Collier
          County, Florida).* M. A. thesis, Florida State University, Tallahassee.
Cockrell, Wilburn A., and Larry Murphy
  1978   Pleistocene Man in Florida. *Archaeology of Eastern North America* 6:1–12.
Coe, Joffre L.
  1952   The Cultural Sequence of the Carolina Piedmont. In *Archaeology of Eastern
          United States,* ed. J. B. Griffin, pp. 301–11. Chicago: University of Chicago Press.
  1964   *The Formative Cultures of the Carolina Piedmont.* Transactions of the American
          Philosophical Society 54(5), Philadelphia.
Cohen, A. D.
  1973   Possible Influences of Subpeat Topography and Sediment Type upon the Devel-
          opment of the Okefenokee Swamp-Marsh Complex of Georgia. *Southeastern
          Geology* 15:141–51.
Cohen, Mark N., and George J. Armelagos (editors)
  1985   *Paleopathology at the Origins of Agriculture.* Orlando: Academic Press.
Collins, Henry B.
  1941   Relationships of an Early Indian Cranial Series from Lousiana. *Journal of the
          Washington Academy of Sciences* 31:145–55.
Collins, M. B.
  1975   Lithic Technology as a Means of Processual Inference. In *Making and Using
          Stone Tools,* ed. E. Swanson, pp. 15–34. Paris: Mouton.
  1993   Comprehensive Lithic Studies: Context, Technology, Style, Attrition, Breakage,
          Use-Wear, and Organic Residues. *Lithic Technology* 18:87–94.
Colman, Steven M., J. P. Halka, C. H. Hobbs III, R. B. Mixon, and D. S. Foster
  1990   Ancient Channels of the Susquehanna River beneath Chesapeake Bay and the
          Delmarva Peninsula. *Geological Society of America Bulletin* 102:1268–79.
Colquhoun, Donald J., and Mark J. Brooks
  1986   New Evidence from the Southeastern U.S. for Eustatic Components in the Late
          Holocene Sea Levels. *Geoarchaeology* 1:275–91.
Colquhoun, Donald J., M. J. Brooks, W. H. Abbott, F. W. Stapor, W. S. Newman, and
          R. R. Pardi
  1980   Principles and Problems in Establishing a Holocene Sea-Level Curve for South

Carolina. In *Excursions in Southeastern Geology: The Archaeology-Geology of the Georgia Coast.* Guidebook 20. Atlanta: Georgia Geologic Survey.

Comuzzie, A. G., and D. Gentry Steele

1988   Maxillary Lingual Anterior Tooth Wear in Prehistoric Hunter-Gatherers from the Texas Coast. *American Journal of Physical Anthropology* 75:197–98.

Conard, Nicholas, David L. Asch, Nancy B. Asch, David Elmore, Harry Gove, Meyer Rubin, James A. Brown, Michael D. Wiant, Kenneth B. Farnsworth, and Thomas G. Cook

1983   Prehistoric Horticulture in Illinois: Accelerator Radiocarbon Dating of the Evidence. *Nature* 308:443–46.

Conaty, G. T.

1987   Patterns of Chert Use during the Middle and Late Archaic in Western Kentucky. *Southeastern Archaeology* 6:140–55.

Conaty, G. T., and E. K. Leach

1987   Resource Patches and Mobility Strategies: Archaic Responses to Climatic Change. In *Man and the Mid-Holocene Climatic Optimum,* ed. N. McKinnon and G. Stuart, pp. 283–301. Proceedings of the Chacmool Conference. Alberta: Department of Archaeology, University of Calgary.

Conn, Thomas L.

1973   *The Utilization of Chert at the Poverty Point Site.* M.A. thesis, Louisiana State University, Baton Rouge.

Connaway, John M., Samuel O. McGahey, and Clarence H. Webb

1977   *Teoc Creek: A Poverty Point Site in Carroll County, Mississippi.* Archaeological Report 3. Jackson: Mississippi Department of Archives and History.

Cook, Thomas G.

1976   *Koster: An Artifact Analysis of Two Archaic Phases in West-Central Illinois.* Prehistoric Research Records 1. Evanston: Archaeology Program, Northwestern University.

Cotterell, Brian, and Johan Kamminga

1990   *Mechanics of Pre-Industrial Technology.* Cambridge: Cambridge University Press.

Cowan, C. Wesley

1985   Understanding the Evolution of Plant Husbandry in Eastern North America: Lessons from Botany, Ethnography, and Archaeology. In *Prehistoric Food Production in North America,* ed. R. I. Ford, pp. 205–43. Anthropological Papers 75. Ann Arbor: Museum of Anthropology, University of Michigan.

1996   Evolutionary Changes Associated with Domestication of *Cucurbit pepo:* Evidence from Eastern Kentucky. In *People, Plants, and Landscapes: Studies in Paleoethnobotany,* ed. K. J. Gremillion. Tuscaloosa: University of Alabama Press.

Cowan, C. Wesley, and Bruce D. Smith

1993   New Perspectives on a Wild Gourd in Eastern North America. *Journal of Ethnobiology* 13:17–54.

Cowan, C. Wesley, H. Edwin Jackson, K. Moore, A. Nickelhoff, and T. Smart

1981   The Cloudsplitter Rockshelter, Menifee County, Kentucky: A Preliminary Report. *Southeastern Archaeological Conference Bulletin* 24:60–75.

Cox, Kim A.

1994   Oysters as Ecofacts. *Bulletin of the Texas Archeological Society* 62:219–47.

Cridlebaugh, Patricia A.

1986   *Penitentiary Branch: A Late Archaic Cumberland River Shell Midden in Middle Tennessee.* Report of Investigations 4. Nashville: Tennessee Department of Conservation, Division of Archaeology.

Crites, Gary D.

1987   Middle and Late Holocene Paleoethnobotany of the Hayes Site (40ML139): Evidence from 990N918E. *Midcontinental Journal of Archaeology* 12:3–15.

1991   Investigations into Early Plant Domesticates and Food Production in Middle Tennessee: A Status Report. *Tennessee Anthropologist* 16:69–87.

1993   Domesticated Sunflower in Fifth Millennium B.P. Temporal Context: New Evidence from Middle Tennessee. *American Antiquity* 58:146–48.

Crumley, Carole L.

1979   Three Locational Models: An Epistemological Assessment for Anthropology and Archaeology. In *Advances in Archaeological Method and Theory,* vol. 2, ed. M. B. Schiffer, pp. 141–73. New York: Academic Press.

Crusoe, Donald L., and Chester B. DePratter

1976   A New Look at the Georgia Coastal Shellmound Archaic. *Florida Anthropologist* 29:1–23.

Curray, J. R.

1965   Late Quaternary History: Continental Shelves of the United States. In *The Quaternary of the United States,* ed. H. E. Wright and D. G. Frey, pp. 723–35. Princeton: Princeton University Press.

Custer, Jay F.

1986   Prehistoric Use of the Chesapeake Estuary: A Diachronic Perspective. *Journal of the Washington Academy of Sciences* 76:161–72.

Danforth, M. E., K. S. Herdon, and K. P. Propst

1993   A Preliminary Study of Patterns of Replication in Scoring Linear Enamel Hypoplasia. *International Journal of Osteoarchaeology* 3:297–302.

Daniel, I. R.

1986   An Analysis of Unifacial Stone Tools from the Hardaway Site, North Carolina. *Southern Indian Studies* 35:3–53.

1992   Early Archaic Settlement in the Southeast: A North Carolina Perspective. In Anderson, Sassaman, and Judge, eds. q.v., pp. 68–77.

1994   *Hardaway Revisited: Early Archaic Settlement in the Southeast.* Ph.D. dissertation, University of North Carolina, Chapel Hill.

Daniel, I. R., and M. Wisenbaker

1987   *Harney Flats: A Florida Paleo-Indian Site.* Amityville, N.Y.: Baywood.

Daniel, I. R., M. Wisenbaker, and G. Ballo

1986   The Organization of a Suwannee Technology: The View from Harney Flats. *Florida Anthropologist* 39:24–56.

Davis, Dave D.

1984   Perspectives on Gulf Coast Prehistory: A Roundtable Discussion. In *Perspectives on Gulf Coast Prehistory,* ed. D. D. Davis, pp. 315–32. Gainesville: University Presses of Florida.

Davis, Richard A., Albert C. Hine, and Eugene A. Shinn
  1992 Holocene Coastal Development of the Florida Peninsula. In Fletcher and Wehmiller, eds., q.v., pp. 193–212.
Debusschere, K., B. J. Miller, and A. F. Ramenofsky
  1989 A Geoarchaeological Reconstruction of Cowpen Slough: A Late Archaic Site in East Central Louisiana. *Geoarchaeology* 4:251–70.
Decker, Deena S.
  1988 Origin(s), Evolution and Systematics of *Cucurbita pepo* (Cucurbitaceae). *Economic Botany* 42:4–15.
Decker-Walters, Deena S., Terrence W. Walters, C. Wesley Cowan, and Bruce D. Smith
  1993 Isozymic Characterization of Wild Populations of *Cucurbita pepo. Journal of Ethnobiology* 13:55–74.
Deevey, Edward S., and Richard F. Flint
  1957 Postglacial Hypsithermal Interval. *Science* 125:182–84.
DeJarnette, David L.
  1952 Alabama Archaeology: A Summary. In *Archaeology of Eastern United States,* ed. J. B. Griffin, pp. 272–84. Chicago: University of Chicago Press.
DeJarnette, David L., Edward B. Kurjak, and James W. Cambron
  1962 Stanfield-Worley Bluff Shelter Excavations. *Journal of Alabama Archaeology* 3, nos. 1–2.
Delcourt, Hazel R.
  1979 Late Quaternary Vegetation History of the Eastern Highland Rim and Adjacent Cumberland Plateau of Tennessee. *Ecological Monographs* 49:255–80.
Delcourt, Hazel R., and Paul A. Delcourt
  1985 Quaternary Palynology and Vegetational History of the Southeastern United States. In *Pollen Records of Late-Quaternary North American Sediments,* ed. V. M. Bryant and R. G. Holloway, pp. 1–37. Dallas: American Association of Stratigraphic Palynologists Foundation.
Delcourt, Paul A., and Hazel R. Delcourt
  1979 Late Pleistocene and Holocene Distributional History of Deciduous Forest in the Southeastern United States. *Veröffentlichungen des Geobotanischen Institute der Eth, Stiftung Rübel* (Zurich) 68:79–107.
  1981 Vegetation Maps for Eastern North America. In *Geobotany II,* ed. R. Romans, pp. 123–65. New York: Plenum Press.
  1983 Late Quaternary Vegetational Dynamics and Community Stability Reconsidered. *Quaternary Research* 13:111–32.
  1987 *Long-Term Forest Dynamics of the Temperate Zone: A Case Study of Late-Quaternary Forests in Eastern North America.* New York: Springer-Verlag.
Delcourt, Paul A., Hazel R. Delcourt, Patricia A. Cridlebaugh, and Jefferson Chapman
  1986 Holocene Ethnobotanical and Paleoecological Record of Human Impact on Vegetation in the Little Tennessee River Valley, Tennessee. *Quaternary Research* 25:330–49.
DePratter, Chester B.
  1976 *The Shellmound Archaic on the Georgia Coast.* M.A. thesis, University of Georgia, Athens.
  1979 Shellmound Archaic on the Georgia Coast. *South Carolina Antiquities* 11(2):1–69.

DePratter, Chester B., and J. D. Howard

 1977   History of Shoreline Changes Determined by Archaeological Dating: Georgia Coast, U.S.A. *Transactions: Gulf Coast Association of Geological Societies* 27:252–58.

 1980   Indian Occupation and Geological History of the Georgia Coast: A 5000 Year Summary. In *Excursions in Southeastern Geology: The Archaeology-Geology of the Georgia Coast*, ed. J. D. Howard, Chester B. DePratter, and R. W. Frey, pp. 1–65. Georgia Geological Society Guidebook 20.

 1981   Evidence for a Sea Level Lowstand between 4500 and 2400 Years B.P. on the Southeast Coast of the United States. *Journal of Sedimentary Petrology* 51:1287–95.

Dickel, David N., and Glen H. Doran

 1989   Severe Neural Tube Defect Syndrome from the Early Archaic of Florida. *American Journal of Physical Anthropology* 80:325–34.

Dickens, Roy S., and Linda R. Carnes

 1983   Preliminary Investigations at Soapstone Ridge, DeKalb County, Georgia. *Southeastern Archaeological Conference Bulletin* 20:81–97.

Dickinson, Martin F., and Lucy B. Wayne

 1987   *Archaeological Survey and Testing Phase I Development Areas, Fairfield Fort George, Fort George Island, Duval County, Florida.* Water and Air Research, Inc., Gainesville, Florida. Submitted to Fairfield Fort George, Jacksonville.

Digerfeldt, G.

 1986   Studies on Past Lake-Level Fluctuations. In *Handbook of Holocene Palaeoecology and Palaeohydrology,* ed. B. E. Berglund, pp. 127–43. New York: John Wiley and Sons.

Dijkerman, J. C., M. G. Cline, and G. W. Olsen

 1967   Properties and Genesis of Textural Subsoil Lamellae. *Soil Science* 104:7–16.

Division of Archives, History and Records Management (DAHRM), Florida Department of State.

 1985   Guana River Cultural Resources Description. In *Guana River State Land Conceptual Plan,* prepared by Florida Department of Natural Resources Division of Recreation and Parks, Florida Game and Fresh Water Fish Commission, and DAHRM, Florida Department of State, pp. A20–A26. Tallahassee.

Dobbs, W. H.

 1988   Vertebral Osteophytosis among Archaic and Mississippian Populations of the Tennessee River Valley in Northern Alabama. *American Journal of Physical Anthropology* 75:204.

Doershuk, John F.

 1989   *Hunter-Gatherer Site Structure and Sedentism: The Koster Site Middle Archaic.* Ph.D. dissertation, Northwestern University, Evanston. Ann Arbor: University Microfilms.

Donisi, Michael P.

 1982   *The Incidence and Pattern of Long Bone Fractures in Selected Prehistoric Human Skeletal Series from the Central Tennessee Valley of Alabama.* M.A. thesis, University of Alabama, Tuscaloosa.

Doran, Glen H., David N. Dickel, and Lee A. Newsom

 1990   A 7,290-Year-Old Bottle Gourd from the Windover Site, Florida. *American Antiquity* 55:354–59.

Doran, Glen H., David N. Dickel, William E. Ballinger, Jr., O. Frank Agee, Philip J. Laipis, and William W. Hauswirth
  1986   Anatomical, Cellular, and Molecular Analysis of 8,000-yr-old Human Brain Tissue from the Windover Archaeological Site. *Nature* 323:803–6.
Douglass, Andrew E.
  1882   A Find of Ceremonial Axes in a Florida Mound. *American Antiquarian and Oriental Journal* 4:100–109.
Dowd, John T.
  1989   *The Anderson Site: Middle Archaic Adaptation in Tennessee's Central Basin.* Miscellaneous Paper 13. Knoxville: Tennessee Anthropological Association.
Duhe, Brian J.
  1976   Preliminary Evidence of Seasonal Fishing Activity at Bayou Jasmine. *Louisiana Archaeology* 3:33–74.
Dunbar, James S.
  1988   Archaeological Sites in the Drowned Tertiary Karst Regions of the Eastern Gulf of Mexico. *Proceedings: Eighth Annual Gulf of Mexico Information Transfer Meeting,* December 1987:418–23. New Orleans: Mineral Management Service.
  1991   Resource Orientation of Clovis and Suwannee Age Paleoindian Sites in Florida. In *Clovis: Origins and Adaptations,* ed. R. Bonnichsen and K. Turnmire, pp. 185–213. Corvallis: Center for the Study of the First Americans, Oregon State University.
Dunbar, James S., S. David Webb, and Michael Faught
  1992   Inundated Sites in Apalachee Bay, Florida, and the Search for the Clovis Shoreline. In Johnson and Stright, eds., q.v., pp. 117–48.
DuPratz, M. Le Page
  1774   *The History of Louisiana.* Facsimile reproduction, published 1975. Baton Rouge: Louisiana State University Press.
Dye, David H.
  1980   *Primary Forest Efficiency in the Western Middle Tennessee Valley.* Ph.D. dissertation, Washington University, St. Louis.
  1993   Initial Riverine Adaptation in the Midsouth: An Examination of Three Middle Holocene Shell Middens. MS on file, Department of Anthropology, Memphis State University.
Ebert, J. I.
  1979   An Ethnoarchaeological Approach to Reassessing the Meaning of Variability in Stone Tool Assemblages. In *Ethnoarchaeology: Implications of Ethnography for Archaeology,* ed. C. Kramer, pp. 59–74. New York: Columbia University Press.
  1992   *Distributional Archaeology.* Albuquerque: University of New Mexico Press.
Ebert, J. I., and T. A. Kohler
  1988   The Theoretical Basis of Archaeological Predictive Modeling and a Consideration of Appropriate Data-Collection Methods. In *Quantifying the Present and Predicting the Past: Theory, Method, and Application of Archaeological Predictive Modeling,* ed. W. Judge and L. Sebastian, pp. 97–171. Washington: U.S. Government Printing Office.

Edmonds, M.
  1987   Rocks and Risk: Problems with Lithic Procurement Strategies. In *Lithic Analysis and Later British Prehistory,* ed. A. G. Brown and M. R. Edmonds, pp. 155–79. British Series 162. Oxford: British Archaeological Reports.
Edwards, Robert L., and K. O. Emery
  1977   Man on the Continental Shelf. In *Amerinds and their Paleoenvironments in Northeastern North America,* ed. B. Salwen and W. Newman, pp. 245–256. Albany: Annals of the New York Academy of Science 288.
Edwards, Robert L., and Arthur S. Merrill
  1977   A Reconstruction of the Continental Shelf Areas of Eastern North America for the Times 9,500 B.P. and 12,500 B.P. *Archaeology of Eastern North America* 5:1–42.
Eleuterius, Lionel N., and Ervin G. Otvos, Jr.
  1979   Floristic and Geological Aspects of Indian Middens in Salt Marshes of Hancock County, Mississippi. *SIDA* 8:102–12.
Elliott, Daniel T.
  1989   *Falcon Field and Line Creek: Two Archaic and Woodland Period Sites in West Central Georgia.* Athens, Ga.: Southeastern Archeological Services.
  1993   *The Clark Hill River Basin Survey.* Watkinsville, Ga.: Lamar Institute.
Elliott, Daniel T., R. Jerald Ledbetter, and Elizabeth A. Gordon
  1994   *Data Recovery at Lovers Lane, Phinizy Swamp and the Old Dike Sites, Bobby Jones Expressway Extension Corridor, Augusta, Georgia.* Occasional Papers in Cultural Resource Management 7. Atlanta: Office of Environment/Location, Department of Transportation, Georgia.
Emerson, T. E., and D. L. McElrath
  1983   A Settlement-Subsistence Model of the Terminal Late Archaic Adaptation in the American Bottom, Illinois. In Phillips and Brown, eds., q.v., pp. 219–42.
Emery, K. O., and Robert L. Edwards
  1966   Archaeological Potential of the Atlantic Continental Shelf. *American Antiquity* 31:733–37.
Ensor, H. B., and J. M. Studer
  1983   Excavations at the Walnut Site: 22IT539. In *Archaeological Investigations in the Upper Tombigbee Valley, Mississippi: Phase I,* ed. J. A. Bense. Report of Investigations 3. Pensacola: Office of Cultural and Archaeological Research, University of West Florida.
Fairbanks, Charles H.
  1942   The Taxonomic Position of Stalling's Island, Georgia. *American Antiquity* 3:223–31.
  1959   Additional Elliott's Point Complex Sites. *Florida Anthropologist* 12(4):95–100.
Fairbanks, R. G.
  1989   A 17,000-Year Glacio-Eustatic Sea-Level Record: Influence of Glacial Melting Rates on the Younger Dryas Event and Deep Ocean Circulation. *Nature* 342:637–42.
Fairbridge, Rhodes W.
  1961   Eustatic Changes in Sea Level. In *Physics and Chemistry of the Earth,* vol. 4, ed. L. H. Ahrens, F. Press, K. Raukawa, and S. K. Runcorn, pp. 99–185. New York: Pergamon Press.

Faught, Michael
 1988   Inundated Sites in the Apalachee Bay of Florida of the Eastern Gulf of Mexico. *Florida Anthropologist* 41:185–90.
Faulkner, Charles A.
 1977   The Winter House: An Early Southeast Tradition. *Midcontinental Journal of Archaeology* 2:141–59.
Faulkner, Charles A., and Major C. R. McCollough
 1974   *Excavations and Testing, Normandy Reservoir Salvage Project, 1972 Season.* Report of Investigations 12. Knoxville: Department of Anthropology, University of Tennessee.
Fenneman, N. H.
 1938   *Physiography of Eastern United States.* New York: McGraw-Hill.
Fenton, James
 1991   *The Social Uses of Dead People: Problems and Solutions in the Analysis of Post Mortem Body Processing in the Archaeological Record.* Ph.D. dissertation, Columbia University. Ann Arbor: University Microfilms.
Ferguson, R. Brian
 1990   Explaining War. In Haas, ed., q.v., pp. 26–55.
Ferguson, Vera M.
 1951   *Chronology at South Indian Field, Florida.* Publications in Anthropology 45. New Haven: Yale University.
Ferring, C. Reid
 1986   Rates of Fluvial Sedimentation: Implications for Archaeological Variability. *Geoarchaeology* 1:259–74.
 1992   Alluvial Pedology and Geoarchaeological Research. In *Soils in Archaeology,* ed. Vance T. Holliday, pp. 1–39. Washington: Smithsonian Institution Press.
Finkelstein, Kenneth, and Marie A. Ferland
 1987   Back-Barrier Response to Sea-Level Rise, Eastern Shore of Virginia. In *Sea-Level Fluctuation and Coastal Evolution,* ed. D. Nummedal. Tulsa: Society of Economic Paleontologists and Mineralogists.
Finkelstein, Kenneth, and C. Scott Hardaway
 1988   Late Holocene Sedimentation and Erosion of Estuarine Fringing Marshes, York River, Virginia. *Journal of Coastal Research* 4:447–56.
Fischer, John W., Jr., and Helen C. Strickland
 1991   Dwellings and Fireplaces: Keys to Efe Pygmy Campsite Structure. In *Ethnoarchaeological Approaches to Mobile Campsites,* ed. C. S. Gamble and W. A. Boismier, pp. 215–36. Ethnoarchaeological Series 1. Ann Arbor: International Monographs in Prehistory.
Fisk, H. N.
 1944   *Geological Investigation of the Alluvial Valley of the Lower Mississippi River.* Mississippi River Commission Publications 52. Vicksburg: U.S. Army Corps of Engineers.
Flannery, Regina
 1943   Some Notes on a Few Sites in Beaufort County, South Carolina. *Bulletin of the Bureau of American Ethnology* 133 (Anthropological Papers 21):143–53. Washington: Bureau of American Ethnology, Smithsonian Institution.

Fletcher, Charles H., and John F. Wehmiller (editors)

1992   *Quaternary Coasts of the United States: Marine and Lacustrine Systems.* Special Publication 48. Tulsa: Society for Sedimentary Geology.

Fogleman, James

1992   Archaic Mounds from South-Central Louisiana. Paper presented at the annual meeting of SEAC, Little Rock.

Ford, James A.

1969   *A Comparison of Formative Cultures in the Americas, Diffusion or the Psychic Unity of Man.* Smithsonian Contributions to Anthropology 11. Washington: Smithsonian Institution.

Ford, James A., and George I. Quimby, Jr.

1945   *The Tchefuncte Culture, an Early Occupation of the Lower Mississippi Valley.* Memoirs of the Society for American Archaeology 2. Menasha, Wis.: Society for American Archaeology.

Ford, James A., and Clarence H. Webb

1956   *Poverty Point, a Late Archaic Site in Louisiana.* Anthropological Papers, vol. 46, pt. 1. New York: American Museum of Natural History.

Ford, James A., and Gordon R. Willey

1941   An Interpretation of the Prehistory of the Eastern United States. *American Anthropologist* 43:325–63.

Ford, James A., Philip Phillips, and William G. Haag

1955   *The Jaketown Site in West-Central Mississippi.* Anthropological Papers, vol. 45, pt. 1. New York: American Museum of Natural History.

Fortier, Andrew C.

1983   Settlement and Subsistence at the Go-Kart North Site: A Late Archaic Titterington Occupation in the American Bottom. In Phillips and Brown, eds., q.v., pp. 243–60.

Foss, John E., and Antonio V. Segovia

1984   Rates of Soil Formation. In *Groundwater as a Geomorphic Agent,* ed. R. G. LaFleur, pp. 1–17. Boston: Allen and Unwin.

Foss, John E., D. P. Wagner, and F. P. Miller

1985   *Soils of the Savannah River Valley: Richard B. Russell Multiple Resource Area, Elbert County, Georgia.* Russell Papers 1985. Atlanta: Interagency Archeological Services Division, National Park Service.

Fowler, Melvin L.

1957   *Ferry Site, Hardin County, Illinois.* Scientific Papers 8(1). Springfield: Illinois State Museum.

1959   *Summary Report of Modoc Rock Shelter: 1952, 1953, 1955, 1956.* Report of Investigations 8. Springfield: Illinois State Museum.

Frankenberg, S. R., D. G. Albertson, and L. Kohn

1988   The Elizabeth Site Skeletal Remains: Demography and Disease. In *The Archaic and Woodland Cemeteries at the Elizabeth Site in the Lower Illinois River Valley,* ed. D. K. Charles, S. R. Leigh, and J. E. Buikstra, pp. 103–19. Research Series 7. Kampsville, Ill.: Center for American Archaeology.

Frazier, D. E.

1967   Recent Deltaic Deposits of the Mississippi River: Their Development and Chronology. *Transactions: Gulf Coast Association Geological Society* 17:287–315.

Frederickson, B. E., D. Baker, W. J. McHolick, H. A. Yuan, and J. P. Lubicky
1984   The Natural History of Spondylolysis and Spondylolysthesis. *Journal of Bone and Joint Surgery* 66-A:699–707.

Frey, D. G.
1954   Regional Aspects of the Late-Glacial and Post-Glacial Pollen Succession of Southeastern North Carolina. *Ecological Monographs* 23:289–313.

Frey, Robert W., and James D. Howard
1986   Mesotidal Estuarine Sequences: A Perspective from the Georgia Bight. *Journal of Sedimentary Petrology* 56(6):911–24.

Fritz, Gayle J.
1990   Multiple Pathways to Farming in Precontact Eastern North America. *Journal of World Prehistory* 4:387–435.
1996   A 3,000-Year-Old Cache of Crop Seed from Marble Bluff, Arkansas. In *People, Plants, and Landscapes: Studies in Paleoethnobotany,* ed. K. J. Gremillion. Tuscaloosa: University of Alabama Press.

Funkhouser, William D.
1939   A Study of Skeletal Remains. In Webb, ed., q.v., pp. 109–25.

Funkhouser, William D., and William S. Webb
1932   *Archaeological Survey of Kentucky.* Reports in Archaeology and Anthropology 2. Lexington: University of Kentucky.

Futato, E. M.
1983   Patterns of Lithic Resource Utilization in the Cedar Creek Reservoir Area. *Southeastern Archaeology* 2:118–31.
1996   A Synopsis of Paleoindian and Early Archaic Research in Alabama. In *The Paleoindian and Early Archaic Southeast,* ed. D. G. Anderson and K. E. Sassaman. Tuscaloosa: University of Alabama Press (in press).

Gaertner, L. M.
1990   *Microwear Analysis of Dalton "Wood-Working Adzes" from Early Archaic Sites in Northeastern Arkansas.* B.A. honors thesis, Ohio State University, Columbus.

Gagliano, Sherwood M.
1963   A Survey of Preceramic Occupations in Portions of South Louisiana and South Mississippi. *Florida Anthropologist* 16:105–32.
1967   *Occupation Sequence at Avery Island.* Coastal Studies Series 22. Baton Rouge: Louisiana State University.
1970a *Progress Report: Archaeological and Geological Studies at Avery Island, 1968–70.* Baton Rouge: Center for Wetland Resources, Louisiana State University.
1970b *Archaeological and Geological Studies at Avery Island, 1967–1970.* Baton Rouge: Coastal Studies Institute, Louisiana State University.
1984   Geoarchaeology of the Northern Gulf Shore. In *Perspectives on Gulf Coast Prehistory,* ed. D. D. Davis, pp. 1–40. Gainesville: University Presses of Florida.

Gagliano, Sherwood M., and Roger T. Saucier
1963   Poverty Point Sites in Southeastern Louisiana. *American Antiquity* 28:320–27.

Gagliano, Sherwood M., and Clarence H. Webb
1970   Archaic–Poverty Point Transition at the Pearl River Mouth. In *The Poverty Point*

Culture, ed. Bettye Broyles and Clarence H. Webb, pp. 47–72. Bulletin 12. Morgantown: Southeastern Archaeological Conference.

Gagliano, Sherwood M., Charles E. Pearson, Richard A. Weinstein, Diane E. Wiseman, and Christopher M. McClendon

1982   *Sedimentary Studies of Prehistoric Archaeological Sites: Criteria for the Identification of Submerged Archaeological Sites of the Northern Gulf of Mexico Continental Shelf.* U.S. Department of the Interior, National Park Service, Division of State Plans and Grants, Contract no. C35003(79). Baton Rouge: Coastal Environments, Inc.

Galloway, Patricia

1991   Where Have All the Menstrual Huts Gone? Paper presented at the annual meeting of SEAC, Jackson.

1994   Prehistoric Population of Mississippi: A First Approximation. *Mississippi Archaeology* 29(2):44–71.

Gardner, Paul S.

1994   Carbonized Plant Remains from Dust Cave. *Journal of Alabama Archaeology* 40(1–2):192–211. Alabama Museum of Natural History, Moundville.

1996   The Ecological Structure and Behavioral Implications of Mast Exploitation Strategies. In *People, Plants, and Landscapes: Studies in Paleoethnobotany,* ed. K. J. Gremillion. Tuscaloosa: University of Alabama Press.

Gardner, William M.

1983   Stop Me If You've Heard This One Before: The Flint Run Paleoindian Complex Revisited. *Archaeology of Eastern North America* 11:49–59.

1989   An Examination of Cultural Change in the Late Pleistocene and Early Holocene (ca. 9200 to 6800 B.C.). In *Paleoindian Research in Virginia: A Synthesis,* edited by J. Mark Wittkofski and Theodore R. Reinhart, pp. 5–51. Richmond: Archaeological Society of Virginia Special Publication 19.

Gauch, Hugh G., Jr.

1982   *Multivariate Analysis in Community Ecology.* Cambridge: Cambridge University Press.

Gero, J.

1991   Genderlithics: Women's Roles in Stone Tool Production. In *Engendering Archaeology: Women and Prehistory,* ed. J. M. Gero and M. W. Conkey, pp. 163–93. Cambridge: Basil Blackwell.

Gibson, Jon L.

1968   Cad Mound: A Stone Bead Locus in East Central Louisiana. *Bulletin of the Texas Archaeological Society* 38:1–17.

1973   *Social Systems at Poverty Point: An Analysis of Intersite and Intrasite Variability.* Ph.D. dissertation, Southern Methodist University, Dallas.

1974   Poverty Point, the First North American Chiefdom. *Archaeology* 27:96–105.

1979   Poverty Point Trade in South Central Louisiana: An Illustration from Beau Rivage. *Louisiana Archaeology* 4:91–116.

1980   Speculations on the Origin and Development of Poverty Point Culture. In *Caddoan and Poverty Point Archaeology: Essays in Honor of Clarence Hungerford Webb,* ed. Jon L. Gibson. *Louisiana Archaeology* 6:321–48. Lafayette: Louisiana Archaeological Society.

1986   Earth Siting: Architectural Masses at Poverty Point, Northeastern Louisiana. In Byrd, ed., q.v., 201–37.

1987a   Poverty Point Reconsidered. *Mississippi Archaeology* 22(2):14–31.

1987b   *The Ground Truth about Poverty Point: The Second Season, 1985.* Report 7. Lafayette: Center for Archaeological Studies, University of Southwestern Louisiana.

1989   *Digging on the Dock of the Bay(ou): The 1988 Excavations at Poverty Point.* Report 8. Lafayette: Center for Archaeological Studies, University of Southwestern Louisiana.

1990   *Search for the Lost Sixth Ridge: Archaeological Excavations at Poverty Point, 1989.* Report 9. Lafayette: Center for Archaeological Studies, University of Southwestern Louisiana.

1991   Catahoula: An Amphibious Poverty Point Period Manifestation in Eastern Louisiana. In Byrd, ed., q.v., pp. 61–87.

1992a   Poverty Point Chronology: The Long and the Short of It. Paper presented at the 34th Caddo Conference, Bossier City.

1992b   Religion of the Rings: Poverty Point Iconology and Ceremonialism. In *Mounds, Embankments, and Ceremonialism in the Mid-South,* ed. R. Walling and R. Mainfort. Occasional Papers. Cobb Institute of Archaeology, Mississippi State University (in press).

1993a   *In Helona's Shadow: Excavations in the Western Rings at Poverty Point, 1991.* Report 11. Lafayette: Center for Archaeological Studies, University of Southwestern Louisiana.

1993b   The Orvis Scott Site: A Poverty Point Component on Joes Bayou, East Carroll Parish, Louisiana. Paper presented at the annual meeting of the Louisiana Archaeological Society, Lafayette.

1994a   Before Their Time? Early Mounds in the Lower Mississippi Valley. *Southeastern Archaeology* 13:162–81.

1994b   Lower Mississippi Valley Exchange at 1100 B.C. In *Exchange in the Lower Mississippi Valley and Contiguous Areas at 1100 B.C.,* ed. Jon L. Gibson. *Louisiana Archaeology* 21:1–12.

1994c   Empirical Characterization of Exchange Systems in Lower Mississippi Valley Prehistory. In *Prehistoric Exchange Systems in North America,* vol. 2, ed. T. G. Baugh and J. E. Ericson, pp. 127–75. New York: Plenum Press.

1994d   Over the Mountain and Across the Sea: Regional Poverty Point Exchange. In *Exchange in the Lower Mississippi Valley and Contiguous Areas at 1100 B.C.,* ed. Jon L. Gibson. *Louisiana Archaeology* 21:251–300.

Gibson, Jon L., and David L. Griffing

1994   Only a Stone's Throw Away: Exchange in the Poverty Point Hinterland. In *Exchange in the Lower Mississippi Valley and Contiguous Areas at 1100 B.C.,* ed. Jon L. Gibson. *Louisiana Archaeology* 21:207–50.

Gibson, Jon L., and J. Richard Shenkel

1989   Louisiana Earthworks: Middle Woodland and Predecessors. In *Middle Woodland Settlement and Ceremonialism in the Midsouth and Lower Mississippi Valley,* ed. R. C. Mainfort, Jr., pp. 7–18. Jackson: Mississippi Department of Archives and History.

Gilman, Antonio

1984   Explaining the Upper Palaeolithic Revolution. In *Marxist Perspectives in Archaeology,* ed. M. Spriggs, pp. 115–26. Cambridge: Cambridge University Press.

Gleason, P. J., and P. Stone

1994   Age, Origin and Landscape Evolution of the Everglades Peatland. In *Everglades:*

The Ecosystem and Its Restoration, ed. S. M. Davis and J. C. Ogden, pp. 149–97. Delray Beach, Fla.: St. Lucie Press.

Goad, Sharon I.

1980   Patterns of Late Archaic Exchange. *Tennessee Anthropologist* 5:1–16.

Goldstein, Marcus

1948   Dentition on Indian Crania from Texas. *American Journal of Physical Anthropology* 6:63–84.

Goggin, John M.

1948   Florida Archaeology and Recent Ecological Changes. *Journal of the Washington Academy of Sciences* 38:225–33.

1952   *Space and Time Perspective in Northern St. Johns Archaeology, Florida.* Yale University Publications in Anthropology 47. New Haven: Yale University Press.

Goodyear, Albert C.

1974   *The Brand Site: A Techno-Functional Study of a Dalton Site in Northeast Arkansas.* Research Series 7. Fayetteville: Arkansas Archeological Survey.

1979   *A Hypothesis of the Use of Cryptocrystalline Raw Materials among Paleo-Indian Groups of North America.* Research Manuscript Series 156. Columbia: South Carolina Institute of Archaeology and Anthropology, University of South Carolina.

1982   The Chronological Position of the Dalton Horizon in the Southeastern United States. *American Antiquity* 47:382–95.

1988   On the Study of Technological Change. *Current Anthropology* 29:320–23.

1993   Tool Kit Entropy and Bipolar Reduction: A Study of Interassemblage Lithic Variability among Paleo-Indian Sites in the Northeastern United States. *North American Archaeologist* 14:1–23.

Goodyear, Albert C., and John E. Foss

1992   The Stratigraphic Significance of Paleosols at Smith Lake Creek (38AL135) for the Study of the Pleistocene-Holocene Transition in the Savannah River Valley. In *Proceedings of the First International Conference on Pedo-Archaeology,* ed. J. E. Foss, M. E. Timpson, and M. W. Morris, pp. 27–40. Knoxville: Agricultural Experiment Station, University of Tennessee.

Goodyear, Albert C., J. H. House, and N. W. Ackerly

1979   *Laurens-Anderson: An Archeological Study of the Inter-Riverine Piedmont.* Anthropological Studies 4. Columbia: South Carolina Institute of Archaeology and Anthropology, University of South Carolina.

Goodyear, Albert C., Sam B. Upchurch, and Mark J. Brooks

1980   Turtlecrawl Point: An Inundated Early Holocene Archaeological Site on the West Coast of Florida. In *Holocene Geology and Man in Pinellas and Hillsborough Counties, Florida,* ed. S. B. Upchurch, pp. 24–33. Guidebook 22. Tallahassee: Southeastern Geological Society.

1993   Turtlecrawl Point: An Inundated Prehistoric Site in Boca Ciega Bay, Florida. Paper presented at the annual meeting of SEAC, Raleigh.

Goodyear, Albert C., Kenneth E. Sassaman, N. Powell, T. Charles, and C. B. DePratter

1990   An Unusually Large Biface from the Phil Neeley Site, 38BM85, Bamberg County, South Carolina. *South Carolina Antiquities* 22:1–15.

Gould, R. A.

1968   Chipping Stones in the Outback. *Natural History* 77:42–49.

Graham, M., and A. Roberts
1986   Residentially Constrained Mobility: A Preliminary Investigation of Variability in
        Settlement Organization. *Haliksa'i: UNM Contributions to Anthropology* 5:105–16.
        Albuquerque: Department of Anthropology, University of New Mexico.

Graham, Russell W., and Jim I. Mead
1987   Environmental Fluctuations and Evolution of Mammalian Faunas during the
        Last Deglaciation in North America. In *Geology of North America,* vol. K-3, *North
        America and Adjacent Oceans during the Last Deglaciation,* ed. W. F. Ruddiman
        and H. E. Wright, Jr., pp. 371–402. Boulder, Colo.: Geological Society of
        America.

Granger, Joseph E.
1988   Late/Terminal Archaic Settlement in the Falls of the Ohio River Region of Ken-
        tucky: An Examination of Components, Phases, and Clusters. In *Paleoindian and
        Archaic Research in Kentucky,* ed. Charles Hockensmith, David Pollack, and
        Thomas Sanders, pp. 153–204. Frankfort: Kentucky Heritage Council.

Grayson, D. K.
1984   *Quantitative Zooarchaeology: Topics in the Analysis of Archaeological Faunas.* New
        York: Academic Press.

Greene, Glen S., and Jennifer Becton
1992   The First Intact Excavated Structure at the Poverty Point Site. Paper presented at
        the annual meeting of SEAC, Little Rock.

Greenwell, D.
1984   The Mississippi Gulf Coast. In *Perspectives on Gulf Coast Prehistory,* ed. D. D.
        Davis, pp. 125–55. Gainesville: University Presses of Florida.

Gregory, Hiram F., Jr.
1991   Terral Lewis: Recapitulation. In Byrd, ed., q.v., pp. 121–28.

Gregory, Hiram F., Jr., Lester C. Davis, and Donald G. Hunter
1970   The Terral Lewis Site: A Poverty Point Activity Facies in Madison Parish,
        Louisiana. In *The Poverty Point Culture,* ed. Bettye Broyles and Clarence H.
        Webb, pp. 35–46. Bulletin 12. Morgantown: Southeastern Archaeological Con-
        ference.

Gremillion, Kristen J.
1993a   Paleoethnobotany. In Johnson, ed., q.v., pp. 132–59.
1993b   Plant Husbandry at the Archaic/Woodland Transition: Evidence from the Cold
        Oak Shelter, Kentucky. *Midcontinental Journal of Archaeology* 18:161–89.
1995   Botanical Contents of Paleofeces from Two Eastern Kentucky Rockshelters. In
        Current Archaeological Research in Kentucky, vol. 3, ed. J. F. Doershuk, C. A.
        Bergman, and D. Pollack, pp. 52–69. Frankfort: Kentucky Heritage Council.
1996   New Perspectives on the Paleoethnobotany of the Newt Kash Shelter. In *People,
        Plants, and Landscapes: Studies in Paleoethnobotany,* ed. K. J. Gremillion.
        Tuscaloosa: University of Alabama Press.

Griffin, James B.
1943   An Analysis and Interpretation of the Ceramic Remains from Two Sites near
        Beaufort, South Carolina. *Bulletin of the Bureau of American Ethnology* 113
        (Anthropological Papers 22):155–68. Washington: Bureau of American Eth-
        nology, Smithsonian Institution.

1945   The Significance of the Fiber-Tempered Pottery of the St. Johns Area in Florida. *Journal of the Washington Academy of Science* 35:218–23.

1946   Cultural Change and Continuity in Eastern United States Archaeology. In *Man in Northeastern North America*, ed. F. Johnson, pp. 37–95. Papers 3. Andover: Robert S. Peabody Foundation for Archaeology.

1952b   Culture Periods in Eastern United States Archaeology. In *Archaeology of Eastern United States*, ed. James B. Griffin, pp. 352–64. Chicago: University of Chicago Press.

1955   Observations on the Grooved Axe in North America. *Pennsylvania Archaeologist* 25(1):31–43.

1967   Eastern North American Archaeology: A Summary. *Science* 156:175–91.

1979   An Overview of the Chillicothe Hopewell Conference. In Brose and Greber, eds., q.v., pp. 266–79.

Griffin, James B. (editor)

1952a   *Archaeology of Eastern United States.* Chicago: University of Chicago Press.

Griffin, John W.

1974   *Investigations in Russell Cave.* Publications in Archeology 13. Washington: National Park Service.

1988   *The Archeology of Everglades National Park: A Synthesis.* Report submitted to the Southeast Archeological Research Center, National Park Service. Contract CX-5000-5-0049.

Grimm, E. C.

1983   Chronology and Dynamics of Vegetation Change in the Prairie-Woodland Region of Southern Minnesota, USA. *New Phytologist* 93:311–50.

1992   Tilia and Tilia-graph: Pollen Spreadsheet and Graphics Programs. *Program and Abstracts,* p. 56, Eighth International Palynological Congress, Aix-en-Provence.

Grimm, E. C., and G. L. Jacobson, Jr.

1992   Fossil-Pollen Evidence for Abrupt Climate Changes during the Past 18,000 Years in Eastern North America. *Climate Dynamics* 6:179–84.

Grimm, E. C., G. L. Jacobson, Jr., W. A. Watts, B. C. S. Hansen, and K. A. Maasch

1993   A 50,000-Year Record of Climate Oscillations from Florida and Its Temporal Correlation with the Heinrich Events. *Science* 261:198–200.

Guccione, M. J., R. H. Lafferty III, and L. S. Cummings

1988   Environmental Constraints of Human Settlement in an Evolving Holocene Alluvial System, the Lower Mississippi Valley. *Geoarchaeology* 3:65–84.

Guilday, J. E., P. W. Parmalee, and H. W. Hamilton

1977   The Clark's Cave Bone Deposit and the Late Pleistocene Paleoecology of the Central Appalachian Mountains of Virginia. *Carnegie Museum of Natural History, Bulletin* 2:1–87.

Guilday, J. E., H. W. Hamilton, E. Anderson, and P. W. Parmalee

1978   The Baker Bluff Cave Deposit, Tennessee, and the Late Pleistocene Faunal Gradient. *Carnegie Museum of Natural History, Bulletin* 11.

Gunness-Hey, M.

1980   The Koniag Eskimo Presacral Vertebral Column: Variations, Anomalies and Pathologies. *Ossa* 7:99–118.

Haag, William G.

1961   The Archaic of the Lower Mississippi Valley. *American Antiquity* 26:317–23.

1975   The Paleoecology of the South Atlantic Coast. *Geoscience and Man* 7:77–81.

1992   The Monte Sano Site. Paper presented at the annual meeting of SEAC, Little Rock.

Haas, Jonathan (editor)

1990   *The Anthropology of War*. Cambridge: Cambridge University Press.

Haeussler, A. M., D. H. Morris, and C. F. Merbs

1990   A Paleoindian Mandible from Warm Mineral Springs. *American Journal of Physical Anthropology* 81:233.

Hajic, Edwin R.

1991   Geomorphology, Stratigraphy, and Landscape Evolution of the Modoc Rock Shelter in the Mississippi Valley. Paper presented at the annual meeting of the Society for American Archaeology, New Orleans.

Hall, C. L., D. S. Amick, W. B. Turner, and J. L. Hofman

1985   Columbia Archaeological Project Archaic Period Radiocarbon Dates. In *Exploring Tennessee Prehistory: A Dedication to Alfred K. Guthe*, ed. T. Whyte, C. Boyd, and B. Riggs, pp. 61–79. Report of Investigations 42. Knoxville: Department of Anthropology, University of Tennessee.

Hall, Robert L.

1977   An Anthropocentric Perspective for Eastern United States Prehistory. *American Antiquity* 42:499–518.

1991   Cahokia Identity and Interaction Models of Cahokia Mississippian. In *Cahokia and the Hinterlands,* ed. T. E. Emerson and R. B. Lewis, pp. 3–34. Urbana: University of Illinois Press.

Hammett, Julia E.

1992   Ethnohistory of Aboriginal Landscapes in the Southeastern United States. *Southern Indian Studies* 41.

Hannant, Owen

1955   Neolithic Grooved Axes of the North American Indian. *Central States Archaeological Journal* 2(4):124–36.

Haskins, Valerie

1992   Recent Dates from the Green River Shell Mound Region. Paper presented at the Kentucky Heritage Council Archaeological Conference, Murray.

Hassen, Harold, and Kenneth B. Farnsworth

1987   *The Bullseye Site: A Floodplain Archaic Mortuary Site in the Lower Illinois River Valley*. Report of Investigations 42. Springfield: Illinois State Museum.

Hayden, Brian

1989   From Chopper to Celt: The Evolution of Resharpening Techniques. In *Time, Energy and Stone Tools,* ed. R. Torrence, pp. 7–16. Cambridge: Cambridge University Press.

Headland, Thomas N., and Lawrence A. Reid

1989   Hunter-Gatherers and Their Neighbors from Prehistory to the Present. *Current Anthropology* 30:43–66.

Heiser, Charles B., Jr.

1985   Some Botanical Considerations of the Early Domesticated Plants North of Mexico. In *Prehistoric Food Production in North America,* ed. R. I. Ford, pp. 57–72. Anthropological Papers 75. Ann Arbor: Museum of Anthropology, University of Michigan.

Hensley, Christine

1991   The Middle Green River Shell Mounds: Challenging Traditional Interpretations Using Internal Site Structure Analysis. In *The Human Landscape in Kentucky's Past: Site Structure and Settlement Patterns,* ed. C. Stout and C. Hensley, pp. 78–97. Frankfort: Kentucky Heritage Council.

1994   *The Archaic Settlement System of the Middle Green River Valley, Kentucky.* Ph.D. dissertation, Washington University, St. Louis. Ann Arbor: University Microfilms.

Heron, S. D., Jr., T. F. Moslow, W. M. Berelson, J. R. Herbert, G. A. Steele III, and K. R. Susman

1984   Late Holocene Sedimentation of a Wave-Dominated Barrier Island Shoreline, Cape Lookout, N.C. *Marine Geology* 60:413–34.

Hicks, S. D., and J. F. Crosby

1974   Trends and Variability of Yearly Mean Sea Level, 1893–1972. *NOAA Techical Memo* 13:7–8.

Hilgeman, S. L.

1985   Lithic Manufacture and Hunter-Gatherer Technology at a Woodland Site in Tennessee. *Tennessee Anthropologist* 10:55–75.

Hinton, Robert J.

1981   Form and Pattern of Anterior Tooth Wear among Aboriginal Human Groups. *American Journal of Physical Anthropology* 54:555–64.

Hockensmith, Charles, Thomas Sanders, and David Pollack

1983   The Green River Shell Middens of Kentucky. National Register of Historic Places Inventory Nomination Form. MS on file, Kentucky Heritage Council, Frankfort.

Hoffman, C. M.

1985   Projectile Point Maintenance and Typology: Assessment with Factor Analysis and Canonical Correlation. In *For Concordance in Archaeological Analysis,* ed. C. Carr, pp. 566–612. Kansas City, Mo.: Westport Publishers.

Hoffmeister, Donald F.

1989   *Mammals of Illinois.* Urbana: University of Illinois Press.

Hofman, J. L.

1981   The Refitting of Chipped-Stone Artifacts as an Analytical and Interpretive Tool. *Current Anthropology* 22:691–93.

1984   Hunter-Gatherers in the Nashville Basin of Tennessee, 8000–5000 B.P. *Tennessee Anthropologist* 9:129–92.

1985   Middle Archaic Ritual and Shell Midden Archaeology: Considering the Significance of Cremations. In *Exploring Tennessee Prehistory: A Dedication to Alfred K. Guthe,* ed. T. Whyte, C. Boyd, and B. Riggs, pp. 1–21. Report of Investigations 42. Knoxville: Department of Anthropology, University of Tennessee.

1986a Eva Projectile Point Breakage at Cave Spring: Pattern Recognition and Interpretive Possibilities. *Midcontinental Journal of Archaeology* 11:79–95.

1986b Vertical Movement of Artifacts in Alluvial and Stratified Deposits. *Current Anthropology* 27:163–71.

1986c *Hunter-Gatherer Mortuary Variability: Toward an Explanatory Model.* Ph.D. dissertation, University of Tennessee, Knoxville.

1992   Defining Buried Occupation Surfaces in Terrace Sediments. In *Piecing Together the Past: Applications of Refitting Studies in Archaeology,* ed. J. L. Hofman, and J. E. Enloe, pp. 128–50. International Series 578. Oxford: British Archaeological Reports.

Holmes, William H.

1992   Stone Implements of the Potomac-Chesapeake Tidewater Province (orig. 1897). In *The Archaeology of William Henry Holmes,* ed. D. J. Meltzer and R. C. Dunnell, pp. 3–152. Washington: Smithsonian Institution Press.

Homburg, Jeffrey A.

1992   Archaeological Investigations at the LSU Campus Mounds. *Louisiana Archaeology* 15:31–204.

1993   Comments on the Age of the LSU Campus Mounds: A Reply to Mr. Jones. *Louisiana Archaeology* 20:183–96.

Hoshina, H.

1980   Spondylolysis in Athletes. *Physician Sportsmedicine* 8:75–79.

House, J. H., and D. L. Ballenger

1976   *An Archeological Survey of the Interstate 77 Route in the South Carolina Piedmont.* Research Manuscript Series 104. Columbia: Institute of Archaeology and Anthropology, University of South Carolina.

House, J. H., and R. W. Wogaman

1978   *Windy Ridge: A Prehistoric Site in the Inter-Riverine Piedmont in South Carolina.* Anthropological Studies 3. Columbia: Institute of Archaeology and Anthropology, University of South Carolina.

Hoyme, Lucille E., and William M. Bass

1962   Human Skeletal Remains from the Tolliferro (Ha6) and Clarksville (Mc14) Sites, John H. Kerr Reservoir Basin, Virginia. *Bulletin of the Bureau of American Ethnology* 182:329–99. Washington: Bureau of American Ethnology, Smithsonian Institution.

Hoyt, William H., John C. Kraft, and Michael J. Chrzastowski

1990   Prospecting for Submerged Archaeological Sites on the Continental Shelf; Southern Mid-Atlantic Bight of North America. In *Archaeological Geology of North America,* ed. N. P. Lasca and J. E. Donahue, pp. 147–60. Centennial Special Volume 4. Boulder. Colo.: Geological Society of America.

Hrdlicka, Ales

1922   *The Anthropology of Florida.* Publications of the Florida State Historical Society 1. Deland: Florida State Historical Society.

Hudson, C., R. Butler, and D. Sikes

1975   Arthritis in the Prehistoric Southeastern United States: Biological and Cultural Variables. *American Journal of Physical Anthropology* 43:57–62.

Hunt, Charles B.

1974   *Natural Regions of the United States and Canada.* San Francisco: W. H. Freeman and Company.

Huntley, B.

1993   The Use of Climate Response Surfaces to Reconstruct Palaeoclimate from Quaternary Pollen and Plant Macrofossil Data. *Philosophical Transactions of the Royal Society of London* B341:215–24.

Hussey, T. C.
  1993   *A 20,000-Year History of Vegetation and Climate at Clear Pond, Northeastern South Carolina.* M.S. thesis, University of Maine, Orono.
Huxtable, J., M. J. Aitken, and J. C. Weber
  1972   Thermoluminescent Dating of Baked Clay Balls of the Poverty Point Culture. *Archaeometry* 14:269–75.
Ingbar, E. E.
  1994   Lithic Material Selection and Technological Organization. In *The Organization of Prehistoric North American Chipped Stone Tool Technologies,* ed. P. Carr, pp. 45–56. Archaeological Series 7. Ann Arbor: International Monographs in Prehistory.
Ingold, Tim, David Riches, and James Woodburn (editors)
  1988   *Hunters and Gatherers,* vol. 1, *History, Evolution, and Social Change.* New York: Berg.
Irish, Joel D., and Christy G. Turner II
  1987   More Lingual Surface Attrition of the Maxillary Anterior Teeth in American Indians: Prehistoric Panamanians. *American Journal of Physical Anthropology* 73:209–13.
Ison, Cecil R.
  1991   Prehistoric Upland Farming along the Cumberland Plateau. In *Studies in Kentucky Archaeology,* ed. Charles Hockensmith, pp. 1–10. Frankfort: Kentucky Heritage Council.
Jackson, D. W., L. L. Wiltse, and R. J. Cirincione
  1976   Spondylolysis in the Female Gymnast. *Clinical Orthopedics* 117:68–73.
Jackson, H. Edwin
  1986   *Sedentism and Hunter-Gatherer Adaptations in the Lower Mississippi Valley: Subsistence Strategies during the Poverty Point Period.* Ph.D. dissertation, University of Michigan, Ann Arbor.
  1991   The Trade Fair in Hunter-Gatherer Interaction: The Role of Intersocietal Trade in the Evolution of Poverty Point Culture. In *Between Bands and State,* ed. S. A. Gregg, pp. 265–86. Occasional Paper 9. Carbondale: Center for Archaeological Investigations, Southern Illinois University.
Jackson, H. Edwin, and Marvin D. Jeter
  1994   Poverty Point Period Earthworks in Arkansas: A Report on the Lake Enterprise Mound (3AS379). *Southeastern Archaeology* 13:153–62.
Jackson, S. T., and D. R. Whitehead
  1993   Pollen and Macrofossils from Wisconsinan Interstadial Sediments in Northeastern Georgia. *Quaternary Research* 39:99–106.
Jacobson, G. L., Jr., and R. H. W. Bradshaw
  1981   The Selection of Sites for Paleovegetational Studies. *Quaternary Research* 16:80–96.
Jacobson, G. L., Jr., T. Webb III, and E. C. Grimm
  1987   Patterns and Rates of Vegetation Change in Eastern North America from Full-Glacial to Mid-Holocene Time. In *The Geology of North America,* vol. K-3, *North America and Adjacent Oceans during the Last Deglaciation,* ed. W. F. Ruddiman and H. E. Wright, Jr., pp. 277–88. Boulder, Colo.: Geological Society of America.

Jahn, Otto, and Ripley P. Bullen
1978   *The Tick Island Site, St. Johns River, Florida.* Florida Anthropological Society Publications 10. Gainesville: Florida Anthropological Society.

Janzen, Donald
1977   An Examination of Late Archaic Development in the Falls of the Ohio River Area. In *For the Director: Research Essays in Honor of James B. Griffin,* ed. Charles Cleland, pp. 123–43. Anthropology Papers 61. Ann Arbor: Museum of Anthropology, University of Michigan.

Jefferies, Richard W.
1979   The Tunacunnhee Site: Hopewell in Northwest Georgia. In Brose and Greber, eds., q.v., pp. 162–70.

1982a   Debitage as an Indicator of Intraregional Activity Diversity in Northwest Georgia. *Midcontinental Journal of Archaeology* 7:99–132.

1982b   The Black Earth Site. In Jefferies and Butler, eds., q.v., pp. 75–451.

1983   Middle Archaic–Late Archaic Transition in Southern Illinois: An Example from the Carrier Mills Archaeological District. *American Archaeology* 3:199–206.

1990   A Technological and Functional Analysis of Middle Archaic Hafted Endscrapers from the Black Earth Site, Saline County, Illinois. *Midcontinental Journal of Archaeology* 15:3–36.

1995   Late Middle Archaic Exchange and Interaction in the North American Midcontinent. In Nassaney and Sassaman, eds., q.v., pp. 73–99.

Jefferies, Richard W., and Brian M. Butler (editors)
1982   *The Carrier Mills Archaeological Project: Human Adaptation in the Saline Valley, Illinois.* Research Paper 33. Carbondale: Center for Archaeological Investigations, Southern Illinois University.

Jenkins, Ned J., and Richard A. Krause
1986   *The Tombigbee Watershed in Southeastern Prehistory.* Tuscaloosa: University of Alabama Press.

Jenkins, Ned J., David H. Dye, and John A. Walthall
1986   Early Ceramic Development in the Gulf Coastal Plain. In *Early Woodland Archaeology,* ed. K. B. Farnsworth and T. E. Emerson, pp. 546–63. Kampsville Seminars in Archaeology 2. Kampsville, Ill.: Center for American Archaeology Press.

Jennings, Jesse D.
1952   Prehistory of the Lower Mississippi Valley. In *Archaeology of Eastern United States,* ed. James B. Griffin, pp. 256–71. Chicago: University of Chicago Press.

Jeske, R. J.
1989   Economies in Raw Material Use by Prehistoric Hunter-Gatherers. In *Time, Energy and Stone Tools,* ed. R. Torrence, pp. 34–45. Cambridge: Cambridge University Press.

1992   Energetic Efficiency and Lithic Technology: An Upper Mississippian Example. *American Antiquity* 57:467–81.

Jeter, Marvin D., and Eugene M. Futato
1994   Notes of Some Alabama Lithic Materials and the Poverty Point Extraction-Exchange System(s). In *Exchange in the Lower Mississippi Valley and Contiguous Areas at 1100 B.C.,* ed. Jon L. Gibson. *Louisiana Archaeology* 21:57–91.

Jeter, Marvin D., and H. Edwin Jackson

1994   Poverty Point Extraction and Exchange: The Arkansas Lithic Connections. In *Exchange in the Lower Mississippi Valley and Contiguous Areas at 1100* B.C., ed. Jon L. Gibson. *Louisiana Archaeology* 21:133–206.

Jeter, Marvin D., Jerome C. Rose, G. Ishmael Williams, Jr., and Anna M. Harmon

1989   *Archeology and Bioarcheology of the Lower Mississippi Valley and Trans-Mississippi South in Arkansas and Louisiana.* Research Series 37. Fayetteville: Arkansas Archeological Survey.

Jochim, M. A.

1989   Optimization and Stone Tool Studies: Problems and Potential. In *Time, Energy and Stone Tools,* ed. R. Torrence, pp. 106–11. Cambridge: Cambridge University Press.

Johannessen, Sissel

1984   Paleoethnobotany. In *American Bottom Archaeology,* ed. Charles J. Bareis and James W. Porter, pp. 197–214. Urbana: University of Illinois Press.

Johnson, Jay K.

1979   Archaic Biface Manufacture: Production Failures, a Chronicle of the Misbegotten. *Lithic Technology* 8:25–35.

1980   Poverty Point Period Social Organization in the Yazoo Basin, Mississippi: A Preliminary Consideration. In *Caddoan and Poverty Point Archaeology: Essays in Honor of Clarence Hungerford Webb,* ed. Jon L. Gibson. *Louisiana Archaeology* 6:251–81. Lafayette: Louisiana Archaeological Society.

1981   *Lithic Procurement and Utilization Trajectories: Analysis, Yellow Creek Nuclear Power Plant Site, Tishomingo County, Mississippi,* vol. 2. Archaeological Paper 1. University: Center for Archaeological Research, University of Mississippi.

1982   Archaic Period Settlement Systems in Northeastern Mississippi. *Midcontinental Journal of Archaeology* 7:185–204.

1983   Poverty Point Period Blade Technology in the Yazoo Basin, Mississippi. *Lithic Technology* 12:49–56.

1984   Measuring Prehistoric Quarry Site Activity in Northeastern Mississippi. In *Prehistoric Chert Exploitation: Studies from the Midcontinent,* ed. B. Butler and E. May, pp. 225–35. Occasional Paper 2. Carbondale: Center for Archaeological Investigations, Southern Illinois University.

1985   Patterns of Prehistoric Chert Procurement in Colbert Ferry Park, Northwest Alabama. In *Lithic Resource Procurement: Proceedings from the Second Conference on Prehistoric Chert Exploitation,* ed. S. C. Vehik, pp. 153–64. Occasional Paper 4. Carbondale: Center for Archaeological Investigations, Southern Illinois University.

1986   Amorphous Core Technologies in the Midsouth. *Midcontinental Journal of Archaeology* 11:135–52.

1987a   Cahokia Core Technology in Mississippi: The View from the South. In *The Organization of Core Technology,* ed. J. K. Johnson and C. A. Morrow, pp. 187–206. Boulder, Colo.: Westview Press.

1987b   Introduction. In *The Organization of Core Technology,* ed. J. K. Johnson and C. A. Morrow, pp. 1–12. Boulder, Colo.: Westview Press.

1989   The Utility of Production Modeling as a Framework for Regional Analysis. In

Alternative Approaches to Lithic Analysis, ed. D. O. Henry and G. H. Odell, pp. 119–38. Archaeological Papers 1. Washington: American Anthropological Association.

1993a North American Biface Production Trajectory Modeling in Historic Perspective. *Plains Anthropologist* 38:151–62.

1993b Lithics. In Johnson, ed., q.v., pp. 36–52.

1994   Prehistoric Exchange in the Southeast. In *Prehistoric Exchange Systems in North America,* vol. 2, ed. T. G. Baugh and J. E. Ericson, pp. 99–125. New York: Plenum Press.

Johnson, Jay K. (editor)

1993c *The Development of Southeastern Archaeology.* Tuscaloosa: University of Alabama Press.

Johnson, Jay K., and S. O. Brookes

1988   Rocks from the Northeast: Archaic Exchange in North Mississippi. *Mississippi Archaeology* 23(2):53–63.

1989   Benton Points, Turkey Tails and Cache Blades: Middle Archaic Exchange in the Southeast. *Southeastern Archaeology* 8:134–45.

Johnson, Lucille Lewis, and Melanie Stright (editors)

1992   *Paleoshorelines and Prehistory: An Investigation of Method.* Boca Raton: CRC Press.

Jones, Charles C., Jr.

1873   *Antiquities of the Southern Indians.* New York: D. Appleton and Co.

Jones, Dennis

1993   The Case of the LSU Campus Mounds Report. *Louisiana Archaeology* 20:169–78.

Jones, Dennis, and Malcolm Shuman

1988   *Archaeological Atlas and Report of Prehistoric Indian Mounds in Louisiana,* vol. 3, *Livingston, St. Helena, St. Tammany, Tangipahoa, Washington.* Report submitted to the Louisiana Division of Archaeology, Baton Rouge.

1991   *Archaeological Atlas and Report of Prehistoric Indian Mounds in Louisiana,* vol. 4, *Acadia, Lafayette, and St. Landry Parishes.* Report submitted to the Louisiana Division of Archaeology, Baton Rouge.

Jones, Joe B., and Dennis B. Blanton

1993   *Phase III Archaeological Data Recovery for Mitigation of Adverse Effects to Site 44HN204 Associated with the VNG Mechanicsville to Kingsmill Lateral Pipeline, Hanover County, Virginia.* Prepared for Virginia Natural Gas, Inc., Norfolk. Williamsburg: Center for Archaeological Research, Department of Anthropology, College of William and Mary.

Jones, Reca B.

1983   Archaeological Investigations in the Ouachita River Valley, Bayou Bartholomew to Riverton, Louisiana. In *Prehistory of the Ouachita River Valley, Louisiana and Arkansas,* ed. Jon L. Gibson. *Louisiana Archaeology* 10:103–69. Lafayette: Louisiana Archaeological Society.

Jones, Volney

1936   The Vegetal Remains of Newt Kash Hollow Shelter. In *Rock Shelters in Menifee County, Kentucky,* ed. W. S. Webb and W. D. Funkhouser, pp. 147–65. Reports in Archaeology and Anthropology 3. Lexington: University of Kentucky.

Jurmain, Robert D.
  1977   Stress and the Etiology of Osteoarthritis. *American Journal of Physical Anthropology* 46:353–66.
  1990   Paleoepidemiology of a Central California Prehistoric Population from ca-ala-329. Part 2: Degenerative Disease. *American Journal of Physical Anthropology* 83:83–94.
  1991   Degenerative Changes in Peripheral Joints as Indicators of Mechanical Stress: Opportunities and Limitations. *International Journal of Osteoarchaeology* 1:247–52.
Kay, Marvin
  1983   Archaic Period Research in the Western Ozark Highland, Missouri. In Phillips and Brown, eds., q.v., pp. 41–70.
Kay, Marvin, Frances B. King, and Christine K. Robinson
  1980   Cucurbits from Phillips Spring: New Evidence and Interpretations. *American Antiquity* 45:806–22.
Keeley, L. H.
  1980   *Experimental Determination of Stone Tool Uses.* Chicago: University of Chicago Press.
  1982   Hafting and Retooling: Effects on the Archaeological Record. *American Antiquity* 47:798–809.
Kelley, Marc A.
  1980   *Disease and Environment: A Comparative Analysis of Three Early American Indian Skeletal Collections.* Ph.D. dissertation, Case Western Reserve University, Cleveland. Ann Arbor: University Microfilms.
  1982   Intervertebral Osteochondrosis in Ancient and Modern Populations. *American Journal of Physical Anthropology* 59:271–79.
  n.d.   Indian Knoll Pathological Data. MS in possession of the author.
Kelley, Marc A., and J. Lawrence Angel
  1987   Life Stresses of Slavery. *American Journal of Physical Anthropology* 74:199–211.
Kelly, R. L.
  1983   Hunter-Gatherer Mobility Strategies. *Journal of Anthropological Research* 39:277–306.
  1988   The Three Sides of a Biface. *American Antiquity* 53:717–34
  1992   Mobility/Sedentism: Concepts, Archaeological Measures, and Effects. *Annual Review of Anthropology* 21:43–66.
  1994   Some Thoughts on Future Directions in the Study of Stone Tool Technological Organization. In *The Organization of Prehistoric North American Chipped Stone Tool Technologies,* ed. P. Carr, pp. 132–36. Archaeological Series 7. Ann Arbor: International Monographs in Prehistory.
Kelly, R. L., and L. C. Todd
  1988   Coming into the Country: Early Paleoindian Hunting and Mobility. *American Antiquity* 53:231–44.
Kent, Susan
  1991   The Relationship between Mobility Strategies and Site Structure. In *The Interpretation of Archaeological Site Patterning,* ed. E. M. Kroll and T. D. Price, pp. 257–68. New York: Plenum Press.

Kilgore, L.

1984   *Degenerative Joint Disease in a Medieval Nubian Population.* Ph.D. dissertation, University of Colorado, Denver. Ann Arbor: University Microfilms.

Kimball, L. R.

1981   *An Analysis of Residential Camp Structure for Two Early Archaic Assemblages from Rose Island, Tennessee.* M.A. thesis, University of Tennessee, Knoxville.

1992   Early Archaic Settlement and Technology: Lessons from Tellico. In Anderson, Sassaman, and Judge, eds., q.v., pp. 143–81.

1993   Rose Island Revisited: The Detection of Early Archaic Site Structure Using Grid-Count Data. *Southeastern Archaeology* 12:93–116.

King, Frances B.

1985   Early Cultivated Cucurbits in Eastern North America. In *Prehistoric Food Production in North America,* ed. R. I. Ford, pp. 73–98. Anthropological Papers 75. Ann Arbor: Museum of Anthropology, University of Michigan.

King, James E., and William H. Allen, Jr.

1977   A Holocene Vegetation Record from the Mississippi River Valley, Southeastern Missouri. *Quaternary Research* 8:307–23.

Klein, Michael J., and Thomas Klatka

1991   Late Archaic and Early Woodland Demography and Settlement Patterns. In *Late Archaic and Early Woodland Research in Virginia: A Synthesis,* ed. T. Reinhart and M. E. N. Hodges, pp. 139–84. Richmond: Archaeological Society of Virginia.

Klippel, Walter E., and Darcy F. Morey

1986   Contextual and Nutritional Analysis of Freshwater Gastropods from Middle Archaic Deposits at the Hayes Site, Middle Tennessee. *American Antiquity* 51:799–813.

Klippel, Walter E., and Paul W. Parmalee

1982a   *The Paleontology of Cheek Bend Cave: Phase II Report.* Report submitted to the Tennessee Valley Authority. Knoxville: Department of Anthropology, University of Tennessee.

1982b   Diachronic Variation in Insectivores from Cheek Bend Cave and Environmental Change in the Midsouth. *Paleobiology* 8:447–58.

Kneberg, Madeline

1952   The Tennessee Area. In *Archaeology of Eastern United States,* ed. James B. Griffin, pp. 190–98. Chicago: University of Chicago Press.

Knight, Vernon J., Jr.

1989   Symbolism of Mississippian Mounds. In *Powhatan's Mantle, Indians of the Colonial Southeast,* ed. P. H. Wood, G. A. Waselkov, and M. T. Hatley, pp. 279–91. Lincoln: University of Nebraska Press.

Knoblock, Byron W.

1939   *Banner-stones of the North American Indian.* Published by the author, LaGrange, Ill.

1954   Banner-Stones Are Ceremonials (orig. 1948, rev.). *Central States Archaeological Journal* 1(3):85–89.

Knox, J. C.

1983   Responses of River Systems to Holocene Climate. In Wright, ed., q.v., pp. 26–41.

Kochel, R. Craig

1988   Geomorphic Impact of Large Floods: Review and New Perspectives on Magnitude and Frequency. In *Flood Geomorphology,* ed. Victor Baker, R. Craig Kochel, and Peter Patton, pp. 169–86. New York: John Wiley and Sons.

Koldehoff, B.

1987   The Cahokia Flake Tool Industry: Socioeconomic Implications for Late Prehistory in the Central Mississippi Valley. In *The Organization of Core Technology,* ed. J. K. Johnson and C. A. Morrow, pp. 151–85. Boulder, Colo.: Westview Press.

Kraft, John C.

1977   Late Quaternary Paleogeographic Changes in the Coastal Environments of Delaware, Middle Atlantic Bight, Related to Archaeologic Settings. In *Amerinds and their Paleoenvironments in Northeastern North America,* ed. B. Salwen and W. Newman, pp. 35–89. Albany: Annals of the New York Academy of Science 288.

1985   Marine Environments: Paleogeographic Reconstructions in the Littoral Region. In *Archaeological Sediments in Context,* ed. J. K. Stein and W. R. Farrand, pp. 5–20. Peopling of the Americas, vol. 1. Orono: Center for the Study of Early Man, University of Maine.

Kraft, John C., and C. J. John

1978   Paleogeographic Analysis of Coastal Archaeological Settings in Delaware. *Archaeology of Eastern North America* 6:41–59.

Kraft, John C., Elizabeth A. Allen, and Evelyn M. Maurmeyer

1978   The Geological and Paleogeomorphological Evolution of a Spit System and Its Associated Coastal Environments: Cape Henlopen Spit, Delaware. *Journal of Sedimentary Petrology* 48:211–26.

Kraft, John C., Robert E. Sheridan, Roger D. Moose, Richard N. Strom, and Charles B. Weil

1974   Middle-Late Holocene Evolution of the Morphology of a Drowned Estuary System—The Delaware Bay. *Memoirs de l'Institut de Géologie du Bassin d'Aquitaine* 7:297–305.

Kuhn, S. L.

1989   Hunter-Gatherer Foraging Organization and Strategies of Artifact Replacement and Discard. In *Experiments in Lithic Technology,* ed. D. S. Amick and R. P. Mauldin, pp. 33–47. International Series 528. Oxford: British Archaeological Reports.

1991   "Unpacking" Reduction: Lithic Raw Material Economy in the Mousterian of West-Central Italy. *Journal of Anthropological Archaeology* 10:76–106.

1994   A Formal Approach to the Design and Assembly of Mobile Toolkits. *American Antiquity* 59:426–42.

Kutzbach, J. E., and T. Webb III

1993   Conceptual Basis for Understanding Late-Quaternary Climate. In *Global Climate since the Last Glacial Maximum,* ed. H. E. Wright, Jr., J. E. Kutzbach, T. Webb III, W. Ruddiman, F. A. Street-Perrott, and P. J. Bartlein, pp. 5–11. Minneapolis: University of Minnesota Press.

Kwas, Mary L.

1981   Bannerstones as Chronological Markers in the Southeastern United States. *Tennessee Anthropologist* 6(2):144–71.

Lallo, J. W.

1973　*The Skeletal Biology of Three Prehistoric American Indian Societies from Dickson Mounds.* Ph.D. dissertation, University of Massachusetts, Amherst. Ann Arbor: University Microfilms.

Lankford, George E.

1992　"Reysed After There Manner." *Arkansas Archaeologist* 31:65–71.

La Rocque, Aurele

1966　*Pleistocene Mollusca of Ohio.* Division of Geological Survey, Bulletin 62. Columbus: Department of Natural Resources, State of Ohio.

Larsen, C. S.

1982　The Anthropology of St. Catherines Island. 3. Prehistoric Human Biological Adaptation. *Anthropological Papers of the American Museum of Natural History* 57:159–270. New York.

1984　Health and Disease in Prehistoric Georgia: The Transition to Agriculture. In Cohen and Armelagos, eds., q.v., pp. 367–92.

Larsen, Curtis E.

1982　Geo-archaeology of the Haw River. In Claggett and Cable, q.v., pp. 145–222.

Larsen, Curtis E., and Joseph Schuldenrein

1990　Depositional History of an Archaeologically Dated Flood Plain, Haw River, North Carolina. In *Archaeological Geology of North America,* ed. N. P. Lasca and J. E. Donahue, pp. 161–81. Centennial Special Volume 4. Boulder, Colo.: Geological Society of America.

Lasley, Scott E.

1983　*Particle Induced X-Ray Emissions (PIXE) Analysis of Trade Items from Poverty Point, Louisiana.* Senior honors thesis, University of Southwestern Louisiana, Lafayette.

Lazarus, William C.

1965　Effects of Land Subsidence and Sea Level Changes on Elevation of Archaeological Sites on the Florida Gulf Coast. *Florida Anthropologist* 18:49–58.

Leach, Elizabeth K., and Michael J. Jackson

1987　Geomorphic History of the Lower Cumberland and Tennessee Valleys and Implications for Regional Archaeology. *Southeastern Archaeology* 6:100–107.

Leacock, Eleanor, and Richard B. Lee (editors)

1982　*Politics and History in Band Societies.* Cambridge: Cambridge University Press.

Ledbetter, R. Jerald

1991　*Archaeological Investigations at Mill Branch Sites 9WR4 and 9WR11, Warren County, Georgia.* Report submitted to J. M. Huber Corporation, Wrens, Georgia. Athens, Ga.: Southeastern Archeological Services.

1995　*Archeological Investigations at Mill Branch Sites 9WR4 and 9WR11, Warren County, Georgia.* Technical Reports 3. Atlanta: Interagency Archeological Services Division, National Park Service.

Ledbetter, R. Jerald, Chad O. Braley, William Moffet, and T. Jeffrey Price

1994　*Archaeological Data Recovery at 9JO6, the Arthur Tarver Site, Jones County, Georgia.* Athens, Ga.: Southeastern Archeological Services.

Ledbetter, R. Jerald, and Lisa O'Steen
    1991   *The Grayson Site, Phase III Investigations of 15CR73, Carter County, Kentucky.* Athens, Ga.: Southeastern Archeological Services.
Lee, Richard B., and Irvene DeVore (editors)
    1968   *Man the Hunter.* Chicago: Aldine.
Lehmann, Geoffrey R.
    1982   *The Jaketown Site, Surface Collections from a Poverty Point Period Regional Center in the Yazoo Basin, Mississippi.* Archaeological Report 5. Jackson: Mississippi Department of Archives and History.
Leopold, Luna B., M. Gordon Wolman, and John P. Miller
    1964   *Fluvial Processes in Geomorphology.* San Francisco: Freeman Press.
Lester, C. W., and Harry L. Shapiro
    1968   Vertebral Arch Defects in the Lumbar Vertebrae of Prehistoric American Eskimos. *American Journal of Physical Anthropology* 28:43–47.
Lewis, T. M. N., and Madeline Kneberg
    1947   *The Archaic Horizon in Western Tennessee.* Tennessee Anthropological Papers 2. Knoxville: University of Tennessee Record Extension Series, 23(4).
    1959   The Archaic Culture in the Middle South. *American Antiquity* 25:161–83.
Lewis, T. M. N., and Madeline Kneberg Lewis
    1961   *Eva, an Archaic Site.* Knoxville: University of Tennessee Press.
Lidz, B. H., and E. A. Shinn
    1991   Paleoshorelines, Reefs, and a Rising Sea Level: South Florida, USA. *Journal of Coastal Research* 7:203–29.
Lindberg, H., and L. G. Danielson
    1984   The Relation Between Labor and Cox Arthrosis. *Clinical Orthopaedics and Related Research* 191:159–61.
Lockshin, M. D., I. T. T. Higgins, H. L. Dodge, and N. Canale
    1969   Rheumatism in Mining Communities in Marion County, West Virginia. *American Journal of Epidemiology* 90(1):17–29.
Lopinot, Neal H.
    1983   Analysis of Flotation Sample Materials from the Late Archaic Horizon. In *The 1982 Excavations at the Cahokia Interpretive Center Tract, St. Clair County, Illinois,* ed. M. S. Nassaney, N. H. Lopinot, B. M. Butler, and R. W. Jefferies, pp. 77–108. Research Paper 37. Carbondale: Center for Archaeological Investigations, Southern Illinois University.
Lundy, John K.
    1981   Spondylolysis of the Lumbar Vertebrae in a Group of Prehistoric Upper Puget Sound Indians at Birch Bay, Washington. *Archaeological Survey of Canada* 106:107–14.
Lurie, R.
    1987   Lithic Analysis. In Bense, ed., q.v., pp. 231–350.
    1989   Lithic Technology and Mobility Strategies: The Koster Site Middle Archaic. In *Time, Energy and Stone Tools,* ed. R. Torrence, pp. 46–56. Cambridge: Cambridge University Press.
Magennis, Ann
    1977   *Middle and Late Archaic Mortuary Patterning: An Example from the Western Tennessee Valley.* M.A. thesis, University of Tennessee, Knoxville.

Magne, M. P. R.

1989   Lithic Reduction Stages and Assemblage Formation Processes. In *Experiments in Lithic Technology,* ed. D. S. Amick and R. P. Mauldin, pp. 15–31. International Series 528. Oxford: British Archaeological Reports.

Malinowski, Bronislaw

1961   *Argonauts of the Western Pacific* (orig. 1922). New York: E. P. Dutton.

Manuel, Joseph O., Jr.

1979   A Radiocarbon Date from the Hornsby Site—16SH21. *Newsletter of the Louisiana Archaeological Society* 6(1):18–19.

1983   The Hornsby Site—16SH21: An Archaic Occupation in St. Helena Parish, Louisiana. MS on file, University of Southwestern Louisiana, Regional Archaeological Program Management Unit III, Lafayette.

Marquardt, William H.

1985   Complexity and Scale in the Study of Fisher-Gatherer-Hunters: An Example from the Eastern United States. In Price and Brown, eds., q.v., pp. 59–98.

1992a Dialectical Archaeology. In *Archaeological Method and Theory,* vol. 4, ed. M. B. Schiffer, pp. 101–40. Tucson: University of Arizona Press.

1992b Recent Archaeological and Paleoenvironmental Investigations in Southwest Florida. In *Culture and Environment in the Domain of the Calusa,* ed. W. H. Marquardt, pp. 9–57. Monograph 1. Gainesville: Institute of Archaeology and Paleoenvironmental Studies, University of Florida.

Marquardt, William H., and Carole L. Crumley

1987   Theoretical Issues in the Analysis of Spatial Patterning. In *Regional Dynamics: Burgundian Landscapes in Historical Perspective,* ed. C. L. Crumley and W. H. Marquardt, pp. 1–18. San Diego: Academic Press.

Marquardt, William H., and Patty Jo Watson

1983   The Shell Mound Archaic of Western Kentucky. In Phillips and Brown, eds., q.v., pp. 323–39.

Marrinan, Rochelle

1975   *Ceramics, Molluscs, and Sedentism: The Late Archaic Period on the Georgia Coast.* Ph.D. dissertation, University of Florida, Gainesville.

Martin, D. L., and N. J. Akins

1994   Patterns of Violence against Women in the Prehistoric Southwest. Paper presented at the Southwest Symposium, Tempe, Arizona.

Martin, D. L., N. J. Akins, and A. Goodman

1993   Health Profile for the La Plata Highway Project. Paper presented at the Fifth Occasional Anasazi Symposium, Farmington, New Mexico.

Mayer-Oakes, William

1955   *Prehistory of the Upper Ohio Valley.* Annals of the Carnegie Museum 34. New York.

Mayr, Ernst

1970   *Populations, Species, and Evolution.* Cambridge, Mass.: Harvard University Press.

McAnany, P. A.

1988   The Effects of Lithic Procurement Strategies on Tool Curation and Recycling. *Lithic Technology* 17(1):3–11.

McAndrews, J. H.

1966   Postglacial History of Prairie, Savanna, and Forest in Northwestern Minnesota. *Memoirs of the Torrey Botanical Club* 22:1–72.

1988   Human Disturbance of North American Forests and Grasslands: The Fossil Pollen Record. In *Vegetation History,* vol. 7, ed. B. Huntley and T. Webb III, pp. 673–98. Dordrecht, Netherlands: Kluwer Publishers.

McAndrews, J. H., and R. Byrne

1975   Pre-Columbian Purslane (*Portulaca oleracea L.*) in the New World. *Nature* 253:726–27.

McCarroll, J. R., J. M. Miller, and M. A. Ritter

1986   Lumbar Spondylolysis and Spondylolisthesis in College Football Players: A Perspective Study. *American Journal of Sports Medicine* 14:404–6.

McCollough, Major C. R., and Charles H. Faulkner

1973   *Excavations at the Higgs and Dougherty Sites: I-75 Salvage Archaeology.* Miscellaneous Paper 12. Knoxville: Tennessee Archaeological Society.

McKee, Edwin D. (editor)

1979   *A Study of Global Sand Seas.* Geological Survey Professional Paper 1052. Washington: U.S. Government Printing Office.

McLearen, Douglas C.

1991   Late Archaic and Early Woodland Material Culture in Virginia. In *Late Archaic and Early Woodland Research in Virginia: A Synthesis,* ed. T. Reinhart and M. E. N. Hodges, pp. 89–138. Richmond: Archaeological Society of Virginia.

McMichael, Alan E.

1982   *A Cultural Resources Assessment of Horr's Island, Collier County, Florida.* M.A. thesis, University of Florida, Gainesville.

McMillan, R. Bruce

1976   The Dynamics of Cultural and Environmental Change at Rodgers Shelter, Missouri. In *Prehistoric Man and His Environments: A Case Study in the Ozark Highland,* ed. W. R. Wood and R. B. McMillan, pp. 211–34. New York: Academic Press.

McMillan, R. Bruce, and W. E. Klippel

1981   Environmental Changes and Hunter-Gatherer Adaptations in the Southern Prairie Peninsula. *Journal of Archaeological Science* 8(3):215–45.

Meltzer, David J.

1988   Late Pleistocene Human Adaptations in Eastern North America. *Journal of World Prehistory* 2:1–52.

Meltzer, David J., and Bruce D. Smith

1986   Paleoindian and Early Archaic Subsistence Strategies in Eastern North America. In *Foraging, Collecting, and Harvesting: Archaic Period Subsistence and Settlement in the Eastern Woodlands,* ed. S. W. Neusius, pp. 3–30. Occasional Paper 6. Carbondale: Center for Archaeological Investigations, Southern Illinois University.

Merbs, Charles F.

1968   Anterior Tooth Loss in Arctic Populations. *Southwestern Journal of Anthropology* 24:20–32.

1983   Patterns of Activity-Induced Pathology in a Canadian Inuit Population. *Archaeological Survey of Canada* 119:1–200.

Merrill, Arthur S., K. O. Emery, and Meyer Rumin

1965   Ancient Oyster Shells on the Atlantic Continental Shelf. *Science* 147:398–400.

Michie, James L.

1974　A Second Burial at Daw's Island Shell Midden, 38BU9, Beaufort County, South Carolina. *South Carolina Antiquities* 6:37–47.

1979　*The Bass Pond Site: Intensive Archaeological Testing at a Formative Period Base Camp on Kiawah Island, South Carolina.* Research Manuscript Series 154. Columbia: Institute of Archaeology and Anthropology, University of South Carolina.

Milanich, Jerald T.

1994　*Archaeology of Precolumbian Florida.* Gainesville: University Press of Florida.

Milanich, Jerald T., and Charles H. Fairbanks

1980　*Florida Archaeology.* New York: Academic Press.

Milanich, Jerald T., Jefferson Chapman, Ann S. Cordell, Stephen Hale, and Rochelle A. Marrinan

1984　Prehistoric Development of Calusa Society in Southwest Florida: Excavations on Useppa Island. In *Perspectives on Gulf Coast Prehistory,* ed. D. D. Davis, pp. 258–314. Gainesville: University Presses of Florida.

Miles, Charles

1986　*Indian and Eskimo Artifacts of North America.* New York: American Legacy Press.

Miller, Carl F.

1949　The Lake Spring Site, Columbia County, Georgia. *American Antiquity* 15:254–58.

Miller, James

1991　*The Fairest, Frutefullest and Pleasantest of all the World: An Environmental History of the Northeast Part of Florida.* Ph.D. dissertation, Graduate Group in City and Regional Planning, University of Pennsylvania, Philadelphia.

Miller, James, and John W. Griffin

1978　*Cultural Resources Reconnaissance of Merritt Island National Wildlife Refuge.* Report submitted to Interagency Archeological Services, National Park Service, Atlanta.

Milner, George R., Eve Anderson, and Virginia Smith

1991　Warfare in Late Prehistoric West-Central Illinois. *American Antiquity* 56:581–603.

Mires, Ann Marie Wagner

1991　Sifting the Ashes: Reconstruction of a Complex Mortuary Program in Louisiana. In *What Mean These Bones?* ed. M. L. Powell, P. S. Bridges, and A. M. W. Mires, pp. 114–30. Tuscaloosa: University of Alabama Press.

Molnar, S.

1968　*Some Functional Interpretations of Tooth Wear in Prehistoric and Modern Man.* Ph.D. dissertation, University of California, Santa Barbara. Ann Arbor: University Microfilms.

1971a　Human Tooth Wear, Tooth Function and Cultural Variability. *American Journal of Physical Anthropology* 34:175–90.

1971b　Sex, Age, and Tooth Position as Factors in the Production of Tooth Wear. *American Antiquity* 336:182–88.

Moore, Clarence B.

1913　Some Aboriginal Sites in Louisiana and Arkansas. *Journal of the Academy of Natural Sciences of Philadelphia* 16(1).

1916　Some Aboriginal Sites on Green River, Kentucky. *Journal of the Academy of Natural Sciences of Philadelphia* 16(3).

Morey, D. F.
1988 *Unmodified Vertebrate Faunal Remains from Stratified Archaic Deposits at the Hayes Site, Middle Tennessee.* Report submitted to Cultural Resources Division, Tennessee Valley Authority, Norris. Contract TV-60066A. Knoxville: Department of Anthropology, University of Tennessee.

Morrow, C. A.
1982 Analysis of Area A Middle Archaic Flaked Stone Technology. In Jefferies and Butler, eds., q.v., pp. 1289–1346.
1987 Blades and Cobden Chert: A Technological Argument for Their Role as Markers of Regional Identification during the Hopewell Period in Illinois. In *The Organization of Core Technology,* ed. J. K. Johnson and C. A. Morrow, pp. 119–49. Boulder, Colo.: Westview Press.

Morrow, C. A., and R. W. Jefferies
1989 Trade or Embedded Procurement? A Test Case from Southern Illinois. In *Time, Energy and Stone Tools,* ed. R. Torrence, pp. 20–33. Cambridge: Cambridge University Press.

Morse, D.
1969 *Ancient Disease in the Midwest.* Reports of Investigations 15. Springfield: Illinois State Museum.

Morse, D. F.
1967 *The Robinson Site and Shell Mound Archaic Culture in the Middle South.* Ph.D. dissertation, University of Michigan, Ann Arbor.
1973 Dalton Culture in Northeast Arkansas. *Florida Anthropologist* 26:23–38.
1975 Paleoindian in the Land of Opportunity: Preliminary Report on the Excavations at the Sloan Site (3GE94). In *The Cache River Archaeological Project: An Experiment in Contract Archaeology,* assembled by Michael B. Schiffer and John H. House, pp. 93–113. Research Series 8. Fayetteville: Arkansas Archeological Survey.
1977 A Human Femur Tube from Arkansas. *Arkansas Archaeologist* 16–18:42–44.
1996 Comments. In *The Paleoindian and Early Archaic Southeast,* ed. David G. Anderson and Kenneth E. Sassaman. Tuscaloosa: University of Alabama Press.

Morse, D. F., and A. C. Goodyear
1973 The Significance of the Dalton Adze in Northeast Arkansas. *Plains Anthropologist* 19:316–22.

Morse, D. F., and Phyllis A. Morse
1983 *Archaeology of the Central Mississippi Valley.* New York: Academic Press.

Mosley, S. A.
1958 The Occurrence of Soapstone in Alabama and Its Use by the Indians. *Journal of Alabama Archaeology* 4(1):9–13.

Muller, J. D.
1978 The Southeast. In *Ancient North Americans,* ed. J. D. Jennings, pp. 281–326. San Francisco: W. H. Freeman.

Munson, Cheryl A., and Thomas G. Cook
1980 The Late Archaic French Lick Phase: A Dimensional Analysis. In *Archaeological Salvage Excavations at Patoka Lake, Indiana,* ed. C. A. Munson, pp. 721–40. Bloomington: Glenn A. Black Laboratory of Archaeology, Indiana University.

Munson, Patrick J.
  1986 Hickory Silviculture: A Subsistence Revolution in the Prehistory of Eastern North America. Paper presented at the conference "Emergent Horticultural Economies of the Eastern Woodland," Center for Archaeological Investigations, Southern Illinois University, Carbondale.

Murphy, James L.
  1977 Radiocarbon Dates from the Globe Hill Shell Heap. *Pennsylvania Archaeologist* 47(1):19–24.

Murphy, Larry E.
  1990 *8SL17: Natural Site-Formation Processes of a Multiple-Component Underwater Site in Florida*. Southwest Cultural Resources Center Professional Papers, Santa Fe, N.M.

Muto, Guy R., and Joel Gunn
  1985 *A Study of Late Quaternary Environments and Early Man along the Tombigbee River, Alabama and Mississippi*. Report submitted to National Park Service by Benham Blair and Affiliates, Oklahoma City.

Nance, J. D.
  1984 Lithic Exploitation Studies in the Lower Tennessee–Cumberland Valleys, Western Kentucky. In *Prehistoric Chert Exploitation: Studies from the Midcontinent*, ed. B. Butler and E. May, pp. 101–27. Occasional Paper 2. Carbondale: Center for Archaeological Investigations, Southern Illinois University.
  1986 The Morrisroe Site: Projectile Point Types and Radiocarbon Dates from the Lower Tennessee River Valley. *Midcontinental Journal of Archaeology* 11:11–50.

Nassaney, Michael S., and Kenneth E. Sassaman (editors)
  1995 *Native American Interactions: Multiscalar Analyses and Interpretations in the Eastern Woodlands*. Knoxville: University of Tennessee Press.

Nathan, H.
  1962 Osteophytes of the Vertebral Column. An Anatomical Study of Their Development According to Age, Race, and Sex with Considerations as to Their Etiology and Significance. *Journal of Bone and Joint Surgery* 44A:243–68.

National Oceanic and Atmospheric Administration (NOAA)
  1990 *Estuaries of the United States: Vital Statistics of a National Resource Base*. Rockville, Md.: National Oceanic and Atmospheric Administration.

Nelson, M. C.
  1991 The Study of Technological Organization. In *Archeological Method and Theory*, vol. 3, ed. M. B. Schiffer, pp. 57–100. Tucson: University of Arizona Press.

Nelson, N. C.
  1918 Chronology in Florida. *Anthropological Papers of the American Museum of Natural History* 22(2):73–103. New York.

Neuman, Robert W.
  1975 *Archaeological Salvage Excavations at the Bayou Jasmine Site, Saint John the Baptiste Parish, Louisiana, 1975*. Manuscript (22–198) on file at the Louisiana Division of Archaeology, Baton Rouge.
  1984 *An Introduction to Louisiana Archaeology*. Baton Rouge: Louisiana State University Press.
  1992 Report on the Soil Core Borings Conducted at the Campus Mounds Site (16EBR6), East Baton Rouge, Parish, Louisiana. *Louisiana Archaeology* 15:1–30.

1993   Reply to Mr. Jones Regarding the LSU Campus Mounds Report. *Louisiana Archaeology* 20:179–82.

Neuman, Robert W., and Jeffrey A. Homburg

1992   The L.S.U. Campus Mounds and the Meso-Indian Era in the Southeastern U.S. Paper presented at the annual meeting of SEAC, Little Rock.

Neumann, H. W.

1967   *The Paleopathology of the Archaic Modoc Rockshelter Inhabitants.* Reports of Investigations 11. Springfield: Illinois State Museum.

Neusius, Sarah W.

1982   *Early-Middle Archaic Subsistence Strategies: Changes in Faunal Exploitation at the Koster Site.* Ph.D. dissertation, Northwestern University, Evanston. Ann Arbor: University Microfilms.

Newman, Christine L.,and Brent R. Weisman

1992   Prehistoric and Historic Settlement in the Guana Tract, St. Johns County, Florida. *Florida Anthropologist* 45(2):162–71.

Newman, Walter S., and Craig A. Munsart

1968   Holocene Geology of the Wachapreague Lagoon, Eastern Shore Peninsula, Virginia. *Marine Geology* 6:81–105.

Newsom, Lee A.

1988   The Paleoethnobotany of Windover (8Br246): An Archaic Period Mortuary Site in Florida. Paper presented at the annual meeting of the Society for American Archaeology, Phoenix.

O'Connell, James F.

1987   Alyawara Site Structure and Its Archaeological Implications. *American Antiquity* 52:74–108.

Odell, G. H.

1980   Toward a More Behavioral Approach to Archaeological Lithic Concentrations. *American Antiquity* 45:404–31.

1985a   Archaic Assemblages from the Stratified Napoleon Hollow Site in Illinois. *Wisconsin Archaeologist* 66:327–58.

1985b   Small Sites Archaeology and Use-Wear on Surface-Collected Artifacts. *Midcontinental Journal of Archaeology* 10:21–48.

1988   Addressing Prehistoric Hunting Practices through Stone Tool Analysis. *American Anthropologist* 90:335–56.

1989   Fitting Analytical Techniques to Prehistoric Problems with Lithic Data. In *Alternative Approaches to Lithic Analysis,* ed. D. O. Henry and G. H. Odell, pp. 159–82. Archaeological Papers 1. Washington: American Anthropological Association.

1994a   The Role of Stone Bladelets in Middle Woodland Society. *American Antiquity* 59:102–20.

1994b   Assessing Hunter-Gatherer Mobility in the Illinois Valley: Exploring Ambiguous Results. In *The Organization of Prehistoric North American Chipped Stone Tool Technologies,* ed. P. Carr, pp. 70–86. Archaeological Series 7. Ann Arbor: International Monographs in Prehistory.

1994c   Prehistoric Hafting and Mobility in the North American Midcontinent: Examples from Illinois. *Journal of Anthropological Archaeology* 13:51–73.

Oetelaar, Gerald A.

1982   An Analysis of Microremains in an Area A Column Sample. In Jefferies and Butler, eds., q.v., pp. 987–1007.

O'Hear, John

1978   Some Thoughts on Late Archaic Settlement-Subsistence Patterns in a Tributary of the Western Middle Tennessee Valley. Paper presented at the annual meeting of SEAC, Knoxville.

Ortner, Donald J., and Walter G. J. Putschar

1985   *Identification of Pathological Conditions in Human Skeletal Remains.* Washington: Smithsonian Institution Press.

Otinger, Jeffrey L., Charles M. Hoffman, and Robert H. Lafferty III

1982   *The F. L. Brinkley Midden (22Ts729): Archaeological Investigations in the Yellow Creek Watershed, Tishomingo County, Mississippi.* Report of Investigations 36. Moundville: Office of Archaeological Research, University of Alabama.

Otvos, Ervin G., Jr.

1979   New Orleans–South Hancock Holocene Barrier Trends and Origins of Lake Pontchartrain. *Transactions: Gulf Coast Association of Geological Societies* 28:337–55.

Owsley, Douglas W., Hugh E. Berryman, and William M. Bass

1977   Demographic and Osteological Evidence for Warfare at the Larson Site, South Dakota. *Plains Anthropologist Memoirs* 13:119–31.

Parkinson, Randall W.

1987   *Holocene Sedimentation and Coastal Response to Rising Sea Level along a Subtropical Low Energy Coast, Ten Thousand Islands, Southwest Florida.* Ph.D. dissertation, University of Miami, Coral Gables.

Parham, Kenneth

1982   *A Biocultural Approach to the Skeletal Biology of the Dallas People from Toqua.* M.A. thesis, University of Tennessee, Knoxville.

Parmalee, Paul W.

1962   Faunal Remains from the Stanfield-Worley Bluff Shelter, Colbert County, Alabama. In DeJarnette, Kurjak, and Cambron, q.v., pp. 112–14.

1963   A Prehistoric Occurrence of Porcupine in Alabama. *Journal of Mammalogy* 44:267–68.

1993   An Archaeological Avian Assemblage from Northwestern Alabama. *Archaeozoologica* 5:77–93.

Parmalee, Paul W., R. Bruce McMillan, and Frances B. King

1976   Changing Subsistence Patterns at Rodgers Shelter. In *Prehistoric Man and His Environments: A Case Study in the Ozark Highland,* ed. W. R. Wood and R. B. McMillan, pp. 141–62. New York: Academic Press.

Parry, W. J.

1994   Prismatic Blade Technologies in North America. In *The Organization of Prehistoric North American Chipped Stone Tool Technologies,* ed. P. Carr, pp. 87–98. Archaeological Series 7. Ann Arbor: International Monographs in Prehistory.

Parry, W. J., and R. L. Kelly

1987   Expedient Core Technology and Sedentism. In *The Organization of Core Technology,* ed. J. K. Johnson and C. A. Morrow, pp. 285–304. Boulder, Colo.: Westview Press.

Pearson, Charles E.

1986   Dating the Course of the Lower Red River in Louisiana: The Archaeological Evidence. *Geoarchaeology* 1:39–43.

Pearson, Charles E., David B. Kelley, Richard A. Weinstein, and Sherwood M. Gagliano

1986   *Archaeological Investigations on the Outer Continental Shelf: A Study within the*

Sabine River Valley, Offshore Louisiana and Texas. Report by Coastal Environments, Inc., Baton Rouge, Louisiana, submitted to Minerals Management Service, U.S. Department of Interior, Reston, Virginia.

Penland, Shea, J. R. Suter, and R. A. McBride
1988   Delta Plain Development and Sea Level History in the Terrebonne Coastal Region, Louisiana. *Coastal Sediments* 1987:1689–1705.

Penland, Shea, Karen E. Ramsey, Randolph A. McBride, Thomas F. Moslow, and Karen A. Westphal
1989   *Relative Sea Level Rise and Subsidence in Louisiana and the Gulf of Mexico*. Baton Rouge: Louisiana Geological Survey.

Perlman, S. M.
1981   Hunter-Gatherer Social Systems and the James River Middle Archaic Lithic Utilization. *Quarterly Bulletin of the Archaeological Society of Virginia* 36:22–28.

Peterson, Drexel
1973   *The Spring Creek Site, Perry County, Tennessee: Report of the 1972–1973 Excavations*. Occasional Paper 7. Memphis: Anthropological Research Center, Memphis State University.

1980   The Introduction, Use and Technology of Fiber-Tempered Pottery in the Southeastern United States. In *Early Native Americans*, ed. D. L. Browman, pp. 363–72. The Hague: Mouton.

Phelps, David Sutton
1964   *The Final Phases of the Eastern Archaic*. Ph.D. dissertation, Tulane University, New Orleans.

1967   FSU-146, Williams Site, Florida. *Radiocarbon* 9:41.

Phillips, James L.
1983   Introduction. In Phillips and Brown, eds., q.v., pp. 1–4.

Phillips, James L., and James A. Brown (editors)
1983   *Archaic Hunter-Gatherers in the American Midwest*. New York: Academic Press.

Phillips, James L., and B. G. Gladfelter
1983   The Labras Lake Site and the Paleogeographic Setting of the Late Archaic in the American Bottom. In Phillips and Brown, eds., q.v., pp. 197–218.

Phillips, Philip
1970   *Archaeological Survey in the Lower Yazoo Basin, Mississippi, 1949–1955*. Papers of the Peabody Museum of Archaeology and Ethnology 60. Cambridge, Mass.: Harvard University.

Phillips, Philip, James A. Ford, and James B. Griffin
1951   *Archaeological Survey in the Lower Mississippi Alluvial Valley, 1940–1947*. Papers of the Peabody Museum of American Archaeology and Ethnology 25. Cambridge, Mass.: Harvard University.

Piatek, Bruce John
1992a   Tomoka State Park Survey and Preliminary Test Excavation Results. *Florida Anthropologist* 45:326–35.

1992b   Archaeology and History at Tomoka State Park. *Florida Anthropologist* 45:314–25.

1994   The Tomoka Mound Complex in Northeast Florida. *Southeastern Archaeology* 13:109–18.

Pickering, R. B.
1979   Hunter-Gatherer/Agriculturalist Arthritic Patterns: A Preliminary Examination. *Henry Ford Hospital Medical Journal* 27:50–53.
1984   *Patterns of Degenerative Joint Disease in Middle Woodland, Late Woodland, and Mississippian Skeletal Series from the Lower Illinois Valley.* Ph.D. dissertation, Northwestern University, Evanston. Ann Arbor: University Microfilms.

Pierce, Lorna K. C.
1987   *A Comparison of the Pattern of Involvement of Degenerative Joint Disease between an Agricultural and Nonagricultural Skeletal Series.* Ph.D. dissertation, University of Tennessee, Knoxville. Ann Arbor: University Microfilms.

Potter, Stephen R.
1993   *Commoners, Tribute, and Chiefs: The Development of Algonquian Culture in the Potomac Valley.* Charlottesville: University Press of Virginia.

Prentice, Guy
1986   Origins of Plant Domestication in the Eastern United States: Promoting the Individual in Archaeological Theory. *Southeastern Archaeology* 5:103–19.

Prewitt, Elton R., and Jeffrey G. Paine
1987   The Swan Lake Site (41AS16) on Copano Bay, Aransas County, Texas: Settlement, Subsistence, and Sea Level. *Bulletin of the Texas Archaeological Society* 58:147–74.

Price, T. Douglas, and James A. Brown
1985b   Aspects of Hunter-Gatherer Complexity. In Price and Brown, eds., q.v., pp. 3–20.

Price, T. Douglas, and James A. Brown (editors)
1985a   *Prehistoric Hunter-Gatherers: The Emergence of Cultural Complexity.* Orlando: Academic Press.

Pullins, S.
1994   Eolian Sandy Sediments and Stratified Deposits at Two Archaic Sites in Southeastern Virginia. Paper presented at the annual meeting of SEAC, Lexington.

Purdue, James R.
1980   Clinal Variation of Some Mammals during the Holocene in Missouri. *Quaternary Research* 13:242–58.
1991   Dynamism in the Body Size of White-tailed Deer (*Odocoileus virginianus*) from Southern Illinois. In *Beamers, Bobwhites, and Blue-Points: Tributes to the Career of Paul W. Parmalee,* ed. J. R. Purdue, W. E. Klippel, and B. W. Styles, pp. 277–83. Scientific Paper 23. Springfield: Illinois State Museum.

Purdy, Barbara A.
1992   Florida's Archaeological Wet Sites. In *The Wetland Revolution in Prehistory,* ed. Bryony Coles, pp. 125–34. WARP Occasional Paper 6. Exeter: Department of History and Archaeology, University of Exeter.

Raab, L. M., R. F. Cande, and D. W. Stahle
1979   Debitage Graphs and Archaic Settlement Patterns in the Arkansas Ozarks. *Midcontinental Journal of Archaeology* 4:167–82.

Rafferty, Janet E., B. L. Baker, and J. D. Elliott, Jr.
1980   *Archaeological Investigations at the East Aberdeen Site (22MO819), Tombigbee Multi-Resource District, Alabama and Mississippi.* Report submitted to the National Park

Service, Southeastern Region, by Department of Anthropology, Mississippi State University.

Ramenofsky, Ann F.

1986   The Persistence of Late Archaic Subsistence-Settlement in Louisiana. In *Foraging, Collecting, and Harvesting: Archaic Period Subsistence and Settlement in the Eastern Woodlands,* ed. S. W. Neusius, pp. 289–312. Occasional Paper 6. Carbondale: Center for Archaeological Investigations, Southern Illinois University.

Rathbun, Ted A.

1993   Trauma at a Late Archaic South Carolina Site: 38BU9. Paper presented at the annual meeting of SEAC, Raleigh.

Rathbun, Ted A., Dean Foster, and Daniel Kysar

1992   Human Skeletal Remains from 38ED9. Report on file, Physical/Forensic Laboratory, Department of Anthropology, University of South Carolina, Columbia.

Rathbun, Ted A., Jim Sexton, and James Michie

1980   Disease Patterns in a Formative Period South Carolina Coastal Population. In *The Skeletal Biology of Aboriginal Populations in the Southeastern United States,* ed. P. Willey and F. H. Smith, pp. 52–74. Miscellaneous Paper 5. Knoxville: Tennessee Anthropological Association.

Reid, Kenneth C.

1983   The Nebo Hill Phase: Late Archaic Prehistory in the Lower Missouri Valley. In Phillips and Brown, eds., q.v., pp. 11–40.

Ricklis, Robert A.

1988   Archaeological Investigations at the McKinzie Site (41NU221), Nueces County, Texas: Description and Contextual Interpretations. *Bulletin of the Texas Archaeological Society* 58:1–76.

Ricklis, Robert A., and Kim A. Cox

1991   Toward a Chronology of Adaptive Change during the Archaic of the Texas Coastal Bend Area. *La Tierra, Journal of the Southern Texas Archaeological Association* 18:13–31.

1993   Examining Lithic Technological Organization as a Dynamic Cultural Subsystem: The Advantages of an Explicitly Spatial Approach. *American Antiquity* 58:444–61.

Ricklis, Robert A., and Rita R. Gunter

1986   Archaeological Investigation at the Means Site (41NU184), Nueces County, Texas. *La Tierra, Journal of the Southern Texas Archaeological Association* 13:15–32.

Robb, N. D., E. Cruwts, and B. G. N. Smith

1991   Is "Lingual Surface Attrition of the Maxillary Teeth (LSAMAT)" Caused by Dental Erosion? *American Journal of Physical Anthropology* 85:345–51.

Robertson, J. A.

1984   Chipped Stone and Functional Interpretations: A Fort Ancient Example. *Midcontinental Journal of Archaeology* 9:251–67.

Roche, M. B., and G. G. Rowe

1952   The Incidence of Separate Neural Arch Coincident Bone Variations. *Journal of Bone and Joint Surgery* 34A:491–94.

Rogers, J., I. Watt, and P. Dieppe
1985 Paleopathology of Spinal Osteophytosis, Vertebral Ankylosis, Ankylosis Spondylitis, and Vertebral Hyperostosis. *Annals of the Rheumatic Diseases* 44:113–20.

Rogers, S. L.
1966 The Need for a Better Means of Recording Pathological Bone Proliferation in Joint Areas. *American Journal of Physical Anthropology* 25:171–76.

Rolingson, Martha
1967 *Temporal Perspective on the Archaic Cultures in the Middle South.* Ph.D. dissertation, University of Michigan, Ann Arbor.

Rothschild, B. M., K. R. Turner, and M. A. DeLuca
1988 Symmetrical Erosive Peripheral Polyarthritis in the Late Archaic Period of Alabama. *Science* 241:1498–1501.

Rothschild, Nan A.
1975 *Age and Sex, Status and Role, in Prehistoric Societies of Eastern North America.* Ph.D. dissertation, New York University, New York.
1979 Mortuary Behavior and Social Organization at Indian Knoll and Dickson Mounds. *American Antiquity* 44:658–75.

Rouse, Irving
1951 *A Survey of Indian River Archaeology, Florida.* Yale University Publications in Anthropology 44. New Haven: Yale University Press

Royal, William D., and E. Clark
1960 Natural Preservation of Human Brain, Warm Springs, Florida. *American Antiquity* 26:285–87.

Ruff, C. B.
1987a Postcranial Adaptation to Subsistence Changes on the Georgia Coast. *American Journal of Physical Anthropology* 72:248.
1987b Sexual Dimorphism in Human Lower Limb Bone Structure: Relationship to Subsistence Strategy and Sexual Division of Labor. *Journal of Human Evolution* 16:391–416.

Ruff, C. B., and Frank P. Leo
1986 Use of Computed Tomography in Skeletal Structure Research. *Yearbook of Physical Anthropology* 29:181–96.

Ruff, C. B., C. S. Larsen, and W. C. Hayes
1984 Structural Changes in the Femur with the Transition to Agriculture on the Georgia Coast. *American Journal of Physical Anthropology* 64:125–36.

Ruppe, Reynold J.
1980 The Archaeology of Drowned Terrestrial Sites, a Preliminary Report. In *Bureau of Historic Sites and Properties Bulletin* 6. Tallahassee: Division of Archives, History, and Records Management.

Russo, Michael
1988a A Comment on Temporal Patterns in Marine Shellfish Use in Florida and Georgia. *Southeastern Archaeology* 7:61–68.
1988b Coastal Adaptations in Eastern Florida: Models and Methods. *Archaeology of Eastern North America* 16:159–76.

1991   *Archaic Sedentism on the Florida Coast: A Case Study from Horr's Island*. Ph.D. dissertation, University of Florida, Gainesville.

1992a   Chronologies and Cultures of the St. Marys Region of Northeast Florida and Southern Georgia. *Florida Anthropologist* 45:107–26.

1992b   *1992 Annual Report for Management Unit 3 Regional Archaeology Program, Department of Sociology/Anthropology, University of Southwestern Louisiana*. Baton Rouge: Division of Archaeology, Department of Culture, Recreation and Tourism, Office of Cultural Development.

1993   *1993 Annual Report for Management Unit 3 Regional Archaeology Program, Department of Sociology/Anthropology, University of Southwestern Louisiana*. Baton Rouge: Division of Archaeology, Department of Culture, Recreation and Tourism, Office of Cultural Development.

1994a   Why We Don't Believe in Archaic Ceremonial Mounds and Why We Should: The Case from Florida. *Southeastern Archaeology* 13:93–108.

1994b   A Brief Introduction to the Study of Archaic Mounds in the Southeast. *Southeastern Archaeology* 13(2):89–93.

Russo, Michael, Ann S. Cordell, and Donna L. Ruhl

1993   *The Timucuan Ecological and Historic Preserve, Phase III Final Report*. Report submitted to the Southeast Archeological Research Center, National Park Service, Tallahassee. Contract CA-5000-9-8011.

Russo, Michael, Barbara A. Purdy, Lee A. Newsom, and Ray M. McGee

1992   A Reinterpretation of Late Archaic Adaptations in Central-East Florida: Groves' Orange Midden (8-Vo-2601). *Southeastern Archaeology* 11:95–108.

Russo, Michael, and Dana Ste. Claire

1992   Tomoka Stone: Archaic Period Coastal Settlement in East Florida. *Florida Anthropologist* 45:336–46.

Sairanen, E., L. Brushaber, and M. Kaskinen

1981   Felling Work, Low Back Pain and Osteoarthritis. *Scandinavian Journal of Work and Environmental Health* 7:18–30.

Salib, Philip

1967   Trauma and Disease of the Post-Cranial Skeleton in Ancient Egypt. In *Diseases in Antiquity,* ed. D. R. Brothwell and A. T. Sandison, pp. 599–605. Springfield, Ill.: C. C. Thomas.

Sampson, C. Garth

1988   *Stylistic Boundaries among Mobile Hunter-Foragers*. Washington: Smithsonian Institution Press.

Sassaman, Kenneth E.

1983   *Middle and Late Archaic Settlement in the South Carolina Piedmont*. M.A. thesis, University of South Carolina, Columbia.

1991   Adaptive Flexibility in the Morrow Mountain Phase of the Middle Archaic Period. *South Carolina Antiquities* 23:31–41.

1992a   Early Archaic Settlement in the South Carolina Coastal Plain. In Anderson, Sassaman, and Judge, eds., q.v., pp. 48–67.

1992b   Lithic Technology and the Hunter-Gatherer Sexual Division of Labor. *North American Archaeologist* 13:249–62.

1992c   Gender and Technology at the Archaic-Woodland "Transition." In *Exploring*

Gender through Archaeology, ed. C. Claassen, pp. 71–80. Madison, Wis.: Prehistory Press.

1993a   *Early Pottery in the Southeast: Tradition and Innovation in Cooking Technology.* Tuscaloosa: University of Alabama Press.

1993b   Hunter-Gatherer Site Structure at Upland Sites in the South Atlantic Coastal Plain. *Southeastern Archaeology* 12:117–36.

1993c   *Mims Point 1992: Archaeological Investigations at a Prehistoric Habitation Site in the Sumter National Forest, South Carolina.* Savannah River Archaeological Research Paper 4. Columbia: Institute of Archaeology and Anthropology, University of South Carolina.

1993d   *Early Woodland Settlement in the Aiken Plateau: Archaeological Investigations at 38AK157, Savannah River Site, Aiken County, South Carolina.* Savannah River Archaeological Research Paper 3. Columbia: Institute of Archaeology and Anthropology, University of South Carolina.

1994a   Changing Strategies of Biface Production in the South Carolina Coastal Plain. In *The Organization of Prehistoric North American Chipped Stone Tool Technologies,* ed. P. Carr, pp. 99–117. Archaeological Series 7. Ann Arbor: International Monographs in Prehistory.

1994b   Production for Exchange in the Mid-Holocene Southeast: A Savannah River Valley Example. *Lithic Technology* 19:42–51.

1995a   The Cultural Diversity of Interactions among Mid-Holocene Societies of the American Southeast. In Nassaney and Sassaman, eds., q.v., pp. 174–204.

1995b   The Social Contradictions of Traditional and Innovative Cooking Technology in the American Southeast. In *The Emergence of Pottery,* ed. W. K. Barnett and J. Hoopes, pp. 223–240. Washington: Smithsonian Institution Press.

1995c   Ed Marshall Site (38ED5). In *Annual Review of Cultural Resource Investigations by the Savannah River Archaeological Research Program, Fiscal Year 1995.* Columbia: Institute of Archaeology and Anthropology, University of South Carolina.

1996   Hunter-Gatherer Land Use as Long-Term History. MS in possession of author.

Sassaman, Kenneth E., and David G. Anderson

1994   *Middle and Late Archaeological Records of South Carolina. A Synthesis for Research and Resource Management.* Columbia: Council of South Carolina Professional Archaeologists.

Sassaman, Kenneth E., and Mark J. Brooks

1990   Cultural Quarries: Strategies for Scavenging and Recycling Lithic Refuse. Paper presented at the annual meeting of SEAC, Mobile.

Sassaman, Kenneth E., Glen T. Hanson, and Tommy Charles

1988   Raw Material Procurement and the Reduction of Hunter-Gatherer Range in the Savannah River Valley. *Southeastern Archaeology* 7:79–94.

Sassaman, Kenneth E., Mark J. Brooks, Glen T. Hanson, and David G. Anderson

1990   *Native American Prehistory of the Middle Savannah River Valley: A Synthesis of Archaeological Investigations on the Savannah River Site, Aiken and Barnwell Counties, South Carolina.* Savannah River Archaeological Research Paper 1. Columbia: Institute of Archaeology and Anthropology, University of South Carolina.

Saucier, Roger T.

1964   Geological Investigations of the St. Francis Basin. *Waterways Experiment Station Technical Report 3-659.* Washington: U.S. Army Corps of Engineers.

1974   *Quaternary Geology of the Lower Mississippi Valley.* Research Series 6. Fayetteville: Arkansas Archeological Survey.

1981   Current Thinking on Riverine Processes and Geologic History as Related to Human Settlement in the Southeast. *Geoscience and Man* 22:7–18.

1994   *Geomorphology and Quaternary Geological History of the Lower Mississippi Valley.* Vicksburg: U.S. Army Engineer Waterways Experiment Station.

Saunders, Joe

1992   *1992 Annual Report for Management Unit 2, Regional Archaeology Program, Department of Geosciences, Northeast Louisiana University.* Baton Rouge: Division of Archaeology, Department of Culture, Recreation and Tourism, Office of Cultural Development.

1994   *1994 Annual Report for Management Unit 2, Regional Archaeology Program, Department of Geosciences, Northeast Louisiana University.* Baton Rouge: Division of Archaeology, Department of Culture, Recreation and Tourism, Office of Cultural Development.

Saunders, Joe, and Thurman Allen

1994   Hedgepeth Mounds, an Archaic Mound Complex in North-Central Louisiana. *American Antiquity* 59:471–89.

Saunders, Joe, Thurman Allen, and Roger T. Saucier

1994   Four Archaic? Mound Complexes in Northeast Louisiana. *Southeastern Archaeology* 13:134–53.

Saunders, Lorraine P.

1972   *Osteology of the Republic Grove Site.* M.A. thesis, Florida Atlantic University, Boca Raton.

Saunders, Rebecca

1994   The Case for Archaic Mound Sites in Southeastern Louisiana. *Southeastern Archaeology* 13:118–34.

Scarry, C. Margaret

1986   *Changes in Plant Procurement and Production during the Emergence of the Moundville Chiefdom.* Ph.D. dissertation, University of Michigan, Ann Arbor. Ann Arbor: University Microfilms.

Schmorl, G., and H. Junghans

1971   *The Human Spine in Health and Disease.* New York: Grune and Stratton.

Scholl, David W., F. Craighead, and Minze Stuiver

1967   Florida Submergence Curve Revisited: Its Relation to Coastal Sedimentation Rates. *Science* 163:562–64.

Schrire, Carmel (editor)

1984   *Past and Present in Hunter-Gatherer Studies.* New York: Academic Press.

Schuldenrein, Joseph, and David G. Anderson

1988   Paleoenvironmental History and Archaeology in the Russell Lake Area. In Anderson and Joseph, eds., q.v., pp. 56–96.

Schuldenrein, Joseph, and Dennis Blanton

n.d.   Pedo-Archaeology Research Strategies for Limited Scopes of Work: A Case Study along the Upper Chickahominy River in the Coastal Plain of Virginia. In *Proceedings from the Second International Conference on Pedo-Archaeology,* ed. Albert C. Goodyear, John E. Foss, and Kenneth E. Sassaman. Columbia: Institute of Archaeology and Anthroplogy, University of South Carolina (in press).

Schumm, Stanley A.

1977   *The Fluvial System.* New York: John Wiley and Sons.

Sears, William H.

1962   The Southeastern United States. In *Prehistoric Man in the New World,* ed. J. D. Jennings and E. Norbeck, pp. 259–87. Houston: Rice University Press.

Sears, William H., and James B. Griffin

1950   Fiber-Tempered Pottery of the Southeast. In *Prehistoric Pottery of the Eastern United States,* ed. James B. Griffin, pp. 2–20. Ann Arbor: Museum of Anthropology, University of Michigan.

Seeman, M. F.

1988   Ohio Hopewell Trophy-Skull Artifacts as Evidence for Competition in Middle Woodland Societies ca. 50 B.C.–A.D. 350. *American Antiquity* 53:565–77.

1994   Intercluster Lithic Patterning at Nobles Pond: A Case for "Disembedded" Procurement among Early Paleoindian Societies. *American Antiquity* 59:273–88.

Segovia, Antonio V.

1985   *Archaeological Geology of the Savannah River Valley and Main Tributaries in the Richard B. Russell Multiple Resource Area.* Russell Papers 1985. Atlanta: Interagency Archeological Services Division, National Park Service.

Semenov, S. A.

1964   *Prehistoric Technology* (trans. M. W. Thompson). Bath: Adams and Dart.

Servello, Frank A.

1984   Cultural Resources Investigations along Route LA 16 between Watson and Amite, vol. 3. Report on file, Louisiana Department of Transportation and Development, Baton Rouge.

Sheets, Payson D.

1975   Behavioral Analysis and the Structure of a Prehistoric Industry. *Current Anthropology* 16(3):369–92.

Shenkel, J. Richard

1984   Early Woodland in Coastal Louisiana. In *Perspectives on Gulf Coast Prehistory,* ed. D. D. Davis, pp. 41–71. Gainesville: University Presses of Florida.

1986   An Additional Comment on Volume Calculations and a Comparison of Formulae Using Several Southeastern Mounds. *Midcontinental Journal of Archaeology* 11:201–20.

Shermis, Steward

1982–84 Domestic Violence in Two Skeletal Populations. *Ossa* 9–11:143–51.

Short, C. L.

1974   The Antiquity of Rheumatoid Arthritis. *Arthritic Rheumatism* 17:193–205.

Shott, M.

1986   Technological Organization and Settlement Mobility: An Ethnographic Examination. *Journal of Anthropological Research* 42(1):15–51.

1989a   Diversity, Organization, and Behavior in the Material Record: Ethnographic and Archaeological Examples. *Current Anthropology* 30:283–315.

1989b   On Tool Class Use-Lives and the Formation of Archaeological Assemblages. *American Antiquity* 54(1):9–30.

Simpkins, Daniel L., and Alan E. McMichael

1976   Sapelo Island: A Preliminary Report. *Southeastern Archaeological Conference Bulletin* 19:95–99.

Smith, Betty A.
  1979   The Hopewell Connection in Southwest Georgia. In Brose and Greber, eds.,
         q.v., pp. 181–87.
Smith, Brent W.
  1976   The Late Archaic–Poverty Point Steatite Trade Network in the Lower Missis-
         sippi Valley: A Preliminary Report. *Newsletter of the Louisiana Archaeological
         Society* 3(4):6–10.
  1991   The Late Archaic–Poverty Point Trade Network. In Byrd, ed., q.v., pp. 173–80.
Smith, Bruce D.
  1986   The Archaeology of the Southeastern United States: From Dalton to de Soto,
         10,500–500 B.P. In *Advances in World Archaeology*, vol. 5, ed. F. Wendorf and A.
         Close, pp. 1–92. Orlando: Academic Press.
  1987   Independent Domestication of Indigenous Seed-Bearing Plants in Eastern
         North America. In *Emergent Horticultural Economies of the Eastern Woodlands*, ed.
         W. F. Keegan, pp. 3–47. Occasional Paper 7. Carbondale: Center for Archaeo-
         logical Investigations, Southern Illinois University.
  1992   The Floodplain Weed Theory of Plant Domestication in Eastern North America.
         In *Rivers of Change: Essays on Early Agriculture in Eastern North America*, by Bruce
         D. Smith, pp. 19–34. Washington: Smithsonian Institution Press.
Smith, Bruce D., and C. Wesley Cowan
  1987   Domesticated *Chenopodium* in Prehistoric Eastern North America: New Acceler-
         ator Dates from Eastern Kentucky. *American Antiquity* 52:355–57.
Smith, Bruce D., C. Wesley Cowan, and Michael P. Hoffman
  1992   Is It an Indigene or a Foreigner? In *Rivers of Change: Essays on Early Agriculture
         in Eastern North America*, by Bruce D. Smith, pp. 67–100. Washington: Smith-
         sonian Institution Press.
Smith, Maria O.
  1982   *Patterns of Association between Oral Health Status and Subsistence: A Study of Abo-
         riginal Skeletal Populations from the Tennessee Valley Area*. Ph.D. dissertation, Uni-
         versity of Tennessee, Knoxville. Ann Arbor: University Microfilms.
  1990   Pattern and Frequency of Forearm Fractures among Prehistoric Populations
         from the Tennessee Valley. *American Journal of Physical Anthropology* 81:296.
  1992   Osteological Indications of Warfare in the Archaic Period of West Tennessee.
         Paper presented at the annual meeting of SEAC, Little Rock.
  1993a Physical Anthropology. In Johnson, ed., q.v., pp. 53–77.
  1993b Intergroup Violence among the Prehistoric Hunter-Gatherers from the Ken-
         tucky Lake Reservoir. *American Journal of Physical Anthropology*, Supplement
         16:183–84.
  1993c A Probable Case of Decapitation at the Late Archaic Robinson Site (40SM4),
         Smith County, Tennessee. *Tennessee Anthropologist* 18:131–42.
  1993d Forearm Trauma and Status in the Archaic. Paper presented at the annual
         meeting of SEAC, Raleigh.
  1995   Scalping in the Archaic Period: Evidence from the Western Tennessee Valley.
         Southeastern Archaeology 13:60–68.
  n.d.   Intergroup Violence in the Archaic Period of West Tennessee: The Osteological
         Evidence. In *Troubled Times: Osteological and Archaeological Evidence of Violence*,
         ed. D. Martin and D. W. Frayer. New York: Gordon and Breach (in press).

Smith, Patricia

1972 Diet and Nutrition in the Natufians. *American Journal of Physical Anthropology* 37:233–38.

Smith, Philip W.

1979 *The Fishes of Illinois.* Urbana: University of Illinois Press.

Smith, Richard Lee

1968 *Test Excavations at the Lock Site (8JE57), Jefferson County, Florida.* M.A. thesis, University of North Carolina, Chapel Hill.

Snow, Charles E.

1948 *Indian Knoll Skeletons of Site Oh 2, Ohio County, Kentucky.* University of Kentucky Reports in Anthropology, vol. 4, no. 3, pt. 2. Lexington: Department of Anthropology, University of Kentucky.

Snyder, Lynn M., and Paul W. Parmalee

1991 *An Archaeological Faunal Assemblage from Smith Bottom Cave, Lauderdale County, Alabama.* Report submitted to the Tennessee Valley Authority. Knoxville: Department of Anthropology, University of Tennessee.

Sollberger, J. B.

1971 A Technological Study of Beveled Knives. *Plains Anthropologist* 16:206–18.

Spaulding, Albert C.

1955 Prehistoric Cultural Development in the Eastern United States. In *New Interpretations of Aboriginal American Culture History: 75th Anniversary Volume of the Anthropological Society of Washington,* pp. 12–27. Washington: Anthropological Society of Washington.

Stafford, C. Russell, and C. Michael Anslinger

1988 Current Research (Indiana State University). *Illinois Archaeological Survey Newsletter* 3(2):11–12.

Stahle, D. W., and J. E. Dunn

1982 An Analysis and Application of the Size Distribution of Waste Flakes from the Manufacture of Bifacial Stone Tools. *World Archaeology* 14:84–97.

Stansbery, David

1970 Eastern Freshwater Mollusks: The Mississippi and St. Lawrence River Systems. *Malacologia* 10:9–22.

Stapor, Frank W., Jr., Thomas D. Mathews, and Fonda E. Lindfors-Kearns

1988 Episodic Barrier Island Growth in Southwest Florida: A Response to Fluctuating Holocene Sea Level? *Miami Geological Society Memoir* 3:149–202.

1991 Barrier-Island Progradation and Holocene Sea-Level History in Southwest Florida. *Journal of Coastal Research* 7(3):815–37.

Steinbock, R. T.

1976 *Paleopathological Diagnosis and Interpretation.* Springfield: C. C. Thomas.

Steponaitis, Vincas P.

1986 Prehistoric Archaeology in the Southeastern United States, 1970–1985. *Annual Review of Anthropology* 15:363–404.

Stewart, T. Dale

1931 Incidence of Separate Neural Arch in the Lumbar Vertebrae of Eskimos. *American Journal of Physical Anthropology* 16:51–62.

1947 Racial Patterns in Vertebral Osteoarthritis. *American Journal of Physical Anthropology* 5:230–31.

1953   The Age Incidence of Neural Arch Defects in Alaskan Natives, Considered from the Standpoint of Etiology. *Journal of Bone and Joint Surgery* 35A:937–50.

1958   The Rate of Development of Vertebral Osteoarthritis in American Whites and Its Significance in Skeletal Age Identification. *Leech* 28:144–51.

1974   Nonunion of Fractures in Antiquity, with Descriptions of Five Cases from the New World Involving the Forearm. *Bulletin of the New York Academy of Science* 50:876–91.

Stoltman, James B.

1966   New Radiocarbon Dates for Southeastern Fiber-Tempered Pottery. *American Antiquity* 31:872–74.

1972   The Late Archaic in the Savannah River Region. In Bullen and Stoltman, eds., q.v., pp. 37–62.

1986   The Archaic Tradition. In *Introduction to Wisconsin Archaeology*, edited by W. Green, J. B. Stoltman, and A. B. Kehoe. *Wisconsin Archaeologist* 67(3–4):207–38.

Stowe, Noel R.

1991   The Gulf Formational Stage on the North Central Gulf Coast. Paper presented at the Midsouth Archaeological Conference, Mississippi State, Mississippi.

Stright, Melanie J.

1986   Human Occupation of the Continental Shelf During the Late Pleistocene/Early Holocene: Methods for Site Location. *Geoarchaeology* 1:347–64.

1988   Inundated Archaeological Sites of the Florida Coastal Region: A Regional Overview. *Proceedings: Eighth Annual Gulf of Mexico Information Transfer Meeting,* December 1987:395–401. New Orleans: Mineral Management Service.

1990   Archaeological Sites on the North American Continental Shelf. In *Archaeological Geology of North America,* ed. N. P. Lasca and J. E. Donahue, pp. 439–65. Centennial Special Volume 4. Boulder, Colo.: Geological Society of America.

Stuiver, Minze, and P. J. Reimer

1986   A Computer Program for Radiocarbon Age Calibration. *Radiocarbon* 28: 1022–30.

Stuiver, Minze, G. W. Pearson, and Tom Braziunas

1986   Radiocarbon Age Calibration of Marine Samples Back to 9000 Cal Yr BP. *Radiocarbon* 28:980–1021.

Styles, Bonnie W.

1986   Aquatic Exploitation in the Lower Illinois River Valley: The Role of Paleoecological Change. In *Foraging, Collecting, and Harvesting: Archaic Period Subsistence and Settlement in the Eastern Woodlands,* ed. S. W. Neusius, pp. 145–74. Occasional Paper 6. Carbondale: Center for Archaeological Investigations, Southern Illinois University.

1993   The Changing Use of Fauna in Human Subsistence Strategies: Faunal Exploitation in the Central Mississippi River Valley. Paper presented at the annual meeting of the Society for American Archaeology, St. Louis.

1994   The Value of Archaeological Faunal Remains for Paleodietary Reconstruction: A Case Study for the Midwestern United States. In *Paleonutrition: The Diet and Health of Prehistoric Americans,* ed. K. D. Sobolik, pp. 34–54. Occasional Paper 22. Carbondale: Center for Archaeological Investigations, Southern Illinois University.

Styles, Bonnie W., and Karli White

1991   Shifts in Archaic Period Faunal Exploitation in the Mississippi River Valley:

Modoc Rock Shelter Revisited. Paper presented at the annual meeting of the Society for American Archaeology, New Orleans.

Styles, Bonnie W., S. R. Ahler, and M. L. Fowler

1983   Modoc Rock Shelter Revisited. In Phillips and Brown, eds., q.v., pp. 261–97.

Sullivan, N. C.

1977   *The Physical Anthropology of Chiggerville: Demography and Pathology.* M.A. thesis, Western Michigan University, Kalamazoo.

Swanton, John R.

1911   *Indian Tribes of the Lower Mississippi Valley and Adjacent Coast of the Gulf of Mexico.* Bureau of American Ethnology Bulletin 43. Washington: Smithsonian Institution.

1931   *Source Material for the Social and Ceremonial Life of the Choctaw Indians.* Bureau of American Ethnology Bulletin 103. Washington: Smithsonian Institution.

Swift, D. J. P., J. W. Kofoed, F. P. Saulsbury, and P. Sears

1972   Holocene Evolution of the Shelf Surface, Central and Southern Shelf of North America. In *Shelf Sediment Transport; Process and Pattern,* ed. D. J. P. Swift et al., pp. 499–574. Stroudsburg, Pa.: Dowden, Hutchinson and Ross.

Taylor, B., M. Brooks, and D. Colquhoun

1994   Holocene Climate and Upland Landscape Evolution in the Upper Coastal Plain of South Carolina. Paper presented at the annual meeting of SEAC, Lexington.

Teltzer, P. A.

1991   Generalized Core Technology and Tool Use: A Mississippian Example. *Journal of Field Archaeology* 18:363–75.

Thanz, Nina R.

1977   A Correlation of Environmental and Cultural Changes in Northeastern Florida during the Late Archaic. *Florida Journal of Anthropology* 2(1):3–22.

Theime, D. M.

1991   Seasonal Specialization, Assemblage Diversity, and the Concept of a Subsistence-Settlement System: A Statistical Analysis of the Riverton Culture. *Midcontinental Journal of Archaeology* 16:85–117.

Theler, J. L., and D. A. Baerreis

1981   A Preliminary Report on Terrestrial Gastropods at Modoc Rock Shelter (11RA501): Environmental and Climatic Implications. MS on file, Illinois State Museum, Springfield.

1991   Environmental and Climatic Implications of Snails at Modoc Rock Shelter. Paper presented at the annual meeting of the Society for American Archaeology, New Orleans.

Thom, B. G.

1970   Carolina Bays in Horry and Marion Counties, South Carolina. *Geological Society of America Bulletin* 81:783–814.

Thomas, D. H.

1983   The Archaeology of Monitor Valley, 2: Gatecliff Shelter. *Anthropological Papers of the American Museum of Natural History* 59, pt. 1. New York.

1989   Diversity in Hunter-Gatherer Cultural Geography. In *Quantifying Diversity in Archaeology,* ed. R. Leonard and G. Jones, pp. 85–91. New York: Cambridge University Press.

Thomas, David Hurst, and Clark Spencer Larsen

1979 The Anthropology of St. Catherines Island, 2: *The Refuge-Deptford Mortuary Complex. Anthropological Papers of the American Museum of Natural History* 56, pt. 1. New York.

Thomas, Prentice M., Jr., and L. Janice Campbell

1991 The Elliot's Point Complex: New Data Regarding the Localized Poverty Point Expression on the Northwest Florida Gulf Coast, 2000 B.C.–500 B.C. In Byrd, ed., q.v., pp. 103–16.

Tippitt, V. A., and W. H. Marquardt

1984 *Archaeological Investigations at Gregg Shoals: A Deeply Stratified Site on the Savannah River.* Russell Papers 1984. Atlanta: Interagency Archeological Services Division, National Park Service.

Torrence, Corbett McP.

1992 More Than Midden: Opening the Shell Around the Late Archaic Lifeways. Paper presented at the annual meeting of SEAC, Little Rock.

Torrence, R.

1983 Time Budgeting and Hunter-Gatherer Technology. In *Hunter-Gatherer Economy in Prehistory,* ed. G. N. Bailey, pp. 11–22. Cambridge: Cambridge University Press.

1989a Retooling: Towards a Behavioral Theory of Stone Tools. In *Time, Energy and Stone Tools,* ed. R. Torrence, pp. 57–66. Cambridge: Cambridge University Press.

1989b Tools as Optimal Solutions. In *Time, Energy and Stone Tools,* ed. R. Torrence, pp. 1–6. Cambridge: Cambridge University Press.

Toth, Alan

1979 The Marksville Connection. In Brose and Greber, eds., q.v., pp. 188–99.

Trinkley, Michael B.

1976 Paleoethnobotanical Remains from Archaic-Woodland Transitional Shell Middens along the South Carolina Coast. *Southeast Archaeological Conference Bulletin* 19:64–67.

1979 Speculations on the Early Thom's Creek Phase Settlement Pattern along the South Carolina Coast. Paper presented at the annual meeting of SEAC, Atlanta.

1980 *Investigation of the Woodland Period along the South Carolina Coast.* Ph.D. dissertation, University of North Carolina, Chapel Hill.

1985 The Form and Function of South Carolina's Early Woodland Shell Rings. In *Structure and Process in Southeastern Archaeology,* ed. R. S. Dickens and H. T. Ward, pp. 102–18. Tuscaloosa: University of Alabama Press.

1986 Excavations. In *Indian and Freedman Occupation at the Fish Haul Site (38BU805), Beaufort County, South Carolina,* ed. M. B. Trinkley, pp. 115–57. Research Series 7. Columbia: Chicora Foundation.

Turner, Christy G. II, and L. M. C. Machado

1983 A New Dental Wear Pattern and Evidence for High Carbohydrate Consumption in a Brazilian Archaic Skeletal Population. *American Journal of Physical Anthropology* 61:125–30.

Turner, Christy G. II, and Nancy T. Morris

1970 A Massacre at Hopi. *American Antiquity* 35:320–31

Turner, Christy G. II, Joel Irish, and L. M. C. Machado

1991 Reply to Robb, Conwys, and Smith, with Additional Remarks on LSMAT. *American Journal of Physical Anthropology* 85:348–51.

Turner, W. B., and W. E. Klippel

1989 Hunter-Gatherers in the Nashville Basin: Archaeological and Geological Evidence for Variability in Prehistoric Land Use. *Geoarchaeology* 4:43–67.

Upchurch, Sam B., Pliny Jewell IV, and Eric DeHaven

1992 Stratigraphy of Indian "Mounds" in the Charlotte Harbor Area, Florida: Sea-Level Rise and Paleoenvironments. In *Culture and Environment in the Domain of the Calusa,* ed. W. H. Marquardt and C. Payne, pp. 59–104. Monograph 1. Gainesville: Institute of Archaeology and Paleoenvironmental Studies, University of Florida.

Van de Plassche, O.

1990 Mid-Holocene Sea-Level Change on the Eastern Shore of Virginia. *Marine Geology* 91:149–54.

Vankat, John L.

1973 *The Natural Vegetation of North America: An Introduction.* New York: Wiley.

Van Nest, Julieann

1993 Geoarchaeology of Dissected Loess Uplands in Western Illinois. *Geoarchaeology* 8:281–311.

Waldron, R., and J. Rogers

1991 Interobserver Variation in Coding Osteoarthritis in Human Skeletal Remains. *International Journal of Osteoarchaeology* 1:49–56.

Walker, P. L., and S. E. Hollimon

1989 Changes in Osteoarthritis Associated with the Development of a Maritime Economy among Southern California Indians. *International Journal of Anthropology* 4:171–83.

Walthall, John A.

1979 Hopewell and the Southern Heartland. In Brose and Greber, eds., q.v., pp. 200–208.

1980 *Prehistoric Indians of the Southeast: Archaeology of Alabama and the Middle South.* Tuscaloosa: University of Alabama Press.

Walthall, John A., and Ned J. Jenkins

1976 The Gulf Formational Stage in Southeastern Prehistory. *Southeastern Archaeological Conference Bulletin* 19:43–49.

Walthall, John A., Clarence H. Webb, Steven H. Stow, and Sharon I. Goad

1982 Galena Analysis and Poverty Point Trade. *Midcontinental Journal of Archaeology* 7:133–48.

Wandsnider, L.

1989 *Long-term Land Use, Formation Processes, and the Structure of the Archaeological Landscape: A Case Study from Southwestern Wyoming.* Ph.D. dissertation, University of New Mexico, Albuquerque. Ann Arbor: University Microfilms.

Waring, Antonio J., Jr.

1968 The Bilbo Site, Chatham County, Georgia (orig. 1940). In *The Waring Papers: The Collected Works of Antonio J. Waring, Jr.,* ed. S. Williams, pp. 152–97. Papers of the Peabody Museum of Archaeology and Ethnology 58. Cambridge, Mass.: Harvard University.

Waring, Antonio J., Jr., and Lewis H. Larson, Jr.

1968   The Shell Ring on Sapelo Island (orig. 1955–60). In *The Waring Papers: The Collected Works of Antonio J. Waring, Jr.,* ed. S. Williams, pp. 263–78. Papers of the Peaboby Museum of Archaeology and Ethnology 58. Cambridge, Mass.: Harvard University.

Warren, Lyman O.

1972   Commercial Oyster Shell of Tampa Bay: 1966 Progress Report. *Florida Anthropologist* 25:49–51.

Warren, Lyman O., William Thompson, and Ripley P. Bullen

1967   The Culbreath Bayou Site, Hillsborough County, Florida. *Florida Anthropologist* 20:146–63.

Waselkov, Gregory A.

1982   *Shellfish Gathering and Shell Midden Archaeology.* Ph.D. dissertation, University of North Carolina, Chapel Hill.

Waters, Michael R.

1992   *Principles of Geoarchaeology: A North American Perspective.* Tucson: University of Arizona Press.

Watson, Patty Jo

1985   The Impact of Early Horticulture in the Upland Drainages of the Midwest and Midsouth. In *Prehistoric Food Production in North America,* ed. R. I. Ford, pp. 99–148. Anthropological Papers 75. Ann Arbor: Museum of Anthropology, University of Michigan.

1992   Discussant comments on the symposium "Archaic Period Mounds in the Southeast." Presented at SEAC, Little Rock.

Watson, Patty Jo, and Mary C. Kennedy

1991   The Development of Horticulture in the Eastern Woodlands of North America: Women's Role. In *Engendering Archaeology: Women and Prehistory,* ed. J. M. Gero and M. W. Conkey, pp. 255–75. Oxford: Basil Blackwell.

Watts, W. A.

1969   A Pollen Diagram from Mud Lake, Marion County, North-Central Florida. *Geological Society of America Bulletin* 80:631–42.

1971   Postglacial and Interglacial Vegetation History of Southern Georgia and Central Florida. *Ecology* 52:676–90.

1975   A Late Quaternary Record of Vegetation from Lake Annie, South-Central Florida. *Geology* 3:344–46.

1980   Late Quaternary Vegetation History at White Pond on the Inner Coastal Plain of South Carolina. *Quaternary Research* 13:187–99.

Watts, W. A., and B. C. S. Hansen

1988   Environments of Florida in the Late Wisconsinan and Holocene. In *Wet Site Archaeology,* ed. B. A. Purdy, pp. 307–23. West Caldwell, N.J.: Telford Press.

1994   Pre-Holocene and Holocene Pollen Records of Vegetation History from the Florida Peninsula and Their Climatic Implications. *Paleogeography, Paleoclimatology, and Paleoecology* 109:163–76.

Webb, Clarence H.

1944   Stone Vessels from a Northeast Louisiana Site. *American Antiquity* 4:386–95.

1968   The Extent and Content of Poverty Point Culture. *American Antiquity* 33:297–321.

1970   Settlement Patterns in the Poverty Point Cultural Complex. In *The Poverty Point Culture,* ed. Bettye Broyles and Clarence H. Webb, pp. 3–12. Bulletin 12. Morgantown: Southeastern Archaeological Conference.

1982   *The Poverty Point Culture.* 2d ed. rev. Geoscience and Man 17. Baton Rouge: Louisiana State University.

Webb, Clarence H., James A. Ford, and Sherwood M. Gagliano

1970   Poverty Point Culture and the American Formative. MS on file, University of Southwestern Louisiana, Lafayette.

Webb, Thompson, Patrick J. Bartlein, Sandy P. Harrison, and Katherine H. Anderson

1993   Vegetation, Lake Levels, and Climate in Eastern North America for the Past 18,000 Years. In *Global Climate since the Last Glacial Maximum,* ed. H. E. Wright, Jr., et al., pp. 415–67. Minneapolis: University of Minneapolis Press.

Webb, William S.

1939   *An Archaeological Survey of Wheeler Basin on the Tennessee River in Northern Alabama.* Bureau of American Ethnology Bulletin 122. Washington: Smithsonian Institution.

1946   *Indian Knoll, Site Oh 2, Ohio County, Kentucky.* Reports in Anthropology and Archaeology, pt. 1, vol. 4, no. 3. Lexington: Department of Anthropology and Archaeology, University of Kentucky.

1950a   *The Carlston Annis Mound, Site 5, Butler County, Kentucky.* Reports in Anthropology, vol. 7, no. 4. Lexington: Department of Anthropology, University of Kentucky.

1950b   *The Read Shell Midden, Site 10, Butler County, Kentucky.* Reports in Anthropology, vol. 7, no. 5. Lexington: Department of Anthropology, University of Kentucky.

1957   *The Development of the Spearthrower.* Occasional Papers in Anthropology 2. Lexington: Department of Anthropology, University of Kentucky.

Webb, William S., and David L. DeJarnette

1942   *An Archaeological Survey of the Pickwick Basin.* Bureau of American Ethnology Bulletin 129. Washington: Smithsonian Institution.

1948a   *The Perry Site Lu25.* Paper 25. Tuscaloosa: Alabama Museum of Natural History, University of Alabama.

1948b   *The Flint River Site, Na–48.* Paper 23. Tuscaloosa: Alabama Museum of Natural History, University of Alabama.

Webb, William S., and William G. Haag

1939   *The Chiggerville Site, Site 1, Ohio County, Kentucky.* Reports in Anthropology and Archaeology, vol. 4, no. 1. Lexington: Department of Anthropology and Archaeology, University of Kentucky.

Webb, William S., and C. E. Snow

1974   *The Adena People.* Knoxville: University of Tennessee Press.

Weigel, Robert D., J. Alan Holman, and Andreas A. Paloumpis

1974   Vertebrates from Russell Cave. In Griffin, q.v., pp. 81–85.

Wells, Calvin

1964   *Bones, Bodies and Disease.* London: Thames and Hudson.

White, Nancy M., and Richard W. Estabrook

1994   Sam's Cutoff Shell Mound and the Late Archaic Elliott's Point Complex in the Apalachicola Delta, Northwest Florida. *Florida Anthropologist* 47:61–78.

Whitehead, D. R.

1965   Palynology and Pleistocene Phytogeography of Unglaciated Eastern North America. In *The Quaternary of the United States,* ed. H. E. Wright and D. G. Frey, pp. 417–32. Princeton: Princeton University Press.

1981   Late Pleistocene Vegetational Changes in Northeastern North Carolina. *Ecological Monographs* 51:451–71.

Whitelaw, Todd

1989   *The Social Organization of Space in Hunter-Gatherer Communities: Some Implications for Social Inference in Archaeology.* Ph.D. dissertation, University of Cambridge, Cambridge.

Wiant, M. D., and H. Hassen

1985   The Role of Lithic Resource Availability and Accessibility in the Organization of Technology. In *Lithic Resource Procurement: Proceedings from the Second Conference on Prehistoric Chert Exploitation,* ed. S. C. Vehik, pp. 101–14. Occasional Paper 4. Carbondale: Center for Archaeological Investigations, Southern Illinois University.

Widmer, Randolph J.

1974   *A Survey and Assessment of Archaeological Resources on Marco Island, Collier County, Florida.* Miscellaneous Projects Report Series 19. Tallahassee: Florida Division of Archives, History, and Records Management.

1988   *The Evolution of the Calusa: A Nonagricultural Chiefdom on the Southwest Florida Coast.* Tuscaloosa: University of Alabama Press.

Wiessner, Polly

1982   Beyond Willow Smoke and Dogs' Tails: A Comment on Binford's Analysis of Hunter-Gatherer Settlement Systems. *American Antiquity* 47:171–78.

1983   Style and Social Information in Kalahari San Projectile Points. *American Antiquity* 48:253–76.

Wilkenson, Richard G., and Karen M. Van Wagenen

1993   Violence against Women: Prehistoric Skeletal Evidence from Michigan. *Midcontinental Journal of Archaeology* 18:189–216.

Wilkins, Gary R., Paul A. Delcourt, Hazel R. Delcourt, Frederick W. Harrison, and Manson R. Turner

1991   Paleoecology of Central Kentucky since the Last Glacial Maximum. *Quaternary Research* 35:224–39.

Willey, Gordon R.

1957   Review of *Poverty Point, a Late Archaic Site in Louisiana,* by J. A. Ford and C. H. Webb. *American Antiquity* 23: 198–99.

Willey, Gordon R., and Philip Phillips

1958   *Method and Theory in American Archaeology.* Chicago: University of Chicago Press.

Willey, Patrick S.
  1990 *Prehistoric Warfare on the Great Plains.* New York: Garland.
Williams, J. Mark
  1994 Archaeological Site Distributions in Georgia: 1994. *Early Georgia* 22(1):35–76.
Williams, Stephen
  1968 Appendix: Radiocarbon Dates for the Georgia Coast. In *The Waring Papers: The Collected Works of Antonio J. Waring, Jr.,* ed. S. Williams, pp. 329–32. Papers of the Peabody Museum of Archaeology and Ethnology 58. Cambridge, Mass.: Harvard University.
Williams, Stephen, and Jeffrey P. Brain
  1983 *Excavations at the Lake George Site, Yazoo County, Mississippi, 1958–1960.* Papers of the Peabody Museum of Archaeology and Ethnology 74. Cambridge, Mass.: Harvard University.
Wills, W. W.
  1992 Plant Cultivation and the Evolution of Risk-Prone Economies in the Prehistoric American Southwest. In *Transitions to Agriculture in Prehistory,* ed. A. B. Gebauer and T. Douglas Price, pp. 153–76. Madison, Wis.: Prehistory Press.
Wilmsen, Edwin M.
  1983 The Ecology of Illusion: Anthropological Foraging in the Kalahari. *Reviews in Anthropology* 10(1):9–20.
Winland, Kenneth J., Natileene W. Cassel, and M. Yasar Iscan
  1993 Demography and Disease in the East Okeechobee Culture Area, Florida. Paper presented at the annual meeting of SEAC, Raleigh.
Winterhalder, Bruce
  1980 Environmental Analysis in Human Evolution and Adaptation Research. *Human Ecology* 8:135–70.
Winters, H. D.
  1968 Value Systems and Trade Cycles of the Late Archaic in the Midwest. In *New Perspectives in Archaeology,* ed. S. R. and L. R. Binford, pp. 175–221. Chicago: Aldine.
  1969 *The Riverton Culture.* Reports of Investigation 13. Springfield: Illinois State Museum.
  1974 Introduction. In *Indian Knoll* by William S. Webb, pp. v–xxvii. Knoxville: University of Tennessee Press.
  1981 Excavating in Museums: Notes on Mississippian Hoes and Middle Woodland Copper Gouges and Celts. In *The Research Potential of Anthropological Museum Collections,* ed. A.-M. Cantwell, J. B. Griffin, and N. A. Rothschild, pp. 17–34. *Annals of the New York Academy of Sciences* 376.
Wood, W. Dean, Dan T. Elliott, Teresa P. Rudolph, and Dennis B. Blanton
  1986 *Prehistory of the Richard B. Russell Reservoir: The Archaic and Woodland Periods of the Upper Savannah River.* Russell Papers 1986. Atlanta: Interagency Archeological Services Division, National Park Service.
Woods, R. J., and B. M. Rothschild
  1988 Population Analysis of Symmetrical Erosive Arthritis in Ohio Woodland Indians (1200 years ago). *Journal of Rheumatology* 15:1258–63.
Wright, H. E., Jr. (editor)
  1983 *Late Quaternary Environments of the United States,* pt. 2: *The Holocene.* Minneapolis: University of Minnesota Press.

Wright, H. T., and M. A. Zeder
  1977   The Simulation of a Linear Exchange System under Equilibrium Conditions. In *Exchange Systems in Prehistory*, ed. T. K. Earle and J. E. Ericson, pp. 233–53. New York: Academic Press.
Yarnell, Richard A., and M. Jean Black
  1985   Temporal Trends Indicated by a Survey of Archaic and Woodland Plant Food Remains from Southeastern North America. *Southeastern Archaeology* 4:93–106.
Yellen, John
  1977   *Archaeological Approaches to the Present: Models for Reconstructing the Past*. New York: Academic Press.
Yerkes, R. W.
  1983   Microwear, Microdrills, and Mississippian Craft Specialization. *American Antiquity* 48:499–518.
  1987   *Prehistoric Life on the Mississippi Floodplain*. Chicago: University of Chicago Press.
  1989a   Mississippian Craft Specialization on the American Bottom. *Southeastern Archaeology* 8:93–106.
  1989b   Lithic Analysis and Activity Patterns at Labras Lake. In *Alternative Approaches to Lithic Analysis*, ed. D. O. Henry and G. H. Odell, pp. 183–212. Archaeological Papers 1. Washington: American Anthropological Association.

Contributors

DANIEL S. AMICK is an assistant professor of anthropology at Loyola University of Chicago. He received his doctorate in anthropology from the University of New Mexico in 1994. His dissertation focused on Folsom dietary breadth, land use, and technology in the American Southwest. He spent several years investigating buried Archaic sites in central Tennessee prior to his dissertation work. His research interests center on lithic technology and hunter-gatherer archaeology. Currently he is investigating Paleoindian occupations in the western United States.

DAVID G. ANDERSON is an archaeologist with the Southeast Archeological Center of the National Park Service in Tallahassee. He is the author of numerous papers and monographs on prehistoric archaeology in various parts of North America and the Caribbean, including *The Savannah River Chiefdoms: Political Change in the Late Prehistoric Southeast*, based on his doctoral research at the University of Michigan. In 1990 he received the first C. B. Moore award for excellence in southeastern archaeology by a young scholar and, in 1991, the dissertation prize of the Society for American Archaeology.

DENNIS B. BLANTON is co-director of the Center for Archaeological Research at the College of William and Mary. He received his graduate training at Brown University and for the last 12 years has been associated with public and private cultural resource management organizations in the eastern and midwestern United States. Dennis has actively pursued research on the mid-Holocene archaeology of the Southeast, often with an emphasis on lithic procurement and use, but more recently he has begun to investigate coastal adaptations. His primary research project now is the study of prehistoric settlement on Jamestown Island, Virginia.

PHILIP J. CARR is a research associate in the Department of Anthropology and Sociology, University of Southern Mississippi. He received his doctorate in anthropology in 1995 from the University of Tennessee. His research interests include prehistoric hunter-gatherers, lithic analysis, and technological organization. He has analyzed chipped stone assemblages from sites in Indiana, Kentucky, Nevada, New York, South Carolina, Tennessee, and Washington. He is currently working with controlled flintknapping experiments to understand prehistoric stone tool technologies better.

CHERYL P. CLAASSEN first excavated in the tenth grade in Oklahoma. Since then she has dug throughout the Southeast, Massachusetts, and New York and in Serbia, France, and Mexico. She received her doctorate in anthropology from Harvard University in 1982. She is a professor of anthropology at Appalachian State University in Boone, North Carolina, and a research associate of the Center for American Archaeology in Kampsville, Illinois. She has organized conferences on archaeology and gender, the lower Illinois River valley, and the Hudson River valley, where she conducted a seven-year-long excavation at the Dogan Point site. The editor and author of six books, she currently coordinates paleoenvironmental reconstruction for an archaeological project in Honduras.

JON L. GIBSON is a professor of anthropology and director of the Center for Archaeo-logical Studies at the University of Louisiana at Lafayette. He received his doctorate from Southern Methodist University in 1973. His dissertation dealt with the Poverty Point cul-ture, and he continues to delve into it and other matters of Lower Mississippi Valley pre-history.

KRISTEN J. GREMILLION is an assistant professor of anthropology at Ohio State Uni-versity. She received her doctorate from the University of North Carolina, Chapel Hill, in 1989. Her research specialties include paleoethnobotany, prehistoric diet and subsistence, and the origins of agriculture. She is currently investigating the development of pre-maize farming systems in the uplands of eastern Kentucky and has recently ventured into the study of dietary remains and DNA from human paleofeces.

ERIC C. GRIMM is a palynologist and paleoecologist at the Illinois State Museum. He received his doctorate in ecology from the University of Minnesota in 1981. His research interests include the ecological dynamics of vegetation change and the rates and timing of broad-scale vegetation and climate change. His current areas of research are in Florida, the Midwest, and the northern Great Plains. He is the coordinator of the North American Pollen Database.

T. C. HUSSEY received graduate training in paleoecology at the University of Maine in Orono. His research focused on the vegetational history of Clear Pond in South Carolina. He now works as a technical computer specialist for Information Systems and Networks Corporation of Durham, North Carolina.

RICHARD W. JEFFERIES is an associate professor of anthropology at the University of Kentucky in Lexington. He received his doctorate in anthropology from the University of Georgia in 1978. He has conducted extensive investigations of Middle and Late Archaic hunter-gatherers of the lower Ohio River valley, primarily focusing on southern Illinois and Kentucky. His research interests include the study of sedentism and the development of social networks during the mid-Holocene.

WALTER E. KLIPPEL is a professor of anthropology at the University of Tennessee in Knoxville. His research interests include prehistoric hunter-gatherers in eastern North America and zooarchaeology in the Mediterranean and eastern North America. Walter has examined subsistence strategies and assessed prehistoric environmental change through analyses of archaeologically recovered faunal remains. He is currently investigating modes of prehistoric bone modification and taphonomic processes that mimic past human activity.

R. JERALD LEDBETTER is staff archaeologist with Southeastern Archeological Services of Athens, Georgia. He has conducted extensive excavations on a number of Archaic sites in the Southeast, focusing his efforts on the recovery of site patterning and architectural data for a variety of site types.

MICHAEL RUSSO is project leader at the National Park Service, Interagency Archeo-logical Services Division, in Atlanta. He received his doctorate in anthropology in 1991 from the University of Florida. His dissertation focused on subsistence patterns and mound construction at the Archaic Horr's Island site. Previously he worked for the Florida Museum of Natural History and the Southeast Archeological Center of the National Park

Service where he investigated coastal and riverine subsistence and settlement patterns in peninsular Florida. Employment at the University of Southwestern Louisiana again led him to investigations of early mound builders with excavations of the Stelly Mounds site.

KENNETH E. SASSAMAN is an archaeologist with the South Carolina Institute of Archaeology and Anthropology. He received his doctorate in anthropology in 1991 from the University of Massachusetts, Amherst. With 15 years experience investigating the hunter-gatherer archaeology of the South Atlantic Slope, Ken focuses his research on technological change and social organization. His current research efforts are divided between excavations of shell middens in the Savannah River valley for the purpose of writing a detailed history of the rise and fall of Stallings Culture and collections research aimed at situating local populations in the social milieu of Late Archaic regional interaction.

JOSEPH SCHULDENREIN is the president and senior scientist of Geoarcheology Research Associates in Riverdale, New York. He has expertise in the methods and applications of geoarchaeology and has undertaken a variety of projects across North America and the Old World. Joe received his doctorate in 1983 from the University of Chicago. His recent research has concentrated on the varied coastal, alluvial, and interior landscapes of the Middle Atlantic and greater Southeast. Recently he joined a Smithsonian Early Man project on the Indian subcontinent. He continues to be involved with research on the relationships between landscape and human settlement during the Upper Pleistocene in the Near East and the Aegean basin.

MARIA O. SMITH is an associate professor of anthropology at Northern Illinois University and a research associate at the Frank H. McClung Museum in Knoxville. She received her doctorate in anthropology in 1982 from the University of Tennessee. Her primary area of research has been the paleopathology of prehistoric populations from the Tennessee River valley, focused on violent trauma. Her research has also broadened to include bio-archaeological analysis of precolumbian populations from the American Southwest.

BONNIE W. STYLES is the director of sciences at the Illinois State Museum. She received her doctorate in anthropology from Northwestern University in 1978. She has participated in archaeological field projects in the Southwest, Midwest, and Plains. A specialist in archaeozoology, she has identified and analyzed faunal remains from over 30 prehistoric sites. Her research interests include Holocene paleoecology, human-land interactions, prehistoric subsistence practices, and human use of fauna. She has published over 40 reports on archaeological and paleoecological themes. Currently she contributes to several long-term projects to document changes in Holocene environments and prehistoric subsistence in the lower Illinois and central Mississippi valleys.

WILLIAM A. WATTS has been a member of the faculty of Trinity College, Dublin, since 1955, and he served as provost of the college from 1981 to 1991. He first visited the United States in 1962 as a research fellow at the University of Minnesota, where he is an adjunct professor in geology. Since then he has returned to the United States on many occasions with periods of residence in Minnesota, at the University of Washington, and in Florida. He has published widely on the vegetation history of the southeastern United States. He maintains an active research program in Florida. His interests are in long records of vegetation and climate from forested regions at low temperate latitudes.

Index

www.ingramcontent.com/pod-product-compliance
Lightning Source LLC
Chambersburg PA
CBHW020653270326
41928CB00005B/96